SAILING DESIGNS

Volume Six

The design reviews of
Robert H. Perry
as published in

ISBN 1-929006-05-5

Library of Congress Control Number
2004095110

Printed in the United States of America

*Information about ordering
this book is available from:*

Port Publications, Inc.
125 E. Main St.
Port Washington, WI 53074

Telephone 1-800-236-7444

CONTENTS

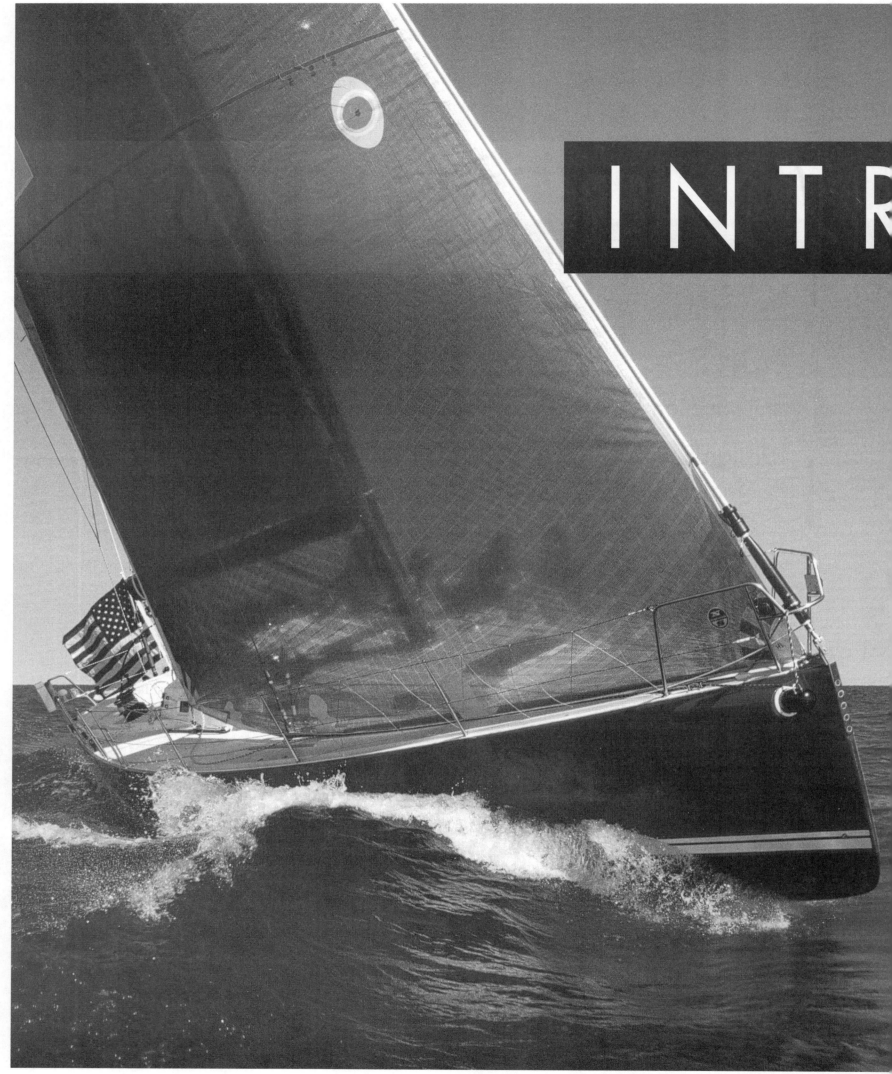

INTR

I feel really good when I walk through a boat show and see one of my reviews from *SAILING* reprinted and mounted on display for a builder. Apparently they must think my review is important and recognized by the industry and the sailing public. I have enjoyed doing these reviews for almost 30 years. It even amazes me.

The success of the reviews is due in a large part to the freedom that *SAILING* publisher Bill Schanen III has given me in expressing my opinions. I don't think there are any other magazines that could afford me that freedom. The cost would be too great in terms of advertising lost. In fact, Bill has stood by me when major advertisers have pulled their advertising over a review.

It's interesting that it's always the builder who gets upset and almost never the designer. One builder was incensed that I called his boat "fat." I called the designer, good old Gary Mull, and explained the situation. Gary said, "It is fat." Still, the builder pulled his advertising and refused for years to let me review his boats.

Another builder claimed he was going to come and "chop off your head." Bill Garden once told someone, "It's easy to find Bob's design office. It's the one with the sand bags piled in front."

On the other side of the coin are all the friends I have made through the reviews and all the new designers I have been able to feature and help get started. Doing the reviews has put me on a first name basis with a lot of designers I respect. I have even had foreign designers come to Seattle and stay at my house.

The focus of the reviews has remained the same since the beginning. These are not boat reviews, but design reviews. I cannot see every boat that is sent for review. In many cases the boat is not built yet and in a surprising number of cases the boat is never built. My job is to look over the design drawings and review the design. If I do have the opportunity to inspect the actual boat I will try to work those observations into the review.

The typical problem I face with reviewing the design is inadequate design drawings, or worse yet advertising agency "renderings" that erase all human designer touches that make designs personal expressions of the designers art.

Ideally I will get a sail plan, deck plan, hull lines and sail plan. Usually these are accompanied by a brochure with a partial list of specs and hopefully some designer comments. I probably get hull lines for 10 percent of the boats I review. Some designers see the hull lines as proprietary, and I understand this for racing yachts. This makes commenting on the specifics of the hull shape difficult, but over the years I have developed ways of intuiting shapes from the other drawings.

I have been studying hull shapes for 44 years now. If I get overly artsy advertising drawings, I just have to do my best with them and hope they are accurate renderings. It is not at all unusual that the figures I get for the dimensions and weight of the boat will differ from one page to another. Sometimes this confusion can be cleared up with a phone call, but other times I have to use my imagination and I often resort to devising my own scale so I can take my own dimensions off a drawing. This does not work for displacement. Confronted with varying displacements for the same design, I will almost always go with the heaviest displacement.

I hope my commentary on these designs helps bring the boats to life and helps the reader in understanding the trade-offs in priorities that accompany any design.

Robert H. Perry

SMALL-BOAT
DESIGNS

Sonatina

Dewitt Dinghy
Daysailer

I think we may all be guilty from time to time of getting too serious about our passion, sailing. I hate the term "a serious cruising boat." If the design is right the cruising should be fun and less serious. In fact, I was thinking of changing the name of my own boat to *Pull My Finger*. "Harbormaster, this is sailing vessel *Pull My Finger* requesting moorage." That'll keep it on the lighter side.

A good way to restore the fun nature of sailing is to sail a dinghy. This is one of my pet areas to promote. Small boats give immediate responses that if not heeded can result in a dunking or, preferably, a

"I can't think of anything much more fun than racing a Dewitt in a fleet of my cronies."

very wet seat. The dinghy experience can help hone your sailing skills, and I assure you there is nothing you will learn on a dinghy that will not translate directly to the skills required to sail your big boat more effortlessly. Cruisers in general, specifically those without any racing experience, can make cruising hard work and in the worst cases, quite dangerous. "Sure Bob, I always run my spinnaker foreguy under the lower lifeline." "Fine skipper. Just give me fair warning so I can duck below when you jibe!"

I just love this Dewitt dinghy. It has great lines, and that's understandable considering the combined sailing-artistic talents of designer Jim Dewitt. Jim's a fabulous painter in addition to being a world-class sailor. At one of the first Atlantic City Boat Shows I was working with the Valiant display. Jim Dewitt had an easel set up about 15 feet away where he was painting an America's Cup scene. It was fascinating to watch him work.

Despite its diminutive 8-foot, 6-inch LOA, I consider this to be far more than a water toy. This boat has some "serious" performance potential. Photos show the Dewitt planing with an adult on board. Now try that on your El Toro or your Optimist. The Dewitt will outsail these boats in any conditions. This dinghy also tows well and can take a small outboard motor, making it an excellent all-purpose tender. Two people are a load for this dink. A built-in dinghy bailer keeps the Dewitt dry in the worst conditions.

Apart from proving an excellent way for old salts to get their sailing kicks, this dinghy makes a superb children's trainer. Among other things, it has enough positive buoyancy to prevent it from swamping. This feature gives it an element of forgiveness sorely lacking in older dinghy designs. A capsized Dewitt rides very high in the water, making it extremely easy to right. The polyethylene Rototuff hull is certainly durable enough to stand the hardest use without requiring costly fiberglass repair.

The rig features a two-piece carbon mast and a zipper-luff mainsail that can be rolled around the mast for reefing. The battens are full-length and have camber inducers to help shape the mainsail. A very handy "halyard pocket" is sewn into the tack of the sail to hold the halyard when the sail is up. I've never seen this before.

You can buy the Dewitt in three different models, the difference primarily being in the sophistication of the sail handling gear. The three models are: Competition, Sport and Resort. The Resort and Sport models have fixed rudder blades while the Competition model has a fold up rudder. To date more than 70 of the Dewitts have been sold.

I can't think of anything much more fun than racing a Dewitt in a fleet of my cronies.

U.S. Dewitt Dinghy Association, 1230 Brickyard Cove Rd. #200, Pt. Richmond, CA 94801. (800) 398-2440. **www.dewittsailboats.com**

October 2000

A dinghy offering performance and fun for all ages.
LOA 8'6"; Beam, 4', Sail Area 56 sq. ft., Hull Weight 90 lbs.

Hunter Xcite and Walker Bay 9 RID
Dinghies

Now we will look at Hunter's latest small boat, the Xcite. Hunter recently acquired controlling interest in JY Sailboats of East Lyme, Connecticut, and this is their first new project. This 10-footer is a car topper designed to keep the kids happy, or, with the choice of the "Turbo" rig, maybe even exciting enough to keep Dad happy.

The Xcite weighs a mere 95 pounds. The key to this is the construction method used, which employs special plastic-injected foam and fiberglass mat, thermoformed into a very durable finished product.

The ergonomics of the deck look good. You sit on the side deck and the cockpit is open at the transom. The daggerboard trunk does not protrude into the cockpit at all.

These are very versatile little boats.

Flip-up rudder and daggerboard make this an ideal boat for off the beach sailing.

Both rudder and daggerboard are high aspect ratio and look very effective to my eye. There are few things worse than a dinghy with inadequate appendages. It's hard to teach someone to sail efficiently to weather if the boat is not up to the task. The Xcite looks to be well suited for performance oriented training.

There are two rigs: training and turbo. The training rig has 34 square feet of sail while the turbo rig has 55 square feet. The difference in the areas of the two rigs appears to be in the amount of roach to the sail. The turbo rig has a full roach with almost a "fat head" plan form while the trainer rig has a straight leach.

This simple, durable boat would be an ideal boat to teach your kids or friends the joys of dinghy sailing.

Jason Rhodes dropped the newest Walker Bay model off at my beach place a couple of weeks ago so I could test it. I own two of the standard 9-footers and I was anxious to see how this new model

performed. I do love the little original 9-footer. It rows, sails and tows very well. However, its performance comes at a price, and that is initial stability. You need to be aware that you are in a small boat at all times and keep your weight centered on the thwart.

Apparently someone brought this to the attention of the Walker Bay family and they have responded with a new 9-foot model called the 9 RID. This model includes inflatable tubes set just beneath the gunwale. These tubes increase the overall beam by 16 inches; each tube being about 9 inches in diameter and tucking under the gunwale detail. Overall length is 9 inches longer than the original 9-footer. The tubes add weight and the RID model weighs 20 pounds more than the original, so if you are carrying your dink up and down the beach this may be a factor. Also, the original still has the advantage of being totally maintenance free.

Under sail the tubes act like outriggers and will alter the entire stability profile of the boat. But they will drag as you heel the boat and this will slow the boat down. Climbing in and out of my Boston Whaler or pulling a crab pot laden with plump, juicy, sweet Dungeness crabs is effortless with the tubes.

I like the looks of the tubed model. The tubes are actually tapered and accent the lovely sheer of the 9-footer nicely. They also lend a more high-tech or current look to the boat while acting as full length fenders.

These are very versatile little boats and make ideal tenders, especially if you prefer to tow your dink.

Hunter Marine, Route 441, P.O. Box 1030, Alachua, Florida 32615. **www.huntermarine.com** *(800) 771-5556.*

Walker Bay Boats, 607 West Ahtanum Road, Union Gap, WA 98903. **www.walkerbay.com,** *(888) 449-2553.*

January 2003

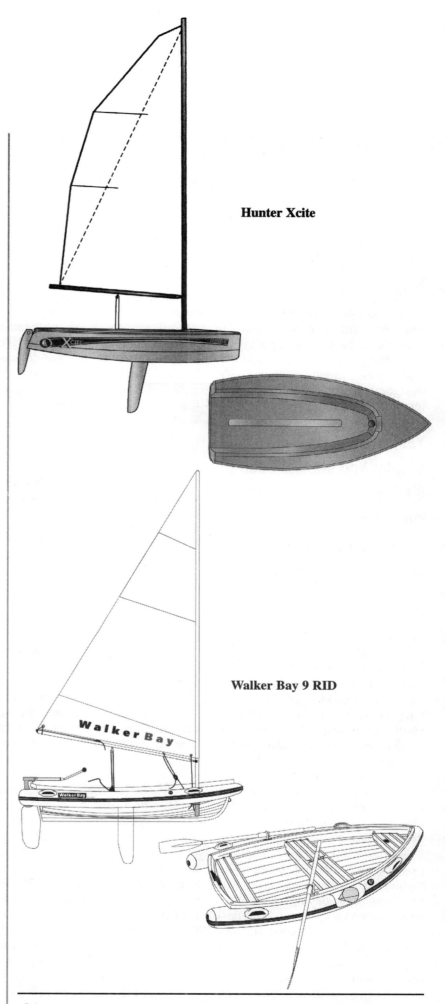

Hunter Xcite

Walker Bay 9 RID

A car-topper that's fun for the whole family and a dinghy with extra stability.

Hunter Xcite
LOA 9'11"; Beam 4'5"; Draft 3'2"; Weight 95 lbs.; Sail area 34 sq. ft. (Training), 55 sq. ft. (Turbo).

Walker Bay 9 RID
LOA 9'; Beam 5'8"; Draft 1'9"; Weight 89 lbs.; Sail Area 39 sq. ft.

X3
Racer-daysailer

If I had two youngsters interested in learning how to sail, I'd be looking hard at this X3. This little boat comes from Australia and has been specifically designed to use a graduated system for introducing sailors to the

Yes, you will capsize this dinghy. You should. I don't think you can learn to ski without falling, and I don't think you can learn dinghy sailing without capsizing.

various complexities of the modern racing dinghy. This is another rotomolded craft. Not only that, it's made from recycled materials.

Aesthetically this boat has the earmarks of a racing dinghy. The stem is almost plumb, and the transom is open. The hull form shows a sharp entry fairing quickly into the topsides to provide plenty of buoyancy. The sections at the stern are a flattened arc for good planing performance. The transom is open for drainage. The centerboard is a deep high-aspect-ratio board that should give this dinghy excellent performance on the wind. The rudder is a kick-up type for beaching. The deck is cambered with a large radius on the inboard edge to make hiking comfortable.

Here's how it works. First you buy the basic hull platform and the "education" sailplan. This is a short cat rig with a fathead-type full-roach main. This is going to look pretty high-tech to your kid compared to the Walker Bay rig, and once your youngster has mastered the main he can graduate to the small asymmetrical chute for better downwind speed. Now your kid's beginning to feel like 49er

champion Jonathan McKee.

Still, there is really no need to rush the chute, since you can have lots of fun with the single sail. It's only 43 square feet, and the gennaker adds another 48 square feet, doubling the horsepower. With a main, gennaker and a 110-pound crew, the SA/D is 38.8. You can also sail the X3 comfortably with two youngsters.

So, after a summer of learning with the education rig your kid can spend the winter bulking up and getting ready for the "fun" rig. This rig adds an additional 19 square feet to the mainsail for a total main area of 62 square feet. The gennaker is also substantially larger with a sail area of 88 square feet. With the bigger rig the downwind SA/D is raised to 58.8, assuming your kid has put on 30 pounds over the winter. To achieve this I recommend Bob's famous Swiss steak recipe with lots of mashed potatoes smothered in Bob's Swiss steak sauce. The X3 with the fun rig is now elevated to true high-performance dinghy numbers and should satisfy the most demanding dinghy sailor.

Yes, you will capsize this dinghy. You should. I don't think you can learn to ski without falling, and I don't think you can learn dinghy sailing without capsizing. Most kids like to capsize, especially on hot days. However, with the short rig this will be a rarity. Really you should instruct your learner in the tricks for righting the dinghy anyway to complete the education process.

Clearly this is a boat I could enjoy.

Sail Extreme Pty. Ltd., 53 Aitken Street, Williamstown, VIC 3016, Australia. 61 3 9399 9009. **www.sailextreme.com**

June 2002

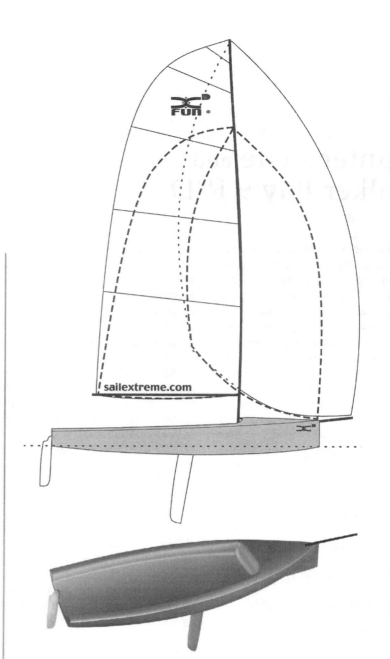

sailextreme.com

Performance dinghy with multiple rigs for all abilities.

LOA 10'2"; Beam 4'11"; Draft 2'11"; Hull Weight 121 lbs.; Mainsail Area 43 sq. ft. (Education), 62 sq. ft. (Fun); Gennaker area 48 sq. ft. (Education), 88 sq. ft. (Fun).

Sunglider and Splash
One-design Daysailers

Here are two small boats for you to consider. One is weird and the other is sensible.

Sail training is more complicated than it used to be. Thirty-five years ago you would put your kid into a Penguin or an El Toro and rest assured they were learning the rudiments of sailing. Today, however, there are a host of powerful planing boats like the Laser and the 29er, which are also vying for kids' attention. It's evident, especially to the Melges crew in Zenda, Wisconsin, that an interim trainer is needed, a boat to introduce the intermediate sailor to the joys of planing performance that isn't too much for intermediate-level sailors under 125 pounds.

Melges Performance Sailboats' solution is the Splash, a shorter and smaller boat than the Laser, and ideally suited as a "foundation" boat to introduce young sailors to the world

The Sunglider is so different you will have to try it to appreciate it.

of high-performance sailing. The brochure says the ideal crew weight for the Splash is between 110 and 155 pounds. This would also make the Splash a better boat for women.

It's a snappy looking little dinghy, with an ergonomically improved cockpit and a splash guard to help keep water out of the well. Draft with the board down is 2 feet, 3 inches.

The one aspect of this design that bothers me is the hull weight of 121 pounds, which is only 19 pounds less than a Laser. That makes it a two-person job to carry the Splash and a real handful for two 100-pound youngsters.

I also object to the overly generous radius on the stem. This is not apparent in the drawing, but is very noticeable in photographs. Maybe this is a buoyancy feature. But the photos clearly show it mushing through the water.

The rig features a long top batten to extend the roach and give the Splash a modern look. The mast is tapered aluminum, with a slot for the luff rope and an external halyard. The brochure says that this boat would make an ideal Christmas present for

your youngster. It might turn out to be one of those presents that Dad wants to play with too.

* * *

And then there's the Sunglider, a hybrid craft combining dinghy and windsurfer features with a unique steering mechanism. Produced by Vanguard of Portsmouth, Rhode Island, the Sunglider appears to be aimed at the sailor who feels the need to stand up while sailing.

Obviously you need to stand on a windsurfer since you are all there is holding the mast up. The Sunglider, however, has a mast that is stepped in the hull, which relieves the sailor of the job of supporting the rig. With this done it would be easy to finish off this design with a rudder and tiller and a place to sit down comfortably and go sailing. But no. The Sunglider sailor will stand, hanging onto an 11-inch-diameter wheel on the end of a long, hinged tube.

Maybe this boat is for sailors who don't like to get their fannies wet. I don't know what the mechanics are for steering this boat, but you do steer it with the wheel and this gives you something to hang onto. I watched a demo sailor sail one of these boats around the Annapolis Boat Show. The boom is high enough so you can duck under it jibing and tacking, but not high enough for a taller person like me to do this with any grace or panache. Standing does give you a good mechanical advantage for hiking. I'm groping here.

I love to see diversity in sailing craft. When I first saw the early photos of this boat I thought, "Now there's a boat I want to try." But now I'm not so sure. Maybe it's a boat for people who want to feel like they are "surfing" and not just "sailing." Maybe it's a boat for people with hemorrhoids.

Clearly the Sunglider is so different that it is one of those boats you will have to actually try to appreciate. I'd like to give it a go, preferably with no one watching.

Melges Performance Sailboats P.O. Box 1, Zenda, WI 53195. (262) 275-1110. **www.melges.com**

Vanguard 300 Highpoint Ave., Portsmouth, RI 02871. (800) 966-7245. **www.teamvanguard.com**

February 2001

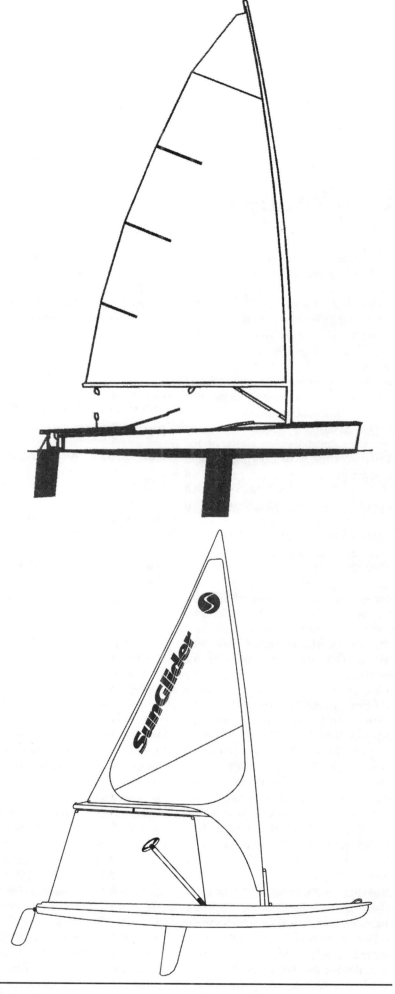

Boats that represent the new and the "unique."

SPLASH
LOA 11'8"; Beam 4'3"; Draft 2'3" (board down); Weight 121 lbs.; Sail Area 60 sq. ft.

SUNGLIDER
LOA 12'6"; Beam 4'5"; Draft 2'10"; Weight 90 lbs.; Sail Area 63 sq. ft.

Chickadee
Scow

I remember the first time I ever took a boat out by myself. It was a calm day on Lake Washington. I was about 14. I rented an 8-foot Sea Scouter dinghy. It weighed about 800 pounds and its only sail was held to the mast with shower curtain rings. I sat on the thwart, sculled my way out of the marina and headed straight downwind for two hours. Stupid, but understandable, considering.

The wind of course died, leaving me up against the lee shore of the Lake Washington floating bridge, known for the nasty square chop that develops there. I could not make that horrible little tub of a boat go to weather at all. Not that I even knew what it took to make any boat go to weather. I recall watching the Star class 24-footers slide by effortlessly in the light breeze maybe 50 feet away from me; to leeward no less. "Why can't I do that?" I ended up rowing the stubby little boat back to the marina with its stubby little oars; all the time the boom banging me upside the head as I didn't have the smarts to lower the stubby little sail. It occurred to me that maybe there was more to this sailing thing than I had suspected.

I love little sailboats. I know I'd get along just fine with this Chickadee designed by Canadian Chris Koper. Chris markets the Chickadee as kits or he would be happy to provide you with plans and patterns along with an instructional video so you can build your own. Chris is passionate about his Chickadee. In fact, it seems to be that the smaller the boat the more passionate the builders are. Maybe it has something to do with the intimate physical connection the sailor makes with a small boat. Regardless, Chris is a zealot for this little trainer. He says it's the perfect next step for a sailor graduating from the Optimist pram.

The basic design is based upon a 12-foot scow designed by Chris's dad Jack in 1956 in South Africa, the Dabchick. They have built 3,500 Dabchicks to date. That's impressive. The scow form on the Chickadee makes for a boat that is quick to plane and quite stable and forgiving. Deadrise is almost constant but flattens out amidships. The increase in deadrise aft prevents the leeward chine from digging in when the boat is heeled. The scow hull form takes a little time to get used to. The squared off bow is not elegant at

There is easily enough performance designed into this boat to keep an expert happy, too.

first glance but can be quite shapely when the plywood is sufficiently tortured. When I brought up the question of scow aesthetics to Chris the sound of hackles rising in Mississauga was clearly audible in Seattle. Like any proud papa, Chris thinks his little scows are beauties. I have to agree. They do have a certain charm.

The rig couldn't be any simpler. According to Chris, the boat sails well with just the main up for beginners or very light crews. The responsiveness of the Chickadee's hull form means that the beginner will get feedback from the boat quickly and technique improvements will be immediately rewarded with better performance. There is easily enough performance designed into this boat to keep an expert happy, too.

The cockpit is a trough type open at the transom. Plywood is bent to an arc to form the cockpit sides and sole. There is a gentle, compound curvature in the foredeck.

I bet if I had been in a Chickadee back in 1962 I wouldn't have had to row back to the marina. It was humiliating in front of those racing dinghies and it took a week for the bruises on my head to heal.

Sea K Designs, #24-3265 South Millway, Mississauga, ON, Canada, L5L 2R3. (905) 608-8994. **www.sea-k-designs.com**

June 2003

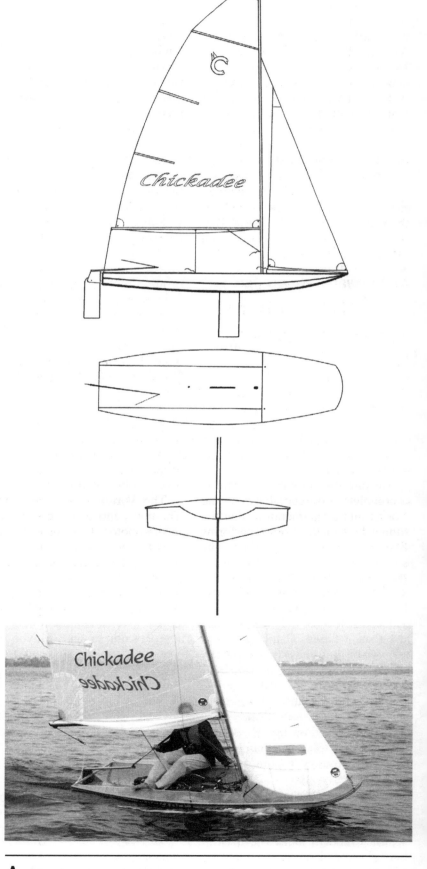

A responsive scow for the Optimist graduate and expert alike.
LOA 12'; Beam 3'11"; Draft 1'3"; Weight 128 lbs.; Sail Area 70 sq. ft.

Laser Vortex
One-design Dinghy

Here's a dinghy that will make easing yourself into the world of performance sailing less traumatic. This British-built singlehander with trapeze was created by International Moth designer Andrew Dixon, brother of Bill Dixon. At first glance the Vortex appears to be a catamaran—in fact, it looks like a cat after several glances—but it's not a cat. It's a tunnel-hulled dinghy.

This shape was prototyped successfully with the Moth class in the '60s and '70s, but proved so dominant the class rules were changed to prevent the tunnel from running the full length of the hull. This reduced the effectiveness of the tunnel so that it disappeared from

As the water enters the tunnel it is forced down the tapered surface producing lift.

the class. As a one-design, however, the Vortex has no such restraints, and there is light at the end of this tunnel with about one square foot of "light" above the flotation plane.

Despite the similarities, there is a complete difference between the Vortex and a catamaran in that the tunnel hull of the Vortex performs like one continuous hydrodynamic surface whereas a cat has two independent hydrodynamic surfaces. This means the interaction of water between the tunnelled hulls enhances performance while the interaction between the hulls of a cat tends to diminish the performance. As the water enters the tunnel it is forced down the tapered surface producing lift. This reduces the drag on the hull and reduces pitching while sailing in waves. The Vortex has one rudder and according to the brochure, "incredible tacking speed."

The Vortex also has two daggerboards that are raked forward and canted inward. As a result, the windward board will be near vertical when the boat is heeled and the leeward board will act like a lifting foil to further reduce drag.

The brochure goes on to say that the shape of the Vortex allows the sailor to get farther outboard on the trapeze due to the hull shape. Well, come on. If beam is near identical how can you get farther outboard? If, on the other hand, you look at the Vector with its pronounced wings and 6-foot beam it's obvious that this winged configuration allows the sailor to get farther outboard. (The beam of the Vector is about a foot greater than the beam of the Vortex.)

Now, having said that you do have to take into consideration the fact that once heeled the Vortex will ride on its leeward hull, and this will push the transverse center of buoyancy to leeward, which will in turn make the righting moment of the sailor on the wire greater. Keep in mind that for the tunnel hull to work optimally you will need to keep both hulls in the water. But then again, with the windward hull lifted clear, it appears the Vortex would behave like a cat. And that's not so bad either if you are looking for speed.

I do think the stability characteristic of this design will be far more forgiving than those of the Vector type. Your Vortex will not tip over at the dock. Kept level this will be a very stable platform.

The Vortex is strange looking. The bows appear to be squared off in the photos. I estimate the "flat" to be about 1.5 inches across. The inner tunnel surface is entirely fair and contiguous. The deck is gently dished, and there is no cockpit per se. The sheer is generously radiused for comfort on the wire. I imagine changing tacks on the Vortex would be a lot easier than it would on the Vector as you pass through that zone of level stability.

The Vortex is gaining in popularity in the United Kingdom. Experienced sailors are quoted in the brochure as saying this is a wonder, an exciting boat. I think, based upon the stability aspect afforded by the tunnel-hull configuration, I hope I get the chance to sail a Vortex and see for myself.

The Laser Centre, 6 Riverside, Banbury, Oxon, OX16 5TL UK. 44 1295 268191. **www.lasersailng.com**

June 2001

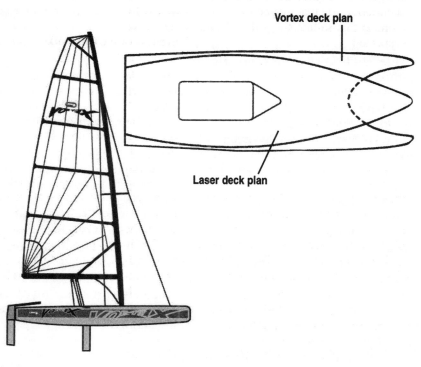

Vortex deck plan

Laser deck plan

An unusual approach to dinghy performance.

LOA 13'9"; Beam 5'; Hull Weight 143 lbs.; Sail Area 113 sq. ft.

Triton
Daysailer

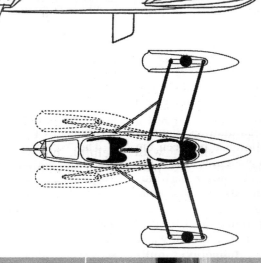

The joys of sailing can often be best experienced in the simplest craft. A windsurfer has always seemed to provide the ultimate and certainly most intimate sailing experience for me. But here in Puget Sound the water never gets above 50 degrees and the breeze only gets steady and strong right at dinnertime, the time when I prefer the comfortable Zen state of cooking to the wet Zen state of windsurfing. A boat like this little Triton trimaran designed by Don Rypinski might do the trick.

This vessel is easily car-toppable and very quick to rig, although it does weigh 200 pounds, which means your wife will have to bend her knees when she picks up her end. There is an optional "stern dolly" designed to aid in car-topping, which I presume would work well as a beach dolly.

The amas hinge inward for a folded beam of 5 feet. With the amas extended the beam is 12 feet, which means hiking will not be a requirement. I don't think you could capsize this tri without a lot of concerted and rigorous effort.

The rudder is activated through foot controls. You can add an electric outboard that attaches to the top of the rudder and will give you two hours of motoring at "up to 5 knots." The electric motor is powered by a 55-pound battery in a compartment aft. You can also paddle the Triton kayak-style with the amas extended.

The rig is essentially a windsurfer rig with a sleeved mainsail that rolls up around the mast for easy and quick reefing. There is a daggerboard between the cockpits to help you sail to weather. The brochure for the Triton says that with a 400-pound load the boat

The joys of sailing can often be best experienced in the most simplest craft.

"will plane in 8 knots of wind and has attained speeds of up to 15 knots maximum in 25 knots."

The single-point, boomless sheeting system for the main will restrict mainsail shape control and would make running and broad-reaching difficult to do effectively. Fore-and-aft trim of the Triton looks fine with two people aboard, but I wonder if the boat wouldn't be stern down with just one crew, as the skipper sits aft.

With an optional forward Lexan "windshield" and an aft cockpit fairing in place, the Triton is a sporty-looking little rig.

Back Bay Boat Works, 629 Terminal Way, Suite #4, Costa Mesa, CA 92627. (949) 515-2733. **www.backbayboatworks.com**.

August 2002

A stable off-the-beach boat for sailing or paddling.

LOA 14'; Beam 12' (outriggers extended) 5' (outriggers retracted); Displacement 200 lbs. (light-ship displacement; Sail area 95 sq. ft.; SA/D 21.3 (with 400-pound crew and gear); Auxiliary electric motor with 50-pound battery.

Skerry & Classic Cat
Beach Cruiser and Catboat

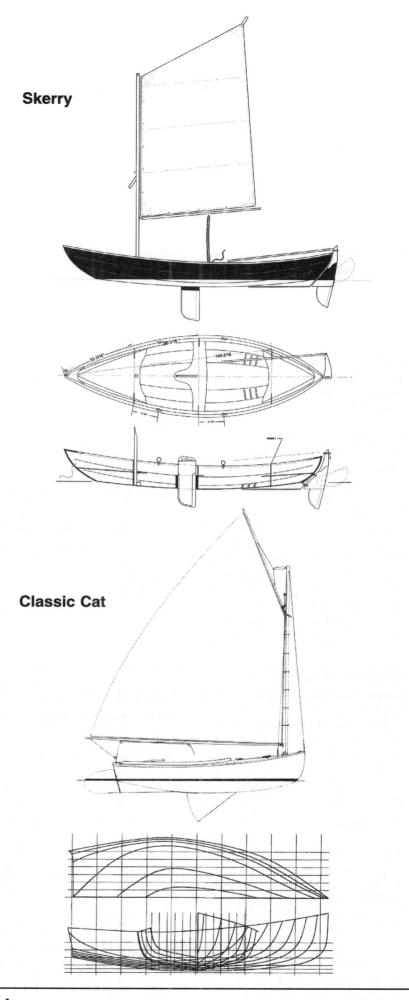

Skerry

Classic Cat

This Skerry is a beautiful boat. It's a classic rowing type with a sailing rig built in a type of lapstrake construction the builder, Chesapeake Light Craft, calls "LapStitch." The promo material calls it a "beach cruiser." I guess I'm old. No, I'm definitely get-

If you have never sailed a good boat with a gaff rig you might be in for a surprise.

ting old. I just can't imagine sailing along with camping gear and pulling my boat up on the beach and setting up camp for the night. There was a time when I could.

There is not an ugly line on this boat. The sheer is beautiful and accented by the lines of the chines. The chines add interest and eye candy to an already appealing boat. The pea pod plan form shape is very traditional and makes this boat row sweetly. I admit to being a sucker for a nice pulling boat. That's what you call them when you are serious about rowing: "pulling boats." It has a good sound. In some ways it's a refined dorylike shape with flared topsides, but more plan form asymmetry. The flared topsides provide stability when the boat is heeled and gives you sufficient buoyancy to go out for an afternoon's sail and return home with a load of herring. "Ahhh, the smell of the sea."

The little sprit rig will move the Skerry along nicely but don't harden up against a Laser. A Sea Scouter would be more fair game. I see myself in the Skerry, Piper perched in the bow, Three Nuns smoldering in one of my vintage Dunhills, silently sailing down the shoreline on a reach trolling for cutthroat trout. Bliss would be mine.

I love small catboats. They are packed with personality and a wee bit quirky. I used to live in a houseboat next to a fellow who rented out Beetle cats. I gave him a hand from time to time and he

let me have unlimited use of his little catboats. This Classic Cat designed by Merv Hammatt is bigger than the Beetle cat and appears to be a very comfortable daysailer.

The hull is the typical Cape Cod catboat model. The waterlines forward are fine and beam has been carried broad to the stern. There is a firm turn to the bilge and about 14 degrees of deadrise. The sheer is springy and essential to that wooden shoe-type profile that sets the catboat apart. The centerboard is a plate type. Lead ballast and foam flotation are both glassed in place. Draft with the board up is 10 inches. Those big, barn door type rudders can be a handful when you bear off onto a broad reach in a breeze. But heck, that's just part of the quirky fun of sailing a catboat. You learn quickly about the effect mainsail pressure has on helm balance.

If you have never sailed a good boat with a gaff rig you might be in for a surprise. If the peak angle of the gaff is high enough you can point just fine. Off the wind the gaff rig exposes a lot of sail area. Obviously, with a rig like this a good vang would be very helpful, but you just don't see them on catboats and that may be a function of the low gooseneck. In a breeze you might find it's more prudent to tack the boat downwind rather than risk the excitement of a flying jibe with that big boom.

I think it's important for anyone interested in the history of sailing yachts to put some time in on a catboat like this Classic. I can guarantee that you will be pleased with the overall performance. No question you will always look very salty. And that's important.

Chesapeake Light Craft, 1805 George Ave., Annapolis, MD 21401. (410) 267-0137. **www.clcboats.com.**

Compass Classic Yachts, P.O. Box 143, South Orleans, MA 02662. (508) 240-1032. **www.compassclassicyachts.com**

June 2003

A sprit-rigged little boat with good pull and a salty-looking catboat.

SKERRY
LOA 15'; Beam 4'6"; Draft 2'6"; Hull Weight 90 lbs.; Sail Area 60 sq. ft.

CLASSIC CAT
LOA 14'2"; Beam 6'10"; Draft 2'6"; Weight 600 lbs.; Sail Area 130 sq. ft.

Small
Daysailer

Antonio Dias is one of those designers who shows his love of the work through the careful attention to the design process. I see some designs where the designer has a good idea for a new boat but the detail drafting is pure drudgery. Although Dias uses a computer for his drafting chores, it's easy to see he has fun with it and produces artlike design drawings. Neat drafting and a good design do not always go hand in hand. Nor does lousy drafting necessarily mean a bad boat. But in the case of Small, we see what appears to be a nice boat nicely drawn.

Dinghies can be divided into three general types: performance one-designs like the Laser and Tasar; trainers like the Hunter 170 and the T15.5; and traditional dinghies based on historical types like the Beetle Cat and Small. I'm big on emphasizing the style aspect of sailing. And if you're not going to race and you want a boat that conjures up images of small-

The hull shape shows shapely ends with a hint of hollow in the entry.

boat sailing when you were a kid, the traditional types are the ticket.

The biggest disadvantage to the traditional types is that they can be heavy and slow. But Dias has combined the looks of the traditional "British day boat" with modern construction techniques to create a dinghy with enough performance to satisfy a seasoned dinghy sailor while providing the panache of a classic type.

This dinghy is available in finished form with a molded fiberglass lapstrake hull or you can assemble it yourself from pre-cut pieces of trim and a bare molded hull. You can also build a Small in timber using glue lap-and-strip-composite construction. William Clements of North Billerica, Massachusetts, is the builder.

The hull shape shows shapely ends with a hint of hollow in the entry and enough hollow in the stern sections to give the dinghy a nice, almost heart-shaped transom, which is accented by a gently curved, solid-rod traveler that goes from gunwale to gunwale.

Centerboard and rudder are carefully designed to optimize performance, and the rudder pivots for trailering. The centerboard is off center so it doesn't interrupt the keelson. A wide and flat caprail makes sitting on the rail to hike easy on the buns.

The rig is called a "Solent Gunter" and is sort of a hybrid between a Marconi-headed sloop rig and a gaff rig. For upwind performance you would want your gaff peaked as high as possible to increase the length of the leading edge of the mainsail. The advantage over a Marconi rig is that you can break the rig down into shorter spar lengths for stowage and you get to say "gunter."

I'd prefer to see longer battens, and the jib sheeting angle is quite wide with the jib sheeting to what appears to be an eye bolt on the caprail. It might be nice to sheet the jib closer, although it might not make much difference with the gunter main anyway. Everything has to be in sync.

This dinghy would make a nice rowboat. Two sets of oarlocks are drawn with the forward rower sitting on the mast partners thwart. For sailing, the seats are about 10 inches below the sheer, which will make you feel like you are "in" rather than "on" the boat. This is also a nice feature when sailing with small kids.

On a nice day, with the sun shining and the wind blowing a steady 12 knots, you can have fun sailing just about anything. Why not do it in style?

Antonio Dias Design, 171 Cedar Island Road, Narragansett, RI 02882. (401) 783-4959. www.diasdesign.com

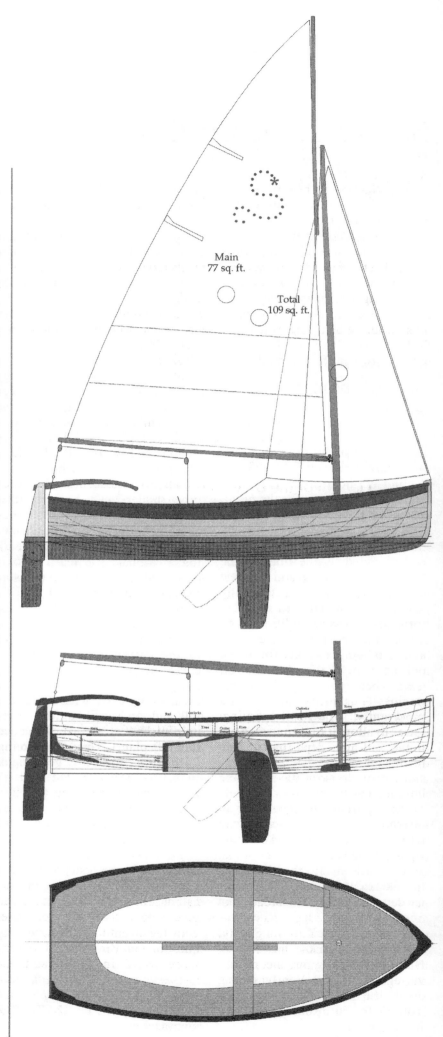

Traditional dinghy with pep.

LOA 14'10"; LWL 13'9"; Beam 5'11"; Draft 7" (board up), 3' (board down); Weight 175 lbs.; Sail Area 95.5 sq. ft.

MegaByte
Daysailer

We tend to think of Bruce Farr as a designer of large offshore racing yachts, but the Farr office has its origins in the world of high-performance dinghies. Bruce drew them and drove them, and he did both jobs well. When Ian Bruce of Performance Sailcraft wanted a quick new dinghy he went to Bruce.

The idea behind the new boat was a dinghy that could combine performance with a greater weight-carrying capacity than

> **"Once you turn the corner, the extra length of the Byte works to make it faster off the wind."**

Performance's The Byte. We are talking serious weight here. In fact, at 225 pounds, I am at exactly the target crew weight for this design. The result is a big single-handed dinghy with a 14-foot, 3-inch LOA and 5 foot, 2 inches of beam. These proportions give the MegaByte stability and, more importantly, the sail-carrying power to allow it to be muscled up in the sail-area department. The displacement of the MegaByte also means you can have friends with you on this dinghy.

The bigger hull (bigger than a Laser's) allows the MegaByte to have a real cockpit with an average depth of 15 inches. The sides of the cockpit well bond to the bottom of the boat, so there is no cockpit sole per se. Side decks are broad and chamfered on the edges and identical to those on the Tasar dinghy. In fact, the entire deck is identical to that of the Tasar. This is a comfortable cockpit and much easier on the knees than the shallow well of a Laser. You will also stay drier on this boat due to the increase in freeboard. Dinghy bailers will keep the cockpit from filling up.

The mast is carbon fiber and the sail is Mylar. There is 20 more square feet to this sail than on a Laser, but hull weights are listed as

identical. Upwind in flat water the Laser can give the MegaByte a run for its money, but once you turn the corner, the extra length of the Byte works to make it faster off the wind. A unique bungy cord in the luff of the Mylar sail allows for good sail draft control. This allows a sail with generous luff roach to match the bendy stick. There is also a traveler. Both the daggerboard and the dagger rudder are built from aluminum extrusions.

The size of this dinghy makes it suitable for family daysailing. As a training boat it has the advantage of allowing both student and instructor aboard at the same time. The boat is fitted with an additional set of hiking straps forward for the crew. I've taught people to sail by putting them into my El Toro and shoving them out and calling out instructions from the beach, but it's much nicer and far more elegant to be able to take those first few rides together so the student can build confidence.

Performance Sailcraft just launched its 150th MegaByte. It has also signed on an additional hull and deck builder (the boats are finished at the Performance Sailcraft plant). This is becoming a popular dinghy.

This is definitely the type of dinghy that can slap you around a bit if you are not diligent with your weight distribution and your sail trim. But that's one of the best ways to learn. A little swim now and then can reinforce good sailing habits. Personally I'm beyond the days when I enjoyed a dunking. In Puget Sound the 49-degree water tends to be a bit too bracing for my attitude, and I'm starting to look really weird in a wet suit. Of course, you can always start out in the light stuff and slowly graduate to planing across the bay in total control.

Performance Sailcraft, 2555 Dollard, Unit 14B, Lasalle, Quebec, H8N 2A9 Canada. (514) 363-5050.
www.megabyteclass.org

October 2000

High-octane dinghy for learning, daysailing or racing.
LOA 14'3"; Beam 5'2"; Draft 3'2"; Weight 130 lbs.; Sail Area 95 sq. ft.

Sonatina
One-design/Daysailer

Kit boats seem to have fallen out of favor in America. This is probably because we have more money than time on our hands so the finished product is attractive. But kits have appeal, especially to youth groups for whom the time-money correlation is reversed.

This handsome little scow has an interesting history and rather than regurgitate it for you I think I'll let Chris Koper, the designer and a veteran Finn sailor, tell it himself:

"My father, Jack Koper, conceived the predecessor design, the Sonnet, of which more than 500

This shapely little rocket would make an excellent family winter project, not to mention a wonderful family dinghy.

have been built in South Africa. The Sonnet was based on the stunning success of the very popular 12-foot Dabchick, a junior trainer that is fleet of foot, yet stable and great fun to sail. That class numbers more than 5,000, and it is still very active; every well-known South African sailor learned to sail and race on a Dabchick. The Sonnet was also derived from the 15-foot Tempo, aimed at the more expert sailor with trapeze and spinnaker.

"When Jack died three years ago I went to be with the family. The weekend after his passing I attended the annual Interschool Regatta and was invited to present the trophy to the winning school team. That gave me an opportunity to tell the latest crop of juniors about how these speedy boats originated when their parents were learning to sail.

"The Interschool event has been run for more than 40 years, and I was one of those who sailed in it back in the late 1950s. The Dabchick has been the core of the event every year since then; today the lineup also includes the Sonnet and the Optimist. I saw then that the Sonnet was also an ideal boat for junior sailing.

The Sonatina is my way of recognizing the amazing influence Jack had on so many lives, and of course my own. I am taking his legacy a step further by offering

North Americans a way to build a wonderful boat and go sailing with the Sonatina. The big advantage is that this enjoyable boat can be built at home with a low level of technical difficulty.

"There is 12 percent more sail area than the Sonnet for more power, and the higher aspect ratio of both the rig and the foils contribute to sparkling windward performance. I narrowed the beam to reduce the wetted surface, then deepened and angled the sides to allow more heeling. That allows one to raise the windward side out of the water and further reduce drag. I then induced a compound double-curve to the bottom panels to provide sweeter lines, and again cut down on wetted surface and drag.

"The prototype is built in plywood covered with epoxy glass for strength and durability, just like the Chesapeake 18 sea kayak I built in the spring. The boat looks stunning in its coat of glossy varnish.

"The hull weighs in at 140 pounds, so it has the advantage of being very quick to plane and it's a lot faster reaching than similar sized dinghies. Compared with Midwest scows, the Sonatina has a much lower displacement, and the V-bottom creates a better hull shape. It's a great feeling to skim over the waves at speed. Juniors and novices enjoy the performance and get hooked quickly."

There are some interesting points that Chris did not mention. The SA/D is a healthy 35.5 if you assume a crew weight of 220 pounds. (I figured one 120-pounder and a 100-pounder.) And there will be an additional rig available soon that provides a more flexible mast for singlehanding, allowing the single sailor to bend the mast to flatten and depower the main. Note that when you heel the Sonatina between 10 and 15 degrees you get the leeward bottom panel about flat with the water, which makes the boat quite stable.

This shapely little rocket would make an excellent family winter project, not to mention a wonderful family dinghy.

Sea K designs, #24-3265 South Millway, Mississauga, ON, Canada L5L 2R3. **www.sea-k-designs.com** *(905) 608-8994.*

June 2002

A dinghy with a history and horsepower that you can build yourself.

LOA 14'6"; Beam 4'6"; Weight 188 lbs.; Sail Area 122 sq. ft. (main and jib).

Active 15
One-design Dinghy

I paid $10 and joined the Corinthian Junior Yacht Club when I was 15 years old. This entitled me to sail a Rhodes-designed Penguin dinghy in local races once I passed the skipper's test. That's another story, but thanks to the weather eye of my mentor Don Miller, I managed to eventually become a "skipper" and I spent many blissful hours piloting Penguins around Lake Washington and Lake Union. Little boats are really cool. Twenty knots of wind, a four-foot steep chop and one boy in a Penguin leave little room for anything but a very steep learning curve.

Phil Morrison is an internationally known high-performance dinghy designer. His International 14s have been the best in the world, and if you can be competitive in that class, let alone dominate, you have to be a master of dinghy design. But I didn't invite you here to talk about I-14s. We are here to look at Phil's new Active 15, a multipurpose high-performance dinghy coming in finished and pre-cut plywood kit form from a South African builder, a GRP hull is also available. The Web site says that sailing in South Africa is in serious decline and the intention of this dinghy is to breathe some life back into the sailing scene by providing an exciting multilevel boat that can be home built.

The Active 15 has been designed to serve dinghy sailors starting from the novice up through the expert. This of course involves some level of compromise in hull and rig design. The Active 15 comes with a choice of four very different rig configurations. The Club is a modest rig aimed at the novice and an ideal boat for introducing a husband and wife team to dinghy racing.

The Race 1 rig has a bigger mainsail with a full roach and a much bigger jib. Add to this an asymmetrical chute on a retractable sprit and a single trapeze and you have upped the performance potential substantially. Then you step up to the Race 2 rig with an even bigger "fat head" type mainsail, a big-

ger jib and a masthead chute. This rig allows two trapezes. There is almost twice the sail area in the Race 2's asymmetrical chute as there is in the Race 1 chute. In terms of only jib and main, the sail area in the Club rig is about doubled for the Race 2 version. There

Sailing in South Africa is in serious decline and the intention of this dinghy is to breathe some life back into the scene.

is also a Regatta version that has slightly less sail area than the Race 1 version.

The hull and foils are fixed for all versions allowing the same basic platform to be used for all the rigs. Deck layouts and hardware will have to change but I would assume that these changes are controlled by the class rules so customization is avoided. However, the Web site is confusing on this last detail and it could be that deck gear variations are encouraged.

The hull is moderately beamy with little flair to the topsides. This will make it more forgiving for the novice. Less beam means the boat will be easier to right after a capsizing. The chine stays wide aft making the 15 a boat that will plane easily and with a sense of stability. The generous waterline beam of the 15 will compromise light air speed and responsive feel but at the same time most beginners are not ready to deal with quite that much "feel" considering it's usually a rather wet feeling. The rig options should compensate for the light air challenges.

Active Sports Boats, P.O. Box 441, Constantia 7848, Western Cape, South Africa. 27 21 715-2531. **www.activesportsboats.com**

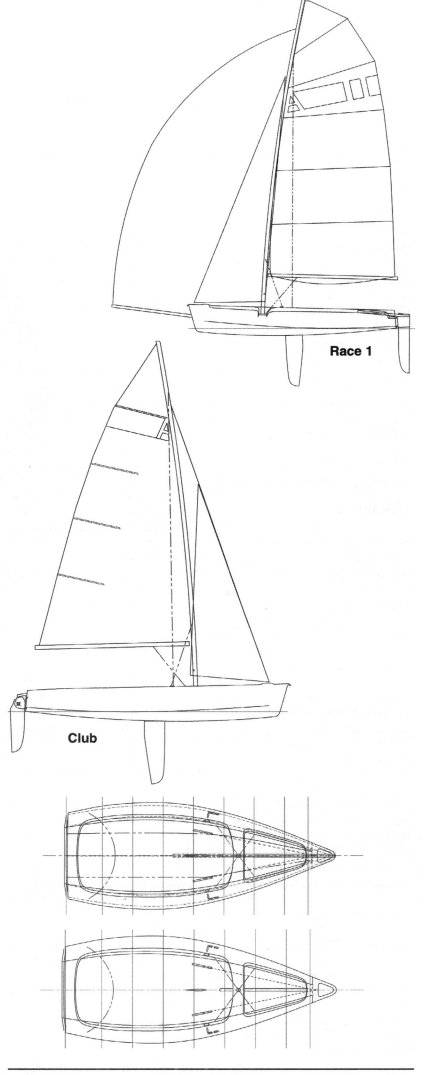

Race 1

Club

LOA 15'; Beam 5'10"; Draft 4'2"; Weight 165 lbs.; Sail Area 110 sq. ft. (Club), 145 sq. ft. (Regatta), 179 sq. ft. (Race 1), 196 sq. ft. (Race 2).

Bongo
Sport Boat

The Bongo is a curious boat best described by a comment by designer Paul Cronin in the promotional material as, "a boat that would satisfy his desire for speed without taxing a body that has already taken some hard knocks." Well, I'm certain many of us can relate to the "hard knocks" part of that statement. Couple that with a less than razor-sharp reaction time and while you may have a mind that's willing, the flesh no longer obeys. Maybe it's time to look at a way to go fast that is not so taxing on the body, a way to sail that allows speed to be reached while relaxing.

Paul's answer to this is the Bongo. It has a drop keel with 100 pounds of ballast so some would argue that it's not really a dinghy, but I'd take that argument on. It was designed primarily for single-handing so just think of that ballast as a 140-pound crewmember who doesn't talk back. Maybe I'd call my Bongo *No Dear*. The hull features a narrow BWL with a chine aft for planing stability and wide wings for comfortable hiking. The cockpit is deep and that makes for a

... a boat that would satisfy the desire for speed without taxing a body ...

comfortable sitting position while hiking and a very comfortable seat in light air. There is a small cuddy cabin big enough to stow your lunch and foul weather gear. You get stirrups and hiking straps to accommodate one of two sailors.

I don't have any drawings for this boat. Usually that would mean no soup for you, Mr. Cronin. But in this case I have a lot of photos and a well written, no-fluff and succinct promo brochure so we'll make do.

I'm not going to address D/L or SA/D for these small boats. Crew weight is too big a variable to make those static calculations meaningful. The Bongo can be sailed by a couple, a 90-pound kid

or a 250-pound singlehander. With a 190-pound crew the first reef goes in around 18 knots. Prior to the main being reefed it's flattened with the multipurchase cunningham that allows you to "blade out" the main by bending the mast tip. Sheet and traveler adjustments can further flatten the sail. The reefing is single line and the Bongo is rigged for two reefs. Sail controls are all led under the deck to a console so adjustments can be made from either side easily.

There is a retractable sprit and a chute launcher in the bow. You hoist the chute with the halyard, adjust the tack line and sheet it in when you feel you are ready for it. When it comes time to drop it you can ease the sheet and tack line and pull the chute into the launching tube with a "bellybutton" retriever line. When things are snug you can retract the sprit. It does not have to be hectic or scary. Besides, if you are single-handling there is no one to yell at anyway.

I like the looks of Cronin's new design. I'm not so old I want to give up planing dinghies, but at the same time I'm not ready to race a 49'er and there was always something about my size-14 shoes and the lines in an I-14 that didn't work. I am very much looking forward to demo-sailing the Bongo when it comes to Seattle this summer.

PC Sailing, P.O. Box 139, Jamestown, RI 02835. (401) 481-3811. **www.sailabongo.com**

LOA 15'2"; Beam 6'6"; Draft 3'11"; Weight 350 lbs.; Ballast 100 lbs.; Sail Area 112 sq. ft. (main) 147 sq. ft. (standard spinnaker).

Vanguard Vector
One-design dinghy

I don't know any sailor who likes to go slow. If that sailor exists I don't want to meet him. Making your boat go as fast as possible is just plain good seamanship in my book. And when it comes to sailing fast and well, there are few ways to better hone your skills than on a racing dinghy.

My own recent experiences racing a Tasar dinghy with my wife were often humbling. But I'm now an even better sailor because of those mind-expanding, ego-deflating moments. If you came to sailing late and your first boat was a 28-footer or a 34-footer, do yourself a favor. Buy, rent, borrow or steal a planing dinghy and go out and put yourself at the low end of the learning curve. You will never regret it, at least not once you dry out.

Maybe the trick is to buy a Vanguard Vector for your kid. Let him go out and learn the boat. Then, when your kid has mastered whatever is needed to keep the Vector upright, you agree to go along as crew.

Better yet, you drive and let your kid go through the athletics of keeping the boat on its pointed little feet. Before long you will have mom out on the trapeze and you will be sitting back tiller in one hand, mainsheet in the other hollering as you blast-reach on a full plane into the marina.

The first thing you need to master with the Vector is how to keep it from capsizing while it sits at the dock. It's hard to look cool while your boat is laying sideways. (I never actually had this happen with my Tasar, but there were moments when I uttered the universal sailor's prayer, "Holy #$%!" as I struggled to belly crawl my way to the dock from a less than stable platform.) The Vector is a light and lively 200 pounds, and you had better keep one hand on the shroud if you want to keep it in a dignified position before shoving off.

Once you're on your way and finished short-tacking through the cut to open water, you finally begin to relax. Now you can get that mainsheet adjusted so the boom is over the quarter. Your mate has finally made it all the way out in the trapeze, and the jib is actually in and not just happily flapping away. Your Vector is begin-ning to accelerate. For pretty much for the first time the boat is under your control. Hardening up slightly you begin to find some real enjoyment. The boat even feels kind of stable as long as your crew adjusts his

It's wet, it's scary at times, but it sure is fun.

position to the changing heel angles. It wants to go in a straight line so you can stop worrying about steering and study your mainsail shape. Maybe it's time to ooch yourself out onto the trapeze so you can sheet in the rest of the main.

Then, finally, you are out on the wire and looking back at the boat almost like you are an observer of the whole thing. You're out here. The boat is down there. You can actually watch the boat move through the water from a removed perspective.

Bearing off you extend the bowsprit and the chute goes up. Then you sheet in the big sail and your Vector accelerates a little quicker than you had in mind. But the funny thing is that as the boat picks up speed things begin to settle down even more. The faster you go the more stable the Vector feels. Before you can say "Uffa Fox" you are planing off on what has become a beam reach.

Back at the marina entrance you look at your mate and after figuring out how to get the chute down you harden up and head up the bay again for another couple more tacks that will take you far enough upwind to get the chute up again. It's wet, it's scary at times, but it sure is fun and you can look right down your nose at the couple in the 35-footer with the jib halyard wrapped around the head-stay and three fenders dangling. Who cares if you capsize the Vector at the dock a couple of times as you unrig the boat. You've earned the right to laugh at yourselves.

Vanguard Sailboats, 300 Highpoint Ave., Portsmouth, RI 02871. **www.teamvanguard.com** *(800) 966-7245.*

June 2001

Walter Cooper photo

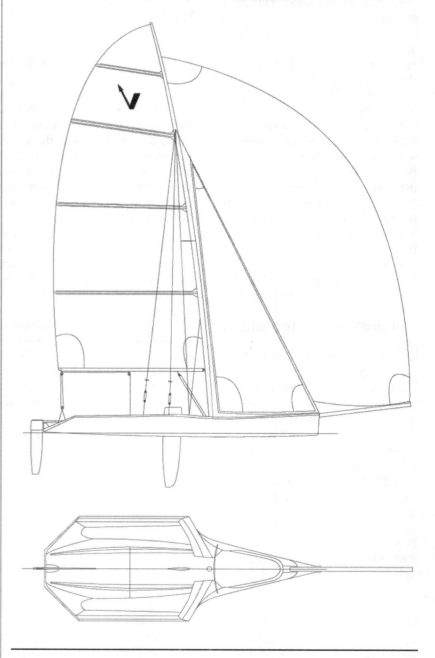

Hang on to your hats. This is not your father's Catalina!

LOA 15'3"; Beam 6'; Draft 4'9"; Hull Weight 180 lbs.; Working Sail Area 160 sq. ft., Spinnaker Sail Area 210 sq. ft.

Fusion 15
One-design dinghy

Here's a dinghy design from Steve Killing, the skilled Canadian designer and author of my favorite book on yacht design, **Yacht Design Explained**. Steve had already generated a series of dinghy sketches when he was approached by Fusion Sailboats for a dinghy that would be "fast, fun and friendly." This means that the new boat would have to fall into that wide gap between the tippy-at-the-dock rockets and the overly fat, stable sluggos that are often shoved on us as "trainers."

This is no tremendous challenge for a good designer, but it does require establishing some benchmarks and then deciding where you will apply the compromises. The first issue to be addressed in designing the hull is stability. My own Tasar was a wonderful boat to sail, but not a boat you would leave unattended at the dock for more than a few seconds. The best way to add stability in an unballasted dinghy is to change the shape of the hull in the area of the beam at waterline. If you give the boat more BWL it will be stiffer but slower. We're talking form stability here.

The shape of Steve's hull for the Fusion 15 shows a firm turn to the bilge extending aft and a moderate amount of deadrise amidships fairing to a flat at the transom. Dockside stability will be excellent without compromising planing potential. I'm not confident offering more insight into this boat's performance without the opportunity to sail it alongside the 15-foot Tasar, with which I am much more familiar. The centerboard is deep and housed in a trunk that only protrudes six inches above the cockpit sole, making it an ideal foot rest.

I don't much care for the shape of the bow, but there is a reason for this almost clipperlike profile. After wrestling with whether to have a spinnaker or not, Killing and Fusion decided to forego the complications of a normal chute and go with an asymmetrical. In order to avoid the bother and expense of an extending bowsprit Steve extended the bow profile enough to pull the tack point of the asymmetrical eight inches forward of the jib. This helps you jibe the chute around the jib stay.

I know this boat is just the type I would enjoy.

Another interesting aspect of this rig is the slick self-tacking jib. There is a single jib sheet that leads up the mast from the self-tacking jib track and then down to a swivel jam cleat just below the boom vang on the mast. You can play with the jib sheet as you tack or you can ignore it. This is essentially the same jib sheet arrangement that I use on my Saga series boats and that you see on the big fancy Wally yachts.

The rolled deck edge works well ergonomically, and the open transom is ideal for a dinghy and will empty the cockpit of water in seconds. Bailers are a drag—both kinds. The open transom forces the builder to use a rudder hump to mount the rudder. Think I'll call it a "rump." This cockpit is extremely clean. The hiking straps are mounted on the centerboard trunk, which puts them at the perfect angle for comfy crew hiking.

I know you can have fun in slow boats. But if you start with a boat that has a reasonable performance potential I firmly believe you and your kids will learn faster. If you enjoy the X-games approach to sailing you can buy a 49er. If you want to sail in a more relaxed style maybe the Fusion 15 is the boat for you. I know this boat is just the type I would enjoy—stable enough to move around in easily and fast enough to scream off on a planing reach when the wind gets over 15 knots.

Fusion Sailboats USA, 1388 Cornwall Rd., Suite D, Oakville, Ontario, L6J 7W5, Canada. **www.fusion15.com** *(416) 543-4772.*

October 2002

A dinghy that offers comfort and speed for both young and old.

LOA 15'8"; Beam 5'6"; Draft 5" (board up), 4' (board down); Hull weight 290 lbs.; Sail Area 142 sq. ft. (jib and main), 79 sq. ft. (spinnaker).

Raider Sport
Sport Dinghy

I always enjoy the Annapolis Boat Show. I've been going now for about 25 years and I still get a kick out of seeing my industry buddies. About five years ago, the Thursday night before the show opened I found a note on the boat I was staying on informing me that I had to be off the boat by Friday to make room for the owner's guests. Right, like I'm going to be able to find a hotel room in Annapolis the day the show opens.

I was depressed and homeless. So with my bags in tow I schlepped my way down the dock without a clue as to where I was headed. Passing a fellow washing down a Valiant 42 I said hello and introduced myself as the designer of his boat. After a brief chat he asked where I was going and I told him, "I have no idea." He replied, "I have a house right here next to the

If you are more interested in sailing than swimming you might prefer the Raider.

boatyard and an extra bedroom. Would you like to stay with us?" You bet I would.

I have stayed with Bob and Barb Schaefer each boat show since. It has made a huge difference. The accommodations have been great and the company has been even better. I FedEx'ed in king salmon and Dungeness crabs this year and cooked dinner for them one night. I think the Annapolis Show is a "must do" for any sailor. Please put it on your calendar for next year.

Although it was tucked in a corner, one of the boats getting some attention at this year's show was the Raider Sport.

Raider Sailboats brings us this new 16-footer aimed at sailors who want to go fast without first acquiring expert level sailing skills. The Raider is available in two models, Raider and Raider Sport. The difference is that the Sport model offers higher tech detailing to further

enhance performance.

You can sail this boat by yourself or with a friend for crew. For single-handing it's a big boat at 16 feet, 2 inches with a 7-foot, 4-inch beam—a function of the wings. Beam at the waterline is quite narrow without being extreme. The bow is narrow and fine then the topsides flair out but not with the concave flair you might expect. The flair to this boat is convex and adds considerable form stability to the craft. It's also drag, and if you are looking for 49er-type thrills this is not the boat for you. But if you are more interested in sailing than swimming you might prefer the Raider.

The Raider also claims to be self-righting, although I'm confused as to what their definition of "self-righting" is.

Hull weight is 200 pounds. The Sport model has a deeper dagger-board with 4 inches more draft.

The deck looks very comfortable. There is a generous roll to the inboard deck edge so you can hike in comfort. The transom is not open, but it's not exactly closed either. There are two huge bailing tubes glassed in to help keep water from accumulating in the cockpit. If you get the Sport model you get a 6-inch longer tiller extension and upgraded Harken deck and sail handling gear.

Additionally, you get a two-piece carbon fiber mast with 18 square feet of extra sail area. The standard model has an aluminum stick. If we go sailing on a Sport model with a friend weighing 140 pounds, we get an all up crew weight of 325 pounds. Add to this the hull weight of 200 pounds, and another 20 pounds for miscellaneous gear, and we get a SA/D of 29.47. If that doesn't keep you moving you can bear off and hoist the big asymmetrical chute that almost doubles the sail area. This could be fun.

Drawbridge Marine, 592 Birch Court, Sebastian, FL 32958. **www.raidersailboats.com** *(561) 388-2832.*

January 2003

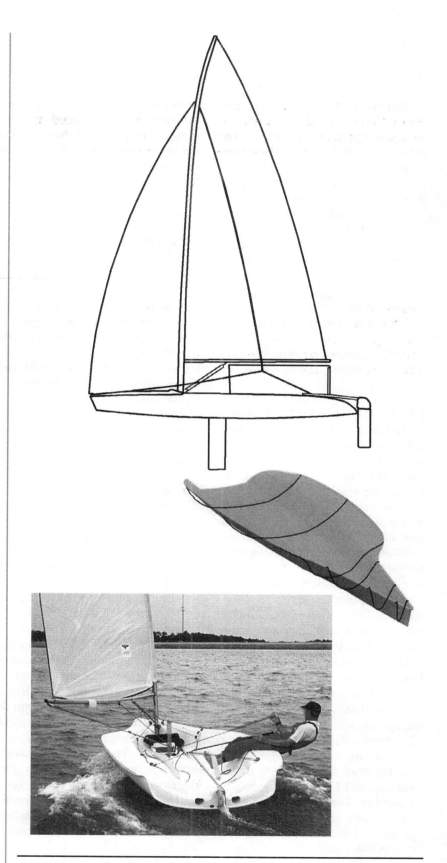

A quick boat that will have you spending more time on the water and less time in the water.

LOA 16'2"; LWL 15'11"; Beam 7'4"; Draft 3'5"; Hull Weight 200 lbs.; Sail Area 123 sq. ft.

Hobie Getaway and Fox
Family Daysailer and Multihull Speedster

Hobie's new entry-level cat, the 16-foot, 7-inch Getaway is designed by Greg Ketterman. This cat involves some crossover technology from the high performance Hobies, but is aimed more at family sailing for those of us whose sea bag doesn't include a crash helmet.

The feature of the Getaway that I first noticed was the lack of any dagger or centerboards. The old Hobie 14s and 16s didn't have boards either, but they did have asymmetrical hulls with exaggerated deadrise to provide resistance to

Of course, the Fox will not be as durable or trouble free as the Getaway, but it will be a lot quicker.

leeway. The Getaway's hulls on the other hand appear to be symmetrical, possibly the result of their roto-molded, polyethylene construction. There is a keel of a sort projecting below the canoe body of this cat, but it's minimal at best, and I think the sailor will have to rely upon the fact that he has the drag of two hulls in the water to prevent leeway. Still, there's leeway and then there's leeway. I can assure you that one sailor's view of acceptable leeway is not always what I would consider acceptable leeway. A test sail in the Getaway against a benchmark boat would help with this evaluation. I have yet to see a boat without any type of board that went to weather well enough to satisfy me. "Hey Bob it's a family daysailer, what do you care?" I care.

Wing seats are an option on the Getaway, and I think they would be a lot of fun. They make it possible to hike without straps and a trapeze apparatus. They also make for very comfortable seating for those of us who get stiff after sitting on a trampoline for two hours. You can always go one step further and rig a trapeze to go with your seats, which would then become "racks." That would allow for some serious hiking.

The rig features a boomless mainsail sheeting to a traveler on the aft crossbeam. This means that you won't do any head bumping as you discover the difference between a tack and a jibe. It also means that downwind there will be nothing to hold out the big mainsail. There is a football-shaped float at the masthead to keep the Getaway from going turtle when you capsize.

* * *

If you have been through the entry-level cat experience and you want to move into something with true performance-cat features and excitement you should look at the Nils Bunkenberg-designed 20-foot Hobie Fox. The Fox weighs a scant 29 pounds more than the 16-foot Getaway while having an additional 66 square feet of sail and the option of an asymmetrical 269-square-foot spinnaker. This is a boat designed for two big men on trapezes. In this case, crew weight equals power.

The weight difference is primarily a function of roto-molding versus the hand-laid-up sandwich/polyester construction on the Fox. Of course, the Fox will not be as durable or trouble free as the Getaway, but it will be a lot quicker.

The Fox meets the class requirements of the Formula 20 class. The unusual hull shape with the volume pushed low in the hulls is an effort to get wave-piercing performance. Flat hull sections amidships and aft will enhance the Fox's ability to plane. Note the reverse rake on the bow profile and the hard knuckle where the stem meets the bottom of the hull. The high-aspect-ratio board is well aft and uses foils developed in the F-18 Hobie Tiger.

Take a look at this rig with the big, fathead mainsail and high- aspect-ratio jib head angle of 20 degrees. If I owned one of these cats I'd name it *Don't Try This At Home.*

Hobie Cat, 4925 Oceanside Blvd., Oceanside, CA 92056. (888) 462-4321. **www.hobiecat.com**

August 2001

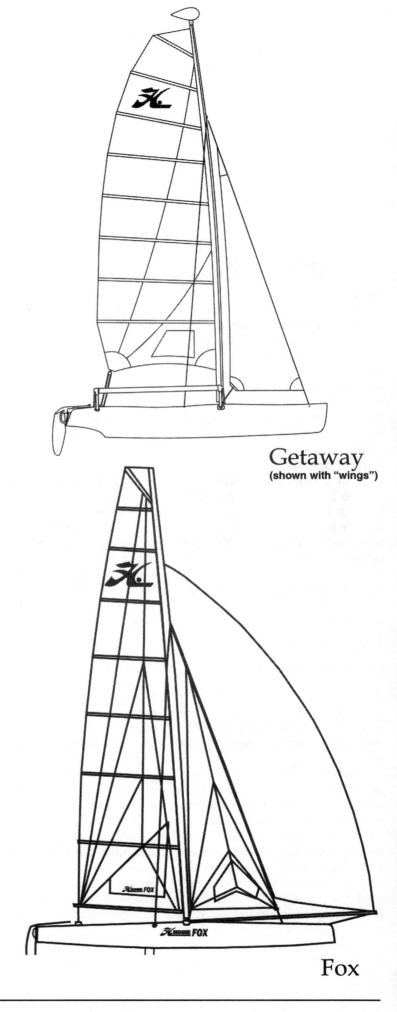

Getaway
(shown with "wings")

Fox

Durable, beginner's daysailer and a high-tech racer.

GETAWAY
LOA 16'7"; Beam 7'8"; Draft 10"; Weight 390 lbs.; Sail Area 180 sq. ft.
FOX
LOA 20'; Beam 8'6"; Draft 6" (board up), 3'9" (board down); Weight 419 lbs.; Sail Area 246 sq. ft.

Hunter 170

Family Daysailer

We have seen sensible daysailers make something of a comeback in the last five years, with a new breed that is high on comfort and stability, while sacrificing blistering planing speeds. If you live in a colder area like Seattle, with its 49-degree year-round water temperature, you will certainly appreciate a small boat you can sail without getting wet.

This is a contemporary-looking boat in keeping with the current Hunter line. I don't think it's particularly good looking. The sheer is flat and the Hunter hull-to-deck

This boat is beamy and deep enough to allow the entire centerboard to be housed below the cockpit sole.

joint with its rubber "rubbing cap" makes for a definite Clorox-bottle appearance. Still it's not bad looking either, and functionally, this boat is very well thought out. Four adults could sail it very comfortably. I'm sure you could sail with six if that's your inclination.

Designed by the Hunter factory design team, this boat is beamy and deep enough to allow the entire centerboard to be housed below the cockpit sole. This has the advantage of giving you a wide open cockpit. There is a raised, molded-in foot rest running down the centerline of the cockpit. The transom is open, allowing easy access to the kick-up rudder and the kick-down 2.5-horsepower electric motor. We could get into a lengthy discussion of auxiliary power on daysailers, but suffice it to say that there are many beginning sailors who will welcome a "no-brainer" way of getting home. I personally would not give up the

fun and challenge of handling a small boat around the docks under sail; sailing in and out of mooring situations can be valuable sailhandling training.

The open transom appeals to me because I need an easy way to haul my 55-pound dog aboard. If I leave the beach without her she'll just swim after me whimpering and snorting up salt water until I heave-to and help her up. I even had a dog cockpit installed in my sea kayak.

The rig is a simple, fractional sloop with swept spreaders. There is no mainsheet traveler and the sheeting is midboom. This is very convenient for the skipper with the tiller in one hand and the main-sheet in the other. It also cleans up the stern of the boat, making access to the open transom easier.

There is a short, about 14-inch, optional stainless tube bowsprit frame on the boat in the photos, part of an asymmetrical chute package. The jib is roller furling, and the mainsail loose footed. Assuming that crew weight is "ballast" and adding four 175-pound crewmembers to the 480-pound boat weight, I come up with an SA/D of 21.49.

There is a nifty covered bow area for gear. With the cover off, this spot would be perfect for a small child or a dog. My dog always wants to drive.

If you have been reading sailing books and magazines for a while and just waiting for the right boat to get you and your family out under sail, now's the time. Try a Hunter 170. You'll love it and you'll be able to say salty things like, "helm's a lee."

Hunter Marine, Rte. 441, Box 1030, Alachua, FL 32615. (800) 771-5556, fax (904) 462-4077. **www.huntermarine.com**

November 1999

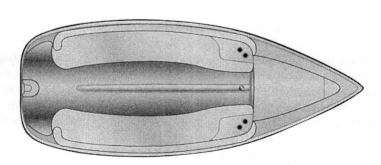

A contemporary daysailer that makes a good starter-boat.

LOA 16'10"; LWL 12'1"; Beam 7'; Draft 6" (board up), 4'6" (board down); Weight 480 lbs.; Sail Area 150 sq. ft.; SA/D 21.49 (with four 175-lb. crewmembers); Auxiliary 2.5-hp electric outboard (optional).

WindRider 17 & Walker Bay 10
Daysailer and Dinghy

WindRider 17

It's been an ongoing theme of mine over the years that you need to be trained in a sailing dinghy in order to truly hone your sailing abilities. It's one thing to blow a jibe in a 38-foot cruiser. You might crash and bang a bit and possibly break part of your traveler assembly. But when you blow a jibe in a small boat in a breeze, you are probably going to get wet, sometimes very wet.

In addition, there's a lot of fun to be had in small boats. I have had some really good sails with my 6-foot, 3-inch 220-pound body press-fit into an 8-foot El Toro dinghy.

I think you would stay pretty dry in this WindRider 17 designed by Jim Brown and the WindRider group. It certainly won't heel with those amas, so your chance of capsize has been

There's a lot of fun to be had in small boats.

greatly reduced compared to that of a monohull. This is a rotomolded boat, so it's pretty much indestructible. This makes it ideal for sailing off the beach especially if your beach is rocky like mine.

The beauty of this 17-footer is that with its trampolines between the main hull and the amas you have a lot of sitting space. You can carry four in comfort with one on each tramp. The helmsman sits aft in a dedicated helm cockpit and steers with his or her feet. Ergonomically the entire WindRider line is designed for comfort with contoured seats and big radiuses on all edges.

We'll forget about D/Ls this month, but we will examine the SA/Ds. To do this with any accuracy we better include the weight of the typical crew with the boat's displacement. A husband and wife crew on a 20,000-pound boat represents only 1.65 percent of the displacement. That same weight on the WindRider 17 will increase the displacement by

100 percent. So, with our 320-pound crew the WindRider 17 has an SA/D of 29.9, if you include the optional jib. If you add two kids to increase the total crew weight to 520 pounds, you reduce the SA/D to 24.9. There is no centerboard or daggerboard on this model, in part because these features do not easily lend themselves to rotomolding.

As for the Walker Bay 10, I already own two of the company's 8-footers. I keep one for my tender and one for my beach dink. I like these boats. They could have easily looked like garbage cans, but with their simulated lapstrakes for stiffening and springy sheers they look quite proper. A little blue tape could provide a nice cove stripe if you just followed a line half an inch above the upper "strake." These boats are injection molded, which requires very expensive tooling, but the result is a far nicer boat than most rotomolded models, while still being light and durable. I just slide mine down the rocks like a sled.

Still, two people is a crowd in my 8-footer, so Walker Bay has introduced a 10-footer that can easily take on two for sailing or three for rowing. And these boats do row well. That along with their aesthetics was their specific appeal for me.

With daggerboard, kick-up rudder and small rig the Walker Bay should sail just fine. It's no Laser, but when you are out there by yourself, speed is relative. With my 220 pounds added to the 115 pounds of the boat, the SA/D is a wee 14.4. But make no mistake, this little boat is no toy.

WindRider Sailing Trimarans, 3761 Old Glenola Rd., Trinity, NC 27370. (800) 311-7245. **www.windrider.com**

Walker Bay Boats, 607 West Ahtanum Road, Union Gap, WA 98903. **www.walkerbay.com** *(888) 449-2553.*

June 2002

Walker Bay 10

A tough, practical dinghy and a fun, stable daysailer.

WINDRIDER 17
LOA 17'; Beam 11'; Draft 1'6"; Weight 320 lbs.; Sail Area 139 sq. ft. (with jib).

WALKER BAY 10
LOA 9'8"; Beam 4'9"; Draft 2'; Weight 115 lbs.; Sail Area 43 sq. ft.

Nomad
Daysailer

When I think back to the 1960s when I began sailing in Seattle the family daysailers in the 17 to 19 foot range that come to mind are the Thistle and the Lightning. Seattle had a small Thistle fleet but a very large and active Lightning fleet partially due to the influence of the Clark family and their boatbuilding efforts.

Both were nice boats and capable of being raced by mom, dad and a kid or two. If you really wanted to go fast you sailed an International 14, but they were and remain demanding boats to sail and expensive boats to own because of the constant need to upgrade in order to stay competitive.

In my opinion the Laser dinghy changed everything—immediately the performance standard was raised. Dinghies were now expected to plane quickly and sailing and swimming were often synonymous.

In the last 10 years there have been efforts to combine modern performance with comfort and stability and this is exactly what Vanguard's Steve Clark and designer Bob Ames addressed in their new 17-footer, the Nomad.

The goals for the new dinghy were an easily driven hull with planing potential, performance sailplan with asymmetrical spinnaker, crew of three to four adults, a sense of comfort and safety, self-bailing cockpit so the boat can live on a mooring, lots of storage and the option of an outboard motor.

The hull of the Nomad features 8 feet of beam at the deck achieved with flared and flanged topsides on a hull with a nominal beam of 7 feet. BWL is moderate, 5.39 feet, for initial stability. Max beam is well aft where you will want the crew weight when you press the boat hard. The entry is fine with a half-angle of entry of 17.5 degrees. Fore and aft rocker is moderate with the chest of the boat farther aft than most other high-performance dinghies. There is a hint of deadrise throughout the bottom of the Nomad.

The deck cockpit of the Nomad is designed so you have the option of sitting in the boat with a short seatback, angled for comfort or you can sit on the rail. The rail is about 8 inches wide aft and that's enough to be comfortable when hiking.

In the last 10 years there have been efforts to combine performance with comfort and stability.

One of the more interesting aspects of this deck is that the seat level continues around the boat making a well of sorts forward of the mast. This provides good safety for kids and makes it very easy to move around on this boat. The cockpit is very clean and control lines have been routed to keep them out of the cockpit. The mainsheet is on a bridle on the transom but from there it leads through the bilge to exit at the top of the centerboard trunk.

The rig is very simple with swept spreaders and a retractable bowsprit. Rig size was chosen with an eye to make one person rigging and de-rigging easy. The jib is on a roller furler and it has been found that it's best to de-power the rig by furling the jib and sailing under main alone. The compression vang also helps keep the cockpit clear during tacks and jibes.

There is a lot of appeal to a dinghy that can be sailed as a catboat. You can get your kids started with the boat using just the main and then let them add the jib when they feel confident.

The Nomad is easily trailerable at less than 700 pounds. You don't need a Hummer to pull this one. I'd like to give this one a go.

Vanguard Sailboats, 300 Highpoint Ave., Portsmouth, RI 02871. **www.teamvanguard.com** *(800) 966-SAIL.*

July 2003

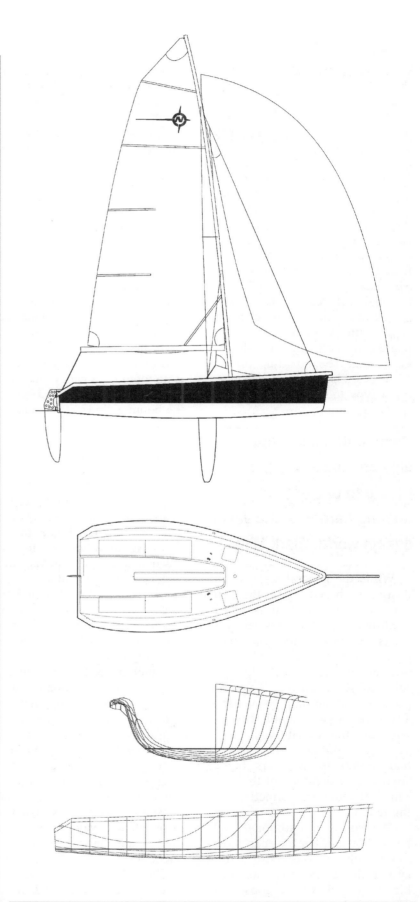

A combination of performance and stability in a family daysailer.
LOA 17'2"; Beam 8'; Draft 4'2"; Weight 665 lbs.; Sail Area 173 sq. ft.

Sun Cat
Pocket Cruiser

If you spend some time digging around in the world of yacht designers you will inevitably come across the name Clark Mills. Best known for his Windmill design, Mr. Mills also designed the Optimist pram. I'm fairly certain that there are more Optimists in the world than any other one-design class.

As you might expect, coming from the Clearwater, Florida, area, Mills' designs are very well suited to shoal-draft restrictions. This 17 foot, 4 inch catboat features a high aspect ratio, stainless steel centerboard that nestles up into a shallow keel-trunk. The board-up draft is 14 inches. The rudder is also a pivoting type to further reduce draft for gunkholing.

Owning this boat would also be a nice way to pay tribute to one of the unsung heroes of the yacht design world, Clark Mills.

While the general style of this design is based upon the Cape Cod catboat model, it is highly modified from the original type. Mills' catboat has the beam pushed forward and less beam at the transom. The bow looks quite full, but you need that if you are going to get any internal volume. The sheer is sweet and in keeping with the traditional type. It's a very good-looking boat. Catboats had plumb stems years before anyone ever dreamed of the IMS. This little boat is all effective sailing length.

The rig is a traditional gaff-headed cat rig, but the spar is outfitted with a "Mastendr" sailing system that allows the mast to be hinged just above the gooseneck. This is helpful for trailering and makes rigging and unrigging the boat very easy. The mast just lays down along the top of the long

boom and rests in a boom gallows on the transom.

The boom is midsheeted to a traveler on the bridgedeck. I'd prefer to see the traveler aft of the cockpit so you would have more of a mechanical advantage controlling the long boom. But the cam cleat and mainsheet fiddle block right on the bridge deck is very convenient. The SA/D of this boat is 18.3.

The cuddy cabin features good-size V-berths and room for a porta potty. There is a large chain locker forward, which you can access from the interior, and two opening ports to help with ventilation. There is no room for a galley, but I would think you could hang a barbecue off the boom gallows. Then again you could always dine on cold fried chicken and potato salad washed down with a crisp German Reisling Spätlese. That works for me.

I like good small cruising boats, although some small cruising boats almost fall into the toy boat category and these bother me. I see folks rigging these at my local marina and then struggling to make any headway at all to weather in our steep Puget Sound chop. Eventually they head back in, thoroughly disillusioned with sailing. You just can't do it safely in one of these toy boats.

Small boats like this Sun Cat, however, are real boats that can take you safely anywhere you choose to go. It just takes an extra measure of planning and a little more time than in a big cruiser.

If you too are attracted to the minimalist approach to sailing the Sun Cat would be a good boat to consider. Owning this boat would also be a nice way to pay tribute to one of the unsung heroes of the yacht design world, Clark Mills.

Com-Pac Yachts, 1195 Kapp Drive, Clearwater, FL 33765. **www.com-pacyachts.com** *(727) 443-4408.*

June 2000

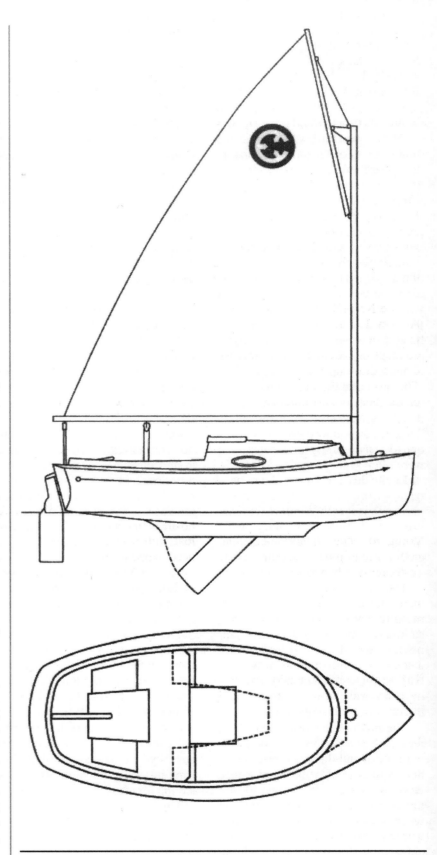

A Clark Mills design for the minimalist cruiser.

LOA 17'4"; LWL 15'; Beam 7'3"; Draft 14" (board up), 4'6 (board down); Displacement 1,500 lbs.; Ballast 300 lbs. (including centerboard and stainless steel tanks); Sail Area 150 sq. ft.; SA/D 18.3; D/L 198; L/B 2.39; Auxiliary outboard.

NorseBoat
Beach Cruiser

There's little doubt in my mind that if I told my wife we were going to take a rowing and sailing trip through the San Juan Islands in an open 17-foot, 6-inch boat she would first look at me strangely, as usual, then just ask, "When do we leave?" She's that kind of gal. She competed in freestyle skiing and was on the Wide World of Sports. She's a jock. The only problem would be that I would have to do it.

Now I need a boat, a good boat that looks salty but is modern enough to reward my hard fought physical efforts with efficient performance. This NorseBoat looks pretty good. It's a Chuck Paine design but I'll manage somehow. It is sexy looking with a sweet sheerline and a shapely bow profile. But the deal clincher is the 12-volt trolling motor snug in the deadwood area.

The NorseBoat is being built by Avalon House on Prince Edward Island in Nova Scotia. The boat is a concept of Kevin Jeffrey, who had Chuck draw up the working plans. The promo material says the weight of the boat is 200 pounds, but that sounds quite optimistic to me. I'm

Just think how smug you could feel as you blow by the bigger cruising boats.

going to need to carry a cooler, cooking equipment, ground tackle, porta-potty, a beach tent, boom tent, two sleeping bags, safety gear, navigational gear and charts, both dogs and clothes for the Northwest's ever changing climate. In the interest of saving weight I will restrict my choice of beverages to water and 151 proof rum. If I add up those weights and include the weight of the crew I get 580 pounds.

Looking at the drawings of the boat I find it hard to believe, even with glass and epoxy construction, that with battery, rig and oars it is going to weigh 200 pounds. Okay, the dogs have to stay home and I will definitely opt for the optional carbon fiber oars. I would believe that ready to go with crew you are looking at 700 pounds before you shove off. That's a lot to row even for two people. How many volts is that motor again?

But as luck would have it there is a nice light breeze blowing.

Unfortunately it's a northerly. But here is where I can be confident that Chuckles Paine has given this boat a shape and a rig that will take it to weather in a dignified and efficient manner. The rig shows a tall gaff mainsail with a carbon mast and a curved gaff. The boom is on one side of the loose-footed main. This means that one tack will be favored unless you want to fuss around with the tack and clew of the mainsail. "Prepare to fuss around." If you are reaching and it's light you can get lots of additional horsepower with the optional screecher that's set off a short bowsprit. With both sails up I'd just bear off and alter my destination so I could lay it on that reach. My hands were sore anyway from just looking at the oars. Reaching along in the NorseBoat with the screecher up would be a blast. Just think how smug you could feel as you blow by the bigger cruising boats.

In typical Northwest summer's day fashion, the wind dies just before twilight and we are left in the middle of the channel battling a 3-knot flood tide. But rowing square to the current we make it into the rocky shoreline where the tide is minimal and the scenery is maximized. As we glide into the small harbor I look longingly at the picturesque bed and breakfast house on the rocks—I imagine meatloaf with mashed potatoes. But who needs a bed when you have been rowing for two and a half hours? We're lucky to find a vacant mooring at the state park nearby and I rig a tether so I can pull the boat off the beach and leave it on the hook for the night.

Well, you get the picture. It could be fun. It's not my idea of a good time. I'm spoiled. But all you have to do is look at the number of voyaging style kayaks sold today to understand that there is a market for this type of boat. If this type of adventure appeals to you I can think of no finer boat for the job than the NorseBoat. If you have no intention of camp-cruising but you are looking for a distinct and yare daysailer I would also recommend that you consider the NorseBoat.

Avalon House, RR1 Belfast, Prince Edward Island, Canada, C0A 1A0. (902) 659-2790. **www.norseboat.com**

Under sail or oar power, a fun boat for beach camping or pillaging.
LOA 17'6"; Beam 5'2"; Draft 3'1"; Weight 200 lbs.; Sail Area 110 sq. ft.

Horizon Cat
Pocket Cruiser

I was surveying the assembled fleet at this year's Perry rendezvous and feeling pretty good when I noticed a smallish catboat setting sail and heading out of the harbor. I've always liked Cape Cod catboats. The have character to burn. They are simple and have a distinct personality that, although quirky at times, is on the whole, endearing. Surrounded by 48 somewhat plush and over-equipped Perry designs, it occurred to me that a 20-foot catboat would be close to my ideal for an "old man's" boat. That could easily be translated into a "smart man's" boat.

The Horizon cat started life as the Herreshoff America, designed by Halsey Herreshoff and built by Nowak and Williams. The Hutchins brothers of Com-Pac

I'd feel a bit shortchanged if my catboat didn't have a manly helm on a reach.

yachts bought the tooling and redesigned the boat to fit it into their family of shoal-draft cruising yachts. The hull form remained the same, but they added a shallow keel and centerboard, and modified the deck and rig. This handsome hull is made even better-looking on paper by Bruce Bingham's skillful and playful drafting. We don't hear much from Bruce these days, so it's good to see him being published once again.

Cape Cod cats were the original fatsos and you can see this in the drawings and the L/B of 2.4. These boats were keelless centerboarders, and it was this beam that gave them stability and carrying capacity.

The 8-foot, 4-inch beam and lack of overhangs coupled with a displacement of 2,500 pounds and a D/L of 200 make this a big 20-footer. This boat is no rocket, but it won't be a pig either. It will go to weather about as well as you would expect a gaff-rigged boat to point, and it will offer a stiff ride for those of you who like to sail on the flat side. I think many of you would be surprised at just how well this cat will sail. Board-up draft is 26 inches. Note the rudder is a kick-up type.

Catboat's traditionally are gaff rigged. This keeps the center of pressure low to help stability and minimizes the complexity of the standing rigging. Some cats even fly a small, high-aspect-ratio jib (a jiblet?) from the forestay. Gaff rigs are fun. The old-timers would just ease off on the peak halyard and let the gaff sag to about 90 degrees when the wind increased in what was called a "fisherman's reef." It sounds awful to me, and you can see here that this 20-footer is rigged with normal reef cringles for a single, traditional reef.

One quirk of catboats is that the weather helm can be a bit sporty from time to time. But the aft location of this centerboard should help keep this cat well balanced. Also, I'd feel a bit shortchanged if my catboat didn't have a manly helm on a reach. It's just part of the fun of sailing a catboat.

Below you have two berths and a forward compartment for a porta potty. I suppose you could put an Origo alcohol stove on one counter in the main cabin. Or, maybe you could just cook on a grill or camp stove in the cockpit.

Four can sit in this cockpit in comfort. There is wheel steering shown on my drawings, but I would prefer a tiller—all the better to experience that helm. Actually the wheel is probably more traditional and a lot more convenient. Boom gallows hold the boom when the sail is lowered and make the boom the ideal ridge pole for a cockpit tent while cruising.

Does your boat have big battery banks, gensets, air conditioners, invertors, refrigeration and all that, that . . . *stuff* people insist on hanging off their stern pulpit-arch-thing? Well, you can't have that on a Horizon Cat. Thirty-five miles will be a darn good day's run in this cat. And what's wrong with that?

Com-Pac builds nice boats. They always have a sparkle to them and show excellent detailing. If you have outgrown your big boat or you want to return to the simple joys of carefree cruising, you might take a hard look at this stylish little hooker.
Com-Pac Yachts, 1195 Kapp Dr., Clearwater, FL 33765. (727) 443-4408. **www.com-pacyachts.com**

October 2002

Carrying on the catboat tradition in a smart new design.

LOA 20'; LWL 17'9"; Beam 8'4"; Draft 26" (board up), 5' (board down); Displacement 2,500 lbs.; Ballast 600 lbs.; Sail Area 195 sq. ft.; SA/D 16.9; D/L 200; L/B 2.4; Auxiliary 9.6-hp outboard or Westerbeke 7-hp diesel; Fuel 7 gals.; Water 10 gals.

Arey's Pond 18
Daysailer

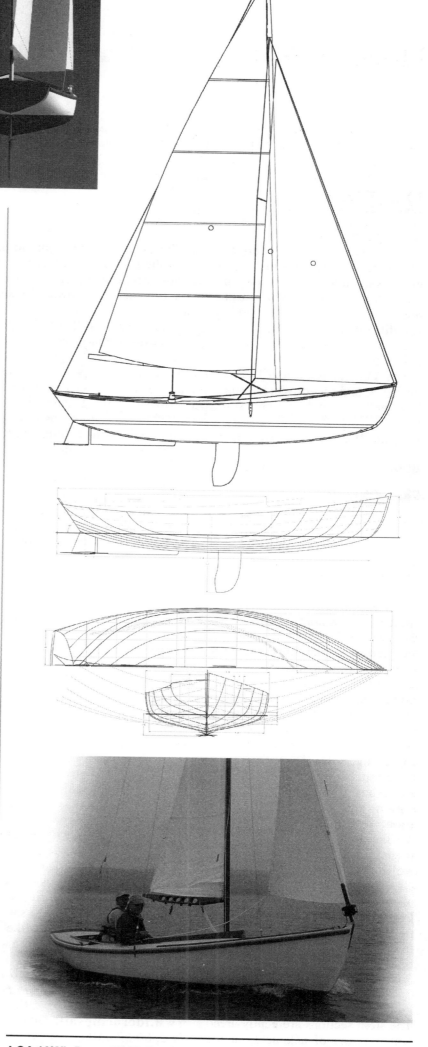

Tony Dias' work is always fun to look at. He has a good eye and his wonderful drawings have always shown an interesting style of presentation. This daysailer was designed for Arey's Pond Boat Yard in Cape Cod. Arey's Pond is best known for its traditional catboats and there is no boat more associated with Cape Cod than the catboat. But this time Tony Davis of Arey's Pond wanted a sloop. If you want to research the history of this type of boat I suggest you find a copy of Howard Chapelle's **American Small Sailing Craft**. It's chock full of beautiful traditional types and it's not much of a stretch to see the origins of Mr. Dias' boat there in several models.

This 18-footer has a high prismatic of .56 coupled with a moderately steep deadrise sectional shape. There is a relatively firm turn to the bilge and this shape should give the boat

One of the nice things about building a small boat is that you have the luxury of trying different appendage design features economically.

good form stability. The lines plan shows that volume has been pushed into the after sections to make the boat more forgiving to varying crew weights and positions.

I can't imagine you have ever heard me say that a boat had too much sheer spring but I think Mr. Dias is pushing the limits with this one. It looks OK on the drawings but in the photos where you have people for scale it looks exaggerated.

The deadrise aft makes for a very pretty transom shape. There is a centerboard that reduces draft from 3 feet, 2 inches to 13 inches. To help with reduced draft performance the rudder is a partially balanced blade with odd scythe-like endplates. Forward of the rudder there is a long skeg but it stops short of the rudder's leading edge, which has some bal-

ance area to it. It's an unusual arrangement and I'm not too keen on that long skeg unless it's there to help the boat sit on the mud at low tide. One of the nice things about building a small boat is that you have the luxury of trying different appendage design features economically. It will be interesting to see if this rudder arrangement stays or eventually morphs into something more conventional. For now it's sure fun to see a designer try something different.

There's not much to say about this rig. The sailplan shows a handsome boat with a perky sheer and low freeboard. While the amount of sheer may be too much for my particular eye I like the way Mr. Dias has sprung his batten. Note how the sheer kicks up at the stern. Too many designers let the sheer just drop off toward the stern. I like the way this rig sits on the boat. It just looks right to my eye.

I'm often asked what the best boat is for a beginner. The answer is always the same, a small boat. I think any boat that is unballasted (my spell-check wants "unblessed") and can capsize will teach you faster than a ballasted boat. The lessons you learn that teach you how to keep a small boat on its feet and under control in heavy going will serve you well in larger boats. Also, the tricks you need to learn to make a small boat go in light air can also be transferred to the larger boat later. Small adjustments to sail trim and weight distribution will be immediately rewarded or punished and you should know immediately if you are doing something wrong. I think this is important.

The Arey's Pond daysailer is a smart looking boat that will find advocates among the lovers of traditional looking small craft.

Arey's Pond Boat Yard, P.O. Box 222, South Orleans, MA 02662. **www.areyspondboatyard.com** *(508) 255-0994.*

LOA 18'8"; Beam 6'11"; Draft 13" (board up), 3'2" (board down); Weight 1,560 lbs.; Sail Area 206.5 sq. ft.

RS K6

One-design

If you were never comfortable in the water or your idea of a good sail doesn't include the individual medley, you might prefer a dinghy with the added stability of a ballasted keel. You could argue that the addition of a ballasted keel takes the K6 out of the dinghy category, and I would probably agree—dinghies don't have ballast; dinghies don't sink.

I really like the idea of a fast and nimble boat that won't capsize.

Still, the K6 is an interesting hybrid. I think it falls into the category of a small sport boat: not quite a regulation keelboat, but certainly not a dinghy. The K6 is designed for a crew weight limit of 440 pounds. That means you can sail with two heavyweights or a crew of three averaging 147 pounds each.

The hull is very sexy looking. The LOA is 19 feet and the all-up weight is 572 pounds. Beam is only 6 feet, 6 inches. As a point of reference, the venerable Lightning, Olin Stephens' daysailer/one-design, first built in 1938, has almost the exact same length and beam, but weighs about 130 pounds more, despite the fact that it's a centerboarder. It gives you an idea of how far we've come in terms of materials. The K6 has 210 square feet of working sail compared to the Lightning's 177 square feet, a function of the K6's ballast-cum-lower-center-of-gravity. It would be interesting to sail the two boats side by side.

The bow of the K6 is fine, with a hint of hollow right at the cutwater. The stern sections are gently arced with no sign of a knuckle at the waterline. The lifting keel shows a curved leading edge and a straight

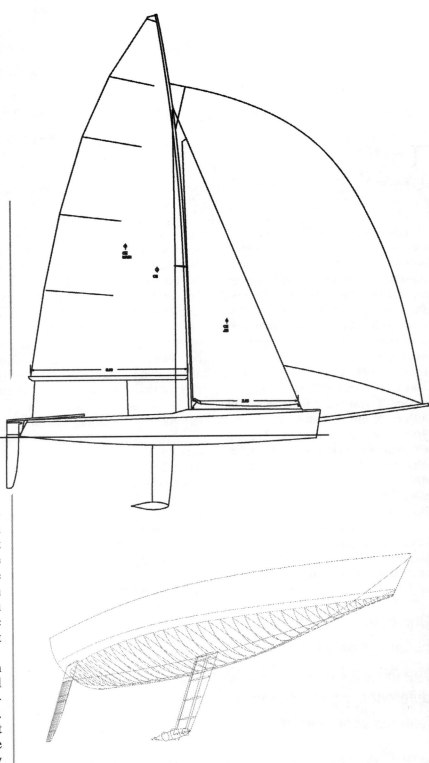

trailing edge. The bulb fairs to the fin at the nose and comprises nearly 50 percent of the displacement. You can raise and lower the keel while you are sailing.

It seems that all these high performance boats use the same promotional jargon: "high stability, low drag" is universal in these types. I'm also surprised the K6 doesn't have a name starting with "V." How about the "Vampire" or in keeping with the times, the "Vegetarian?"

The brochure promises "low sheet loads" for the K6. I know from my own designing experiences that in small boats you reach a point where you don't really need winches for the sheets, but it would sure be nice to have them. With the addition of winches, however, you increase not only the ergonomic challenges, but also the weight and the cost.

The K6 has a powerful rig with a 310-square-foot asymmetrical chute (compared to a 300-square-foot spinnaker on the Lightning). And it's not just the sail area that you are dealing with here, since the K6 has the stability to carry sail in heavier conditions, which will further increase sheet loads. The asymmetrical chute is launched through a tube in the bow. The mast is carbon fiber. The jib is self-tacking with a furling drum located below the deck.

I really like the idea of a fast and nimble boat that won't capsize. The K6 seems to fit the bill perfectly. I would have to sail the boat first to see if it felt like too much of a handful in terms of controlling the sails.

RS Racing Sailboats, Trafalgar Close, Chandlers Ford, Eastleigh, Hants S0 53 4BW, UK. **www.ldcracingsailboats.co.uk** *44 2380 27 4500.*

June 2001

Dinghy-keelboat hybrid may offer the best of both worlds.

LOA 19'; Beam 6'6"; All-up weight 572 lbs.; Ballast 265 lbs.; Sail Area 210 sq. ft. (working sail), 310 sq. ft. (spinnaker).

T590
One-design

My Mum was a Kiwi and so is this new dinghy, called the T590 and designed by the notable New Zealand naval architect Steve Thompson. Steve designs a lot of very fast boats and created this one with his own needs in mind. The aim was to separate the thrills from the fear of sailing a fast boat.

Now here is where we get on thin ice. Is it a dinghy when it has a ballast keel? The T590 has a nifty, whalelike bulb at the bottom of its lifting fin. This bulb weighs 290 pounds and is pinned to the fin so it can be easily removed for shipping. Technically speaking, I think the fact that this boat is ballasted takes it

> **The unusual hull form is capped by an unusual rig, for there is no jib on this boat.**

out of the dinghy category. But for all intents and purposes this is a dinghy. The 19-foot LOA and 780-pound all-up weight also make this one push hard against the dinghy categorization. The benefit of the ballasted keel is that the T590 is self-righting. It's also unsinkable, with two buoyancy tanks in the bow.

This is an unusual boat starting with the hull form. Rather than orient this boat toward planing performance, Steve designed a hull that would be happy going to weather. This means the stern is a little narrower than you would find on most planing dinghies, while the topsides flare amidships to little wings to aid hiking. This gives the boat a pumpkin-seed-shaped hull form with the wings hiding a deceptively narrow BWL and a very fine bow for piercing a chop. I had a boat like this once, a Wylie Wabbit, and it was an incredibly wet boat to sail at high speeds. It

was like someone had a fire hose on you. The wings on the T590 prevent the bow wave from spraying up into the crew's face.

There is quite a marked arc to the sections at the stern as opposed to flatter planing-type sections. The keel is retractable for shipping and is left down once the boat is in the water. There isn't a lot of form stability to this design.

The unusual hull form is capped by an unusual rig, for there is no jib on this boat. In fact, it's a bit like the X3. There's a big main, without the extended fat-head-type upper roach, and an asymmetrical chute or gennaker that flies from a retractable bowsprit, which is about 5 feet long. The gennaker is launched from a tunnel in the bow with an endless halyard so it can be easily raised and doused. The same line that raises the chute hauls it back down into the tunnel. According to the designer it was a cost issue to go with the single-spreader mast. An all-carbon mast could have avoided the spreaders, but it was too expensive. The SA/D is 38.7 with main alone and over 100 when you add the gennaker. I did not include crew weight as this boat is ballasted. The T590 is built in E-glass and epoxy.

I have no trouble envisioning the 590 sitting on my buoy. This boat would be easy to singlehand in our light Pacific Northwest winds. My aesthetic inclinations would lean toward a Herreshoff 12½, but my performance expectations would draw me to the T590. I think I would rather scoot along looking ordinary than sit glued to one spot looking good. Come to think about it, just going fast is a pretty sight in itself. I'll take the T590.

Tboat, P.O. Box 34540, Birkenhead, Aukland, New Zealand. 649 419 6032. **www.tboat.com**

June 2002

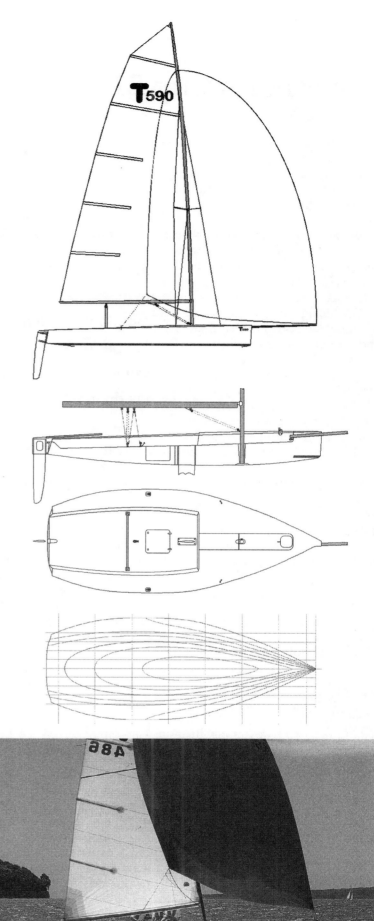

Unconventional speed machine from New Zealand.

LOA 19'; LWL 17'; Beam 7'5"; Draft 5'2"; Weight 780 lbs.; Bulb weight 290 lbs.; Sail Area 205 sq. ft. (main only), 588 sq. ft. (main and spinnaker).

Governor's Cup 21
One-Design

It's always great to get an Alan Andrews design to review. Alan works down in Long Beach, California, just down Pacific Coast Highway from Hermosa Beach where I like to shop for shirts at Jack's Surf Shop then grab a burger at the In and Out Burger joint. Alan and his small crew quietly turn out exciting performance-oriented boats.

This design was commissioned by the Newport Balboa Sailing and Seamanship Association and is intended not as a trainer but as a sprightly little keelboat for match- and fleet-racing events. That's a broad set of parameters but Alan produced a design that appears to be a mini version of the world's hottest offshore monohulls. Maybe much of this involves aesthetics but it's important to produce a boat that performs and in every way looks current, and Alan has done this.

The goal was a good course-racing boat. Light air speed was paramount, but blinding off-the-wind speeds were not. Light air speed is handled by a medium-light boat with low wetted surface and a big rig. Bow waterlines are straight with no hollow and the topsides are flared. BWL is moderately narrow. The D/L is 120 and L/B is 2.59. At this LOA you need the beam for stability and sail carrying power. The hull rocker shows a flattening amidships but this is to compensate for the keel volume. The run kicks up enough to prevent dragging the transom in less than 3 knots. The keel trailing edge is vertical but there is a hint of taper added by the slight sweep of the leading edge.

When I first saw this boat I questioned the cute cuddy cabin. I thought just maybe the boat would have been better with a longer cockpit as the cabin is not big enough to offer much of anything other than stowage space. So I called Alan and said, "What's with the cuddy?" I was quickly informed that the cuddy was important for a variety of pragmatic reasons, not the least being the room it afforded for getting "into" the boat to attach hardware, tighten keel bolts, bond the mast bulkhead, etc. The small cuddy also offers some protection for a hypothermic crewmember, Alan insisted. Whatever my objections and whatever Alan's reasons it was clear that he had given the cuddy a lot of thought, so I think it's best we give him the benefit of

Maybe much of this involves aesthetics but it's important to produce a boat that performs and in every way looks current, and Alan has done this.

the doubt on this one. I like its looks. It adds interest to the profile of the boat. The racing crew will be three or four people.

The rig is a single swept spreader type with masthead, symmetrical chute. The mainsail is loose-footed and the roach overlaps the backstay by about 12 inches. The mainsheet traveler is mounted on the cockpit sole within easy reach of the helmsman. Chainplates are outboard as the jib sheets inboard of the chainplates with minimal overlap. The SA/D is 26.26.

Another interesting connection I have with this project is that the builder is Leif Beiley of Bravura Yachts in Costa Mesa. Leif is a designer and builder and is responsible for the Bravura 29, B-25 and B-32 boats. Leif and I go way back to the early 1970s when I began designing for Islander Yachts. It was Leif's job to take my "funny papers" and turn them into shop-working drawings. Leif's experience with small, fast boats makes him the ideal builder for this new boat.

The Governor's Cup 21 is not an ultralight, one-way, hold-on, planing rocket. It's a medium-light boat designed to be fast all the way around the course in light to medium air. This boat should find fans in all race areas. It would also make a fabulous family daysailer.

Alan Andrews Yacht Design, 259 Marina Drive, Long Beach, CA 90803. (562) 594-9189. e-mail andrewsyacht@compuserve.com.

October 2003

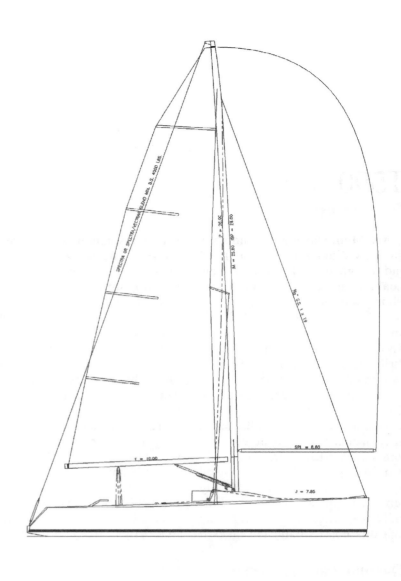

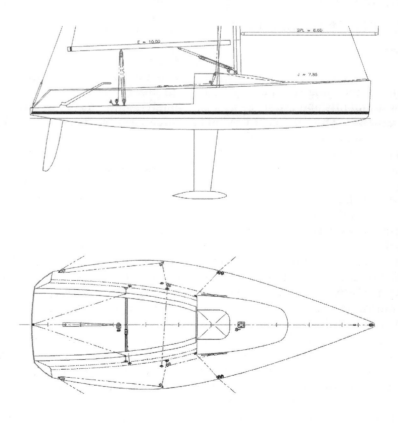

A competitive course racer with the looks of an offshore speedster.

LOA 21'; LWL 18'5"; Beam 8'1"; Draft 5'; Displacement 1,670 lbs.; Ballast 650 lbs.; Sail Area 326 sq. ft.; SA/D 26.26; D/L 120; L/B 2.59.

Hunter 216
Family Daysailer

Hunter went to Glen Henderson for the design of its new family daysailer. Glen is known for his fast sport boats. The key to this design is its lifting keel. The keel is lead and is raised with a hydraulic ram that is recessed into the cockpit sole. The keel up draft is a scant 12 inches, while the keel down draft is still only 3 feet, 6 inches. The keel shows a squatty plan form, but I suspect this was done to keep the VCG of the lead as low as possible. The rudder is what we call in my office a "cassette" type—the brochure calls it a "VARA" type. This lifting rudder detail has been around for years and involves an oversized bearing cylinder with a diameter sufficient to capture the entire chord length of the rudder foil. The parallel-sided rudder profile allows the

> **This freeboard does allow the cockpit to be deep, so you get the feeling you are 'in' the boat rather than 'on' the boat.**

rudder to pull up vertically through this large bearing when you want to reduce draft or trailer the boat.

The D/L is 85 and the L/B is 2.71, so we can safely consider this design beamy. This will help with initial stability and cockpit volume. Overhangs are basically nonexistent. The sheer is flat and freeboard is generous and looks too high to me despite the careful attempt at lowering the visual freeboard with stripes. But this freeboard does allow the cockpit to be deep, so you get the feeling you are "in" the boat rather than "on" the boat. There is "1,500 pounds of positive flotation." I don't know what that means. I suspect it means a total of 1,500 pounds of flotation to float the hull, at 1,250 pounds, plus a crewmember. Sometimes specs like this need elaboration.

The cuddy cabin (my spell-check always wants to change this to cruddy cabin) is sufficient for a couple of berths, a portable head and some stowage space. I don't think many people would take this boat cruising, but you could. With a boom tent for sun and rain you'd be set, and with the variable draft feature you could gunk some shallow holes in this boat. You would certainly have access to the anchoring spots the bigger boats couldn't reach.

The rig is a simple sloop with a hinged mast for trailering and getting under low bridges. Without any crew weight the SA/D for this boat is high at 34.75 but I suspect strongly that this sail area of 252 square feet includes the roach of the mainsail and all the area of the jib and not just the fore triangle. That throws this figure off but I think the rig is plenty big for some fun sailing.

Hunter Marine, Route 441, P.O. Box 1030, Alachua, FL 32615. **www.huntermarine.com**, *(800) 771-5556.*

November 2003

A fun daysailer capable of some serious gunkholing.

LOA 21'6"; LWL 18'9"; Beam 7'11"; Draft 1' (board up), 3'6" (board down); Weight 1,250 lbs.; Sail Area 252 sq. ft.; SA/D 34.75; D/L 85; L/B 2.71

Capri 22
Daysailer

If we move a notch or two down in our performance expectations and a notch or two up in terms of comfort we would come out right at the new Capri 22 by Catalina. Designed by the in-house Catalina team, the new 22 replaces the old Capri 22. The changes are significant. This is not one of those cosmetic redesign jobs. This boat is new from the hull on up.

Addressing comfort first, the Capri has a head. Yes-sir-ee that old Wayside Chapel can come in handy sometimes, especially if you don't have the Kevlar blad-

The clean almost classic good looks of this 22-footer will keep it looking fresh and handsome for years to come.

der of a 19-year-old. This head is not enclosed, but tucked between the V-berths. You can pull a curtain for privacy if you need it.

The Capri also offers the advantage of having berths. This is not exactly what I would call a cruising layout, but with some careful packing and stowage, a family of four could cruise this boat. Even better, a couple of teenagers could throw their gear on the V-berths and sleep aft and cruise in enough comfort to keep them happy.

This is a true keel boat with a D/L of 123. You can have your choice of standard fin keel with 700 pounds of lead, or the wing keel with 650 pounds of lead. Draft with the fin keel is 4 feet and with the wing 2 feet, 8 inches. I can't imagine sailing a boat with 2 feet, 8 inches of draft, and I hope I never get the chance to try it. Beam is 8 feet, 2 inches for ease of trailering.

The changes over the previous model include a more pronounced knuckle at the forefoot, a finer bow, more beam aft, a new rudder planform and much

less rocker. In short, the new 22's hull looks much more modern in its overall shape. I wonder which would be the faster boat if the boats were equipped identically. I know on paper the new version should outsail the older version. But strange things can happen in the wonderful world of yacht design. The numbers are virtually identical. The new keel is smaller in wetted surface, and the rudder is deeper. I'm sure the additional 2 inches of beam on the new model is only at the deck.

The cabintrunk has been redesigned too. The new cabintrunk is sleeker and less angular than the original. I like the long cockpit of this design. This cockpit is as big or at least as long as many you will find on boats over 28 feet. I could comfortably lay down on these cockpit seats.

The rig is the same as the old 22. Okay, they did change to an angled halyard exit block for a better fairlead on the new 22. Comparing the two drawings, old and new, I do see some changes, but they are not reflected in the spec sheet. The SA/D is 21.66. The new rig has a taller "I" dimension and either a shorter "E" dimension or a different traveler placement. The boom also looks lower on the new 22.

I have always been a fan of the Catalina line. Maybe it's because I'm a West Coast guy, but there is something I relate to in the general design focus of the Catalinas. I once owned a Catalina 27 and was quite happy with it. I taught my wife to sail in that boat. I applaud Catalina for not following the herd down the Euro styling path or is it the path of "Eurine." The clean almost classic good looks of this 22-footer will keep it looking fresh and handsome for years to come.

Catalina Yachts, 21200 Victory Blvd., Woodland Hills, CA 91367. **www.catalinayachts.com** *(818) 884-7700.*

June 2001

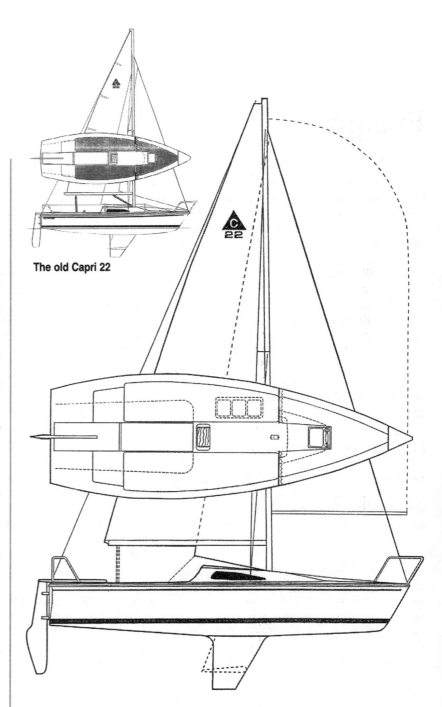

The old Capri 22

Catalina modernizes a daysailing classic.

LOA 22'; LWL 20'; Beam 8'2"; Draft 4' (fin keel), 2'8" (wing keel); Displacement 2,200 lbs. (fin keel), 2,250 lbs. (wing keel); Ballast 650 lbs. (fin keel), 700 lbs. (wing keel); Sail Area 229 sq. ft. (standard rig), 250 sq. ft. (tall rig); SA/D 21.66 (standard rig/fin keel); D/L 123 (fin keel), 125 (wing keel); L/B 2.69.

Ensign
One-design

In 1962 Carl Alberg designed the Ensign as a family daysailer and one-design racer. The Ensign design was a development of a previous Alberg design called the Electra, which had larger accommodations but a smaller cockpit.

If you are not familiar with Carl Alberg I can tell you that he distinguished himself as the designer of capable and fast boats back in the days when the line between racer and cruiser was not so distinctly drawn. The conventional-looking Alberg 35 is today sought after as a tough cruising boat. In 1963, how-

I used to fantasize about sending my two boys off to go cruising on a boat like this.

ever, many races were won in Alberg 35s. Alberg was not a very adventurous designer. His boats all tend to look the same, i.e., flat sheers, cutaway full keels, long overhangs and slablike topsides with firm bilges.

With 1,776 Ensigns built by Pearson between 1962 and 1983, interest in the boat waned and production was stopped. But as the market filled up with daysailers that required life jackets and crash helmets, the search for a safe and sane daysailer resulted in renewed interest in the Ensign. Today there are 45 active fleets in the United States.

In 1995 Zeke Durica of Dunedin, Florida, set up a shop, Ensign Spars Inc., to supply replacement parts to the aging fleet of Ensigns. This led to the purchase of the original molds and, this past year, the taking of orders for new Ensigns. The new Classic Ensigns began at hull number 2,000 and are available on a semicustom basis. Two are currently in the water with numbers three and four on the way.

If you wonder what has made the Ensign such a durable design I would have to say it boils down to that big, deep cockpit, the generous displacement and the stiffness of the boat in terms of stability. This stiffness comes from a hull shape with a wide BWL, a firm turn to the

bilge and 1,200 pounds of internal lead ballast. That's a ballast-to-displacement ratio of 40 percent. Interestingly, the original construction drawing from 1962 calls for 2,000 pounds of ballast.

The long overhangs are an artifact of the old CCA rule where a boat's sailing length was approximated by a waterline taken 7-percent of beam above the DWL. This rule produced short DWLs with the justification that once a boat heels over its sailing length is increased. Well, in some cases maybe. Nonetheless this was once the look du jour and pretty much reigned until the IMS reintroduced short ends and longer DWLs. The D/L of the Ensign is 213.

Take a look at that keel. It sure is long, but if you go back a few decades and look at 12-meters like *Vim* and *Columbia* you will see a family resemblance, although the Ensign keel is proportionally much longer.

The original drawings show a head nestled between the V-berths. If you do go cruising in your Ensign you will have to cook in the cockpit. You might also want to consider the optional doors for the cuddy cabin. (my computer's spell check always wants that to be "cruddy cabin"). There is enough room below to put a small table between the berths. But I'm not sure there is sufficient sitting headroom to make the table useful. I suspect not. Oh well, a toasted cheese sandwich and a bowl of tomato soup can be cradled in your lap easily. If the rain you can hope for an invite over to the Swan 65 anchored nearby.

I used to fantasize about sending my two boys off to go cruising on a boat like this. Now they just tell me, "We're taking the boat out, Dad," and there goes my boat. I couldn't be more proud. I think proper seamanship is best learned when you reduce the mechanical-electrical variables.

I wish Zeke the best of luck with his new Classic Ensign.

Ensign Spars Inc., 736 Scotland St., Dunedin, FL 34698. (727) 734-1837. **www.ensignspars.com**

October 2001

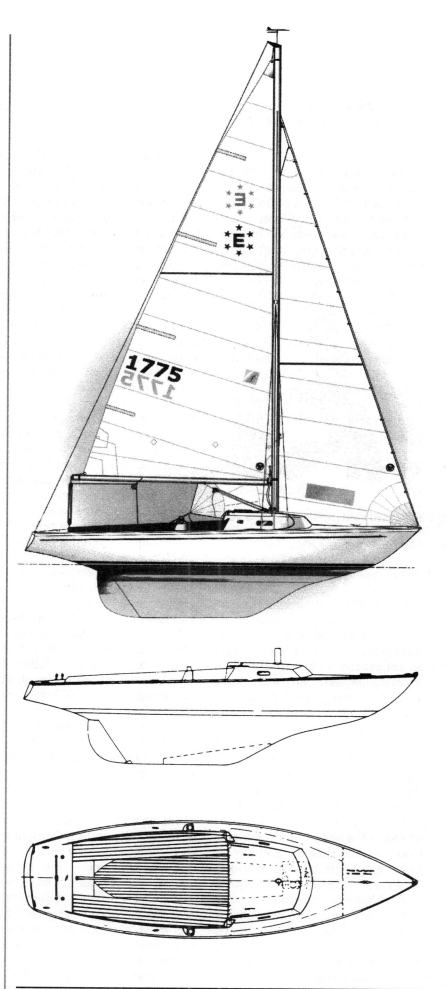

This classic Pearson is back in production after an 18-year hiatus.

LOA 22'6"; LWL 16'9"; Beam 7'; Draft 3'; Displacement 3,000 lbs.; Ballast 1,200 lbs.; Sail Area 201 sq. ft.; SA/D 15.4; D/L 213; L/B 3.21.

Blue Heron 23
Daysailer

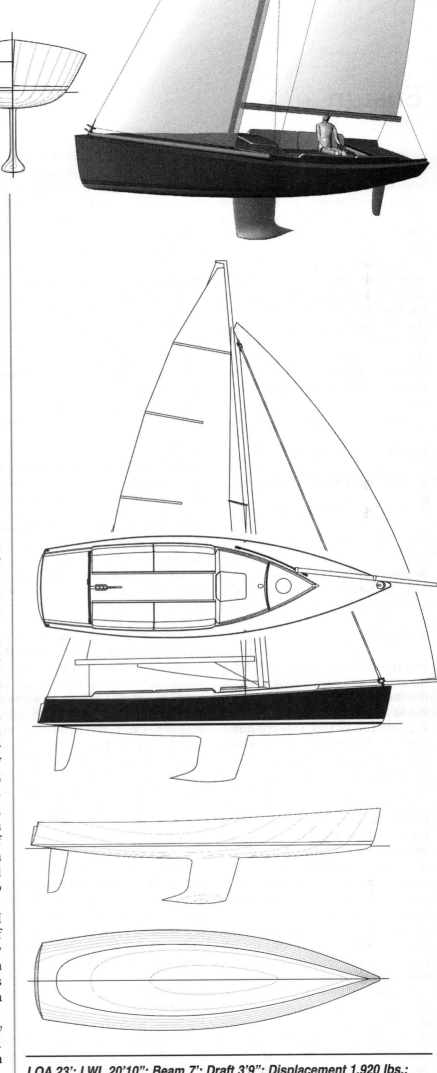

I think this is our first look at a Paul Coffin design and I like it. Here's a boat that pays attention to modern design concepts while still managing to have what I would call traditional good looks. OK, we can go on and on about how beautiful long overhangs are, but they don't work. If you buy into the "give me everything and make it fast in light air and fast in heavy" you are going to need DWL. Granted some of you

The boat was designed around the cockpit to ensure comfortable family daysailing.

don't need boat speed and would gladly sacrifice a knot for a romantic and nostalgic look, but I look back at the legions of traditional types that had short overhangs and I have no trouble at all seeing beauty in the short ended boats of today. Keep in mind that the original long-ended yachts were products of rating rules that penalized DWL. It's almost ironic that the inspiration for this design came from the old Herreshoff 12 1/2.

At 23 feet LOA this is a moderate-shaped boat with an L/B of 3.28. The sections show a narrow BWL with no hollow at the entry. Angle of entry is 15 degrees. There is a slight V to the most forward sections but this fares out quickly to a shape that goes tangent at centerline. I hesitate to call this a flat bottom because it's really not flat anywhere. There is just no "crease" or corner at centerline. The keel shows a lot of planform. I probably would have gone with less area in the fin, saved some weight and added it to the bulb. Draft is only 3 feet, 9 inches and the designer says a centerboard model will be added to the line once production is underway.

The boat was designed around

the cockpit to ensure comfortable family daysailing. The seat benches are eight feet long and artfully designed with toe space below them and high seat backs for comfort and security. The cockpit sole area below the seats is angled and will provide a near level place for footing when the boat is heeled. The wood extension of the seat back will extend about eight inches above the deck, giving the boat a traditional look. This wood rail detail extends forward of the mast where it terminates in a sharp "breakwater-like" shape. There is a track for a self-tacking jib on the forward edge of the cuddy cabin-top. There is a small deck area aft where kids can sit while underway. The tiller emerges from under this deck. The mainsheet traveler is on the forward edge of this aft deck. There is room in the cuddy cabin for a porta-potti and a small V-berth. This is a very well thought out deck design.

The sailplan shows a simple single spreader rig with swept spreaders and a standing backstay. The clew of the jib is kept as low as possible. I know I said I was going to ignore SA/Ds this month but let's take a look at this one assuming a family is out for a day on the bay. Our family of four weighs a cumulative 556 pounds. This brings total displacement up to 2,476 pounds, and if we use the actual sail area for main and jib we get a SA/D of 22.47. So if we discount the area of mainsail roach we would still be around 20, and that's plenty to keep the family grinning.

I look at some of the boats I review and I can't see myself enjoying them even though they may be wonderful designs. I can see myself really enjoying this boat, but I'd have to go with a custom 7-foot keel.

C Design, 13113 Brandon Way Rd., Gaithersburg, MD 20878. **www.blueheronyachts.com** *(301) 926-1755.*

June 2004

LOA 23'; LWL 20'10"; Beam 7'; Draft 3'9"; Displacement 1,920 lbs.; Ballast 1,000 lbs.; Sail Area 257 sq. ft.; SA/D 26.6; D/L 94.8; L/B 3.28.

Yarmouth 23
Pocket Cruiser

The Yarmouth is right out of the 10-year-old boy's (me) daydream. With any luck at all you can prevent the world from beating that dream out of you, and while my eyes may be blackened, at 55 I can still see the appeal of this type of boat. If cruising involves style points, you have to give the Yarmouth the advantage.

Built by The Yarmouth Boat Company in Yarmouth on the Isle of Wight, this little gaffer was

This boat will be at its best receiving admiring glances from the rest of us.

designed by the Wyatt and Freeman office to be a modern antique and is available either complete or in kit form.

This hull has what you would call a raised sheer. Note how the sheerline aft rises to the aft end of the cabintrunk where it continues to the bow. This provides volume below and looks quite good. There is a deep well-deck forward and a narrow, straight-line trunk, which adds headroom to what is almost a flush-deck design. Note how your eye picks up the rubrail as the visual sheer of the boat. Photos of the boat show some awkward aesthetic points in this design as fiberglass construction meets traditional detailing. But from a cost perspective, these are very hard to avoid. All in all I find this a handsome vessel.

Let's do away with the performance question right off. With a full keel and a draft of less than 35 inches I think we can assume that this boat will not be at its best on the wind. Actually, with a D/L of 429 and an SA/D of 15.42 (including topsail) the Yarmouth will not be at its best off the wind either. Performance, however, should not be an issue with this boat. This boat will be at its best receiving admir-

ing glances from the rest of us.

The layout features an enclosed head aft with a corner-mounted wash basin. On the starboard side there is a nice galley with a two-burner gas stove, a sink and some small lockers. There is even what appears to be an icebox outboard of the stove, although it must be very small. As I said earlier, on my boat I'm in favor of using a cooler, which I stow on the quarter berth. I like being able to take it home to load it and clean it. This way I also avoid having stinky water drain into my pristine, dry bilge. I don't pump my bilge, I vacuum it.

The settees on the 23 appear too short, but in fact they extend through the forward bulkhead and under the V-berths so that they are full length for sleeping. The drawings show V-berths dimensioned at 5 feet, 6 inches when measured parallel to centerline. If we measure the length of the V-berth down the center of the angled berth we get about 5 feet, 9 inches, which is not long enough. This is a thoughtful interior (sans wet locker), but I would be very uncomfortable trying to sleep on a 5 foot, 9 inch berth. I'm also not especially keen on sticking my feet into a hole in the bulkhead. It would be like sleeping in stocks. Still, it's cozy. Cozy is a good for cruising boats in the Pacific Northwest.

Sailing the Yarmouth would be a lot of fun. If the enjoyment you get out of sailing is in direct proportion to the number of strings you have to pull this is the boat for you. It takes a throat halyard and a peak halyard just to get that gaff up and peaked at the right angle. Now add mainsail sheet, jib sheets and flying jib-sheets, and you have a lot of fine adjustments you can play with.

The Yarmouth Boat Company Ltd., Saltern Wood Quay, Yarmouth, Isle of Wight, PO41 OSE, England. 44 1983 760521. **www. yarmouth23.com**

October 2001

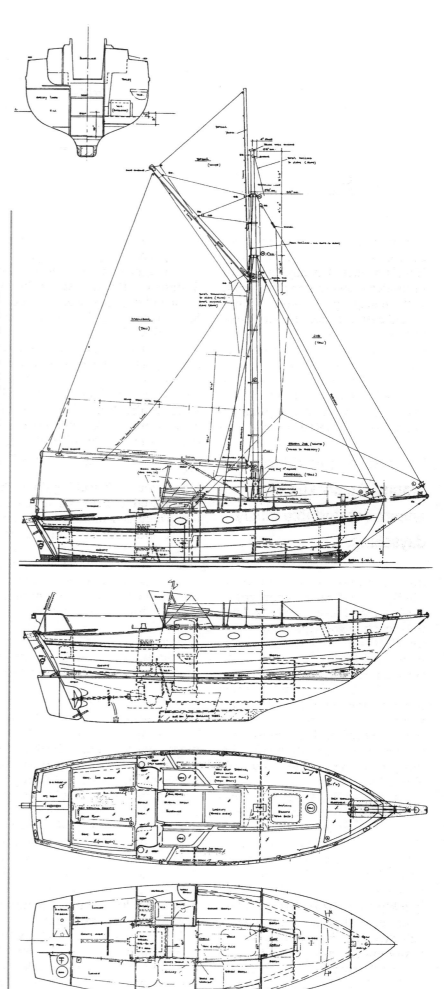

A modern "antique" with panache to spare.

LOA 23'; LWL 18'; Beam 7'6"; Draft 2'11"; Displacement 5,588 lbs.; Ballast 2,000 lbs.; Sail Area 304 sq. ft. (including topsail); SA/D 15.42; D/L 429; L/B 3.06; Auxiliary 13.5-hp diesel; Fuel 11 gals.; Water 20 gals.

CRUISING DESIGNS

Eastsail 25
Bluewater Cruiser

Maybe Frers and Holland are not right for Mozart. I hate to see Mozart reduced to the level of mortals. Frers and Holland have had it too professionally easy. We need some torment here. Mozart struggled his whole life to find patrons. He changed his music to suit the area he was in and did his best to find even moderate financial success.

The Eastsail yard is a little bit like this. As a builder, it has a vision of the type of boat it wants to build. Now the trick is to find buyers who want that type of boat. The little cabintrunk Offshore 25 model has not taken off like the company would have liked so it has modified it into this "all-weather" model with pilothouse.

Look at the sailplan. This is a strong sheerline.

While this little sloop isn't exactly a custom design, it is a semicustom boat using a stock hull and deck and an interior to the owner's specs. Designed by Eliot Spalding, this little full-keel cruiser weighs 7,500 pounds for a D/L of 413. It's a very traditional looking design with a raised quarter rail and clipper bow. Outboard rudder, boomkin and bowsprit complete this aesthetic. Draft is 3 feet, 8 inches. That's just not enough draft for me, but this is not the type of boat in which you would attempt a long and challenging beat.

Look at the sailplan. This is a strong sheerline. You can get away with it on a design like this where such an exaggerated element seems almost apropos. I don't know if it's right to call a design like this "traditional" because I can't think of any specific tradition that it builds from. Maybe you can draw a faint line from this boat to the Friendship Sloop. But even that's a stretch. It's a character boat.

Now the styling trick is to make that pilothouse with its baseball cap coachroof blend with the clipper-bowed hull form. I know only one designer who could do this successfully and that's Bill Garden. Old Bill has some magic in his pencil. To my eye Mr. Spalding's blend looks a little awkward. But putting an aesthetically pleasing pilothouse on any boat is a challenge, let alone a 25-footer.

Note that the mast is deck stepped on a "bridge" that eliminates the support post interfering with the interior.

The interior features an inside steering position and a very small head. I once took my tape measure into the head on a commercial jet. I figured Boeing should have head minimums down by now. I measured the distance from the front of the toilet seat to the bulkhead and door to be 22 inches, which works, just barely. I don't see 22 inches here.

Maybe, as the builder points out, you would be better off moving the head to a place under the V-berth. It's not an elegant head solution, but it does open up the pilothouse area. This would allow another quarter berth. The dining table fits between the V-berths and the small seats aft of the berth. Headroom forward of the pilothouse is 5 feet, 4 inches.

As these are semicustom boats, you can arrange your layout any way you like. Note that the mast is deck stepped on a "bridge" that eliminates the support post interfering with the interior. Certainly the big windows of the pilothouse would open up this interior.

The auxiliary is a 20-horsepower diesel that should push the Offshore 25 along at 5.25 knots with ease burning around .25 gallons an hour.

I hope this different boat finds an appreciative audience.

Eastsail Yachts, 553 Rte. 3A, Bow, NH 03304. (603) 224-6579. **www.eastsail.com**

September 2000

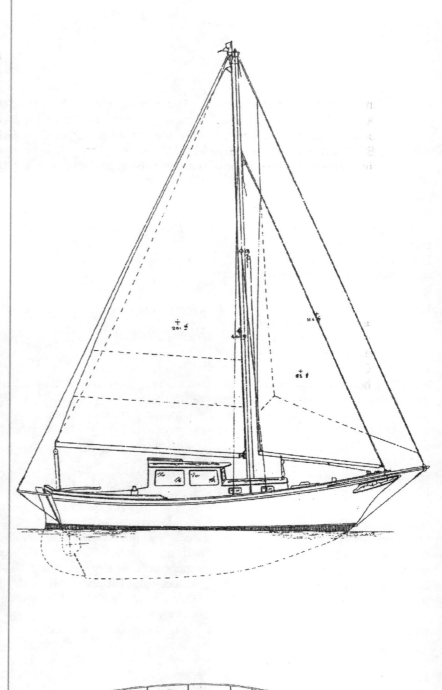

Sturdy cruiser for both coastal and bluewater passages.

LOA 25'; LWL 20'10"; Beam 8'6"; Draft 3'8"; Displacement 7,500 lbs.; Ballast 2,300 lbs.; Sail Area 400 sq. ft.; SA/D 16.7; D/L 413; L/B 2.94; Auxiliary 20 hp diesel; Fuel 20 gals.; Water 35 gals.

Brewer 25
Pocket Cruiser

Sometimes I like to play a game where I line up famous composers with famous yacht designers. Phil Rhodes would be Handel. Bill Atkin is Gluck. Bill Garden would be J.S. Bach. Olin Stephens would be Haydn. Chuck Paine would be Verdi, and Bruce Farr would definitely be Richard Wagner.

I'd settle for Bob Dylan, but I desperately want to be Beethoven. Ron Holland and German Frers can fight over Mozart for now. But Ted Brewer is certainly Woody Guthrie, and if you knew Ted, you would know that he would take this as a compliment.

I'll tell you my favorite Ted story. Ted flew in to Seattle to speak at Evergreen College, a very liberal, liberal arts school. He was picked up at the airport by three students for the hour drive back to the campus. On the way a student asked if Ted minded if they smoked. Ted said, no, he didn't mind and then watched as the student began to roll a smoke. Ted had rolled his own tobacco for years so he became frustrated with the student's inept attempts to roll a cigarette. "Hey, let me show you how to do that." Ted quickly realized that he wasn't rolling tobacco, but finished the job anyway. I'm sure that was an interesting if long ride.

This 25-footer from Ted shows a perfect sheer. It's perky without exaggeration. It's balanced with the low spot well aft. It's ideal in every way. Even the painted whale strip below the sheer is perfect. Note how it does not strictly parallel the sheer but slightly and slowly converges with the sheer toward the stern. Ted's patron for this design wanted a traditional design that he could sail from his home in the Bahamas. The design is pure whimsy but based upon traditional types. This design is not about tenths of a knot. This design is about looking cool.

The hull lines show a very shapely hull with a hint of hollow at the entry and a broad stern. The transom is wineglass shaped. You can't have a big conventional transom and not have some wineglass hollow to it. Well, you can, but it

will look horrible.

This is a centerboard boat for the shoal waters of the Bahamas. There is an honest, barn door outboard rudder. The D/L is 262. The hull is beamy with an L/B of 2.6. Ballast is 2,200 pounds of internal lead. Board-up draft is a scant 2-feet, 6 inches.

The design is pure whimsy but based upon traditional types. This design is not about tenths of a knot. This design is about looking cool.

The rig is a Bahama-style sloop with a big, loose-footed gaff mainsail and overhanging boom. The gooseneck is almost right down on the deck. The bowsprit projects 6 feet, 8 inches off the nearly plumb stem. The gaff is peaked almost vertically, and it's easy to see the technical progression from this rig to the "leg o'mutton" main we use today. The SA/D is 19.2. There are no spreaders, no battens, no backstay and no winches shown. Mainsail panels are shown running parallel to the leech and I suppose with today's fabrics you could do this without undue stretch.

The accommodation plan shows a cuddy cabin with three berths. There is no head and tankage will be jerrycans "to suit." There is an outboard well tucked in the stern.

Go ahead, buy a Melges 24. Then once or twice a week go out and get your butt kicked all over the place by some kids who have no lives off the race course. Come home humbled, bruised and most probably bleeding. Or, get Covey Island Boatworks to build you one of these Brewer beauties and get back to the romantic essence of why we sail. Hats off to Ted's client.

Brewer Yacht Design Ltd., P.O. Box 48, Gabriola Island, BC Canada, VOR 1XO, **www.tedbrewer.com** *(250) 247-7318.*

September 2000

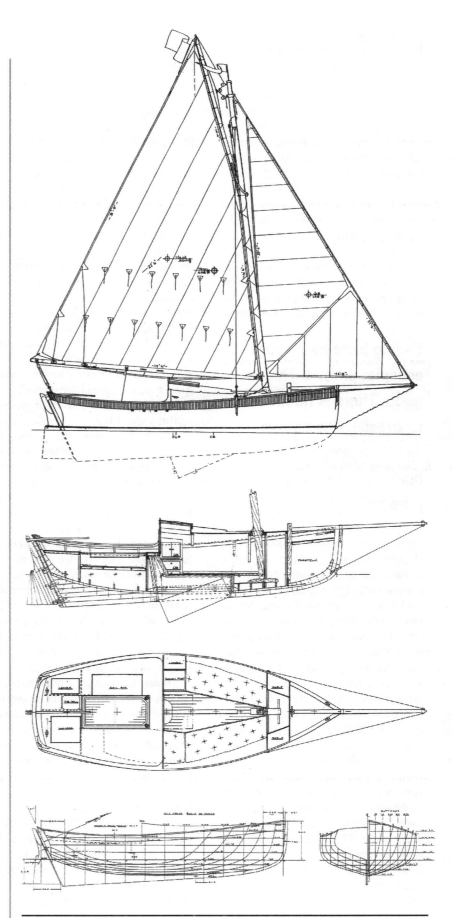

Shapely cruiser for thin water in the Bahamas.

LOA 25'2"; LWL 23'1"; Beam 9'8"; Draft 2'6" (board up); Displacement 7,200 lbs.; Ballast 2,200 lbs. (internal); Sail Area 448 sq. ft.; SA/D 19.2; D/L 262; L/B 2.6; Auxiliary outboard motor; Water Jerrycans "to suit."

Alerion 26
Daysailer

As a boy I read the story of the Herreshoff brothers. There is no doubt that the world has never seen a talent like Nathanael G. Herreshoff when it comes to designing yachts. Today, if you want an authentic Nathanael G. Herreshoff boat, you can either get lucky through brokerage or you can call Barry Carroll at Carroll Marine. Barry says this is the only "real Herreshoff production boat in the world today." A close inspection will reveal a carefully wrought hybrid.

The first two things that come to my mind when I look at this boat are the elegance and romance of sailing. They probably go together. If we leave behind the world of late Friday

Sailing becomes a pure escapist pursuit. This is good. There is no modem to wrestle. The screen won't mysteriously go blank. You can bask in a pure analog world.

night phone calls to round up crew, skipper's meetings at 8 a.m., jibe sets at the weather mark, torn chutes and protest meetings at 6 p.m., we might find ourselves in the kinder, gentler world of pleasure sailing. Beating Joe to the mark is irrelevant. Finding that extra 10th of a knot on the reach is meaningless. What is left after we strip away the hassle of racing is the pure joy of doing something as disconnected from our cyber world as possible. Sailing becomes a pure escapist pursuit. This is good. There is no modem to wrestle. The screen won't mysteriously go blank. You can bask in a pure analog world.

Now you are sailing just for your own amusement. So, how do you want to do it? How do you want to look out there on the water? What kind of picture would you like to paint on the water? Imagine sailing the boat that N.G. Herreshoff designed for his own use in 1912. The new boat was redesigned by Halsey Herreshoff along with A. Sidney DeWolffe Herreshoff and Isaac B. Merriman. The scale of the original design was changed and

"contemporary selective refinements were employed to facilitate modern construction while remaining essentially faithful to the original."

That means it's a hybrid.

Changes include the use of a full keel over the original centerboard model. Of course modern construction means fiberglass for the hull and deck. The cockpit has house details crafted in teak to preserve the classic look. All hardware is as close to the original Herreshoff patterns as possible, including cast-bronze coaming knees. Sail-handling hardware is modern with the idea that even Captain Nat would have chosen the best sailing gear available. This includes Lewmar winches and a Harken traveler along with a spar system by Hall Spars. You'd have to be a nut to want Egyptian cotton sails.

The cuddy cabin (don't you just love that term, cuddy cabin?) is fitted with a 6-foot, 8-inch V-berth and a compact galley with optional stove. The head is tucked under the end of the V-berth. This boat is primarily a daysailer, but it's always good to have a head. There is room below for comfortable cruising for two if you don't mind close quarters. The graceful lines of the cuddy add appreciably to the beautiful look of this little yacht. With the jib on a club this rig is selftending. A roller-furling jib could be added for even more convenience. The SA/D is 16.87.

I know the picture I want to paint on the water, and this boat would suit me just fine. I remember taking my two young sons out on a Buzzard's Bay Boy's Boat. They were fascinated by the whole concept. I'm sure in many conditions this boat would give more modern designs a good run for their money in terms of boat speed. In terms of pure sailing style points the Alerion 26 would win hands down. If I were introducing grandchildren to sailing, this is exactly the boat I would want.

Herreshoff Design, 1 Burnside Street, Bristol, RI 02809. (401) 253-5001.

January 2000

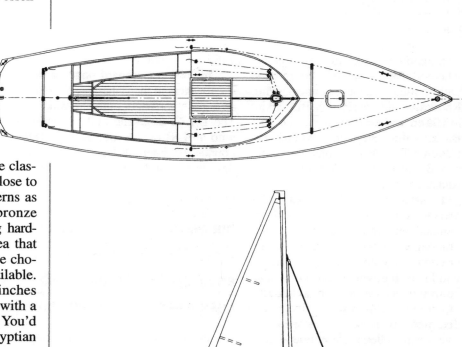

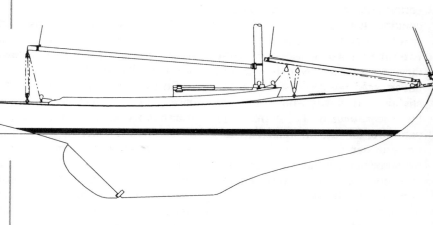

Elegant Herreshoff design is reborn using modern building techniques.

LOA 25'4"; LWL 20'; Beam 7'2"; Draft 3'7"; Displacement 4,800 lbs.; Ballast 2,500 lbs.; Sail Area 300 sq. ft.; SA/D 16.87; D/L 267; L/B 3.53; Auxiliary Yanmar diesel.

MacGregor 26
Motorsailer

Did you hear the story about the sailor sailing singlehanded in his MacGregor 26 when he had a heart attack? He put the pedal to the metal and powered back to the dock at speeds in excess of 20 knots where he was met by paramedics. He thinks the MacGregor saved his life. In my own 26-footer he would have powered back at a sedate 5.5 knots and probably died en route.

But we have a new MacGregor 26 now. The new 26 has been modified and improved for even better performance and comfort. Roger MacGregor does all the design work for his plant. Roger was kind enough to send me a 48-inch long model with the brochure for this review. Thanks, Roger.

"Sails better than a powerboat and powers better than a sailboat," they say. In fact the new 26 is a respectable sailer. I have a client who, after owning an original 26, fell in love with sailing and bought a Saga 35. If the 26 had been such a bad boat he would

All the proportions are there for a decent sailing boat.

have never bought another sailboat. While the aesthetic package may not be to your liking and the 50-horsepower outboard auxiliary may be contrary to what you think of for a sailboat, don't underestimate these boats. To a great degree they are designed to entice powerboaters who think they might like sailing into giving it a try. More than 6,000 26s have been sold to date. That's about three a day for six years. The boats are EEC-approved and about a third of the production is shipped overseas.

The new 26 has more shape to the hull and an additional 300 pounds of internal lead ballast. Deadrise has been increased from 8 degrees to 13 degrees to give the boat a softer ride and get the VCG lower for stability. The deep chest of the 26 flares to a flat run for planing performance. The original 26 had a centerboard and that has now been replaced by a high-aspect-ratio daggerboard. The

smaller slot of the daggerboard has reduced drag and improved speed under power and sail. This deep daggerboard should work to give the 26 good on-the-wind performance as long as you keep the boat on its feet. The brochure says 22 mph under power.

If I use 2,750 pounds as displacement I get a D/L of 101. L/B is a modest 3.25. Draft with board up is 12 inches and with board down 5 feet, 9 inches. The internal ballast is augmented by 1,150 pounds of water ballast in a tank that runs on centerline from the daggerboard trunk to the transom. Built-in foam flotation will keep the 26 afloat in case of damage. Before you begin casting asparagus at the performance of this boat just imagine the boat with 10 inches less freeboard and a more svelte cabintrunk. All the proportions are there for a decent sailing boat.

The layout is clever and uses a big mirror forward of the galley to give the effect of a totally open, bulkhead-less layout. In fact, the head is enclosed, so there are bulkheads. Roger has worked two double berths into this layout, settees and a mini galley. There is no privacy for sleeping but I think adding more bulkheads and doors would have destroyed this interior. It's designed for small families where privacy is not required. The cockpit is large but that little wheel, while I'm sure it works, looks too small for me.

"But what about those aesthetics, Bob?" I think the boat looks fine. While I would not call it beautiful or handsome I do prefer the new model with its stepped cabintrunk. The look is more interesting and there is better headroom below. I wouldn't put this boat alongside the latest Chuck Paine design and compare the aesthetics. The 26 shows a hybrid power/sail look that won't work on many boats. The wraparound windows and lack of side decks are right out of the powerboat school. I think you have to put this boat into an aesthetics genre of its own.

MacGregor Yacht Corp., 1631 Placentia, Costa Mesa, CA 92627. **www.macgregor26.com** *(949) 642-6380 .*

November 2003

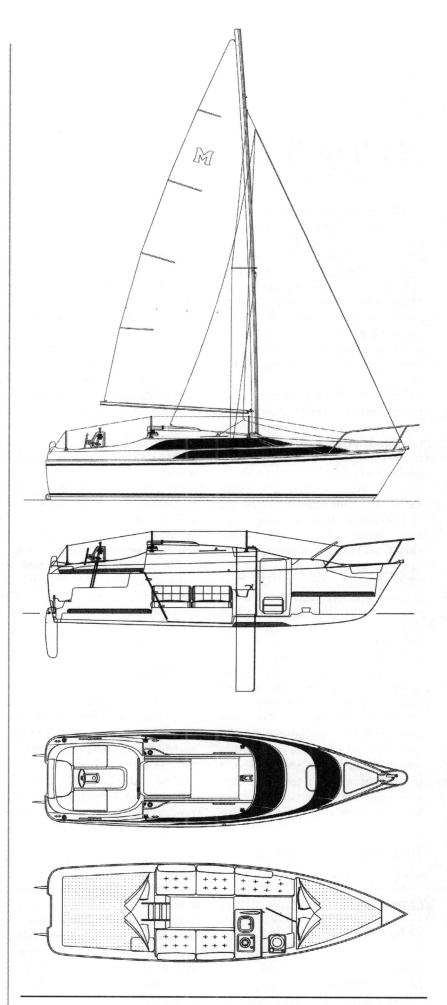

A new version of the classic design perfect for reformed powerboaters.

LOA 25'10"; LWL 23'2"; Beam 7'9"; Draft 12" (board up), 5'9" (board down); Displacement 2,550 lbs.; Ballast 1,450 lbs.; Sail Area 300 sq. ft.; SA/D 25.7; D/L 101; L/B 3.25; Auxiliary 5- to 50-hp outboard; Fuel 24 gals.; Water 5 gals.

Hadley 27
Coastal Cruiser

The Hadley 27 was designed by my pal Dieter Empacher and originally built by Bristol, the Hadley 27 is now semicustom built by Triangle Marine Engineering Ltd. in North Kingstown, Rhode Island. This is a true little yacht capable of sailing anywhere. The only limitation will be the skipper's. If you want to rendezvous with your friends in their bigger boats just leave a day earlier.

This boat looks like a mini-Little Harbor, which should come as no surprise considering Dieter was head designer at Hood's office for years. The proportions are classic with shapely overhangs and a nice sheerline punctuated by a teak toerail and handsome bow casting.

The hull form is a cutaway, full-keel design with centerboard. Dieter has probably designed more centerboard cruising boats than any other American designer. The prop is in an aperture, and that usually means challenging performance in reverse. The D/L is 381.5. I think you can assume this boat will be stiff and carry a gentle helm.

If I have one complaint with this design, it is that, given the cockpit size and rudder location, you could not fit in tiller steering. The tiller swing would be too intrusive. It's a shame to steer a small boat with a wheel. It may look "yachty," but a tiller gives a better feel. The singlehander can tuck a tiller between his legs, freeing up both hands for

This interior layout has no tricks or angles, just good common sense application of space.

raising the sails and tacking and jibing maneuvers.

This interior layout has no tricks or angles, just good common sense application of space. The head can be enclosed and is quite large. The galley is just fine, and the quarter berth will make an excellent place for an additional

ice chest or your guitar: You could even store your extra sails there at night to free up the V-berth.

The only hanging locker I see is outboard of the w.c., and I think this design would benefit from a dedicated wet locker to starboard instead of a second sink. Stowing wet gear on a small cruiser is a tough problem. Wet gear needs to have air circulation if it is to have any chance of drying. In Seattle this is important. Two sinks on a boat this size is too luxurious a use of space.

This interior will have a good feel to it. Meaning? It will feel like a boat.

The displacement of this boat is sufficient to allow for a pair of 25-gallon water tanks and a 24-gallon holding tank. There is also a 20-gallon fuel tank. This is lots of tankage for a little boat and will help make the Hadley self-sufficient for extended periods. Fifty gallons of water will last a couple a week easily.

The engine can be either an 18-horsepower, two-cylinder Westerbeke diesel or a three-cylinder 27-horsepower diesel. I would think that the 18-horsepower model would be more than enough power. Two 12-volt 80-amp-hour batteries provide a bountiful electrical system for this small cruiser.

The SA/D is 16.42. That won't win you any bragging rights at the rendezvous, but it will be comforting in a breeze. The drawings show end-boom sheeting, but the photo shows midboom sheeting. You know how I feel about that. Put the traveler on the bridgedeck where it belongs. If you can't step over it take up golf. Of course you could argue that the endboom sheeting would allow for a dodger, but I've never owned a boat with a dodger. The hood on my Helly Hansen is my dodger.

Triangle Marine Engineering Ltd., P.O. Box 208, North Kingstown, RI 02852. (401) 846-2039. **www.trimareng.com**

November 1999

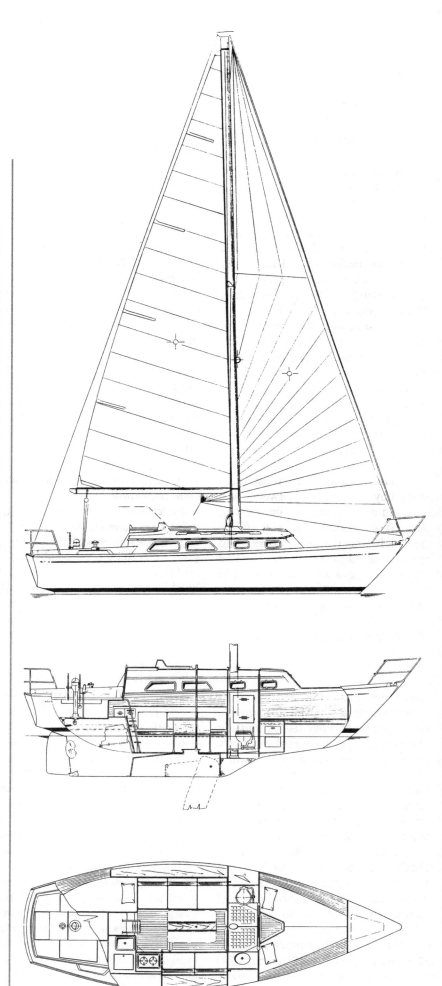

Hardy, well-outfitted cruiser designed to sail anywhere.

LOA 27'3"; LWL 20'9"; Beam 9'5"; Draft 7' (board down), 3' (board up); Displacement 7,635 lbs.; Ballast 3,818 lbs.; Sail Area 397 sq. ft.; SA/D 16.42; D/L 381.5; L/B 2.89; Auxiliary Westerbeke 18-hp or 27-hp diesel; Fuel 20 gals.; Water 50 gals.

ETAP 26i
Coastal Cruiser

I like this little Belgian boat. It's about the same size as my own boat so I can relate easily to the design trade-offs. Designed by Mortain and Mavrikios, the ETAP 26i is distinguished by beautiful joinerwork detailing and the fact that it is "unsinkable." ETAP has been building unsinkable boats for 30 years and appears to have this niche to itself. The main reason for this is the cost of construction. The building technique required to make the ETAPs unsinkable also makes them cost about 30 percent more than comparably sized boats. That's quite a premium, but then again, having a boat that can sustain major damage and stay afloat is a definite advantage.

This unsinkable feature is accomplished by filling voids between the hull skin and the interior liner with injected polyurethane foam. The same technique is applied to the area between the deck and the molded headliner. The down side of this is that a good part of the boat's potential stowage volume will be displaced by foam.

This is a beamy hull with an L/B of 2.85. Any time you get an L/B under 3 you have a beamy boat. The beam is carried aft to a broad transom in contemporary fashion. Overhangs fore and aft are minimal. The D/L is 175. You can have a deep-draft keel drawing 4 feet, 11 inches or a shoal draft keel at 3 feet, 9 inches. I would certainly recommend the deeper keel. There is also the interesting option of an ETAP "tandem keel," which is comprised of two foils and a single bulb.

The interior is quite unusual in that the dinette is pushed as far forward as possible and wraps around in a U-shape. You can drop the table to turn the dinette into a double V-berth if you like, although there will be a mast compression in the middle. There is another double berth in its own enclosed area aft. The head is to starboard and includes a space for hanging wet gear. The galley is minimal, but what do you expect on this size boat? I think this is a fine layout, although I'm not sure I'd want to sleep in that constricted area aft.

I like the looks of this boat. It has a purposefulness to its look.

The short and abrupt house has windows forward that let in a lot

There is a no-nonsense look to this boat that I admire.

of light. Side decks are generous and the use of a self-tacking jib eliminates the need for genoa tracks. I would have liked to see the self-tacking jib track go farther outboard to cope with reaching sheet leads. I'd have run that track clear to the rail. There are stand-up blocks on each side adjacent to the front of the house, but they look to me to be too far forward to sheet the genoa that is shown on some of the drawings.

The cockpit is big and divided by the mainsheet traveler. Some of you will see this as a disadvantage, but this is exactly where the traveler belongs. It is also removable so it will be out of the way when you are relaxing at anchor. There is a nice swim step aft with fold-down boarding ladder. There is an anchor well forward.

The rig is fractional with a full-batten main and a self-tacking jib. The jib sheet runs up the mast then goes down to exit at the deck-stepped mast base and leads back to the cockpit. The short bowsprit holds the anchor roller and allows for an asymmetrical chute tack point. The single spreaders are swept 27 degrees with chainplates out at the rail. The self-tacking jib is convenient for shorthanded sailing.

There is a no-nonsense look to this boat that I admire despite the lackluster computer drafting job. The photos show a very handsome vessel. You know by now that I like small, capable and strong boats. You don't cruise in ultimate comfort on a small cruiser, but after a 20-mile, 20-knot beat I don't need much to be comfy. A bite, a book, a Bach, a Balvenie and a berth. Yep, that's all I need.

ETAP-USA, 9 Timber Ridge, Freeport, ME 04032. (866) 382-7872., www.etap-usa.com

November 2002

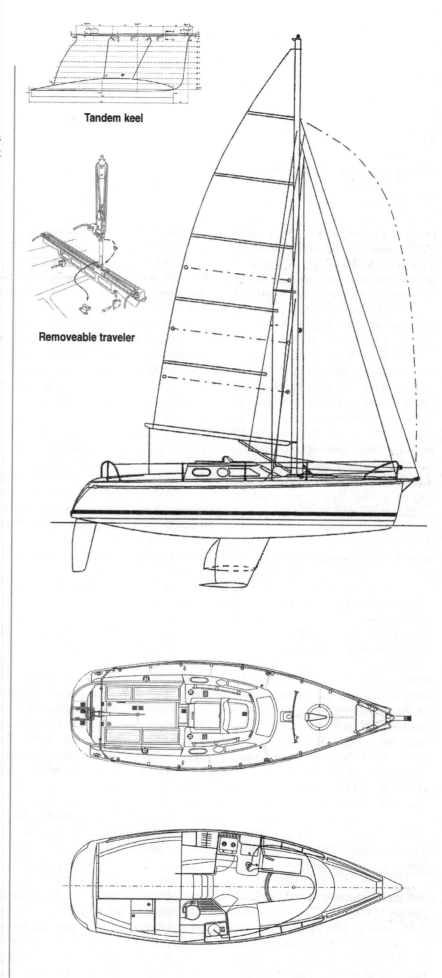

Tandem keel

Removeable traveler

A certified unsinkable cruiser with top-quality detailing.

LOA 27'8"; LWL 23'6"; Beam 9'2"; Draft 5'1" (standard), 3'9" (shoal); Displacement 5,066 lbs.; Ballast 1,432 lbs.; Sail Area 324 sq. ft.; SA/D 17.6; D/L 175; L/B 2.85; Auxiliary Volvo-Penta 10-hp; Fuel 13 gals.; Water 21 gals.

Finngulf 28E
Family Cruiser

I am a fan of compact cruising boats, and the new Finngulf 28E is a good example of the type. It's a handsome boat by Strahlmann Yacht Design, presumably in Finland, and built by Finngulf Yachts.

Starting with the interior, however, I do have two gripes with this design. First, there is a door separating the double quarter berth from the main cabin. This essentially puts the berth in a box. To my eye this is just way too small a space to be shut in by a door. Privacy? Who are you kidding? I don't think there is room in

I like the overall style of this good looking boat.

that compartment sufficient to allow you to pull your pants on anyway. Note how the V-berth is butted right up against the bulkhead at the forward end of the main cabin so that anyone occupying the V-berths will have to get dressed and undressed in the main cabin. Cruising on this boat is best either for a couple, a couple with two kids, or two couples that are very intimate friends.

My second gripe is that the nav station, although nice, isn't necessary on a boat this size. What I really think this boat needs is more hanging-locker space. If you cruise in a rainy area like Seattle you will find that you need room to stow wet gear. Believe me, Henri Lloyd and Helly Hansen aside, by nightfall everything you have on will be damp.

The galley is better than adequate and includes fresh and saltwater foot pumps at the sink. This designer has even managed to get counter space on each side of the two-burner range as well as two drawers just aft of the range. The interior finish is kind of like a mini-Swan with solid teak trim, teak veneer and a teak-and-holly sole. It's an impressive look.

The hull is of the beamy, short-ended type that dominates the market today. The L/B is 2.96 and the D/L is 171. Draft is moderate at 5 feet, 5

inches, with the lead ballast hung on a deep GRP sump. The spade rudder looks quite big to my eye, but there is nothing wrong with a big rudder on a cruising boat. You could argue against the added wetted surface and drag from the thicker section, but I'd take those any day in exchange for excellent handling in close quarters and a boat that tracks well. Small boats, by virtue of their size, are not great trackers so the larger rudder may help keep the boat on course while you go below for a sandwich.

Looking at the sailplan we see this is a fractionally rigged boat. This means that the boat will have a longer boom, which in this case allows the mainsheet to come down to a traveler aft of the tiller head. This helps clean up the compact cockpit. There is a small bowsprit that contains the anchor roller. This is a thoughtful addition and will keep the anchor from clanking against the stem when you raise it.

The chainplates are external, which is a little unusual but well done in this case. The fact that this is a fractional rig with a minimally overlapping jib—I'd say about 110 percent—means you can sheet the jib inboard of the shrouds to cabintop tracks. This is helped even further by the 16-degree sweep to the spreaders.

I like the overall style of this good looking boat. I like the swim step on the transom, and I like the nearly plumb bow. In many ways this design reminds me of my own boat. We get some pretty awful small cruising boats these days, a situation that is all the more troubling since, as we get accustomed to them and they eventually begin to look okay, they pave the way for an even worse looking bunch of boats. The Finngulf 28E gives us an effective combination of features in a very attractive package put together by a clever design team.

Finngulf Yachts/R.B. Yacht Sales, P.O. Box 9204, 145 Pearl St., Noank, CT 06340. (860) 536-7776. **www.finngulf.com**

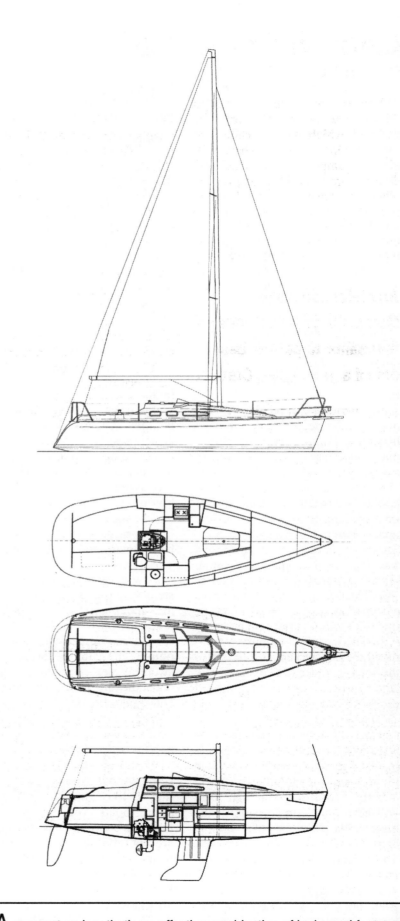

A compact cruiser that's an effective combination of looks and features.

LOA 28'3"; LWL 25'3"; Beam 9'6"; Draft 5'5"; Displacement 6,930 lbs.; Ballast 1,980 lbs.; Sail Area 450 sq. ft.; SA/D 19.8; D/L 171; L/B 2.96; Auxiliary Volvo Penta MD 2010; Fuel 10 gals.; Water 36 gals.

Cornish Crabber 30
Coastal Cruiser

I think one of the fascinating things about sailing is the variety of ways in which we can choose to enjoy it. On one hand we have foil-borne, composite-built machines doing more than 40 knots; on the other we have fat little hookers struggling to sustain 4 knots. At the end of the day the pilot of the 40-knotter and the skipper of the 4-knotter can both say, "We are

Any idiot can make a Mumm 30 go fast. It takes a real sailor to get the best out of a gaff-rigged Crabber.

sailors." That's probably where the discussion should end because there is not going to be much more those two can agree on when it comes to sailing.

There's a sailing world where tenths of a knot mean nothing, and VMG is measured in smiles on the skipper's face. "Going to weather" means anything shy of 45 degrees apparent. Getting there quickly is not as important as getting there in style. Welcome to the world of the Cornish Crabbers. These cutters have been built at the mouth of the Camel Estuary in North Cornwall for more than 25 years and have a very strong following. The company's current models range from a 12-footer to the new 30-footer designed by Roger Dongray.

This is a full-keel design. There is no distinction between where the forefoot ends and the keel begins. Draft is 3 feet, 6 inches, but there is a plate centerboard you can lower that adds another 21 inches to the draft. This centerboard is housed entirely below the cabin sole. Beam is moderate with an L/B of 3.15. The beam is carried into the ends. The plumb stem also means that volume is carried into the bow. The LOD of 30 feet is deceptive. This is a big 30-footer. The D/L for the gaff rig is 366 indicating what you would imagine to be a rather heavy boat. But it isn't. Its displacement

is moderate. The wide "planks" of the fiberglass hull form give the Crabber almost a multi-hard-chine look. These lines accentuate the shapeliness of the hull and enhance the vintage look. I love the perky sheer spring of this design.

My favorite feature of this rig is the traditional way the bowsprit is set off center, passing alongside the pronounced stem timber. Photos in the brochure show that the outboard end of the bowsprit is on centerline, but the inboard end with its samson post fixture is off-set to starboard. In the old days these bowsprits were reefable.

You can choose either a Bermuda-rigged Crabber or a gaff-rigged Crabber. As long as you are going with this type of boat you might as well go with the gaff rig. I suspect the Bermuda rig will be faster upwind and the gaff rig faster downwind. The gaff rig has 34 square feet more sail area than does the Bermuda rig. With flying jib, staysail, mainsail and main topsail you will have plenty of strings to pull on this boat. Look at that sailplan. This is a great looking boat. Any idiot can make a Mumm 30 go fast. It takes a real sailor to get the best out of a gaff-rigged Crabber.

The accommodation plan is laid out for four cruisers. The settees are shorter than what I would consider berth length but the V-berth and quarter berths are generous. Finished in all mahogany this interior is stunning. The entertainment center is the liquor cabinet.

If you go with the optional teak deck you can go wild with the varnish and create a real vintage look. Add the wine-red sails, throw the GPS overboard and you can easily imagine yourself transported back to 1912. Come to think of it, that's a really appealing idea right now. Although I think I'll hang on to the GPS.

Cornish Crabbers/Britannia Boats, P.O. Box 5033 Annapolis, MD 21403. (410) 267-5922. **www.britanniaboats.com**

March 2002

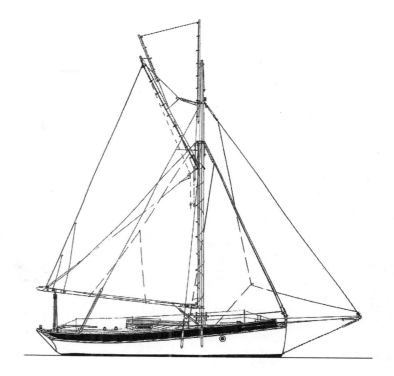

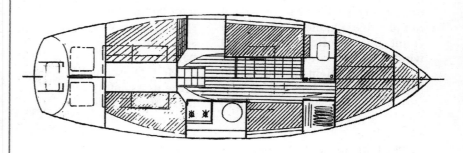

Small cruiser that measures VMG in smiles instead of knots.

LOD 30; LWL 25'9"; Beam 9'6"; Draft 3'6" (board up) 5'3" (board down); Displacement 14,000 lbs. (gaff rig), 15,680 lbs. (Bermuda rig); Ballast 5,500 lbs.; Sail Area 600 sq. ft. (gaff rig) 566 sq. ft. (Bermuda rig); SA/D 15.6 (gaff rig), 14.5 (Bermuda); D/L 366 (gaff rig) 409 (Bermuda rig); L/B 3.15; Auxiliary Yanmar 3GM20 diesel: Fuel 23 gals.; Water 29 gals.

Truth
Traditional Cruiser

Truth was designed by Antonio Dias of Harbor Island, Rhode Island. The builder is Briio Reiff in Brooklin, Maine, and the owner is Mr. David Pratt of Larchmont, New York. A quick look tells you that this custom design is the antithesis of just about every production yacht available. Just imagine a lineup of Sabres, J Boats, Hunters, Tartans and Catalinas, and then throw in Truth. You get the picture. Clearly this owner wanted something different. Mr. Dias has risen to that challenge and produced a very

This shape produces a boat with a lovely motion.

traditional-looking little cutter that could have come off the pages of a 1952 *Rudder* magazine. We don't see enough of these designs today.

I can hear most of you, "Yeah Bob, but it's slow." Maybe you're right, but consider this. Cruisers generally choose not to beat to weather. I don't know if this is a function of owning slow boats, not knowing how to make their boats go or just plain laziness. The fact remains that they usually motor to weather unless the conditions are perfect. This leaves reaching and running. This cutter will reach and run just fine. On the wind you can count on an effective apparent wind angle of around 38 to 40 degrees. You might be able to do better than this, but I think the gaff-headed mainsail will begin to fall off at the peak and be the controlling factor.

The hull shows slack bilges and a high degree of deadrise—around 31 degrees—almost going as far as a hollow garboard. In laymen's terms this means the hull is very V-ed in section and approaches the "wineglass" shape of old wooden boats where the hull section fairs gently into the keel section. This shape produces a boat with a love-ly motion but very little stability, so this boat will show tenderness. On the other side of the coin, this shape produces boats with a high degree of ultimate stability. A parabolic leading edge is better. The D/L is 233.

The accommodations include a quarter berth aft to port. Ahead of this there is an icebox that I presume doubles as a chart table. To starboard is the galley.

The settees are quite narrow, but they pull out for additional depth when needed.

The most interesting aspect of this interior is the Swedish composting head. It's big and it's high, standing 30 inches off the cabin sole. However, this unit is self contained and, according to the designer, in wide use in Scandinavia. "A solar powered fan keeps it running properly and the end product is a small amount of odorless humus suitable for garden use."

Sometimes these small-scale interior drawings are hard to read, but keep in mind, dear reader, that designers have to balance the need to present a clear and easy-to-read drawing with the need to produce a technically accurate drawing. Most of the time the technically accurate drawing is too cluttered with notes and dimensions to be intelligible when reduced to the small image you see on these pages.

Mr. Dias has given us a healthy dose of imagination and based it loosely upon historical types to create a romantic image.

Thanks, Mr. Dias, for sharing this lovely flight of fancy.

Antonio Dias Design, 171 Cedar Island Road, Narragansett, RI 02882. (401) 783-4959.

January 2000

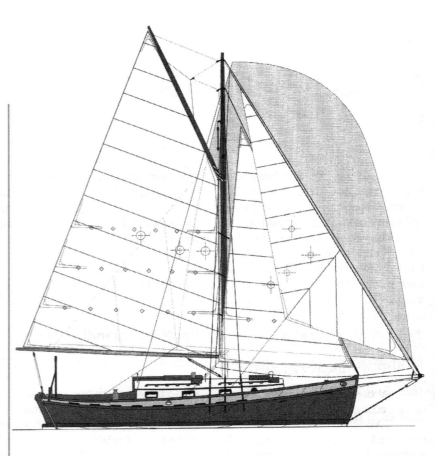

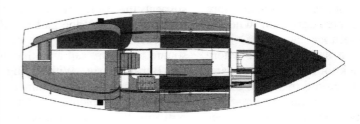

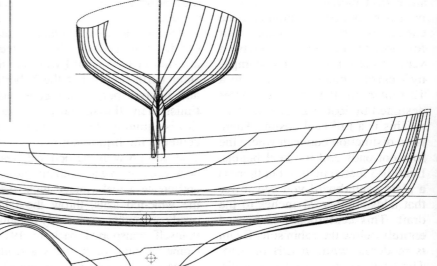

Gaff cutter makes a statement that sets it apart from the crowd.

LOA 30'8"; LWL 27'5"; Beam 9'9"; Draft 4'11"; Displacement 10,900 lbs.; Ballast 4,845 lbs.; Sail Area 624 sq. ft.; SA/D 20; D/L 233; L/B 3.18; Westerbeke 12-hp diesel.

Hanse 311
Family Cruiser

In any of the major cruising destinations it's easy to be distracted by the megayachts. They are imposing and many of them even manage to be beautiful. It is another world. I remember one day musing: "What if I was moored in Porto Fino on my megayacht, sitting comfortably on my leather upholstered seat with an exotic drink in my hand and …" I was depressed. Now what? I don't think a megayacht ensures happiness.

For some of us the pursuit of happiness involves reducing life to the minimal elements. Of course we are, at the core, sailors, so we need our boats. (And I think "need" is the correct word.) But being truly self-sufficient on your boat can make you happy. Now we could argue about what "self-sufficient" means, but indulge me here and imagine it means snug on the hook, the dog walked, dinner on the two-burner, a glass of Dalwhinnie and the comforting sound of a Schubert piano sonata coming from your Sony water-resistant portable stereo. You could even remove the scotch and the stereo and replace them with a good book—about Schubert. Small boats can make you happy.

The Hanse 311 seems to have everything you would need. The design is by Judel-Vrolijk, and the hull is contemporary but conservative. The beamy hull has short ends, a broad stern, large rudder and a bulb-type fin. Designed to be a family cruising boat or what we would call in the old days a "cruiser-racer," this boat reminds me of countless Ericsons, Rangers, Islanders and Pearsons. It's just a good, all round design. The D/L is 204.

The layout has a double quarter berth that has a door on the compartment. (I hesitate to call it a "stateroom.") The head is fine with access to the port lazarette adjacent to the cockpit where the drawings show a pipe berth. Access to this pipe berth is tight. I'm not as flexible as I once was, and I was never very flexible, so this does not look like a place I would want to sleep. A "charter" layout is also available and comes with two mirror-image double quarter berths.

The main cabin has opposing settee berths that extend into the forward chainplate bulkhead. I have never been too keen on these "foot pock-

This boat reminds me of countless Ericsons, Rangers, Islanders and Pearsons. It's just a good, all round design.

ets." The forward V-berth looks short, but fine for children. Hey! It's a 31-foot boat. You can't expect everything. Galley and nav table look functional. Headroom is 6 feet, 1 inch.

Fractional rigs dominate modern designs. Why? I'll tell you why I think this is. It's better to have the bigger sail on the boom where it is easier to handle. Big, overlapping genoas are hard to handle and of dubious value. You could extend this argument with rating rule benefits, but that doesn't really fit our discussion. Putting the mast farther forward also probably results in a more manageable helm and better feel to the boat. Plus, with the main moved forward you can sail more effectively under main alone, although I'm not sure why you would do this. The spreaders are swept and the mainsail roach clears the backstay. I don't have I, J, E and P so I can't tell you the exact SA/D. My guess is that it's around 19.

Built by Germany's second largest sailboat builder, Yachtzentrum Greifswald, the Hanse is made with a balsa-core hull and deck and all iso resins. The keel design was awarded second place at the the 2001 Bricola de Oro Design competition.

Hanse North America, Brewer Wickford Cove Marina, 65 Reynolds St., North Kingston, RI 02852, **www.hanseyachts.com** *(401) 423-9192.*

March 2002

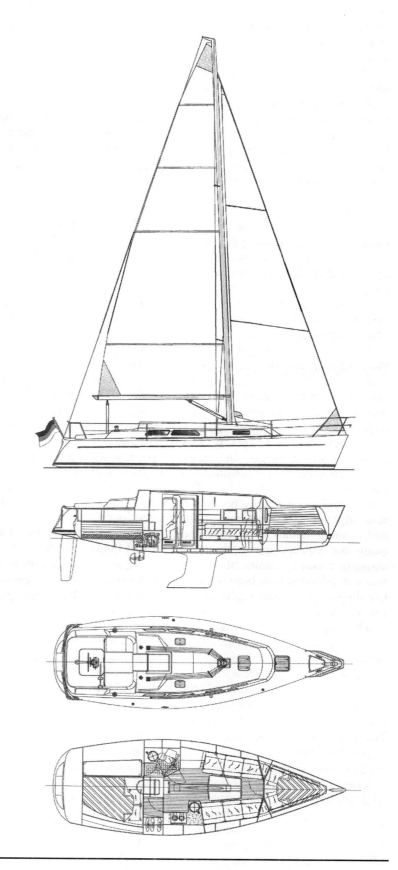

All you need for a satisfying adventure out on the water.

LOA 31'7"; LWL 26'6"; Beam 10'6"; Draft 5'8" (deep keel), 4'6" (wing keel); Displacement 8,500 lbs.; Ballast 2,800 lbs. (deep keel), 3,090 (wing keel); Sail area 536 sq. ft.; SA/D 19; D/L 204; L/B 3.0; Auxiliary 19-hp Volvo Penta 2020: Fuel 15 gals.; Water 30 gals.

Perry 32
Traditional Cruiser

I got a call from a local retired jack-of-all-trades who had owned a series of unusual boats. His last two boats were the Schumacher-designed Alerion Express (spell-check calls it the Algerian Express) and a J/109. He races with a local club every weekend, 52 weeks a year. He often goes out singlehanded. He was beginning to think the J was not the most suitable boat for singlehanded racing in the winter when he saw an article on an old wooden double-ender built in England 100 years ago. He was immediately smitten with this 28-foot, 16,000 pound, lapstrake, internally ballasted, 11-foot beam, gaff-rigged cutter. Mr. Ulysses Cheng called me and asked if I would like to talk about designing an updated version of this classic double-ender. Are you kidding?

The trick in a design job like this is to preserve the original character of the boat while updating the performance and the method of construction. The aesthetic goal is everything.

The new boat is 32 feet in LOA and 11 feet, 2 inches in beam. Displacement is 13,000 pounds for a D/L of 238 and an L/B of 2.85. The parent model was beamy because it was originally a fishing boat and it had internal ballast. It needed the beam for volume and stability. I chose to retain the beam because it was critical to the look but I reduced the displacement and replaced the full keel with a fin.

The outboard rudder was a feature we mulled over but decided to keep because it was so important to the look of the boat. How can you resist that flagstaff mounted off the side of the rudder cheeks and the lantern mounted on the rudder head? These are strong visual elements. Sculpted stem and sternpost features were de rigueur.

This is a big hull but it has only 27 inches of freeboard. Add to this the fact that the cabintrunk was originally 5 feet wide but I widened it to 6 feet. Yet even with that you don't have a lot of useable interior volume. There will be sitting headroom below but just only. There will be 5 feet, 8 inches of headroom at the galley. We may still shove the head farther forward and put a couple of berths just aft of the head. I copied the "Z leg" dining table from an old Ray Richards design. It allows you to swivel the table around for clearance even while it is set.

If we went with a Marconi rig we would gain performance but lose the look we were after. I drew both

How can you resist that flagstaff mounted off the side of the rudder cheeks and the lantern mounted on the rudder head?

Marconi and gaff rigs. As soon as we saw the finished gaff rig we agreed that it looked good. To pull off this gaff rig we will need a carbon mast, boom, off-center bowsprit, gaff and topmast. We can detail the carbon spars with carbon reproductions of vintage wooden spar features. It will not be cheap but it will look good while dramatically lowering the VCG and improving performance. I expect we will have to settle for an upwind apparent wind angle of close to 40 degrees with the gaff rig. But this boat will not be a pig. I will do everything I can to make this boat a good performer. We have enough sail area to drive the boat in the light airs of Puget Sound.

We will build the boat in cold-molded timber construction. We preferred the look of the lapstrake, but it presented challenges we chose not to confront. I don't know what we will do for an auxiliary yet. This design will change before construction begins next May on Bainbridge Island, a ferry ride away from Seattle. I will play with the sheer some more. Maybe take some sheer spring out aft. I'll continue to fiddle with the freeboard and the overall hull shape nuances will be in constant flux until the day I have to deliver the Mylar patterns to the builder. I really like this little hooker. I'll have lots of fun with this one.

Robert H. Perry Yacht Designers, 5801 Phinney Ave., N. Suite 100, Seattle, WA 98103. **www.perryboat.com** *(206) 789-7214.*

November 2003

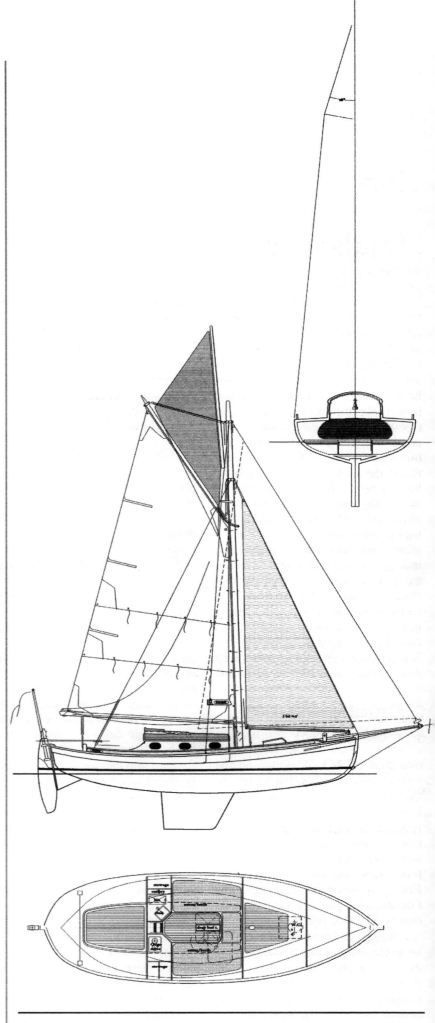

A classic double-ender with a few modern updates.

LOA 32'; LWL 29'; Beam 11'2"; Draft 6'; Displacement 13,000 lbs.; Ballast 5,100 lbs.; Sail Area 674 sq. ft.; SA/D 19.5; D/L 238; L/B 2.85; Auxiliary 18-hp diesel; Fuel 20 gals.; Water 15 gals.

Shoalsailer 32
Shoal-water Cruiser

At the Annapolis Sailboat Show, I was happy to see Walter Schulz sitting on his newest project, the Shoalsailer 32. Now if you are reading this on the West Coast I can assure you that you probably do not have a clear appreciation of just how important shoal draft is to East Coast sailers. Shoal-draft keel versions will outsell their deep-draft brothers four to one. On the East Coast the primary cruising concern has to be "is there enough water there for me to get in?" The Shoalsailer 32 is designed to eliminate that concern.

The patent-pending hull shape was drawn by Walter with help on the rudder and daggerboards from George Carter. This hull is no whim or arbitrary attempt at something different. There are more than five years of testing prototypes behind this final hull shape. A lot of this testing involved chined ver-

Compared to other shoal-draft boats, I think this boat will do better than hold its own.

sions of the hull that had disastrous handling characteristics. The basic midsection that slowly evolved is a flared shape above the DWL, with a deep center section. The extremely slack and narrow bilges rise to a very hard turn (but not a chine) just above the DWL. It's kind of like a beamy light hull sitting on top of a deep and narrow light boat.

The L/B of 2.54 indicates a very beamy boat. From maximum beam to the transom there is almost no taper. All the ingredients are here for a really ugly boat. But surprise, once you get over the beam at the transom this is a very handsome and conventional-looking boat.

Bow profile, entry, sheer and cabin-trunk contours are artfully drawn. The D/L is 157.

There are two daggerboards well off center and raked forward. These are short, low-aspect-ratio boards that do not increase the sailing draft of the boat when down. Walter said that you do not even need them until the breeze gets over 18 knots. This means you can really forget about draft most of the time. There are twin lifting, beachable rudders that work well with the shoal-draft approach.

The photos of the boat under sail show a good portion of the transom dragging and this is never fast. However, compared to other shoal-draft boats, I think this boat will do better than hold its own. Walter tells me that they hold their own against a deep-draft C&C 30, but they are not as fast or close-winded as a J/30. I think that indicates very respectable performance against recognized benchmarks.

The interior is well laid-out and pretty comparable to what you would find in any 32-footer. The big difference is that this boat offers 6 feet, 5 inches of headroom. There are three hanging lockers in this boat and a good-sized galley.

The deck takes advantage of the ultrabeamy stern to use a two-wheel cockpit configuration. This allows a clear walk-through to the transom swim step. Under sail you can sit well outboard and get a clear view of the jib luff.

Shoal-draft boats usually don't excite me. I know their limitations despite brochure claims. Walter and George may have a new, successful breed of shoal-draft boat here. I predict success for this effort.

Shannon Yachts, 19 Broad Common Rd., Bristol, RI 02809. **www.shannonyachts.com** (401) 253-2441.

December 2000

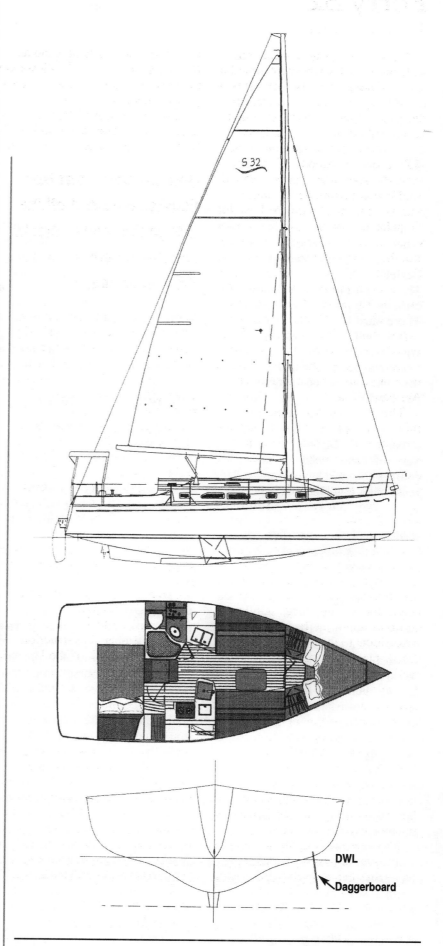

Innovative thin-water cruiser.

LOA 32'5"; LWL 30'; Beam 12'9"; Draft 2'9"; Displacement 9,532 lbs.; Ballast 2,200 lbs.; Sail Area 540 sq. ft.; SA/D 19.2; D/L 157; L/B 2.54; Auxiliary Westerbeke 38-hp diesel; Fuel 25 gals.; Water 60 gals.

Beneteau 323
Coastal Cruiser

This new Beneteau is a combined design effort of Group Finot/Conq with designer Jean Berret's new pivoting wheel detail. The design target is a comfortable cruising boat for two couples. There must be an echo in here.

The hull form is classic French with a very wide stern and plenty of maximum beam. The L/B is 3.08 and the "buttwater-to-beam ratio" is 82 percent. Of course the benefit to this wide stern is a huge cockpit and volume aft for the big queen-sized quarterberth. The D/L is 152. Ends are very short and freeboard is generous. Still it's not a bad looking hull and the hull-house combination looks good to my eye. You can choose from a deep keel drawing 5 feet, 11 inches or a shoal keel drawing 4 feet. There is also talk of a lifting keel being available next year.

The deck design shows a house with a raised portion aft so I would presume that full headroom disappears as you go past the galley. But while this house treatment compromises headroom it maximizes aesthetics and I like this look. All the interior areas that require headroom are aft anyway. The cockpit is broad and a hinged portion of the helm seat allows it to swing down for clear access to the swim step. The traveler seems very short and I would prefer a long traveler whenever possible on any boat. There is deck access to a large sail stowage bin to starboard in the cockpit. There is virtually no fo'c'sle but there is a shallow anchor well in the foredeck. There are teak handrails and teak covering on the cockpit seats. I'm all for reducing maintenance. The real trick to this deck design is Berret's new wheel, which pivots 90 degrees to allow you to walk past it to the swim step.

The rig is fractional with only one set of spreaders that are highly swept. The mast is deck stepped. There is an option of in-mast furling.

This requires a loose-footed mainsail. But with the mainsheet mid-boom and a rigid vang I would prefer to see mainsail loads spread out across the entire boom with a non-loose-footed design. With leach loads concentrated on the outboard end of the boom and luff loads taken solely by the tack fitting, it's not hard to see that it would take little to bend

The real trick to this deck design is Berret's new wheel pivots 90 degrees.

this boom. A stout boom section will be required. The SA/D is 18.93.

I find this layout interesting. Look at the amount of interior volume devoted to the head. This is a big head for a 32-foot, 10-inch boat. It would be a nice head on a 40-footer. The head is bigger than the galley. The galley on the other hand is minimal with no counter space except for the corner where the refer is. "How would you like your Spam tonight?" Of course, any design attempt to add to the galley would run into conflicts with the quarter stateroom and I don't see any way you could cut that down.

With lots of windows and hatches letting light and air below the 323 should be a comfortable boat to cruise. I think the design pedigree speaks for itself and the numbers indicate a stiff boat that should move in light air as long as you keep the pointy end in and the fat end out to minimize that wetted surface.

Accommodation preferences are subjective and I'm sure many of you will feel comfortable in this layout.

Beneteau USA, 1313 Highway 76 West, Marion, SC 29571. **www.beneteauusa.com** *(843) 629-5300.*

May 2004

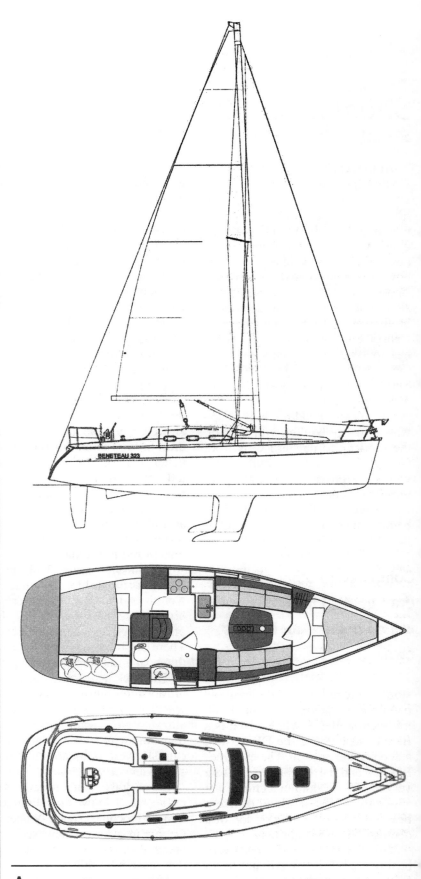

A comfortable couples cruiser with a clever wheel design.

LOA 32'10"; LWL 29'2"; Beam 10'8"; Draft 4'9" (Standard), 5'11" (Deep); Displacement 8,448 lbs.; Ballast 2,258 lbs.; Sail Area 492 sq. ft.; SA/D 18.93; D/L 152; L/B 3.08; Auxiliary Yanmar 18-hp; Fuel 17 gals.; Water 42 gals.

Brewer 33
Family Cruiser

It's fun to own a distinctive boat. I like it when people ask me about my boat. Of course, the ultimate in distinctive is to own a one-of-a-kind, custom boat. Ted Brewer found such a client and chose Tony Grove, an instructor at the Silva Bay Shipyard School in British Columbia, to build it in the cedar strip planking method. If you're looking for a project to fill up your free time, you can also buy the plans direct from Ted. Ted has designed a great looking little cutter for his client that should be an object of envy in any harbor. Maybe it would be fun to approach this review from the angle of just what makes this boat distinctive.

To begin with look at that sheerline. No wimpy, flaccid, spineless sheer here. This sheer has strength in its spring. The boat is pretty beamy, so it can stand a lot of sheer, which is accentuated by the 4-inch-high bulwark and cove stripe. Note that an echo of the sheer spring is carried over to the upper line of the bootstripe. Sheer gives boats character. Think of the boats you find really beautiful, and I'll bet you can trace that appeal straight back to the spring of the sheer. No matter how you detail a yacht, an ugly sheer will always be the kiss of death.

I like Ted's bow profile too. It has strength in its curvature.

I love outboard rudders, but I would have preferred to see this one with more "meat" in the area directly above the rudder blade. This one looks anemic, weak aesthetically to my eye. Fortunately the lure and appeal of the sheerline is so strong that your eye is not really drawn to the rudder.

Looks are one thing and performance is another. Considering that this boat is a cruiser and will be sailed by a cruiser you might as well throw out Mumm 30-styled performance goals. This client won't sail like that. You could argue that by raising the freeboard forward you increase windage. You could argue that the spoonlike convexity to the bow profile makes for fuller forward waterlines. But I'm certain that in both cases the client would say, "So what? I want a good looking boat!" The quality of time spent cruising is not necessarily always a function of boat speed. This becomes a matter of personal style.

Ted's hull lines show a hull with marked deadrise running full length. This gives the boat a sharp forefoot and a shape aft that almost approaches the old "bustle" shape. The waterlines reflect that deadrise and are quite symmetrical fore and aft indicating a boat that should maintain nice balance through a wide range of heel angles.

The deadrise at the transom gives a nice shape to the transom, which is accentuated by a bit of tumblehome. This transom may not be exactly the shape of speed, but

We don't build production boats like this. Not anymore.

it's a looker. If you choose to couple modern performance-dictated sectional shapes aft with a traditionally raked transom you will get a terrible looking stern. You have to have a pretty fanny on your boat.

The interior layout is fine, if you like dinettes and individual seats. I'd prefer settee berths with a drop-leaf table. I can hear Ted saying "Well Bob, when you build yours we'll do it like that." This would be an easy change to make in the plans. Note the diesel fired "fireplace" to starboard directly ahead of the seat. I don't like this galley. There is no counter space on either side of the sink. This would not suit my style of cooking at all. Where do the dirty dishes go? Where do the clean dishes go? Where does the clean lettuce go while I wash the rest? Why is Eric Clapton's new CD so bad? These are all important questions. But heck, this is what makes custom boats wonderful.

We don't build production boats like this. Not anymore. Financially it's too scary. Tooling, plugs and molds are very expensive. Today's production boat has to be an everyman's, one-size-fits-all type of boat that will have universal appeal not necessarily derived from its direct links to classic yacht beauty. We are losing these optimistic, unique expressions of one sailor's life on the water. Nice job Ted.

Brewer Yacht Design Ltd., P.O. Box 48, Gabriola Island, BC, Canada, VOR 1X0. (250) 247-7318. **www.tedbrewer.com**

July 2001

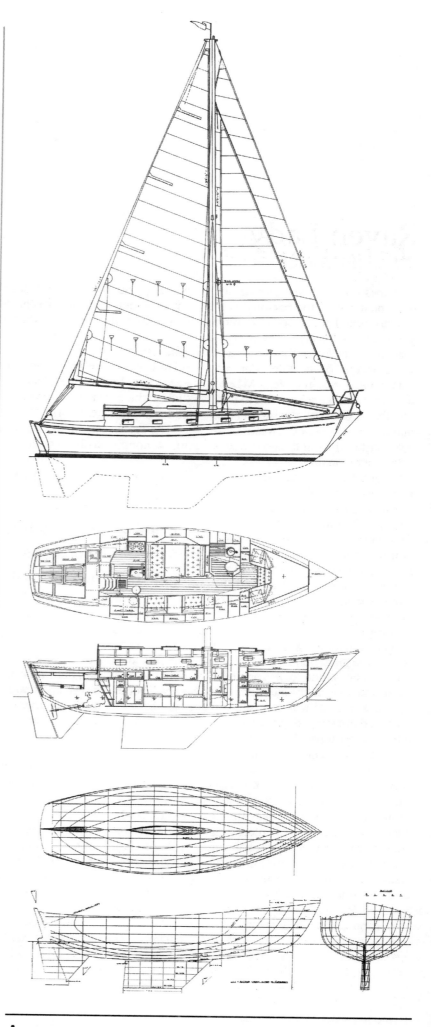

A custom cutter that's distinctive from its pretty fanny to its beautiful sheer.

LOA 33'1"; LWL 28'3"; Beam 10'7"; Draft 5'6"; Displacement 13,900 lbs.; Ballast 4,750 lbs.; Sail Area 613 sq. ft.; SA/D 16.9; D/L 275.2; L/B 3.11; Auxiliary Yanmar 3 GM 30 F; Fuel 40 gals.; Water 47 gals.

Raven Lady
Coastal Cruiser

"Does it make sense to sacrifice pure boat speed for personality?" For cruisers I think so, providing you preserve enough upwind performance to keep the boat and yourself out of trouble. For my part I need respectable VMG to weather to make a boat fun to sail. Ideally, the clever designer can maintain today's performance targets while infusing the boat with a distinct personality.

Raven Lady is the first design I have seen from Canadian designer Mike Camp of Comox, British Columbia. The boat is designed as a cat schooner, which is not the most weatherly of rigs since both sails have big round poles at their leading edges. Considering the performance potential of this hull, however, this rig is appropriate.

The stayless rig is clean and will be cheap to build with solid fir poles. The plans call for these masts to be deck stepped, but that's a tough way to support unstayed masts. I'd prefer to see the spars go through the deck and be securely stepped on the keel. The SA/D of this rig is 16.3, and considering that there are no headsail options to increase this ratio, I think this boat will be less than a rocket in light air. An interesting aspect of this rig is that, according to the designer, it requires no winches. Both sheets are 3:1 purchases, although in a blow I think a winch located on the aft end of the cabintrunk might come in handy.

The hull is a multichine (not "chime" and while I'm at it, there is no "n" in bowsprit) type for steel construction. Steel is certainly the most durable of hull materials, but it is the least designer-friendly in terms of shape and detailing. This hull shows a strong sheer spring and a pugnacious bow profile. There's plenty of lateral plane to the full keel, but draft is shy at 4 feet. The rudder is an outboard barn-door type with rack-and-pinion steering. The designer notes that you can add optional bilge keels to this design that will keep the boat upright when it "takes the mud." But bilge keels add a lot of wetted surface.

The layout is simple and comfy for a couple with two guests. I

Which reminds me of the scene in the "Rocky Horror Picture Show" when Dr. Frankenfurter declares, 'I didn't build him for you!'

don't think there is room at the dinette for all four crew to eat at once, and that is a problem. There's plenty of available cabin sole in this layout, but I'd prefer to see a better conversation area in the main cabin. Of course if the intended crew is two people, this will work just fine.

Clearly this design is aimed at the minimalist sailor who prefers simplicity and low cost over pure boat speed. A skilled and patient sailor could make this boat go to weather, but it would not be my ride of choice. Which reminds me of the scene in the "Rocky Horror Picture Show" when Dr. Frankenfurter declares, "I didn't build him for you!"

That's the beauty of custom designs. They have no need to appeal to everyone. This is a handsome vessel that would add interest and beauty to any anchorage.

Mike Camp Designs, General Delivery, Comox, British Columbia, Canada V9N 8A1. (250) 339-5521, fax (250) 339-5855.

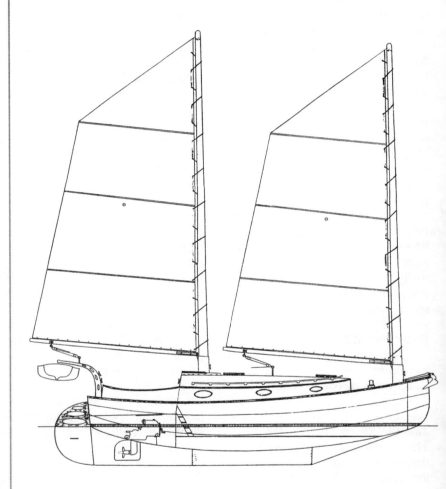

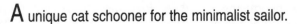

A unique cat schooner for the minimalist sailor.

LOA 33'5"; LWL 32'; Beam 11'; Draft 4'; Displacement 18,000 lbs.; Ballast 5,000 lbs.; Sail Area 700 sq. ft.; SA/D 16.3; D/L 245; L/B 3.03; Auxiliary Yanmar 27-hp saildrive.

Falmouth Cutter 34
Traditional Cruiser

When I was a kid I fell in love with a boat in one of Uffa Fox's books. It was *Dyarchy*, a big, noble 45-foot Channel Cutter designed by Roger Pinkney. Face it, you either like these traditional types or you don't. I'm not going to tell you they are fast because by today's standards they are not. The detailing required to pull them off aesthetically means they will require a lot of maintenance. But, even if these boats are not your cup of tea, it might be worthwhile to stop and take a look at one of the very few traditional types that still enjoys considerable popularity. This new Channel Cutter is built by Bryan Gittins in Cedar, on Vancouver Island in British Columbia. The original design was by Lyle Hess and is based upon his work with the type, including the Pardey's *Taleisin*.

There is a lot of boat here in 34 feet of LOA. The DWL is 30 feet, 10 inches and the D/L is 289. This sounds heavy but any time you have a full keel design with a D/L below 300 you have a relatively

> **It's impossible for me to be objective about boats like this. Cruising is such a personal thing.**

light design—relatively. The hull is beamy with an L/B of 2.93 and there is a firm turn to the bilge that you don't see on the older slack-bilged Channel Cutters. It should firm up initial stability. The bow sections of this model are much fuller than typical with the fullness added above the DWL so the angle of entry is not affected. I measure the angle of entry as 18 degrees and that's quite fine, perhaps even finer than the HR 37. The sections are wineglass type with hollow garboards and the ballast is internal. The outboard "barn door" rudder is essential to the look.

The galley is big. There is a pilot berth and a quarterberth that should prove ideal offshore. I can keep my guitar on that pilot berth ready for any emergency. The head is generous and includes a wet locker. The double berth forward looks like it's minimal but adequate. A fireplace

can sit snugly on the counter ahead of the starboard settee. Heck, what's a boat like this for if not for a Charley Noble? You will have to duck as you go by the head area as there is no headroom there, but the scuttle-type hatch over the forward berth gives headroom in that area and looks very cool.

The rig is big and should keep this hooker moving in light air. My pal Bernie claims his Channel Cutter is deceptively fast in light air. The mast is well forward in this hull, and with the bowsprit, it brings the center of pressure even farther forward. I'm certain this boat will show fingertip balance in all conditions. The long boom allows the mainsheet bridle to be mounted on the transom but there is no traveler. A short A-frame-type boomkin aft allows the backstay to clear the roach. Chainplates are outboard so sheeting won't be tight but it will be in concert with the hull form.

It's impossible for me to be objective about boats like this. Cruising is such a personal thing. As long as a boat has no genetic flaws that would make it dangerous I can't tell you a boat is "wrong." A boat should be an extension of the owner's personality. Mr. Gittins' construction style is traditional, beautiful and totally in keeping with the type. Maybe the perfect cruising boat is one that makes you feel good. Maybe it's not about tenths of a knot or pointing ability or blistering light-air speed. Maybe cruising is an aesthetic lifestyle statement. I just can't help feel that if you were anchored in your plain white sloop and you watched a Channel Cutter like this one slip into the harbor and drop anchor (all under sail of course) you would be a wee bit jealous. I know I would.

Uffa wrote in 1930 that *Dyarchy* represented "the quintessence of the English cutter—one of the last of her line." Well, not if Mr. Gittins can help it.

Channel Cutter Yachts, 3300 Bissel Rd., Ladysmith, British Colombia V9G 1E4, Canada. **www.channelcutteryachts.com** *(250) 722-3340.*

February 2004

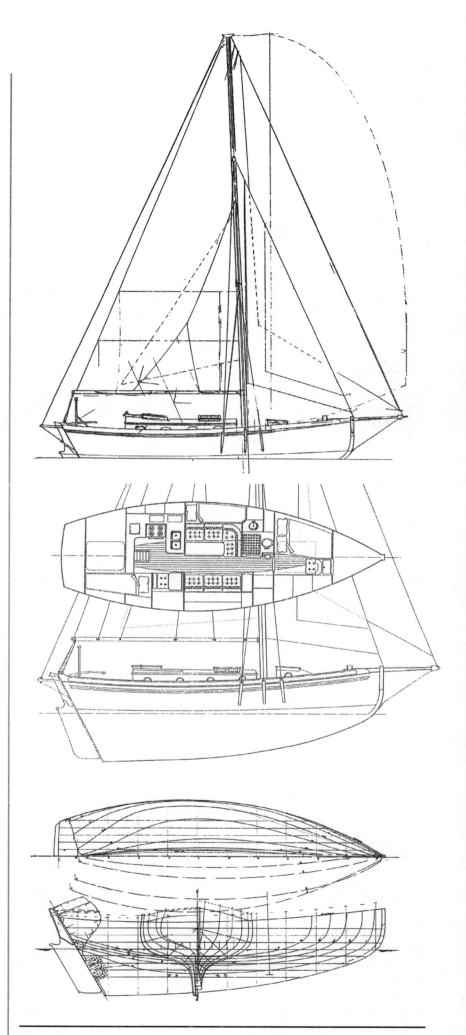

Tradition lives on in this pretty Channel Cutter.

LOA 34'; LWL 30'10"; Beam 11'7"; Draft 5'1"; Displacement 19,000 lbs.; Ballast 6,600 lbs.; Sail Area 800 sq. ft.; SA/D 17.98; D/L 289; L/B 2.93; Auxiliary Yanmar 40-hp; Fuel 75 gals.; Water 90 gals.

Seaward Eagle 32
Coastal Cruiser

This boat is not a motorsailer. It's a shoal draft, lifting-keel sloop that you can trailer behind the family's stout SUV. The brochure shows the boat nestled up to a white sandy beach. The lady holding onto the stern is in calf-deep water. Now this type of convenience is not too important in deep-old Puget Sound, but I know a lot of you live where water depths over 7 feet are a luxury. If you are one of those sailors this boat should get your attention. I know my swimming-crazy dogs would love this boat.

I saw this boat at the Annapolis Boat Show. You should really go to that show. I don't know of any other show that gets the sheer numbers of different models collected in one

It's good to see a designer with the chutzpa to put a healthy spring in the sheer.

extended marina. I thought this was a handsome boat with a perky, near-plumb stem, nice accenting rubrail and well-sculpted deck structures.

What I don't like about his design is the way the sheer spring has been exaggerated aft. This is a great example of why you need to think of these lines in three dimensions. The sailplan shows this strong sheerline, and it looks just fine. But in the water, it appears to my eye that there is some conflict with the sheer's low point and the distribution of beam. The kick in the sheer aft is just too exaggerated for my eye. Still, it's good to see a designer with the chutzpa to put a healthy spring in the sheer. It certainly gives this boat a distinct personality, and nit-picking aside I like this boat. The sheer is even further accentuated by the integral extension of the GRP bowsprit. The design work was done by the company president, Nick Hake. The new model is a development of the company's fixed-keel Eagle, which was introduced in 1988.

This is a shapely, dinghylike hull with a hard knuckle at the forefoot and the deepest part of the canoe body well forward. The fin and bulb keel fully retract so that only the bulb is visible, which reduces the draft from 6 feet, 6 inches to 20 inches. The keel is raised with an electric

winch operated from the cockpit. If the winch fails you can use the mainsheet to raise the keel. The cleverly designed outboard rudder kicks up. Rudder and propeller are well above the low point of the retracted keel. Displacement is 8,300 pounds with a 30 percent ballast-to-displacement ratio. The point of maximum beam is very far aft in this design. Using the typical 10-station breakdown of hull shapes, most boats show max beam around station 6. In this case, however, it has been pushed aft to around station 8. The D/L is 129.

Like many small production cruising boats, this model is built with a molded GRP liner. The Seaward Eagle's interior is very nicely detailed with laminated teak joiner accents. The layout has been carefully balanced to provide a good-sized dinette to port with small seats to starboard in the main cabin. There is a double quarter-berth to port and a V-berth makes another double. The head has a shower stall and this is quite unusual on a 32-footer. The lifting-keel trunk is neatly worked into this layout, so its impact is negligible, if even noticeable.

The rig features a fathead mainsail with extended headboard to maximize the main area while keeping the overall mast height minimized. I suspect this may have been done to help with the trailering aspect of the design. A long crane at the masthead pulls the backstay aft so it clears the roach of the main. SA/D is 17.95 and that should be plenty to give the Eagle good speed in all conditions. The mast is lowered and raised using the exposed upper keel arm as a gin pole. I wondered what that strange stainless tubing feature shown in the photos was on the stern until I realized it's a crutch to hold the mast when it's lowered for trailering.

On deck the Eagle is detailed in yachtlike fashion, and this boat has a very capable look to it. The transom is open to allow direct access to the rudder lifting mechanism. There is 65 gallons of water tankage, 24 gallons of fuel and 30 gallons of holding. The auxiliary is a 28-horsepower Yanmar.

Hake Yachts, 4550 SE Hampton Ct., Stuart, FL 34997. (561) 287-3200. www.seawardyachts.com

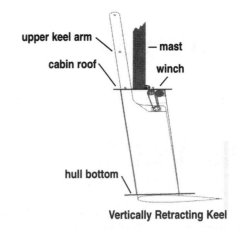

Vertically Retracting Keel

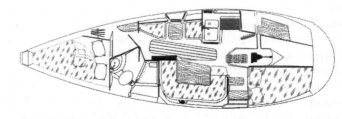

Innovative shoal-draft sloop.

LOA 34'7"; LWL 30'7"; Beam 10'6"; Draft 6'6" (keel down), 20" (keel up); Displacement 8,300 lbs.; Ballast 2,500 lbs.; Sail Area 460 sq. ft.; SA/D 17.95; D/L 129; L/B 3.29; Auxiliary 28-hp 3GM30 Yanmar; Fuel 24 gals.; Water 66 gals.

Babson Island 35
Daysailer

Regular readers will know by now that I'm big on boats being playful extensions of our personal approaches to life on the water. In short, have some fun with it. Leave the tenth of a knot stuff to the hardcore racers and get a sailboat that allows you to exercise the subjective side of sailing. This doesn't mean you forget about performance, you just balance it with some art.

I like nostalgic boats. They remind me of all the things that attracted me to sailing when I was a kid. This new boat from the Brooklin Boat Yard in Maine is a perfect example. It's hardcore nostalgic but you had better think twice before you harden up on it and expect to blow it away on a stiff beat up the bay.

The real fun part of this project was just how it got started. A lady came by the yard and asked if they could build a boat that she could give to her husband as a wedding gift. She thought he might like a nice big daysailer. What a gal! The yard said no problem and off it went. Total time for this transaction was five minutes. It appears to me that she made a wise choice.

The chief designer for the Brooklin yard is Robert Stephens and he has carefully hand drawn a lovely design. The hull shape shows high deadrise with an angle amidships of 20 degrees. Beam on deck is 9 feet, 4 inches while BWL is 7 feet, 9 inches. There is a lot of shape to the topsides. The transom has a gentle heart shape to it that shows some hollow in the garboards. This hollow garboard shape is reflected in a slight hollow in the counter aft. The D/L is 181 and the prismatic is .54. The deep, bulb fin gives this slack-bilged boat the stability it needs to stay on its feet. The L/B is 3.79.

The sailplan shows off the sweet sheer of this vessel. The cabintrunk is built with the sides angled outboard in reverse to what we are used to seeing in modern designs that need to be released from a fiberglass mold. This is a quaint and traditional look. The rig fea-

The real fun part of this project was just how it got started.

tures a self-tacking jib with the single jib sheet led up the mast so it can be brought down and led to a convenient winch on the cabintop. The SA/D is 21.8.

The interior shows about 4 feet, 6 inches of headroom. There is an enclosed head and a small galley in addition to V-berths. I don't see a dining table and I don't see any hanging locker. Given that this boat is a daysailer, the emphasis has been on the cockpit and not the interior. However, I'd at least like to see a spot where a couple could sit comfortably and dine.

The Babson 35 is built in 5/8-inch cedar strip planking skinned with 6-ounce unidirectional carbon fiber inside and out. Cored panels were used in the interior to save more weight. This provides a light and stiff hull with a good ballast-to-displacement ratio.

Think of the times you spent daysailing your boat. Cruising around the bay with your friends crammed into a small cockpit while you drag around sleeping accommodations for six. This is exactly the reverse of what many of us really need. The Babson 35 addresses the concerns of daysailing first and does it in a stylish manner. If I had a long dock in front of my house I'd put a Babson 35 on it. I'd just take a chair, a cup of tea and my pipe down in the morning and relax looking at the boat. It would be good for my blood pressure.

Brooklin Boat Yard, P.O. Box 143, Brooklin, Maine 04616. (207) 359-2236.

May 2003

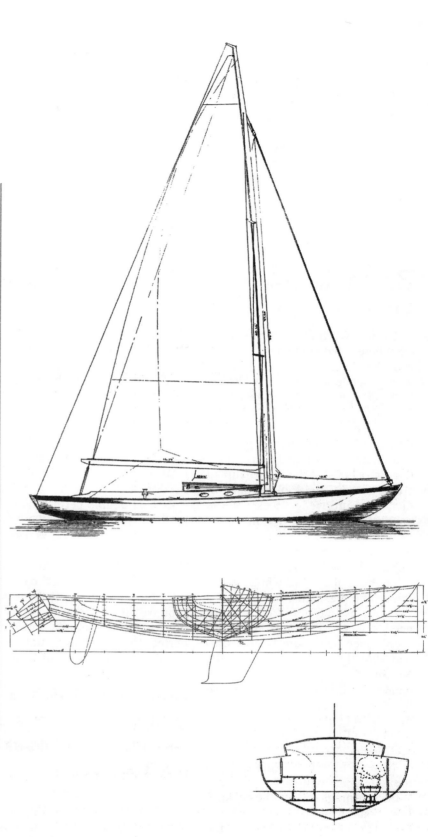

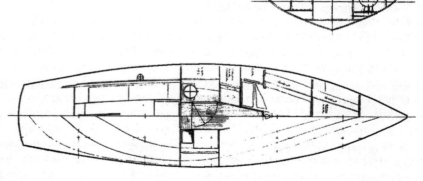

A retro design made for relaxing daysails.

LOA 35'4"; LWL 27'; Beam 9'4"; Draft 6'; Displacement 7,544 lbs.; Ballast 3,850 lbs.; Sail Area 544 sq. ft.; SA/D 21.8; D/L 181; L/B 3.79; Auxiliary Yanmar 18hp: Fuel 9 gals.; Water 9 gals.

Bavaria 34
Family Cruiser

Clearly we find ourselves in an era where "character boats" are out, and the focus is on Euro-styling with a general high-tech design look. This is okay, but it gets a little boring after a while. Obviously if you use a modern hull form, i.e. plumb stem, broad stern, high freeboard and highly raked transom for a swim step, it will be difficult to create a traditional-looking boat. In fact, the Euro/wedge-deck style is your only reasonable option.

With that as a given, the designer must draw a sleek-looking cabintrunk that will provide headroom throughout the boat while at the same time presenting the look of a voluminous interior. You do not need a wide cabintrunk for headroom since headroom is only crucial directly over the cabin sole. Making the trunk wider, however, creates the illusion of more useable interior volume, although at a cost of less side deck area and more windage. Teak accents this nicely sculpted deck.

Now with the cabintrunk defined the designer will need to wrap some coamings around the cockpit. Low coamings will look great and provide excellent sheet leads to the winches. But if you get the coaming any lower than 10 inches above the seat level, it will dig into your kidneys and provide little security or overall comfort.

The Bavaria shows a good way of dealing with high coamings. They are stepped down as they go aft and this breaks up the overall bulk. With emphasis on cockpit size, the coamings on the Bavaria are carried all the way to the transom but are scooped out to make them lower as they go across the top of the transom. This cockpit opens directly to the swim step. I should mention that there are numerous discrepancies between the details as drawn and as shown on the

photos. There's no problem with this other than the fact that they make reviewing the boat difficult.

You can choose between two layouts. One has the head forward and two double quarter berths aft, and the other has the head aft and one bigger quarter double berth. In the head-forward model, the V-berth is truncated on the port side making it, to my eye, less than a full-sized double berth. The galley is tiny. You have to stand your Vegemite sandwich on end in this galley. I think a 35-foot, 5-inch boat should offer a better galley. But it's all a matter of balancing priorities. You can call them compromises if you like. Certainly the big, opposing, straight settees are perfect for entertaining and dining, just don't expect a leg of lamb.

I think this boat will be a good performer if you avoid the shoal keel that draws only 4 feet, 5 inches.

The hull and rig are so typical I think I'll combine my comments on them into one paragraph. The D/L is 207 and the SA/D is 18.98. The hull form is normal with a near plumb stem. There is a nice indented whale stripe in the topsides to accent the sheerline. The spreaders are swept and there are no runners. I think this boat will be a good performer if you avoid the shoal keel that draws only 4 feet, 5 inches.

This model fits the Mediterranean charterboat type well.

Bavaria Yachts, P.O. Box 3415, Annapolis, MD 21403., (410) 990-0007, **www.bavariayachts.com**

May 2000

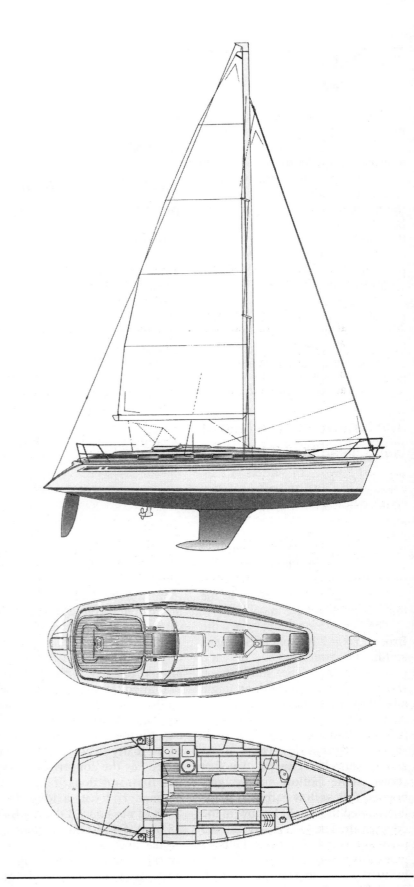

Euro-style cruiser is a strong entry in a competitive market.

LOA 35'5"; LWL 27'8"; Beam 11'5"; Draft 4'5" (shoal), 5'11" (deep); Displacement 9,920 lbs.; Ballast 3,086 lbs.; Sail Area 545 sq. ft.; SA/D 18.98; D/L 207; L/B 3.1; Auxiliary Volvo 19 hp MD 2020; Fuel 40 gals.; Water 80 gals.

Elan 36
Family Cruiser

Rob Humphreys is the designer of this 36 and he's one of my favorites.

The overall hull proportions are similar to those of the Sun Odyssey with an L/B of 3.05 and a D/L of 209, although the hull profile shows a small "fin of mystery" ahead of the raked rudder.

The forward berth is kind of weird. I can't tell if it's a full-sized double berth or a 'half-double.'

Generally I like to keep the keel as far aft as possible. If you combine this keel and rig location with the fact that the rig is drawn with substantial rake, you might imagine a beamy boat that is difficult to balance through a wide range of heel angles.

Two keels are offered drawing 4 feet, 7 inches and 6 feet, 5 inches. I don't like the square facing on the stem. If you are going to cut the water cleanly it seems to me a radiused or sharper cutwater might be desirable. The stern is very, very broad. The sheerline shows that attractive perkiness that distinguishes Humphreys' designs.

This rig also has swept spreaders (24 degrees) and a babystay forward. Sailmakers love babystays. They tear away at the leech of the genoa every time you tack. The SA/D of this 36-footer is 18.75. Note that the mainsheet traveler is in the cockpit with the track on the bridgedeck. This pre-

cludes a dodger, but it sure makes handling the mainsail easier.

The Elan also has two staterooms aft with double berths. I like the nook-styled nav station of this design.

The galley is adjacent to the large dinette, and while this may not be ideal for offshore, it certainly is appealing for cooking at rest. I'd like to cook in this galley. Again, I don't see any galley drawers. Drawers are expensive to build, but they are definitely the most efficient way to stow kitchen utensils.

The forward berth is kind of weird. I can't tell if it's a full-sized double berth or a "half-double." Clearly the port side is not long enough for an adult, and I can't see how a filler piece could be used to turn this into one large double. Maybe this is a berth for kids, and the adults will sleep aft.

The beamy stern of this design allows for a big cockpit, although it does not open to the transom swim step. Inboard shrouds and genoa tracks keep the side decks clean, and the teak decking, which will provide excellent non-skid, is raised to provide a deep waterway along the rail. This time, the aluminum toerail has holes. There is a well in the foredeck for ground tackle.

The Elan appears to have been designed with the charter trade in mind.

Elan Marine, 4275 Begunje na Gorenjskerm, Slovenija. + 386 64 75 10, fax + 386 64 751 386 **www.elan-marine.com**

April 2000

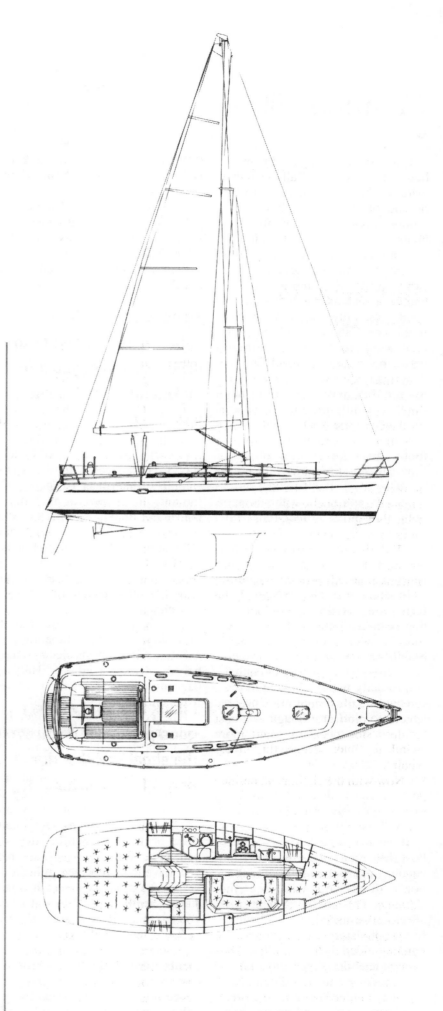

Rob Humphreys' design combines a beamy hull with extra sail power.

LOA 35'11"; LWL 30'8"; Beam 11'9"; Draft 4'7" (shoal keel), 6'5" (deep keel); Displacement 12,760 lbs. (shoal keel), 12,100 lbs. (deep keel); Ballast 5,500 lbs. (shoal keel), 4,840 lbs. (deep keel); SA/D 18.75; D/L 209; L/B 3.05; Auxiliary Yanmar 28 hp; Fuel 23 gals.; Water 66 gals.

Catalina 350
Cruiser

Catalinas are designed by an in-house team that by all available evidence has truly tapped into the psyche of the American cruising family. Look at the numbers of boats they produce. That should be evidence enough. I have given talks to Catalina owners' groups and I can't think of a more satisfied bunch of owners. In fact, some of them have only owned Catalinas. In this new Catalina 350 I see a perfect example of the synthesis between the Euro approach and the American approach, although to my eye they have swayed this new Catalina a little too far toward the Euro side of the design coin.

With 13 feet of beam on a 36-footer we have an L/B of 2.77. From any point of view you have to see that as fat. If I do some quick scaling I get a beam at the corners of the transom of 11 feet, four inches. I can think of older 36-footers that had less than that. But all this beam has a purpose—volume below and cockpit volume on deck.

In defense of this type of hull form you should also remember that beam adds stability and we all like a stable or "stiff" boat. Stability equals sail carrying power and affords the option of sailing comfortably without having to reef or change sails frequently. You can get a fin keel drawing 6 feet, 8 inches or a wing-type keel drawing 4 feet, 6 inches. My guess is that while 4 feet, 6 inches of draft may sound nice, you will give up a lot of performance with this shoal keel no matter how big those wings are. The D/L is 199.

If when you go below you like a boat that smells of diesel fuel, fried bacon, wet wool and old cordage I don't think you will like the Catalina. This sparkling interior is all gloss varnished teak and sumptuous upholstery set off by a clean white molded headliner. There is enough teak detailing in this interior to make you forget you are looking at a molded interior liner boat. The layout is focused on two-couple cruising with comfort to burn. There is an athwartships double quarterberth that looks huge. The nav area is neatly tucked outboard of the aft leg of the port settee. A generously large television is mounted over the chart table

("Where are we?" "I don't know but come below, the "Anna Nicole Show" is about to start.")

Speaking of Anna Nicole, the galley looks great with plenty of stowage and a microwave mounted directly above the range.

The rig is pure American classic masthead type. There are fore and

There is enough teak detailing in this interior to make you forget you are looking at a molded interior liner boat.

aft lower shrouds and a split backstay to ease access to the swim step. The mainsheet is once again too much midboom for me but this placement of the mainsheet opens up options for the dodger while eliminating clutter from the cockpit. The SA/D is 17.18.

The beam of the 350 allows for wide, unobstructed side decks with the chainplates and genoa track well inboard. Halyards are lead aft to winches at the companionway and there is even an electric main halyard winch available. Halyard bags are provided to keep the lines from spilling into the cockpit.

The cockpit itself is huge. It's wide enough so that there is room for a drop-leaf table in the middle. It's fun to eat in the cockpit, so a permanent table there is great and on a boat this beamy it helps break the wide open spaces of the cockpit up into more secure spaces. I'm not keen on those robotlike steering pedestals. Why does all the nav gear have to be repeated right at the helm? You can only see it when you stand directly abaft (I love it when you talk like that) the pedestal. This pedestal has room for a chartplotting screen, all the sailing instruments, the engine instruments, engine controls and a compass. It's a wee bit on the bulky side for my delicate eye, but I'm confident it's exactly what the buyers want.

Catalina Yachts, 21200 Victory Blvd., Woodland Hills, CA 91367. **www.catalinayachts.com** *(818) 884-7700.*

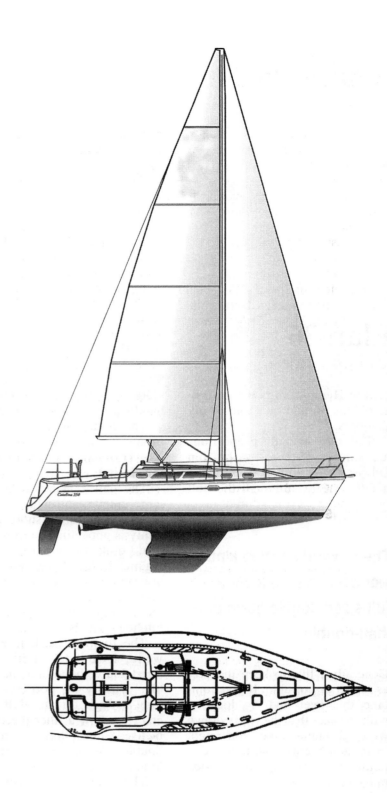

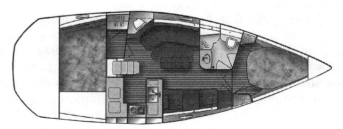

Mixing American and European styles in a family cruiser.

LOA 36'; LWL 31'3"; Beam 13'; Draft 6'8" (deep), 4'6" (shoal); Displacement 13,635 lbs.; Ballast 5,835 lbs.; Sail Area 613 sq. ft.; SA/D 17.18; D/L 199; L/B 2.77; Auxiliary Universal M35; Fuel 39 gals.; Water 88.5 gals.

Southerly 110
Coastal Cruiser

If you want to wreck a designer's day just tell him you want your new boat to be shoal draft. From a designer's outlook, draft makes a lot of performance options viable. Lowering the keel drops the VCG, and that adds sail-carrying power. It also ensures a good "grip" on the water to allow the boat good VMGs to weather.

Of course in some areas shoal draft is a prerequisite if you want to venture out of the dredged channel. So with that in mind it's no surprise that a builder like Southerly in England has come up with a complete line of retractable-keel cruising yachts.

The leeward rudder will maintain its effectiveness even when the weather rudder is lifting.

Let's start by identifying some of the problems with a retractable keel. First, it's an additional mechanism and that should lead to maintenance considerations. Second, the keel trunk can intrude upon the accommodation volume. And third, by matching the keel-up draft with the depth of the rudder you can end up with a small and shallow rudder that cavitates at low angles allowing the boat to round up in the puffs.

Probably the biggest concern, especially with today's "Ooooh, am I going to tip over?" mentality, is the question of stability. When the keel comes up so does the bulk of the ballast and a higher CG means less stability. These are all reasonable considerations. Let's see how Southerly dealt with them.

Southerly started on the right foot by hiring one of my very favorite designers, Rob Humphreys. We've never met but I'm going to call him Rob. Rob's design work combines both racing and cruising types and that gives him an edge on performance. I usually love his sheerlines, and even in this stubby design, there is some perkiness to the relatively flat sheer.

The mechanism of this lifting keel is very clever. It combines a grounding plate comprising 66

percent of the ballast, with a large-diameter stainless steel pin to pivot the keel. The keel trunk is hidden in the interior by combining it into the galley-dinette area. And the "silly little rudder" problem has been handled by using two rudders, so that the leeward rudder will maintain its effectiveness even when the weather rudder is lifting to the point where it will suck air.

Stability? Okay, here's where I raise my right eyebrow. The brochure claims that with the keel raised this design has in excess of 140 degrees of positive righting moment. But I'd have to have more data on exactly how that righting moment was calculated before I trusted it. This is not a heavy boat (D/L 221) and this is not a narrow boat (L/B 3.04). In fact, for a cruising boat it's relatively light and wide, and I would estimate the VCG of this design at about 6 inches above the DWL. Perhaps they included the volume of the entire deck, maybe even the mast. That's just fine, but it's not the way the IMS does it, which is the standard for stability comparison in this country if you want to enter an offshore race in many areas. Either way, my eyebrow is still up at that jaunty angle.

The layout is very Euro, with a big double berth tucked under the cockpit, and a head accessed from the galley area or the aft cabin. The galley looks good to me, but I wonder about those cute little round sinks. Being the cook I also like to do the dishes so that I'll know everything is clean to my standards before I prepare the next meal. It's a personal problem.

I don't have I, J, E and P for this design so I can't give you a precise SA/D but from the look of the rig it's small. Using the areas for full mainsail and genoa I get 16.05. Without genoa overlap and mainsail roach the actual SA/D must be down around 14. That's approaching motorsailer ratios.

This would be a good San Francisco boat.

Northshore Yachts Ltd., Itchenor, Chichester, West Sussex, PO 20 7AY, United Kingdom. +44 1243 512611. www.northshore.co.uk

June 2000

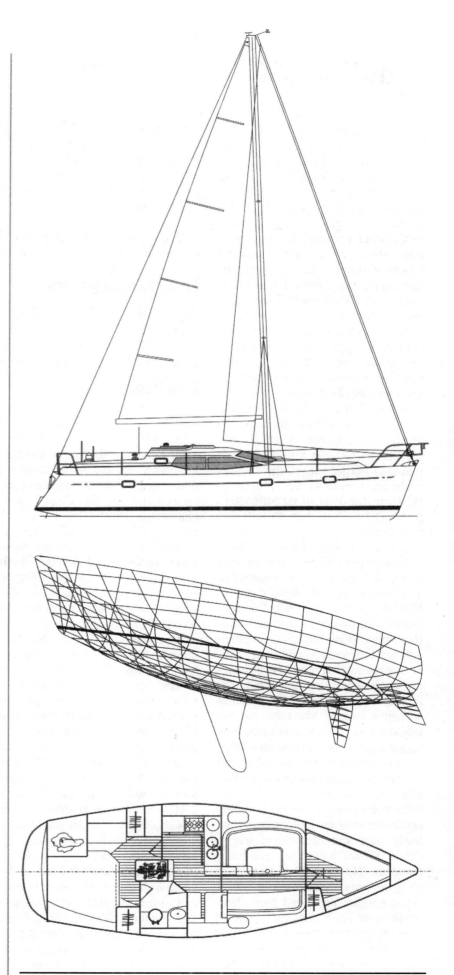

Shoal-draft cruiser from Rob Humphreys.

LOA 36'; LWL 30'3"; Beam 11'10"; Draft 2'4" (board up), 7'2" (board down); Displacement 13,750 lbs.; Ballast 6,765 lbs. (including board); Sail Area 576 sq. ft. (including genoa overlap); SA/D 16.05 (for full genoa); D/L 221; L/B 3.04; Auxiliary Yanmar GM30 27-hp; Fuel 40 gals.; Water 45 gals.

Morris 36
Traditional Cruiser

Sometimes I like to dig through my pile of old *Yachting* magazines to top up my creative well. I even like the smell of the old magazines. From time to time we see an effort to recreate the look of the boats of the early 1950s. I find most efforts unsatisfactory with the end result being neither fish nor fowl. But when it comes to aesthetics I'm about as picky a critic as you will find. Materials have changed. Detailing of decks has

I'm sure this boat will have a lot of you drooling. It should.

changed. Rigs and rig hardware have changed. And more than anything else our expectations have changed. Headroom in the 1950s was 5 feet, 11 inches at most. It's all different today. Headroom today is 6 feet, 6 inches, and you had better not hit your head.

The biggest impact of these changing expectations can be seen in the freeboard of this new Morris Yachts and Sparkman & Stephens project, the Morris 36. It's a handsome boat … but it would be far more handsome if you chopped the freeboard off where the cove stripe is and then lowered the cove stripe. But the first thing you would lose would be sitting headroom over the settees. In a relatively light boat like this 36 with a D/L of 220 and a shallow canoe body, the cabin sole can only go so low.

Then there is the issue of cabin-trunk height. You need the cabin-trunk to be high enough to mount opening ports. This dimension is the same for a 24-footer and a 74-footer, about 10 to 12 inches depending upon the exact portlight you are using. If you are working from a headroom requirement and a cabin sole location you can lower the freeboard, but you will have to raise the cabintrunk, which could then look too high and stubby. The best aesthetic solution is what you

see on the Morris—keep the trunk as low as possible. But now you are stuck with that freeboard. So what I'm trying to say here is that I would like to see less freeboard, but given contemporary requirements I don't think there is any way you can do it. If you really want vintage proportions you would be safer working out these relationships on a 70-footer or revising your own ergonomic expectations.

The DWL of the Morris 36 is really short at 25 feet on a LOA of 36 feet, 3 inches, which results in long overhangs. Note the concavity in the counter aft. This hollow will give the transom a pretty shape. The keel and rudder are up to date and should ensure good handling and decent speed to weather for the DWL. Of course the overhangs will contribute some to the sailing length once the boat is heeled over.

You could cruise this boat very comfortably. The layout would work well for two people sleeping on the settees. There is a huge fo'c'sle for stowage. The cockpit is really nice with all lines led to winch pods located on each side of the wheel. The helmsman will be able to make any required sail adjustments without getting up. The cockpit benches appear long enough to sleep on.

The SA/D is a healthy 24.6 and this should give the 36 good light air speed. The jib is self-tending. One benefit of that long stern overhang is that it allows the backstay to be far enough aft to clear the mainsail roach.

I'm sure this boat will have a lot of you drooling. It should. Morris will do a superb job of building it and it will look fabulous on the end of your dock or sliding down the line for the start of a club race. I find this a very pretty design. She'll be a head turner.

Morris Yachts, P.O. Box 395, Grandville Rd., Bass Harbor, ME 04653. **www.morrisyachts.com** *(207) 244-5509.*

February 2004

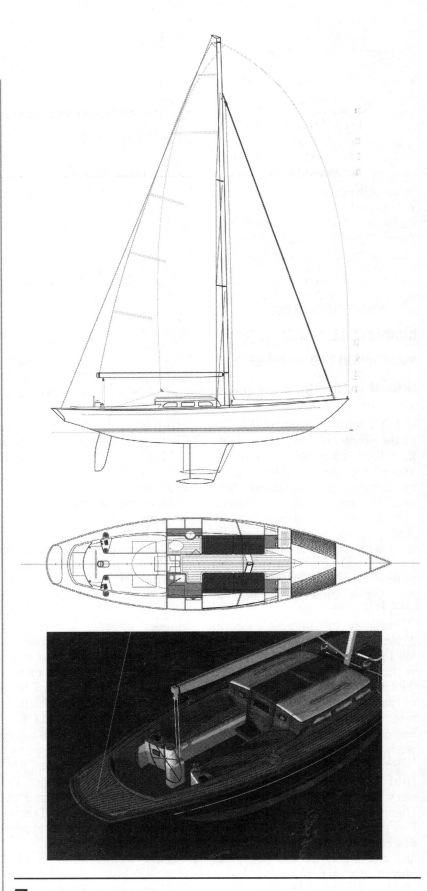

The best mix of old and new in 36 feet LOA.

LOA 36'3"; LWL 25'; Beam 10'1"; Draft 6'6" (Standard), 5'3" (Shoal); Displacement 7,700 lbs.; Ballast 3,750 lbs.; Sail Area 599 sq. ft.; SA/D 24.6; D/L 220; L/B 3.6; Auxiliary Yanmar 18-hp; Fuel 12 gals.; Water 20 gals.

Nauticat 37
Motorsailer

Siltala Yachts of Finland builds a well-thought-out line of motorsailers. The line is divided into two styles. The earlier Nauticats were designed by S&S and are boxy and traditional looking. The newer models, like this one designed by Kaj and Patrick Gustafsson, show a more svelte Euro approach to motorsailer aesthetics.

I'm not sure I would go so far as to say the new 37 is good-looking. A lot of boat has been packed into 37 feet, and accommodation pressures have produced a high freeboard, which is further exaggerated by a raised quarterdeck. Once you have studied the Procrustean nature of these layouts, however, you will better understand the profile of the 37. And given these pressures, I wouldn't say this boat is *bad*-looking either. It's a 37-foot, center-cockpit motorsailer with a pilothouse, and this is a challenge to any stylist. I don't have any photos to refer to, but based on the drawings I have, the 37 looks to be an interesting hybrid of performance and comfort types.

The hull shows plenty of fore and aft rocker. The keel is a small fin with a draft of just over 6 feet. The rudder is on a partial skeg, and the ends of this hull have been cut off as much as reasonably possible. The bowsprit extension will be needed to get the ground tackle away from the stem. I know it's in vogue to have minimal bow overhang, but it makes me wonder if in this case the designers would not have been better off adding some overhang to take the stem out to where the end of the bowsprit is. That would have eliminated a costly detail, the bowsprit, while adding a smidge of sailing length. It would have also added considerably more deck space forward while producing a dryer if slightly more old-fashioned-looking boat. The D/L of this design is 235.

There are three interiors available for the 37, with the aft stateroom staying pretty much the same with a double berth and small head in all but one. You can have inside steering with a wheel or an extended chart table. Keep in mind that you could still steer with an autopilot remote if you went with the extended chart table version. Forward, you can have one stateroom with a large head or two staterooms with a smaller head. I find three separate

staterooms on a 37-footer hard to imagine, but you can have it here. The optional guest stateroom has only one berth and tucks under the dinette.

How did you like that word "Procrustean?" It comes from a Greek robber who used to take his

Clearly Nauticat is a master of this type of boat.

victims home then stretch or cut off their limbs until they fit his bed. I find it perversely appropriate when applied to compacted interiors like these. Classical myths aside, all three layouts appear to me to be well designed.

When I look at this sailplan, I get the idea the designers had in mind a hybrid between a modern racing yacht and the boat's older Nauticat siblings. The rigs have fore and aft lowers, and in-line spreaders. What's wrong with that, you ask? Among other things, swept spreaders would require only one chainplate rather than three and would be cheaper to build. Also the forward lower shroud can get in the way when tacking. Other than those issues, if you equip this boat with a good, stout mast section and a backstay adjuster, you will be fine. Still, I think I would have preferred the simplicity of a swept-spreader rig. The SA/D is 18.

The cockpit sits above the raised quarterdeck of this design, giving you a feeling of being really high up when you steer this boat. The cockpit is fine, with room enough for a large-diameter wheel and small bench seats forward. There is a flush anchor well forward, but no aft deck-access storage that I can see. The big pilothouse windows are aluminum framed safety glass.

Clearly Nauticat is a master of this type of boat. The company's quality is always top-notch. It has had a lot of practice bringing us capable motorsailers. While the motorsailer as a type lacks the romance of some of the racier approaches, it just may be the boat we need for all-weather comfortable cruising.

Siltala Yachts OY, Lallintie 92, FIN-21870, Riihikoski, Finland. 358 2 486 400. **www.nauticat.com**

July 2002

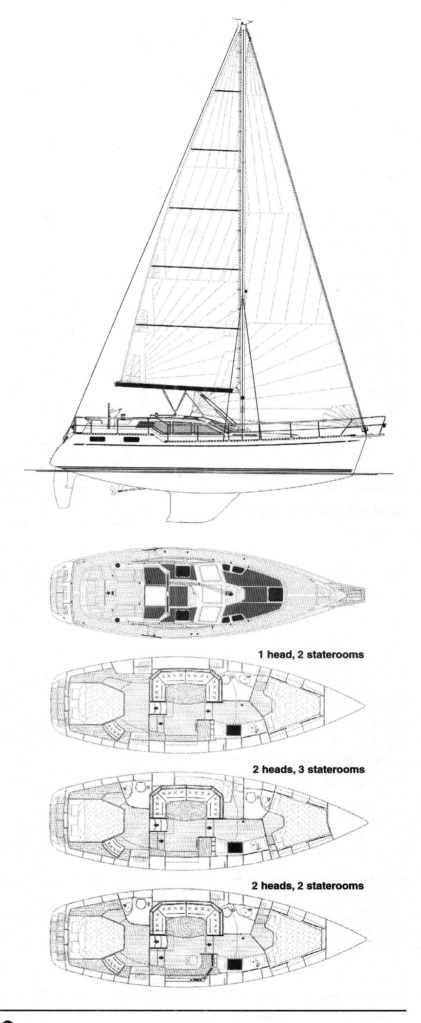

1 head, 2 staterooms

2 heads, 3 staterooms

2 heads, 2 staterooms

Sturdy all-weather motorsailer from Scandinavia.

LOA 36'10"; LWL 33'1"; Beam 11'11"; Draft 6'; Displacement 19,200 lbs.; Ballast 6,700 lbs.; Sail Area 807 sq. ft.; SA/D 18; D/L 235; L/B 3.08; Auxiliary Yanmar 4JH3-E; Fuel 115 gals.; Water 105 gals.

Etap 37
Bluewater Cruiser

I like these Belgian Etap boats. They always appear to be purpose designed and are more handsome than beautiful. This design is by Mortain and Mavrikios, but the drawings we have all come from the factory design team. The main sales point of the Etap line is that its boat are built with a double skin and they are certified as unsinkable. The double skin also helps eliminate condensation.

The hull of the 37 has a D/L of 188 and an L/B of 2.92. Anytime you get an L/B under 3.00 you have a beamy boat and I would be inclined to call it fat. Based upon the drawings I have the hull form looks very regular with the de rigueur short ends and broad transom but in this case the transom beam is not exaggerated. You can choose from a deep keel drawing 6 feet, 5 inches or you can go with the tandem shoal keel drawing 4 feet, 5 inches. These tandem keels have been around for years and

A big part of the Etap 37's good looks, in my opinion, is the quasi-flush deck configuration.

they do have some structural and pragmatic advantages but remember, there is no substitute for draft when it comes to performance. Of course, any boat with its keel imbedded in the mud is very slow. Curiously, the drawings show a deep rudder that goes with both keels and the rudder draws more than the shoal keel. I hope this is a drafting error.

At first glance there is not much in this interior layout they could not have accomplished with a more narrow boat. But if you look care-

fully you will see that with the stateroom aft and the head aft the additional beam allows better access to those areas while not hurting the galley or the nav area.

A big part of the Etap 37's good looks, in my opinion, is the quasi-flush deck configuration. The cabin sole steps down preserving most of the headroom. There is a wedge running forward of the cabintrunk that helps with headroom. It's not really a flush deck but it looks like one. The cockpit has long seats that are nipped aft to make room for the wheel. Genoa tracks and chainplates are inboard leaving the side decks clear. There is a deep, deck-accessed anchor well in the bow.

The rig is tall and fractional with swept double spreaders. Is there an echo in here? The drawings show the optional inner forestay that allows a hanked on storm jib to be flown while the primary genoa is rolled up on the headstay. It's not much fun to have to beat to weather in a breeze with a big sausage right in front of your jib's leading edge, but it is convenient. The sailplan shows two full-length battens at the top of the mainsail and partial battens below. This is my preferred way to rig a mainsail. I like the sensitivity you gain in the sail by keeping the lower battens short and the long upper battens will support the roach just fine. The SA/D of this design is 17.62.

The Belgian Etaps differ from most French boats in that they do not seem to care if the model fits the charter scene. While this layout does little for me I remain a fan of the Etap line at least for their distinct approach and aesthetics.

ETAP-USA, 9 Timber Ridge, Freeport, ME 04032. (866) 382-7872. **www.etap-usa.com**

October 2003

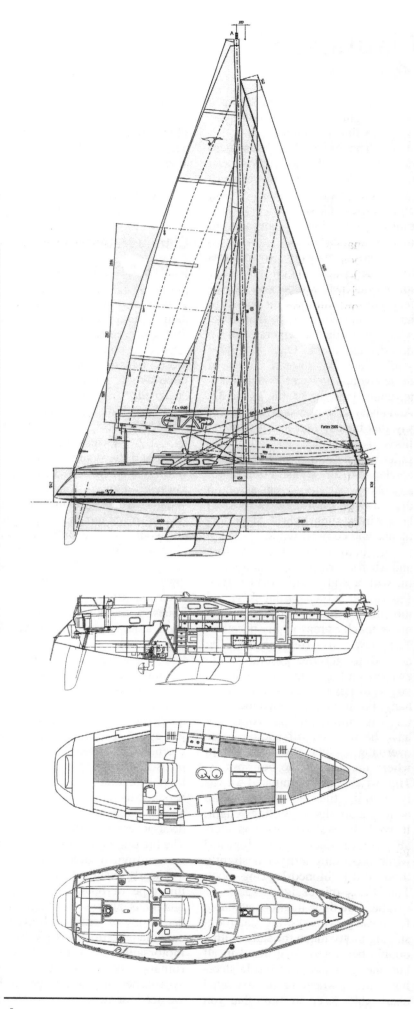

A handsome boat designed for serious cruising.

LOA 36'11"; LWL 32'6"; Beam 12'8"; Draft 6'5" (Standard), 4'5" (Shoal); Displacement 13,987 lbs. (Standard); Ballast 4,405 lbs. (Standard); Sail Area 657 sq. ft.; SA/D 17.62; D/L 188; L/B 2.92; Auxiliary Volvo Penta 2030; Fuel 30 gals.; Water 65 gals.

Hallberg-Rassy 37

Bluewater Cruiser

This is an amazing design. With 37 feet, 2 inches of LOA, German Frers and the Hallberg-Rassy crew have managed to get an interior into this boat that would do justice to any 40-footer. This in itself is not surprising given the center-cockpit configuration of this boat. What does surprise me is that the designers have done it while producing a good-looking boat with moderate proportions.

The freeboard is on the high side but it's nicely blended with a perky sheer spring and short overhangs giving the hull a muscular look as opposed to the graceful look of the Morris 36. The L/B is 3.19 and that indicates a beamy boat. The D/L is 196. The rudder is a semibalanced blade with a half skeg. Even with the skeg the designers have managed a rather high-aspect-ratio combination. The keel is outside lead hung below a deep, molded-in sump. When you combine this with a bulb-type keel fin you get a low VCG, and with the beamy hull this should provide good stability.

You don't see too many rigs today with fore and aft lowers but this new HR has them. It's a conservative way to rig a boat and with some fiddling with the relative tension on the aft and forward lowers you can still get some useful mast bend. These shrouds come down to chainplates smack in the middle of the side deck. This makes for a 16-degree sheeting angle and that's a bit wide for my taste. If the chainplates had been moved inboard they would have cleared up the side decks and allowed for higher pointing but made a mess out of the saloon settee arrangement. So you won't point 29 degrees apparent in this boat but you will foot right along. The SA/D is 18.07.

At first glance this layout seems to lack nothing. There are comfortable berths for four or five. The galley is well laid out. Wet lockers are conveniently located and there is a dedicated engine room, unheard of in most boats under 45 feet. The reefer box in the galley is quite small and the head is small. I don't mind the small head. We could pick some more but overall this is a great layout.

The downside is a lack of deck-accessed stowage. There is a small well above the foot of the aft double berth, but it hardly qualifies as a lazarette. There's also a well deck forward but it's no fo'c'sle. "Prepare to deflate the fenders."

Combine this with a bulb-type keel fin you get a low VCG, and with the beamy hull this should provide good stability.

There is that big engine room and you can access that from a seat hatch in the cockpit. I suppose with some clever method of dividing that space up you could stow quite a bit of gear there. But then it's not a dedicated engine room anymore. Where would you stow a spinnaker or two and a light air genny on this boat?

The cockpit seems more than adequate and there is a removable panel in the cockpit sole to get the engine out if ever required. HR uses its standard windshield for this design and that lends itself to a good dodger. I grew up looking at sailboats with windshields; Bill Garden did several, so this does not bother me aesthetically at all. The small swim step will work but only barely.

Looking at the sailplan I am struck with what a good-looking boat this is. There is a nice balance between cabintrunk height, freeboard, short ends and sheer spring. This design shows the HR/Frers team to be at the top of their form. Nice boat.

Hallberg-Rassy, Vars AB, Hällavägen 6, S-474 31, Ellös, Sweden. www.hallberg-rassy.com

In the U.S. contact Eastland Yachts, 33 Pratt St., Essex, CT 06426. www.eastlandyachts.com *(860) 767-8224.*

February 2004

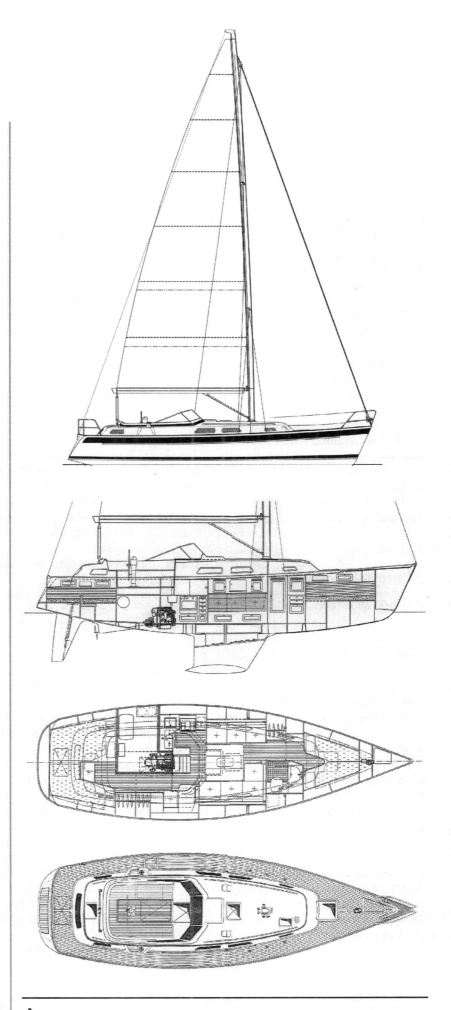

Another strong design from the team of German Frers and Hallberg-Rassy.

LOA 37'2"; LWL 33'6"; Beam 11'8"; Draft 6'3"; Displacement 16,500 lbs.; Ballast 7,100 lbs.; Sail Area 732 sq. ft.; SA/D 18.07; D/L 196; L/B 3.19; Auxiliary Volvo Penta D2-55; Fuel 83 gals.; Water 96 gals.

Sun Odyssey 37
Family Cruiser

The Juneau Sun Odyssey 37 was designed by Jacques Fauroux and the Jeanneau Design group. All in all this is a very typical example of the modern French cruising boat. In terms of image and styling this boat is indistinct. It's a handsome design, but there is nothing to set it apart from a lot of other boats.

The sailplan shows moderate freeboard with an almost flat sheer and short overhangs. The double-spreader rig features spreaders swept to 21 degrees and a babystay forward. The deck plan clearly shows forward lowers. It's unusual to need a

The real highlight of these interiors is the beautiful joinerwork detailing.

babystay when you sweep the spreaders to this degree. The compression on the swept spreaders will normally take care of that forward bending moment. The SA/D for this sloop, using I, J, E and P, is a very moderate 15.56, almost underpowered by today's standards.

This is a beamy boat with an L/B of 3.09. Any number below 3.25 indicates a beamy boat. This beam is used by the designers for interior volume, cockpit volume and good initial stability. The D/L is 188, and the stern is very wide. There are two keels offered: a shoal keel drawing 4 feet, 9 inches and a deep keel drawing 6 feet, 4 inches. Note the vertical rudder stock and the large, shapely rudder blade.

There are two layouts: one with a single quarter stateroom aft, and another with two mirror-image staterooms aft. Of course, if you choose the two-stateroom model you sacrifice your lazarette and any cruiser knows that you can never have enough lazarette. The single stateroom also has a nicer head. The nav table can be used from a seat aft or

the short settee forward. This is a clever detail.

The real highlight of these interiors is the beautiful joinerwork detailing, which features rich veneers and a lighter wood trim. There are plenty of lockers, but I don't see any galley drawers. Note that none of the lockers under the side decks come up to the deck head, and there is a three-inch to four-inch gap in between. This allows the builder to finish almost the entire interior before the deck is put on. It's an efficient manufacturing technique, but the lockers lose valuable volume. Still, this is a very impressive interior.

This is a sleek-looking boat with teak decks accented by an unusual aluminum toerail that has no holes. I don't know about you, but I like the holes in my "holy rail," although this "nonholy rail" looks clean and trim. There is a well in the foredeck to stow anchor tackle and an optional windlass just aft of the well. The stem fitting features double rollers.

All halyards are led aft, and there is an aluminum track where you can attach the dodger. The cockpit is huge and opens to the transom swim step. I know I'm old fashioned, but I don't like these big obtrusive, robot-like steering pedestals. I prefer the simple binnacle type. Still, with owners wanting so many instruments within reach at the wheel, we are forced to use these amorphous-looking towers of tech. I sailed my Valiant 40 with only a knotmeter, depth sounder and VHF, and never once felt in imminent danger.

The 37 will make an excellent all-around coastal cruising boat and should have great appeal to charter companies.

Jeanneau North, America 105, Eastern Ave., Suite 202, Annapolis, MD 21403. (410) 280-9400. **www.jeanneauamerica.com**

April 2000

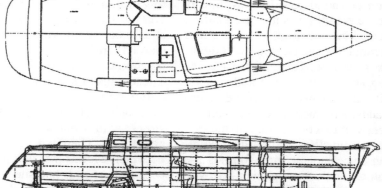

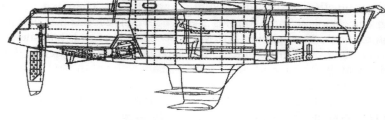

Comfortable and affordable French cruiser.

LOA 37'4"; LWL 31'9"; Beam 12'1"; Draft 6'4" (deep keel), 4'9" (shoal keel); Displacement 13,448 lbs.; Ballast 4,057 lbs. (deep keel), 4,453 lbs. (shoal keel); Sail Area 550 sq. ft.; SA/D 15.56; D/L 188; L/B 3.09; Auxiliary 40-hp diesel; Fuel 36 gals.; Water 85 gals.

Bavaria 36
Bluewater Cruiser

J&J designed this new Bavaria model and to my eye it looks like a direct attack on our current crop of Euro-produced cruising boats. It's a handsome boat in profile, despite the generous freeboard. I think the prominent feature stripe will help hide that freeboard on the finished product.

The hull shows a very full, suppository-like shape in plan view. Plan view is designer talk for looking down on the boat. The stern is broad and to my eye the bow looks puffed out. Of course this fullness buys interior volume and can be very helpful when it is present at berth top heights or counter heights.

Unfortunately fullness in the topsides, while providing some additional stability, can also be slow. For instance, in order to keep the half-

Bavarias are nicely detailed boats that always appear to be very well styled.

angle of entry low for a fine entry and good performance on the wind, a high performance boat today might have a half-angle of deck plan as low as 14 degrees. This same angle on the Bavaria is 23 degrees. This just means that the Bavaria will not exactly knife its way to weather. On the other hand, when you bear off onto a reach the fullness forward can add to your hull speed.

With an L/B of 3.04 this design can be considered quite beamy. The profile shows a very normal distribution of volume with short ends for a D/L of 184. You can choose from standard draft at 5 feet, 1 inch or deep at 6 feet, 5 inches.

The 36 comes in two layouts. You can have three staterooms with mirror image, double berth staterooms aft with the head forward, or you can have two staterooms with one stateroom aft and the head aft on the starboard side. If you go with two staterooms aft and the head moved for-

ward, the available space for the forward stateroom is impacted and eats up part of the lazaretto. The galley, nav area and dining areas remain the same for both versions.

To my eye the dual stateroom version is the most appealing as it preserves the lazarette and makes the forward stateroom much bigger. The galley is on the small side with a "cooling box" adjacent to the sinks that I think would be inadequate. Of course, in this case, there would be no way of expanding the cooling box without sacrificing room in the aft stateroom or the settee area, so this compromise seems to be balanced. The dining table is shown as stopping about four inches short of the edge of the settee. I like to see table edges lap the settee edges by three inches. I have no photos of this interior but in the drawings there are no surprises here. It's a standard layout meant to appeal to those wanting a charter boat or a family cruiser.

The deck plan shows the transom opens up so you walk from the cockpit to the swim step. The cockpit seats are long enough to stretch out on and are nipped away at the wheel to allow for a large diameter wheel. There is an anchor locker forward.

The rig is a fractional type with midboom sheeting and swept spreaders. I don't have I, J, E and P so I can't give you a SA/D but it looks to me to be in the 18 to 19 range.

This category of boat has become very popular. If you are looking for a 36-footer with a lot of accommodations you will have several well-known builders to choose from. The Bavarias are built in Germany. My impression of the Bavarias based upon those I have seen is that they are nicely detailed boats that always appear to be very well styled.

Bavaria Yachts USA, PO Box 3415, Annapolis, MD 21403. www.bavariayachts.com (410) 990-0007.

February 2003

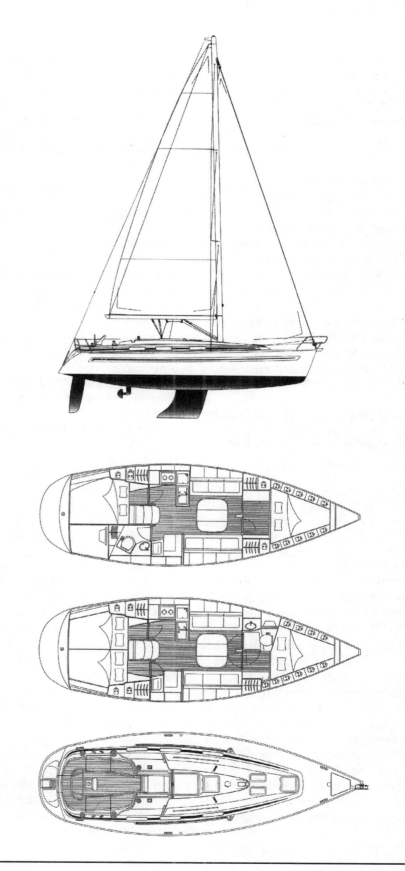

A popular design for a family or charter cruiser.

LOA 37'5"; LWL 30'10"; Beam 11'10"; Draft 5'1" (Standard) 6'5" (Deep); Displacement 12,100 lbs.; Ballast 3,300 lbs.; Sail Area 610 sq. ft.; SA/D 18.6; D/L 184; L/B 3.04; Auxiliary Volvo-Perkins MD2030: Fuel 40 gals.; Water 80 gals.

Najad 373
Family Cruiser

This 37-footer is a little different in that it is a center-cockpit design. The builder is Sweden's Najadvarvet AB. A center-cockpit design under 40 feet could be a designer's worst nightmare aesthetically, but it's obvious that the designers, Najadvarvet AB and Judel/Vrolijk, did a great job with the overall look of this compact cruising yacht. The name on the drawings is E. Segerlind. I would presume Mr. Segerlind is Najad's in-house designer.

The advantage of this design is that it offers the privacy of an aft cabin separated from the rest of the interior by the length of the engine room. Of course with the engine located directly below the cockpit sole, access is much better than in the aft-cockpit designs where the engines are tucked under the companionway steps. The disadvantage to the center-cockpit approach is that the cockpit has been reduced to mini hot-tub proportions.

This Judel/Vrolijk hull is more shapely than the previous two. The stern is less broad, and with an L/B of 3.13, the boat is not as beamy. Certainly this reduction in beam is offset by the increase in displacement to a D/L of 249.

The rudder is a partially balanced spade on a half skeg. Again two keels are available drawing 6 feet, 3 inches and 5 feet, 2 inches. The keels show outside lead on a shared, molded-in root sump. This configuration provides a useful deep sump area and also helps get the VCG of the lead down. Neither keel is bulbed, but they both are slightly flared at the tip with dead-flat bottoms, which may help prevent some crossover flow at the tip. The nicely sprung sheerline of this design is accented by a raised bulwark topped with a teak caprail.

This is an impressive interior layout showing very little evidence of having been squeezed into the boat. I like the layout of the saloon, which was obviously helped by spreading the galley down alongside the cockpit well. There are six drawers in this galley, drawers below the chart table and a pletho-ra of lockers. The beautiful joinery, all done in African mahogany, is given a fine satin finish.

The double V-berth forward and the aft double berth both look more than adequate. The head is tight, but hey, it's the head. I like the opposing

I haven't seen many boats under 40 feet finished as well as this one.

settee and drop-leaf table arrangement. While the lazarette has been sacrificed to the aft cabin, there is a large locker amidships just aft of the head. Being in the middle of the boat, this deck-accessed locker may have more useable volume than would a lazarette. I haven't seen many boats under 40 feet finished as well as this one.

This rig confuses me with its 16-inch offset between the headstay and the backstay. The brochure calls it a fractional rig, but I can't imagine what so small an offset is supposed to accomplish. Perhaps it's to make the mast easier to bend. But considering that the boat has both aft and forward lower shrouds, this doesn't look probable; fore and aft lowers make it harder to bend the mast. Maybe the idea is to keep the lower mast panel fixed so all the mast bend will be above the lower spreaders. Maybe the idea is to allow room above the headstay to fly a masthead chute with the offset leaving some room for the sock. I'm confused. I think a simple masthead rig would have been better.

I find this boat very good looking. The cabintrunk-sheer interaction is ideal. Even the windshield looks good and will make a great base for the dodger. Certainly in terms of deck detailing and displacement I think this boat would be a suitable offshore cruising boat.

Najad, Najadvaret AB, SE-473 31 Henan, Sweden. + 46 304 360 00, fax + 46 304 311 79. www.najad.com

April 2000

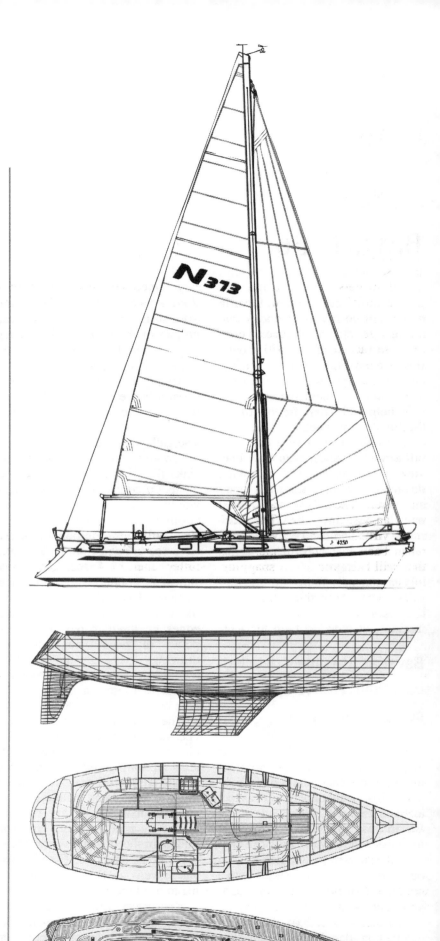

An attractive design with an impressive interior.

LOA 37'8"; LWL 32'; Beam 12'; Draft 6'3" (deep keel), 5'2" (shoal keel); Displacement 18,260 lbs.; Ballast 6,820 lbs.; Sail Area 705 sq. ft. (with 110-percent); SA/D 16.27; D/L 249; L/B 3.13; Auxiliary Yanmar 53 hp; Fuel 40 gals.; Water 69 gals.

Island Packet 370
Coastal Cruiser

Island Packet Yachts and its founder/designer Bob Johnson have been marching to the same drummer for the past 25 years. The drum has changed a bit but the beat is the same. IP and its loyal following of owners adhere to the full keel principle of design, and if number of boats built are an accurate gauge, they are successful in this approach. The new 370 is pure IP but it does show a few subtle evolutionary changes from the older models.

The boat is at the heavy end of the current D/L range with a D/L of 315. Any time you go with a full keel it is hard to get the D/L down under 300, because there's so much volume in the keel envelope itself. The 370 is beamy, too, with an L/B of 2.89. The keel starts virtually at the cutwater and rakes back at a nice gentle angle that will help you avoid snagging lobster pots.

The keel stops short, leaving a large space for the prop, and the rudder is attached to the keel with a long shoe that I presume is stainless steel. The rudder shows a hint of balance. Certainly with the hull and long keel monocoque you have a very strong boat to resist damage from grounding. The stern of the 370 is proportionally wider than previous models. This, of course, buys you accommodation volume and a better cockpit. By sticking with this long keel approach, Johnson ensures that his boats are well separated from the rest of the cruising boat pack.

The sail plan is a true cutter with the mast well aft and a staysail on a Hoyt boom. It's not much fun to drag a genoa around an inner forestay but if you leave the staysail up it works like a kind of baffle that helps guide the genoa around, so long as you leave the staysail sheeted to weather as you pass through the tack. With the Hoyt boom I don't think you have control over this. It will tack automatically, which of course is one of its benefits when it's blowing. With the 370 the gap between the inner forestay and the headstay is pretty big, so the pain will not last long.

Staysail and genoa together is not the most close-winded of combinations, as the staysail ends up gasping for clean air unless you bear off, but with a keel like this you are not going to point 30 degrees apparent anyway. Once you bear off onto a close reach both headsails will work well together. The 370 has a single spreader rig and an in-

By sticking with this long keel approach Johnson ensures that his boats are well separated from the rest of the cruising boat pack.

mast furling system. SA/D is listed in the brochure as 17.1 for the cutter and 14.4 for the sloop, indicating that they have added the sail areas of the genoa and staysail together to get the sail area of the cutter. I prefer using I, J, E and P for sail area with 100 percent of the fore triangle. That way there is no confusion.

The 370 is laid out for two couples with double berths forward and aft. The galley is big and very well laid out. The nav station is in the port quarter cabin. The bulkhead separating the quarter-cabin from the saloon has a big open window that closes with a removable panel. There is a head with a shower stall. Twisting that port double quarterberth 50 degrees opens up the port quarter lazarette area and makes use of space under the cockpit sole where it's almost impossible to access for stowage anyway. This seems a good compromise to my eye. Headroom throughout is 6 feet, 5 inches.

Bob Johnson's evolutionary approach to the design of his line has worked well for him. With its nipped transom profile and big swim step the 370 is as up-to-date a full keeler as I think you will find.

Island Packet Yachts, 1979 Wild Acres Road, Largo, FL 33771. **www.ipy.com** *(727) 535-6431.*

March 2004

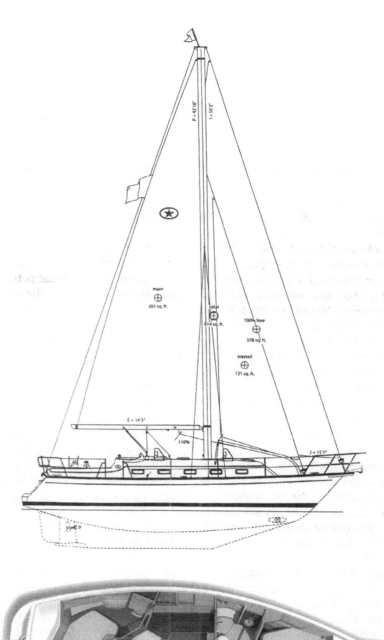

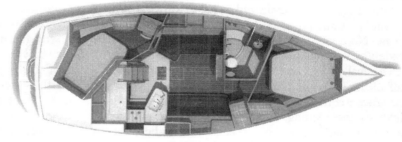

A comfortable cutter with a sensible layout.

LOA 37'10"; LWL 31'; Beam 13'1"; Draft 4'3"; Displacement 21,000 lbs.; Ballast 8,400 lbs.; Sail Area 814 sq. ft. (cutter rig); SA/D 17.1; D/L 315; L/B 2.89; Auxiliary Yanmar 56-hp; Fuel 75 gals.; Water 160 gals.

38-foot Schooner
Coastal Cruiser

Steve Killing is one of those designers who works quietly behind the scenes on some very high-tech projects and once in a while produces an exquisite design. In this custom design for a Canadian East Coast client we see an unusual combination of features that are certainly never to be found on a production-built yacht. The design parameters included, first and foremost, the desire for easily accessed twin engines. I also get the impression, reading Steve's designer comments, that the owner has his own ideas on just about every other feature of this design, from table height to deck layout. In my experience, tough owner requirements, while testing the designer, can help breathe life into a design and give it personality.

There is nothing particularly unusual about this hull. It's a full-ended, short-overhang boat with a cruising fin keel and skeg-hung rudder. There is a trim tab on the trailing edge of the keel, which is certainly unusual for cruising boats. Note also that the rudder blade itself is quite small.

The ballast occupies the lower half of the large fin, and the D/L is 285. Beam is moderate, and there is plenty of sheer spring. Pay attention here. Sheer spring tends to give boats a real identity "stamp," which may be something to avoid if you are trying to produce 600 boats that appeal to the masses. With the boats we are looking at this month, we see strong, confident sheer statements.

This is a staysail schooner rig. Why? It's a personal thing. Some owners want two masts. You could argue that it keeps the overall rig height down. You could also argue that it keeps the individual sails smaller for easier handling.

Note that these two masts are stayed independently without the use of a connecting triatic stay. This is accomplished by sweeping the spreaders of the foremast dramatically, 42 degrees. Now if you were to lose one of the masts it would not drag the other one down with it.

Three of the sails are on self-tacking booms, and in a real breeze, you might find it goes well with only the

fore and main staysails up. I don't think this is a particularly fast rig—the big sail, the mainsail, will have to operate in the backwind of the three smaller sails, which will affect pointing ability—but it sure is a photogenic. The SA/D is 16.8.

This is a strange interior. The engines are located well forward under the galley counter on the port side and under the head counter on the starboard side. These two engine locations preclude any standard approach to the layout. There is a double berth aft just forward of a stand-up chart table and a combination settee and

This boat is tiller steered with a sister tiller to control the trim tab on the keel.

berth to port. In between is a drop-leaf table. The mainmast comes down right in front of the companionway, which is slightly off to port, so you'll come below and immediately be met with the mast and the dining table. There is a reading chair adjacent to the galley. The forward V-berth is pierced by the foremast. I'm not sure how you access the starboard side of this berth or if you are even intended to. This layout is so specialized that I think its appeal will only be to the owner. But hey, "I didn't build it for you!"

This boat is tiller steered with a sister tiller to control the trim tab on the keel. There is a deep anchor well forward. Construction was done at the capable Covey Island Boatworks in Nova Scotia. The building method was Covey Island's typical epoxy strip plank method, with the hull planked in clear white cedar.

I like boats that defy identifying. They make you need to ask, "What kind of boat is that?" This handsome Killing design is bound to be a conversation piece in any harbor.

Steve Killing Yacht Design, RR#1 Midland, Ontario, Canada L4R 4K3.

Covey Island Boatworks, RR#1, Petite Riviere, Nova Scotia, Canada B0J 2P0. (902) 688-2591.

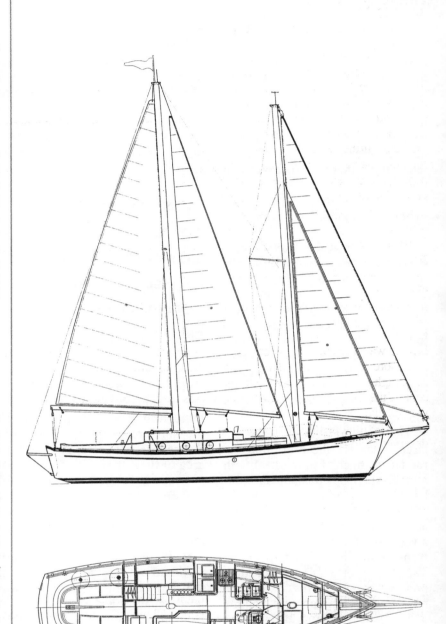

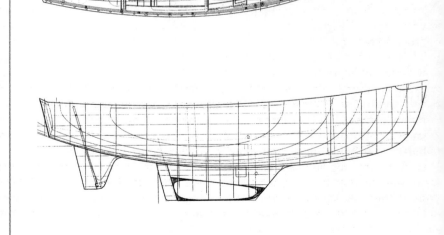

Custom-built schooner with many interesting features.

LOD 37'11"; LOA 45'; LWL 31'9"; Beam 11'5"; Draft 5'6"; Displacement 20,000 lbs.; Ballast 8,000 lbs.; Sail Area 774 sq. ft.; SA/D 16.8; D/L 285; L/B 3.32; Auxiliary two 42-hp Peugeot diesels.

Rogers 38
Coastal Cruiser

The people who commission these custom designs are not really clients. They are "patrons of the art." There are any number of production boats under 50 feet that would do the job, but these owners want something unique. Furthermore they want the fun and entertainment of creating the boat with a designer. The finished product will carry the owner's own stamp as prominently or even more prominently than the designer's. Common sense does not tell you to go get a custom boat built. I praise the spark of creativity that glows within these owners.

This owner had a raging fire inside when he commissioned Simon Rogers of Lymington, England. In fact, it was a group of owners, so it was more of a brush fire. They wanted a high-performance boat reminiscent of the old gaff-rigged yawls similar to the traditional Itchen ferry types. The final result is a hybrid that deserves a close look.

This boat is about as distinct as you can get, combining very different rig and hull ideas. I'm not so sure how it will work. But that's what custom boats are all about, i.e. not pleasing everybody. I do know I'd love to see this boat under sail.

What a rig! Don't worry, the weight aloft is being addressed by the use of home-built carbon fiber spars. Starting at the end of the 15-foot widowmaker bowsprit we have: flying jib, jib and staysail. The mizzen is either a standing lug or a dipping lug sail. I suspect it's a standing lug. If you get bored off the wind, you can hoist a mizzen staysail just for fun and extra horsepower. Standing rigging shows deadeyes and channels on the gunwale. Jibs can sheet inboard of this.

On the main the gaff is as long as the boom and will twist off to leeward when you try to put this boat on the wind. The topsail will go with the gaff, and both these sails will end up looking like bags anyway due to insufficient sheet tension.

The designer is going to try and control gaff twist with an "alpha line" leading from the end of the gaff to the top of the mizzen mast. But I don't care whether you use alpha lines or unobtainium for the spars; I can't see any way this rig will be close-winded

or will produce the "blistering" performance that the designer's notes call for. I see the blisters all right.

In defense of this design it was the owner's wishes to have all the family members kept busy. On a beam reach, when all six sails are finally in proper trim, this yawl should take off.

In a perfect world this boat would beat the pants off the latest Bruce Farr boat.

At 17,600 pounds, this is not a light boat by today's standards, and the D/L is 177. The designer says this boat will "plane," but I'm not so sure. A brief white-knuckled surf from time to time is about all you can expect out of a boat of this weight at this length. The hull form shows minimal fore and aft rocker and minimal overhangs. The keel and rudder are both retractable. The keel and its "box" are being built at The Lymington Forge. Draft with the keel down is 7 feet, 6 inches and 3 feet, 1 inch with the keel up.

The accommodation plan is also different. There is a small galley aft, and enough berths, including the main settees, to sleep eight crewmembers. There is actually a bath tub under the aft end of the V-berth. Obviously this interior's mission in life is to sleep a crowd: a clean crowd. After playing with all that running rigging all day I suspect the crew will need a bath. It's a custom design. What can you say?

I can tell from the comments accompanying the drawings for this special design that all involved are very proud of this vessel. It's a labor of love built in Cleethorpes by Farrow and Chambers using their cedar "speedstrip" method. Finish work will be done by a group of the owners.

In a perfect world this boat would beat the pants off the latest Bruce Farr boat. But, I've got sand in my shoes, and my hair looks funny today. It's not a perfect world.

Rogers Yacht Design, 68 High Street, Lymington, Hants SO41 9AL, England. 44-1590-672000. www.rogersyachtdesign.com

September 2000

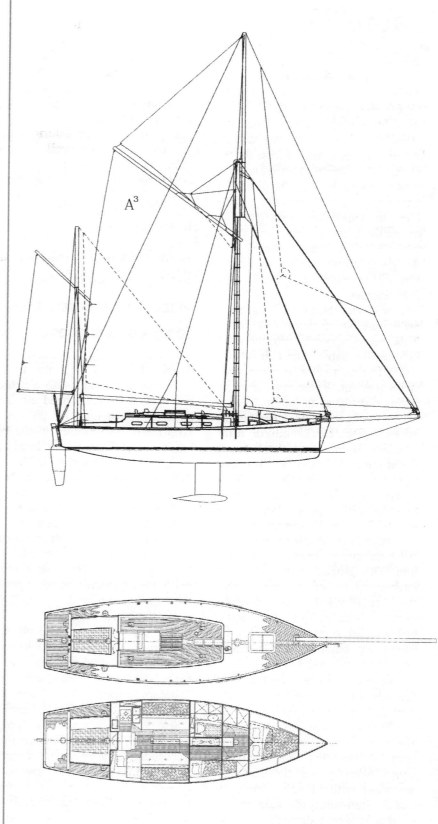

A blend of tradition and state-of-the-art from the UK.

LOA 38'; LWL 35'5"; Beam 11'8"; Draft 7'6" (keel down), 3'7" (keel up); Displacement 17,600 lbs.; Ballast 6,800 lbs.; Sail Area 1,425 sq. ft. (all sails drawn); SA/D 33.6; D/L 177; L/B 3.3; Auxiliary Kubota Beta 38 hp; Fuel 60 gals.; Water 160 gals.

Sabre 386
Luxury Cruiser

This new Sabre model was designed by Jim Taylor and the "Sabre Design Team." When I see this I wonder, "Fine, who did what?" In most cases it's safe to assume the designer of record, Jim in this case, drew the hull, keel and rudder lines, the rig, the structure and probably the laminate schedule. This leaves the exact contours of the deck and the interior layout for the Sabre design team. This design is aimed at cruising comfort for two couples (there's that echo again).

Jim Taylor quietly works away producing some very fast boats. This has to carry over into the work he does for Sabre. The L/B ratio is 3.05. The buttwater-to-beam ratio is 68 percent. Remember in measuring buttwater-to-beam we are taking the beam at deck right at the aft end of the DWL and not at the transom. If we used the transom beam the ratio could be a function of overhang aft. The D/L is 220.

The hull sections show flattish topsides with a gentle but definite turn to the bilge to improve stability. There is no deadrise anywhere. All sections go tangent at centerline. This smooth bottom is only interrupted by the elongated skeg structure forward of the rudder. I know it adds stiffness to the hull bottom and it probably helps the boat track, but I doubt it's needed with the large rudder.

You can get a winged bulb keel drawing 4 feet, 10 inches or a deep keel drawing 6 feet, 10 inches.

This is a handsome boat. The sheer has about 3.68 inches of spring to it but that's enough to prevent it from looking flat. The ends are short without being truncated and the transom is elevated enough so that it won't drag through the water when the boat heels.

The sailplan shows a carefully sculpted and well-proportioned house. The sailplan also shows a double-spreader rig with minimal sweep to the spreaders. The SA/D is 18.5. This is sort of an older-style rig with long J and a large foretriangle.

It surprises me that so many boats in this size range are now designed for two couples with double berths in both ends of the boat. Not too long ago we would have seen V-berths with a filler to turn the berths into a

The cabintrunk is relatively narrow on this boat and that's good. Most designers make the trunk wide, but headroom over berths, settees and counters doesn't do anyone any good.

double. In this design the master stateroom is forward with a centerline double with the head aft. This requires Velcro on your pillows to keep them from falling off the bed but it works. There is one head and it's aft with a shower stall. The nav station uses the settee for a seat. Note how most of the bulkheads are designed to be perpendicular to the hull shell. The galley is adequate.

The cockpit is designed around a large, 40-inch diameter wheel. I like big wheels. This one doesn't pivot but I think if you can't get by the wheel you probably should not be on the boat.

The cabintrunk is relatively narrow on this boat, and that's good. Most designers make the trunk wide, but headroom over berths, settees and counters doesn't do anyone any good. You only need headroom where you walk and stand. Large, uncluttered side decks are far more important. They give you the sheeting angles you need to be close winded and anything you can do to reduce the bulk of the house is probably good. This design gives the impression the genoa sheets were laid down first then the house was drawn, and that's the way is should be.

Sabre Yachts, PO Box 134, South Casco, ME 04077. **www.sabreyachts.com** *(207) 655-5050.*

May 2004

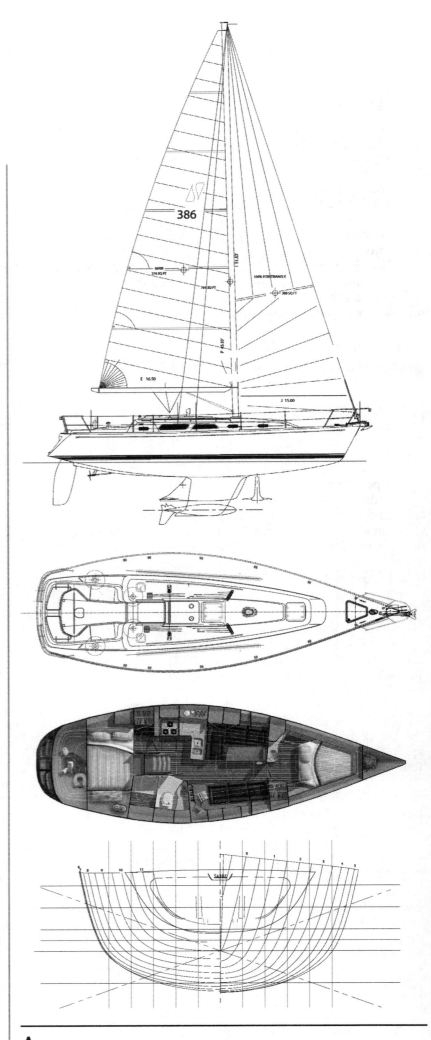

A handsome design from Jim Taylor and the Sabre crew.

LOA 38'7"; LWL 32'6"; Beam 12'8"; Draft 6'10" (fin keel), 4'10" (wing keel); Displacement 16,950 lbs.; Ballast 6,250 lbs.; Sail Area 763 sq. ft.; SA/D 18.5; D/L 220; L/B 3.05; Auxiliary Yanmar 40-hp; Fuel 40 gals.; Water 90 gals.

Vilm 116
Motorsailer

Designed by yacht designer Georg Nissen and built by Bootsbau Rugen in Germany the Vilm 116 is an all-weather cruising boat. This is one brochure that doesn't show bikini-clad youngsters enjoying a sun-drenched blue sea. This is a brochure that has photos of men in foul weather gear sailing on a slate-gray sea. You get the idea that perhaps this design

The more I studied this design the more I liked it.

was never intended for the tropics. Living in Seattle I can relate to that. Wolfgang Dietrich, the importer, says that this boat is a motorsailer with the emphasis on the sailing side of performance.

The design is dominated by a hard dodger that almost entirely closes in the cockpit. The best I can gauge is that the opening to get out of the cockpit is about 30 inches long. I do like this design. It's a very good-looking boat. But I wonder if I wouldn't feel a little too closed in with that hard dodger.

The wheel is forward and mounted on the bulkhead, powerboat style. This gets the wheel out of the way in the cockpit but also greatly limits the way you can sit at the wheel. This wheel placement feature really gives this boat the feel of a motorsailer. There are fold-up seats on both sides of the cockpit to give you an unobstructed view forward. Seat backs appear to be quite high. You can add a canvas extension to the hard dodger to fully enclose the cockpit or just use the top for a bimini.

The hull shape is very moderate in its proportions with an L/B of 3.19 and a D/L of 278. The forefoot is deep enough for a bow thruster. The fin keel is well forward on the boat, and with this in mind I would favor the optional bowsprit to help keep the boat well balanced. The rudder is a semibalanced spade on a partial skeg. The prop shaft is contained within a nacelle, so no strut is needed. The attractive sheer of this design is accented by a colored wale stripe (not shown in the drawings) and the rubrail.

It's sure hard to do an aesthetically acceptable center-cockpit boat under 40 feet, but I think the Vilm is

a good-looking boat. The secret here is that the designer has made no attempt to connect the forward accommodations with the aft accommodations. You access the aft stateroom with its two single berths from the cockpit. There is no head aft, but I suppose you could nestle a head between the two berths if you really needed it. I wouldn't. There is a pull-out table aft with chart stowage. This is the way center-cockpit boats were in the past. I mean the "real" past, i.e., the '50s and '60s. You just didn't try to walk through a passageway from the forward accommodations to the aft cabin. Add that connecting passageway and you have an entirely different design problem. I like this layout with the isolation of the aft cabin, and I bet your kids would love it too.

The forward accommodations feature a head to port and a very good U-shaped galley to starboard. The settee berths are generous, and there are two hanging lockers in the V-berth stateroom. This is an amazing layout when you consider the 39-foot LOA of this design. The photos in the brochure show beautiful joinerwork detailing in mahogany. The Vilm has the look of a hand-built yacht.

The rig is modest in size with slightly swept double spreaders. The standard rig has the headsail tack about 8 inches aft of the stem. As I mentioned earlier, you can add a short bowsprit to get the tack forward. I would recommend that option. The drawings show a rather ungainly looking profile with awkward window selections. But the photos show that the boat as built with a far nicer look. The odd-looking large cabintrunk windows have been replaced with smaller, more standard shapes that improve the look immensely. The overall detailing to the deck and deck strictures is excellent. With a low bulwark capped in teak and teak decks this is a very handsome boat.

The more I studied this design the more I liked it.

Bootsbau Rugen/International Yachting Center, Hwy. 64 West, Columbia, NC 27925. **www.inter-yacht.com** *(252) 796-0435.* **www.vilm.de**

March 2002

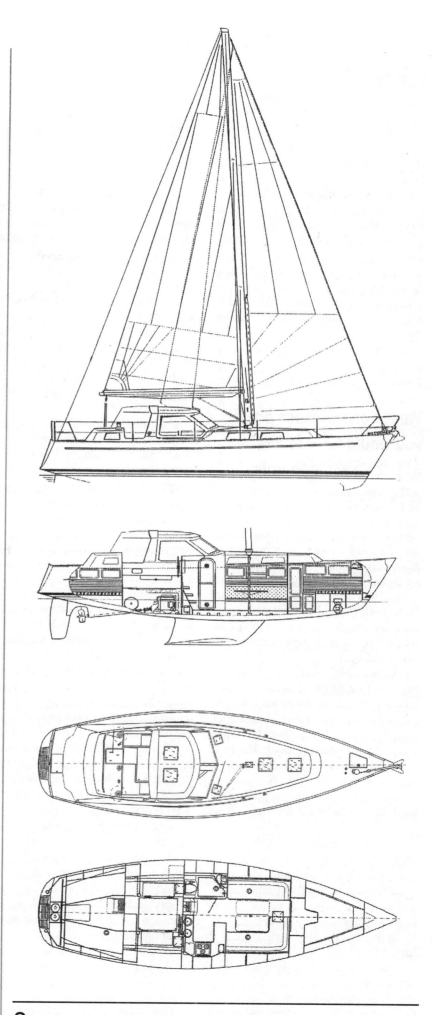

Sturdy motorsailer for cruising in inclement weather.

LOA 38' 11"; LWL 32' 10"; Beam 12' 2"; Draft 4' 11"; Displacement 22,000 lbs.; Ballast 6,800 lbs.; Sail area 720 sq. ft.; SA/D 14.7; D/L 278; L/B 3.19; Auxiliary Volvo 50-hp MD22L: Fuel 80 gals.; Water 80 gals.

One 40
Coastal Cruiser

I'm wading my way through the classic book **Thayer's Life of Beethoven, Vol. 1**. Much is made of Beethoven's relationship with Haydn. Haydn took Beethoven on as a student, but they didn't get along. Haydn thought Beethoven was a young upstart regurgitating his original ideas. Beethoven thought Haydn was an old fart. Beethoven had his own problems with younger composers. He wouldn't even let little Schubert in the door.

Thayer reminds us that we tend to place the significant examples from our formative years on a near-

This is one of those boats you would have to live with for a while to truly appreciate.

sacred plane as we age. Those boats we admired as kids become icons. It's a trait I know I personally have to fight. "Well sonny, that Cal 40 was a real boat." I try to listen to Nine Inch Nails but they just don't do it for me. It's getting to the point where I feel I sometimes need to pry my mind open.

"Creeeeeek." That's the sound of my mind being pried open. Built by One Boats AB of Storebro Sweden and designed by Finnish designer Guy Lonnegren, the One 40 is not your father's cruising boat. The hull is very dish-shaped in section with a narrow BWL—8 feet, 6 inches— and a very fine entry. In plan view the hull is very broad with an L/B of 2.65. That's 14 feet, 9 inches of beam on a hull with an LOA of less than 40 feet. The D/L is 88.

The keel is a hydraulically controlled centerboard that hinges up to be carried below the canoe body. Board-up the draft is 3 feet, 1 inch. With the board fully down, draft is 9 feet, 11 inches.

I was not sure exactly what I was reading so I read it several times, but the promotional brochure says you can just drop your centerboard down into the mud when you want to take a break from sailing. The illustration shows jagged rocks, where the lowered keel will act as an "anchor." I bet.

There is an internal, sliding piece of lead that goes from side to side allowing the keel ballast to be reduced for a given righting moment. The brochure is sketchy on this feature, and I don't know what provision there is to make sure this sliding piece of lead is always on the weather side. There is also water ballast to increase stability: 170 gallons or 1,400 pounds, to each side.

A wide, flat boat like this has high initial stability but a low degree of ultimate stability. Combine that with the possibility of broaching with both the water ballast and the sliding ballast on the wrong side, and you could end up looking silly, wet and scared.

The interior is unusual and the styling looks similar to the interiors you might see on fancy Euro powerboats. The interior contours are all swervy, curvy, softened and rounded. The saloon is raised and visibility looks great.

The deck and the rig are fairly conventional once you get past the amorphous deck contours. There is a small sprit for the asymmetrical chute. Maybe you will need that keel for an anchor, because I don't see any sign of an anchor roller.

There is a tremendous amount of room in the cockpit, but I don't see much seating area. The small arcing cockpit seats may not be comfy when the boat is heeled over. Every single photo of the boat sailing shows the helmsman standing at the wheel.

"Slam!" that's my mind closing again. This is a strange and unique boat. It's hard to evaluate this design from our recognized benchmarks. This is one of those boats you would have to live with for a while to truly appreciate. For me, sailing is a hobby that speaks to a lot of different parts of my psyche. This design would not satisfy some of those deeply subjective needs I satisfy with some sailing boats. That said, I do appreciate the chance to look at such an innovative design, and I trust that this design will excite some of you enough to pursue some follow-up information.

One Boats AB, Box 45 SE 590 83 Storebro, Sweden. +46 492-303-40 **www.oneboat.com**

January 2001

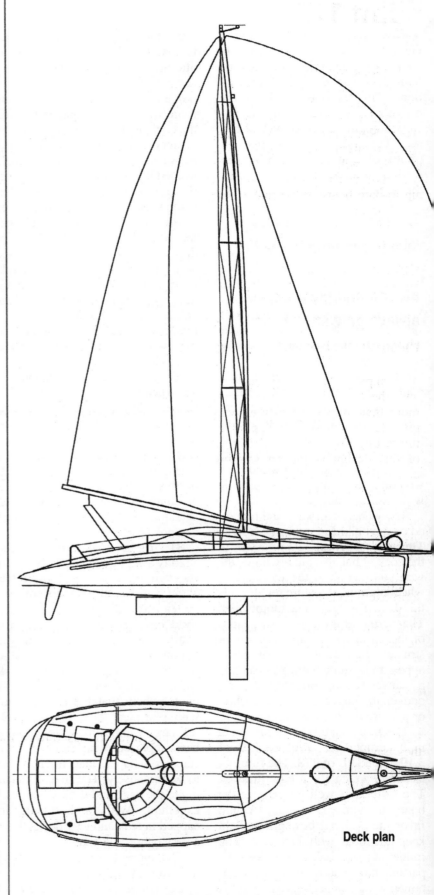

Deck plan

Mind-stretching new design from Finland.

LOA 39'2"; LWL 37'5"; Beam 14'9"; Draft 9'11" (board down), 3'1" (board up); Displacement 10,400 lbs.; Ballast 3,300 lbs. (keel weight plus moveable ballast); Sail Area 870 sq. ft.; SA/D 29.2; D/L 88; L/B 2.65; Auxiliary Volvo Penta 28-hp MD 2030S; Fuel 31 gals.; Water 52 gals.

Vilm 117
Motorsailer

If I look for something different to highlight in this design by Georg Nissen, I think I would be inclined to call this design a motorsailer. Not in the old 50/50 manner, but a modern motorsailer. I think this boat will sail well and motor well but that's typical of today's up-to-date boats. What makes this say "motorsailer" to me is the style

Given the choice of a trip through the cockpit to go aft and an ugly boat, I'd always go with the trip through the cockpit.

of cockpit with its wheel position and the hard dodger that covers more than 50 percent of the cockpit and the short rig. The other interesting and more novel feature of this design is the aft steering position. Now that's different.

If you feel too closed in by the hard dodger while you are steering in the cockpit you can move to the aft wheel that is mounted proud on the stern. The aft helm seats are in the quarters and attach to the stern pulpit. It would certainly work and it probably feels just fine but it sure looks weird. New things do tend to look weird and I would not want to be accused of epoch-centrism. I'll try to pry my mind open.

The rest of the deck layout is standard with the mainsheet traveler on the top of the aft house and halyards lead aft alongside the cabintrunk moving through a tube where they traverse the edge of the cabintrunk. There is a flush anchor locker forward. The vertical transom rules out a swim platform but makes the aft helm position possible. If you really wanted a swim step I'd just do a stainless powerboat-style swim platform. They can look just fine.

The hull form is quite moderate with a D/L of 256. The L/B is 3.2 and buttwater beam ratio is 67 percent. The hull profile shows a boat with max hull depth forward and a deep forefoot. The sheer is not a straight line but there is only about 4 inches of spring to it. I like sheer spring. That deep-chest-

ed profile would most probably pull the Longitudinal Center of Buoyancy forward, which would partially explain why this keel appears to be well forward on the hull. I find it better to design for a more aft keel position as it gives you more freedom with the rig geometry and helm balance issues. Draft is 5 feet, 8 inches.

The layout is unusual in that there is no passageway from the forward accommodations to the aft stateroom. This would have been common 30 years ago but today the two areas are almost always connected and in a boat of this size that connection almost always results in awful aesthetics. In this case the cockpit coaming is low, the cockpit itself is low with tall seatbacks and the look of the boat remains relatively svelte. Forward accommodations include a large head, a nice U-shaped galley, a dining and settee area, and forward stateroom with V-berths. If you had the dodger extension, as shown on the sailplan, you would avoid having to walk out in the rain as you went aft for the night. Either that or you move to California. Given the choice of a trip through the cockpit to go aft and an ugly boat, I'd always go with the trip through the cockpit.

The rig is conservative with double spreaders and fore and aft lowers. The mast is deck stepped. Note the inboard position of the backstay so it clears the helmsman standing at the aft steering station. The SA/D is 13.83.

The Vilm yard is on the island of Ruegen in what used to be East Germany. The yard was started in 1900. Prior to unification, Vilm built GRP boats that never reached the United States but achieved a reputation for the very finest quality and detailing.

I like this boat. It's different. It would work well in Puget Sound. People will look at you and wonder what kind of boat that is. I like that.

International Yachting Center, Hwy. 64 West, Columbia, NC 27925. **www.inter-yacht.com** *(252) 796-0435.*

April 2004

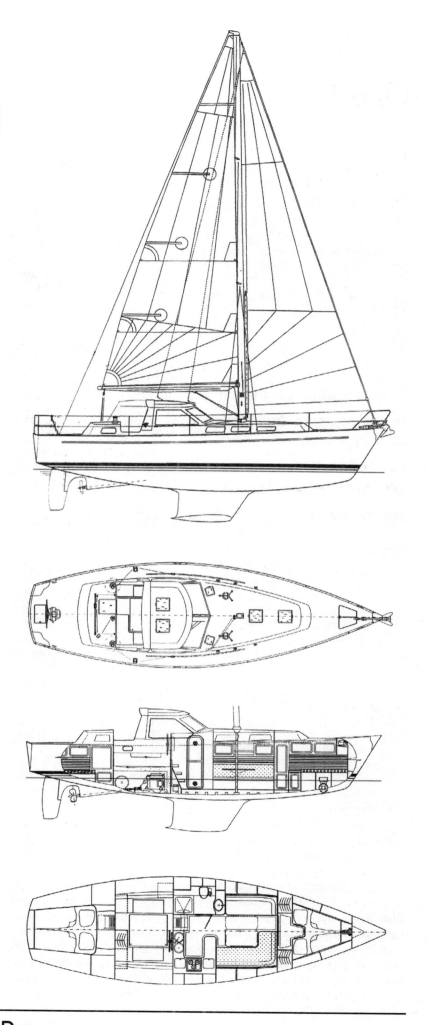

Double helms makes for comfortable driving.

LOA 39'5"; LWL 32'8"; Beam 12'2"; Draft 4'11" (Standard), 5'8" (Deep); Displacement 20,000 lbs.; Ballast 7,600 lbs.; Sail Area 637 sq. ft.; SA/D 13.83; D/L 256; L/B 3.2; Auxiliary Volvo Penta D2-55; Fuel 115 gals.; Water 110 gals.

Etap 39
Bluewater Cruiser

Designed by J&J Design, the Etap 39, built in Malle, Belgium, is promoted as an "unsinkable" yacht. The design itself is quite normal, pedestrian even, and a typical family cruising boat in the European style. The difference is that the Etap is built with what the brochure calls a "ship in ship" method, i.e., an outer hull and an inner hull with what the company describes as "polyurethane foam with a mini-

If you are after 'unsinkable sailing pleasure' this may be the boat for you.

mum of 95-percent closed cells" injected between the two hulls. This increases the displacement of the structure to the point where the boat will not sink, even when holed. There are additional flotation cambers in the bow and the stern. I think what the company is telling us is that this is a liner-built boat with foam injected between the hull and the liner. While the term "double skinned" may be factually accurate, it may also be misleading. The "unsinkable" term makes me nervous. It's like tempting fate.

The deck of the Etap features a "coffee can" type hull-to-deck joint. In this case the joint is not actually at the sheer but about six inches down the topsides. The sheer is less than crisply defined, although an unusual tubular toerail seems to accent it well.

The hull form is pretty standard. The ends are short. Freeboard is generous and disguised by the dropped hull-on-deck joint. Beam is moderate. Displacement is moderate, with a D/L of 184. The ballast-to-displacement ratio is 32 percent. You can have either 4 feet, 11 inches or 6 feet, 6 inches of draft. The stern is broad but not as exaggerated as we see on other European boats. It's a fine looking, normal hull. The brochure lists a "prebalanced elliptical section rudder." Maybe there's a translation problem here.

The accommodation plan can be ordered with either two staterooms aft or a single double stateroom to starboard. The single stateroom model has a larger double quarter berth and an excellent lazarette. In this model you also get a shower stall. The double stateroom model has virtually no lazarette.

The saloon features the entire galley on the port side with a U-shaped dinette to starboard. This makes for a nice galley, but with no secure place for the cook to stand while at sea. Then again, this may not be that type of boat. There is a little center-island seat for an additional diner. I don't think six could eat at this table but the sixth guest could eat at the chart table. The photos show a nicely finished interior with lots of wood veneers and very little of the interior liner visible.

The rig is a moderately tall, fractional type with spreaders swept 18 degrees. The unusual thing about this rig is that the mainsheet traveler, while end-boom and where it should be in the middle of the cockpit, is removable. You can just pop a couple of pins and then take the traveler entirely out of the cockpit to make room for the cockpit dining table. The main reefing system is a one-line type led to the cockpit. A Stak Pak-type lazy jack and sail bag system is standard. There is a removable Solent stay inside the headstay that allows you to fly a heavy air headsail without removing the roller furled genoa.

While studying the sailplan, note the windshield on the deck. Etap does a nice job with this detail. The windshield makes a convenient place to start your dodger, although I'm not sure with this mainsheet traveler location you could really use a dodger.

In most ways this is a very "normal" design. It appears well executed. I think it's a smart move to fill the cavity between liner modules and the outer hull with foam. According to the brochure, if you are after "unsinkable sailing pleasure" this may be the boat for you.

Etap Yachting N.V., Steenovenstraat 2, BE-2390 Malle, Belgium. (U.S. distributor Sail La Vie LLC. **www.sail-la-vie.com** *(207) 865-1855).*

February 2001

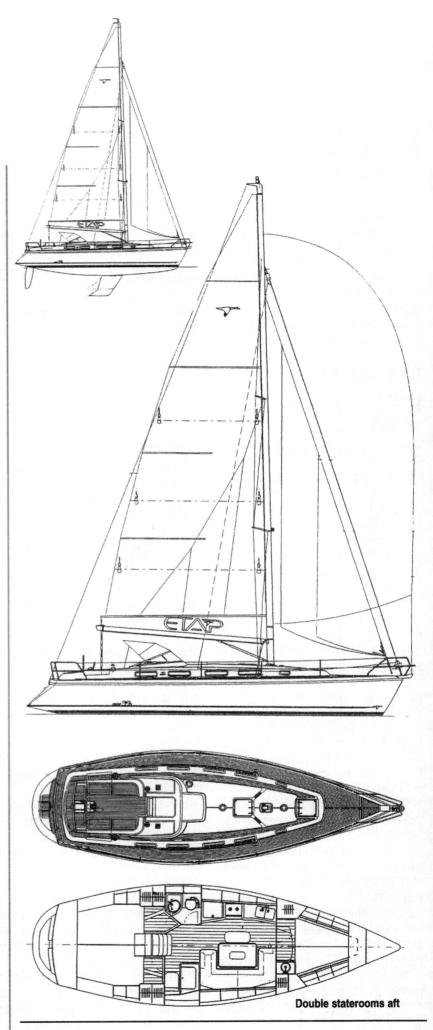

Double staterooms aft

Unsinkable safety from Belgium.

LOA 39'7"; LWL 33'5"; Beam 12'7"; Draft 4'11" (shoal), 6'6" (deep); Displacement 14,978 lbs. (shoal), 15,418 lbs. (deep); Ballast (keel weight) 4,515 lbs. (shoal), 4,956 lbs. (deep); Sail Area 825 sq. ft. (main and genoa); SA/D 21.3 (deep draft); D/L 184 (deep draft); L/B 3.08; Auxiliary 40-hp diesel; Fuel 37 gals.; Water 92 gals.

Catalina 387
Family Cruiser

There's no doubt that people will recognize your Catalina. These are immensely popular boats and boast one of the most loyal bands of owners anywhere. When I talk to Catalina owners' groups I am always amazed by how many have only owned Catalinas. Thirty years ago I owned a Catalina 27. I think the aim of the Catalina line is simple. It is to provide cruising sailors with the most comfort possible in any given LOA.

This is a beamy boat with an L/B of 3.23 and a buttwater-to-beam max ratio of 73 percent. The D/L is 249. This is not a light boat. The ballast to displacement ratio is 36 percent, and along with the beamy hull, that should provide good stability. You can choose from a fin keel drawing 7 feet, 2 inches or a wing drawing 4 feet, 10 inches. Let's compare the half-angle at the deck of the Catalina with that of the Dixon-designed Moody. The Catalina has a half-angle at deck of 24 degrees compared to the 26 degrees of the fuller Moody.

Belowdecks you get accommodations for two couples with the option of a centerline double berth or a giant athwartships double berth aft. Despite the fact that this berth is tucked under the cockpit it still looks like there's enough room around it to prevent you from feeling closed in. You can access the head from either the saloon or the aft cabin. The galley looks good to me. It has a top- and front-loading refer. There is ample counter space on each side of the range and the sinks. Yes!

But I hate those chairs. What is it with chairs in the saloon these days? I think you can lower that table and convert these two chairs into a berth, but why not just start out with a settee/berth and then you could use the volume under it for a tank. There is just something un-nautical about chairs below. "You are in my chair, Mr. Christian." Nope. But I know for sure Catalina would not put those chairs there if the market had not demanded them. It's a simple lay-out but it works well and has plenty of elbowroom.

I imagine Catalina's focus for the rig is "make it easy to sail." With that in mind the rig is on the short side with a SA/D of 16.15. The deck-stepped mast is well forward in the boat to make the helm forgiving and the boom is short allowing the mainsheet traveler to go forward on the cabintop. There are in-line cap shrouds, aft lowers and a babystay. The babystay is a pain to drag a genoa around but so are forward lowers. The babystay has a better vector for keeping the mast

What is it with chairs in the saloon these days?

supported than forward lowers, and from a builder's viewpoint it's only one chainplate to install, not two.

This boat has a big cockpit with a table that folds off the pedestal. There is a short door opening up the cockpit to the swim step but neither the drawings nor the pics I have show enough detail on this door for me to fully understand it. On the drawings it looks like it goes down to the cockpit sole. Genoa tracks are on bosses up off the side deck to help keep the side deck clear. There is an anchor well forward and minimal lazarette space aft.

This design appears to my eye to be a blend of Euro and American styling tricks and the look just does not grab me. I will say that the deck tooling shows superb detailing. If you compare the sailplan with photos of the boat you will see that the designers have carefully not shown the bulwark. Either that or they have not shown the rub strip that defines the hull-to-deck joint. This makes the boat in the drawing look sleeker than the boat in the photos.

I'm certain that Catalina will sell a lot of these boats. It always does.

Catalina Yachts, 21200 Victory Boulevard, Woodland Hills, CA 91367. (818) 884-7700. **www.catalinayachts.com**

April 2004

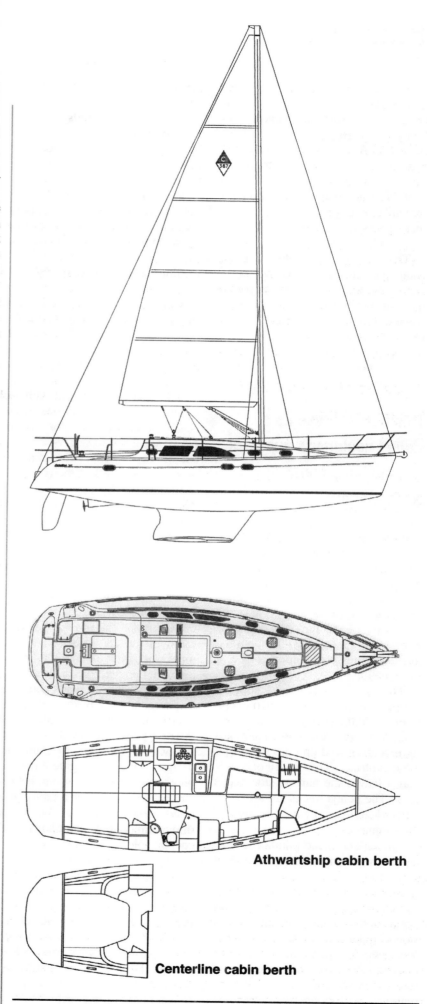

Athwartship cabin berth

Centerline cabin berth

The most comfort per foot in a cruiser.

LOA 39'10"; LWL 32'5"; Beam 12'4"; Draft 7'2" (fin keel), 4'10" (wing keel); Displacement 19,000 lbs.; Ballast 6,800 lbs.; Sail Area 719 sq. ft.; SA/D 16.15; D/L 249; L/B 3.23; Auxiliary Yanmar 3JH3BE; Fuel 37 gals.; Water 102 gals.

Buizen 40
Motorsailer

This design comes from a long-time reader of this column, a designer living in Australia named Paul Stanyon. The Buizen 40 is being built by Eddie Buizen. Photos show the boat going through sea trials off Pittwater, north of Sydney. I used to visit Pittwater when I was a kid. I remember eating oysters right off the rocks and wishing I was big enough to race a VJ-class sloop.

This boat is a true motorsailer, but what does that mean today? Forty years ago motorsailers were sometimes called 50/50s. That meant 50 percent sail and 50 percent power. Doesn't that sound lovely?

Today we have learned to give a boat excellent performance under both sail and power with really no

This boat represents a skilled designer's quest for an ambitious blend of performance.

compromise at all. We can thank lightweight construction for this. We can also thank modern, full-sterned hull forms and lightweight, high powered diesel engines. What makes this design stand out is the fact that the designer—I'll call him Paul because I know he'd prefer that—has pushed this design toward the power side of the equation.

This involves reducing the side-deck width and increasing the volume inside the pilothouse. This cabintrunk is so wide the chainplates have been moved up onto the top of the cabintrunk. The beauty of this is that it leaves the narrow side decks clear. The genoa tracks are also well inboard and up against the side of the cabintrunk.

The height of the pilothouse may take some getting used to, on paper at least. But it is very nicely proportioned and the photos show the sides tucked in ever so slightly at the lower cabintrunk edge to create the impression of reduced bulk. No, you cannot see over the pilothouse from the cockpit, but you can easily see through the windows. This high pilothouse allows for only two steps going below and a tremendous amount of volume in the bilge for the engine and tankage. Paul makes the point that this is a true "full pilothouse" and not a "deck saloon."

With 13 feet of beam, this boat is

not a fatso, but it's not svelte either. As we push and push for more interior volume, beam tends to grow. In terms of performance this is not good. Skinny boats are "better" boats. They may be wetter, tippier and more confined, but boy do they sail nicely.

Still, competition among cruising-boat marketing groups has pushed beam to levels that would have been considered obese in the old days, and by today's standards I'd call this one medium with an L/B of 3.07. This hull is quite full in both ends. There's enough volume aft for each quarter cabin to have a double berth. Paul, however, knows hull shapes. His boats have been race winners. I suspect this full-figured beauty performs just fine.

The interior is laid out with three staterooms, two aft and one owner's stateroom forward. The forward double is not the standard V-berth type, but off to one side. This stateroom also features a desk, although I'm not sure I know why you would want a desk on a boat. "Take the wheel, I'm going below to pay the bills."

The pilothouse features a settee and dinette with 360-degree visibility, just like a motorboat. There is also inside steering while a pair of "boxes" come off the back side of the pilothouse to intrude into the cockpit space and provide headroom in the aft cabins. As in most designs like this, the lazarette has been eroded to the point where it only holds your fenders, and only if you deflate them! "Blow up the fenders dear. We're approaching the dock." That's funny, but not fair to Paul. This design, with the engine under the pilothouse sole, has room between the two aft cabins for a pretty good-sized lazarette that can be reached through an inconvenient hatch in the cockpit sole.

This boat represents a skilled designer's quest for an ambitious blend of performance and comfort. I'd be surprised if we saw the 40 marketed in the United States, but it would make a very nice boat for my own drizzly Puget Sound. Bring one up Paul. We'll throw a cougar on the barbie and I'll show you the Northwest.

Stanyon Marine Design, Gold Coast City Marina, Coomera Qld 4209, Australia. 07-5573 6300. **www.stanyonmarine.com.au**

April 2001

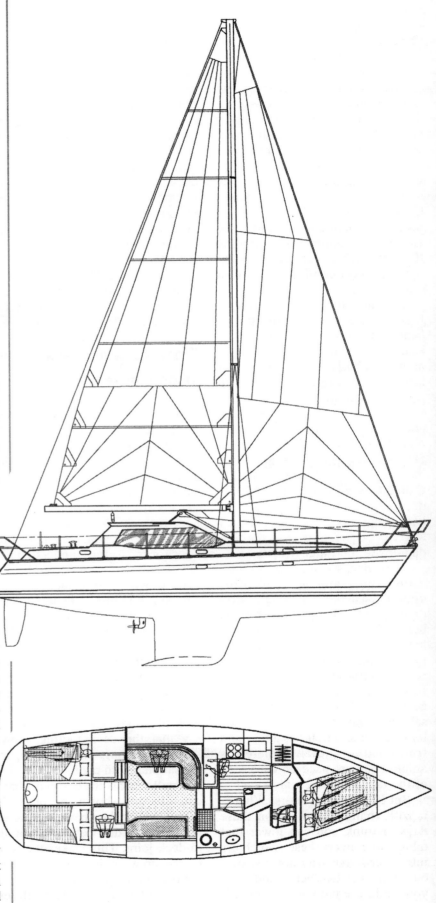

The best of both worlds with plenty of volume.

LOA 40'; LWL 34'6"; Beam 13'; Draft 6'4"; Displacement 19,800 lbs.; Ballast 7,700 lbs.; Sail Area 828 sq. ft. (with genoa); SA/D 18.1; D/L 215; L/B 3.07; Auxiliary Volvo MD 22p; Fuel 117 gals.; Water 117 gals.

Najad 400
Bluewater Cruiser

As a kid I would get up in the morning, pour myself the first of many bowls of cereal totally covered in white sugar and chomp away while studying the designs of Bill Garden, Bill Atkin, Bill Tripp, Phillip Rhodes and my all time favorite, K. Aage Neilsen.

It's no wonder I developed a reverence for the presentation of a design. Those guys could make the drawings talk to you. The boat would come alive on the paper. Garden's little cat schooner *Bug* had a guy asleep on the berth with a bottle of whiskey cradled in his crossed arms. The lacelike quality of Neilsen's line weights gave the boat an implied three-dimensional vitality and the exaggerated line weight shading of Phil Rhodes drafting style also lent a 3-D look

This length challenges good designers spatially and aesthetically.

to drawings. These drawings captured my heart. Compare these Judel/Vrolijk drawings of this new Najad 400 model with the drawings for the Ocean Star and you will see what I mean.

Forty feet is short for a center-cockpit boat. This length challenges good designers spatially and aesthetically. J/V has done an excellent job with this design. The freeboard is on the high side but that helps with accommodations by allowing the cabin sole to come up, and as the sole rises it gains area. The sailplan shows a good looking boat with a fixed windshield and a low cockpit coaming rising above the long cabintrunk. The spinnaker pole will be carried on the mast when not in use. This not only eliminates the necessity of struggling around the deck with the pole in your arms but in this case there is very little free deck space to stow the pole on deck without it being a major obstacle. It causes weight and windage aloft stowed on the mast but it is convenient.

Using I, J, E and P, I get a SA/D of 14.13. This is very close to that of the Ocean Star. Maybe we are

starting to see a reaction to the towering cruising rigs with SA/D ratios in excess of 20. Lots of sail area is fun when it's light but not fun in a blow. If you want light air speed and pointing ability the 53-horsepower Yanmar should do it.

You can choose from three interiors with the major options being in the way the boat is arranged aft of the cockpit. The standard layout shows a centerline double berth aft and one head accessible from the saloon. You can have outboard single berths aft or you can even go with two staterooms aft. It looks like you have to walk through one stateroom to get to the other. The galley extends down the passageway and there is no room for dishes on either side of the sinks. Of course this is no problem when you are heeled over because you'll put the dishes in the sinks. You can have a settee berth to starboard or you can go with Streisand chairs. It's a lot of interior for 40 feet and you give up fo'c'sle and lazarette to get it. There is one deep cockpit locker but it looks to me like this space, while big, would be hard to use efficiently. There are also small, saddlebag-style lockers in the quarters but there is no voluminous lazarette. Najads are built to order so some customization is possible.

The deck has no surprises for us. The cockpit is on the small side as you would expect from a 40-foot center-cockpit design. There is a flush hatch on the foredeck for access to the small fo'c'sle. Chainplates are smack in the middle of the side deck. I know you hate this but it's really where they need to go in most cases if you want to be able to sheet a genny in and go to weather. Sorry.

The Najad would make a great cruising boat for a couple with two kids.

Najad, Najadvarvet AB, S-473 31 Henån, Sweden. 46(0)304 360 00. **www.najad.se**

In the U.S. contact Seacraft Yacht Sales, 927 N. Northlake Way, Suite 100, Seattle, WA 98103. (206) 547-2755. **www.seacraft.com**

July 2003

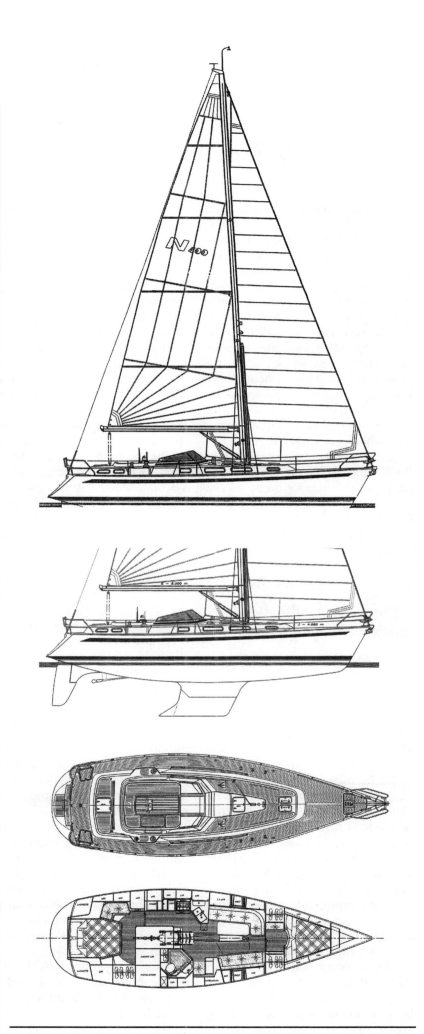

Spacious accommodations in a center-cockpit design.

LOA 40'; LWL 34'3"; Beam 12'7"; Draft 6'7"; Displacement 26,840 lbs.; Ballast 8,800 lbs.; Sail area 796 sq. ft.; SA/D 14.13; D/L 299; L/B 3.18; Auxiliary Yanmar 4JH3; Fuel 51 gals.; Water 132 gals.

Wauquiez Centurion 40
Bluewater Cruiser

Wauquiez boats are built by a division of the Beneteau group. You could look at it like Wauquiez is Beneteau's premier line. I think some of the finishing details have been cross-pollinated but other than that the Centurions are distinctly different boats than Beneteaus. This new Centurion was designed by Berret/Racoupeau and, like 85 percent of the boats I review these days, is a boat showing some race boat heritage combined with a comfy interior.

The underbody looks exactly like what you would expect. The rocker shows the canoe body pulled down around station 7.5 and this gives a little steeper angle to the run. There are shoal and deep draft keels drawing 5 feet, 10 inches and 7 feet, 8 inches respectfully. The deep draft keel shows a pronounced

> **There is a monster quarter-berth to starboard. You could sleep lying fore and aft or athwartships on this berth.**

leading edge/hull fillet. The rudder is a deep spade. L/B is 3.22 and the D/L is 131. The hull shows a nearly flat sheerline and very short ends. In plan view the drawings show a broad transom. There's that echo again. The trick for the designer is to make the boat look like it's ready to race but at the same time emphasize features that will aid in the layout. I wish we could go back to a universally accepted rating rule so we could see some boats designed with less attention paid to interior volume.

I like this layout. The galley shows working counter space on both sides of the sink and the range. I wonder how big the icebox is. There is enough seating space in the settee and at the dinette so you can spread out after dinner. The large head aft includes a stall shower and wet locker. "Does my foul weather gear smell funny?" The chart table laps over the foot of the edge of the settee but I can't see what is gained by this detail. They apparently don't need it for length. There is a monster quarterberth to starboard. You could sleep lying fore and aft or athwartships on this berth. Forward there is another stateroom with a smaller double berth, vanity and hanging locker. It's a good layout for two couples but not so good if you are a couple with children of opposite sexes. I think if I were cruising this boat with my wife I would be inclined to use the stateroom for stowage as the aft berth is larger. But I'd have to see which area was best ventilated and I would guess that would be the bow.

There must be something to this tall, fractional swept spreader rig. The masthead rig has all but disappeared. I can remember when you couldn't find a fractional rig on a modern boat. I think the first modern fractional rigged boats we saw, dinghies aside, were the Kiwi ton boats back in the mid 1970s. Today everyone wants a small foretriangle with the biggest sail on the boom where it's easier to control. Personally, I don't care if I ever see another 160-percent genoa again. My boat is fractional rigged. The Centurion has a keel-stepped mast. The SA/D is 20.42. You can choose either rod or wire rigging. I like rod.

The Centurion carries 105 gallons of water in two tanks and 58 gallons of fuel. That's plenty for the type of cruising most of us do. Engine choice ranges from a 40- to 56-horsepower Volvo with sail drive. Go with the big one. When you have to motor it's best to get it over with quickly.

This is a good looking boat. The cabintrunk is sleek and the orthogonal big windows are dramatic looking.

Wauquiez International, ZI Du Vertuquet, 59535 Neuville-en-Ferrain Cedex, France. www.wauquiez.com

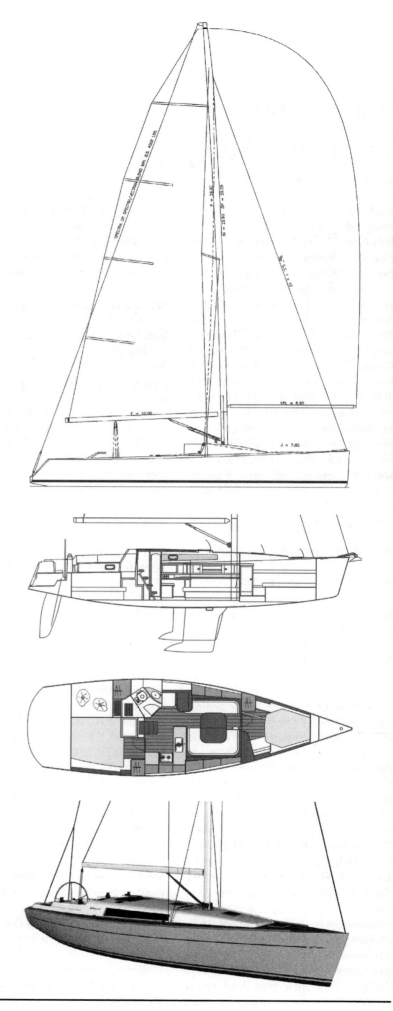

A comfy cruiser with thoroughbred styling.

LOA 40'6"; LWL 38'6"; Beam 12'7"; Draft 7'8" (Standard), 5'10" (Shoal); Displacement 16,750 lbs.; Ballast 5,950 lbs.; Sail Area 836 sq. ft.; SA/D 20.42; D/L 131; L/B 3.22; Auxiliary Volvo 40-hp or 56-hp; Fuel 58 gals.; Water 105 gals.

Hallberg-Rassy 40
Bluewater Cruiser

There are few designers in this business with a better eye than German Frers. His sheerlines are usually exquisite. However, I find this 40-footer to be boxy looking and not particularly attractive. It's certainly a subjective call. The freeboard is high, the ends are snubbed off and there is little change in contour to the long cabintrunk. You could take the windshield off and reduce the visual height of the profile, but Hallberg-Rassy loves those hard windshields. In the end the design is probably right the way it is and when you come to an understanding of exactly why certain features are used they can, in time, grow on you. In the end, what works well starts to look good.

D/L is 234 based upon 22,000 pounds of displacement. B/L is 3.25 and I'd call this moderate beam. Just for fun I measured the half angle in plan view at the deck and I got exactly 20 degrees in comparison to the 23 degrees of the Bavaria and the sub-13 degree half angle of a typical America's Cup yacht. Draft is 6 feet, 3 inches and no shoal draft keel option is available. The rudder is mounted on a half-skeg. I draw half-skegs myself but mainly they are for owners who are not psychologically ready to accept a full spade rudder. The half-skeg certainly does not protect the rudder. It allows for a lower bearing and that in turn allows for a smaller diameter rudder stock.

There are two interior layouts. You can have a centerline double berth aft or you can have the double off to port and a single berth to starboard. I think the centerline double will look better and it does offer at least the impression that you can access the berth from either side. In both cases the berths are taken so far aft that there is no volume left for a lazarette and I think big lazarettes are a must on any cruising boat. As with most center cockpit layouts this one has the advantage of offering a separate engine room. The rest of the layout looks fine. The V-berths are a bit pointy at the toe. You can have chairs in the saloon or a settee berth to port. I'd go

with the versatile settee berth version.

The shrouds are in line and there are two spreaders. The headstay does not go to the masthead and my drawing shows no provision for a

Hallberg-Rassy is one of the few builders dedicated to providing true offshore-suitable sailing yachts.

staysail. I think staysails are one of the most abused sails on board but they seem to be considered de rigueur for serious cruising. It's nice to be able to shift gears in a blow and sail under main and staysail, but in many cases this gear shifting takes you from fifth gear down to second gear in one jump. Another benefit of the center cockpit configuration is that it allows for the mainsheet traveler to be aft of the cockpit and the mainsheet can be at the end of the boom. The SA/D of this design is a sedate 16.44.

In terms of efficiency and convenience, the pros and cons of center cockpit deck arrangements are subjective and revolve around your appreciation of the interior layout options. If we eliminate interior considerations, the aft cockpit deck plan, to my eye, is the best in that sheet leads are easier and you sit lower in the boat. Choice of aft or center cockpit boils down to accommodation priorities.

Hallberg-Rassy is one of the few builders dedicated to providing true offshore-suitable sailing yachts. Their boats command high resale prices and are very much in demand. The build quality is first rate and they are very clever with the construction detailing. If you were asked to buy groceries, pack a sea bag and just go, you couldn't go wrong with a Hallberg-Rassy.

Hallberg-Rassy Varvs AB, Hällavägen 6, SE-474 31 Ellös, Sweden. **www.hallberg-rassy.com** *46 304-54 800.*

February 2003

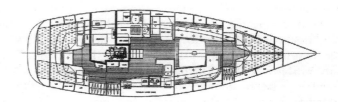

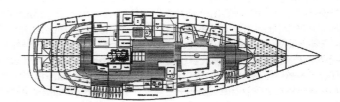

A 40-footer for the serious offshore cruiser.

LOA 40'8"; LWL 34'9"; Beam 12'6"; Draft 6'3"; Displacement 22,000 lbs.; Ballast 9,100 lbs.; Sail Area 807 sq. ft.; SA/D 16.44; D/L 234; L/B 3.25; Auxiliary Volvo Penta D2-55; Fuel 107 gals.; Water 98 gals.

Friendship 40
Family Cruiser

Here's a design with aesthetics taken from another era. This design is by Ted Fontaine and is the smallest design I have seen from Ted. Ted's got "the eye." This is a handsome design and I like just about everything. It's not going to be a rocket in any conditions but that was not the idea. (It won't be a pig either.) The idea was to provide an elegant daysailer or weekend cruiser that could be handled with ease. That said, there is nothing about this boat that would prevent you from sailing it anywhere you wanted.

Spoon bow, elevated counter, heart shaped transom and beautiful springy sheer all combine to give this design a vintage look. It's a heavy boat with a D/L of 388. This displacement is reflected in the generous fore and aft rocker to the hull. This is a boat that will hit its hull speed at about 7 knots and sit there. Any attempt to drive this boat much above 8 knots will result in the hull just digging a big hole in the water. That's okay. It's just the price you pay for having overhangs and copious displacement. Draft is a scant 3 feet, 11 inches with the board retracted and 10 feet, 3 inches with the board down. Beam is wide with an L/B of 3.18. This boat will be stiff. If I was going to nitpick I'd mention that it's hard to carry off these aesthetics while using the freeboard required to get today's required headroom and accommodation volume. The old boats had low freeboard and this boat does not. Ted has carefully not drawn the DWL on the profile so as to confuse our eye into thinking the freeboard is low. I'm not fooled.

The rig is where the innovation is. Ted has devised what he calls the Sail Stick. This is a device that controls the mainsail with a joystick. Push the stick up and the mainsail goes up. Push it down and the sail is retracted into the furling boom. Push the stick to one side and the mainsheet is eased. Push it the other way and the mainsheet is pulled in. It reminds me a bit of when I bought my first Peugeot. It took me a while to get used to the "joysticks" on the wheel. I would approach a corner, wash my windshield, engage the cruise control, disengage the cruise control, turn on the windshield wipers, turn off the windshield wipers, then turn on the turn signal. Well maybe it's not that bad and I'm sure there are some of you who want the physically demanding aspects removed from sailing. I'm not there yet. I'd

The rig is where the innovation is.

go for oversized winches before I'd go the joystick route. This is not a big boat. I don't think it needs so much power assistance. At least I don't think that today. Talk to me again in 15 years or on a day when my back is acting up.

The jib is self-tacking and on a hydraulic furling unit. These functions are again controlled by a joystick. Of course I can remember laughing at powered sheet winches years ago in the pre-ibuprofen days. The SA/D of this design is 17.24. The three spreaders are swept and the headstay does not go to the masthead. On a boat of this weight I might prefer to see less sweep to the spreaders so I don't impale the mainsail so quickly when it is eased.

The cockpit is huge. This is where you will live on this boat. You can dine in the cockpit at the big folding table. You can entertain those sleepy friends very comfortably in this cockpit. They can even fall asleep on those long seats. A dodger would be easy to mount for rainy weather sailing. Imagine the volume below this cockpit for stowage. This is really the cockpit of a 50-footer connected to the interior of a 30-footer. Given the ratio of time spent in the cockpit to time spent below I would agree with this allocation of space.

This is an appealing boat. It's great looking and unique in its approach to comfort. It's giving me visions of luxurious, well-fed, singlehanded cruising. Where would I put my Martin?

Fontaine Design Group, 92 Maritime Dr., Portsmouth, RI 02871. (401) 682-9101. www.fontainedesigngroup.com

March 2003

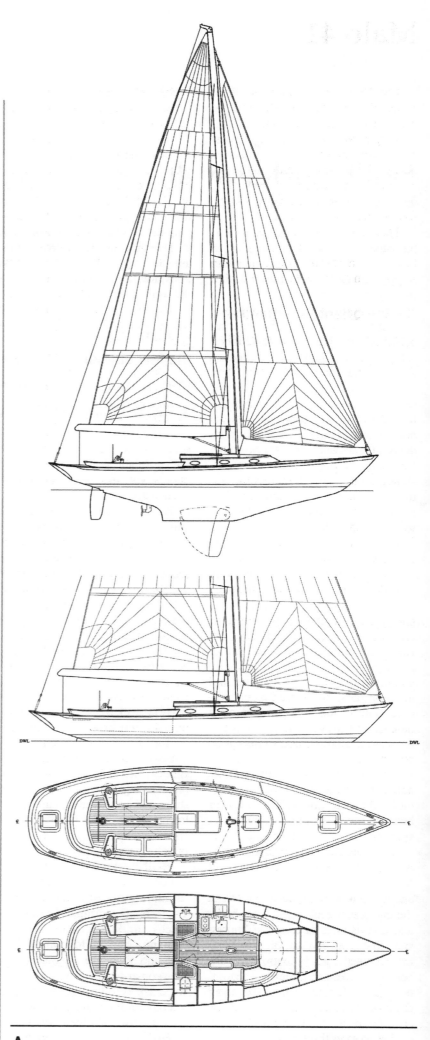

Another classic looking cruiser with a very modern sail system.

LOA 40'11"; LWL 29'7"; Beam 12'10"; Draft 10'3" (keel down), 3'11" (keel up); Displacement 22,500 lbs.; Ballast 7,600 lbs.; Sail Area 859 sq. ft.; SA/D 17.24; D/L 388; L/B 3.18; Auxiliary Yanmar 40-hp; Fuel 25 gals.; Water 60 gals.

Malo 41
Family Cruiser

The Malo 41 comes to us from Sweden's Malo Yachts. Much of the design work was done in-house with the help of Mr. Hans Leander. At first glance you can see strong similarities between this design and the boats produced by Halberg-Rassey. The intent is a strong, capable and comfortable family cruising yacht.

There are actually two versions of the Malo 41's hull. You can get this boat with a reverse transom, swim step and an LOA of 41 feet, 11 inch-

It's important to remember the virtues of the modestly proportioned family yacht.

es or with a traditional transom and an LOA of 43 feet, 2 inches. While it sure is nice to have additional deck space aft I think the advantages of the boarding platform are preferable. Aesthetically my eye prefers the traditional transom version, but this sheerline is so bland it really does not make much difference. Let's face it. This is not a very sexy boat. There is little sparkle to this design on paper.

Still, here's a case where the yard has added enough sparkle in the form of teak decks and a teak overlay to the cabinhouse top that the finished boat is quite striking. I even like the practical fixed windshield that dead-ends on the mainsheet arch. I recognize that aesthetics are primarily a personal thing, but I find it hard to not recognize some universal parameters for beauty. The workmanship shown in the accompanying photos looks good by any standards.

The hull is a very conventional shape with moderate overhangs in the ends and an arclike midsection. The bow is on the full side, which should give good volume forward but will slow the boat down when beating into a chop. The bottom never quite goes flat at centerline. The L/B is 3.27, which makes the Malo borderline beamy. Displacement is a moderate 23,100 pounds for a D/L of 243. This is right in the middle of "medium" displacement. Draft is a moderate and sensible 6 feet, 5 inches.

I have drawings for four different layouts for this design, and I get the impression that the Malo yard will do semicustom interiors on order. You can have port and starboard aft quarter berths, or you can have a nice big lazarette and one quarter berth. Within these berths you can have over-and-under stacked quarter berths or a single

double. The saloon is available in a variety of configurations including settees with a nav station; chairs and dinette with no nav station; and chair with nav station and dinette. The forward head is probably a one-piece molded unit so it stays the same as does the V-berth. You know how I feel about chairs so I guess it shouldn't surprise you that I like the one shower, dinette with bench settee and nav station. Whichever you choose, the layouts are all beautifully executed in mahogany veneer and solid mahogany trim.

The sailplan shows a very conventional masthead sloop rig with swept spreaders and fore and aft lower shrouds. The mast is well forward in the boat, and I would estimate that this boat will balance very nicely. The mainsheet arch is practical and gets the traveler out of the cockpit. The only problem with this traveler location is that it makes the traveler itself quite short, and I can't see from the photos how you would adjust it from the cockpit. The sheet itself dead-ends on the boom then goes through three blocks to lead down the side of the arch where it turns 90 degrees to go to a winch. The big standard equipment rigid vang shown should take care of the short traveler length. Malo offers the option of a main that stows inside the mast. I know this is very convenient, but it makes getting a good shape out of your mainsail so hard. If you need a furling main you would be better off with in-the-boom furling. Many owners of in-mast furling systems love them. It just boils down to one of those sailing "style" things.

Today we are bombarded with increasing ratios and exaggerated hull proportions. A lot of these are attractive on paper, but it's important to remember the virtues of the modestly proportioned family yacht. The Malo 41 is just that type of boat, i.e., predictable and reliable in performance. There is enough displacement in this design to give the engineer a free hand for strength making it perhaps the perfect cruising boat for you to face the challenges of life on the water. As Dr. Gizmo says, "To recognize the beauty of the sea you must actively engage the sea and wrestle with it." You should be safe doing your wrestling aboard the Malo 41.

Malö Yazchts AB Kungsviken, S 47399 Henan, 46-304-59-600. Discovery Yachts, 1500 Westlake Ave. N., Suite 108, Seattle, WA 98109. (206) 301-9104 **www.discoveryyachts.com**

May 2001

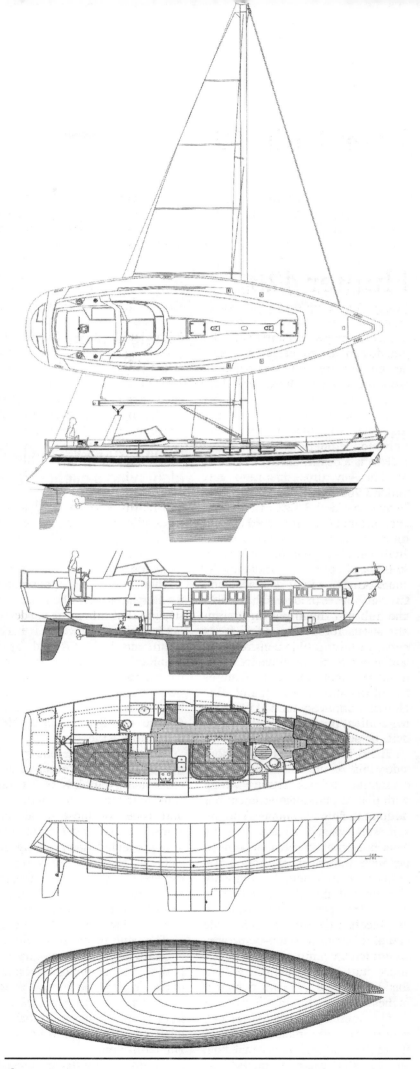

A cruiser of sound design and excellent workmanship.

LOA 41' 11"; LWL 34'11"; Beam 13'1"; Draft 6'5"; Displacement 23,100 lbs.; Ballast 9,350 lbs.; Sail Area 1,000 sq. ft. (with genoa); SA/D 19.7; D/L 243; L/B 3.27; Auxiliary 80-hp diesel; Fuel 97 gals.; Water 170 gals.

Hunter 426
Bluewater Cruiser

Here is a new cruising boat from the design group at Hunter. The design is very much in keeping with the current Hunter range. I went aboard a new Hunter at the Seattle boat show and I was very impressed with the level of fit and finish to the interior.

This is a beamy hull with an L/B of 2.9. Any time this ratio gets under 3 you are dealing with a very beamy boat. Beam buys you accommodations, stability and room on deck. But if you look at almost any handicap rule, beam per se is always on the slow side of the equation along with displacement. Cruisers have to decide just how much they want to pay in accommodations for performance. It's a personal sailing style consideration and there is no formula to determine the right balance of features for everyone. A company like Hunter works very hard at identifying a client profile and tailoring its design specifically to that profile.

The D/L is 178 and I would consider this on the light side for a cruiser but there's nothing wrong with that. Lighter displacement has nothing to do with a boats ability to sail well when loaded with gear. This boat probably has a pounds-per-inch immersion of about 1,500 pounds. This would be probably the same if the boat weighed an extra 8,000 pounds. Although the displacement may change, the actual footprint or water-plane area would remain similar. You can get a shoal-draft keel drawing 5 feet or the deeper keel drawing 6 feet, 6 inches.

The interior is designed for two couples to cruise in comfort. While the profile and deck plan of the boat show an aft cockpit design, the interior layout shows more of a center cockpit type configuration. To my eye this means that there are going to be some headroom compromises in the aft cabin. The galley is won-

derful with lots of uncluttered counter space. The reefer and freezer are both front loading. The forward head has the basin outside the head area and many clients of mine prefer this. The starboard settee

Hunter works very hard at identifying a client profile and tailoring its design specifically to that profile.

looks too short to be another berth.

Hunter continues its adherence to the Bergstrom rig. The mast is deck stepped, but the lower panel, without benefit of belowdecks "bury," is reinforced and stiffened by two stainless struts. Deck-stepped masts have advantages, I have one on my own boat. A keel-stepped mast can be a big funnel to deliver rainwater down to the bilge, and in Seattle this is a serious issue.

The triangulated geometry of this rig provides for a rigid spar that needs no forward lowers. The disadvantage is that off the wind you can quickly impale the mainsail on the spreaders. The SA/D is 16, but this does not include the generous mainsail roach shown on the drawings. In this case area added by the roach would be significant. Note the mainsheet is led to a traveler on a stainless arch that bridges the cockpit.

The styling of this Hunter is strong. The variety of windows and port shapes has a big effect on the overall look of the boat, as does the prominent hull-to-deck joint feature. It's a unique look that obviously continues to find favors with Hunter's clientele.

Hunter Marine, Route 441, Alachua, Florida 32615. **www.huntermarine.com** *(800) 771-5556.*

May 2003

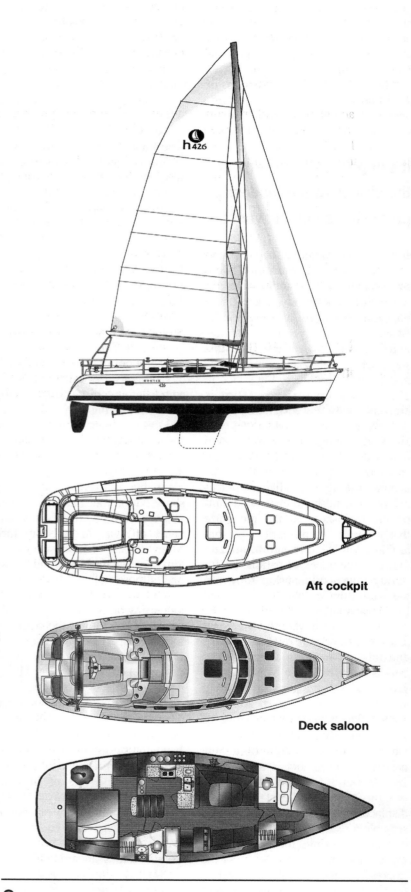

Aft cockpit

Deck saloon

Strong styling marks this comfortable cruiser.

LOA 42'1"; LWL 39'2"; Beam 14'6"; Draft 6'6" (deep), 5' (shoal); Displacement 23,936 lbs.; Ballast 7,237 lbs. (deep), 7,389 lbs. (shoal); Sail Area 834 sq. ft.; SA/D 16; D/L 178; L/B 2.9; Auxiliary Yanmar 56hp; Fuel 51 gals.; Water 125 gals.

Gib'Sea 43
Coastal Cruiser

I think it's time once again to go over the basic format of these design reviews. I've had 25 years to consolidate my philosophy of design reviews. It's key to remember that I'm only reviewing the design. In most cases I have not seen the actual boat, and in many cases the actual boat has not been built yet. I will tell you when I have had a chance to see or sail the boat in review. The rest of the time my comments will be restricted to the design as it's presented to me on paper.

This means that sometimes I have awful advertising agency "renderings" to work from. These seldom convey the nuances of the

"The extra-broad stern makes it possible to get two staterooms aft."

designer's work. Once in a while I get almost a full set of designer's drawings and that's always nice. Too often I get a sailplan and an accommodation drawing with maybe a deck plan included. Hull lines are rare but, now that I think about it, more frequent than in the past.

This Gib'Sea 43 came with the basic three drawings (advertising renderings) and an additional, optional interior layout.

"You seem to like all the boats you review." I hear this frequently. I always have the option of rejecting a boat the editor has asked me to review, and I have rejected a handful. Sometimes the design is too amateurish or I feel from my own experience that we are looking at the beginnings of a "bad boat." I do review boats that I don't personally like. They may not be bad boats, but they may be the type that I am not fond of personally. In these cases I try to put on my objective hat and restrict my comments to an evaluation of how the boat stacks up against the rest of its breed.

I've grown tired of being chased around boat shows by irate builders over a not-so-glowing review, so I've tried to soften my criticism over the years. That takes care of about half my irate pursuers. I have

no idea why the rest are after me. Designers seem to agree with my reviews even when I am critical, but builders usually take it all very personally. Sometimes, if a boat doesn't knock me out, it's better to just change the subject and talk about cooking or wine or music.

I think this Gib'Sea was designed for the charter market. It certainly has the layout for it. You can get this boat with four staterooms or three. It's only a 42-footer but with 14 feet of beam they have accomplished these layouts with minimal compromise. The extra-broad stern makes it possible to get two staterooms aft. There is no apparent lazarette and the fo'c'sle is minimal. The saloon arrangement with its island J-shaped settee works with this beam. This opens up the starboard side for a good-size galley with plenty of counter space. I don't see what the appeal is of the small settee added to the forward stateroom. I think it's better to have the small extra stateroom that can accommodate more guests or better yet, be a great stowage area.

Beam helps again when it comes to laying out the cockpit. Note the twin wheels on this design. This does a couple of things: It opens up the cockpit well so you can walk through to the swim step, and it gets the helmsman farther outboard where he can see the sails or the dock easier.

The rig is generous for a charter-type boat with an SA/D of 21.48. The spreaders are swept and there is a babystay forward. I don't like babystays. They get in the way when tacking. I also don't understand what's with the forward moment on the mast that the swept spreaders produce, why you would need another stay pulling the center of the mast forward. I'd prefer runners if I needed an extra wire.

The D/L of this long waterline hull is 177. Draft is 5 foot, 7 inches. The brochure credits Olivier Poncin for "development" and J&J Design for the "Design."

Dufour Yachts USA, 1 Chelsea Court, Annapolis, MD 21403. (410) 268-6417, fax (410) 268-9739, www.dufouryachts.com.

October 2000

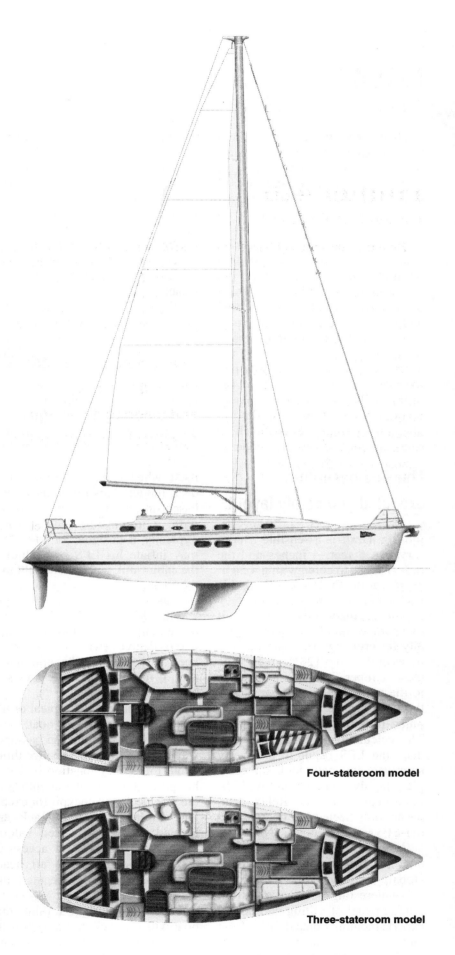

Four-stateroom model

Three-stateroom model

A roomy cruiser with plenty of sail power.

LOA 42'8"; LWL 35'9"; Beam 14'; Displacement (light) 18,081 lbs.; Draft 5'7"; Sail Area 925 sq. ft., Mainsail Area 408 sq. ft.; SA/D 21.48; D/L 177; Hull Length 42'1"; Keel Weight 6,174 lbs.

NW43
Bluewater Cruiser

Here's a very nice design from the Sparkman & Stephens office, built in Barcelona, Spain. Joinerwork, detailing and overall finish quality make this a first-class yacht. The designers have done an excellent job of preserving good looks while managing to fill this boat with an extensive interior layout in the raised-saloon style.

The hull is certainly not svelte by any standard. The L/B is 3.04 and the D/L is 225. The overhangs are minimal with enough overhang forward to make handling the anchor less hazardous. I really like the shape of the fore-and-aft rocker of this hull. It's very clean looking, giving the boat a long and flat run aft. Note the huge rudder. No client ever calls me and says his rudder is

This is a beautifully executed and comfy layout.

too big. Draft is a sensible if conservative 6 feet, 4 inches and the rudder looks to come within 4 inches of that depth. I would think this yacht sails very well.

Much is made today of the Limit of Positive Stability, which generally for cruising boats is a number between 115 and 128 degrees. I see these numbers inflated in some ads to the point of incredibility. I also think the typical buyer puts far too much importance on this number. The calculations required to produce the LPS result in an overly simplistic and static look at a complex, highly dynamic and multidimensional problem. "Relax dear, we are only heeled 122 degrees and our LPS is 125 degrees." Not.

A recent study done in Australia after the calamitous 1998 Sydney Hobart race came up with some very interesting observations from a large panel of sailing and design experts including data derived from tank tests involving various simulated wave types and combinations. You can read a synopsis of this study in the February issue of the British magazine *Seahorse*.

After extensive testing the article says the experts came up with three major observations: first,

and most obviously, that lowering the boat's VCG will result in an increase in the LPS; second that the bigger the boat the more resistant it is to capsize; and third, in the words of crewmembers caught in the Sydney Hobart storm, that in those conditions "It wouldn't have mattered what boat we were in, we were going to capsize." Exactly.

When assessing a boat's safety the focus should be not on when you go over but how quickly the boat can right itself. If everything about your boat looks relatively "normal" then you are going to have a "normal" stability profile.

The article goes on to say that the additional immersed volume provided by a cabintrunk in fact hindered a boat's ability to right itself when compared to a flush-deck model. This observation was based on tank tests using a model with a removable coach roof. Typically a designer or a builder may inflate his LPS by including the cabintrunk with the thought that the boat is now going to show increased stability.

The IMS-derived LPS for this design is an honest and acceptable 120.6 degrees with the standard keel. If you go to the optional 4 foot, 6 inches shoal keel your stability will be reduced.

This layout is very typical of the modern, center-cockpit boat, with the galley tucked into the passageway to the aft cabin. The nice thing about this galley location is that it has portlights looking out onto both the side deck and cockpit for excellent ventilation and light. Tanks are located under the raised saloon sole. There is excellent access to the engine through the aft head. This is a beautifully executed and comfy layout.

I like this design. I think this boat will sail well and transport its crew safely and in comfort with uncommon style.

The North Wind Group, 100 Second Ave. S., Suite 200, St. Petersburg, FL 33701. (727) 709-0611. www.yachtmarketinggroup.com

April 2001

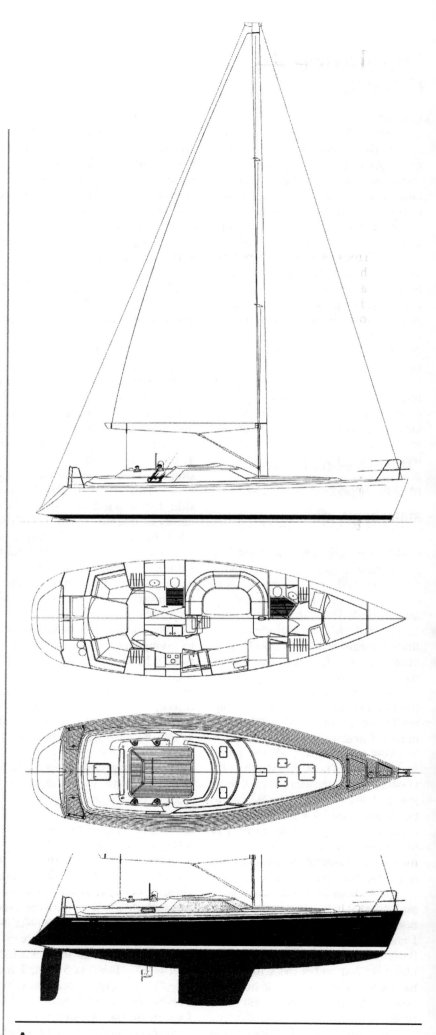

A solid, roomy cruiser with good performance.

LOA 43'; LWL 37'; Beam 14'1"; Draft 6'4"; Displacement 25,000 lbs.; Ballast 8,500 lbs.; Sail Area 1,087 sq. ft. (with 150% genoa); SA/D 20.3; D/L 225; L/B 3.04; Auxiliary Yanmar 56-hp diesel; Fuel 90 gals.; Water 145 gals.

Freelance 44
Coastal Cruiser

Garry Hoyt always wants to do it different and he's not always successful. Remember the Manta? As they say, you can always tell the pioneers. They are the guys with the arrows sticking out of their backs. Garry will show you the scars.

Still Garry doesn't lack for confidence, and I happen to own two boats with the Garry Hoyt boom system, which I assure you works beautifully. Garry's strength, besides his creativity, is that he's a sailor's sailor and he knows the difference when it comes to performance. Garry's new design, produced with some help on the hull lines and general aesthetics from Carl Schumacher, is a development of the boat that started Garry's career: the Freedom 40 cat ketch. Garry considers this latest design as an answer to what he sees as the proliferation of powerboats. We can probably trace the entire movement of free-standing cat rigs back to

Hats off to Garry for once again stirring the pot and sharing his vision.

Garry's work with the Freedom 40.

There is no denying that this design is different in every area. Let's begin with the rig. Using Hoyt booms on carbon fiber, rotating masts, Garry has given us a cat ketch with sails that roll up around the outside of the spars. This allows infinite reefing and makes it easy to get under way since there are no halyards.

The Hoyt booms eliminate the need for a vang as they cannot rise as you ease the sheet. This makes for an efficient sail off the wind. Upwind the clean leading edge of the sleeve-type sail is also effective. Garry has minimized the diameter of the masts to help keep the leading edge clean.

The Achilles heel of this rig is poor performance to weather in light air. A normal sloop would just hoist a bigger genoa and the race would be over. But you can't do that here. As a solution Garry proposes wire-luff staysails in addition to the two working sails to increase sail area and create a more efficient jib-type leading edge. If you add a staysail between the main and the mizzen, however, I'm not sure what you do when you tack. The drawings do not show these sails so we will just wait and see. To me, they seem a clumsy solution,

especially if you consider the need for additional halyard winches and sheet winches. Garry says these additional sails would only be used in winds under 12 knots, which means 85 percent of the time here in the Pacific Northwest. The SA/D with the working sails is a healthy 20.6. That's enough for me. I'd forget the staysails.

As long as we are looking at the sailplan we might as well tackle the question of aesthetics. To my eye this design looks like an SUV towing a house trailer. The aft house is almost flush with the sides of the hull, which plays havoc with our sense of visual "balance." People tend to like what is familiar, and this shape ain't familiar. That doesn't necessarily make this an ugly boat, but it does mean that we have to put it into a separate aesthetic category. I'm ready to say that this will be an awkward-looking boat by most standards. However, given the design parameters of this project, a truly graceful aesthetic solution seems a tall order.

This divided accommodation plan is obviously aimed at a warmer, drier climate than we enjoy in Seattle. The sleeping accommodations are all forward, with two near-identical staterooms and two heads. This way the noisy, partying crew aft would not disturb the early-to-bed guys like me. A boom tent would help in Seattle.

Aft there's an expansive saloon with 360-degree visibility and access to the "back porch," which is an expanded swim step that's roomy enough for a hard dinghy. Once the hook was down and the dinghy launched this area would be wonderful.

The rig of this boat is very well thought out and has undeniable advantages. The accommodations are novel. The overall look of the boat, to my eye, needs some work. I'd start with a total break with traditional shapes. (Who asked you?) I think the concept has a lot going for it. We'll just have to wait and see if the marketplace is receptive to it and a builder is bold enough to tool up for production. Hats off to Garry for once again stirring the pot and sharing his vision.

Newport R & D, One Maritime Dr., Portsmouth, RI 02871., (401) 683-9450. **www.alerionexpress.com**

November 2000

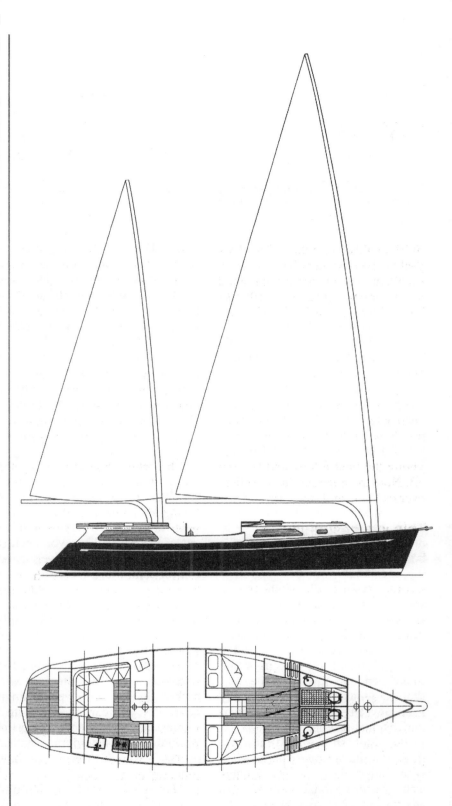

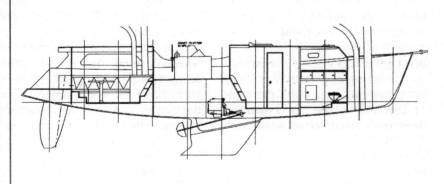

A new look in cruising yachts from the creator of the Freedom 40.

LOA 43'3"; LWL 38'; Beam 13'1"; Draft 5'11"; Displacement 18,000 lbs.; Ballast 7,300 lbs.; Sail Area 884 sq. ft.; SA/D 20.6; D/L 260; L/B 3.30; Auxiliary Honda 44-hp diesel; Fuel 100 gals.; Water 100 gals.

Sun Odyssey 43 DS
Coastal Cruiser

This 43-footer was designed by Daniel Andrieu and is built by Jeanneau. The company has used a pretty broad brush with this design trying to hit as wide a target as possible. There are six different accommodation plans and two different keels. I'm surprised there is only one rig offered.

This is a raised-saloon type of design, which seems to be in vogue these days, for good reason I suppose due to the visibility and feeling of light and air you get below. On deck the house is a bit of an obstruction, which in this case is exaggerated by putting the helmsman down in a shallow well behind the wheel. This makes no sense to me on paper. I'd have to see the boat in person to understand why this was done.

Despite the bulk of the house and the steep angle to the "windshield," I like the looks of this design. The blocky house goes well with the blocky short ends of the hull and the near straight sheer. There's enough contour in the deck shapes to make this deck look sexy from any angle other than a two-dimensional profile.

The hull shows the extra fat fanny we have come to associate with French designs. Here it buys us huge accommodation volume aft and an immense cockpit. Cockpits often get short shrift in cruising boats. This cockpit will be perfect when you are anchored but is so wide that you won't be able to brace your feet against the leeward seat while heeling (a small price). It opens onto a broad swim platform.

The deck is punctuated with teak decking to give the boat a rich look. Teak decks can become a problem down the line, but they look great when they are new, and teak does make an excellent nonskid surface. There is a well in the foredeck for lines and fenders, but the windlass is mounted at deck level. The lazarette is tiny as is the forepeak. This makes me think this boat must be aimed at charter groups primarily.

The DWL is 37 feet, 5 inches, which would give this design a D/L of 175. Beam is 13 feet, 8 inches for an L/B of 3.17. This is a beamy boat. I think this would be a very stiff boat if you went with the deep-keel option. The rudder looks dinky to my eye and appears to have been designed so as to not exceed the depth of the shoal keel. This is a good idea although in a wide-sterned

This boat would make an ideal warm weather cruising boat.

boat you can pull a lot of the rudder out of the water when you heel, so extra rudder depth can be very effective for control in a breeze.

The accommodation plans all use the same saloon design with an elevated dinette and opposing built-in elevated chairs. Forward of the saloon you have the choice of a head and a single stateroom, two staterooms, or one stateroom with both a double berth and a single berth. Aft you can choose from a single stateroom with a centerline double or two staterooms. Maxed-out for berths this design can have four staterooms.

There is no dedicated nav center, although you could use the little table to port in the saloon or the desk in the single forward stateroom model.

I'm always amazed at the beautiful interior finish of these Jeanneaus. There is plenty of satin-varnished teak in this interior, and the overall look is quite impressive. Forward the hull sides are lined with teak veneer. Fixed hull ports let in more light.

This boat would make an ideal warm weather cruising boat.

Jeanneau America Inc., 105 Eastern Ave., Suite 202, Annapolis, MD 21403. (410) 280-9400. **www.jeanneauamerica.com**

November 2000

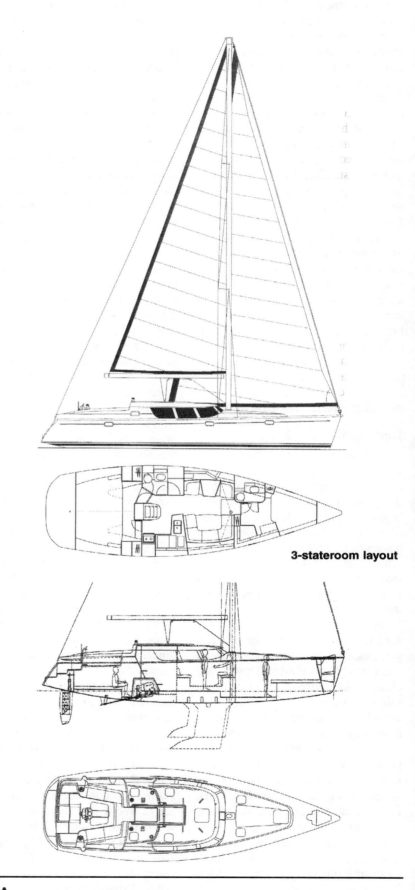

3-stateroom layout

A great boat for having fun in the sun.

LOA 43'4"; DWL 37'5"; Beam 13'8"; Draft 6'6" (deep), 5'2" (shoal); Displacement 20,503 lbs.; Ballast 6,515 lbs. (deep), 6,967 lbs. (shoal); Sail Area 770 sq. ft.; SA/D 16.45; D/L 175; L/B 3.17; Auxiliary 75 hp diesel; Fuel 55 gals.; Water 146 gals.

Beneteau 42
Bluewater Cruiser

Here's an interesting design from Group Finot for Beneteau. I find interesting the fact that this design is not especially "Euro" in its styling. In fact, it's sort of American looking and good looking too. So, let's examine this profile in detail.

The transom is traditionally raked as opposed to reversed. This eliminates the standard swim step we see so often. But Beneteau has countered this with a drop-down platform that extends about a foot beyond the transom. This platform is raised and lowered by block and tackle. A sliding flush-deck hatch covers the steps when they are not in use. This is an elaborate and very well thought out transom detail that will allow you to bring your dinghy up next to the boat without threatening the gelcoat on the transom edge.

This traditionally raked transom really drives the look of this boat. It certainly affects the character of the sheer. I would have liked to see a bolder sweep to this sheer, but it's fine as is. Note how the tip of the transom is at the waterline. This,

This is one boat I'll definitely board at Annapolis.

combined with the short bow overhang, produces a long sailing length. I think the designers have done a good job of blending the deck structures with the hull.

The D/L of this design is 183. L/B is 3.38, making this a moderately beamy boat on the lighter side of medium displacement if we choose 200 to be the middle of current D/Ls for cruising boats. The keel is a bulbed fin giving 5 feet, 11 inches of draft. Note the deep forefoot on this design and the straight line to the canoe body profile. All in all this is a handsome and moderate hull.

The interior shows a two-head, two-stateroom layout with the galley in the passageway to the aft cabin. The galley is spread out fore and aft, but it looks to me like there is still plenty of working room. The aft cabin has a large double berth and symmetrically arranged lockers and settees. Why settees? Well, they look good and occupy volume that is not much good for anything else

due to the shape of the hull.

There is a head with shower stall adjoining the aft cabin. The saloon has a dinette, which to my eye looks on the minimal side. I suppose you could seat four for dinner if you had to, but it would be a tight squeeze. The forward stateroom has a double berth with the toe end cut away to make room for the forward head. I'm not sure how this berth would work for a couple. Obviously, the biggest advantage to center-cockpit boats is the separation of the sleeping accommodations. There is space below the cockpit for the engine room.

Putting the cockpit in the middle of the boat allows the designer to place the mainsheet traveler at the end of the boom and place the traveler where it will not interfere with the cockpit layout. This rig is well forward and shows swept spreaders with forward lower shrouds. Unfortunately, the sailplan we have is not carefully drafted so it doesn't do much for the look of the boat. The photos also show a staysail. This is a very nice looking boat.

The windshield is fixed and, while obtrusive in the drawing, looks just fine in the photos. I'm not too keen on the wheel position. It is a bulkhead-mounted wheel offset to starboard, much like we see on cruising catamarans. This means you will sit in one position at the wheel without the benefit of being able to turn 90 degrees or change sides.

This wheel arrangement does free up the rest of the cockpit and puts the helmsman securely under the dodger. A teak-capped bulwark adds a rich look to the deck.

Beneteau's boats always deserve a close look. The company obviously puts a lot of market research into its new models. In this case the company has given us a well-designed boat with some unusual features. This is one boat I'll definitely board at Annapolis.

Beneteau USA Inc., 1313 Highway 76 W., Marion, OH 29571. **www.beneteauusa.com** *(843) 629-5300.*

October 2002

Drop-down platform

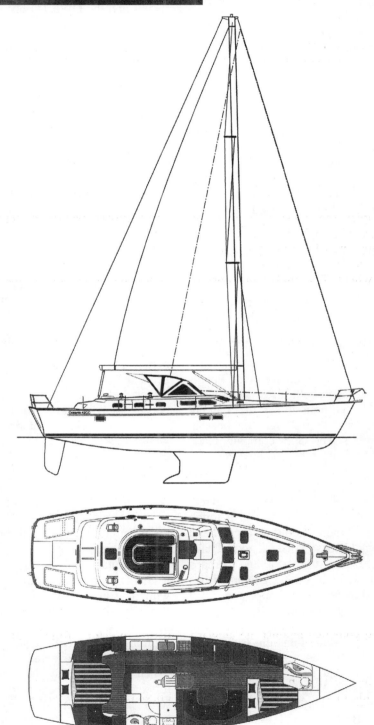

Ν ew French-built cruiser with a distinctly American look.

LOA 43'6"; LOD 41'10"; LWL 36'4"; Beam 12'10"; Draft 5'11"; Displacement 19,841 lbs.; Ballast 5,556 lbs.; Sail Area 878 sq. ft.; SA/D 19.1; D/L 183; L/B 3.38; Auxiliary 53-hp Yanmar; Fuel 63 gals.; Water 153 gals.

Amaryllis II
Traditional Cruiser

When I was a kid I collected so many old yachting magazines my parents thought the floor of my bedroom was going to fall through. My favorites were the oldest ones. I can still vividly remember their smell. If you go back to before the '60s you will find the world of yachting populated with a tremendous variety of

This review puts me in a tough place.

vessels. Today, science has eliminated the oddballs and given us a bland world of near-look-alike racing yachts. The same thing threatens the world of cruising boats. In my perfect world the harbor is full of varied yachts of individual, pronounced and proud character that in most cases echo the character of the owner.

One of my very favorite designers was Laurent Giles of Britain. His designs always carried a unique stamp that was best exemplified by his Channel cutters.

In 1937 Giles designed *Amaryllis* for a retired sailor. The boat was raced and cruised, and when World War II started, used to smuggle French resistance fighters across the English Channel. The boat was cruised through the '50s and eventually, in 1987, was bought by veteran sailor Simon Phelps and restored. Phelps was so taken with his restored yacht that he commissioned the Laurent Giles firm to redesign the boat in fiberglass. The Giles company made the boat bigger, but retained the original character of the lines. The boat is currently being built by Rock Run Yachts of Plymouth, Devon, England.

This review puts me in a tough place. Sometimes old is just old and being old doesn't make it good. I have never sailed this boat and perhaps *Amaryllis* has sailing characteristics belied by her general appearance. I'll leave room for that. But, with so many fabulous looking boats back in the '30s, I don't think this is the one I would have chosen to resurrect. I wonder what good old dead Laurent Giles is thinking? While the look of *Amaryllis* is certainly that of a traditional Bermuda yawl, I don't find the lines that attractive. It's hard for me to put my finger on why. I just don't see the level of harmony I need in a hull shape here. Maybe it's in those anemic ends. Okay, wash my mouth out with soap.

The bow of the original is almost straight in profile, which was unusu-

al in a day of exaggerated spoon-bow profiles. This straightened stem would give *Amaryllis* a finer entry. Curiously, I see that on the redesigned version the designers have added some fullness to the bow sections. I prefer this aesthetically, but I can't help thinking that fine bow had something to do with the performance of the original. The stern overhang about equals that of the bow overhang. The LOA is 43 feet, 7 inches and the DWL is only 30 feet, 9 inches. When you couple this with a displacement of 30,240 pounds you get a D/L of 464. Beam is narrow by today's standards at 11 feet, 10 inches.

The rig has a large mizzen that is stayed independently of the mainmast, i.e., there is no triatic stay connecting both masts. The long stern overhang makes sheeting the mizzen easy and keeps the sail out of the cockpit. The SA/D is around 15.5. The mizzen makes a great riding sail for when you are at anchor and the sail should be built with full-length battens. This may look out of place, but will prolong the life of the sail.

The layout for the new *Amaryllis* is very conventional with quarter berths and V-berths. There is one head, a big wet locker, a large nav center and a nice galley. The doghouse has port and starboard seats. It's a very workable interior and it would look great outfitted in wine-colored, velvetlike upholstery. Sure it will be dark below, but to some of us that's the appeal of this type of boat. Going below should have that "back to the womb" feel. A wee nip of a good single malt should brighten things up sufficiently.

The vintage look is so seductive—it's hard to resist that abrupt doghouse with its squared off windows—but I'm afraid it will be hard to carry off in fiberglass. The new, boxed cockpit coaming will not help. That's the rub with these resurrected antiques. When you take away the traditional timber detailing it's easy to end up with an aesthetically awkward hybrid. I hope the builders of *Amaryllis II* can avoid this.

I can still taste that soap.

Simon Phelps, Primrose Cottage, 23 Above Town, Dartmouth, Devon, England, TQ6 9RG. 44 1803 835 242. **www.amaryllis.uk.com**

March 2001

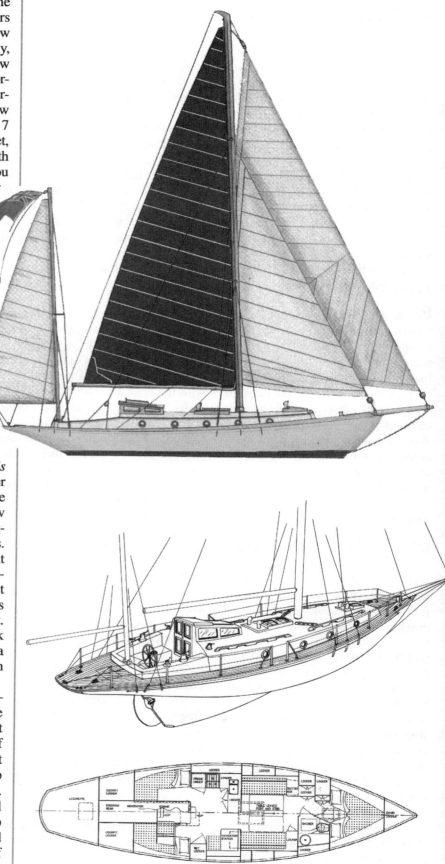

A classic cruiser reborn in fiberglass.

LOA 43'7"; LWL 30'9"; Beam 11'10"; Draft 6'6"; Displacement 30,240 lbs.; Ballast 12,000 lbs.; Sail Area 940 sq. ft. (jib, main and mizzen); SA/D 15.5; D/L 454; L/B 3.69; Auxiliary diesel-hydraulic; Fuel 48 gals.; Water 53 gals.

Barracuda 43
Coastal Cruiser

Here is a very interesting boat from French designer Gilbert Caroff, best known for his shoal-draft sailing yachts. Production is in aluminum at the company's yard in Fort Lauderdale. The brochure information says that Barracuda yachts "is the only manufacturer utilizing new technology to accomplish anti-electrolytic manufacturing." It uses a process that would reduce the effects

This is a pure cruising boat designed specifically for those with draft problems.

of electrolysis in aluminum by coating the hull inside and out with an epoxy-based enamel.

This is a pure cruising boat designed specifically for those with draft problems. There is a fixed keel version available that draws a very modest 5 feet, 7 inches. The D/L is 196. Beam is generous at 14 feet, 3 inches. The ends are very short and consequently the waterline is long. Beam is carried well aft. I'm not wild about this type of hull. There is a lot of wetted surface aft. Judging by the useable amount of cabinsole area, I would guess this boat has a firm turn to the bilge. This would again increase wetted surface while increasing initial stability.

The downside to this shape is that with the ballast located in the "belly" of the hull, the VCG will be high. Combine this with a wide beam and hard bilges and you usually get low ultimate stability. There is a huge skeg-type fairing that protects the prop strut and adds even more wetted surface. There are two shoal rudders to enhance the shoal-draft ability of the boat. Draft with the board up is 2 feet, 11 inches. Having two rudders again increases wetted surface. Dragging all that wetted surface around means that this boat will not be a light-air flyer. That may not be important for a cruising boat. Most cruisers motor in light air anyway.

Take a look below and maybe the lack of emphasis on light-air speed is better understood. There, on the starboard side and ahead of the galley, is an inside steering station. The dinette is raised so you will get a good view out the big windows when seated. I'll warn you that in this size range this feature comes at a price, and that price is side-deck width.

There are two staterooms with double berths and one large head aft. Forward, with its own access from the deck, is another stateroom with V-berths. To get to the head at night, people using this forward stateroom will have to go on deck and access the head through the main companionway or walk through the center stateroom. You could always add another head tucked between the notch of the V-berths.

This is a conservative and very traditional sloop rig. There is a "Solent stay" forward to allow the setting of a reasonably proportioned staysail for heavy air. Most staysails are too small and have too narrow a head angle to be of much use. No, you cannot fly your genoa and your staysail at the same time. The inner stay is removable. There are two sets of spreaders and fore and aft lowers. The brochure says the Barracuda has 1,506 square feet of sail area and I know that can't be right unless they are including the area of a 150 percent genoa, so there's no use in calculating an SA/D. To my eye the rig looks short, but that is certainly in keeping with the hull form and the inside steering station. The truth is that most cruisers neither want nor can handle tall, flexible rigs. The rig of the Barracuda is sort of a back-to-basics type and I find it refreshing.

If aluminum construction makes you nervous you should relax. Properly built, an aluminum hull offers some very real advantages. Next to steel, it is the most durable hull material around. You can beat up an aluminum hull and still maintain watertight integrity. It also frees the designer from the weight and shape constraints of steel construction. I like aluminum.

If you live where draft is a major consideration, the Barracuda might be your answer to comfortable cruising.

Barracuda Yachts Inc. (954) 327-9888, fax (954) 791-6555.

August 1999

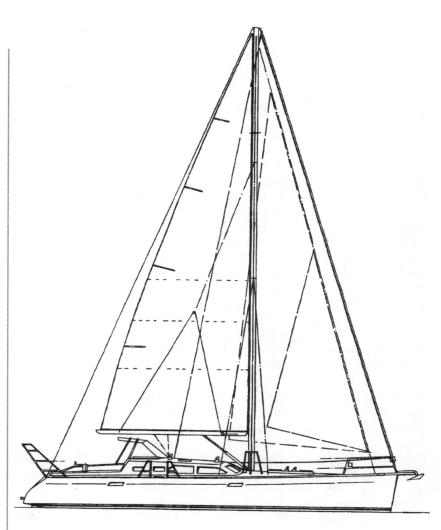

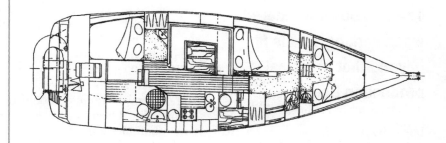

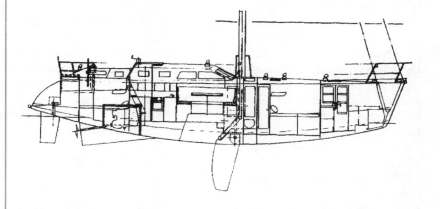

Centerboard design for shallow water.

LOA 43'11"; LWL 39'9"; Beam 14'3"; Draft 5'7" (keel version), 7'11" (centerboard down), 2'11" (centerboard up); Displacement 27,600 lbs.; Ballast 9,300 lbs. (centerboard version), 8,830 lbs. (keel version); D/L 196; L/B 3.1; Auxiliary 48-hp Volvo or 52-hp Yanmar; Fuel 132 gals.; Water 264 gals.

Silver Phantom
Bluewater Cruiser

I had an early connection with this project. The client came to my office, picked my brain and then went to Bill Dixon for the design. Hmmmmm. "Now be objective Bob." No problem. I'll do my best. I saw this boat on a cold, wet and blustery Seattle day at the marina. My views here will reflect what you can see in the drawings and what I saw during that visit.

My first impression on seeing this hull was that it was awkwardly full forward, and this fullness is very evident in the drawings. There is a lot of "roundness" in the topsides and this full shape is carried well into the bow sections. This is not the shape of speed. Take a look at the fast boats of today and you will see rapier-fine bows designed to minimize drag. Still, considering that this boat is not a racer but a comfy cruiser you could justify the puffy

The SP shows wonderful woodworking details far beyond that of typical production boats.

bows by their impact on internal volume. I see this basic shape on most Dixon designs so apparently it's a shape that he prefers.

With an L/B of 3.08 you can classify this boat as quite beamy. You can choose either a shoal keel drawing 5 feet or the standard keel drawing 6 feet, 8 inches. Considering the beam of this boat and the fullness in both ends, I'd prefer to see the keel farther aft for better helm balance. That's just my eyeball judgement. The D/L is 236.

The layout, with its aft stateroom, offers the advantages of a center-cockpit configuration while preserving a large aft cockpit. The owner's stateroom is forward with an adjoining head, shower and "office" area. This office area is probably a spacious nav station, but I think the volume might have been better used by contracting the nav area a bit and

using the extra volume for more storage. Show me a boat with too many lockers. I dare you.

The inside steering station is very well laid-out with excellent visibility forward but no visibility at all aft. The raised dinette is rounded in form, and regular readers will remember that I favor corners in my settees. I think we unconsciously seek corners when we relax. The galley features great counter space and looks like a cook's delight. Of course, the raised sole of the pilothouse means that stowage volume under the side decks is minimal. Built in New Zealand the SP shows wonderful woodworking details far beyond that of typical production boats.

On deck the SP is beautifully detailed with some of the best custom fabricated deck fittings I have ever seen. The bulwark chocks are works of art. These chocks blend a stainless half-oval rub strip with a well-proportioned teak caprail. The result is a very handsome boat. Note the prerequisite Euro stripes aft of the pilothouse windows.

The SA/D is low at 15.16. The SP will not be a light air flyer, but the 76-horsepower Yanmar should help in that area. Given the motorsailer-type configuration of this boat I think a lowish SA/D is prudent. The main is an in-the-boom furling type by Leisure Furl.

The SP is built with a Kevlar layer in the laminate and a Herex foam core. The laminate is heat cured. The rudder stock is carbon fiber. There is tankage for 120 gallons of fuel and 184 gallons of water.

My pals Dave and Laura did not leave on their world cruise this fall after Laura found out she had leukemia. They will instead cruise the Pacific Northwest. The SP would be the perfect boat for them, providing comfort, visibility and shelter from our pervading drizzle.

Silver Phantom Yachts, 244 Parfitt Way SW, Bainbridge Island, WA 98110. **www.silverphantom.com** *(206) 780-2391.*

December 2001

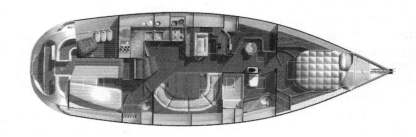

Center-cockpit cruiser with a spectacular finish.

LOA 44'; LWL 37'5"; Beam 14'3"; Draft 5' (shoal), 6'8" (standard); Displacement 24,250 lbs.; Ballast 9,039 lbs. (shoal), 8,488 lbs. (standard); Sail Area 794 sq. ft.; SA/D 15.16; D/L 236; L/B 3.08; Auxiliary Yanmar 76-hp 4JH3-THE; Fuel 120 gals.; Water 184 gals.

HR 43
Bluewater Cruiser

Here is the newest Hallberg-Rassy cruising boat designed by Frers. This is a very conventional center cockpit sloop designed to be a comfortable voyager and replace the venerable HR 42. Hallberg-Rassy is one of the few companies that offers sailing yachts designed specifically for offshore work. This is how HR made its mark. In looking at this new design let's have some fun and see if we can spot the compromises.

Considering that this design will have to be your home for very extended periods let's begin with the layouts. There are two. You can have

If you are considering offshore sailing, don't get carried away with big SA/D numbers.

one double berth aft or a smaller double to starboard and a generous single berth to port. If you were serious about heading offshore I think the two aft berths would make more sense. For live-aboard and coastal cruising I'd go with the larger double berth and settee layout. You also have the option of Streisand chairs to starboard or a straight and far more sensible settee/berth.

I can't figure this out. What's with the small reefers on these new boats? I always work with the idea that you need the biggest reefer you can get and hopefully it will have both reefer and freezer sections. This 43-footer has a reefer that appears to be no bigger than the Swan or IMX reefers. Not that I don't like warm tuna fish sandwiches, but stowage room for cold food and frozen food is of paramount importance for distance cruising.

Note there is counter space on each side of the sink and counter space on each side of the stove. There isn't a lot of counter space, but then 43 feet is pushing the lower limit for a center cockpit boat, and considering that this design has an actual engine "room," this tight galley is no surprise.

The rest of the layout is fine. There are plenty of hanging lockers, two shower stalls and a nice, big chart table, as well as lots of small lockers. Lockers are expensive to build but very important to orderly stowage for cruising.

A serious consideration with any center cockpit boat designed for offshore is the lack of a lazarette. This can be accounted for if the forepeak is large, but in this case it is not and the lazarette is almost nonexistent. Now think of all the stuff you need to take with you on your yearlong trip. It can't all go below. Sure you could fill up one of the shower stalls, but that's not very elegant. Extra anchors, extra rode, crab pot, gasoline tanks for the outboard, the outboard, drogue, fenders, extra lines, buckets, hoses: All these things need specific, dedicated stowage spaces, and I'm just scratching the surface. I think you will be hard-pressed to find that stowage volume on this boat. Of course, in a boat show environment, stowage volume does not sell boats. Dried plants, macraméed whisky bottles and doilies sell boats.

I can remember going several rounds with John Neale years ago over what made for a good offshore cruising boat. He was attacking the Valiant 40 as being too "radical" with its separated keel and skeg-hung rudder. Today John sails an HR and I know he doesn't consider the V-40 radical any more. In fact, by V-40 standards, this new HR is radical. The D/L is 216 compared to the V-40's 260. The keel is shorter in chord length and the rudder has only half a skeg.

The 43 rig is the epitome of conservatism. The spreaders are in-line and there are fore and aft lower shrouds. The masthead location of the forestay will make this an easy rig to set up and a no-brainer once the initial tuning is finished. The SA/D is 17.35. This is a low number by today's standards, but it does have its benefits. I advise you, if you are considering offshore sailing, don't get carried away with big SA/D numbers. Big SA/D numbers can give you a very fast boat that sails very well in light air. But this same boat may require reefing at 18 knots apparent when the HR is comfortable with full sail at 22 knots apparent.

The HR boats are full of nice, thoughtful touches. These are well-thought-out boats that have few peers.

Hallberg-Rassy, Hällavägen 6, SE-474 31 Ellös, Sweden. **www.hallberg-rassy.com** *46 304 54 800.*

September 2001

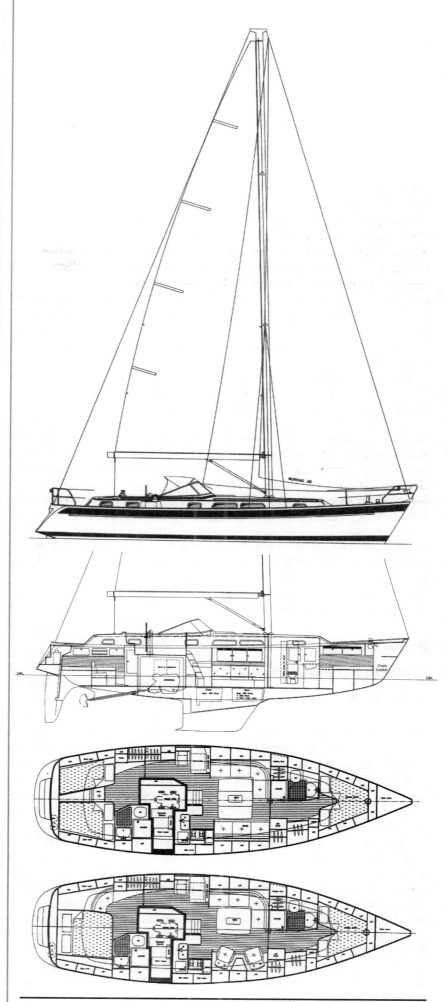

A center-cockpit cruiser designed for bluewater voyaging.

LOA 44'6"; LWL 38'7"; Beam 13'5"; Draft 6'7"; Displacement 28,000 lbs.; Ballast 10,500 lbs.; Sail Area 1,000 sq. ft.; SA/D 17.35; D/L 216; L/B 3.32; Auxiliary Volvo Penta TMD 22; Fuel 105 gals.; Water 174 gals.

IP 420
Bluewater Cruiser

This new 420 from Island Packet has an LOA of 44 feet, 7 inches, but I think the LOD (length on deck) is 42 feet. Designed by Bob Johnson, the 420 is classic IP all the way and is a natural extension of its well-received series.

This hull defines the modern full-keel boat. Look at the way the forefoot and the leading edge of the keel blend together so there is no distinction between the two. This is what I consider to truly be a full keel, although we generally think of any boat with the rudder attached to the keel as being "full keel."

The 420 has plenty of planform to its keel. The upside of this is probably good directional stability. On the downside, I can't imagine that, with any amount of rudder blade, the 420 will be quick to

IP does a really nice finishing job with its interior joinerwork.

respond to the helm. Another positive to this keel is the protection it affords in grounding situations. The prop is well tucked away. Of course another downside is wetted surface, your prime enemy in any light air sailing.

Note there is a shoal-keel version and a deep-keel version although the difference is only 6 inches. I don't believe that you would lose much performance with the shoal version. The D/L, based upon the brochure's displacement of 28,400 pounds, is 244.

The rig is the standard IP cutter type, with the mast well aft. There are fore and aft lowers and an intermediate backstay coming from the staysail hounds. I've used these intermediate backstays myself, but I don't think they do much at all other than add to the

compressive load on the mast. I'd prefer to see runners that can be deployed when needed.

The Gary Hoyt staysail club works well and adds a vanging vector to the club as the sheet is eased. SA/D is listed as 18.9. But by my calculations that figure includes both 100 percent of the foretriangle and the area of the staysail.

I'm sure you can sail upwind with both headsails set, but I don't think it's a very effective way to sail. When reaching, however, you can use both headsails simultaneously to great effect. The IP sheets its genoa to the rail, so I don't think the company is after a very close-winded boat. This type of sheeting angle is consistent with the full-keel approach.

You'll be comfy in this interior. It's laid out for two couples, with a double-berth stateroom with an adjoining head in each end of the boat. The forward head is unique and features a large shower stall off to starboard. The aft double is a canted athwartships berth. The galley is big with lots of reefer volume and counter space. Note the side deck location of the propane tanks. The port settee pulls out to make another double berth. IP does a really nice finishing job with its interior joinerwork.

If you're a member of the "Crab Crusher Club" you'll appreciate the thought that Johnson puts into refining the full keel approach to hull design. It's not everyone's cup of tea, but it has proven very effective for IP, and the IP owners I've spoken to love their boats. The IPs are handsome, well outfitted off-the-shelf and capable of taking you anywhere.

Island Packet Yachts, 1979 Wild Acres Rd., Largo, FL 33771. (727) 535-6431, fax (727) 530-5806.

October 1999

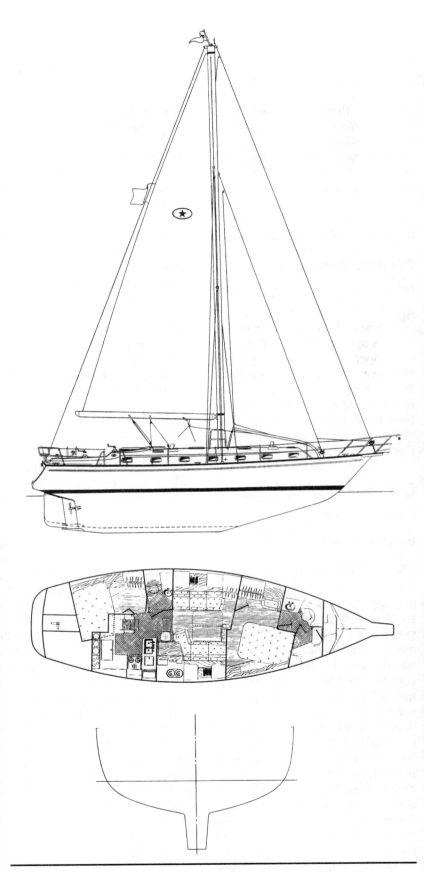

The latest full-keel IP cruiser.

LOA 44'7"; LWL 37'4"; Beam 14'3"; Draft 4'10" (standard), 4'4" (shoal draft); Displacement 28,400 lbs.; Ballast 12,700 lbs.; Sail Area 1,088 sq. ft. (with staysail); SA/D 18.9; D/L 244; L/B 3.16; Auxiliary 75-hp Yanmar; Fuel 160 gals.; Water 250 gals.

Barge Yacht
Coastal Cruiser

As the Monty Python crew would say, "and now for something completely different." It's 45-feet LOA so it fits with this month's theme. Designed by Andrew Wolstenholme of Norfolk, United Kingdom, this unusual canal barge design presents a startling alternative. It's a little wacky initially, but the more you study this design the more you realize it may be a very sensible alternative to the stock or semistock offerings. I find this a great-looking boat. Even Phil Rhodes designed a barge yacht.

Built in steel, this design is a true barge with boxlike midsection. The ends are carefully sculpted through the use of flat-plate-developed surfaces to provide effective sailing lines once this hull is heeled a few degrees. The result is a shapely hull, handsome from every angle.

Lateral plane is provided by port and starboard leeboards, kind

Clearly the owner of the barge would not be out to optimize performance as we understand it.

of clunky but very effective when you lower the leeward board. The D/L is 296. Where our other boats this month weigh in the upper 20,000-pound range, this barge weighs 60,352 pounds. On the other hand, it's all waterline.

Clearly the owner of the barge would not be out to optimize performance as we understand it. This owner would be out to optimize style points. The boxlike midsection and draft of 2 feet, 6 inches (boards up) will give this boat tremendous initial stability, but I would guess ultimate stability will be around 110 degrees. Given that, it should be understood that this type of design was never intended as a "bluewater cruiser" but a canal crawler and bay crosser. No, this will not be a light-air rocket.

Given the boxy sections and displacement, you might think this

boat would have a huge interior. But, the old saying that accommodations are a function of displacement is wrong. LOA is the determinate of accommodations and the barge has about the same useable interior space as do our other designs this month. The big difference would be in anchorage and storage areas. The barge has a mammoth lazarette. It's really a dedicated engine room!

The rig is pure traditional with topmast, topsail, gaff main, sprit mizzen and retractable bowsprit. The rig is low enough not to need any spreaders. I would guess that "hard on the wind" means an apparent wind angle of around 45 degrees. The SA/D of 12.39 brings this rig down into the area of 50-50 motorsailers. Still, it's quite picturesque and I like it.

There are three layouts but I'll concentrate on the one called "Live-aboard." The galley is big, (whoopee!) and you know what that means, pot roast stuffed with cranberry dressing for dinner. There are two heads, one with a shower stall. The saloon features opposing settee berths with pilot berths outboard. The owner's stateroom has a queen-size berth. The fo'c'sle is divided from the rest of the boat with a watertight bulkhead and has plenty of room for two crew berths. This would make a great family cruising layout.

Charlie Ward Traditional Boats Ltd. Of Norfolk builds these barges. You can have any interior you can fit in. A 82-horsepower Perkins will push this boat along at 8.5 knots and huge tanks will keep you self-sufficient. With a retractable bowsprit and outboard rudder, this may be the biggest boat you can physically get into a 45-foot slip.

I like everything about this boat.

Charlie Ward, Traditional Boats Ltd., Tide's Reach, Morston, Nr Holt, Norfolk NR25 7AA, 44 1263 740377, 44 1263 741424 (fax).

March 2000

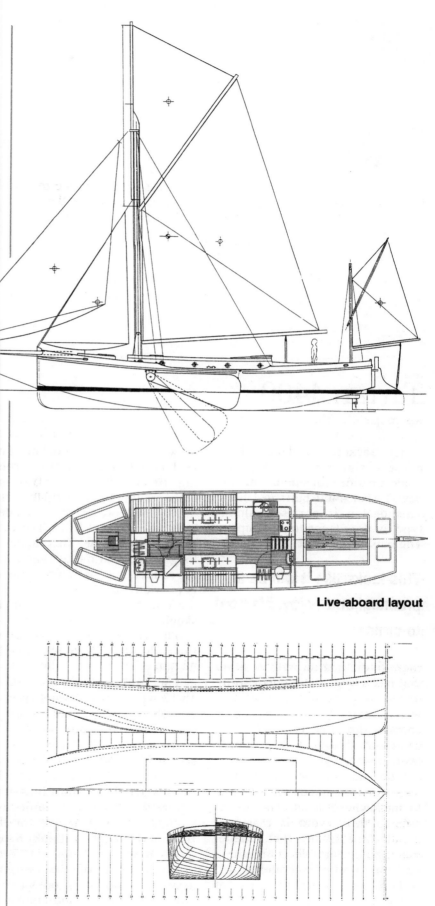

Live-aboard layout

Traditional and practical approach to coastal cruising.

LOA 45'; LWL 42'; Beam 13'; Draft 2'6" (boards up), 8'2 (boards down); Displacement 60,352 lbs.; Ballast 8,000 lbs.; Sail Area 1,192 sq. ft.; SA/D 12.3; D/L 296; Auxiliary Perkins Sabre M90 82-hp; Fuel 80 gals.; Water 120 gals.

Tartan 4400

Family Cruiser

Tim Jacket, president and in-house designer for Tartan, has made a major move in having this new Tartan 4400 built in China. This design is a raised-saloon-type laid out for two couples. There is a head aft and a state-

This looks like it will be a practical and enjoyable boat to cruise.

room in the quarterberth position that has a large double extending under the cockpit well. The forward stateroom is very spacious and has direct access to its own head and shower. On the upper level of the layout you have the dinette and nav station. The galley is forward and down, adjacent to the owner's head. The downside to this layout is that four people will fill up that dinette, making comfortable entertaining on board a bit of a challenge.

Tim has designed lots of Tartans, so he knows what he's doing with hull shapes. This hull shows a broad stern, traditional transom and short bow overhang. The traditional transom eliminates the stern boarding step and gate, but it does allow the cockpit to move aft in the boat, and these

drawings show a big cockpit. The keel is a low-aspect-ratio cruising fin with a beavertail-type bulb on the tip to help get the VCG down. Note the extended trailing-edge keel fillet. The rudder is a spade type. This rudder is long in chord at the tip, and it's a big rudder, but it's depth, or span, is restricted by the 5-foot, 6-inch draft of the boat. There is a small skeglet preceding the rudder.

The D/L is 203 based upon the published displacement of 24,000 pounds.

The sailplan shows an SA/D of 18.13 with double, swept spreaders. The small spritlike extension of the hull is more for ground tackle than it is for the rig. I don't see much harmony in the juxtaposition of the hull lines and cabintrunk geometry. But I fully recognize that this is very subjective so I will trust your eye for the final judgement. I think Spam tastes good.

My opinion of the design's aesthetics aside, this looks like it will be a practical and enjoyable boat to cruise.

Tartan/Fairport Marine, 1920 Fairport Nursery, Fairport Harbor, OH 44077. (888) 330-3484. **www.tartanyachts.com**

July 2002

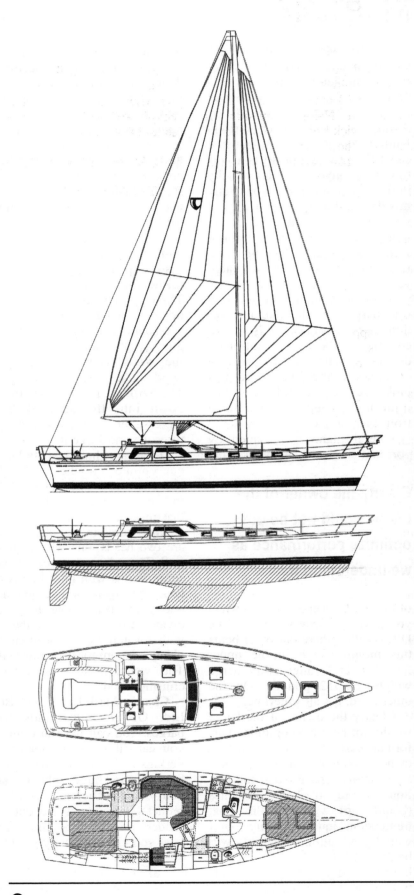

Comfortable raised-saloon cruiser with traditional transom.

LOA 45'; LWL 44'; Beam 14'1"; Draft 5'6"; Displacement 24,000 lbs.; Ballast 9,000 lbs.; Sail Area 943 sq. ft.; SA/D 18.13; D/L 203; L/B 3.19; Auxiliary 75-hp diesel; Fuel 80 gals.; Water 200 gals.

Morris 46
Bluewater Cruiser

I'll tell you one of my favorite Chuck Paine stories. In 1973 Chuck and I both worked for Dick Carter in Nahant, outside of Boston. Dick had a fabulous house right on the water and our office was in a 14-foot-square, concrete, five-story, submarine watchtower. Each floor measured inside 12 feet by 12 feet and we used ladders to get from floor to floor above the second floor. We had an amazing view of the Atlantic. Chuck worked on the fifth floor and Mark Lindsay and I worked on the third floor with Yves Marie Tanton. My take-home pay was $157 a week, but I was sure happy drawings those Carter designs.

One day I was looking over Chuck's shoulder as he worked on a drawing. I was silently marveling at his drafting skills.

"I love the way you draw," I said. "I try to make my drawings look like your drawings."

Chuck replied, "Oh really? I try to make my drawings look like your drawings."

That was probably one of the nicest compliments I ever received of my work. In those days before CAD, hand-drafting skills were very important to both Chuck and me. Pencil or keyboard are both only tools so it's really not important, but I thought I'd bring it up because these drawings, excluding the deckplan, are obviously hand drawn. You have to look very carefully but I assure you the hand of man is at work here. Analog rules. Vinyl forever!

This Morris 46 has Maine written all over it. The styling is absolutely classic Northeastern yacht. The overhangs are drawn out. The transom is small. The sheer is strong and the bow has a delicate spoon profile. The center cockpit configuration poses some aesthetic problems to the designer and I don't think Chuck conquered all of them. Few designers ever do. Given headroom requirements and the constant battle with cockpit volume and seatback height requirements, the end product is always an aesthetic compromise.

Hand me a pencil. I'll fix this profile in a heartbeat. Of course you will loose headroom. The cockpit will look like a mini hot tub and the seat back will hit you

This Morris 46 has Maine written all over it.

right in the kidneys. One solution is to raise the freeboard, flatten the sheer and adopt a more contemporary look all together. But that's not this boat, and the styling tone of this boat is its moderate freeboard and strong sheer spring.

Another critical consideration for you armchair designers is the fact that when you pull the entire boat into one flat plane as a two-dimensional representation, you loose aesthetic three-dimensional accuracy. While the drawing may be technically accurate, it's still aesthetically misleading. Photos of the Morris 46 show a great-looking boat. It's a Paine design. Of course it looks good.

The interior layout shows the galley in the passageway leading to the aft cabin. This is a well laid-out galley with plenty of counter space on each side of the sinks and the range. The nav station is generous in size. The staterooms in the ends of this boat are not huge and remind us that we are dealing with a boat with DWL 2 inches longer than a Valiant 40. There is a good-sized lazarette.

The D/L of this design is 288 and the L/B is 3.6. Draft is minimal at 5 feet, 6 inches. There is very little "balance" to the deep skeg-hung rudder. In plan view you can see that there is far less beam aft in this design than in most new designs. This shape is part and parcel of the approach. A big, wide transom on this design would look awful.

Morris Yachts will undoubtedly do a fabulous job on this design.

Morris Yachts, P.O. Box 395 110 Grandville Rd., Bass Harbor, ME 04653. (207) 244-5509. **www.morrisyachts.com**

April 2003

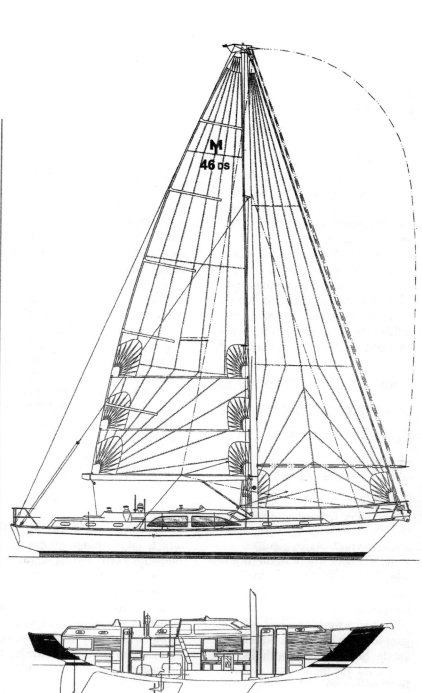

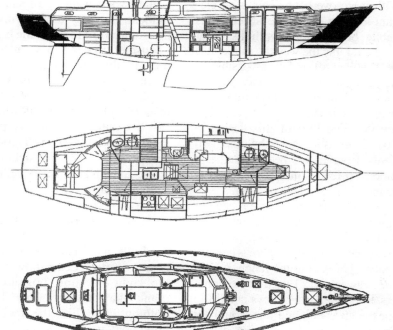

Traditional Down East looks are nicely blended with oceangoing capability.

LOA 45'11"; LWL 34'6"; Beam 12'9"; Draft 5'6"; Displacement 26,500 lbs.; Ballast 8,200 lbs.; Sail Area 998 sq. ft.; SA/D 19.1; D/L 288; L/B 3.6; Auxiliary Yanmar 4JH 3-CE 52-HP; Fuel 100 gals.; Water 150 gals.

J/46
Performance Cruiser

When I first looked at the drawings for the J/46 it was like someone had eavesdropped on my dreams of the perfect boat. Deck plan to interior plan to aesthetics to rig, this boat suits me just fine. The J/46, to my eye, looks to be designed for the ex-racer who wants to go cruising while not losing any of the performance features of a racing boat. This is a very subjective balancing act, but I look at it this way: It's more fun to cruise a race boat than it is to race a cruising

There's nothing quite like the feel of a good boat, well set up, cleaving the water on the rhumbline

boat. The trick is to manipulate the allocation of features and weights so that the word "compromise" never enters the boat's description.

Rod Johnstone draws fast boats with clean hulls. The DWL to LOA percentage works out to 88 percent, but the J/46 has the look of a boat with more overhang. This is an elegant-looking hull. The sheerline is subtle but beautiful with its point well aft. I like the way the rudder has been pulled aft as far as possible. It may ventilate more easily in this location, but it will also make the boat track better and steer easier in reverse. The D/L of this design is 164. Beam is less than the other two boats. I prefer less beam. Draft is a modest 6 feet, 2 inches. That seems to me a very sensible number.

I like this interior. There is counter space on each side of the sinks. The reefer features both top-opening and front-opening doors. There is counter space right next to the range. I don't see drawers, and I need some drawers in the galley. My boys could flip for the aft cabin, and one would get the pilot berth. I love pilot berths. They just look yare. (It's an old word and means yachting perfection or something like that.) When my wife and I cruise, I would put my guitar on the pilot berth. The opposing settees make for a wonderful conversation area where you really feel like you are in a boat. What's wrong with feeling like you are in a boat? I'm not wild about two heads. When my second son was born, I was given the job of always cleaning around the WC. I'd prefer one head, but this layout works better with two. I like the big double forward that does not cram the toe of the berth right up into the point of the bow.

The rig features a headstay pulled down from the masthead enough to allow for a spinnaker sock. I'm really old fashioned and had one of the first-generation Spinnaker Sallys (an open hoop arrangement prior to socks). I'm probably strange, but I'd rather wrestle with the chute than fiddle with a sock. If I don't have enough help on board to safely fly my chute, I'm going to wing out my genny. It's not enough to get the chute up and down. You have to keep the chute from coming down shredded.

The SA/D of this design is 19.4, which takes it out of the snoring range and keeps it just short of the white-knuckle range.

There are lots of reasons to own boats and many styles of boat usage. Some owners want the romance of a sailboat, but they aren't willing to invest the effort to make the boat go. I consider myself a lazy sailor, and for me that means getting there quickly and with the least amount of effort. I prefer that the boat do most of the work. I want a pointer and a footer. I can do my part if things are designed well and laid out properly. And in fact, if my efforts are well rewarded, I'll tweak a good boat all day long. Forget novelty rig features. Get a good, basic sloop rig like this J/46. Learn how and when to reef. Get good headsails and don't go crazy on genny overlap. Learn how to find the right sheeting position and crank that hummer in. There's nothing quite like the feel of a good boat, well set up, cleaving the water on the rhumbline to the anchorage.

Remember, you are what you sail.

J Boats Inc., P.O. Box 90, Newport, RI 02840. (401) 846-8410, fax (401) 846-4723. **www.jboats.com**

September 1999

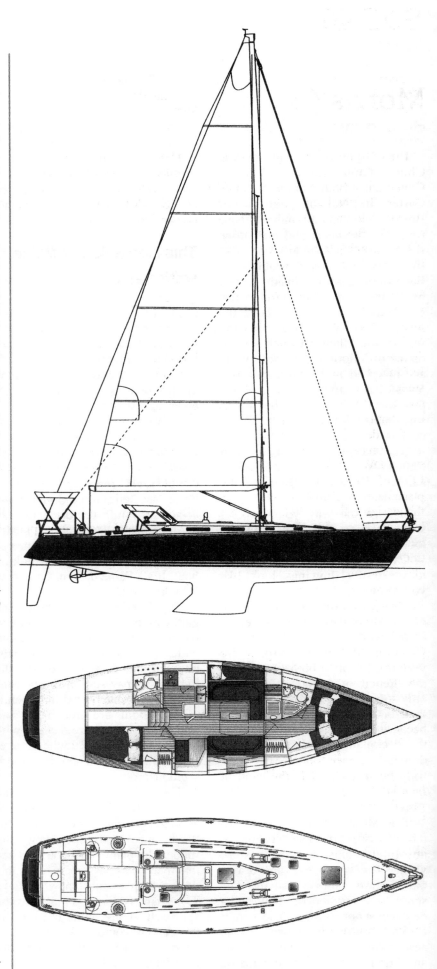

Sleek, fast performance package.

LOA 46'; LWL 40'6"; Beam 13'10"; Draft 6'2"; Displacement 24,400 lbs.; Ballast 9,350 lbs.; Sail Area 1,020 sq. ft.; SA/D 19.4; D/L 164; L/B 3.33; Auxiliary Yanmar 4JH-TE 76-hp turbo; Fuel 90 gals.; Water 120 gals.

S&S 46
Traditional Cruiser

There is a yacht builder in Denmark called Walsteds Baadevaerft. It has been building yachts for more than 50 years and builds, unquestionably, some of the most exquisite yachts in the world. K. Aage Nielson, one of my boyhood designer heroes, used to have almost all his designs built at Walsteds. I once tried to visit Mr. Nielson when I moved to Boston, but when he asked if I was coming to his office to spend money and I answered no, he turned me away. I was crushed. Mr. Nielson knew that if you wanted the very best you went to Walsteds. You still do, and S&S is lucky enough to count Walsteds as one of its clients. In this 46-footer S&S has given us a great-looking, capable cruising boat well suited for offshore work. You can count on this boat being the epitome of yacht-building perfection.

The design is very classic in its overall proportions. The ends are long with a DWL of 34 feet, 1 inch on an LOA of 46 feet. A "light-ship" displacement of 27,000 pounds gives this design a D/L of 304, which is a bit on the heavy side. Draft is 6 feet, 3 inches, but there is an optional shoal-draft keel. Distribution of beam is classic too, with the stern being on the narrow side and the spoon-bow profile being reflected in a fuller deck-plan line forward. All these proportions have to work together. You can't choose a spoon bow and then ask the designer for a concave entry. You'd end up in geometry hell. Executed in flawless, bright finished mahogany, as will be the case with boat No. 1, this hull will be very beautiful.

This is a simple layout and in many ways as classic as the hull form. The galley is bigger than it would have been 20 years go. But you still get pilot berths outboard of the settee berths. The quarter berth is a double. The fo'c'sle is big enough to push the V-berth aft so the toes won't be too confined. This is a very good galley layout. Note the counter space on each side of the sinks and on each side of the range. The engine box is under the centerline galley counter leg. There is a Luke, wood-burning fireplace nestled into the forward end of the engine box. Interior joinery is all mahogany.

The deck plan shows a cockpit that stops short of the transom, which is unusual these days, but necessary because the stern overhang is far greater than on most current designs. The mainsheet traveler is aft. Genoa tracks are long to provide options for correct sheeting of the genoa in different rolled-up configurations in addition to staysail sheeting options. There is an outboard track for heavy air or reaching staysail sheeting. The cockpit is long. Side decks are broad and uncluttered. There is a "butterfly"

These drawings don't do justice to the detailing that Walsteds will apply.

hatch over the main cabin. I'll bet Walsteds' butterfly hatches don't leak. These drawings don't do justice to the detailing that Walsteds will apply. There is a world of boatbuilding skill just in the way the teak toerail is shaped.

The construction features a cold-molded hull of mahogany and western red cedar, the outer layer being the finest red cedar available for matched grain. The deck will also be red cedar and mahogany, planked with 12-mm teak, set in epoxy. There will be no fastenings in the teak deck. The cabintrunk will be uninterrupted mahogany planks. The top of the cabintrunk will be planked in Oregon pine. The auxiliary will be a four-cylinder Yanmar, and there will be a 3.5-kW gen set. Handling around the dock will be aided by a Max Prop hydraulic, retractable bow thruster. The photos I have show a boatbuilding shop that is pristine in its cleanliness and order. There isn't a single wood shaving on the deck. Maybe like mother cats these workers just lick the boat clean as they go. Many of Walsteds' workers have been there for their entire working careers.

There is a second version of this boat planned. It will be a raised-freeboard model with a flush deck forward and white painted topsides. I'd take either one. I don't know what else to tell you about this boat and its builder. I think you will need to track down a Walsteds boat and take a look for yourself.

Sparkman & Stephens Inc., 529 Fifth Ave., New York, NY 10017. **www.sparkmanstephens.com** *(212) 661-1240.*

May 2002

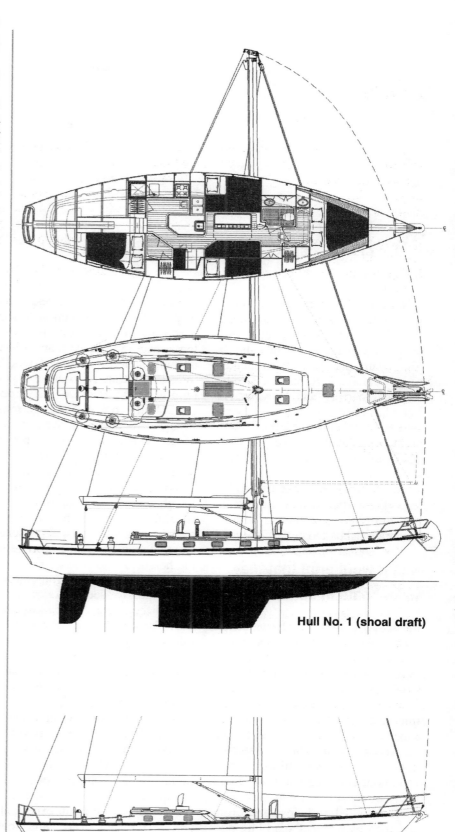

Hull No. 1 (shoal draft)

Hull No. 2 (deep draft)

Classic design built to an impeccable finish.

LOA 46'; LWL 34'1"; Beam 13'; Draft 6'3"; Displacement 27,000 lbs.; Ballast 9,000 lbs.; Sail Area 1,050 sq. ft.; SA/D 18.7; D/L 304; L/B 3.54; Auxiliary 75-hp Yanmar; Fuel 95 gals.; Water 65 gals.

Tayana 460
Motorsailer

This new Robert Harris design was built by my old friends at Ta Yang in Taiwan. I have spent many a happy day puttering around the Ta Yang yard and have been treated royally at fabulous dinners hosted by the yard owner, Nan Hi Chiu. Ta Yang has been one of the most consistent and busiest sailing yacht builders in Taiwan for over 20 years. The yard excels in beautiful teak joinerwork.

I was driving from the yard to the airport one afternoon in a torrential rainstorm. It was raining so hard the driver almost had to pull off the road

Isn't it wonderful that they make boats in all flavors?

for lack of visibility. I innocently asked if he thought my plane would take off in this weather. "No problem. Chinese pilot very brave." Cool.

We had better clear up some terminology. Exactly what is a "motorsailer" and how does it differ from a pilothouse sloop? This is a subjective area so you can call these boats just about anything you want. I call boats motorsailers when they have been designed with inside steering and it's obvious that sparkling performance under sail was not paramount in the design objectives. Another designer I know defines a motorsailer as "any boat that has three 17,000 BTU air conditioners."

We know that freeboard is windage, and this boat has a lot. We also know that copious deck structures add to windage. There is a very good reason for this high appearance, and we will get to that when we discuss the accommodations.

The D/L of this design is 364. This is a heavy boat, and considering the amount of interior in it, that should come as no surprise. The

ends are moderately long especially if you go with the optional sugar scoop transom. The keel is a long, low-aspect-ratio fin with an elongated bulb at the tip. Ballast will be internal. The ballast-to-displacement ratio is on the low side at 23.8 percent. Draft is 6 feet. The large semi-balanced rudder is set well aft and supported at the bottom by a power-boatlike keel extension that is bolted onto the trailing edge of the keel.

There are three interiors available for this boat, all featuring inside steering in the pilothouse. Headroom throughout is 6 feet, 5 inches, and that would partially account for the height of the profile. I have no favorite layout here. You know I don't like to see sinks right up against the range. Maybe Layout B with the orthogonal settee in the saloon would work best for me. Both forward and aft heads have their own generously proportioned shower stalls. I like the large lazarette to starboard.

Side decks are minimal on this boat, and they disappear as you go aft. Note the step in the deck adjacent to the pilothouse. This provides more usable volume below. The cockpit looks to be small, but the seats scale out to be in excess of 6 feet, 10 inches long, and that's enough to lay down on. I think it would bother me to sail behind that large pilothouse, although I know from experience that you don't look over or around a pilothouse like this. You look through it. The windows are big enough to provide better than adequate visibility.

Isn't it wonderful that they make boats in all flavors?

Imagine Yachts Ltd., 980 Awald Drive, Suite 201, Annapolis, MD 21403. **www.imagineyachts.com** *(410) 268-0102.*

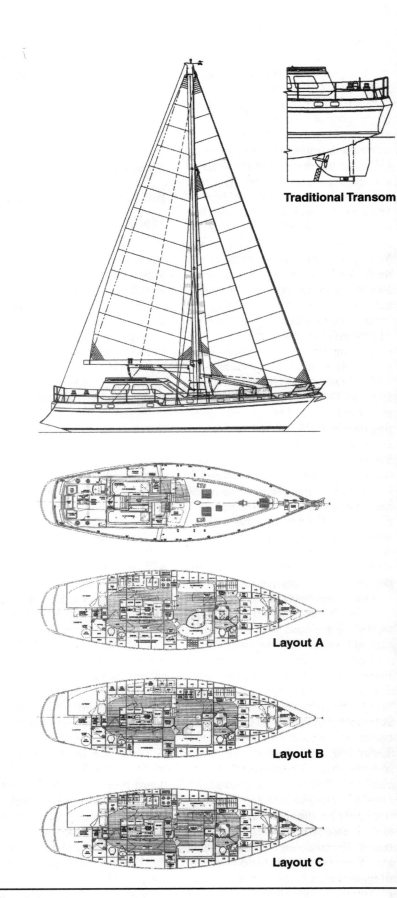

Traditional Transom

Layout A

Layout B

Layout C

Sturdy cruiser with plenty of room.

LOA 46'; LWL 37'2"; Beam 13'7"; Draft 6'; Displacement 42,000 lbs.; Ballast 10,000 lbs.; Sail Area 1,425 sq. ft.; SA/D 18.9; D/L 364; L/B 3.4; Auxiliary 100-hp diesel; Fuel 325 gals.; Water 240 gals.

Hunter 460
Coastal Cruiser

The Hunter 460 appears to be aimed at the pure cruiser with the accent on ease of sail handling and cockpit comfort.

Hunter designers once again used what I call the "grab bag" approach to windows and portlights, but it works. Hull ports never look good to me, although owners love them. The Hunter's hull ports are big but with more freeboard they look in proportion. The long, wedgelike cabintrunk extending forward on the Hunter gives this boat a sleek look.

The D/L of this design is 208 and our DWL to LOA percentage is 87 percent. Overhangs are disappearing in favor of sailing length and—even more important — more interior volume. The keel is a bulbed fin drawing 5 feet, 6 inches. This should keep those in shallow areas happy, but won't do much for upwind VMG. Note the extended trailing edge fillet on this keel design. In plan form the hull looks very full in the ends, which will also help with interior volume.

There are two interior layouts available. You can have three staterooms with double berths or you can eliminate one aft stateroom and substitute an officelike space. There are Barbara Streisand chairs, adjacent to the dinette. "Why do you call them Barbara Streisand chairs, Bob?" Once I did chairs like this and the client took me sailing, made me sit in a chair and put on a Barbara Streisand CD. He insisted that I sit there and listen to the music while we sailed along. To him this was the ultimate sailing experience. To me it was torture. Even though I draw them when asked, I really think a straight settee is a far more versatile interior component. Once you design a wraparound dinette with a center island seat you have the dilemma of what to do with the other side of the boat. My own taste in interiors runs more toward the "argh matey" school of interior design. I must say that photos of the Hunter's interior, finished in teak veneer with solid teak trim, look very nice.

I can't remember when Hunter did not use swept spreaders. In fact the rig Hunter uses is called a Bergstrom-Ridder rig after the original designers. There are struts coming from the spar about 8 feet above the deck to the chainplates to support the lower panel. This gives you a very stiff and rigid stick that you will not bend to affect sail shape. The drawback is that when you bear off and ease the mainsheet you will impale the main on the spreaders quickly. The SA/D is 16.6.

I think Hunter really shines in the area of deck design and tool-

I think Hunter really shines in the area of deck design and tooling.

ing. The cockpit features a steering pedestal employing a large cockpit table. The wraparound cockpit seats look comfy, but I'd prefer to see more seat back height. There is a recessed anchor well forward with windlass. I like Hunter's overhanging stern pulpit seats; a lot of builders are copying these seats, and I can see why. Note the unusual mainsheet arrangement. The mainsheet traveler is on top of the aluminum bimini arch. This gets it totally out of the cockpit while keeping the sheet at the end of the boom. It does appear strange on the drawings, but looks fine on the photos.

Hunter Marine Corporation, Route 441, P.O. Box 1030, Alachua, FL 32615. (904) 462-3077, fax (904) 462-4077. **www.huntermarine.com**

September 1999

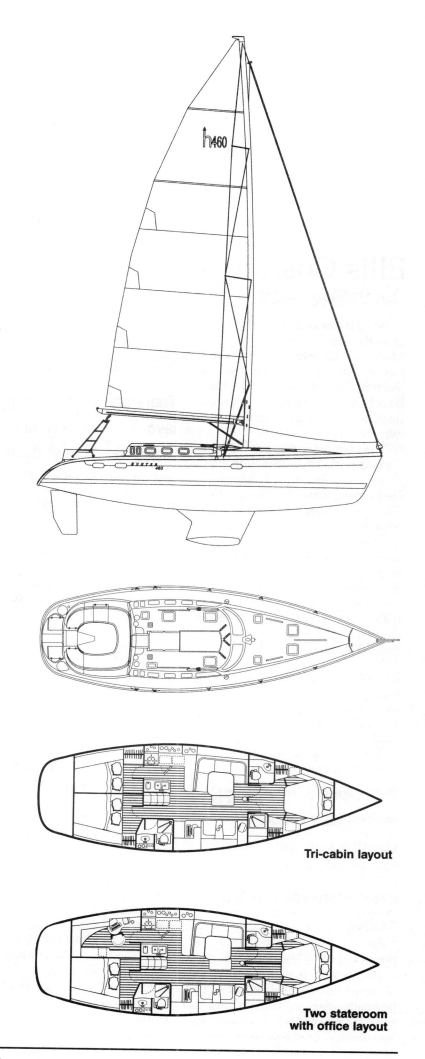

Tri-cabin layout

Two stateroom with office layout

A comfortable, good-looking cruiser.

LOA 46'1"; LWL 38'8"; Beam 14'; Draft 5'6"; Displacement 27,000 lbs.; Ballast 9,500 lbs.; Sail Area 932 sq. ft.; SA/D 16.6; D/L 208; L/B 3.29; Auxiliary Yanmar 62-hp diesel; Fuel 100 gals.; Water 200 gals.

Ellis Custom 47
Family Cruiser

An aft-cockpit cruising boat from the Mark Ellis' design office. Mark has "the eye." No, you can't buy it. I'm not even sure you can teach it. I find the lines of the Ellis boat very harmonious. I can't see a line I would change. This design is pure eye candy.

The clients for this custom boat wanted a classic yacht with bold sheer and conventional shapes on deck. Mark gave them a sweeping sheer accentuated by a teak cap. Note how the short bowsprit carries the eye forward, adding visual length to the sheer. The stern features an elegantly raised counter and traditionally raked transom. The bow profile is a slight spoon with a hint of a knuckle just above the DWL that straightens out as it nears the sheer.

The hull shape is vintage Ellis, with the keel set well forward. The keel plan form is moderate aspect ratio. The run is clean and the rudder takes advantage of this by going right up to the canoe body for some endplate effect help. Note

With modern, monocoque, carbon fiber rudder construction, you would tear the back end off this boat before you broke the rudder.

the amount of balance on this spade rudder. I would guess it's about 12 percent. This gives you a huge advantage in that you have in effect a "power assist" working on your helm. The autopilot will work easier and you will work easier steering this boat. With this type of rudder and the prop well forward, I would bet that this boat will back up like a champ.

Is the rudder vulnerable because it is not protected by a skeg? A bit. Is the rudder weak because it is not supported by a skeg? Not at all. With modern, monocoque, carbon

There are no tricks to this layout, no angles, no razzle-dazzle, just good common-sense application of available volume.

fiber rudder construction, you would tear the back end off this boat before you broke the rudder. I have seen too many boats that had skegs that were held on by the rudders.

This layout features accommodations for two couples. I assume both berths can use filler pieces to become doubles. The aft head has a big shower stall. The galley is big and has the sinks near centerline. The dinette is big and integrated with the opposite settee. I would prefer to see some counter top to each side of the stove. But otherwise this will be the perfect interior to sit around and share stories with friends. If I could change anything I'd add a guitar locker. There are no tricks to this layout, no angles, no razzle-dazzle, just good common-sense application of available volume.

The rig is very normal, and the spreaders are swept to help eliminate the need for runners with the staysail. The SA/D is 18.97, which is a very sensible number for a mom-and-pop cruiser.

Custom built by Bruckmann Custom Yachts of Opakville, Ontario, this one is a guaranteed head turner.

Mark Ellis Design Ltd., 77 Bronte Rd., Oakville, Ontario L6L 3B7. **www.markellisdesign.com** *(905) 825-0017.*

March 2000

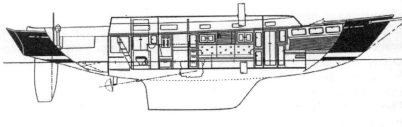

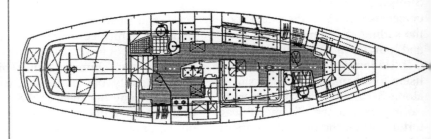

Well-designed and attractive cruising sloop.

LOA 46'6"; DWL 35'8"; Beam 13'3"; Draft 6'; Displacement 25,000 lbs.; Ballast 9,950 lbs.; Sail Area 1,014 sq. ft.; SA/D 18.97; D/L 246; L/B 3.3; Auxiliary Yanmar 63-hp diesel; Fuel 90 gals.; Water 140 gals.

Ocean Star 48.1
Bluewater Cruiser

Sometimes I visit the various sailing Web sites. I'm always keen on picking up on the comments made about the *SAILING* reviews. It seems that there is a need to remind you, dear readers, that I am only reviewing the material I receive. In a few cases I can see the actual boat and in even fewer cases I may get the chance to sail a boat I am reviewing. But usually I am just looking at drawings. Having been drawing boats for the past 43 years, I do feel qualified in this area.

The Ocean Star 48.1 is built by Ocean Yachts in Hellas, Greece. I understand the design is done in-house, but I would have preferred to see a little more effort put into shaping the deck structures. That truncated vertical ending to the coamings aft is a wee bit hard on my eye. Of course this is compounded by the distinctively bland drafting style. There is just no life to this image. I'm not saying it's a bad design, I'm just less than impressed with the design presentation.

The most distinctive thing about this hull form is the reverse to the counter profile aft. There is a definite hook to the counter. The benefit to this is that it makes the stern bigger and that would give you a bigger swim platform. But why didn't the designer just eliminate the hook and give the boat a longer DWL? That way he would have a faster boat with even more volume aft. It's academic anyway, the drawings show no swim step. I'm inclined to think that there will be one but showing it on the drawings was not deemed vital to the appreciation of the design.

The D/L is 216. The keel looks too far forward to my eye. If the keel were moved aft about two feet I think the ballast could be reconfigured to take care of the trim issues while producing a boat that was less prone to weather helm. The rudder is a partially balanced spade on a half skeg.

The accommodation layout is aimed at charter groups. There are four staterooms with double berths and three heads. This layout looks well thought out. The trick with squeezing two staterooms in forward is the access to the rooms. Leaving room for those two doors eliminates options with your saloon layout.

But why didn't the designer just eliminate the hook and give the boat a longer DWL?

The sailplan shows an almost IOR-like ribbon mainsail, one that's very short on the foot. This will help with the helm balance. Ribbon mains aren't much fun off the wind. In this case the mainsheet is well forward on the boom and the short foot helps with this. The sailplan drawings shows a lot of sweep to the spreaders, certainly in excess of 20 degrees. There are also forward lower shrouds, which is desirable when you have swept spreaders on a deck-stepped mast. You can't induce pre-bend with a deck-stepped mast without forward lowers.

The SA/D is 14.3. I checked this number a couple of times to make sure it was correct and it is. This is a low SA/D and indicates that this boat will not be a light air flyer. However, we would have to know where the boat is intended to be sailed before commenting further. If this boat is going to be sailed in an area where they get a steady 20 knots every day this rig will be perfect.

The deck plan shows a large cockpit with two wheels. This layout is perfect for direct access to a large swim step carved into the transom but again, it doesn't show on any on the drawings I have.

I like to think that in person this boat will have more appeal than it does in these simplistic drawings.

Ocean Yachts, 6 Afxediou Str., Alimos 174 55, Greece. 30 210-985 5518. **www.ocean-yachts.com**

July 2003

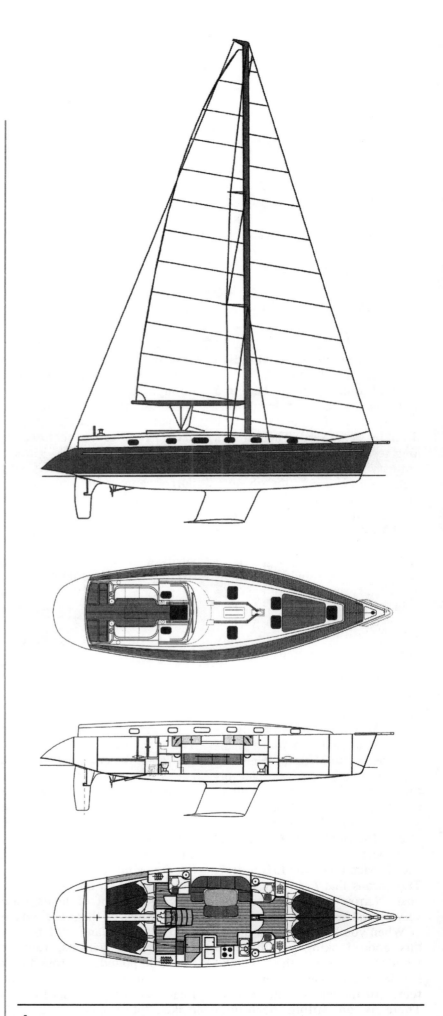

A comfortable boat for chartering.

LOA 46'6"; LWL 37'9"; Beam 13'9"; Draft 6'3"; Displacement 26,432 lbs.; Ballast 8,960 lbs.; Sail area 783 sq. ft.; SA/D 14.3; D/L 216; L/B 3.38; Auxiliary Yanmar 75hp; Fuel 94 gals.; Water 208 gals.

Lena
Traditional Cruiser

Imagine an owner walking into the boatyard and asking for a boat to "sail quickly from bed and breakfast to bed and breakfast." That's what happened at the Brooklin Boat Yard. Then after a long series of seven different preliminary proposals the 46-foot, 7-inch *Lena* emerged. It's a beautiful boat, drawn by Robert Stephens and built at the Brooklin Boat Yard in cedar strip planking reinforced with carbon fiber.

The hull sections show lots of deadrise, a V-ed and gently hollowed entry and a hint of concavity in the counter sections aft. This concavity in the sections reduces effective sailing length but it sure helps to produce a pretty transom. If you remove this hollow you will gain a fraction of a fraction of a knot but end up with a bland and boring transom shape.

The keel is big with a moderate aspect ratio and a bulb-ish treatment at the tip. The root is long enough to make it easy to get this fin securely fastened to the hull so that loads are spread out in case you hit a rock. Draft is moderate at 7 feet. The rudder shows a moderate aspect ratio and is a semibalanced spade type. The L/B is 5.17. This means that *Lena* is a narrow boat. Narrow boats tend to have very neutral helms. The D/L is 112.

When you look at a boat that is this good looking you have to wonder what's the catch? Headroom, my friend. *Lena* has 4-feet, 10-inches of headroom. There is no sitting headroom under the side decks. Of course, all this could have been cured by adding another 14 inches of freeboard, but the overall aesthetic proportions of the boat would

have been destroyed and I would have been grinding my teeth all through this review. I think it was wise old Uffa Fox who once said, "If you want to stand up, go on deck." The head is enclosed. You can sleep on the wide settees if you can't find a B&B. A single burner camp stove could heat up a can of the "brotherhood of man" and with the right bottle of wine you'd be living like a king.

The tall, fractional rig shows a small working jib with minimal overlap. The jib is hanked on the

When you look at a boat that is this good looking you have to wonder what's the catch?

same way I do it on my own boat. The mainsheet traveler is aft of the cockpit coaming and that keeps it out of the way. The spreaders are slightly swept and no runners are shown on the sail plan. I might want runners, but that would depend upon just how stiff the carbon spar was. The SA/D is a muscular 25.1.

I look out on our beautiful bay and I see a lot of boats sailing today. Most of them are only out for the day. Many will be dragging around gensets, refrigeration, 500 pounds of ground tackle and home theater systems. Beautiful, simple boats like *Lena* make a lot of sense.

Brooklin Boat Yard, P.O. Box 143, Brooklin, ME 04616. (207) 359-2236.

December 2003

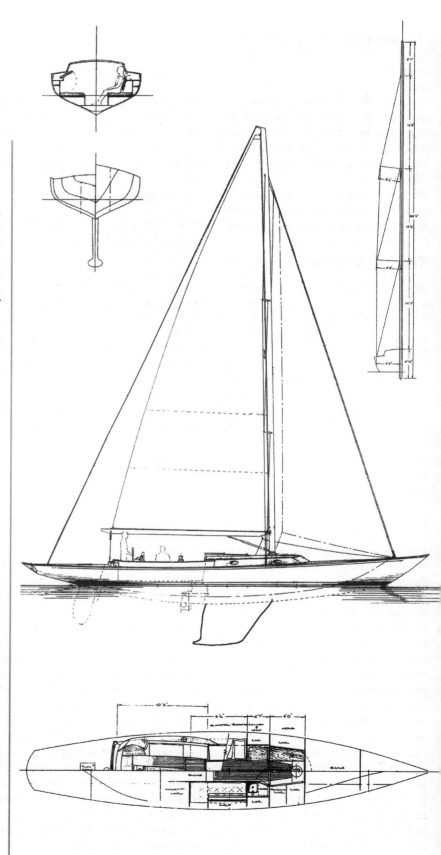

Sail from inn to inn in style.

LOA 46'7"; LWL 34'6"; Beam 9'; Draft 7'; Displacement 10,300 lbs.; Ballast 5,150 lbs.; Sail Area 744 sq. ft.; SA/D 25.1; D/L 112; L/B 5.17; Auxiliary Yanmar 27-hp; Fuel 14 gals.; Water 14 gals.

Beneteau 473
Family Cruiser

I saw this boat at the Annapolis boat show. I couldn't walk by without thinking what a great looking boat it was. One of my cronies said he couldn't walk by without thinking how ugly it was. There you have it, different tastes. I thought the boat had a strong, masculine look and while not on the pretty

The three-stateroom layout would be close to ideal for family cruising with two kids.

side, was aesthetically well integrated and well done. It certainly has a look of its own and not just a "unique" look bordering on plain weird like some novel efforts. The designer of this boat is Groupe Finot. In profile this boat reminds me of one of my own older designs, the Norseman 447.

The hull form is French all the way. The ends have been truncated and the stern is about as wide as you would dare go on a conventional hull. The overall beam is not as wide as the smaller French models. L/B for the 473 is moderate at 3.31.

The bow is quite full in plan view, but this is just an effort to push the forward accommodations as far into the bow as possible. The D/L of the 473 is 144. Standard draft is 5 feet, 6 inches, and there is an option for 6 feet, 11 inches of draft with 882 pounds less ballast.

Note the unusually flattened fore-and-aft rocker to the canoe body. I'm not sure if this is a design feature or just a function of the less-than-sensitively drawn profile that I have.

The sailplan shows a modest SA/D of 16.22. This would be an ideal rig for a breezy area like our winter months in the BVI. Summer in Puget Sound would find this rig gasping for breath, but easy to handle.

There are two layouts. The three-cabin layout has mirror image dou-

ble quarter berths that look huge. The compromise in this three-cabin layout is that the starboard quarter cabin intrudes into the area of the galley, forcing the range up against the bulkhead. You are left with virtually no lazarette and limited counter space. I like to see counter space on each side of the range when possible. In both galleys the reefer space looks minimal.

There are two heads and the forward head has a shower stall. The nav station looks generous. The saloon has one of those center island seats that I don't care for in boats of this size. They seem to break up the saloon area too much for my taste. On the plus side they do allow for six people to squeeze into the dinette for some real cozy dining. The forward stateroom is quite spacious with its own access to the forward head.

Despite the compromise to the galley, the three-stateroom layout would be close to ideal for family cruising with two kids. A three-couple charter would also work. Given the size of those quarter doubles I would think two kids could easily share each berth. I would miss that lazarette though. Ventilation is provided by 10 opening hatches, including the companionway. There are eight opening hull ports.

The deck plan is distinguished by an immense cockpit, as you might expect when the stern is this wide. There are two wheels and plenty of room to walk between them. The primary sheet winches are located aft where the helmsman can easily reach them. There is a removable drop-leaf table in the forward part of the cockpit. There is a recessed windlass well in the foredeck.

Its distinctly handsome looks alone would be enough to give this boat a closer look.

Beneteau USA, 1313 Highway 76 West, Marion, SC 29571. (843) 629-5300. **www.beneteauusa.com**

January 2001

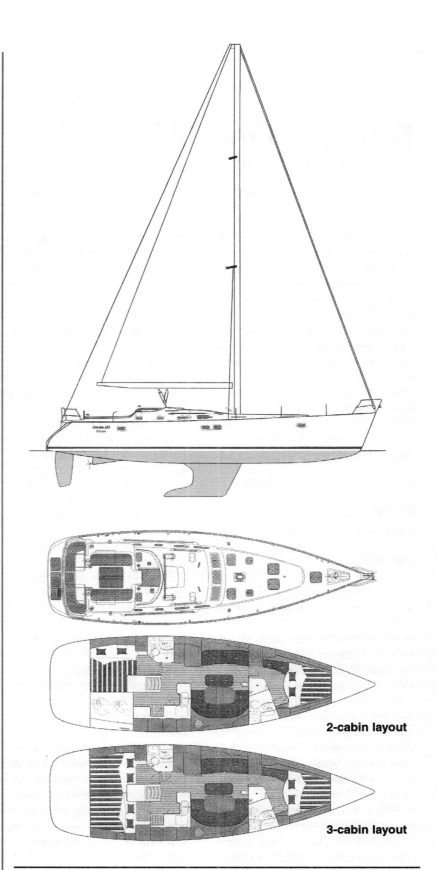

2-cabin layout

3-cabin layout

A big cruiser with its own, distinctive look.

LOA 46'11"; LWL 43'10"; Beam 14'2"; Draft 5'6" (standard), 6'11" (deep draft); Displacement 27,072 lbs.; Ballast 8,157 lbs. (standard), 7,275 lbs. (deep draft); Sail Area 914 sq. ft.; SA/D 16.22; D/L 144; L/B 3.31; Auxiliary 63-hp diesel; Fuel 52 gals.; Water 220 gals.

Beneteau First 47.7
Performance-cruiser

If you go back to the late '60s and '70s you'll find that most production boatbuilders built dual-purpose or racer-cruiser types. This approach died a natural death as pressure on racing boats increased—partially due to the IOR system of rating, and partially due to the new, more intense style of campaigning. This Farr-designed 48-footer takes us back toward the dual-purpose type.

With a D/L of 161 this is not a light boat, but it's far from heavy. This D/L is pretty normal for a

The canoe body shows the typical IMS-style profile going flat through the mid-sections and kicking up at the ends.

modern, performance-oriented boat. Beam is generous with an L/B of 3.21. To my eye the deck plan indicates a boat with fairly full ends. For fun let's divide the DWL by the LOA to see how much static sailing length each designer gets out of his LOA. In this case it's 87 percent. The canoe body shows the typical IMS-style profile going flat through the midsections and kicking up at the ends.

The rudder is very deep and about half the planform of the keel fin. You have your choice of 7 feet, 6 inches, or 9 feet, 2 inches of draft. Consider that there is probably nothing you can do to any boat that will affect its performance more than increasing draft. Note the large fillet radii at both ends of the keel root.

There are several interior layouts available that vary the number of staterooms and berth types.

You also have your choice of galley layout. You can have the galley moved forward and adjacent to the elliptical dinette, or you can move the galley aft alongside the starboard side of the companionway steps. This choice is subjective. You lose a settee with the galley forward, and the galley aft is more of a wraparound style for convenience offshore.

You can have four staterooms, which would make a good charter layout. You can have three staterooms, and you can have two spacious double staterooms. There are two heads, with one all the way forward. When you look at the sailplan you may be struck with how far forward the cabintrunk goes, but considering the forward head you should understand why. It's a tough feature to make look good, and you inevitably end up with a fore "deckette."

The sailplan is almost masthead. The small offset of the headstay may be to make room for the spinnaker sock. The spreaders are swept. There are two rigs available: a standard rig, and an "S" rig. The S rig is bigger by 108 square feet. This increases the SA/D from 18.89 to 20.89.

There can be little doubt that combining the skills of one of the world's best design offices with one of the world's best production builders will provide a very successful end product.

Beneteau U.S.A, 1313 Highway 76 West, Marion, SC 29571. **www.beneteauusa.com** *(843) 629-5300.*

Editors note: The 47.7 was scheduled to make its debut in fall of 1999 and all dimensions were subject to change.

September 1999

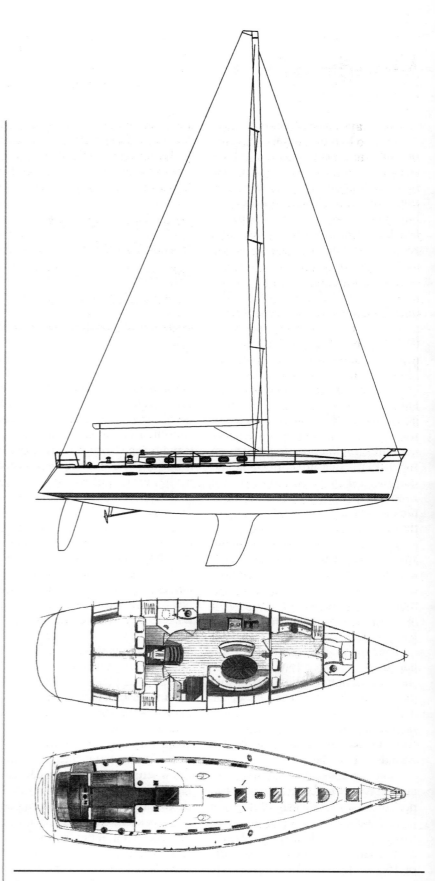

New Farr design harks back to dual-purpose cruisers.

LOA 47'7"; LWL 41'4"; Beam 14'10"; Draft 7'6" (standard), 9'2" (deep); Displacement 25,353 lbs. ("light" displacement); Ballast 8,3609 lbs.; Sail Area 1,019 sq. ft. (standard), 1,127 sq. ft. ("S"); SA/D 18.89 (standard), 20.89 ("S"); D/L 161; L/B 3.21; Auxiliary 50 to 85 hp; Fuel 66 gals.; Water 185 gals.

Moody 47
Bluewater Cruiser

The way I usually start each review is to look at the design and try to determine what it is about this boat that makes it noteworthy or different from other boats with similar design targets. All too often I see nothing that sets the boat apart, but that does not make the design a bad design, so off I go trying to make something about the boat sound reasonably interesting.

My editors never force me to review a boat I dislike. At the same time there are moments when I have to restrain my own subjective reaction to a boat so that I don't find myself forcing my own "personal problems" down the throats of readers. When I look at this new Bill Dixon-designed Moody the first thing that strikes me is that it's a beamy boat with the beam pushed forward resulting in a very full bow. But Mr. Dixon seems to favor this shape so it does not surprise me.

The L/B is 3.22, which makes the boat beamy by numerical definition. But, just for fun, let's take the beam max and divide it into the beam at the aft end of the DWL (buttwater?). This will give us a relative reading of how wide the stern is. In this case the beam at the buttwater is 80.01 percent of beam max. Note how full the bow is on this boat. Of course, we only have the deck plan and accommodation plan as indicators but I think they are enough. If I measure the half-angle of the bow at the deck I get 26 degrees. Compare that to a modern racing yacht with a deck half-angle of 14.5 degrees or 13 degrees for an America's Cup boat.

OK, the design parameters are totally different but we do know that finer bows are faster. In a design like this Moody, performance sometimes takes a back seat to accommodations. The D/L is 241 and the ballast-to-displacement ratio is 30.65 percent. You can get a deep keel drawing 6 feet, 9 inches or a shoal keel drawing 5 feet, 3 inches.

This is a three-stateroom boat designed for two couples with the third stateroom more suited for children. The amazing thing is, the third stateroom doesn't impact the rest of the layout appreciably at all. The galley is spacious and down a step from the saloon. This is good as it opens up

So you give up light air speed. But what do you get back? You get to sail along with full sail while your overpowered pals are reefing.

the area under the side decks for bigger galley lockers. The companionway ladder is too steep for my dog. Unfortunately there is no way you could reduce the steepness of the ladder without closing up the passage to the nav area. The head of the forward berth appears to be a little more than 36 inches wide. That's tight. But the design push is always to get more into less and with that in mind, Mr. Dixon has done his job well.

The SA/D is only 14.25. While that appears really low for a modern boat consider how most people cruise today. If your boat speed falls below 4 knots you are probably going to motor. You have a nice, big motor and you will cruise along under power at 8.5 knots in this Moody, so light air performance ceases to be very important. So you give up light air speed. But what do you get back? You get to sail along with full sail while your overpowered pals are reefing. The Moody has an inner forestay so you can fly a self-tacking staysail in heavy air.

I like the looks of this boat. It's a bit blocky on paper in two dimensions but the pics show it to be a good-looking Euro-styled boat.

Moody America, 335 Lincoln Street, Hingham, MA 02043. **www.moody-america.com** *(781) 749-8600.*

April 2004

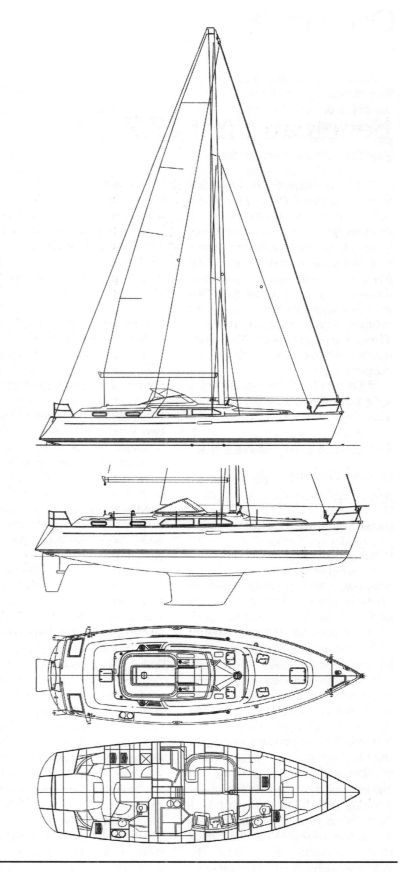

An accommodations-driven cruiser.

LOA 47'8"; LWL 39'4"; Beam 14'5"; Draft 6'9" (Standard), 5'3" (Shoal); Displacement 32,890 lbs.; Ballast 10,340 lbs.; Sail Area 942 sq. ft.; SA/D 14.25; D/L 241; L/B 3.22; Auxiliary Yanmar 4JH3; Fuel 114 gals.; Water 168 gals.

Orphan 38
Coastal Cruiser

Patrons come and patrons go. Sometimes, right in the middle of an absorbing design, they find another, already built boat that will "do the job." So what can a designer do? Here I sit with an orphaned design of my own forcing me to do the work of a surrogate parent. I designed this boat for an East Coast client who wanted a traditional 38-foot yawl. I've become quite attached to the little hooker. We have bonded.

The hull is moderate beam and displacement on the light side of moderate with a D/L of 213. The entry is slightly hollowed and overhangs are minimized for sailing length. I gave this hull some deadrise because deadrise makes for a natural bilge sump. I consider this hull capable of good performance, but I wouldn't square off against a Mumm 36.

The owner wanted a 6-foot, 4-inch draft, but now that I am the foster parent I have altered the draft to 7 feet, 6 inches. I like a boat that will stand up to its sail and tenaciously claw its way to weather. In Puget Sound draft is not an issue. The rudder is a carbon fiber partially balanced spade.

I struggled with this sheerline. I didn't want to exaggerate it and get the boat looking like a cartoon. On the other hand I wanted a strong sheer statement. The computer can't do it on a design like this. You have to draw the sheer by hand and then transfer the data to the computer. When I look at Ted's sheer on his Bahama sloop I think I'd like to draw this sheerline again.

The rig is a yawl. I drew standing rigging on the mizzen but I think it would be nice to do the mizzen as a carbon fiber freestanding spar. The bowsprit is a pipe frame type that incorporates the anchor rollers. Note the Chuck Paine headstay offset from the masthead. Chuck will chuckle over this, but dammit, it just looks right on this design.

The mizzen will be furled when sailing upwind in any breeze over 10 knots. Mizzen included, the SA/D is 21.05. Chainplates will be inboard to allow the use of a 140-percent genoa. (I added that for Seattle's light air.) The mizzen will make a nice riding sail when the boat is anchored.

The interior is laid out for a couple. The galley is big. My galleys are always big. My client wanted the trash bin where you see it in the drawings, but it really should be closer to the sink. The centerline sinks will work well. The settees are 6 feet, 9 inches long and deep enough to make comfortable berths in a pinch.

I didn't expect to find this baby in a basket sitting on my doorstep when I came to the office that Thursday.

Note the large fo'c'sle and expansive lazarette. I'm not wild about fore-and-aft chart tables, but in this layout it's the only way I could get a decent-sized chart table in. The key will be to have a good swing-away seat built. An extra 2 feet of LOA would remedy this. Headroom is 6 feet, 5 inches.

Construction could be in a wood composite method or all composite GRP. I prefer all GRP, and with this healthy D/L ratio you can afford to build this boat strong and durable. Tankage would be 60 gallons of fuel and 120 gallons of water. I would have no genset and only two batteries. I would keep the boat as simple and as light as possible. The auxiliary would be a saildrive Yanmar 51-horsepower 4JH2CE.

I didn't expect to find this baby in a basket sitting on my doorstep when I came to the office that Thursday. But it's a handsome little fellow, and I think it would make someone a darn good and satisfying cruising boat.

Robert Perry Yacht Design 5801 Phinney Ave. North, Suite 100 Seattle WA 98103. (206) 789-7212. **www.perryboat.com**

September 2000

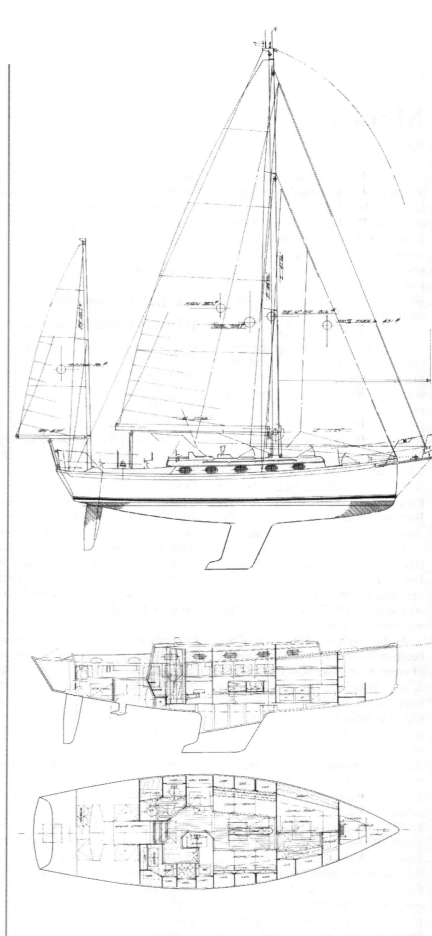

A long lost design in search of a good home … sniff!

LOA 48'8"; LOD 47'8"; DWL 33'9"; Beam 12'6"; Draft 7'6"; Displacement 18,400 lbs.; Ballast 6,500 lbs.; Sail Area 904 sq. ft.; SA/D 21.05; D/L 213; L/B 3.09; Auxiliary 51-hp Yanmar; Fuel 60 gals.; Water 120 gals.

Sun Odyssey 49
Bluewater Cruiser

This new model built by Jeanneau is part of its Sun Odyssey line and is a successor to its previous Sun Odyssey 45. The design work is a combination effort from the Philippe Briand office and the designers at Jeanneau. I can't tell who did what but the hull, appendages and the rig probably came out of the Briand office.

This is a good-looking boat but it sure looks like a lot of other boats. You can trace the origins of this styling genre back to the early Swans with their wedge-like deck structures. It was always a good look. The printed material that came with the drawings has an interesting slant on the styling: "A sailboat's primary function is its aesthetics." I think they may be spot on here. They go on to say, "lines have been designed to complement an identity which combines boldness with reassurance. The superstructure blends the dynamic tension of the longitudinal lines with the confidence of the curved transversal sections." I thought "dynamic tension" had more to do with Charles Atlas.

I have always respected Briand's work and I would anticipate that this hull would be a good performer. The D/L is quite low at 165 and beam is moderate with an L/B of 3.35. There is nothing distinctive about this hull form that I can discern from these drawings. It's a pretty normal looking modern boat. Beam at the transom is about as wide as you would dare get it but that's not unusual these days. In plan view the ends look quite full, but of course you can't see what is happening at the DWL without a set of lines.

This boat comes with two layouts. The charter layout features four staterooms and four heads. One head is bigger and this head has access from the main cabin and the port aft stateroom. The main cabin has the galley to port and dinette with a centerline island seat to starboard. I don't think a boat like this really needs a U-shaped galley. This looks like a good galley to me for cooking when you are on the hook. I think the dinette seating arrangement is tight but six sailors can certainly dine comfortably there. I'd just like to see more room for spreading out after dinner.

I would anticipate that this hull would be a good performer.

If you don't need four staterooms you can go with the three-stateroom version. In this layout you retain the two staterooms aft and the day head but the starboard, smaller head is gone. This recaptured space is now devoted to a spacious nav center. The entire area forward of the mast is given over to a nicely laid out master stateroom. The galley and saloon stay the same.

The 49 has a huge cockpit with twin wheels and a large center console for stowage and a drop leaf table. Including the companionway hatch there are 12 deck hatches. The opening ports in the cabintrunk are tucked under visors for better sun protection. The material I have says "portholes" but I'm wondering if they do not mean those large and long main windows. It makes little sense to recess the two small ports per side while leaving the large windows unprotected. This feature does not show on the drawings. I need to see it in person.

The rig is very ordinary in that it's a tall, fractional rig with double swept spreaders. The headstay is pulled off the stem about 16 inches. It's a handsome boat despite the lackluster drafting. I'm sure this boat will be turning up soon in the charter fleets.

Jeanneau America, 105 Eastern Avenue, Suite 202, Annapolis, MD 21403. (410) 280-9400. **www.jeanneauamerica.com**

October 2003

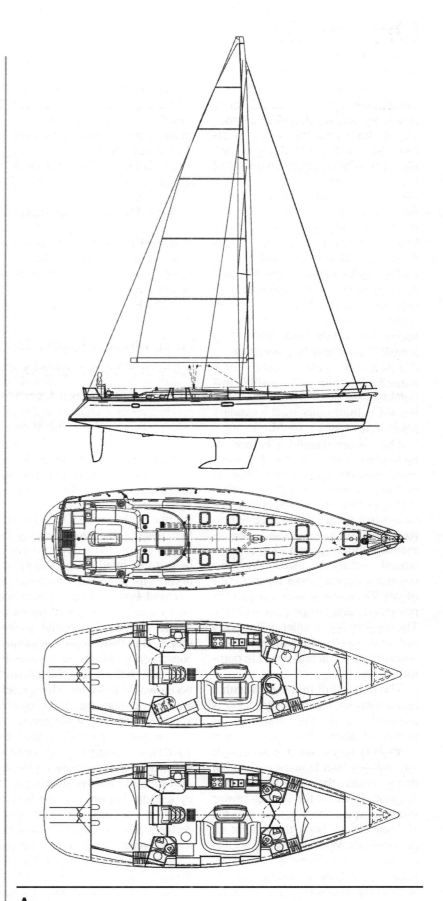

A "dynamic" cruiser coming soon to a charter fleet near you.

LOA 49'1"; LWL 42'3"; Beam 14'8"; Draft 7'; Displacement 27,888 lbs.; Ballast 8,267 lbs.; Sail Area 928 sq. ft.; SA/D 16.15; D/L 165; L/B 3.35; Auxiliary Yanmar 75-hp; Fuel 63 gals.; Water 185 gals.

Bruckmann 480
Motorsailer

The yachting fraternity lost an icon recently, Bob Derecktor, builder/designer and tough individualist. I never met Mr. Derecktor. But I did hear a story once that I doubt is true, but is such a good story. Mr. Derecktor's yard was building a Britton Chance-designed 12-meter. The workers were putting the finishing touches on the trailing edge of the rudder and they needed to know how to radius off the aft, lower corner of the rudder blade. According to legend, as builder and designer pondered the feature, Chance pulled out his pocket slide rule and began calculating (calculating what, I have no idea). After a few minutes of Chance's slide ruling Mr. Derecktor grew impatient and pulled off his ever present cloth cap, laid the bill down on the aluminum, traced a line around the bill and said "Cut here!" It's a good story. It's hard to manufacture originals.

Mark Ellis draws nice boats, always has. This new motorsailer combines Mark's eye with the building skills of another near legendary yard, Bruckmann's of Mississauga, Ontario. This design is a development of another smaller Ellis motorsailer, the Northeast 400. There is nothing wrong or derogatory about calling a boat a motorsailer. It just means that parameters affecting performance under sail and performance under power have been almost equally balanced. We have come a long way from the old days of 50/50s when it was 50 percent powerboat and 50 percent sailboat. The modern motorsailer will usually sail quite well while allowing the owner to motor at hull speed in comfort all day long.

The hull is full in the ends with a broad transom. Canoe-body rocker is minimal, and the transom is immersed about 9 inches to help boost hull speed under power. True this will not be a light-air rocket, but that's what the 140-horsepower Yanmar diesel is for. Under power you can expect cruising speeds in the 10-knot range. Now that's light-air performance. With an L/B of 2.99 this can be considered a beamy boat. The large, semibalanced rudder extends beyond the hull aft. I like the swim platform that will hit the dock before the rudder blade. The D/L is a moderate 262. The ballast-to-displacement ratio is a sensible 36 percent.

There's a lot going on in this interior. There are three staterooms, and the two heads share a shower stall. The galley is down, nicely laid-out and open to the pilothouse. The pilothouse features an inside steering station and a large dinette. Two reading chairs are on the starboard side. I suspect that the Bruckmann yard would

The modern motorsailer will usually sail quie well while allowing the owner to motor at hull speed in comfort all day long.

be willing to do a custom layout if you don't like this one.

The cockpit is huge. A permanently mounted table with stowage lockers is on centerline and the bench seats are well over 6 feet long. There is a transom door to access the swim platform. One of the benefits of beam on a design like this is that while preserving interior volume in the pilothouse you still have the luxury of designing adequate side decks. Narrow side decks are not fun.

If you accept the fact that designing a motorsailer means forgoing light-air speed under sail you can easily live with an SA/D of 13.86. In fact, despite the astronomically high SA/Ds we see these days, this rig will be just fine in all but ghosting conditions. I'm not keen on in-the-mast mainsail furling. I have yet to see a boat rigged this way that has what I would call an acceptable mainsail shape. But there is no denying the convenience. Maybe a Leisure Furl system with the main rolling up in the boom would be better. The spreaders are swept, and the short bowsprit allows you to carry a big genoa.

I've got to go sailing this afternoon. It's 52 degrees and sprinkling with vigor. The forecast calls for drizzle turning to showers turning to rain by tonight. It's Seattle. The boat I'm going to sail doesn't even have a dodger. Mark's Bruckmann 480 is looking pretty good to me right now.

Bruckmann Custom Yachts, 2265 Royal Windsor Drive, Mississauga, Ontario L5J 1K5 Canada. (800) 254-7618. Mark Ellis Design Ltd. **www.markellisdesign.com** *(905) 825-0037.*

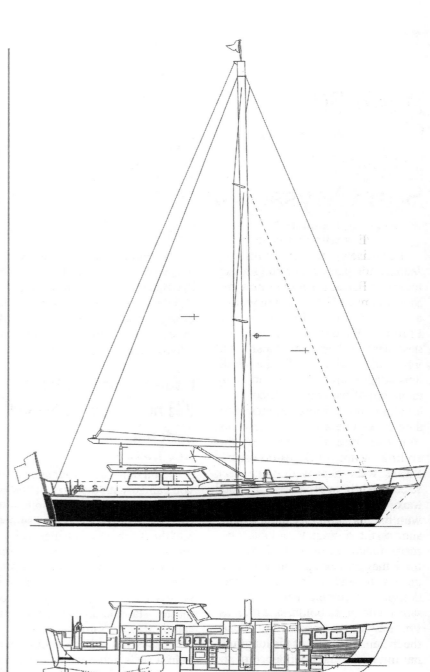

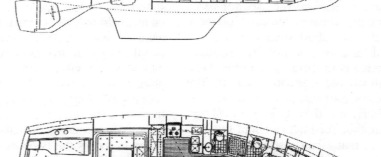

Comfort and performance in one solid package.

LOA 49'4"; LWL 46'2"; Beam 15'5"; Draft 6'; Displacement 44,000 lbs.; Ballast 16,000 lbs.; Sail Area 1,080 sq. ft.; SA/D 13.86; D/L 262; L/B 2.99; Auxiliary 140-hp Yanmar; Fuel 200 gals.; Water 240 gals.

Atoll 50
Coastal Cruiser

Let's get this out, right up front. The French builder Dufour has given us a strange-looking boat. Its aesthetic appears to have been derived by crossing French catamaran styling with megayacht features. This is not so surprising when you consider the designer is Philippe Briand. But before you pass judgment, I would ask you to consider that you need to evaluate a boat's appearance from two aspects. First, how does it look from the outside. Then, how does it look from the inside. If we were to step aboard the Atoll 50 and look out those vertical windows, the entire picture might change.

It doesn't matter where we start, everything about this boat is different, with the exception of the rig. The deck has a deep well-deck forward. This depression, or well-in-the-deck, is about 16 inches deep and about 6 feet long. Aft, the cockpit has been turned into a combination cockpit and saloon area, with shelter provided by the house overhang. There is no saloon below, so this area is it. This saloon-cockpit area is on the same level as the galley in the pilothouse. You could comfortably seat a crowd in this cockpit. This is very much like a catamaran layout and obviously designed for a dryer and warmer area than Seattle. There is a folding canopy that allows the saloon area to be enclosed. Twin wheels leave the middle of the cockpit open for access to the swim step.

The interior follows through on this cat-type design approach. Look carefully and you'll see the advantages and disadvantages of a catamaran layout. The boat is laid out in two mirror images. From the galley area in the pilothouse you step down steep ladders port and starboard into the hull where there are quarter cabins aft with double berths. Leaving the galley and going down forward, you enter an area that opens to four staterooms, each with a double berth. A special ventilation system has been designed to bring fresh air to these "buried" staterooms. There are four heads on this boat.

Combining the cockpit, saloon and galley on the same level will make this interior feel big. As an exercise in spatial manipulation, this is an ingenious layout.

The hull shape shows a deep midsection that kicks up sharply at the stern. As you might expect, the beam has been pushed to the max, and the L/B is 3.03. That's just too beamy for me. The beam is carried

When evaluating any boat it's important to find valid benchmarks for comparison. That's a tough order with this boat.

to the transom. There is little doubt in my mind that this is a case where the hull was wrapped around an interior layout. That's fine in itself, but you can't expect a boat with these proportions to be a swift sailer. I doubt speed was in the design brief.

The D/L is 170. I look at this ultrawide hull and the forward placement of the keel, and I get concerned about this boat's ability to balance well. Draft is 5 feet, 11 inches. The rudder is a spade, with plenty of balance area.

The rig is a tall fractional-type with swept spreaders. The SA/D is 20.6. This is enough to provide reasonable off-the-wind speed to this unusual boat.

When evaluating any boat it's important to find valid benchmarks for comparison. That's a tough order in this case. I can think of no other boat that offers this combination of features in a similar configuration. In a recent National Public Radio show featuring European pop music, the comment was made that Americans are too conservative. I immediately took this as a slam. But now I'm not so sure. I appreciate the opportunity to review such a radical departure.

Dufour Yachts U.S.A., 326 First St., Ste. 14, Annapolis, MD 21403. (410) 268-6417, fax (410) 268-9739. www.dufouryachts.com

December 1999

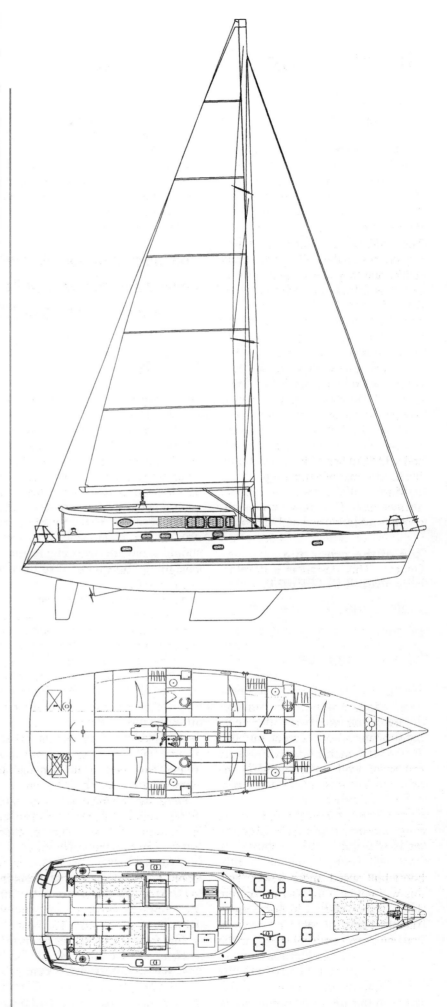

Unorthodox design blends features from catamarans and monohulls.

LOA 50'; LWL 43'4"; Beam 16'6"; Draft 5'11"; Displacement 30,940 lbs.; Ballast 9,945 lbs.; Sail Area 1,268 sq. ft.; SA/D 20.6; D/L 170; L/B 3.03; Auxiliary 85-hp; Fuel 180 gals.; Water 390 gals.

Contest 50CS
Bluewater Cruiser

Center cockpit-raised saloon boats seem to be the rage now. This new Contest 50CS is a good example of the breed. Center cockpits offer division of accommodations and nice staterooms aft. They also work perfectly for engine location and dedicated engine rooms. Raising the saloon lets in light and makes space in the bilge for tankage. Now, the first trick is to integrate those heights and spaces so the interior is not too chopped up. The second trick is to find an aesthetic solution to the multi-heights that will not make the boat look like a wedding cake. Let's see how designer Georg Nissen handles the challenge.

The hull is very normal looking with a wide stern and deep forefoot. The sheer is quite flat and there's plenty of freeboard. This freeboard allows for a 4-inch bulwark amidships increasing to about 6 inches at the bow. The D/L is 227

One of the attractive advantages of center cockpit boats is that they can get the mainsheet traveler aft at the end of the boom.

and the L/B is 3.27. Both are textbook "moderate" numbers. You can choose from two keels; the deep one drawing 7 feet, 1 inch, and the shoal keel drawing 6 feet, 5 inches. The shoal keels are winged bulbs designed by Piet van Oossanen, and as I recall, he was part of the design team responsible for the wing keel on *Australia II*. The rudder is unusual in that it shows on the drawings to have about 25-plus percent balance area forward of the stock centerline. Most sailing yachts have rudders with between 10 and 17 percent balance. This is a huge rudder.

This is a three-stateroom layout with a traditional V-berth all the way forward, upper and lower berths in the stateroom adjacent to the mast and a big double berth aft. That upper and lower berth stateroom will be very tight and best suited to kids. The galley is linear and runs down the passage to the aft cabin. It looks fine to me

but I don't see much space for reefer and freezer. On the raised saloon level you have a big dinette and the nav station. I just would not want to be the first one into that dinette. I'd feel trapped and I worry abut how much room there is below that table for all the pairs of legs involved. The aft stateroom looks comfy. Note how the double berth is tucked between lazarette areas port and starboard. The engine room looks tight but it's a lot better than an engine tucked under a cabin sole. Layouts are subjective for the most part. We all have out priorities and personal space requirements. Old-fashioned elbow room is what I like, but I don't see much here.

The rig is masthead and the mast is forward. The lower shroud chainplates are inboard at the edge of the cabintrunk and the cap shroud chainplates are outboard just inboard of the bulwark. This provides a clear side deck and should allow the working 105-percent jib to sheet inboard of the cap shroud for a nice, close sheeting angle. There are three spreaders and they are very slightly swept while the mast is drawn with prebend. Halyards are lead aft under the deck and exit at the cockpit. One of the attractive advantages of center cockpit boats is that they can get the mainsheet traveler aft at the end of the boom.

Aesthetically I think this boat is successful. The lines of the deck house blend well with the flattish sheer and short ends. With the hull painted dark blue you don't even notice the ports in the topsides. Visibility from the large cockpit forward is excellent. There is a lot of clear deck space on this design. Large, flush hatches aft give access to the lazarettes. The brochure photos show this to be a very handsome boat.

Contest, Overleek 3, 1671 GD Medemblik, Holland. 31 227-543 644. www.contestyachts.com

In the U.S. contact Contest Yachts N.A., Box 12-B, The Swan Building, Suite 2, Washington Blvd., Stamford, CT 06902. www.contestyachtsna.com (203) 348-9100.

March 2004

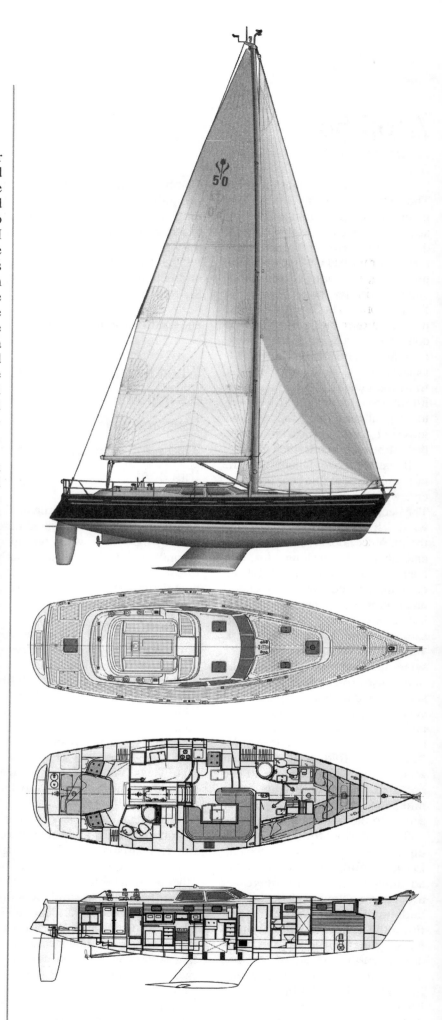

Elegant lines make this center cockpit design a pleasant cruiser.

LOA 50'; LWL 42'4"; Beam 15'; Draft 7'1" (Standard), 6'5" (Shoal); Displacement 38,573 lbs.; Ballast 13,445 lbs.; Sail Area 1,339 sq. ft.; SA/D 18.76; D/L 227; L/B 3.27; Auxiliary Yanmar 4JH3; Fuel 154 gals.; Water 176 gals.

Farr 50
Cruiser

There was one more self-indulgent thing I wanted to talk about this month. About a half hour's drive from Bruce Farr's design office—at 380 Log Canoe Circle, Stevensville, Maryland, to be precise—is the Paul Reed Smith guitar factory. Last year after touring the factory, Paul and I sat down to discuss his ideas for a new boat. After we had covered just about everything, Paul asked if I would be interested in bartering some of the design work for a new guitar. After thinking it over for about a nanosecond, I said yes. The *LA Times* called Paul's guitars "one of the 10 most collectable things in the world." Two weeks ago I got my new PRS guitar. She's a beaut; perfect in every way and right in time for playing in the group at the annual Perry Rendezvous. Once or twice a day I sit down, grab hold of guitar perfection, play and smile.

So out Paul's circular driveway and across the bridge back to Annapolis, we find the busy Farr design office. Bruce and his team of designers drew this boat for Boat Sales International, and the boats are built by BSI Marine in Sweden. A quick look at the sailplan will show this 50-footer to be very similar in concept to the Wauquiez Pilot Saloon 40. But the Farr office had an additional 10 feet to work with, and that makes a difference.

Consider this: A 50-footer is 25 percent longer than a 40-footer using LOA. But if we use displacement as a measurement of useable volume, in this case 37,400 pounds for the 50-footer vs. 22,075 pounds for the 40-footer, the difference is almost 70 percent. And that's just below the waterline. When we talk about "size" in boats, displacement must be considered right along with LOA. In short, the displacement or "size" of the boat increases in proportion to the cube of its length.

Now let's see what Farr did with this additional volume. There are two layouts available, and they both represent a break from the typical layouts we see in center-cockpit 50-footers. To begin with, this boat has a large fo'c'sle and a large lazarette. These are not features that will add to the boat's boat show dazzle, but they sure will make the boat easier to live with while cruising. The other interesting feature of these layouts is the way the aft double berth has been moved forward to tuck under the cockpit where

we would often find an engine room. In this case the engine is under the pilothouse sole. Sure, this is not as good as a dedicated, walk-in engine room, but it does open up a lot of volume for additional accommodations.

Both layouts have three heads with the amidships head being the day head, which you have access to without going through any of the staterooms. These are complex layouts with a lot of small spaces. I like

This is a handsome boat, plain and simple but well proportioned.

the aft cabin. Note that the designers have used the volume under the starboard, raised dinette to work in that small double berth. This layout clearly shows the same limiting pilothouse effects that we see on the smaller Wauquiez.

This is a handsome boat, plain and simple but well proportioned. The sheer is almost flat, like other Farr sheers, but its low point is back around station 8, where you would usually find it, as opposed to being pushed forward as is the case with many Farr designs. Either way, the photos show that this sheer is attractive and effective, hiding a 4.5-inch bulwark capped with teak. The hull is very much like a larger version of the Wauquiez hull with an L/B of 3.25 and a D/L of 198. The keel is a winged fin with full tip-chord-length wings. I think at this point we can trust the Farr office to produce a very good sailing hull.

There are two rigs. If you want in-mast furling you get extra P, no roach and vertical battens. I'd go with the shorter P and in-boom furling if it were my boat. I don't have much faith in vertical battens. I like mine the old fashioned way, horizontal. Spreaders are in-line, and there are runners and a babystay. The SA/D is a safe and sane 18.27.

The engine is a 100-horsepower Yanmar turbocharged diesel and with tankage for 198 gallons of fuel and 140 gallons of water.

Boat Sales International, Hamble Point Marina, School Lane, Hamble, Southampton, S031 4NB, England. **www.farr-pilothouseyachts.com** *44 23 8045 7966.*

November 2001

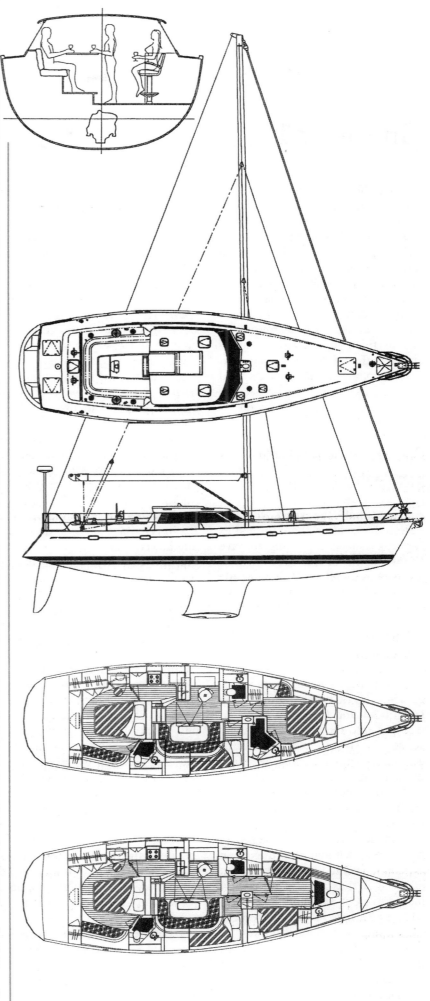

Cruiser with an unconventional raised-saloon layout.

LOA 50'6"; LWL 43'10"; Beam 15'5"; Draft 7'6"; Displacement 37,400 lbs.; Ballast 13,200 lbs.; Sail Area 1,277 sq. ft.; SA/D 18.27; D/L 198; L/B 3.25; Auxiliary 100-hp Yanmar 4J3-DTE; Fuel 195 gals.; Water 132 gals.

Gib'Sea 51
Cruiser

I like the brochure for this boat. It says, right out, that the directive to the designers, J&J, was to design "the most spacious cruising yacht in her size." That certainly simplifies our quest for understanding in this new design. Obviously, there is a market for boats with maximized accommodations, and in this case you can cruise with a crew of 10 people, five couples. This design is aimed at the charter trade, and several companies ordered boats prior to introduction. I don't even know four other couples I'd want to cruise with.

Charter companies will gobble this one up.

About half the specs for this design have after them in italics "approx" so we are going to have to take some of our ratios with a grain of sea salt. I don't fault the builder for this. Actually most builders should publish their specs the same way.

The length on deck of this design is 48 feet, 11 inches so I would estimate the DWL to be 45 feet, 3 inches. This gives us a D/L of 154. The boat is beamy with an L/B of 3.1 and the beam is pulled well out into the ends. There is no sense in trying to maximize accommodations if you don't maximize beam.

The brochure calls this bow a "dolphin nose" bow. Clearly this molded effect is intended to get the ground tackle away from the nearly plumb bow without resorting to an expensive welded bowsprit. On the other hand, maybe an additional 24 inches of LOA and more bow overhang could have accomplished the same thing with a touch more elegance. Draft is 6 feet, which would qualify as shoal draft in a boat of this size.

The brochure shows two layouts with five staterooms and one with four. The problem with these layouts is that the only way you can access the forward stateroom is by going through the master stateroom in the four-stateroom layout

or one of the other guest staterooms in the five-stateroom layout. Perhaps this forward stateroom is intended as a stateroom for paid crew who will access their space through a deck hatch.

Looking at the dinette I estimate that seven can sit comfortably for a meal. The galley is minimal for a boat this size with very little counter space. If you use the reefer lid for counter space you will have to move the food when you want to access the reefer. Why should I care, anyway? I'm on an all-tofu diet.

The aft staterooms have big double berths. I've got an idea. We need to come up with a name for the maneuver you have to do in the middle of the night to get out of a berth without waking your partner. It's impossible for me to do so with any kind of panache given my general inflexibility, and it usually results in my crashing to the cabin sole with a charley horse in my thigh.

There are five heads on this boat if you choose the five-stateroom layout. Apparently there is a three-cabin layout on the drawing board.

The simple rig is masthead and short. The mainsheet is a midboom type, which frees up the large cockpit. There are two wheels, and of course, the photo in the brochure shows at least half the crew trying to crowd around the wheels. I don't know about you, but I have a problem with people who insist on sitting as far aft as possible.

There is a fixed table with an icebox in the middle of the cockpit. This cockpit is so big it needs something like this to break it up so you can't fall all the way to the leeward seat.

I can see this boat's virtues if you want to go cruising with a large group of friends. My guess is that charter companies will gobble this one up.

Gib'Sea/Dufour Yachts, 1 Chelsea Court, Annapolis, MD 21403. **www.dufouryachts.com** *(410) 268-6417.*

December 2001

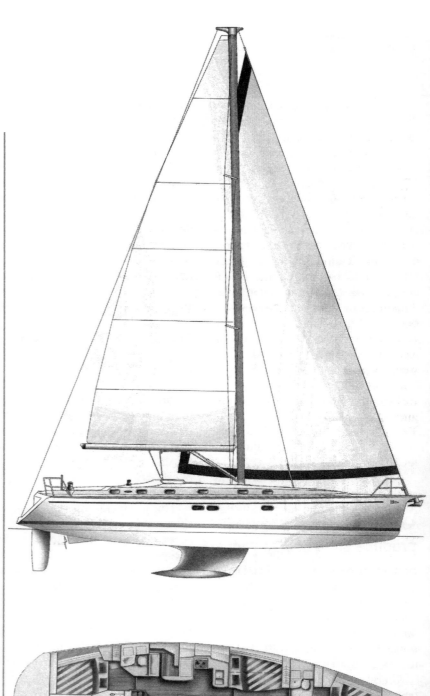

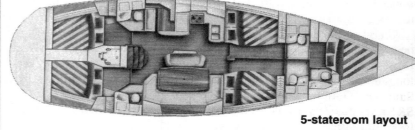

5-stateroom layout

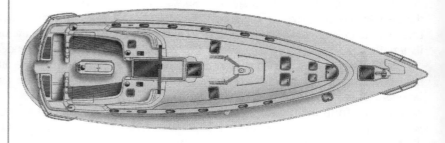

A cruiser built big enough for all your friends.

LOA 51'10"; LWL 45'3"; Beam 15'9"; Draft 6'; Displacement 31,900 lbs.; Ballast 10,670 lbs.; Sail Area 1,377 sq. ft.; SA/D 21.9; D/L 154; L/B 3.1; Auxiliary 78-hp Volvo; Fuel 130 gals.; Water 275 gals.

Seguin 52
Bluewater Cruiser

I flew to Maine last weekend to visit the Lyman Morse yard in Thomaston for an open house held mainly to introduce its new Sparkman & Stephens 52-footer being built for Ken Sawyer. A trip to this yard is a feel-good experience. Lyman Morse is as good as it gets, period. I was joined at the yard by a covey of other designers including my old pals Chuck Paine and Dieter Empacher along with Jim Taylor, Doug Zurn, Ward

There is no doubt that this design, combined with Lyman Morse detailing, will produce an exquisite yacht reminiscent of the classics from the 1950s.

Setzer and reps from David Pedrick's office and S&S. Chuck and I stroked our gray beards and assured each other that they were on the verge of "getting it right" but not quite. Dieter and I had a long conversation about 100-foot Samoan racing longboats. The S&S guys took umbrage with my last *SAILING* review and Jim Taylor schmoozed potential clients so we didn't have a chance to chat. All in all it was a wonderful time.

Ken Sawyer is a true patron of the arts in the old sense like Count Lichnowski was to Beethoven. Ken just loves to participate in yacht projects and doesn't mind having multiple projects going at once. He owns a fleet of boats but he enjoys fine tuning the designer's efforts and creating new boats that reflect his taste, knowledge and experiences at sea, racing and cruising. I wish we had more Kens.

The mission Ken gave S&S for the new 52 was a boat in the classic S&S style that would be built on a semi-custom basis. Look at that long flush deck. It's impossible not to love that look. While

Greg Matzat, the head designer at S&S, and I sparred over sheer nuances, there is no doubt that this design, combined with Lyman Morse detailing, will produce an exquisite yacht reminiscent of the classics from the 1950s like the S&S Bolero and one of my all time favorites, the Rhodes-designed *Carina*.

The hull is moderate in beam with an L/B of 3.5. The buttwater-to-beam ratio is 67 percent but looks much lower due to the long overhang aft. With 52 feet of LOA this design has only 38 feet of DWL. The D/L is 301. This model will certainly outperform the original vintage models.

There are pilot berths in the saloon along with a fireplace and comfortable settees. The galley is great. There is a seat at the chart table that wraps around so you can sit at the wet locker to change your boots. To truly appreciate this layout you have to imagine it detailed in the Lyman Morse style with sculpted mahogany trim accenting the veers and painter raised panels.

Ken is still fine-tuning the cockpit area to maintain classic styling while being functionally comfortable for today's helmsman. The flush deck will be festooned with dorade vents and hatches with the saloon hatch being a butterfly type and the foredeck hatch being a raised sliding type.

The immediate impression will be one of a beautifully maintained older boat. Good work, S&S. Mission accomplished, Ken.

Designer: Sparkman & Stephens, 529 Fifth Ave., New York, NY 10017. (212) 661-1240. **www.sparkmanstephens.com**
Builder: Lyman Morse Boatbuilding, 82 Water Street, Thomaston, ME, 04861. **www.lymanmorse.com** *(207) 354-6904.*

May 2004

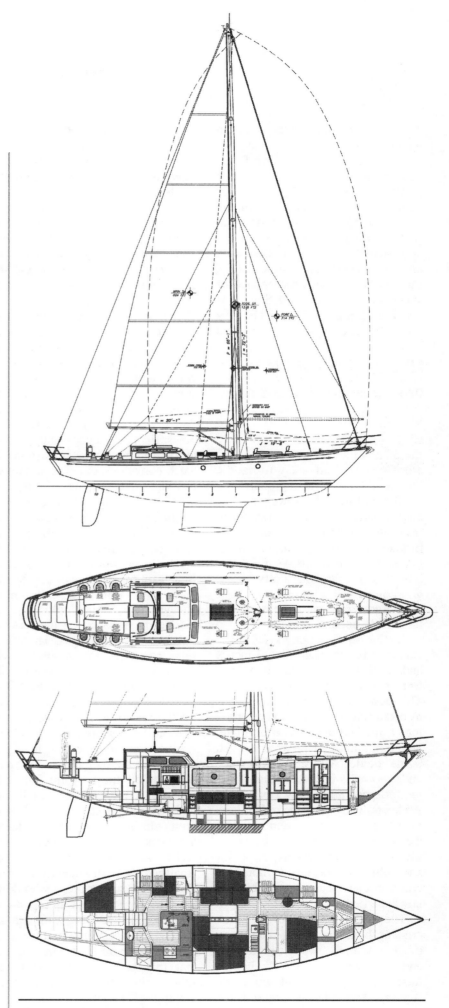

A classic designed for a true art patron.

LOA 52'; LWL 38'; Beam 14'7"; Draft 7'8"; Displacement 37,000 lbs.; Ballast 14,000 lbs.; Sail Area 1,378 sq. ft.; SA/D 19.8; D/L 301; L/B 3.5; Auxiliary Yanmar 100-hp; Fuel 260 gals.; Water 260 gals.

Saga 48
Bluewater Cruiser

Back in the mid-1990s, at a time when a lot of boatbuilders were biting the dust, Scotsman Alan Poole decided to start Saga Marine and produce a line of sailboats initially conceived as counterpoints to the overly beamy cruising boats that were dominating the market. Alan approached me to do the designing and I signed on immediately. Pundits gave Saga little chance of surviving. That was 50 Saga 43s ago and 12 Saga 35s ago. The new 48 is the next logical step beyond

I like the looks of this boat. If I didn't I would have changed it.

the Saga 43 and is intended to be a comfy, fast and easy-to-handle "mom and pop" cruising boat.

The hull form borrows the short ends and nearly plumb stem from my Saga 43 and 35, although this time I have chosen to go with more beam. The L/B of the 48 is 3.47 so the 48 is still far from a fatso when you compare it to many other contemporary cruisers, some of which have L/Bs under 3.

A fine entry combined with a waterline length of 43 feet, 7 inches and a D/L of 160 ensures good performance under both sail and power. This design recognizes that most of us end up motoring a lot when cruising. I just had a weekend on Puget Sound of 3-knot tides combined with light, fickle winds. Performance under power is important. I am looking for speed under power of around 9.5 knots. The big, spade rudder is as far aft as I could put it and will give the 48 good tracking characteristics. The keel is a moderately shoal fin-and-bulb type designed more for cruising convenience than blazing upwind speed.

The concept was for a quick cruising boat capable of navigating the ICW with the happy couple snug and cuddly, so I gave the boat a raised, double helm seat and inside steering. The galley is big and that suits me just fine. There is lots of counter space and a very large reefer/freezer unit. The dinette is not raised but extends outboard under the side deck. This dinette is 7 feet,

6 inches long and more than adequate for four to dine in comfort. The two heads share a shower stall. There is a nav station adjacent to the aft head. Note the large hanging locker. The forward stateroom is spacious and features a double berth that is 6 feet wide across its widest point. The plumb stem affords us the volume for a large fo'c'sle and the aft cockpit layout leaves plenty of room for a huge lazarette.

On deck we chose a two-wheel arrangement for the cockpit in order to have a clear walk-through transom opening to the swim step. The wheel areas feature sculpted consoles to house instruments and computer screens. Just like with the other Sagas, we went with a pipe frame bowsprit that houses the ground tackle rollers. There is a foredeck hatch that allows direct access to the fo'c'sle. I like the looks of this boat. If I didn't I would have changed it. I do find it ironic that while I rail against Euro-styling from time to time, my Saga 48 looks more Euro than the Group Finot-designed Beneteau reviewed next. The Sagas, with their truncated ends, have always had a distinct look.

The rig is based on the rigs we did for the other Sagas. There is a self-tacking jib with a single sheet that goes up the mast from the jib track and then down to a coaming-mounted winch. There are tracks for the masthead genoa, which is a light-air or reaching sail. The best way to tack the genoa on this rig is to just bite the bullet and roll it partially or all the way up. You can squeeze it through the small slot without rolling it up, but it ain't pretty. In any wind above 8 knots the tremendous convenience of the self-tacking jib overcomes the small reduction in sail area. There is also a taller rig for those who don't have to worry about going under bridges. The SA/D is 19.98 with the tall rig. This is on the high side for a mom and pop boat, but consider that this boat is designed to be sailed primarily with the nonoverlapping self-tacking jib.

Saga Marine, St. Catharines, Ontario, Canada. (800) 560-7242. **www.sagayachts.com**

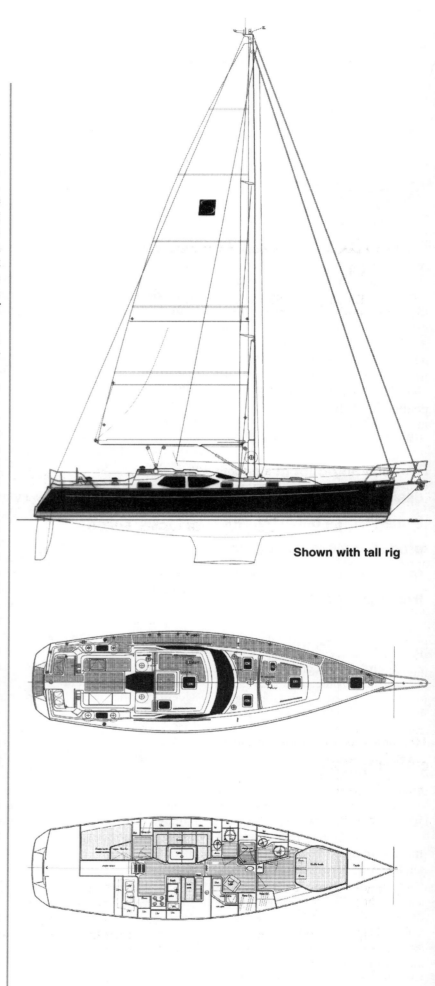

Shown with tall rig

The third in a line of fast and comfortable cruisers.

LOA 52' 3"; LOD 47' 10"; DWL 43' 7"; Beam 13' 9"; Draft 6'; Displacement 30,000 lbs.; Ballast 9,850 lbs.; Sail area 1,206 sq. ft.; SA/D 19.98; D/L 160; L/B 3.47; Auxiliary 75-hp Yanmar; Fuel 183 gals.; Water 180 gals.

Empacher 52-footer
Family Cruiser

Dieter Empacher's 52-footer, designed for Kanter Yachts in Canada, is a typical Empacher design. It's moderately heavy at 47,250 pounds. But with a waterline length of 46 feet the D/L is only 217. This includes 20,000 pounds of ballast. On the ever-moving D/L scale, 217 can be considered medium.

The keel is a long, low-aspect-ratio fin, giving the boat a 6-foot draft. Wings have been designed that stretch almost the entire keel tip length. The wings will help lower the VCG and, properly designed, should increase the apparent aspect ratio of the fin; although I wonder if they will act like the world's biggest Bruce anchor when you ground in sand.

The rudder shows an unusual profile with a little nipple on the trailing edge heel. I would guess this rudder has about 20 percent balance area. This is a lot, the most I have ever seen on a sailboat.

The sailplan is almost a true cutter rig. Note the mast is well aft leaving plenty of room for the staysail.

Beam is modest. This hull type will be at its best in a good blow with the wind ahead of the beam, and it will be a soft and confident ride.

The sailplan is almost a true cutter rig. Note the mast is well aft leaving plenty of room for the staysail. There are fore and aft lower shrouds and two spreaders.

I know the hardtop takes a little getting used to—it's eye spinach—but keep in mind that this feature was probably a requirement of this design. Once on board you can't stand back and admire the profile anyway, so this feature will soon endear itself to the owners and crew due to its uncompromised function.

Note the mainsheet traveler on top of the hardtop. You will need either a Leisure Furl-type boom or in-the-mast furling on this boat, since there is no way you can reach the foot of this sail easily for furling. The SA/D is 14.84.

The forward staterooms are spacious and have plenty of locker space.

The interior is laid out with accommodations for a couple aft and two staterooms forward for kids or crew. The galley is great with plenty of counter space and a huge reefer-freezer unit. The reefer is above the counter level and front-opening.

Adjacent to the galley, on the other side of the cockpit well, is a large nav center. The dining area looks skimpy, but I suppose you could pull up a couple of folding captain's chairs. The table looks small for seating six people for a meal.

The forward staterooms are spacious and have plenty of locker space. Note the location of the shower stall ahead of the staterooms. This makes sense to me although I'm confused as to how the starboard staterooms' access to the shower works. The drawing is ambiguous on this detail. There is a small lazarette aft and a big fo'c'sle forward.

This vessel will be built in aluminum and will carry 210 gallons of fuel and 210 gallons of water.

Dieter Empacher Designs, 75 Evans Rd., P.O. Box 194, Marblehead, MA 01945. (781) 631-5705, fax (978) 744-2440. www.dieterempacher.com

July 2000

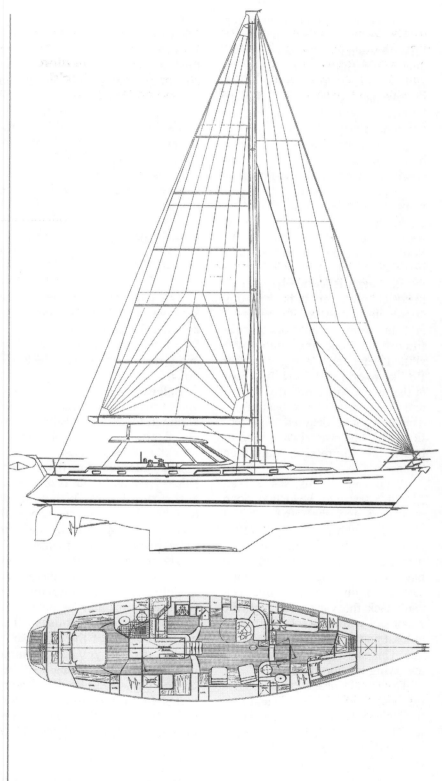

Comfortable cruiser for six or more.

LOA 52'4"; DWL 46'; Beam 14'10"; Draft 6'; Displacement 47,250 lbs.; Ballast 20,000 lbs.; Sail Area 1,212 sq. ft.; SA/D 14.84; D/L 217; L/B 3.52; Auxiliary 110-hp Yanmar 4LH-TE; Fuel 210 gals.; Water 210 gals.

Shannon 47
Bluewater Cruiser

I've known Walter Schultz for more than 20 years, and as long as I have known him, Walter has produced a premium quality yacht. About 25 years ago I got word at the Annapolis show that Walter Schultz was looking for me to "punch Perry in the nose." Apparently he did not like my review of his 37. I immediately went over to the Shannon display and introduced myself. "I hear you want to punch me in the nose."

We had a nice, long, almost friendly chat. My argument with Walter's approach to boatbuilding is that he does his own design work. There is certainly enough historical precedent to back up this approach, but I think both the 37 and this design would have benefitted from some fine tuning by a skilled designer. Having said that I'd like to add that I saw this boat at the recent Annapolis Boat Show and it is certainly a beautifully executed yacht, detailed to perfection. The line was always long to board the impressive, dark-blue Shannon 47.

Walter calls this his "scutter" rig, and it uses two headstays, one masthead and the other almost masthead, with just enough difference so that the roller furling gears have clearance. The idea is that you have your entire headsail inventory, sans storm jib, up all the time. You can't tack the yankee through the small slot without a lot of effort or at least partially rolling up the yankee. This is no problem unless you are trying to short tack a bay.

This small slot also precludes flying both headsails at once and puts the bulk of the rolled yankee where it will interfere with the genoa, especially when going to windward. In evaluating this rig, you have to balance the need for convenience with the need for efficiency, and depending on the owner's sailing style, I can see this going either way. The 47 comes in either a "scutter" or a "sketch" rig using the same headsail arrangement.

The hull form is moderate in every aspect, and the D/L is 227. There is an unusual hollow to the sections at the stern that are a function of a faired-in skeglike area directly above the rudder and a long bustle area preceding the actual skeg. The skeg itself is long at the tip and interrupted by a propeller aperture. My experience with rudder-skeg combinations like this has shown that they usually produce a boat that is hard to handle in reverse.

The 47 comes in either a 'scutter' or 'sketch' rig.

You have the option of a fixed keel with 6-foot, 6-inch draft or a keel-and-board combo that draws 5 feet, 7 inches with the board up and 9 feet, 7 inches with the board down.

Ballast is internal and Walter is very strong on that feature, although there again, I think there are plenty of excellent arguments for external lead ballast.

The interiors for the 47 are "ideas" and no layout is offered as a standard layout. Walter builds each boat like a custom yacht with each interior specifically laid out to the owner's requirements.

The problem with aft-cockpit boats of this size is that there is no graceful way of getting more than two staterooms into the boat without severe compromises. The biggest benefit of the Hull No. 1 layout is that you get a large lazarette, and no cruising boat ever has too big a lazarette. If you converted this design to a center-cockpit layout you would gain accommodation volume but you would lose storage space.

I think Walter Schultz is rightfully very proud of this boat and the reception it is getting.

Shannon Yachts, 19 Broad Common Rd., Bristol, RI 02809. (401) 253-2441. On the Web: **www.shannonyachts.com**

March 2000

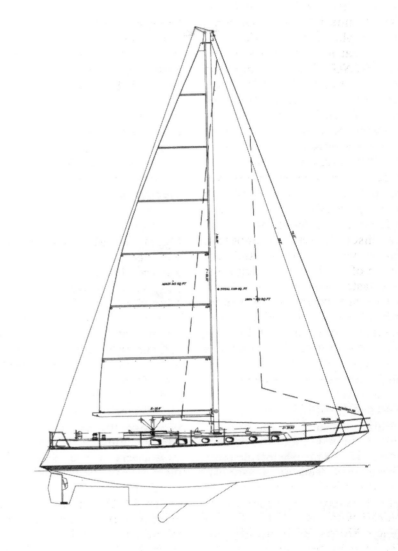

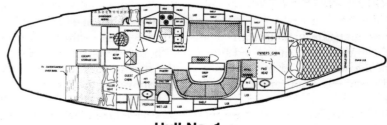

Hull No. 1

Sturdy, long-range cruiser with a unique rig.

LOA 52'7"; LOD 47'6"; LWL 42'7"; Beam 14'3"; Draft 6'6" (fixed keel), 5'7" (centerboard up), 9'7" (centerboard down); Displacement 35,500 lbs.; Ballast 13,500 lbs.; Sail Area 1,200 sq. ft. ("scutter" rig), 1,173 sq. ft. ("sketch" rig); SA/D 17.5; D/L 227; L/B 3.33; Auxiliary 82 hp; Fuel 130 gals.; Water 230 gals.

Perry 53-foot MS
Motorsailer

I was having a quiet dinner with Laurie Davidson in Auckland, New Zealand, enjoying the local whitebait fritters along with some excellent local Savignon Blancs. We were having a good time talking about boats and people. Then Laurie mentioned that he had seen a review in *SAILING* of one of my own designs, a big double-ender. I told him that, yes, that was the Shrontz boat. All excited, I asked him what he thought of it.

"I thought it was bloody awful" he blurted. "I pulled out a piece of sketch paper, laid it over the drawing in *SAILING* and drew a new bow on the boat and my bow improved the boat immensely." Laurie appeared happy with himself and his choice of sav blanc. I thought the wine tasted a little bitter.

This new design of mine is for an East Coast client with a love of traditional old boats. When we began this project he sent me a

My hope is for a wolf in sheep's clothing.

book to illustrate his ideas of what a beautiful boat should be. He likes stalwart traditional craft that almost border on workboat traditions. This new boat makes a stark contrast with the yacht styling of Paine's Morris 46. Ironically, this new motorsailer will be built in Maine at Lyman-Morse.

The plumb bow came from another design of mine, the one Laurie had mentioned. Despite Laurie's criticism of this shape, I am using it again. I think it fits the look and buys us a lot of DWL. Compare this boat to the Morris. The DWL of the Morris is 34 feet, 6 inches while my motorsailer at 53 feet has a DWL of 49.42 feet. That gives the Morris a hull speed of 7.9 knots and my 53-footer a hull speed of 9.5 knots using a speed-to-length ratio of 1.35. But my boat is not only about boat speed. It's also about creating a vintage look, which is why the boat is a double-ender and has a plumb stem. In fact, if you look very carefully you'll see this stem actually

curves back, beyond plumb. I admit, it's a strong look. I love big, bold and earthy cabernets, too.

The L/B is 3.58 and the D/L is 203. We are using a modern fin-and-bulb-type keel and a semi-balanced spade rudder with a carbon stock. Given that we chose the double-ended hull form for aesthetics we have done what we could with this hull to ensure excellent speed under sail. My hope is for a wolf in sheep's clothing. I also like lamb.

There was never any intention of filling this entire hull with accommodations. That would have put pressure on the aesthetics that would have compromised the overall look of the boat. The layout features two staterooms with the owner's forward. There are two heads and the owner's head is all the way forward with a big shower stall.

The pilothouse has a large dinette raised so you can see comfortably out the big windows. The galley is sunken to extend the counter and lockers outboard under the side deck. The steering station is in the aft starboard corner. It's unusual to put the pilot station aft but it works and allows us to line up the settee with the dinette.

The rig is big for a motorsailer with a SA/D of 17.89. The working jib will be self-tacking and the mainsail will be on a Leisure Furl boom. A self-tacking staysail will be used for heavy air. Note on the profile that the pilothouse top extends aft of the aft bulkhead to allow for some sheltered seating in the cockpit. Wide side decks and a small overall cabintrunk should add to the vintage look of this boat.

When the client and I started this project the idea was to try to have some fun with it. Make a real distinct design statement. Do a boat you would never see at a boat show. That's what custom boats are all about.

Robert Perry Yacht Design, 5801 Phinney Ave. Ste. 100, Seattle, WA 98103. (206) 789-7212. **www.perryboat.com**

April 2003

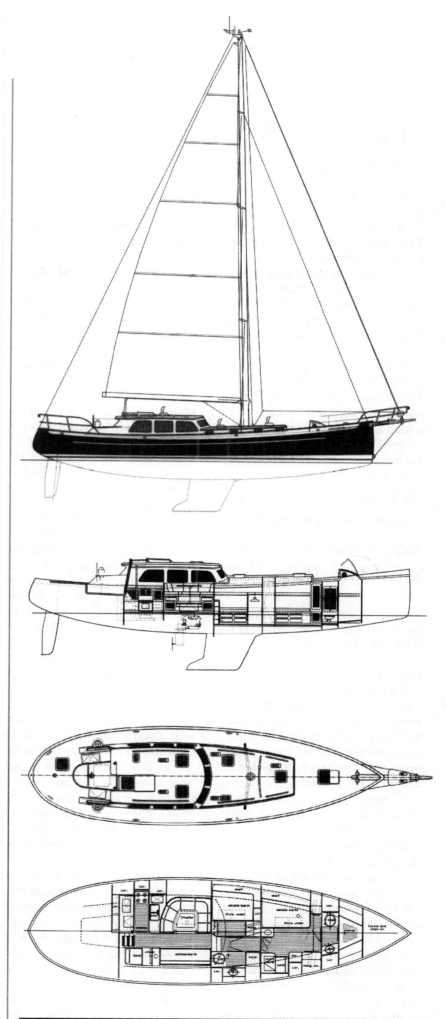

Swift, traditionally styled motorsailer with a sense of fun.

LOA 53'; DWL 49.42'; Beam 14.8'; Draft 8'; Displacement 45,000 lbs.; Ballast 18,000 lbs.; Sail Area 1,415 sq. ft.; SA/D 17.89; D/L 203; L/B 3.58; Auxiliary Yanmar 4JH 3-CE 95-hp; Fuel 300 gals.; Water 200 gals.

Discovery 55
Family Cruiser

This Ron Holland-designed Discovery 55 is evidence of the Oyster impact on cruising boats. I'm not saying Oyster invented the type. I'm just saying the company has promoted it to the point where it's impossible to separate Oyster's identity from the raised-saloon center-cockpit design. Of course, Beethoven used themes by Mozart for inspiration so what's wrong with a Ron Holland piece based on an Oyster theme? The Discovery 55 is another comfy and fast cruising boat designed for owners with a high level of expectation.

The drawings from Ron's office are beautiful. True, they are all com-

While this interior is basically normal in its components, I think it shows a heightened level of design finesse.

puter generated, but they show the hand or finger of someone intent on producing the design as art.

The hull form is moderate with U-shaped sections forward and a small amount of deadrise aft at the transom. BWL is broad. There is a slight hint of reverse to the counter aft. There is a deep, molded-in sump in the way of the external lead keel. The keel is longish with a bulb. The rudder is hung on a half skeg with a considerable amount of balance area. Compare this to the Oyster rudder with no balance. The D/L is 246. This design shows a beautiful sheerline.

The sailplan shows an SA/D of 17.9 and you can arrange your foretriangle any way you like. All options include a self-tacking jib or staysail. Sailplan B is my favorite with an almost full-hoist, 90-degree self-tacking jib with a furling masthead genoa tacked to the stem.

In all cases the triple-spreader rig has spreaders swept to 23 degrees. The sheeting angle from the stem to the outboard edge of the self-tacking track is 10 degrees. This works on the wind,

but once you bear off, it would be nice to have an additional 5 degrees to maintain a proper jib shape.

Ken Freivokh did the interior design work. If you read the megayacht magazines you will have heard of Ken's work. He's a master stylist. There are almost no surprises in this interior, a three-stateroom layout with two heads.

The galley is big and would be fun for a cook. The dinette shows rounded contours, but it also has some straight stretches. This will certainly work better than the nearly circular dinette.

Surprise! There's a pilot berth tucked under the side decks to starboard in the saloon. This is a sea berth and very unusual in this type of boat.

As usual with center-cockpit boats, the lazarette has been eroded to the point where it almost doesn't exist. The fo'c'sle is adequate but not big. Note the location of the bow thrusters. Two bow thruster options are shown. While this interior is basically normal in its components, I think it shows a heightened level of design finesse without being novel.

The deck shows narrow side decks. I like broad side decks, but in a design like this they interfere with the interior and particularly the layout of the center cockpit. This cockpit is big and, like the Oyster's, divided into two sections, although the Discovery 55 has only one wheel. One particular advantage of the narrow side decks can be seen in the room on the cabintrunk in way of the cockpit where there is sufficient space to get in hatches between the two winches. Overall deck styling is straight out of the Oyster book. It's a good-looking boat that to my eye has a little more snap and appeal than the Oyster.

Discovery Yachts Ltd., Harbour Close, Cracknore Industrial Park, Marchwood, Southampton S040 4AF UK. 44 2380 86 5555. **www.discoveryyachts.co.uk**

July 2000

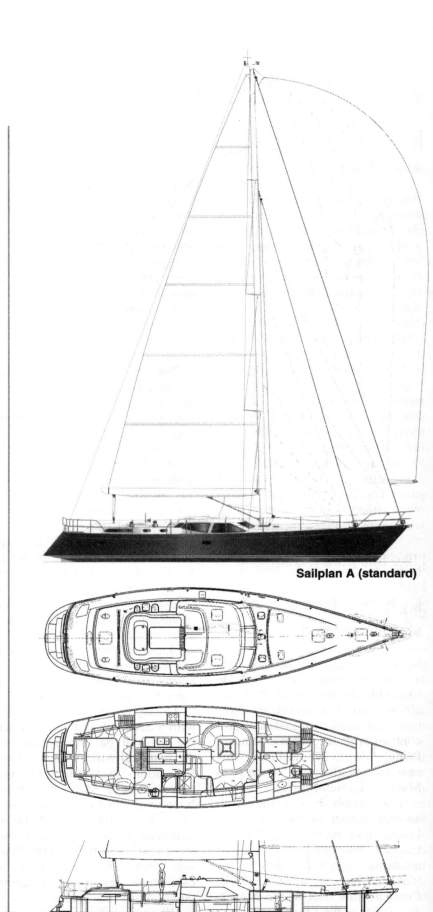

Sailplan A (standard)

A sophisticated variation on an elegant theme.

LOA 54'9"; LWL 44'9"; Beam 15'8"; Draft 7'3" (standard), 6' (shoal); Displacement 49,500 lbs.; Ballast 20,900 lbs.; Sail Area 1,510 sq. ft.; SA/D 17.9; D/L 246; L/B 3.49; Auxiliary 110-hp Yanmar; Fuel 210 gals.; Water 206 gals.

Kay Cottee 56
Bluewater Cruiser

Here's a design from Australia prepared by the first woman to sail nonstop unassisted around the world, Kay Cottee. Cottee will market this boat, and Aussie Scott Jutson, known for his fast boats, did the design work on this project. It's hard to do a complex design like this justice in this review format so forgive me if I miss some areas that might be of interest to you.

It's a great looking boat. The freeboard is high and the ends are short. Max beam is well aft and looks a little odd to my eye. The L/B is 3.45 and the D/L is 178. Draft is variable with the hydraulically-lifted bulbed keel going from 5 feet, 6 inches in the up position to 9 feet down. The wide stern requires two rudders to

I like this galley. Someone involved with this project cooks.

insure that one rudder is always in the water when the boat heels. Note how far aft the keel fin is. It makes me wonder if the keel position was dictated to some degree by the cabin sole heights, structural considerations and the interior layout. In fact, maybe that's why we see the beam so far aft. It might be moved aft in order to move the Longitudinal Center of Buoyancy aft to support the keel weight. If you put these individual characteristics together they seem to make sense.

The rig is a masthead type with well-swept triple spreaders, about 20 degrees. The staysail is self-tacking. The SA/D is 17.17. The spar is aluminum and the standing rigging is Dyform. The boom is the Leisure Furl model. If the conservative SA/D bothers you, don't fret—there is a 140-horsepower Yanmar to push the boat along in the light stuff.

There are accommodations on this boat for three cruising couples. One couple gets upper and lower berths while the other two

enjoy spacious doubles. The owner's stateroom is forward and has its own head with shower stall attached. The aft staterooms also have their own heads but only the starboard stateroom has a shower stall. All three staterooms are more than adequate and in fact are very comfortable. The drawings show "viewing ports" through the bottom of the hull right next to the heads in both quarter cabins. Hmmmmmm. "That's a funny looking fish, Mommy."

I like this galley. Someone involved with this project cooks. You can pass dishes right over the bulkhead dividing the galley from the dinette and conveniently deposit them in the sinks. There are front-loading refers and a top-loading freezer. There's lots of counter space. Most guests will dine in the raised saloon at the big dinette, but if you have guests who chew with their mouths open, you can make them eat at the mini-dinette adjacent to the galley. The aft starboard head is also accessible from the saloon. There is a large fo'c'sle with a workbench.

I like the styling of this deck. It's Euro but the shapes are well defined and that suits my eye. The cockpit is huge. There are two wheels and room to walk between them directly to the broad swim step with its hidden swimming ladder. Forward of the wheels is a fixed, drop-leaf table for dining. The mainsheet traveler is on the housetop. The windlass is in a flush well forward. The self-tacking jib track allows for up to a 16-degree sheeting angle. This is good.

This boat is launched and sailing and the pictures show the interior looking marvelous in rich veneers. Fixtures and fittings are all Italian in chrome or gold-plated brass. You can be certain of both looking good and feeling comfortable on this cruiser.

SailAus Pty. Ltd., P.O. Box 323, Maclean NSW, Australia 2463, 61 2 6645 5088, www.kaycottee.com

April 2003

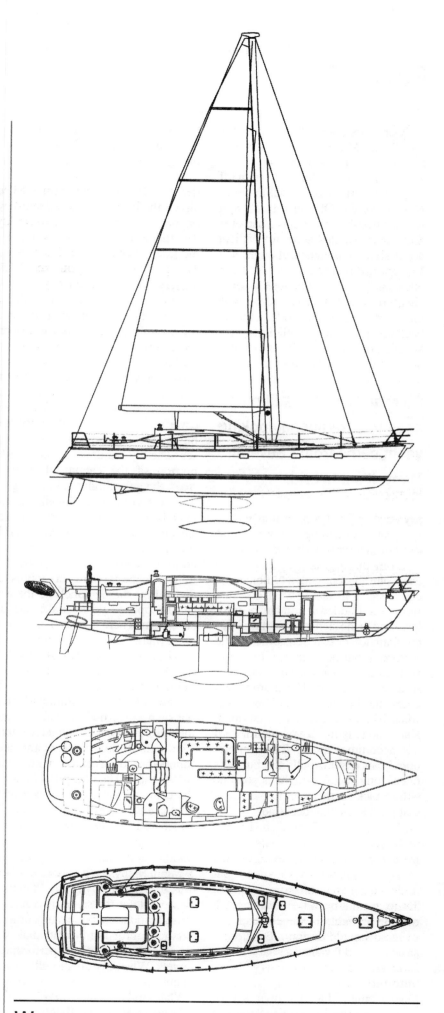

Well-thought-out offshore passagemaker from Down Under.

LOA 56'; LWL 48.75'; Beam 16.25'; Draft 5'6" (keel up), 9' (keel down); Displacement 20.66 tons; Ballast 19,800 lbs.; Sail Area 1,375 sq. ft.; SA/D 17.17; D/L178; L/B 3.45; Auxiliary 140-HP Yanmar diesel; Fuel 264 gals.; Water 264 gals.

Perry 56
Bluewater Cruiser

Four years after getting the bum's rush from Mr. K. Aage Nielson I heard he was hopping mad. He accused me of "stealing" the stern off his Walsteds-built double-ender *Holger Danske*. Of course I stole it. It was the best-looking fanny I had ever seen, and I wanted it for my Valiant 40 design, although I thought the Vikings had invented it, not K. Aage Nielson. So, six months ago when a client from Utah approached me with ideas for a big double-ender I fought back my inclination to sell him on the benefits of the transom and pulled that handsome stern out of my mem-

So exactly what tradition does this traditional-looking yacht come from? Several. Many. It's a hybrid.

ory once again. Think of it as whimsy. That's something we are in dire need of in today's yachting world.

From the beginning I planned to use a plumb stem with a tumblehome canoe stern. In fact, I went one step further and added a smidge of tumblehome to the stem profile. I find this combination of end treatments a little dissonant, but heck, as any musician will tell you, controlled dissonance is what it's all about. The plumb stem gives me the sharp entry I want for weatherliness along with additional waterline length and volume forward for accommodations. The tumblehome canoe stern pulls the buttocks out as long and as straight as possible before tucking them up into a shape that goes tangent at deckline.

As sectional shapes go, I stuck with high deadrise amidships to give me the displacement I needed for true cruising tankage. This is a boat designed for long offshore passages. There would be little advantage in making it light. I wanted displacement so I could design a bulletproof structure, and I wanted a boat with the internal volume to carry large amounts of cruising stores. Displacement has its own set of virtues for cruising boats including a comfortable motion at sea. With generous displacement—60,300 pounds—I could get a D/L of 192 and have plenty of displacement left over in the weight study to give me a

ballast-to-displacement ratio approaching 40 percent. This translates into good stability and excellent ultimate stability figures in excess of 128 degrees. The long-planform fin keel allows the lead to be placed very low on the fin to further enhance stability. The rudder is on a partial skeg to get the safety factor of a lower bearing. The half angle of entry is 17.75 degrees. The prismatic is high at .554.

The interior is laid out with the owner's stateroom aft with access to the owner's head and shower to port. Adjacent to the engine room and to starboard is a pilot berth that does double duty as a workbench. Its proximity to the engine room makes this feature ideal. There is a washer and dryer below the berth. The galley is big and U-shaped for efficiency at sea. The big windows in the raised portion of the cabintrunk will make the galley light and inviting. Note the convenient hanging locker directly aft of the nav station. The saloon is spacious, and with two additional folding chairs can dine six in comfort, eight in discomfort. The mirror-image forward staterooms are divided by sliding panels so the area can be opened up to make one big stateroom. There is a head and shower forward.

The look I was after is rooted in the English yachts of the 1930s through the 1950s, as seen in the designs of Douglas Phillips-Birt or our own Phil Rhodes. There is a 4-inch-high bulwark capped in teak. The cabintrunk corners are well rounded and accented with "eyebrow" trim. The cockpit is long and the coaming is broken on centerline aft for easy access to the mainsheet winch and the main traveller winch.

So exactly what tradition does this traditional-looking yacht come from? Several. Many. It's a hybrid. My hope was to achieve a vaguely "familiar" look while at the same time making an individual styling statement in an offshore cruising yacht that was designed to hit modern performance targets. When my client pulls into an anchorage I want sailors to ask, "What kind of boat is that?"

Robert H. Perry Yacht designers Inc., 5801 Phinney Ave. North, Suite 100, Seattle, WA 98103. (206) 789-7212. **www.perryboat.com**

May 2002

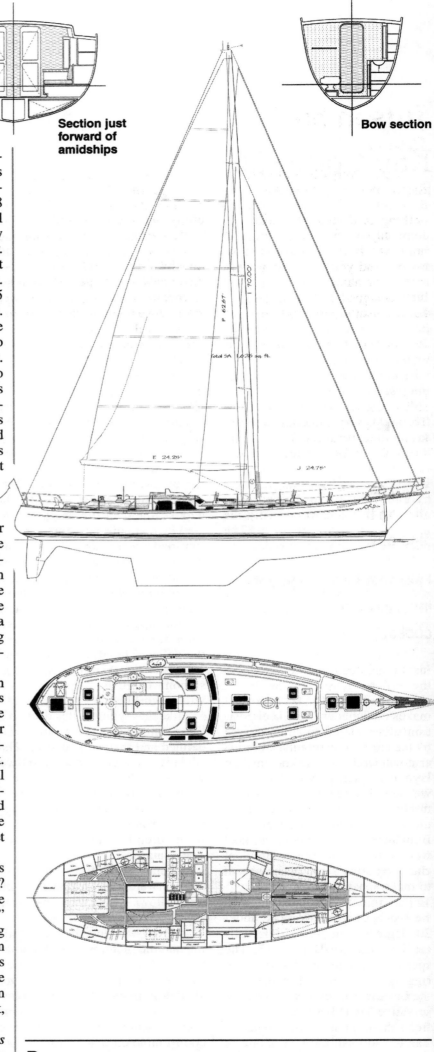

Section just forward of amidships

Bow section

Double-ender represents an amalgam of traditional types.

LOA 56'; DWL 52'; Beam 15'6"; Draft 7'; Displacement 60,300 lbs.; Ballast 23,000 lbs., Sail Area 1,626 sq. ft.; SA/D 17; D/L 192; L/B 3.6; Auxiliary 113-hp Lugger; Fuel 250 gals.; Water 200 gals.

Jutson 56
Cruiser

Here's another hybrid-style 56-footer, this time from Australian designer Scott Jutson. There is nothing usual about this boat. Hull form, layout, rig and deck are all unusual. It's very Euro in its styling and you'll probably either love it or hate it. To my eye it's well designed and good looking, but it doesn't quite tickle my sailboat appreciation nerve endings. But, of course, that's why we have different designers.

This Jutson 56, at 48,730 pounds, is a heavy one, although it still manages to keep its D/L at 157. The hull is very deep and the lifting keel is quite far aft. In fact, from the viewpoint of the longitudinal center

I dug as hard as I could for dirt on the rig, but I couldn't find any.

of gravity, I don't know how they got it that far aft. The distribution of beam shows a boat that could easily be stern heavy, and this should push the ballast forward. It must be the weight of the Carbospar and the jet ski combined with lots of heavy ground tackle. Still, to my eye it doesn't look quite right. Don't forget the weights associated with the large dinghy stowed in the lazarette. There are two stubby little rudders that will work with the keel-up draft of 5 feet, 6 inches. Keel-down draft is 9 feet, 2 inches. Beam is 16 feet, 5 inches for an L/B of 3.42.

The layout features a pilothouse with inside steering and dinette. The dinette is not raised, but the deep windows of the Jutson should allow for visibility while seated. Engine space and the keel trunk are below the pilothouse.

There is another large dinette on the lower level forward adjacent to the galley. The galley is big. Forward of the galley are upper and lower berths for four guests, who will share a forward head. The owner's stateroom aft has a head to starboard and a large shower stall to port. The fo'c'sle area is taken up by ground tackle stowage and a bow thruster. There is no general stowage forward that I can see. With the dinghy in the

laz I don't see any general stowage aft either. I'd like to see far more deck access to large multipurpose stowage areas.

The deck plan shows minimal side decks and a large cockpit. I'm from the old school I guess, and I like broad side decks. This boat has a very wide stern and the cockpit takes advantage of that with two wheels and two wraparound seating areas forward with tables.

The driver will sit on an elevated powerboat-style helm chair so he can see over the pilothouse. The dinghy will launch with an extendable crane/davit from the large garage in the stern. There is a nest on the foredeck for a jet ski. I tried this a couple of times with my dog sitting between my arms. She liked it better than I did, and after 15 minutes I got bored and quit. I hate the noise and would just as soon see them all end up rusting in carports. The last thing I want in a secluded anchorage is a fool on a jet ski.

Oops, got off the track there.

The cockpit uses a tubular wrapover arch structure to form a Bimini. Pulpits and lifelines are integrated into a stout pipe rail system.

The Aerorig by Carbospars is interesting. I am currently using one on an 85-footer. I dug as hard as I could for dirt on the rig, but I couldn't find any. I contacted Bill Dixon in the UK. He's used them several times and the best I could determine was that the darn things work very well. They seem to lack some power for light-air sailing, but I don't think light-air speed is part of the target with this type of boat. Some owners of early Aerorigs are coming back for a second Aerorig. It turns sail-handling into virtually a one-sheet exercise. There are no shrouds or sheet tracks, and the rig is very effective off the wind. The main can furl Leisure Furl style in the boom. It's odd looking, but that can change with time as you gain appreciation for its virtues.

Jutson Yacht Designs, P.O. Box 132, Manly, New South Wales, Australia. www.jutson.com *61 2 9948 1512.*

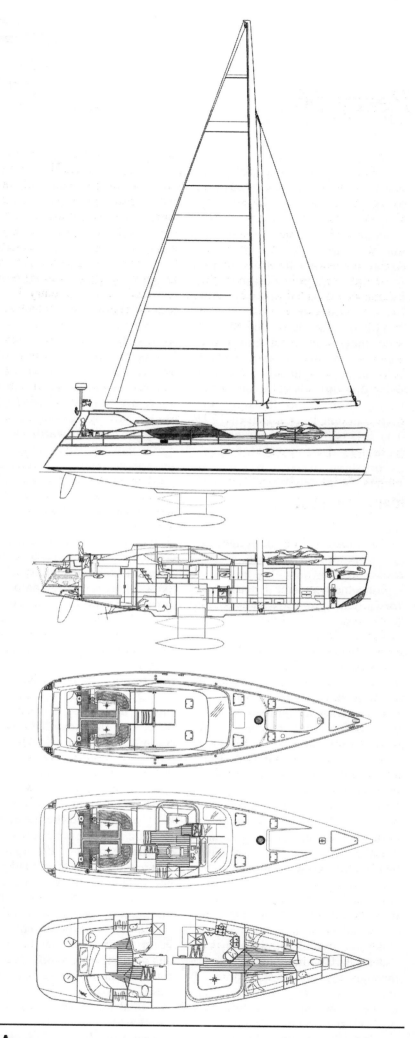

An innovative yacht for the cruising public.

LOA 56'2"; LWL 51'7"; Beam 16'5"; Draft 9'2" (keel down), 5"6" (keel up); Displacement 48,730 lbs.; Ballast 15,620 lbs.; Sail area 1,162 sq. ft.; SA/D 13.9; D/L 157; L/B 3.42; Auxiliary 165-hp Lugger L668T; Fuel 312 gals.; Water 130 gals.

Beneteau 57
Bluewater Cruiser

Give Beneteau credit; its brochures are marvelous works of art. The illustrations are very well done and unusual in this day of computer-rendered images in that they are hand drawn. This design is by the Farr office and it is obviously a boat designed for the charter trade or cruising with two guest couples.

This is an attractive hull with a nice sheer and short ends. The transom is conventional but there is a unique swim step arrangement that unfolds to reveal steps up the stern. Using the lightship displacement I get a D/L of 177. The L/B is 3.45. You can choose from deep draft at 8 feet, 6 inches or shoal draft at 6 feet, 10 inches. While that is not shoal draft in my book it should give the boat good performance on the wind.

Two layouts are offered. You get three guest staterooms and one crew stateroom. The choice is whether the owner's stateroom is forward or aft. Most would opt for having the owner aft but having the owner aft puts the stateroom in the traffic pattern of returning crew when you are moored stern to. It might be 1 a.m. and the crew might not be as sure-footed and nimble as they were before dinner. They could make a lot of noise.

If you go with the two staterooms aft you have to walk through the galley to get to the port stateroom and that is less than optimal. The galley is huge in both models but the designer still put the sinks up against a bulkhead. If you go with the two staterooms forward they have their own heads but they share a centerline shower stall. Note the small day head right next to the crew stateroom, which allows guests to use a head without having to go through any of the staterooms. I see no reason why life would not be very comfortable aboard this big, volume-oriented design.

This deck plan has some unusual features. There are large hatches port and starboard aft to access the big lazarette. Lazarette volume is compromised by the stairs that lead down to the fold-up swim platform. The transom folds down to form the swim platform and there is a large sliding hatch in the deck to open up the stairway. Beneteau has a patent on this

This deck plan has some unusual features.

feature. It's quite clever but only necessary with a conventional transom. One version of the cockpit features a wraparound settee aft and this is made possible by moving the helm position off to port and forward. This feature is usually used on multihulls and powerboats. It does have some advantages in that it clears the steering console out of the middle of the cockpit but I would not like to drive heeled over from that helm seat. It just can't be very comfortable. But you have to balance this drawback against the advantages, and for on-deck dining this layout would be perfect. You do have the option of a centerline, traditional-type steering pedestal. I think I'd want to try the offset helm before deciding. It's very convenient.

The rig is straightforward. The jibstay does not go to the masthead and this may be to allow room to fly a spinnaker in a sock without having the sock hang up on the headstay. The spreaders are swept 20 degrees and the mast is keel stepped. There are sissy bars around the mast. These provide some sense of security but they can get in the way when you are working with a spinnaker pole. The SA/D is 18.68. The mainsail of the 57 is smaller than the main of the O/C Open 40.

This is a big boat. The accent is on volume but the Farr office has given the 57 a hull, keels and rig that should make it an interesting boat to sail. I can imagine this boat being very sought after for charter operations.

Beneteau USA, 1313 Highway 76 West, Marion, SC 29571. **www.beneteauusa.com** *(843) 629-5300.*

September 2003

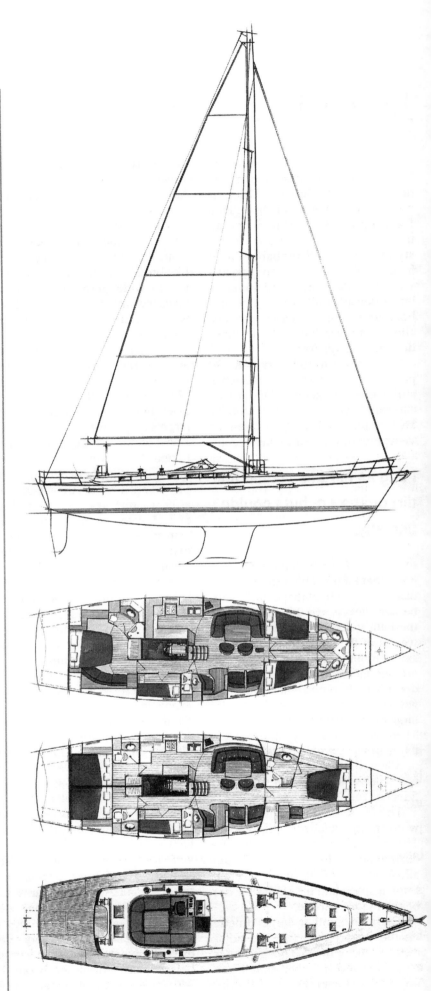

Farr-design built for comfort cruising with performance features.

LOA 57'9"; LWL 56'5"; Beam 16'4"; Draft 8'6" (deep), 6'10" (shoal); Displacement 47,300 lbs.; Ballast 15,169 lbs. (deep keel); Sail Area 1,890 sq. ft.; SA/D 18.68; D/L 177.4; L/B 3.45; Auxiliary Yanmar 160-hp; Fuel 125 gals.; Water 260 gals.

Northwind 58
Bluewater Cruiser

I've seen these Spanish-built boats at boat shows. They are beautifully built. The designs are all by Sparkman & Stephens, as is this new 58-foot model. The look is Euro and the intent appears to be comfy family cruising or chartering. The 58 is a stretch of an earlier model, the Northwind 56. This model makes an interesting comparison with the Beneteau 57, also in this month's reviews.

Stretching a boat is not unusual. It most frequently involves adding a conventional stern to a boat that was originally designed with a reverse transom. This can often upset the balance of the sheer to my eye. In the case of the Northwind 58 the sheer looks just fine with its new transom. The sheer is pretty flat on this design and that helps. I like the way the snubbed-off bow plays against the aft overhang. It's a nice, conservative looking hull with a D/L—based upon a "minimum" displacement—of 210. I'm not sure what "minimum" displace-

> **It's a very simple layout but it's a layout that will work well. Curves and angles do not always make an interior better.**

ment is. In my office we have what we call an "out of the box" displacement but once the boat hits the water and the outfitting starts that displacement is not relevant. I'd prefer to use a realistic "as the boat sits at the dock in typical load condition" displacement. Draft is a healthy 7 feet, 8 inches. The rudder is a large plan form, semibalanced spade.

The advantage to stretching the boat is that now the boat can have an aft cabin and a lazaretto. You also gain considerable space on deck aft of the cabintrunk. In this case there are large, flush doors to access the lazarette on the aft deck. Of course you give up the sugar scoop-style swim platform with this transom. I see no swim step provision on these drawings. I like swim steps more and more as I get older and less agile.

The layout is pretty much standard for this size of center-cockpit boat. The galley is in the passageway aft. The owner's stateroom is aft and the adjoining head is huge with a large shower stall. The mirror image guest quarters forward share a centerline shower stall. Forward of these two staterooms are the crew's quarters with adjoining head. The saloon looks like a nice place to entertain and relax. It's a very simple layout but it's a layout that will work well. Curves and angles do not always make an interior better.

The deck plan shows a cockpit split by the mainsheet traveler. Or you can see it as two cockpits. There are gates through the coaming for the forward cockpit.

With the stern extended on this design the rig appears to be well forward in the boat. But using a 10-station breakdown of the DWL you can see that the aft side of the mast is about 4 inches forward of station 4. This is very normal. The triple spreaders are swept. The SA/D, based again upon minimum displacement, is 17.02.

As usual the designers at S&S have given us a nice looking boat that promises to be a capable sailer.

North Wind Yachts, Pso Juan de Borbón s/n, Moll de Llevant, 08039 Barcelona, Spain. 34-93 221 6056. **www.northwindyachts.com**

In the U.S., contact Mason Yachts International, 400 Harbor Drive, Suite C, Sausalito, CA 94965. **www.masonyachts.com** *(415) 332-8070.*

September 2003

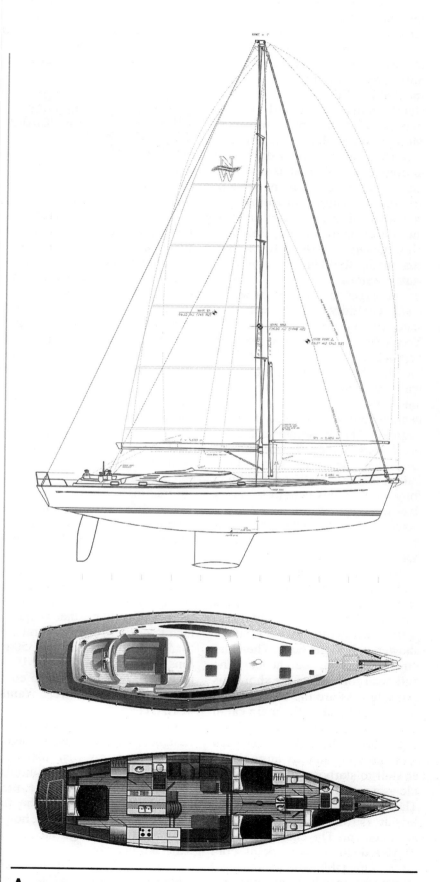

An S&S-designed cruiser offering a simple but comfortable interior.

LOA 58'; LWL 48'; Beam 17'; Draft 7'8"; Displacement 52,082 lbs.; Ballast 20,445 lbs.; Sail area 1,551 sq. ft.; SA/D 17.02; D/L 210; L/B 3.4; Auxiliary Yanmar 140-hp; Fuel 208 gals.; Water 260 gals.

Perry 60
Bluewater Cruiser

We did two designs for this European client, and while both boats are very similar in size, over time his choice of preferred features changed. This boat is built with aluminum at the Jachtbouw Fulmer yard in the Netherlands. We worked closely with our Dutch contact Marinus Meijers to coordinate the conversion from our computer drawings to computer 3-D models to allow the entire structure to be nested and precut. The result to my eye is a work of art, all shiny in aluminum prior to sandblasting and highlighting the skill level that has made the Dutch aluminum yards famous.

The target for this design was a fast, seakindly, all-weather offshore cruiser for a family of five. The hull form is narrow with an L/B of 3.52 and the D/L is 166. The sections show a soft, arclike shape with low wetted surface. The half-angle of entry at the DWL is 15 degrees and at the deck it is 19 degrees. The buttwater beam-to-beam max number is 75 percent. Draft is moderate at 7 feet and the ballast is all internal. The keel fin is long to allow this boat to sit on its keel when hauled and provide sufficient volume to get the lead down low in the fin along with 400 amp-hours of batteries.

This interior evolved from our first design for this client. As his family grew and moved his needs changed. The owner's stateroom is forward with head and large shower stall in the bow. There are three watertight bulkheads. The bulkhead forward of the shower is watertight as are the bulkheads at the forward end of the main cabin and the aft end of the quarter staterooms. There is another head aft to port and another large shower stall to starboard that will double as a wet locker when offshore. The most unusual feature of the layout is the double nav table arrangement. The chair will swivel 180 degrees to work at both tables. One table will be dedicated to navigation while the other for more domestic- and business-oriented desk uses. Each quarter stateroom has stacked berths, a large hanging locker, copious

stowage under the pilothouse sole and a sink.

The pilothouse seats are long enough to use as berths. The aft cockpit is on the small side and all

The most unusual feature of the layout is the double nav table arrangement.

lines will be led aft so they can be reached from the wheel. The focus in this area was on safety and comfort in cold weather cruising areas. Inboard and outboard genoa tracks are provided for a variety of sheeting options. There is a track for the self-tacking staysail. The life raft is stowed in a locker accessible from the swim step.

The sailplan shows a handsome boat by my eye. There is a deep, full-length bulwark and a large swim platform aft. Hull ports are fixed while deck ports are opening. The boat will be sailed as a fractional rig much of time with the help of the self-tacking staysail. The SA/D is 18 with the 100-percent foretriangle and 17.6 with the fractional rig.

The aluminum construction features a skin thickness of 7 millimeters to just above the DW where it increases to 8 millimeters. The keel shoe is 20 millimeters. This is very durable construction. It's also easier to get a fair hull when you work with plating more than a quarter-inch thick. There are integral tanks for 520 gallons of fuel and 350 gallons of water. There is 19,000 pounds of lead ballast. The engine is a 120-horsepower Yanmar 4LHAHTP.

Of course I like this boat. I designed it along with the help of Ben Souquet, my right-hand man, and Marinus Meijers. I think it may represent one of the nicest boats I have designed. The final judgment will have to wait, however, until I can gauge the owner's satisfaction level.

Perry Yacht Design, 5801 Phinney Ave. North #100, Seattle, WA 98103. (206) 789-7212. **www.perryboat.com**

April 2004

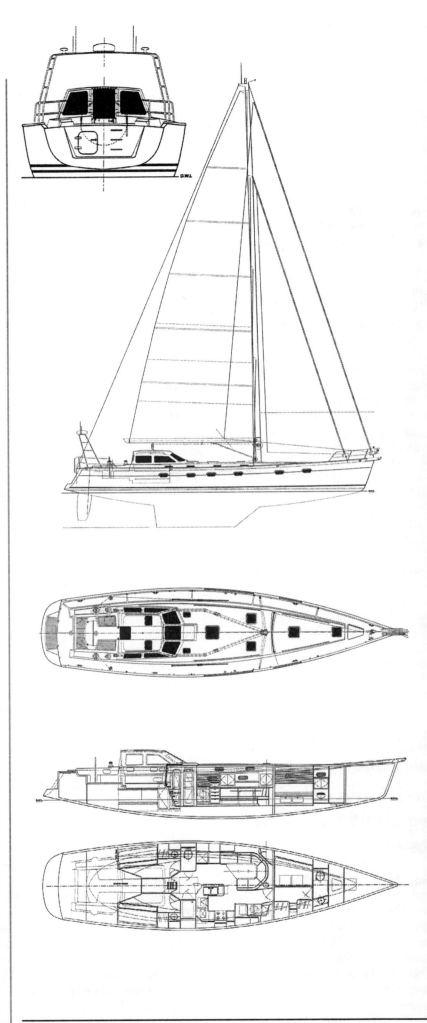

Dutch craftsmanship distinguishes this design project.

LOA 60'; LWL 54'; Beam 15'4"; Draft 7'; Displacement 58,520 lbs.; Ballast 19,000 lbs.; Sail Area 1,696 sq. ft.; SA/D 18; D/L 166; L/B 3.52; Auxiliary Yanmar 4LHAHTP; Fuel 520 gals.; Water 350 gals.

Amelia³
Bluewater Cruiser

Here's a beautiful boat designed by Ted Fontaine. That name probably won't ring a bell, but I can assure you that you've seen Ted's work many times on these pages. Ted was the head designer for Ted Hood's Little Harbor design group for 22 years, taking over when Dieter Empacher left the firm. When Hinkley bought out Little Harbor the design group was one of the first things to go. But no worries for Ted.

The sailplan shows a traditionally handsome boat.

He just set up his own shop and took over the projects in progress. Ted has a good eye. His boats are very conservatively styled in what I would call a Northeast style, a.k.a. Little Harbor, Alden and Hinkley. *Amelia³* is a perfect example of this American style.

Amelia³ was designed for a sailor who has owned two other Hood designs, so it's no surprise the new boat would be a shoal-draft, long-ended, relatively heavy boat. The graceful overhangs fore and aft leave a DWL of only 47 feet, 9 inches, which combined with a displacement of 60,000 pounds gives a D/L of 246. Draft with the board up is 6 feet, 6 inches, and board-down draft is 14 feet, 2 inches. L/B is moderate at 3.81.

Note the way the canoe body droops below the profile of the counter. In the old days we called this droop a bustle. I don't think it has any hydrodynamic advantages, but it allows the designer to pull volume aft to increase the useable cabin sole area in the aft cabin while maintaining that elevated counter look. This elevated counter may be pretty, but I just see it as wasted sailing length. The rudder is a semibalanced spade on a dead vertical stock.

The promotional material that came with this design calls *Amelia³* a "high-performance cruiser," although placed next to the aggressive Tripp 77 that definition loses its teeth. I'm sure the boat will sail very well, just not on the same level as a short-ended, lighter design. The good news is that the displacement of *Amelia³* will reward the owner with a comfortable ride at sea, copious tankage and good stability. Clearly with his experience

with two other Hood boats the owner was after a refinement of similar performance characteristics. For cruisers high performance remains a moving target.

There is nothing not to like about this interior layout. First off, the builder, Lyman-Morse is known for impeccable joinerwork so you can be sure that visually the interior will be a knockout. There is a pilothouse with raised settees and a nav station. Armed with an autopilot remote you could control the boat from here with good visibility.

Below there is a wonderful saloon, which is ideal for entertaining and dining with a nav station tucked aft on the port side. Forward there are mirror-image accommodations with two staterooms with upper and lower berths and two heads. There are crew quarters forward. The galley is in the passageway to the owner's stateroom aft. There are better places for galleys where they are not in the traffic pattern, but you have to balance this feature against the other benefits of this layout, and in that context it makes good design sense to me.

Note how the sinks and the range are in direct line with each other. They should be offset. Note also the huge reefer/freezer compartments aft and the copious counter space to each side of both sink and range. I'm already getting visions of pot roast stuffed with cranberry dressing. The owner's stateroom has direct access to the deck, a large double berth, a settee berth and an adjoining head and shower stall.

The sailplan shows a traditionally handsome boat with a conventionally stayed rig with fore and aft lowers babystay and running backstays. The main is drawn for an in-the-mast furling system with vertical battens in the leech of the main. I remain opposed to this kind of rig, but I know it does have its supporters. In this case the additional weight of the in-the-mast furling is partially offset by using a GMT carbon fiber mast.

Lyman-Morse and Ted Fontaine have combined talents to bring us a very attractive boat.

Fontaine Design Group, 92 Maritime Dr., Portsmouth, RI, 02871. (401) 682-9101. www.fontainedesigngroup.com

September 2002

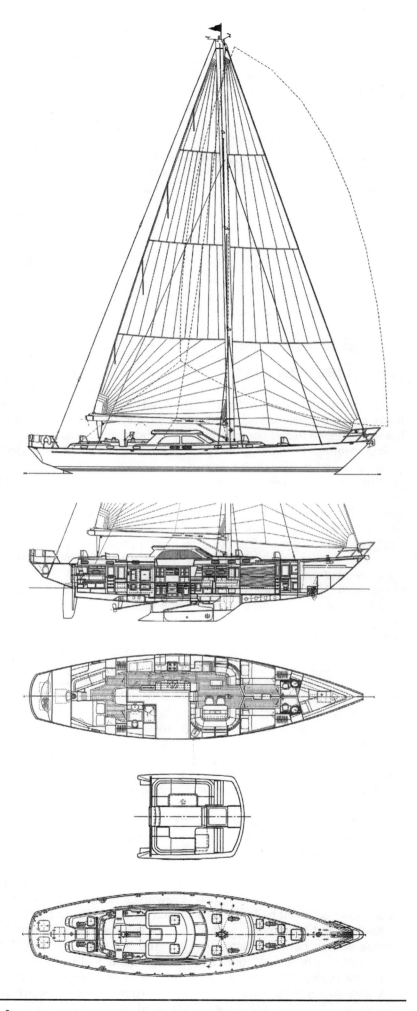

Another example of American's "Northeast" style.

LOA 62'11"; DWL 47'9"; Beam 16'6"; Draft 6'6" (board up), 14'2"; Displacement 60,000 lbs.; Ballast 22,000 lbs.; Sail Area 1,870 sq. ft.; SA/D 19.5; D/L 246; L/B 3.81; Auxiliary Westerbeke 170-hp; Fuel 330 gals.; Water 300 gals.

63-foot *ALCA i*

Motorsailer

About 25 years ago the door to my small office flew open and in burst George Buehler looking wild and woolly smoking a pipe with a broken stem repaired with a wad of black electrical tape. Under his arm was a large can of Sir Walter Raleigh tobacco. After brief introductions George launched into a tirade based upon the premise that "your boats are silly. My boats are sensible." I was new in business,

This will be a stout and stalwart passagemaker.

not tremendously secure and genetically a little on the combative side, but we managed to end our meeting before coming to blows. George harangued and puffed on his crippled pipe while I puffed on one of my cherished, immaculate Dunhills probably packed with imported Escudo cut navy plug. Yep, we certainly were two different flavors.

A year later settling down on *Ricky Nelson* for a quiet night on the hook in Eagle Harbor, I noticed a perky double-ender drop anchor across the bay. It was George. I finished dinner, grabbed a fresh bottle of single malt and rowed my dinghy toward the dim yellow kerosene light in George's cabin. I don't think we finished that bottle of scotch that night, but I remember making a good dent in it. George and I were now friends.

George reminds me of Van Morrison, the Irish singer. You may not like everything he does, but you have to admire a man who for many years is faithful to his own unique vision of his craft. I like just about all of George's boats. They are rough and ready, and they border on workboat aesthetics. This one, called *ALCA i*, was designed for a couple who will build the boat themselves and have the fortune of owning an oak farm for materials. They wanted a boat they could use for marine biological research. This is a true motorsailer with a true pilothouse. This is a manly boat.

The hull style harkens back to the North Sea lifeboat types with its strongly curved ends and its boldly sprung sheer. This boat is heavy at 94,443 pounds. But with a waterline length of 59 feet, 6 inch-

es the D/L is only 212. George favors an almost symmetrically balanced hull form fore and aft. Deadrise is almost constant throughout, and both ends are on the full side. Not surprisingly, this full-ended shape gives an exceptionally high prismatic coefficient of .622. This would indicate less than great performance in light air and good speed when the big, six-cylinder auxiliary kicks in. In fact, with 1,066 gallons of fuel, this boat will go 4,000 miles at 9 knots without the aid of sails. There is essentially no salient keel to this design. The high-deadrise-angle canoe body is well over 4 feet deep amidships. Draft is only 6 feet and that precludes even reasonable upwind performance. This boat is designed to motor to weather.

George calls this rig a "three-masted schooner." I think not. If it were a schooner the last mast should be no less in height than the mast forward of it. Hell, I don't know. It's 2002! I'm going to call it a "gooner."

Given the size of this boat and the fact that it will have a crew of two you have to break the rig down into small-sized sails. Of course, you could use all the modern gizmos like Leisure Furl and hydraulic roller-furling headsails, but Van Morrison wouldn't use a drum machine, would he? I'll bet this rig has galvanized wire standing rigging. The low center of pressure afforded by this handsome rig will couple well with the boat's 11 percent ballast-to-displacement ratio.

There's a lot of cabin sole in this boat. It is refreshing to look at an interior that is not the five pounds of marbles in the two-pound-bag type.

Solidly built, the hull is all white oak with a laminated keel, double sawn frames and 2³/₈-inch-by-2¹/₂-inch strip planking. This will be a stout and stalwart passagemaker.

You are what you sail. I'd feel really good sliding into a remote harbor in this rugged beauty. But I still wouldn't wrap electrical tape around one of my Dunhills.

George Buehler Yacht Design, P.O. Box 966 Freeland, Whidbey Isl., WA 98249. (360) 331-5866. www.georgebuehler.com

January 2002

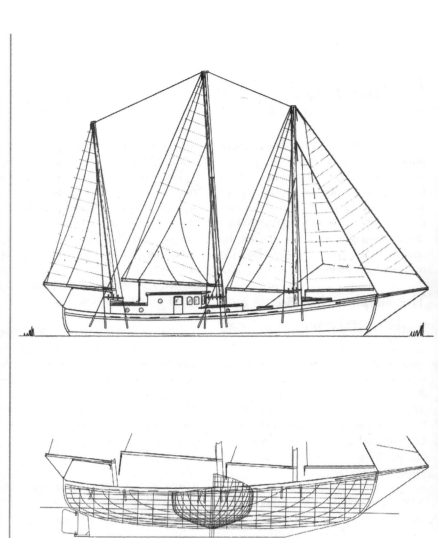

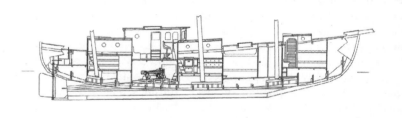

A design with character and strength.

LOD 63'; LWL 59'6"; Beam 16'6"; Draft 6'; Displacement 94,443 lbs.; Ballast 11,000 lbs.; Sail Area 1,328 sq. ft.; SA/D 10.2; D/L 212; L/B 3.72; Auxiliary 6-cylinder diesel; Fuel 1,066 gals.; Water 100 gals.

Oyster 62
Luxury Cruiser

"Like an Oyster." It's become a generic qualification similar to "like a Swan." Oyster yachts have come to almost define center-cockpit, raised-saloon boats. This new 62 combines the design talents of Rob Humphreys for the hull shape and rig, Dick Young for the interior layout and the Oyster Design Team for the styling and detailing. We have come to expect the best from Oyster.

I pored over these drawings looking for nits to pick. It's a difficult task. This boat is big and laid out for uncompromised comfort. You can choose from a layout featuring three double-berth staterooms or a layout with five staterooms including two double-berth staterooms. If you are contemplating a paid hand or two you would want the five-stateroom layout. Suffice it to say, you will be comfy in either. Big spaces, copious lock-

I would hope all your troubles would disappear while cruising this beauty.

ers, huge galley, three heads, what's not to like?

Well, since you asked, take a look at that rounded dinette. I know they look sexy on paper, but try and find a spot to stretch out and you just end up ooching around the entire seat area until you drop out on the floor at the other end. If you are going to entertain six guests with some movies why have the TV on the starboard side so only the two people in the Streisand chairs can see the TV set? And what about an engine room? This layout gives all its volume over to accommodations and gives machinery space short shrift. I suppose you could just go ashore and stay at the Negresco while they take the boat apart to get at the machinery.

I really do like the separate companionway for the aft cabin. These are good layouts. I want my Montrachet at 58 degrees damn it, not 59 degrees!

The hull shape is pretty normal,

with no surprises. In plan view the ends look on the full side, but that just increases the working room on deck. The D/L is 188 based upon an optimistic displacement of 70,550 pounds. Draft is 8 feet, 6 inches and the keel is a fin-and-bulb type quite small in plan form. There is the option of a 6-foot, 6-inch keel. The rudder is deep and hung on a full-length skeg.

The deck design shows a big center cockpit broken down into two spaces. There is room aft for two wheels. The dual mainsheet winches are located just off center-line between the two wheels. Forward of the steering area is the rest of the cockpit with a nice drop-leaf table and plenty of room for lounging. I'm sure all the winches are powered.

Forward of the sculpted raised house there is a wedgelike house extension and a deck-access anchor well. The extension looks good and helps the eye to make the transition to the high house. It's a very handsome boat but perhaps a bit heavy on the sculpted styling for my conservative eye.

The rig is a three-spreader sloop with staysail. There are fore and aft lower shrouds shown on one sailplan and aft lowers with a babystay shown on the other. It might be easier to drag your genoa around one babystay rather than two forward lowers. The SA/D is 17.28. The headsails are on Harken hydraulic furlers. Note the amount of rake designed into this rig.

If you feel lazy and don't want to sail, you can push your Oyster 62 along at an easy 9.5 knots with a 225-horsepower Perkins-Sabre tur-bocharged diesel driving a 3-bladed Max prop. Three hundred gallons of fuel should get you there and 264 gallons of water will make plenty of ice.

I would hope all your troubles would disappear while cruising this beauty.

Oyster Marine Ltd., Fox's Marine, Wherstead, Ipswich, Suffolk, 1P2 8SA. 44 1473 68 88 88. **www.oystermarine.uk.com**

July 2000

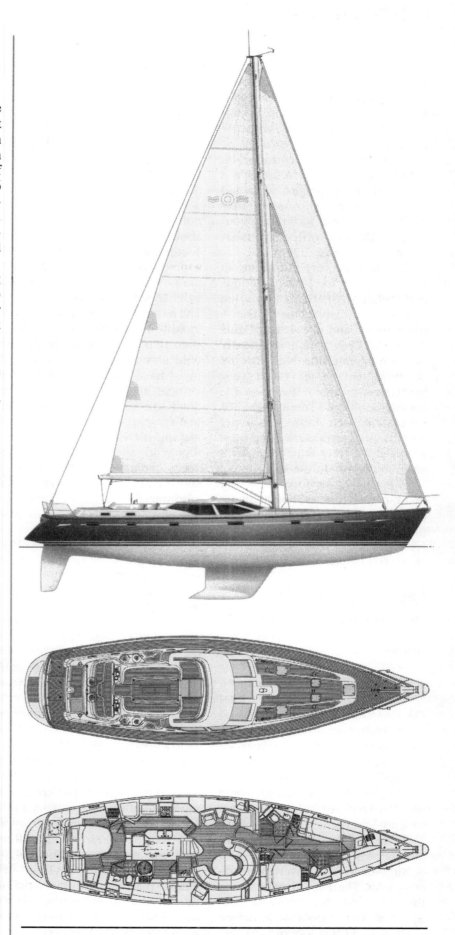

The latest in the Oyster tradition.

LOA 63'3"; LWL 55'1"; Beam 17'8"; Draft 8'6" (standard), 6'6" (shoal); Displacement 70,550 lbs.; Ballast 20,700 lbs. (standard) 22,700 lbs. (shoal draft); Sail Area 1,845 sq. ft.; SA/D 17.28; D/L 188; L/B 3.49; Auxiliary 225-hp Perkins-Sabre; Fuel 300 gals.; Water 264 gals.

Moody 64
Luxury Cruiser

Bill Dixon designed the new Moody 64 and a handsome vessel it is. Built in Southampton, England, the Moody is a luxury cruising yacht. Moody's brochure is fabulous and includes a lot of technical drawings of construction details we rarely get to see. It's a far cry from the grapes, wine and bikinis that often promote new models. This is a technical document. Dixon's office produces beautiful technical drawings.

The hull is very moderate in shape with arclike, deep sections and a D/L of 193 if I use the "tanks full" displacement. Dixon likes beam and the L/B of this design is 3.62, which is actually on the moderate side. Note that the beam is carried aft for a very broad transom that shows the same double-cambered detail as the Swan. This just means the upper corners of the transom have been radiused off to provide an elegant shape transition to the sheerline.

The keel looks forward to my eye but this type of boat can get heavy aft easily and put pressure on the designer to get the ballast forward. The rudder is on a half skeg. You can choose from 6 foot,

I see marvelous culinary delights coming out of this galley.

6 inch draft or 8 foot, 6 inch draft.

The interior detailing is by Roel Degroot Design and the pictures I have show beautifully detailed joinerwork. The drawings I received include the most amazing interior computer rendering I have ever seen. It truly takes some study to realize that you are not looking at a photo.

Two couples will be very comfy on this boat. There are sparse crew accommodations forward with its own head. There are four heads on this boat. When my second son, Spike, was born my wife informed me that I had just inherited latrine duty for life, so I favor as few heads as possible.

The owner's stateroom aft is palatial with symmetrical settees, a queen-sized berth and adjoining head with shower. I'm not sure

what that small desk and seat are for in the passageway. Maybe it's a workbench as it is adjacent to the engine room door. Maybe it's an office. The galley is a step down from the saloon level and is wonderfully laid out. I see marvelous culinary delights coming out of this galley.

Crew quarters aside there is nothing minimal or cramped about this layout. Of course accommodations like this come at a price and you can see in the plan view that lazarette and fo'c'sle are minimized.

The sailplan reveals a good looking boat with a nice profile. I even like the windshield. I'm not wild about in-mast mainsail furling. I have not lived with the new vertical battens but I'm a nut for good sail shape. There is a track just forward of the mast for a self-tacking jib. The sheeting angle to this track is 13 degrees and the specs indicate that this track is specifically for the staysail. The working jib is a high-clewed yankee type. The SA/D is 17.03 using the tanks full displacement.

The center cockpit shows two wheels with contoured helm seats. The traveler is just aft of these seats. The lounging area of the cockpit is wide. The styling of the deck is very well done. There is a swim step that folds up into the transom. This offers the advantages of a molded-in swim platform without detracting from the volume available for the lazarette. The deep bulwark is capped with teak.

My only complaint with this deck design is the lack of opening ports. There are plenty of deck hatches though. I prefer to see more possibilities for cross ventilation but it goes without saying that most of these boats will be equipped with air conditioning.

I like Dixon's styling. It's almost Euro but with more definition of shapes and crisper detailing. This boat will certainly be a head turner in any harbor.

Moody America, Inc., 335 Lincoln Street, Hingham, Massachusetts 02043. (781)749-8600. www.moody-america.com

May 2003

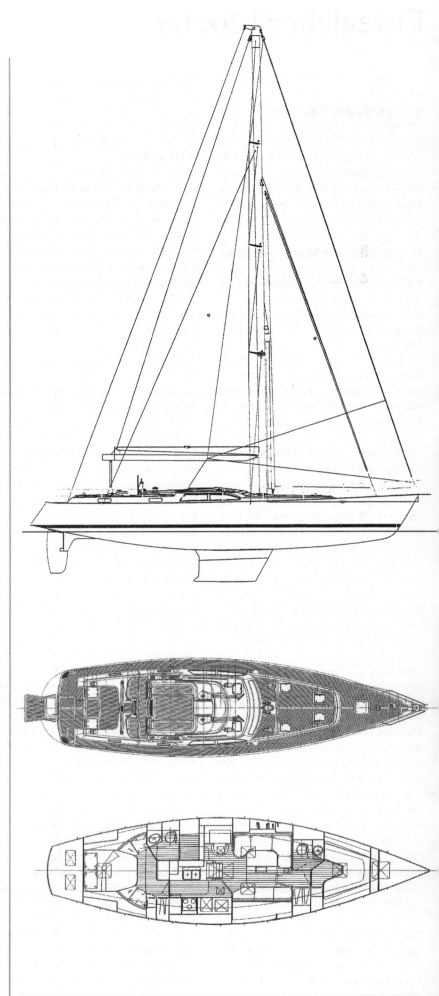

A modern cruiser with gracious accommodations.

LOA 63'5"; LWL 54'3"; Beam 17'6"; Draft 8'6" (fin), 6'6" (shoal); Displacement 69,080 lbs.; Ballast 22,000 lbs.; Sail Area 1,794 sq. ft.; SA/D 17.03; D/L 193; L/B 3.62; Auxiliary Yanmar 4LHA-STE; Fuel 565 gals.; Water 363 gals.

Erdevicki 64-footer
Motorsailer

If you have been reading these reviews for the past five years you may recall that this is where Ivan (pronounced "Eevaan") Erdevicki (pronounced "Erdevechk") had his first two designs reviewed. Ivan, who is from Montenegro, and I became friends and I was able to help him get a job in Seattle with Delta Marine. In the spirit of the true designer, howev-

In a utilitarian way, this is a very good looking boat.

er, Ivan chafed at working in a large design office and is now establishing his own office. Over dinner and a little too much wine I got the feeling that Ivan felt the only thing standing between himself and truly great design work was the client. We all feel that from time to time. Couple Ivan's 6-foot, 5-inch ex-professional water polo player frame with his accent and intensity and you can easily imagine Ivan glaring at the client and saying, "You don't like my sheer! No soup for you, two years!" Ivan's a good guy and a talented designer.

This is a very interesting design prepared for a Seattle client who wanted an aluminum motorsailer built as simply as possible. Ivan chose to use a single chine with flat plate conically developed so that there are no compound curves. This makes fabrication easier and cheaper but puts pressure on the designer to not let the geometry take over too much of the job of shaping the hull. This, however, is a great looking hull. The ends are short and this gives it a bit of a pugnacious look, accented by the flattish sheerline. The chine runs right above the DWL, and there is about 10 degrees of deadrise amidships fairing out to around 8 degrees at stern. The topsides are pretty slabby, but that's what you would expect with a single-chine shape. The D/L is a low and probably optimistic 67.7. The prismatic coefficient is a textbook 54.8. This means the volume in the ends of the boat is neither full nor fine. Beam is narrow with an L/B of 4.4.

You have the choice with this design of going with port and starboard daggerboards or a single, centerline daggerboard. The keel is stubby with a board-up draft of only 4 feet. The rudder appears to be a work in progress. It will have to retract too.

The rig drawing shows a ketch rig with short, deck-stepped masts and lots of roach on the main and mizzen. The masts are independently stayed and there is provision for a mizzen staysail to be tacked to the aft end of the house. Off the wind this rig will work well but upwind you have the problem of a catboat chasing a sloop. Can you hear that wheezing? That's the sound of the mizzen gasping for clean air. Still, considering that this boat is a motorsailer, it will spend very little time on the wind under sail, anyway, and upwind work will be done with the "iron genny."

The jib will be self-tacking and once again I would not have stopped that track short of the rail especially for a reaching boat. I'd carry it as far outboard as physically possible. The on-deck bowsprit can be angled 20 degrees to weather to help the asymmetrical chute. The SA/D is 21.

The layout is a bit unusual in that there are two staterooms but enough berths to sleep six without even using the saloon settee and dinette. The heads are roomy and have generous shower stalls. There is an inside steering position to starboard in the saloon. Note the handy wet locker next to the companionway. Ivan has given plenty of volume to the engine room, with room to walk around the engine, although headroom will be compromised by the cockpit well.

The deck plan shows minimal side decks and a large cockpit. The deck is raised aft into a quarterdeck, which provides headroom in the aft cabin. (You can call it the poop deck if that makes you happy.) I know Ivan was not too keen on the long line of rectangular windows in the house, preferring something sexier I suspect. But I find the windows as drawn just fine. In a utilitarian way, this is a very good looking boat.

The engine is a Perkins Sabre 215-horsepower diesel. Cruising speed under power will be about 10 knots. Performance under power is important in the Pacific Northwest where we have strong tides and light winds.

Ivan has done a beautiful job preparing these plans. Everything was done on the computer, but that didn't stop the artist in Ivan from coming through loud and clear. This unusual, shoal-draft motorsailer will make a very interesting cruising boat.

Ivan Erdevicki, 400-1200 West Pender St., Vancouver, BC, V6E 2S9, Canada. (604) 879-0363. www.ivanerdevicki.com

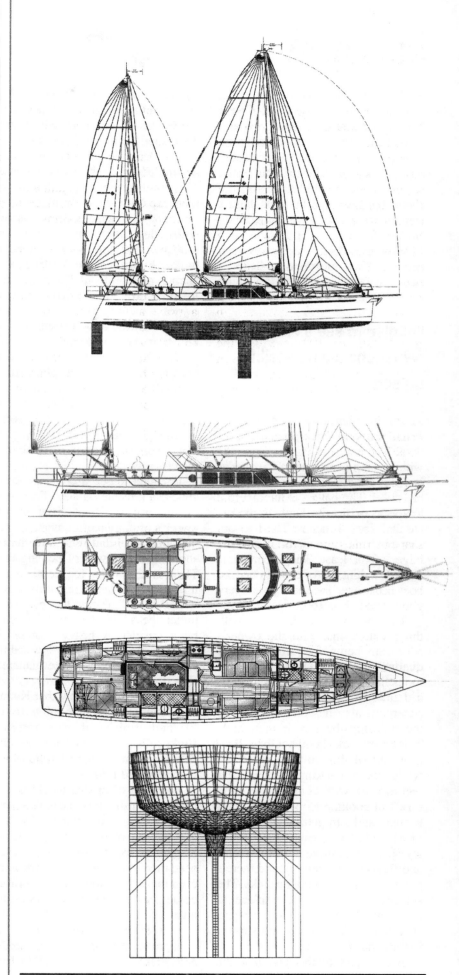

Sturdy, practical motorsailer with some unique features.

LOA 64'; LWL 63'2"; Beam 14'6"; Draft 13' (keel down), 4' (keel up); Displacement 38,000 lbs.; Ballast 12,600 lbs.; Sail Area 1,380 sq. ft.; SA/D 21; D/L 67.7; L/B 4.4; Auxiliary 215-hp Perkins; Fuel 600 gals.; Water 300 gals.

May 2001

Kanter 64
Bluewater Cruiser

Here's another nice cruising boat from the Kanter/Paine team. Chuck Paine's boats always look good and combined with Kanter's aluminum construction they have a clean and businesslike appearance. This is the second Paine/Kanter boat for the client, but this time he went bigger and chose a cutter rig rather than another ketch.

With an L/B of 3.82 this boat can be considered moderate in beam. I think "narrow" boats start with an L/B of 4. I don't have any hull lines

I'm glad to see a cruising owner choose a sensible rig size.

for this boat but it seems to be pretty much textbook Paine in its proportions. The ends are on the short side without being truncated. The rudder is about as far aft as you could possibly put it. The ballast is internal in a low-aspect-ratio fin. Draft is moderate at 7 feet, 4 inches. The transom shape indicates a moderate turn to the bilge, aft at least. The sheerline is almost straight, but of course once the boat heels over the sheer looks very good. The D/L is 160.

This 64-footer is laid out with three staterooms, with the owner's stateroom being forward. The port quarter stateroom has a berth that looks like it can be configured to be a double or two snug singles. This stateroom also has direct access to the amidships head with its bathtub. The galley looks good but there is no room aft of the stove to put a pot while you're cooking, and with 64 feet to work with I can't understand this. But cooking's one of my ways to relax and I'm getting rigid in my ideas about what makes a good galley. On the positive side the reefer and freezer areas are big and there's plenty of room around the sinks. The saloon looks like a nice place to relax with friends. The forward stateroom with its head and shower is very spacious.

A nice part of this layout is the raised pilothouse. There is a dinette to port that is raised up two steps. I know this is high but it has to be two steps in order to put the eyes of the people in the dinette in the middle of the window. One step is not enough. To starboard there is an inside steer-

ing station and navigation center. The helm chair is straight out of the space shuttle and a big computer screen dominates the forward console.

The deck plan shows 13 hatches not including cockpit seat hatches. This will provide ventilation, as there are only two opening ports aft in the cabintrunk. Side decks are wide and the chainplates are inboard. I'm not too keen on the bulky looking stem fitting and anchor platform but I suppose it's form following function as the owner wants two 160-pound anchors on the bow. I think it's the fact that they wrapped the toerail around this bow structure that bothers my eye. The swim platform is big and opens to the cockpit with a low door. The cockpit itself is split for two wheels and there is some overhang to the pilothouse to provide more protection for the on-watch crew.

I'm glad to see a cruising owner choose a sensible rig size. The SA/D of this rig is 16.48. One of the owner's primary requirements for the new boat was that it be stiff, and a short rig is one way of helping that. There is no traveler for the main and it is bridled to the edges of the pilothouse. I've done this too but I still prefer the additional control offered by a traveler. A heavy-weather jib tacks to the front of the low cabintrunk. Two headsails are permanently rigged at the stem.

The pics I have show that Kanter has done its usual nice job with the fit and finish of the interior. Bulkheads are white but joinery details are in varnished solid wood with sculpted fiddles.

For most of us this would be the ultimate cruising boat. I can't see anything lacking; 400 gallons of fuel and 370 gallons of water. You could go bigger but pretty soon you would need more than your wife as crew and even this boat without a bow thruster could prove challenging in close quarters. "Push dear!"

Designer: Chuck Paine & Associates, P.O. Box 763, Camden, ME 04843. (207) 236-2166. **www.chuckpaine.com**

Builder: Kanter Yachts, 9 Barrie Blvd., St. Thomas, Ontario N5P 4B9, Canada. (519) 633-1058. **www.kanteryachts.com**

February 2004

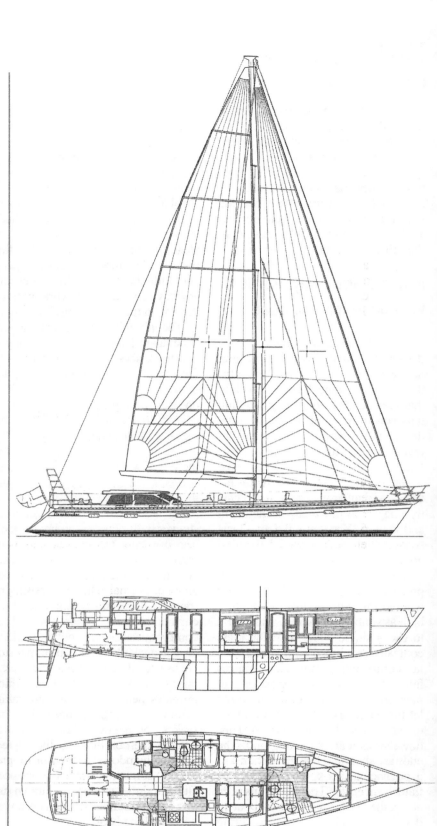

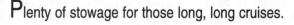

Plenty of stowage for those long, long cruises.

LOA 64'; LWL 55'; Beam 16'9"; Draft 7'4"; Displacement 63,000 lbs.; Ballast 19,000 lbs.; Sail Area 1,631 sq. ft.; SA/D 16.48; D/L 169; L/B 3.82; Auxiliary Yanmar 140-hp; Fuel 400 gals.; Water 370 gals.

S&S 65-footer
Coastal Cruiser

This design from the S&S design group headed by Bruce Johnson and Greg Matzat will be constructed by French builder CNB and uses the unusual AeroRig. The idea is to produce an easily handled performance cruising yacht. Is there an echo in here?

This is an unusual-looking sheerline—fitting I suppose considering it goes on an unusual boat. The low point or nadir of this sheer spring is right in the middle of the boat. I'd prefer to see the nadir of the sheer farther aft, but this would give the boat a more conventional look and perhaps the designers were not after that. To my eye this boat looks stern high.

The hull features a hydraulic, retractable fin and bulb keel. This allows the draft to be reduced from 11 feet, 6 inches to 6 feet. Twin rudders help reduce the draft. I suspect the twin rudders are also intended to open up the middle of the stern so they could put in the garage for the 15-foot Sea-Doo tender. The D/L is 160 based upon a preliminary half-load displacement of 69,312 pounds.

The interior is set up for three couples. The aft guest staterooms are mirror images. These aft staterooms share a head to starboard and a shower stall to port. Where do you undress for the shower? Do you wear your clothes into the shower and then toss them out into the passageway so they don't get wet? Do you undress in your stateroom, peek out the door to see if the coast is clear, then bolt buck-naked for the shower stall? This needs more thought.

The raised saloon features a raised dinette for seated visibility. This is always nice, but you can see the volume that was lost outboard of the pilothouse perimeter. This is inevitable with this type of design. The designers have cleverly worked in the daggerboard trunk so that it has very little impact on the interior layout. The lower saloon combines a comfy dinette with a superb galley design. However, if you were seated in the dinette and you looked aft you just might be able to see a naked person busting a move to the shower.

The owner's stateroom is forward

and the forward head has a shower stall tucked into the bow. This looks like a comfy stateroom, but might have been better with a centerline double that allows equal access to either side of the berth.

I don't know much about the AeroRig. I have seen one in person and I did not find it aesthetically pleasing, although if things work well they soon start to look good. Some people think the unstayed AeroRig is the ultimate in simplicity

Where are the winches and the flying elbows? With the AeroRig the winches are gone.

and ease of handling. Eventually I'll get the chance to sail one and then I might have something to say. The SA/D of this design is 18.36. This is a nice, normal number, but keep in mind you can't add a genoa to help with light-air performance.

This is a highly sculpted deck design. There are two wheels aft in a helming cockpit. Forward of this there is a lounging cockpit. Where are the winches and the flying elbows? With the AeroRig the winches are gone. The single sheet winch is a recessed reel-type hidden below the deck. This means in addition to no sheet winches there are no jib tracks, blocks or running rigging cluttering up the deck. There is a hydraulically activated transom door giving access to the tender.

This boat will be built with Kevlar, E-glass and resin-infused vinylester resin with Baltek Superlite balsa. The engine is a Yanmar 170-horsepower diesel. There are 300 gallons of water and 350 gallons of fuel. There will be a hydraulic, tunnel-type Lewmar bow thruster.

S&S has been the most prestigious of all the American design offices. It's nice to have one of its new designs to review.

Sparkman & Stephens Inc., 529 Fifth Ave., New York, NY 10017. (212) 661-1240, fax (212) 661-1235. **www.sparkman-stephens.com**

July 1999

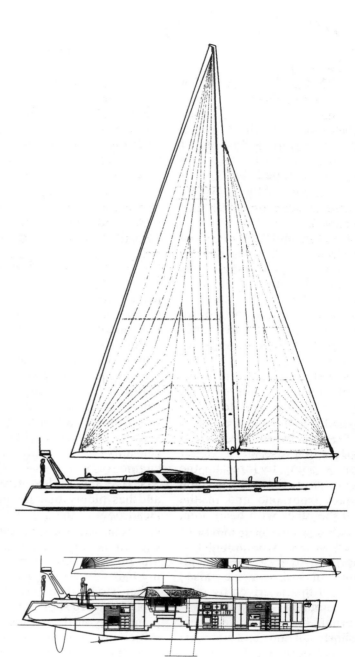

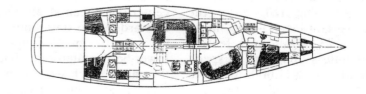

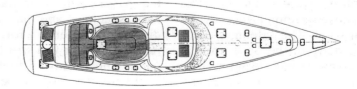

Custom cruiser with an innovative rig and design.

LOA 65'; LWL 57'11"; Beam 17'5"; Draft 6' keel up, 11'6" keel down; Displacement 69,312 lbs.; Ballast 22,250 lbs.; Sail Area 1,956 sq. ft.; SA/D 18.36; D/L 160; L/B 3.73; Auxiliary Yanmar 4LH-DTE 170-hp diesel; Fuel 350 gals.; Water 300 gals.

Hylas 66
Luxury Cruiser

Hylas yachts are built at the Queen Long yard in Taiwan. I like that yard. Years ago on a cold morning I stopped by Queen Long for a visit and they gave me some strange, grayish drink to warm me up. I like the way Queen Long build their boats. They were one of the first Taiwan builders to adopt a more stark, Euro-style of joinerwork.

Hylas yachts are designed by the German Frers office in Buenos Aires. These are handsome boats with lots of freeboard and top hamper, but it's all carried off well by the careful interplay of lines and curves. You really can't judge the looks of this type of boat by comparing it to a low freeboard, aft-cockpit boat. Just the use of a center cockpit is going to force up the height of the cabintrunk so you can walk from one end of the boat to the other with headroom. Now add the vertical pressure of a raised saloon. Compound this by the need to raise the cockpit so you can see over the raised saloon. All this is driven by interior requirements.

The hull form is conventional with shortened ends and a moderately broad stern. The L/B is 3.69 indicating the 66 is on the slightly narrow side of medium, but as LOA increases L/B also typically increases. The D/L from the Hylas "preliminary, light" numbers is 173. Draft is 9 feet, 2 inches unless you want to spend an additional $31,000 to get a hydraulically raised centerboard that will give you a board-up draft of 6 feet, 10 inches.

At first glance you assume this is a raised-saloon type layout. But it's not. The saloon is down where it would be on a normal, non-raised saloon design. There is a "mezzanine" level to this layout just aft of the saloon. There is 6 feet, 2 and a half inches of headroom on this mezzanine level and 9 feet, 2 inches of headroom in the saloon.

The mezzanine level includes a generously sized forward-facing nav station with a worktop extending aft from the chart table. This worktop provides the headroom for the accommodations directly below the mezzanine level. On the port side there is a settee that is pulled inboard with a pilot berth outboard and

I think you will be quite comfy aboard this 66-footer.

up at the top of the seatback level. This pilot berth provides the headroom for the galley, which is on the saloon level. Are you still with me? Raising the mezzanine sole provides room below it for the engine, which can be accessed from the stateroom on the port side. It's not a walk-in engine room but it would certainly be an ample crouch-in engine room.

I like the galley. It's roomy and has plenty of counter space. Headroom in the galley is 6 feet, 3 inches. That means that, depending upon just how high I pile my Roy Orbison pompadour, my hair will hit the overhead. I'd rather stoop than have my hair rub. If you are shorter than 6 feet, 3 inches you'll be fine. I'm not criticizing as much as I am trying to point out the Chinese puzzle aspect of this type of layout.

Sleeping accommodations are aft in a stateroom with an almost centerline queen-sized berth and forward in two staterooms. There is also the smaller upper and lower berth stateroom adjacent to the galley. Each stateroom has its own head. The forward heads share a shower and the aft most forward head is accessed from the passageway. The saloon is very spacious and has a large dinette to port with chairs inboard. I think you will be quite comfy aboard this 66-footer.

I suspect Hylas will be as successful with this model as they have been with the rest of their line.

Hylas Yachts Ltd., E5-7 Westminster Business Square, Durham St., London, SE11 5JH, UK. 44 (0) 20 7834 8651. www.hylasyachts.com

February 2003

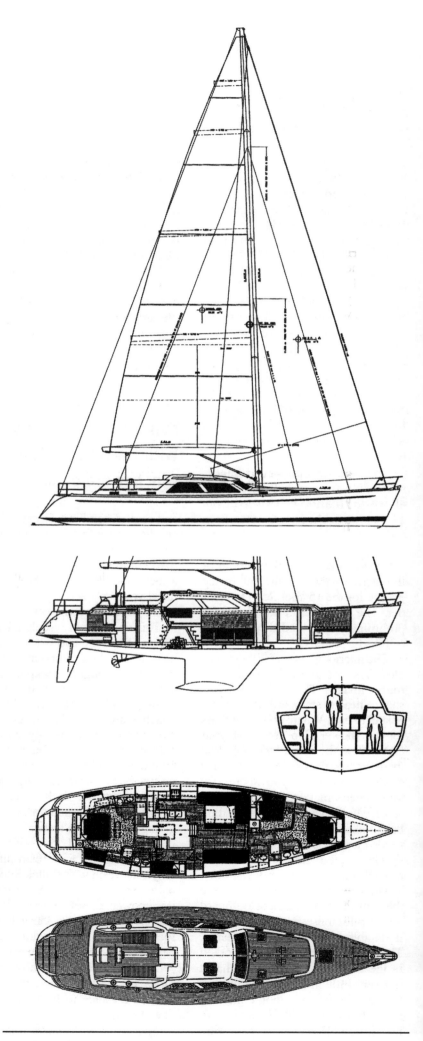

This Frers-designed cruiser features an interesting layout.

LOA 66'5"; LWL 58'1"; Beam 18'; Draft 9'2"; Displacement 76,060 lbs.; Ballast 30,864 lbs.; Sail Area 2,045 sq. ft.; SA/D 18.21; D/L 173; L/B 3.69; Auxiliary Yanmar 200 horsepower; Fuel 650 gals.; Water 300 gals.

Gumboot 56
Traditional Cruiser

Here's what you get when you combine a picky client, in this case John Steele, owner of Covey Island Boatworks, and a designer skilled in traditional types, Nigel Irens of the UK. John knew exactly what he wanted. He wanted a schooner to replace the 1893 cutter *Marguerite T* he had cruised with his family during a yearlong sabbatical. The new boat was to carry over a lot of *Marguerite T*'s design features and most assuredly be designed and built according to a faithful traditional schooner model.

This 56-footer weighs 85,800 pounds. If we assume a DWL of 45 feet this gives us a D/L of 420. John says he understands the bene-

Covey Island is very good at this type of boat. John's a lucky man.

fits of a heavy boat, and I assume he means comfort at sea and safety in terminal conditions. I don't think you can add speed to that list. Performance, however, can mean many things. This full-keel hull carries a total of 31,000 pounds of ballast, 17,000 pounds of which is internal ballast in the form of concrete in the bilge. The external ballast consists of 14,000 pounds of lead. This boat will be very stiff and have good directional stability. But it won't turn on a dime, and I'll wager that a bowthruster gets installed at some point.

To my eye the most interesting aspect of this hull is the stern. We go from a nearly slab-sided midsection with very full garboards (the better to house that internal ballast) and copious deadrise to a stern shape that appears to be neither a transom type nor a double-ender nor a fantail-type, but some type of hybrid. According to John, he battled Irens over this stern and won because this is exactly the stern shape he had on the *Marguerite T*. It's a devilish stern shape to plank in wood, and I happened to be talking to John the day they were planking it. The rest of the hull shape is predictable with fair and attractive waterlines showing a hint of hollow at the entry. I

don't care for the cut in the bulwarks, and I think the sheer is a little flat aft.

The rig is pure schooner with a topsail on the mainmast. I'm fascinated by the little minibowsprit or "spritinni" above the real bowsprit. It even appears to have its own little bobstay-inni. Note that the real bowsprit is off centerline passing alongside the stem without interrupting it. I love that feature. In the old days these bowsprits were often reefable.

Chainplates are external. The working jib is on a self-tacking boom. I have two sailplans, a "traditional" sailplan with two topsails and three headsails, and a "rationalized" sailplan with a topsail and two headsails. If we use the sail area figure on the traditional plan, we get an SA/D of 17.71, but I would assume that includes the area of all the headsails shown on the sailplan rather than I and J. Imagine what that inner jib, the staysail, would say if it could talk: "Help me, I'm suffocating!"

The engine is a Perkins 85-horsepower 4-236. If you have become accustomed to 85 Yanmar horses I need to tell you that these English Perkins horses are of a different breed. Instead of pounding their little hooves off at 3,000 rpm to get 85 horses, the Perkins' big, brawny English horses will do it at less that 2,500 rpm, and do it at a low, comfortable and reassuring frequency.

The interior is laid out specifically for John's family. There are three staterooms and one big head with a bathtub. The fo'c'sle is huge and could easily be used as additional crew quarters. The galley is up in the small pilothouse area aft along with the dinette and nav station. Across from the owner's stateroom is the "office/library." I just don't see one big area where everyone on board could gather for conversation.

Covey Island is very good at this type of boat. John's a lucky man.

Covey Island Boatworks, Petite Riviere, Nova Scotia, Canada BOJ 2PO. (902) 688-2843. www.coveyisland.com

July 2002

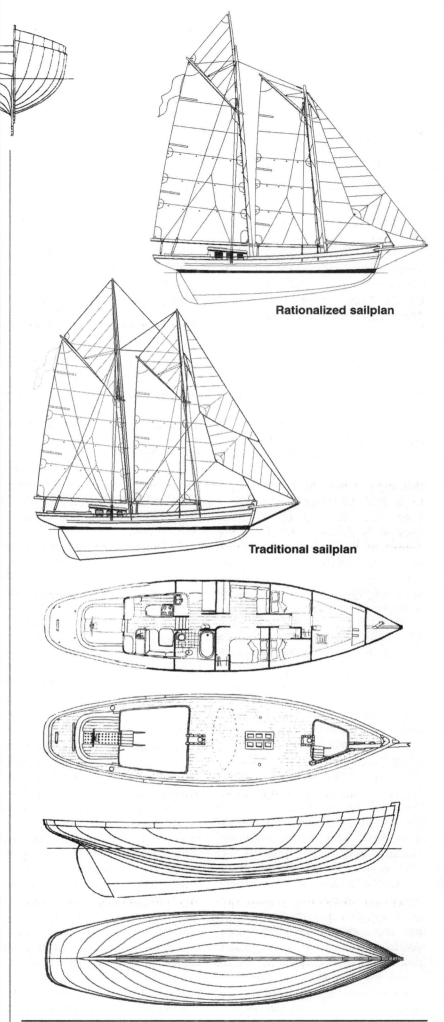

Rationalized sailplan

Traditional sailplan

A boat that says tradition from keel to trunk.

LOA 68'6"; LOD 56'; DWL 45'; Beam 15'; Draft 8'; Displacement 85,800 lbs.; Ballast 31,000 lbs.; Sail Area 2,154 sq. ft. (traditional), 1,835 sq. ft. (rationalized); SA/D 17.71; D/L 420; L/B 3.73; Auxiliary Perkins 4-236; Fuel 265 gals.; Water 330 gals.

Sonny
Bluewater Cruiser

This beautiful 70-footer comes to us from Dieter Empacher in Marblehead, Massachusetts. *Sonny* is his third design for this client, Albert Phelps. The design directive called initially for an aluminum boat, but the owner's desire for a recessed cove stripe led to the exploration of other methods. Eventually Steve White's Brooklin Boat Yard in Maine convinced the owner that a cold molded boat would be the best way to achieve the desired aesthetic ends. The result is a boat that is beautiful from every angle. You wouldn't change a single line on this design. I think as we go through this review we should concentrate on what makes this boat so aesthetically successful.

Clearly a major contribution to any boat's looks is the yard. Ugly boats can be built by insensitive builders working with beautiful drawings. Conversely, beautiful boats can be built by a skilled and aesthetically sensitive yard from not-so-beautiful drawings. If you have any doubts as to the Brooklin yard's abilities take a look at the Joel White W-class boat *Wild Horses*. It's a masterpiece.

While short ends may make sense to a VPP run intended to get the most knots out of a given LOA, short ends are seldom pretty. Short-ended boats can look handsome, brutish, powerful and businesslike, but I don't think I've ever seen one I would call beautiful. Dieter has given *Sonny* plenty of bow overhang and a generous amount of stern overhang. In fact, working with an LOA of 69 feet, 10 inches, the DWL is only 58 feet. That's almost 12 feet devoted to overhangs. Overhang forward can work well for a cruising boat. It gives you greater deck area forward, keeps the anchor well away from the stem and makes for a drier boat in a seaway.

Dieter's sheerline for *Sonny* is strong in its amount of sweep and yet gentle enough not to be too detracting. Beam is modest at 16 feet, 6 inches for an L/B of 4.23. The D/L is on the low end of "medium" at 175.6. The 8-foot draft is complimented by a large wing starting at around the 30-percent position on the tip chord. Obviously with 70 feet to work

with you can do a flush deck design without exaggerating the freeboard. Flush deck designs tend to highlight the sheerline. In this design there is very little that is going on to distract your eye from the sweep of the sheer. Looking at the sailplan you can see

Dieter's sheerline for Sonny is strong in its amount of sweep and yet gentle enough not to be too detracting.

the small structure that provides the height for the cockpit coamings and the companionway. This blends in well with the hull. The lines of this structure are very simple.

The rig shows triple, swept spreaders and in-boom furling for the mainsail. There is provision made for a self-tacking staysail for heavy air, and with a flush deck forward, there is nothing to stop the self-tacking track from going as far outboard as needed to give the staysail a good shape on a close reach. Actually I'd like to see this one even wider to give more sheeting options. There is a clew board on the staysail to allow for varying the lead angle. Winches are Harken hydraulic. Better get your thumb in shape. Pushing those buttons can be grueling.

This is a wonderful and comfortable layout, although I'm not wild about circular dinettes. They look great on the drawing, but I prefer some corners to wedge into. Note the huge "navigatorium" on this layout. I like the berth arrangement aft. There is a double to starboard and a single berth to port. The other staterooms forward have upper and lower single berths.

If Mr. Phelps calls you and asks you to go cruising with him on *Sonny* I suggest you accept.

Dieter Empacher Designs, P.O. Box 194, Marblehead, MA 01945. **www.dieterempacher.com** *(781) 631-5705.*

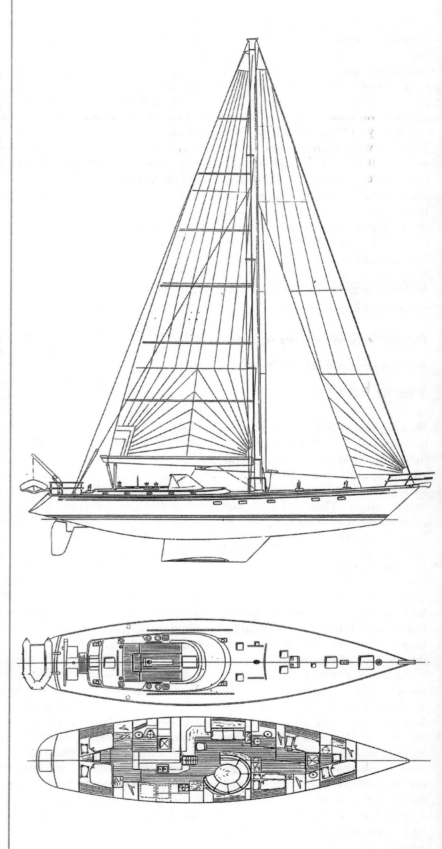

A classic cruiser with great curves.

LOA 69'10"; DWL 58'; Beam 16'6"; Draft 8'; Displacement 76,750 lbs.; Ballast 28,000 lbs.; Sail Area 2,170 sq. ft.; SA/D 19.2; D/L 175.6; L/B 4.23; Auxiliary 230-hp Yanmar; Fuel 550 gals.; Water 430 gals.

Spirit 70
Bluewater Cruiser

This is a spectacular looking design from UK designers Sean McMillan and Mick Newman. The boat is currently under construction and is being promoted as "the most beautiful bluewater cruiser available."

Clearly these drawings are hand drawn. There is a delicacy and sensitivity to the line weight that is very hard to get with a computer. I like this style of drafting. It's fun to look at. I'm not wild about the design though.

From hull shape to joinery detailing this is a vintage type design and the builder appears to be doing a wonderful job of carrying that look through.

Here is a 71-foot, 10-inch boat with a DWL of 50 feet, 6 inches and that means 21 feet, 4 inches of overhangs. That means there will be a lot of boat not contributing to sailing length. Of course you will pick up some sailing length as the boat heels but it would be far more effective as static waterline length. Of course, then you would lose your attractive overhangs.

The spoon-bow profile means that the forward waterlines will be rather full. Note that there is no defined forefoot or "chin" on this design. Look back at the Finngulf and you will see what I mean. Right at the DWL or the cutwater there is a distinct knuckle. The sections of the bow as they approach that knuckle become almost conelike in shape resulting in a soft, U-shaped section at the entry. You can see this on the AC boats as it is exaggerated in the bow forward of the Davidson knuckle. Given the bow profile and lack of distinct knuckle in the profile I have to assume that these bow sections are very V-shaped.

Now look at the heart shape of the transom. This is a pretty shape but requires hollows in the aft sectional shape. The keel bulb looks very full forward to my eye. I'll agree that these shapes may be attractive in the same way a 1958 Oldsmobile is attractive.

These boats are custom built so it makes little sense to nitpick on the interior drawings. Owners can have the layout they want. The interior shown here has the disadvantage of having the galley accessed from the aft end away from the dining area. Maybe if you have a paid chef you want to isolate them from the owner and his guests.

The deck plan features an oval cockpit coaming surrounding twin cockpits. The steering cockpit aft shows the seat being tapered away almost to nothing exactly where I think I would want to sit. There's no way my fanny is going to be comfortable on a seat 14 inches wide. I'd want to see that widest part of the seat on the sides where you are most likely to sit. I find I almost never sit on centerline when I am sailing.

One important feature of this deck plan is the aft well for the big inflatable dinghy. There are huge, flush deck hatches to access this area but there is no indication on the drawings as to how the dinghy is lifted, deployed and retrieved.

The Spirit is built with Brazilian cedar planking over a male mold. The planking is epoxy bonded and bronze fastened. This planking is then skinned in two layers of 3-millimeter Khaya laid 45 degrees to the planking and again epoxy bonded. Keelson, stem, horn post and stern post are all Brazilian mahogany. Floors, engine bed and mast support are Iroko or mahogany. All plywood used is Bruynzeel with major joinerwork components bonded to the hull for more support. The photos I have of the boat under construction are very impressive. It does look marvelous.

From hull shape to joinery detailing this is a vintage type design and the builder appears to be doing a wonderful job of carrying that look through. While the design itself may not be my cup of tea there can be little doubt that this boat will be a head turner in any harbor, in any fleet, in any year.

Spirit Yachts Ltd., Ipswich Haven Marina, New Cut East, Ipswich IP3 0EA. 44 1473 214 715. **www.spirityachts.com**

March 2003

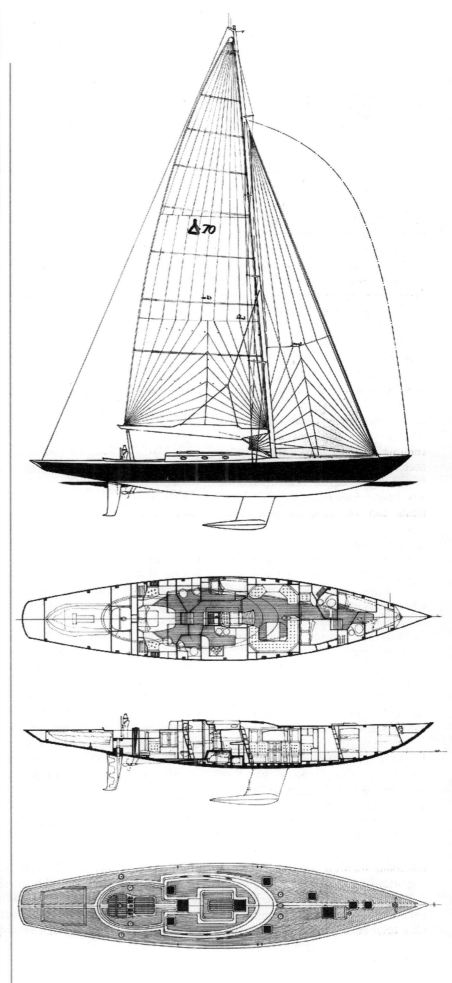

Elegant detailing adorns this classic head turner.

LOA 71'2"; LWL 49'6"; Beam 15'2"; Draft 9'5"; Displacement 48,000 lbs.; Ballast 21,600 lbs.; Sail Area 1,680 sq. ft.; SA/D 20.4; D/L 177; L/B 4.69; Auxiliary Yanmar 100-hp; Fuel 104 gals.; Water 99 gals.

Pelagic II
Expedition Cruiser

This design by Tony Castro deserves a close look. It's not a particularly good looking boat, but Tony Castro has a good eye and can and has drawn beautiful boats. In this case Mr. Castro has drawn a very purposeful looking design for Skip Novak who intends to take the boat to the most remote and demanding cruising areas. Maybe the aesthetics of this boat are better understood if we think of this design as a workboat and not a "yacht."

At 110,000 pounds of displacement this is a heavy boat, but with a DWL of 64 feet the D/L is only 187. Beam is moderate with a L/B of 3.77 and a centerboard allows the minimum draft to be a modest 3 feet, 9 inches. The wedge-shaped board closes up the slot to reduce drag and eliminates the chance of something getting stuck in the slot. The rudder will hinge up dinghy-style to allow the boat to function in shoal waters. The bow is knuckled above the DWL to allow it to ride over the ice. The vertical transom provides for max sailing length and maximum length on deck. There is tumblehome amidships to help protect the deck edge. There is 26,400 pounds of lead ballast in the bilge of this boat for a ballast-to-displacement ratio of 24 percent. The limit of positive stability is 130 degrees.

This interior is different and I really like it. Aft there is the "great cabin." "I'll meet you in the great cabin." This large cabin aft features a big wraparound settee and two tables that can be linked to form one big table so the entire crew can congregate and share a meal in comfort. There is almost no labeling on this drawing so I guess that's a fireplace on centerline facing aft in the great cabin. The galley is perfect. Note that the galley range is forward and mounted 90 degrees to the centerline. I'm not sure if it's gimbaled or not.

This layout starts with a pilothouse with inside steering and a nav station. You go down forward from the pilothouse to enter the sleeping area where there are six staterooms divided by the large centerboard trunk, two heads and a

workshop. You can access the great cabin by going through the starboard aft stateroom or you can go back up into the pilothouse and access the great cabin from there. There are five watertight doors in this layout including one to the engine room. There is a huge forepeak and a large lazarette.

As you might expect, given the task, the rig for this boat is on the small side with a SA/D of 16.37. All three headsails will be carried on roller furling. The masthead

This cabin aft features a big wraparound settee and two tables so the entire crew can congregate and share a meal in comfort.

genoa has plenty of overlap. There is a high-clewed yankee inside of that and a staysail for heavy air inside of the yankee. The spin pole will be stowed on the mast. Chainplates are outboard.

The cockpit sole is the main deck. You can see over the pilothouse when standing and the pilothouse top extends over the forward part of the cockpit for shelter. There is a two-pronged, boxlike structure running forward of the pilothouse for deck stowage lockers. This structure allows a dinghy to be nestled in. There is a pedestal winch just aft of the mast between the prongs and I wonder if it is for raising the centerboard but I also see halyards are lead to it.

In order to build a boat of ultimate "toughness," Novak and Castro chose aluminum, which they will leave unpainted. If all goes well with *Pelagic II* this will be the first in a series of charter boats. The more I studied this design the more I liked it and the better it looked.

Tony Castro Ltd., Rio House, 76 Satchell Lane, Hamble, Southampton SO31 4HL, England. **www.tonycastroyachts.co.uk** *E-mail: designoffice@tonycastro.co.uk. 44 23 80 45 47 22.*

January 2004

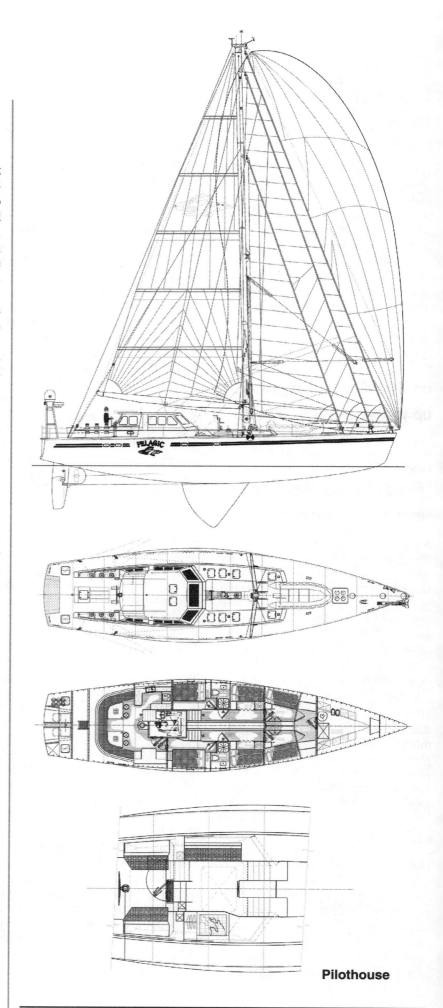

Pilothouse

A workboat designed for harsh Southern Ocean conditions.

LOA 74'2"; LWL 64'; Beam 19'8"; Draft 12'6" (board down), 3'9" (board up); Displacement 110,000 lbs.; Ballast 26,455 lbs.; Sail Area 2,368 sq. ft.; SA/D 16.5; D/L 187; L/B 3.77; Auxiliary Cummins 250-hp; Fuel 1,717 gals.; Water 265 gals.

Swan 75 RS
Luxury Cruiser

Let's just say you want a comfortable daysailer but you also want comfort below and you have a really long dock. Well, then you need to trade in your Babson Island 35 for a new Swan 75. This boat does it all, and talk about style. The hull and rig design is by German Frers and I think the deck and interior design is done by the Nautor team of in-house designers. There are two versions, the Flush Deck and the Raised Saloon. While the flush-deck version is spectacularly beau-

If you are not comfortable on this boat you better give up yachting.

tiful in every way I'm going to restrict my commentary to the raised-saloon version because to my eye it's more challenging to design and more interesting.

This 75 marks the beginning of Swan's new line of cruising boats. These boats have been designed to optimize cruising comfort and performance. The hull profile shows a hull with deeper forward sections for a softer ride when on the wind, according to the brochure. The ends are short without appearing truncated. The D/L is 165 using the "loaded" displacement. The L/B is 3.91 and the draft loaded is 9 feet, 10 inches. By today's standards this is a modest draft for a boat of this size. The ballast-to-loaded-displacement ratio is 27 percent. If we use the "light" displacement the ballast-to-displacement ratio is 32 percent.

I think with this pedigree you can be assured that the performance of this boat will be just fine. Frers' sheers are always perfect. While the sheer is quite flat there is still a subtle balance to its spring. Note the trademark double-cambered transom on this Swan. This makes for an attractive transom. I used the same detail on my 65-footer *ICON* but I did feel some degree of guilt.

Yeah, yeah, yeah, the deck is great. Let's go below. What's not to like down here? The crew goes forward with a stateroom right next to the galley. There is a crew's mess and head along with upper and lower berths. The galley is huge.

"Would that be white or dark bread with that tuna fish sandwich, sir?" I can't tell from the drawing what everything is in the galley but I think it's safe to assume that everything is there. The saloon is captured within the trace of the deckhouse so you lose the use of the volume outboard but in this case the boat's so big it really doesn't matter.

The port dinette is mammoth and I'd guess it's about 10 feet long. There is a deep settee to port and large navigation center. There is a "mud room" directly aft of the companionway where you can shed your wet gear before entering the real accommodations. There are two staterooms aft with the owner's cabin in the stern with a big queen-sized double berth. Both aft heads have shower stalls. There is another stateroom adjacent to the galley and I'm not sure if this is for a guest or for the captain. Either way it has its own head and shower and is very spacious. If you are not comfortable on this boat you better give up yachting.

The rig is barely fractional to make room for the head of the asymmetrical chute when jibing. There are four spreaders with 29 degrees of sweep. The chainplates are well outboard, allowing the jib to sheet inboard. The sailplan shows no big overlapping jibs. A carbon fiber mast with Park Avenue boom is standard. I like the look of this boat. The house is prominent but attractive in its proportions.

The deckplan shows a giant cockpit with symmetrically opposed dinettes forward and twin wheels and contoured helm seats aft. The working part of the cockpit is separated from the lounging part of the cockpit.

The drawings show some strange contours to the cockpit seatbacks but I suppose if I see the boat in person they may make sense. Try as I might, I have picked the only nit I can find.

For most of us the Swan 75 is as much a fantasy as is the Babson 35. The scales are different. That's all.

Nautor Swan New York, Swan Building 12-B, Foot of Washington Blvd., Stamford, Connecticut 06902. **www.nautorgroup.com** *(203) 425-9700.*

May 2003

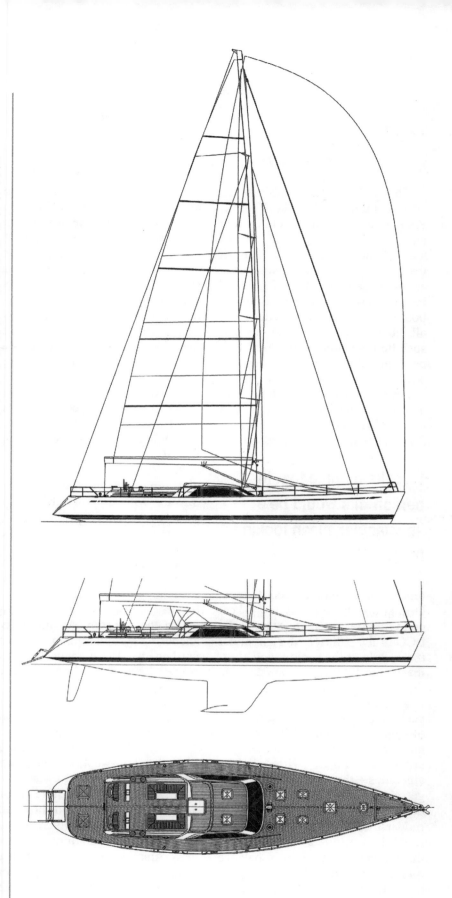

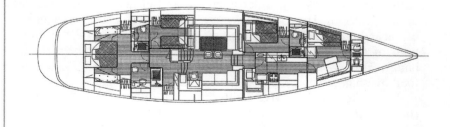

Another attractive design from Nautor.

LOA 74'6"; LWL 64'; Beam 19'; Draft 9'2"; Displacement 83,800 lbs.; Ballast 26,500 lbs.; Sail Area 2,632 sq. ft.; SA/D 22.1; D/L 165; L/B 3.9; Auxiliary Cummins 180hp: Fuel 400 gals.; Water 317 gals.

Baltic 79
Bluewater Cruiser

This new Baltic combines the design talents of Judel/Vrolijk, R&J Design, Vismara Yacht Design and the Baltic in-house design team. That's enough to ensure all the details are covered. This boat is about the same length as *Pelagic II* but obviously it's a very different boat. That's what custom design is all about—specific solutions for specific client requirements. I suspect this client wanted something sleek, comfortable and fast.

Judel/Vrolijk did the hull, keel and rudder shapes. The D/L is 95.5 and the L/B is 4.02. Draft is 9 feet, 2 inches with the board up and 14

> **I would imagine that in person this would be a spectacular, clean looking boat.**

feet, 9 inches with the board down. One of the benefits of the T-keel configuration is that it puts the LCG of the ballast bulb right under the middle of the keel fin and eliminates most twisting moments on the fin. Of course it does make for a wonderful kelp catcher so I suspect there will have to be some type of kelp cutter device. Clearly if you have a light boat—outfitted for cruising comfort with all the amenities—the only way you can get good sail carrying power is to do a fin-and-bulb-style keel. The rudderstock is near perpendicular to the hull profile at the stock and there appears to be a lot of balance on this big rudder. With my eye I'd estimate close to 20 percent. In plan view the hull is very typical with perhaps a slightly wider than normal transom. The transom is cut off near vertical. This boat has a total of 6 feet, 6 inches of overhangs. That's 2 feet, 6 inches less total overhang than a Cal 40.

The interior has five staterooms but I don't see a double berth anywhere. The customer obviously did not care about double berths and once again that's what custom design is all about. There is a big engine room with standing headroom. The galley is on the small side for a boat this

size and it's aft in an area set aside for paid crew. There is direct access to the aft cockpit from the crew's area. Note the dining counter adjacent to the galley and the on centerline nav station. The guest staterooms are separated by the lifting keel trunk. Each stateroom has its own head and shower stall. The owner's stateroom is all the way forward and the berths look bigger than single berths but smaller than full doubles. The saloon looks like a nice place to hang out and enjoy a meal. I think that is a bar shown on the starboard side just aft of the big dinette.

The deck plan shows two cockpits separated by the mainsheet traveler with the forward cockpit removed from sail handling activities. Halyard winches are mounted on the deck at the mast. Sheet winches are flanking the aft cockpit with its two wheels. There is an extra large flush hatch to access the big fo'c'sle. The dinghy will stow inside the transom. An innovative anchoring system remains invisible until needed. I'm not wild about the overall look of this boat on paper but I would imagine that in person this would be a spectacular, clean looking boat. The styling was done by Vismara Yacht Design.

The SA/D of this design is 26.12. Spreaders are swept 26 degrees and there is a cutter stay forward. The boom will be a "canoe-style" boom designed to catch and hold the mainsail when it is lowered.

The hull is built from a carbon, glass, Aramid, epoxy composite over Core-Cell foam, vacuum bagged and post-cured for 16 hours at 122 degrees. The deck is all carbon over Core-Cell and cooked at 122 degrees. "Is that deck I smell cooking?"

If the owner of the Baltic 79 offers to let you take it north for a couple of weeks I suggest you jump at the chance.

Baltic Yachts Ltd., Balticvägen 1, FIN-68555 Bosund, Finland, 358 6 7819 200. In the U.S. contact Baltic Yachts USA, 53 America's Cup Avenue, Newport, RI 02840. **www.balticyachts.com** *(401) 846-0300.*

January 2004

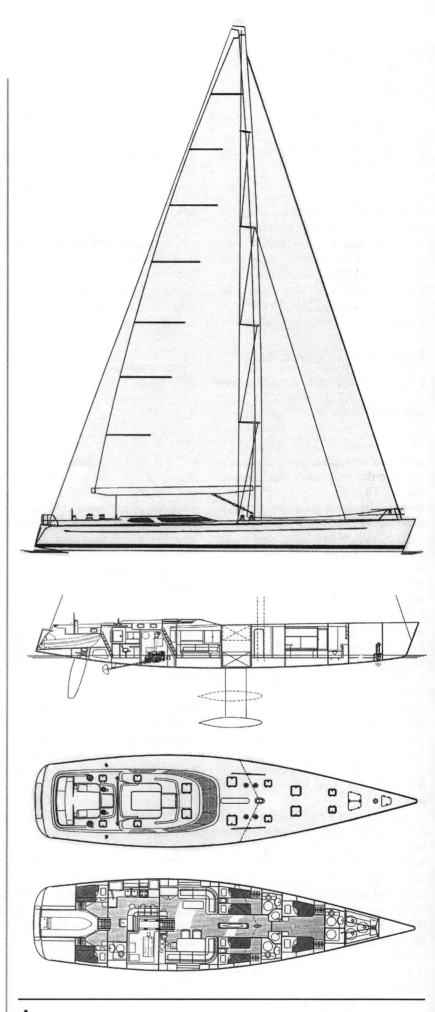

A sleek looking semicustom design for world cruising.

LOA 78'9"; LWL 72'2"; Beam 19'7"; Draft 14'9" (keel down), 9'2" (keel up); Displacement 80,469 lbs.; Ballast 31,636 lbs.; Sail Area 3,042 sq. ft.; SA/D 26.12; D/L 95.5; L/B 4.02; Auxiliary Yanmar 6LP-STE; Fuel 660 gals.; Water 530 gals.

Christoffel's Lighthouse
Traditional Cruiser

Let's just ignore the fact that this cutter is 90 feet long for a moment and reflect on the fact that, like John Steele's schooner, this Gerry Dijkstra design is also a traditional-looking boat, similar to the Channel cutter type and actually based on the 1886 America's Cup contender *Mayflower*. Where this design fundamentally differs from the Irens design is that it combines a traditional topsides look with a very modern underbody. This is my very favorite kind of boat, and Mr. Dijkstra has done a beautiful job with this design. "Of course," you could say. "It's 90 feet on deck!" That's true, but still, I can't find a line I'd change on this design. Well …

The hull, which will be built in aluminum, shows attractive arclike sections (No, not Noah's) with a wide BWL, extended stern counter and dead-plumb stem. The keel lifts hydraulically to reduce the draft from 14 feet, 2 inches to 8 feet, 6 inches. The rudder is hung on a skeg. The D/L is 185. Deadrise increases as you go aft giving the transom almost a heart shape. In a design like this I think it's appropriate to compromise performance a tiny bit to make the transom shape look beautiful.

The all-carbon rig is well forward and carries a self-tacking working jib along with a larger genoa tacked to the end of the bowsprit. The SA/D is 22. The mainsail will furl into the boom. All winches will be hydraulic, and I would imagine that the sheet winches will be captive-type reel winches.

To my eye this design has the look of a good-sailing boat. The design goal was a rig that could be handled by two people (sure, as long as everything is going fine). While looking at the sailplan, notice the way the lines of the hull work together. There is that accent line at deck level, which is not quite parallel with the sheer. Then there's that rub strip just below deck level, which isn't parallel with either the sheer or the deck line.

Each new line gives the clever designer another possibility to control and add sophistication to the look of the boat. Even the boxy deck structures look perfect.

The owner is planning a trip to the Arctic for this boat so the interior is designed with cold weather in mind. Now here's a boat with room for the entire crew to gather

This is one of the most attractive designs I have seen in some time.

in one place. There is a big dinette in the pilothouse along with an extensive navigation station. There is access to the owner's stateroom from the pilothouse, and this stateroom features split head and shower compartments, settees, a queen-sized berth, lots of lockers and direct access to the cockpit.

If I'm reading the drawing correctly, the keel trunk divides the saloon area with a conversation nook to port aft of the wraparound galley. The galley is big enough for me to prepare my famous Scottish apple pie. No, the apples aren't Scottish. I just pour Scotch over the apples before I put them in the pie crust. The big dinette is to starboard with four separate chairs and room for at least eight to dine. There are three more staterooms forward along with three more heads. There are crew berths shown in the lazarette. The engine room with its 300-horsepower Lugger is below the pilothouse.

Clearly this is a world-class yacht. I find nothing about it not to like, except the price. This is one of the most attractive designs I have seen in some time. I much prefer this traditional approach to styling over the more prevalent Euro poodle-puller look.

Gerard Dijkstra & Partners, Kruithuisstraat 21, 1018 WJ, Amsterdam, Holland. 31 20 670 95 33. www.gdnp.nl

July 2002

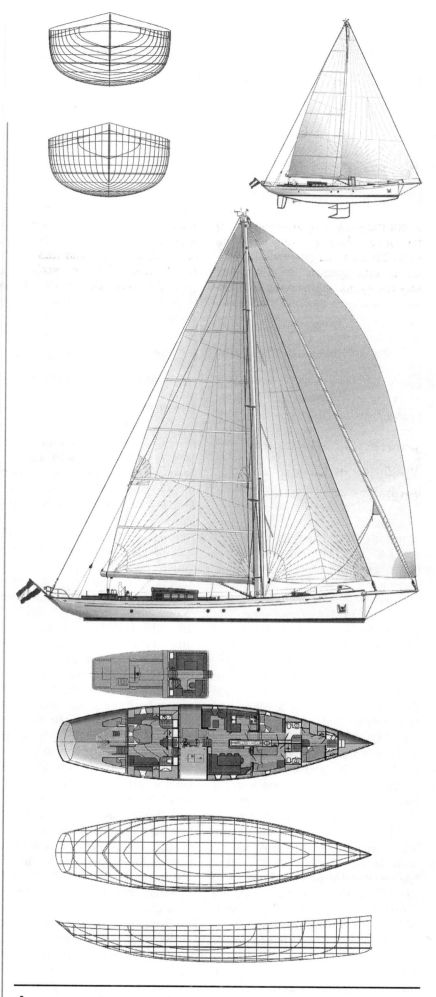

A deceptively modern cruiser based on classic lines.

LOA 106'; LOD 90'; LWL 76'9"; Beam 22'4"; Draft 8'6" (keel up), 14'2" (keel down); Displacement 187,000 lbs.; Ballast 48,000 lbs.; Sail Area 4,500 sq. ft.; SA/D 22; D/L 185; L/B 4.02; Auxiliary 300-hp Lugger; Fuel 730 gals.; Water 520 gals.

Paraiso
Luxury Cruiser

This 108-footer from the Ted Fontaine office represents, in my opinion, yacht design at its finest level. This design is exquisitely drawn whether you like the type or not. The boat is being built in New Zealand by Alloy Yachts and is scheduled for launch in spring.

Ted calls this hull shape "the proprietary Delta Form hull." I'm not sure what makes it proprietary, it just looks like a deep, heavy boat to me. The basic hull form is similar to that used for years by Ted Hood, who Ted Fontaine worked for. Draft with the board up is 7 feet, and with board down it's 18 feet, 9 inches. The rudder has a blade that extends its span when the centerboard is down. The D/L is 274 and the L/B is 4.11. The long overhangs give this design an elegant and classic look. Note the hint of concavity in the counter profile aft. Just to help you put this design in perspective, there are 104,600 pounds of ballast.

The layout puts the crew quarters and galley forward. There are two crew cabins with over and under berths, a crew's mess and two heads that share a shower stall. The owner's party goes aft and there are two staterooms with double berths and one with two single berths. Each stateroom aft has its own head with shower and the owner's head has a bidet and what looks to me like a small tub. The owner's stateroom has a walk-in closet, large desk, locker for an exercise bike and access to the aft cockpit. I guess if all the winches are powered you will need that exercise bike.

You can lounge in the lower saloon. You can lounge in the raised saloon. You can lounge in the deck-level saloon. "Where did I leave my drink?" With all this lounging the exercise bike is making more sense. The nav station is in the deck-level saloon. There is a real bar with bar stools in the raised saloon. With that

paid crew doing all the work you might as well hit the bottle. Formal dining will be in the lower saloon while informal dining can be at the dinette in the deck-level saloon. The crew has their own access through a hatch

I guess if all the winches are powered you will need that exercise bike.

directly forward of the mast. This is a really nice layout but on a boat of this size I would expect a nice layout. If I had to nitpick, and I feel the need, I'd pick on the seven different levels required to carry this layout off.

The deck layout features a small cockpit aft with direct access to the owner's stateroom. There is no forward stateroom. Where the "cockpit" would be there is deck-level accommodations with twin wheels forward of seats that appear to be about 7 feet long. The rest of the "cockpit" seating is under the covered area where there are two dinettes and the nav station. The two large winches aft are probably to help with stern-to docking in addition to being available for the chute. Genoa and mainsheet winches will undoubtedly be captive type and hidden away. I'm struck by how few hatches there are on this design. I suppose that's a reflection of the quality of the air conditioning. Still, I like hatches and I like at least trying to live in the ambient air temperature as long as possible without mechanical assist. If it were too hot for me I would just sail somewhere else.

There's not a line out of place on this boat. Job well done, Ted.

Fontaine Design Group, 92 Maritime Dr., Portsmouth, RI 02871. (401) 682-9101. **www.fontainedesigngroup.com**

March 2004

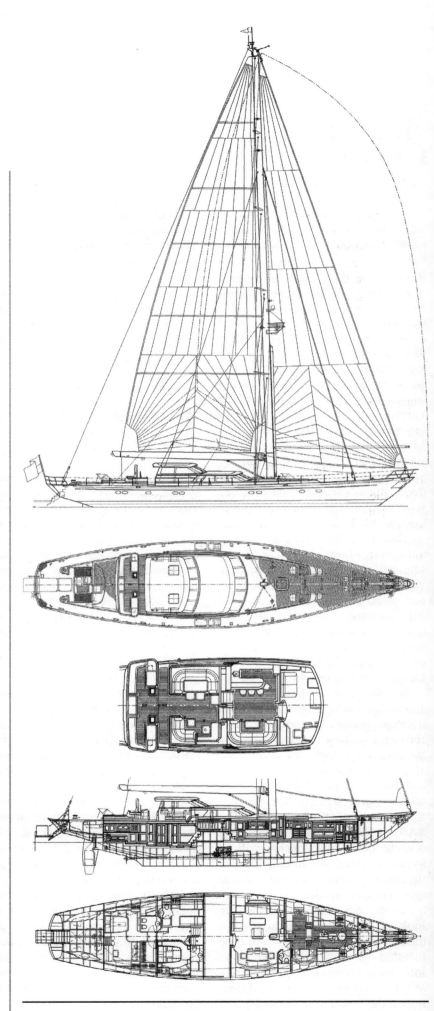

There's room for lounging aboard this classic Fontaine design.

LOA 108'2"; LWL 82'1"; Beam 26'3"; Draft 7' (board up) 18'9" (board down); Displacement 340,000 lbs.; Ballast 104,600 lbs.; Sail Area 5,180 sq. ft.; SA/D 17; D/L 274; L/B 4.11; Auxiliary Lugger 6108 A2 (double); Fuel 2,450 gals.; Water 1,800 gals.

Aventura

Luxury Cruiser

If you want to take your family world cruising and you want to be comfortable look no further. Ted Fontaine has designed this handsome 109-footer that should fit the bill. Face it, if you are not comfortable on this boat you are just not going to be comfortable. Period. This is an ultimate boat. I suppose if we added another 25 feet to LOA we could have a theatre or maybe a disco. But I'm not sure I'd want a disco on my own boat. I disco better in strange ports surrounded by total strangers.

This is a beautiful design in the classic yacht style. Ted used to run the Ted Hood design office so you can easily see the origins of this aesthetic approach. Ted nails the aesthetics. Ted calls the hull form the "Delta" form, which is a deep deadrise hull shape; the type we used to call a whale body. This high deadrise shape produces a hull that creates lift on its own, and performance on the wind, even with the centerboard up, can be respectable. I sailed a similar Hood boat and I was surprised at how well the boat sailed with the board up. Draft with the board up is 8 feet, 2 inches. The overhangs are long but it suits this style. The D/L is 169 based upon a displacement of 319,665 pounds. Just to put this in perspective, consider this boat has 121,252 pounds of ballast.

This interior is laid out with seven changes in cabin sole height. There is a mezzanine level immediately as you come below. This is the pilothouse and there is an inside steering station and nav center. Big wraparound settees will make this a prime spot for relaxing and watching the looky-loos walk up and down the dock.

From the pilothouse it's down five steps to saloon level. There is a giant dinette to port and a conversation area to starboard. Forward of the saloon and on the same level is the galley and crew dinette. I could cook in this galley. It's perfect. Down one step from the galley are the crew staterooms. There is a double berth forward of the saloon and on the

stateroom to port and a stateroom with upper and lower berths to starboard. Both crew staterooms have adjoining heads and shower stalls. There is plenty of hanging locker space for the crew's matching outfits. "Today I'd like the Gilbert and Sullivan suits, tomorrow the Star Wars suits." This crew will live comfortably.

I could cook in this galley. It's perfect.

Going down six steps aft from the saloon you enter the area of the owner's party staterooms and directly to port is an engine room workshop space. There are four staterooms here. The two staterooms on the starboard side share a head and shower stall. There is no day head in this boat. All the heads have to be accessed through a stateroom. I would want this feature changed—I have to pick on something.

The owner's stateroom is palatial and has its own access to the afterdeck. All in all you could sleep 12 on this boat. The lazarette and forepeak are huge. I might like to see this layout tried with fewer changes of level. The profile would probably suffer though.

All sail handling gear has been kept out of the cockpit area. The sheet winches are all aft of the cockpit. There is no mainsheet traveler. The cockpit is in two levels with the aft level raised so you can see over the pilothouse. A hard top bimini will shield those who choose to eat on deck at one of the two large cockpit dinettes.

Most of us would love to go world cruising with our families. It's a dream. For this lucky owner it will come true in this fabulous custom yacht built to perfection by Danish Yacht of Skagen, Denmark. I'd be just as happy with a 107-footer.

Fontaine Design Group, 92 Maritime Drive, Portsmouth, RI 02871. (401) 682-9101. **www.fontainedesigngroup.com**

September 2003

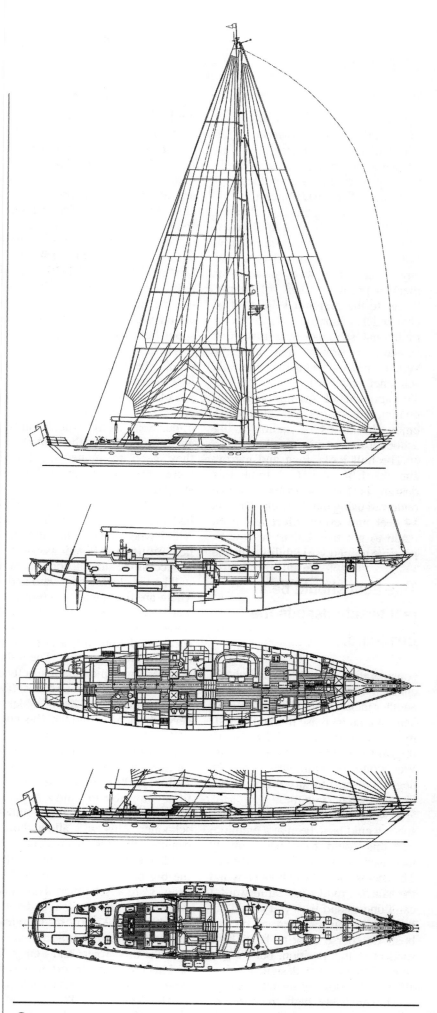

Classic aesthetics define this stately 109-footer.

LOA 108'11"; LWL 84'4"; Beam 26'4"; Draft 8'2"; Displacement 319,665 lbs.; Ballast 121,252 lbs.; Sail Area 5,272 sq. ft.; SA/D 18; D/L 169; L/B 4.12; Auxiliary Scania 420-hp; Fuel 2,860 gals.; Water 1,300 gals.

Aruna
Coastal Cruiser

About five years ago I was hired to design a large powerboat for wheelchair-bound charter clients in Alaska. It was one of the most fascinating projects I have ever done.

Today, Tom MacNaughton of Maine is designing this big schooner for sailors with physical disabilities. This includes sailors in wheelchairs, sailors who are sight-impaired and any other sailor with mobility or medical problems. This, of course, brings to the design a unique set of challenges. I suppose the choice of a traditional schooner was made for aesthetic reasons. There are few sights more beautiful than a schooner under a full press of sail. The thought of giving physically challenged sailors the chance to enjoy the thrills of sailing a big schooner makes my spirit soar.

The hull looks long and narrow and the L/B is 5.56. I think this design is the narrowest I have reviewed using that formula. Draft is 14 feet and every effort has been made to get the ballast as low as possible to increase stability, a prime

This boat should be a real beauty despite the freeboard.

consideration for sailors in wheelchairs. I, however, would have taken another tack. I would have increased beam for an increase in initial stability. A narrow boat with a low center of gravity can still be initially tender. We wouldn't want the first 15 degrees of heel to turn this ride into the wheelchair X-games.

I would also have thought deck space would have been at a premium and this could have been greatly increased if the beam were greater. The keel is cut away in both ends and the attached rudder is well forward. I can't understand why you would put the rudder this far forward on any boat. Of course a lot of boats have rudders in this position, but 99 percent of them were designed before 1955. But enough of the nit-picking.

The relatively high freeboard of this design is intended to provide deep bulwarks for safety. The stern fairs to a shapely transom with marked tumblehome. The D/L for this design is 123. I think the listed

displacement, considering the published ballast-to-displacement ratio of 40 percent, is on the optimistic side.

The rig is an "all inboard" schooner rig, i.e., there is no bowsprit and the main boom does not overhang the transom. The staysail is shown on a wishbone to make it self-tacking. The strange shape below the wishbone was a scuttle hatch, but that has been removed and replaced with a lower hatch. Using the total working sail area and not I, J, E and P—I get an SA/D of 26. With this proud spoon bow and the sweeping sheer this boat should be a real beauty despite the freeboard.

The accommodation plan for wheelchair sailors presents a special challenge. It's not the actual dimensions of the wheelchairs that are a problem but the turning radii they need to maneuver. Luckily there are well proven architectural standards that establish minimums for these clearances, and Tom has had the benefit of working closely with a wheelchair-bound architect to help refine these solutions.

Access to the accommodations will be via elevators forward and aft. There are four guest staterooms forward and some crew accommodations. There are additional crew accommodations aft, a large pantry and a captain's cabin. The saloon features three pilot berths outboard of extra-long, 23-foot settees. Twin port and starboard dining tables are very wheelchair friendly. This layout will be "transformable" so it can be tailored to the unique needs of individuals and groups.

Tom and his crew have the benefit of being able to build a 25 percent scale model of this unusual schooner. This will allow them to evaluate the design concept and if needed, even move the rudder aft on the big boat. The test "model" will be a 33-foot schooner. This model will also be taken on tour and used as a promotional tool to help raise money for the final project.

I like this project and I envy Tom and his group the opportunity to participate in such a creative challenge.

MacNaughton Yacht Designs Post Office Box 190, Eastport, ME 04631. (207) 853-6678. www.macnaughtongroup.com

April 2001

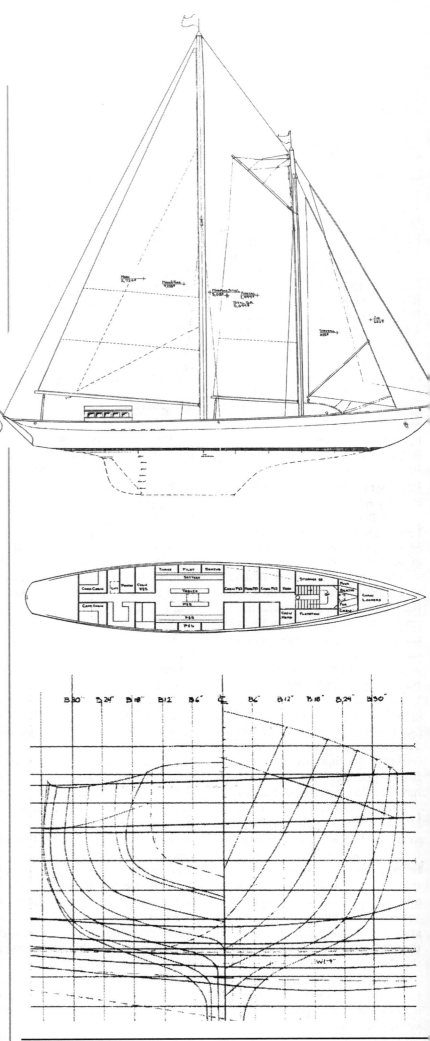

A special schooner for handicapped sailors.

LOA 133'6"; LWL 91'; Beam 24'; Draft 14'; Displacement 200,000 lbs.; Ballast 80,000 lbs.; Sail Area 5,699 sq. ft.; SA/D 26; D/L 118; L/B 5.56; Auxiliary 426-hp diesel.

Baltic 147
Bluewater Cruiser

For real comfort and privacy combined with boat speed you need something like this new Baltic 147. There's just nothing quite like 147 feet of LOA to pull all the various competing components together.

The design work on a big boat like this is a collaboration of several teams. This design team included Reichel/Pugh of San Diego, R & J Design and Design Unlimited, which worked on the interior and deck styling.

The hull shows that flattened canoe-body profile we see so often today. Note how the rocker seems to flatten around the keel. There could be several reasons for this, but I think it's done to push more volume toward the end of the boat to increase potential surfing speeds. In a boat of this size I can't imagine it's any rule-induced feature.

The D/L of this boat is 58. The L/B is 4.9. Compare this to the 2.54 of the little Shoalsailer. This is a skinny boat.

There is a lifting keel that provides 21 feet, 9 inches of draft in the down position. "Keel-up" draft is 13 feet, 1 inch. It takes a little mental adjustment, but the specs list the ballast at 97,000 pounds and that's probably shared between the stainless steel fin and the lead bulb.

Clearly this will be a very fast boat. I'm sure it will give the Wally boats a run for their money at the maxi-yacht regattas.

I think a yacht of this size should be spectacular, and not simply as a

These will truly be at least queen-size berths, probably king-size.

function of its size. I can't think of any reason why huge yachts should not be the most beautiful yachts. They are free of all the pragmatic considerations and restrictions that aesthetically challenge small boats. Freeboard is obviously not an issue. LOA restrictions don't exist. Headroom doesn't require an invasive cabintrunk.

Given those aesthetic freedoms, I just don't see the "poetry" in this design. The sheer is boring. It's essentially flat and that may be what you want with this narrow

hull shape, but I still like to see some statement in the sheerline.

The IMS snubbed-off bow treatment may give you the maximum sailing length for a given LOA but, hey, who are we kidding here.

There's no doubt that looking down on this monster from the dock it will be spectacular: Size alone dictates that. Still, I'd like to see an element of elegance that I feel is missing from this boat. Maybe the reason for this styling can be found in the owner's original requirement that the boat have the appearance of a lightweight racing yacht.

It's kind of funny when you read in the specs that this boat is designed for three couples in the owner's party. I can think of several 45-footers that could say the same, although these couples will have far larger staterooms. One stateroom is shown with twin berths rather than a double, but I'm sure that could be fixed. These will truly be at least queen-size berths, probably king-size.

The owner's stateroom is amidships. Unfortunately this puts the stateroom right below the center cockpit where it might be noisy. The forward staterooms are divided by the extensive lifting keel trunk. All staterooms have adjoining heads and showers.

The deck is designed with four cockpits: two for the guests who may want to steer the boat from time to time but don't care to tail a sheet (assuming this boat has winches that even need tailing), one for the twin wheels, and one for sailhandling with an arch overhead to carry the mainsheet traveler. There is a companionway leading down to the skipper's nav station in this last cockpit.

This hull will be built with Nomex honeycomb core and pre-preg carbon fiber. The auxiliary engine is a 700-horsepower diesel.

Next time I'm down scrubbing my boat, getting that grunge out that accumulates along the toerail, I'm going to be glad it's not 147 feet long.

Reichel/Pugh Yacht Design, 2924 Emerson St., Ste. 311, San Diego, CA 92106. (619) 223-2299. **www.reichel-pugh.com**

December 2000

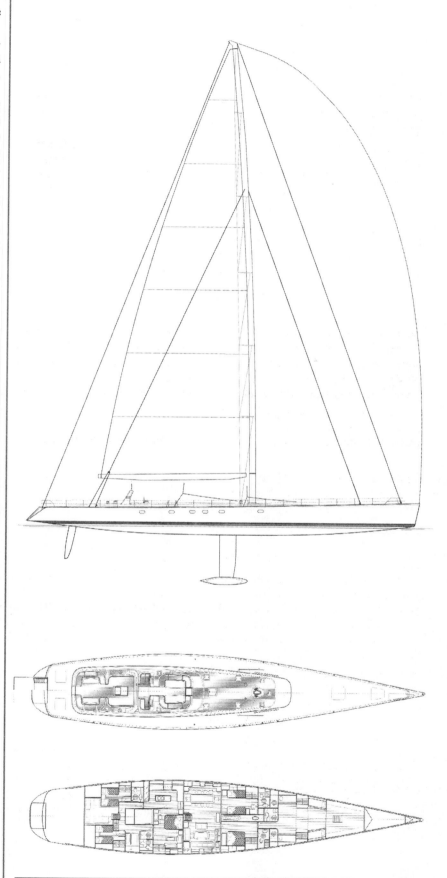

A megayacht in every sense of the word.

LOA 147'; DWL 121'; Beam 27'2"; Draft 21'9" (keel down), 13'1" (keel up); Displacement 230,000 lbs.; Ballast 97,000 lbs.; Sail Area 10,000 sq. ft. (with genoa); SA/D 42.6 (with genoa) ; D/L 58; L/B 4.9; Auxiliary 700-hp diesel; Fuel 1,500 gals.; Water 1,300 gals.

CRUISING-RACING
DESIGNS

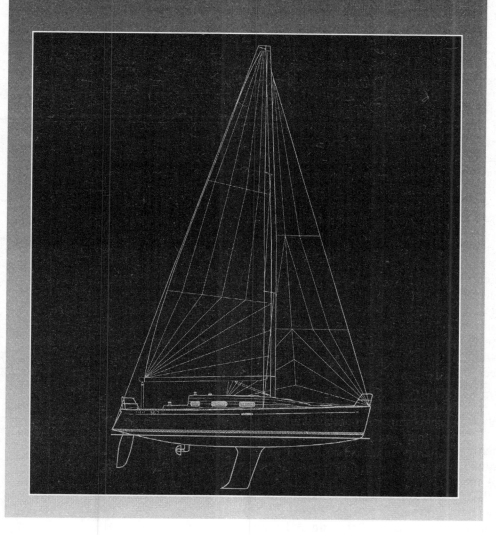

Ultimate 24
Racer-Cruiser

Pocket cruisers are close to my heart. My own cruising boat is 26 feet long and I love it. I'm a firm believer in keeping things simple and preserving the unique sailing lifestyle that initially attracted me. I don't need a hair dryer on board. I can survive without a microwave. I certainly don't want a TV on board, and—wonder of wonders—I have even found ice to be a trouble-free way of keeping my food and drinks cold.

Jim Antrim's Ultimate Sailboats-built Ultimate 24 has performance written all over it, and it was probably conceived more as a race boat than a cruiser. But that won't stop us from looking at it through a cruiser's eyes. This model was designed to fit in between Jim's Ultimate 20 and the Antrim 27, two boats that are also designed with speed in mind. The hull is short-ended to maximize sailing length with a D/L of 96. The keel can be raised and lowered for trailering, but you will leave it down while sailing. Keel-down draft is 5 feet, 6 inches. The keel foil is carbon fiber and the bulb is lead. With the keel up and the rudder removed you can launch this boat from a ramp.

Below there are quarter berths port and starboard, which extend forward to the forward end of the keel trunk. Forward of the keel trunk there is a counter to starboard with a sink and another counter to port with a locker outboard. The head is a porta potty type and located under the V-berths. I have this same arrangement on my own boat. It is inconvenient if your friend is a lady and she insists on using the head during the night. But a better solution would be hard to find. For me there's a certain cavalier appeal to breaking the stillness of the night

with a tinkle over the stern. "Ooh look, phosphorescence!"

I don't much care for this layout. I would prefer to see the galley aft where you could benefit from the unlimited headroom of the open companionway hatch. Of course,

This sporty little packet has performance written all over it.

this would interfere with at least one of the quarter berths. The other shortcoming of this interior, is the paucity of hanging lockers. A decent hanging locker would take a 24-inch-long chunk out of this layout. Cruising in the Pacific Northwest means you will get wet, and having a place to hang wet gear would be very convenient. My own boat has hanging space outboard of the settees and while the gear doesn't hang straight down (it drapes against the hull) at least it is out of the way.

The rig of the 24 shows a mainsail with lots of roach and a loose foot. The deck-mounted carbon bowsprit extends to fly a large asymmetrical chute. If you include the mainsail roach you get an SA/D of 35.3. If you base the SA/D on I, J, E and P with 100 percent of the foretriangle you get 27.96.

The 24 has an outboard for the auxiliary, but given the high SA/D and the general nature of this design I can't imagine that you would need to motor very often.

Ultimate Sailboats, 565 McQuaide Drive, La Selva Beach, CA 95076. (800) 724-5820. **www.ultimatesailboats.com**

October 2001

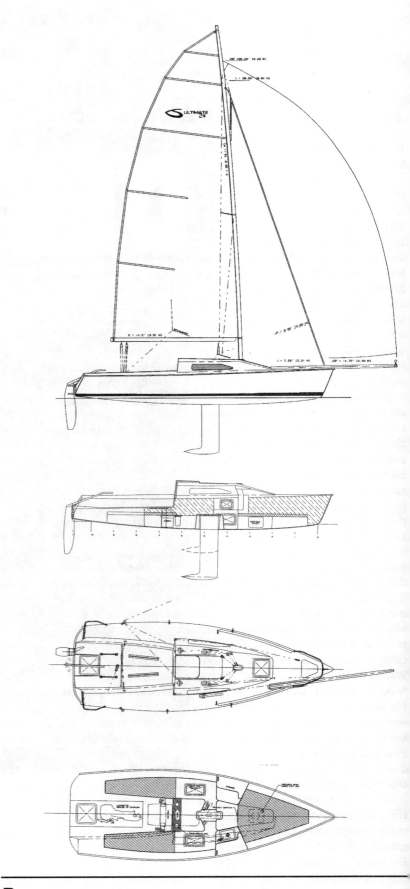

Performance cruiser with plenty of performance.

LOA 24'5"; LWL 21'2"; Beam 8'6"; Draft 5'6" (keel down), 2'11" (keel up); Displacement 2,040 lbs.; Ballast 750 lbs.; Sail Area 355 sq. ft. (plus roach); SA/D 35.3; D/L 96; L/B 2.88; Auxiliary 5-hp outboard.

Elan 31
Performance Cruiser

The interesting thing about this no man's land of handicap rules we seem to be in now is that we are seeing a return of dual-purpose boats much like the boats of the late 1960s and early 1970s.

This new Elan 31 designed by Rob Humphreys is another obvious attempt to do one boat that appeals to both racers and cruisers. I have always been a fan of Humphreys' work. The line of Elan models all have one thing in common—the Humphreys' trademark perky sheerline. I have the benefit of some photos of this boat and I can tell you confidently that this is a good looking boat. It looks a little bit "lumpy" in the drawings but as built it has a sweet appearance.

The hull profile shows the same skeg that we saw in the Sabre but this time it's proportionately much shorter and does not fair into the canoe body profile as it does on the Sabre. The rudder is on a vertical stock and the keel shows a large bulb. Overhangs are minimal and there appears to be a slight convexity to the bow profile. With a L/B of 2.94 this design breaks the 3 barrier and qualifies as a beamy boat. This fullness is carried out into both ends. The D/L is 190. Your draft choices are 6 feet and 4 feet, 11 inches. The keels are cast iron. There are no surprises in this hull shape that I can see other than an apparent fullness forward as indicated by the trace of the V-berth in plan view. Clearly Mr. Humphreys can draw a faster boat with an LOA of 30 feet, 10 inches, but in this case he had a variety of interior accommodation pressures to deal with and I think that is behind this beamy hull form.

It's pretty amazing when you look at this interior plan and consider what was considered adequate in a 30-footer 25 years ago. But if you added both bow and stern overhangs similar to what you would have seen in 1969 you would be looking at a 35-footer at least. The Elan is laid out with a huge double quarterberth that is enclosed to port. There is a head to

starboard with a wet locker. The nav area looks big enough and the galley does not. However, it's only a 30-foot, 10-inch boat. The V-berths convert to a double berth with a filler piece. This basic lay-

I can tell you confidently that this is a good looking boat.

out has become widely used. If I'm reading the brochure and converting from metric accurately, there is only 6 feet of headroom in the saloon and galley. I can put up with less than standing headroom anywhere in a boat with the exception of the galley. This is a tough call on a 30-footer where the designer wants to keep the profile as low as possible.

The deck plan shows a large cockpit with the mainsheet traveler bisecting the cockpit well. A tiller is drawn and the specs do not list a wheel as an option. I like tiller steering and I have one of those handy tiller-activated autopilots for my own tiller-steered boat. It works very well and can be stowed away easily when not needed.

This cockpit is open to the swim step aft. Note that the cockpit coamings are cut away aft where the helmsman will sit. This seat area is angled to make it level when the boat is heeled about 15 degrees, making for a very comfy helming position. Teak pads on the deck here will have a good grip on the seat of your pants. Genoa tracks are well inboard and the decks are clear. There is an anchor well forward with a flush hatch.

The rig is the standard of the day—the swept-spreader, fractional type. The mast is deck stepped. The SA/D is 18.31. The Elan 31 is built in by Elan Marine in Slovenia.

Elan Marine, SI-4275 Begunje na Gorenjskem. Slovenia. 386 4 535 13 70. **www.elan-marine.com**

December 2002

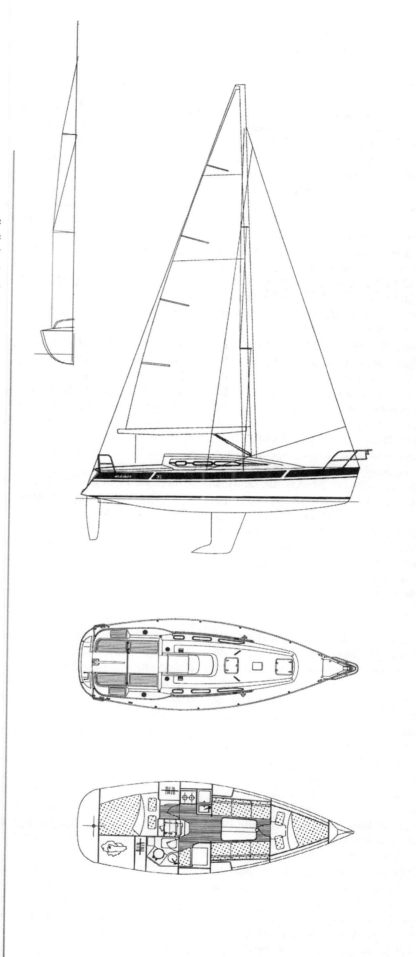

Another racer-cruiser that doesn't skimp on accommodations.

LOA 30'10"; LWL 27'; Beam 10'6"; Draft 6' (deep), 4'11" (shoal); Displacement 8,140 lbs.; Ballast 2,860 lbs.; Sail Area 462 sq. ft.; SA/D 18.31; D/L 190; L/B 2.94; Auxiliary diesel 18 hp; Fuel 18 gals.; Water 39 gals.

Sun Odyssey 32
Performance Cruiser

We cross the border from Belgium to France to check out this new 32-foot Jeanneau model designed by Philippe Briand. This good-looking boat is designed to be a dual-purpose boat with enough comfort to be qualified as a cruiser and enough performance to be effective and fun on the PHRF race course.

Let's start with the hull and aesthetics. It's a shapely hull with short ends and a strong spring to the sheer. With this much beam—10 feet, 9 inches and an L/B of 2.92—you can carry more sheer spring due to the additional linear length of the actual sheerline. The entry appears slightly hollow in the photos and BWL is broad. The stern is very wide with a moderate turn to the bilge aft. The forefoot or "chin" is immersed and there is considerable fore and aft hull rocker as you would expect with a D/L of 207. This is on the light side of "medium" displacement. Draft is on the shy side of moderate at 4 feet, 11 inches. While this will be very convenient for many of you, I would prefer to see a 6-foot draft for better VMGs.

I like the way the designer has blended this house with the hull shape. The house is bullet-shaped forward and slowly fairs to a straight-sided shape at the cockpit. This is a complex shape and was first done years ago to perfection by the original C&C designers, Cuthbertson and Cassian. The fixed windows are big and separated by an opening port. Freeboard is generous but well disguised by lowering the cove stripe, which pulls your focal point down. Raising the double bootstripes also helps reduce the apparent freeboard. Given the challenging overall proportions of this design I still cannot find an ugly line anywhere.

The evolution of the modern production boat interior took a leap forward when Joe Artese designed the layout of the original Alan Gurney-designed Islander 36 in the early 1970s. The next leap in accommodation design came via the French designers with their beamy boats and wide sterns. All of a sudden there were new areas of the boat opened up to accommodations. I think you have to assume the broad-sterned shape was initially driven by the quest for interior volume and the lure of staterooms. But if you compare these sterns to the skinny-minny sterns of the old IOR boats, there is definitely a performance benefit to all that added beam and volume aft. Specifically, you have added sailing length, increases in stability and more directional stability at hull speed. Unfortunately, these days we see this added beam aft taken to extremes in order to maximize useable interior and cockpit volume.

I cannot find an ugly line anywhere.

This interior illustrates what I'm talking about perfectly. Look at the size of that quarterberth. I even hesitate to call it a quarterberth. I can't imagine it's easy to get in and out of this berth, but once you are in, it's very spacious. The head can be accessed from either the saloon or the quarter stateroom.

This galley is big for a 32-footer. It's U-shaped and a snug place for the cook if you ever need to prepare meals while under way. The aft-facing nav station uses the settee for a seat. There is some compromise in the V-berth area with the port side of the V being truncated to make room for a hanging locker. This means that the shorter of the two V-berth occupants will take the port side. The brochure shows impressive wood joinerwork and trim detailing.

The rig is an almost-masthead fractional type with swept single spreaders and about five inches of prebend to the mast. The SA/D is 16.56. This is a wee bit low for aggressive racing in my light-air region, but it's enough to keep cruisers moving and it certainly reduces the need to reef early. Jeanneau is also marketing a Sun Fast version that uses the same hull but a deeper keel and taller rig.

With our racing world floundering around looking for a handicap or rating rule that is universally accepted, we are beginning to see more and more dual-purpose boats. It's kind of like the early 1970s. I see this as a healthy trend and this Sun Odyssey 32 as an excellent example of the type.

Jeanneau America, 105 Eastern Ave., #202, Annapolis, MD 21403. **www.jeanneauamerica.com** *(410) 280-9400.*

Sun Fast 32i

Sun Odyssey 32

A performance cruiser with an evolved interior.

LOA 31'5"; LWL 27'11"; Beam 10'9"; Draft 4'11"; Displacement 10,103 lbs.; Ballast 3,020 lbs.; Sail Area 485 sq. ft.; SA/D 16.56; D/L 207; L/B 2.92; Auxiliary 19-hp diesel; Fuel 19 gals.; Water 45 gals.

C&C 99
Racer-Cruiser

Tim Jacket shows us two distinct design styles with his work as both president of the company and designer of record for the C&C and Tartan lines. These two brands are quite different, and I applaud his effort at maintaining the aesthetic elements that distinguished the original C&Cs. I still think C&C gave us some of the very best looking production boats. I can't walk by an old C&C 39 without marveling at its good looks. The new C&C 99 is also very good looking, and according to sailing reports, is an exciting performer. "C&C" stands for Cuthbertson and Cassian, the Canadian design team that started the original company.

This is a very beamy hull with an L/B of 3.01. When an L/B gets close to 3 you have a beamy boat. This beam is accentuated by being carried dinghylike to the transom.

It wasn't too long ago when 40-footers had layouts like this. There is nothing missing in this layout.

In plan view this is a very wedge-shaped boat. While we could argue the performance aspects of this design feature there is no doubt that it affords the designer the best shape for the interior layout and cockpit layout, while resulting in a lot of wetted surface and weight aft. The D/L is 168.

Draft is either 6 feet, 6 inches or 5 feet, 3 inches depending on your choice of keel. The deep fin shows an extended trailing edge fillet, which I would assume is to facilitate the mating surface at the hull for both keel models. The keel leading edge is near vertical. The rudder shows a shape that lacks any significant taper but has plenty of area. Big rudders are nice.

The midsection has 13.8 degrees of deadrise and a firm turn to the bilge for good initial stability. While the overall styling is right out of the old C&C design handbook Tim's approach to hull shapes is entirely his own.

Boy! When you look at this interior you have to do a double take considering that this boat is only 32 feet, 6 inches long. It wasn't too long ago when 40-footers had layouts like this. There is nothing missing in this layout. The aft double berth is a little on the tight side and some of the other features show some "compression," but it's an amazingly complete layout for a 32-foot boat. Tim likes angles in his layouts. I applaud the use of a saildrive for the auxiliary.

The SA/D of this masthead rig design is 20.38. The spreaders are slightly swept. The mainsail has enough roach on the drawings to overlap the backstay by about 8 inches. Sailmakers will inevitably go even farther than that.

The deck design is all facets and angles producing a very chiselled look that I find appealing. The cockpit is not long, but it is wide thanks to that extremely broad transom. The cockpit is open to the swim step, but there is a hinged piece that drops into place to close it off and provide a helm seat. The traveler is right in front of the binnacle, and I like that. The large-diameter wheel will make steering the 99 fun.

This boat reminds me of the racer-cruisers of the early '70s. The speed was there, combined with comfort. It's a very sensible approach. This would be a great family boat if you were the type of family that enjoyed some local races between cruises.

Fairport Yachts Ltd., 1920 Fairport Nursery Rd., Fairport Harbor, OH 44077. (440) 354-3111. www.c-cyachts.com

February 2002

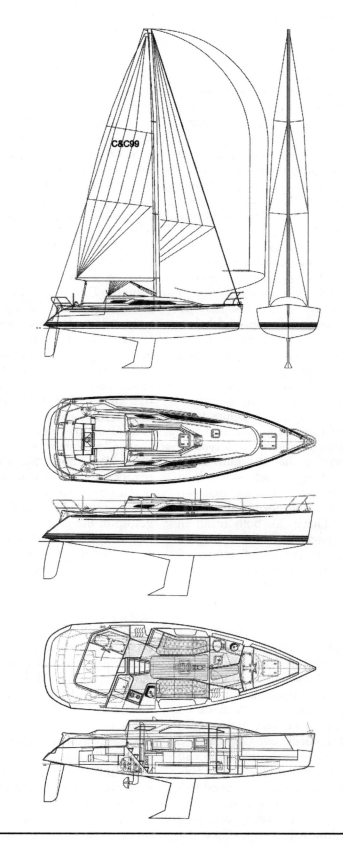

The C&C tradition continues in a new racer-cruiser.

LOA 32'6"; LWL 29'1"; Beam 10'10"; Draft 6'6" (deep fin), 5'3" (shoal); Displacement 9,265 lbs.; Ballast 3,200 lbs.; Sail Area 562 sq. ft.; SA/D 20.38; D/L 168; L/B 3.01; Auxiliary 19-hp Volvo MD2020; Fuel 20 gals.; Water 40 gals.

Quest 33
Racer-Cruiser

Designed by Rodger Martin the new Quest 33 is another racer-cruiser that shares in intent at least some of the same goals shown by *Icon* and the J/145: that is, speed for cruising and speed for racing in one package. Given the common target, the Quest goes about achieving that target with a very different approach to hull design.

While the J/145 has marked deadrise and *Icon* has minimal deadrise, the Quest has an arclike midsection with no deadrise. I grabbed my circle template to check this midsection, and below the DWL at the midsection, this shape is almost exactly a portion of an arc. The topsides are very full and this fullness is accentuated by the large radius at the sheerline. The overall effect is a suppository-like hull form very soft in shape. One nice thing about this type of hull form is that the hull shape doesn't change much as the boat heels. Still, it's amazing that two so diverse hull forms, the J/145 and the Quest 33, both result in fast and manageable boats. I would like to see curves of immersed areas for both boats. While the hull forms can be wildly different, the immersed volume curves can be identical.

The Quest shows short ends with a plumb bow. This boat is all sailing length. With an L/B of 2.86, the Quest will be shopping in the "husky" department for sure. The plan view of the deck shows the Quest to be very full in both ends at the deck, but keep in mind that the beam at the waterline will be much narrower. The D/L is 106. Note that the keel fin is raked forward 2 degrees. I've done this on two boats with very successful results. You will need a kelp cutter to keep the fin clean, and I don't see one on this design.

The rig is a tall fractional one with a masthead chute flown from a retractable bowsprit. The spreaders are swept 16 degrees.

The mainsail is loose-footed, and there is about 12 inches of roach overlap on the backstay. The SA/D is 33.6 and that ought to keep you on your toes and your boat on its ear. You will need to sail this wide boat flat.

It's a handsome boat, although I'd like to see more shape in the cabintrunk. Still, the amorphous lines of the cabintrunk blend with the hull shape.

What do you want to do when you go below in this light 33-footer? Do you want a nice roomy berth for cruising? Do you want adequate head and a wet locker? Do you want a comfortable place to sit, eat and entertain, and an efficient and spacious galley? Well, four out of five ain't bad. The bulbular lines of the hull and deck have been carried below into the interior shapes, and these seem to work well. You know me, I'd like a bigger galley. I also wonder how much fun it would be sleeping in the aft double berth and having to get up in the night.

The deck plan shows a raised portion of the deck where you sit (to keep your seat dry) but no cockpit coamings. This is fine for racing, but I like to find a nook to nestle into when I want to sit in the cockpit on the hook and read. This cockpit is nestle-and-nookless.

The short traveler is mounted on the cockpit sole. I'd like to see the traveler raised to deck level and go much farther outboard. You can get either wheel or tiller steering with this boat. You can also get optional water ballast.

I think that if you want to do some racing and some cruising in a 32-foot, 6-inch boat you could do it with some insurance of performance in this shapely little design.

Holby Marine Co., 97 Broad Common Rd., Bristol, RI 02809. **www.holbymarine.com** *(401) 253-1711.*

May 2000

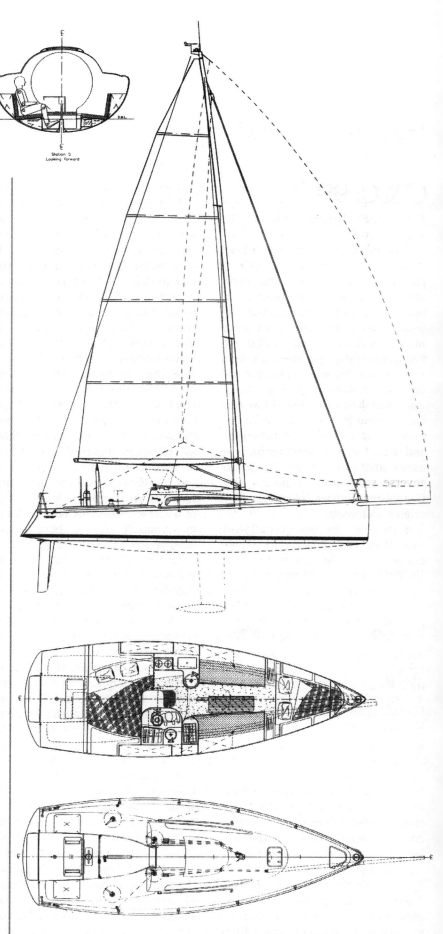

Sail area and plenty of beam result in a high-powered package.

LOA 32'6"; LWL 29'4"; Beam 11'4"; Draft 6'11"; Displacement 6,000 lbs.; Ballast 1,950 lbs. (bulb and fin); Sail Area 694 sq. ft. (with 150-percent jib); SA/D 33.6; D/L 106; L/B 2.86; Auxiliary Yanmar 2GM with saildrive; Fuel 14 gals.; Water 20 gals.

Synergy 1000
One-Design

Here's a boat built right down the street from my office by a new yard called Timeless Marine. Its first project is this Carl Schumacher-designed sport-type boat. It's a very handsome looking little boat and should find favor with racers who are looking for speed in an easily handled package.

The hull shape shows a reverse sheer. This has advantages. It reduces windage in the bow, and puts the max freeboard where it will do the most good, below in the accommodations. There may also be a structural advantage to reversing the sheer as it then opposes the hull's fore and aft bending loads. I know that Tom Wylie uses the reverse sheer for this precise reason. It doesn't look bad either.

The D/L of this design is 79. The keel is a steel fin engineered by my old roommate Craig Goring of Friday Harbor. There is a 1,850-pound lead bulb molded onto the bottom of the hollow steel fin. Note the keel is well aft on this design, helping to balance the huge mainsail. Draft is 7 feet. The hull form

With its near masthead asymmetric chute this boat wants to start to plane in 10 knots of true breeze.

looks on the full side from the deck plan, but I can assure you this hull is anything but full. The entry is hollow and topsides are flattish and flared. It's a very fast-looking shape.

The rig is big and designed specifically to be used without genoas in the light airs that dominate Seattle's summer. The spreaders are swept aft 22 degrees. The rig is carbon fiber. The SA/D is 33.96—say 34. This is a lot of horsepower per pound. I would guess this boat would be very fast accelerating off the starting line. With its near masthead asymmetric chute this boat wants to start to

plane in 10 knots of true breeze.

Obviously this is not a cruising boat. I'm not sure why they bother with accommodations at all except you might want to sleep part of your crew while you are away at a race week. Maybe you want to cruise for a couple of weeks. There is no reason why you couldn't cruise this boat. This is a little boat. The head is in the V-berth area and there is really no galley. There is a nice big chart table so you will know exactly where you are when you starve. My 26-footer has at least as comfortable a layout as this 32-footer. To be fair my 26-footer weighs an additional 1,200 pounds.

One of the cleverest features of this design is the auxiliary. The Honda Four Saildrive 280 is a 12.5 horsepower, four-stroke, gasoline-powered Honda outboard motor head with a saildrive unit. This is a quiet, smooth and especially light way to power this boat. It weighs 110 pounds, everything included. The Honda drives the Synergy effortlessly at 8 knots. Note this month that three out of the four reviews use saildrives. Saildrives offer the lowest drag of any propeller installation.

Construction uses a male mold and composite construction with wood, foam, carbon fiber and glass. This produces a very strong and stiff sandwich with panel weights around 1.5 pounds per square foot.

Regular readers will know by now what I think of one-designs. If there is to be any momentum behind a new class it will come from boat performance and not ad hype. People will flock to a new, hot boat. They won't buy a dog just because they think there will be another 10 of them on the starting line. From all I can see at this early juncture, the Synergy 1000 will attract a vital group.

Timeless Marine Inc., 5355-C 28th Ave. NW, Seattle, WA 98107. (206) 782-4650, fax (206) 782-4066.

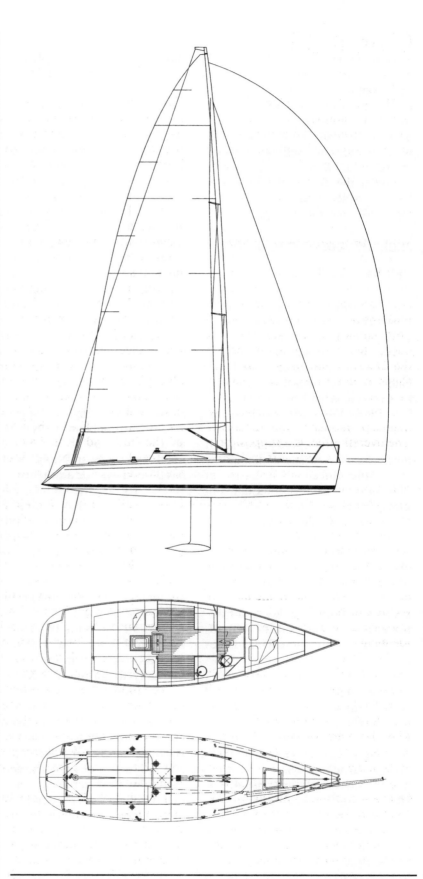

A high-powered, lightweight one-design.

LOA 32'10"; LWL 29'2"; Beam 9'9"; Draft 7'; Displacement 4,400 lbs.; Ballast 1,850 lbs.; Sail Area 589 sq. ft.; SA/D 33.96; D/L 79; L/B 3.36; Auxiliary Honda 12.5 hp gas with saildrive; Fuel 12 gals.

X-332
Racer-Cruiser

Niels Jeppesen has added another attractive boat to his potent fleet of X boat models. The intent of this model according to the brochure is to be a "mid-size offshore one-design." To date the boat has been winning races and selling very well in the United States.

Given the fact that this model has a complete and luxurious looking teak interior I suppose you

Niels Jeppesen has a good eye for aesthetics.

could consider this a dual-purpose boat. You could cruise it, but a 13.2-gallon fuel tank and 31.7 gallons of water might take the X-332 out of your "serious cruising boat" category. I see this boat primarily as a race boat with weekend cruising capabilities, and for many of us that's all we really need.

The hull looks pretty normal. It might be nice to see someone try something different in terms of hull form but I don't think that's in the cards. Even at the America's Cup level hull shapes seem to be fairly uniform in terms of volumetric distribution. Again for fun, I checked the half angle in plan view of the deck edge and the angle for the X-332 is 21.5 degrees. The keel shows large leading and trailing edge fillets and draft is a modest 5 feet, 11 inches. This makes me think there must be a performance keel available but I don't see one listed anywhere. If the boat is showing race winning performance with a 5-foot, 11-inch draft, I am truly impressed. The D/L is 177. Note that the rudder stock is almost vertical and not perpendicular to canoe body as it usually is. Note also the small skeglet preceding the rudder.

This interior is typical of many European boats this size. The double berth aft is big but not particularly easy to access. The galley is adequate but the icebox is small and there is very little counter space for food preparation. "What! Pickled herring for dinner again?" The two sinks are barely big

enough for a full-sized plate.

In contrast the nav station is generous in size and in fact takes up as much boat as the entire galley. The head is tight but it includes a small wet locker. The photos I have of this interior show a beautifully detailed boat with rich teak veneers and solid trim. Curves are used to soften the components and the round stool for the nav station that the drawings shows is really a comfy, built-in helm seat.

On deck the cockpit is long and divided by the mainsheet traveler. The tiller looks really short but you can go with the wheel option. There is a shallow swim step notched into the transom. The companionway is slightly recessed into the aft side of the cabintrunk providing an ideal surface for halyard bags directly outboard of the hatch. Decorated with big, multiple bootstripes the freeboard of the X-332 is disguised and this is a really good looking boat. Niels Jeppesen has a good eye for aesthetics.

The rig is fractional, as you would expect for a racing boat. There are double sweptback spreaders. The headstay is pulled about 10 inches off the stem. Using their sail areas with full main including roach, I would assume, and 100 percent jib I get a SA/D of 22.43.

While I can think of better galleys on bigger boats, I'm sure after a brisk beat up the sound I'd be ready to forgive the X-332 its shortcomings. This is a great boat for racing and occasional cruising. It's a size where things will not get overpowering when the wind pipes up. Considering the 33 feet, 10 inches of LOA the accommodations are impressive and I'd much rather have a design tilted toward performance than interior volume.

X-Yachts, Fjordagervej 21, Box 104, 6100 Haderslev, Denmark, 45-74-521022. **www.x-yachts.com**

In the U.S. contact X-Yachts USA, Foot of Washington Blvd., Stamford, CT 06902. (203) 353-0373.

February 2003

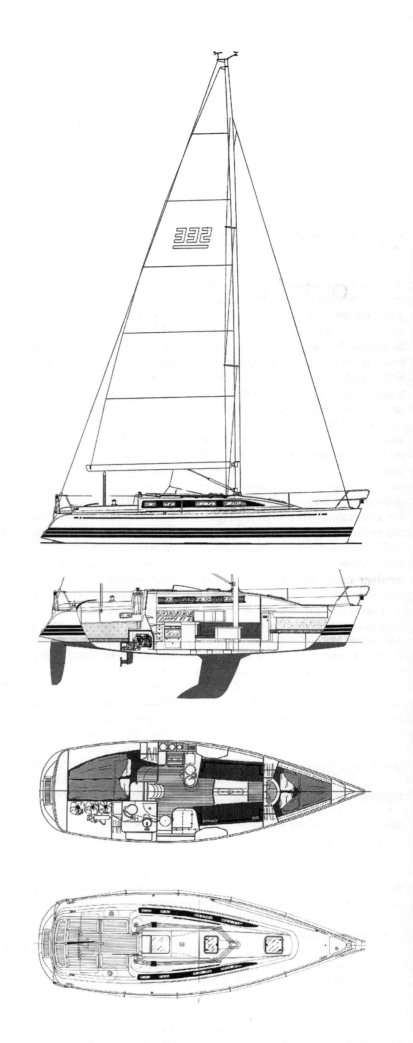

The racer will feel at home aboard this boat.

LOA 33'10"; LWL 28'11"; Beam 10'10"; Draft 5'11"; Displacement 9,590 lbs.; Ballast 3,968 lbs.; Sail Area 633 sq. ft.; SA/D 22.43; D/L 177; L/B 3.13; Auxiliary Yanmar 18hp; Fuel 13 gals.; Water 31 gals.

Dufour 34
Performance Cruiser

From designers Umberto Felci and Patrick Roséo comes this new 34-footer built in France by Dufour. It's another cruiser-racer, a type we are seeing more frequently. This is a very nice looking boat. Like many in this category, its styling looks derivative of the early Nautor boats, with wedgelike cabintrunk profiles and low cockpit coamings.

The L/B of this design is a very beamy 3.02. This clearly puts this model in the cruiser-racer category and not the racer-cruiser category. Beam increases interior volume, and that's probably why we are seeing it on this design. The D/L from my estimated DWL of 31 feet is 148. You can have either a shoal-draft keel drawing 4 feet, 7 inches or the deeper keel drawing 5 feet, 11 inches. The deep keel is very shapely, but I'm not sure why it is this shape.

You can choose from two interiors. There is one model with mirror-image double quarterberth cabins and the head forward. The other layout has one double quarterberth cabin and the head aft. The head-aft version makes for a bigger forward stateroom and offers a reasonable sized lazaretto. You wouldn't call this boat roomy; after all it's only 34 feet, 5 inches LOA. The galley and nav areas are minimal.

But if you ignore the missing inches here and there this layout is very complete and should make for comfortable cruising. The wet locker immediately aft of the nav station appears to be 10 inches wide. Note that if you go with the head-forward model, the double V-berth has one side truncated to accommodate the volume of the head. So, if your wife is 6 feet, 3 inches tall I suspect this layout will not work.

Rigs have become so generic

these days that it reminds me of the late 1960s when all we saw were masthead, single-spreader rigs with big foretriangles. Somehow I don't miss the old 180 percent genoas or those 15.5 SA/D ratios. The rig of today for

The deck is beautifully sculpted.

either racing or cruising is a fractional rig with at least two spreaders, preferably swept, and a short, overlapping genoa.

Mainsails have enough roach to them today to overlap the backstay. The bigger the mainsail in proportion to the overall size of the rig, the less importance you will have to place on jib selection. Ideally, all your sail reductions and depowering would be done with the mainsail and you would only use one size jib. You might carry jibs of different weights but the same size for varying wind speeds. With a furling boom and furling genoa this would be a very easy rig to handle. The SA/D is 17.8.

The deck is beautifully sculpted. The mainsheet traveler is right in front of the big wheel on the cockpit sole. There are coamings forward in the cockpit but they are cut down aft in the way of the wheel. There is a flush anchor well forward and a short swim step cut into the cockpit.

The hull is vacuum bagged with Kevlar, glass and PVC foam. The deck is "vacuum injected" for a claimed weight savings of 30 percent.

Dufour Yachts USA Inc., 1 Chelsea Court, Annapolis, MD 21403. (410) 268-6417, (877) 698-2195. www.dufouryachts.com

April 2003

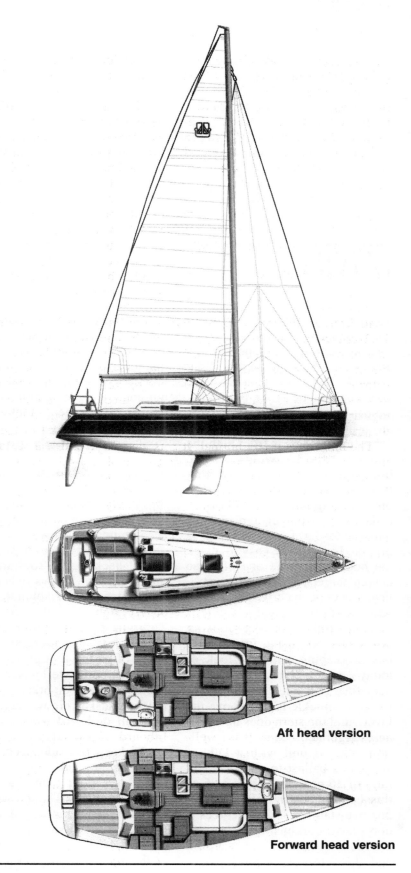

Aft head version

Forward head version

Stylish and seakindly addition to the French builder's line.

LOA 34'5"; LWL 29'11"; Beam 11'10"; Draft 4'7" (shoal), 5'11" (deep); Displacement 9,900 lbs.; Ballast 3,300 lbs.; Sail Area 657 sq. ft.; SA/D 17.8; D/L 148; L/B 3.02; Auxiliary Volvo Penta 20-HP diesel; Fuel 27 gals.; Water 70 gals.

J/109
Racer-Cruiser

This new J Boat is unique for the company in that it first went into production in Europe and was unveiled at the Southampton Boat Show in England. The brochure does not list a designer, but I think we can assume it was the work of an in-house team headed by Bob Johnstone. It's clear from both the text and the drawings in the brochure that J Boats is marketing this boat as an answer to everyone's sailing needs. It's a cruiser, a daysailer a one-design racer, a live-aboard, a floor wax and a grappa. It should be easy to attack the boat on at least one of these design targets, but I really can't. From my perspective the J/109 seems to fill all these bills.

The J/109 is an okay-looking boat, a wee bit bland for my eye, but in keeping with the look of today's racing boats. The sheer is very flat. The ends are short. The forefoot knuckle is just above the DWL, and the stern does not show an exaggerated beam. It's a well-proportioned hull with a D/L of 165 and a ballast-to-displacement ratio of 36 percent. L/B is 3.06 so this boat is beamy. The limit of positive stability is 123 degrees. I don't have sections, but I can see the run is quite flat at the transom and the forefoot is gently V-ed. The keel is a lead fin with bulbed tip, generous in planform and drawing 7 feet.

The layout drawings and photos make the interior look very comfy, finished in what looks like either

teak or mahogany. The overall layout is tight. The galley is small with a two-burner range and minimal icebox. The head is small and has access to the lazarette. Still, nothing is miniaturized and the double quarter-berth looks really

I've always been a fan of J Boats' deck plans.

big. Given 35 feet of LOA to work with, this is a well-thought-out accommodation plan.

I've always been a fan of J Boats' deck plans. To start with, the company knows where the mainsheet traveler belongs, in the cockpit right in front of the wheel. This would preclude tiller steering on this boat, but there aren't too many of us left that prefer tillers. The cockpit well is narrow enough so you can brace your feet to leeward. The big wheel lets you get well outboard when steering. Inboard chainplates and genoa tracks keep the side decks clear. Halyards are led aft to winches and clutches on each side of the companionway. There's a bowsprit for the asymmetrical and the SA/D is a safe, sane 21.

The J/109 is another example of the healthy trend back to good, all-around boats.

J Boats Inc., P.O. Box 90, 557 Thames St. Newport, RI 02840. (401) 846-8410. **www.jboats.com**

May 2002

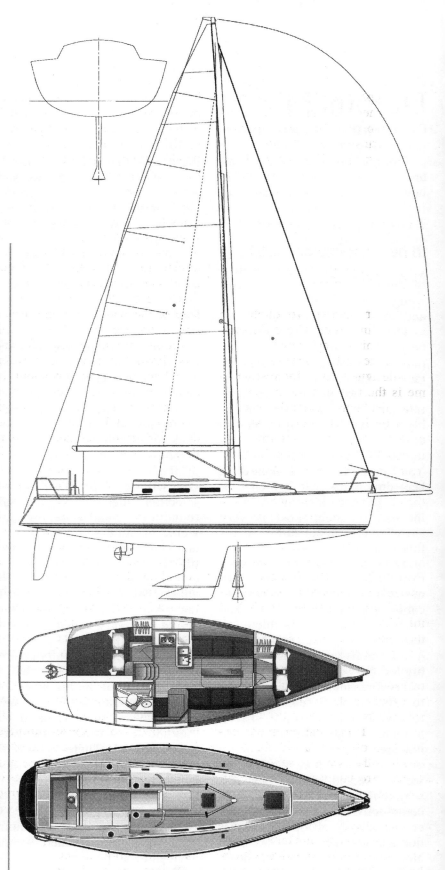

A well-designed 35-footer that does it all.

LOA 35'3"; LWL 30'6"; Beam 11'6"; Draft 7'; Displacement 10,900 lbs.; Ballast 3,900 lbs.; Sail Area 644 sq. ft.; SA/D 21; D/L 165; L/B 3.06; Auxiliary Volvo MD 2030; Fuel 20 gals.; Water 35 gals.

Beneteau First 36.7
Racer-Cruiser

If we count boats over 32.66-feet LOA, Beneteau has at least 13 different models to choose from. The company works with a variety of designers and breaks its boats down into "racer-cruiser," "performance cruisers" and "center cockpit" categories. I'm not positive, but I would imagine Beneteau builds more sailing yachts than

To my eye this appears to be a handsome, good all-round boat.

any other builder. To quote my favorite line from "Close Encounters": "This is important."

The newest Beneteau is this Farr-designed 36.7. Interesting to me is the fact that the brochure's specs list "Farr" under the heading "hull design." I think it's safe to assume that a company like Beneteau employs a gaggle of in-house designers to take care of interiors, decks and structural details. Rigs, keels, rudders and hulls are best left to the "out house" designer of record.

This model was inspired by the highly successful, Farr-designed First 40.7. The 40.7 has earned an enviable race record in some of the world's toughest fleets. The hull of the 36.7 shows what we might call the current generic racing shape, i.e., no overhangs, moderately light displacement, broad stern and fine entry. It's not an especially distinctive looking design in any way. It really looks like the rest of the racing fleet. I miss the divergent racing fleets of the '70s with those all-out pigs that were so much fun to whip. (Are you racing?!) The performance range of most fleets is dramatically narrowed today.

The D/L is 185 based on a "light ship" displacement. The 36.7 is on the beamy side with an L/B of 3.1. You have your choice of a deep keel drawing 7 feet, 2 inches and weighing 3,748 pounds, or a more shoal keel drawing 5 feet, 11 inches and weighing 4,034 pounds.

The interior layout certainly is oriented toward the family cruiser. There's a massive double quarter berth to port and a single quarter berth to starboard, both within their own enclosed spaces. The galley is on the skimpy side, but there is little else you can do when you want two quarter staterooms. The nav station is generous. It takes up as much space as does the galley. Looking at this layout makes me wonder if there isn't a race version of the interior. This Beneteau model, like the C&C 99, works hard to be both racer and cruiser.

The deck design takes advantage of the wide stern and uses a large-diameter wheel. The cockpit coamings are cut away aft, and this allows the mainsheet traveler to extend out to within about 10 inches of the rail. Note that there is a teak toerail on this model. There is a handy well in the foredeck for ground tackle. As usual, Beneteau has done a superlative job with its deck tooling. The cockpit seats are veneered in teak. The cabintrunk is highly radiused for a low-windage shape.

The rig is fractional with two sets of swept spreaders. The SA/D is 20.6. I find it curious that whoever drew the sailplan I am looking at tried very hard not to let the mainsail roach overlap the backstay. Usually sailmakers will ignore what the designer drew for sails unless you are working closely together on a custom project.

There is tankage for 79 gallons of water and 20 gallons of fuel. The standard auxiliary is a 29-horsepower Volvo diesel saildrive. Construction features a solid fiberglass hull as opposed to the typical cored hull you see in most boats of this type. The deck is balsa cored. The rudder, stock and blade are composite.

To my eye this appears to be a handsome, good all-round boat.

Beneteau USA Inc., 1313 Highway 76 West, Marion, OH 29571. (843) 629-5300. **www.beneteauusa.com**

February 2002

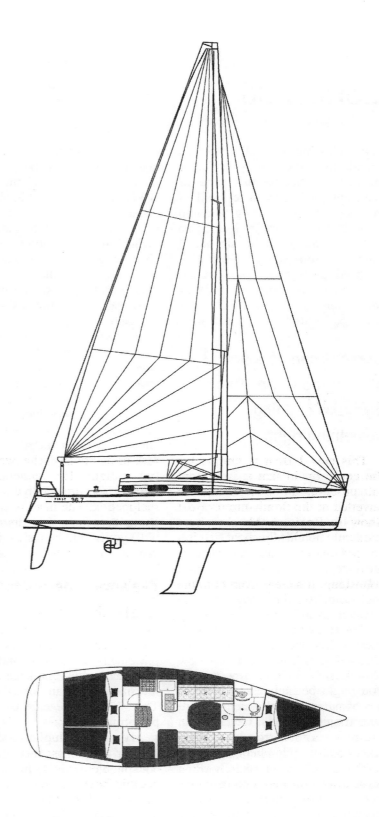

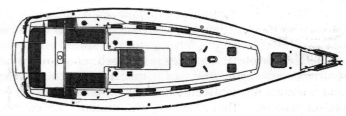

Racer-cruiser from the Farr office.

LOA 36'; LWL 30'4"; Beam 11'7"; Draft 5'11" (shoal), 7'2" (standard); Displacement 11,552 lbs.; Ballast 4,034 lbs. (shoal), 3,748 lbs. (standard); Sail Area 665 sq. ft.; SA/D 20.6; D/L 185; L/B 3.1; Auxiliary 29-hp diesel; Fuel 20 gals.; Water 79 gals.

Corsair 36
Performance Cruiser

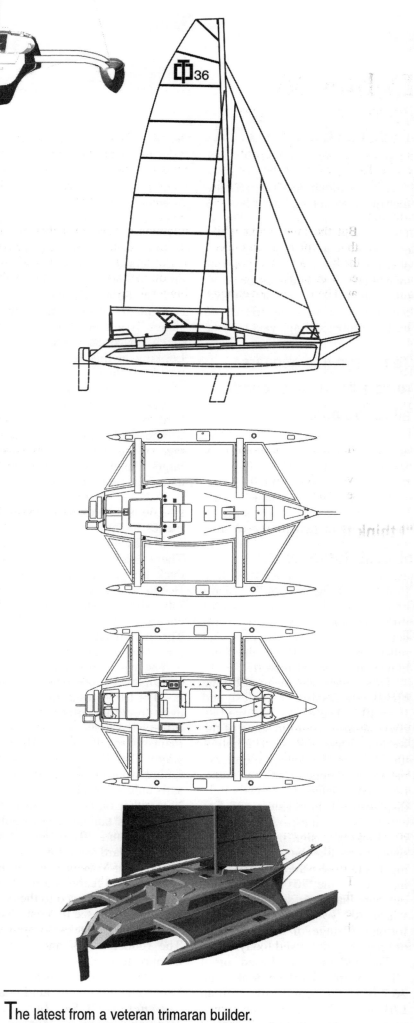

It's blowing a steady 20 knots outside the office today, which is unusual for Seattle this time of year, but perfect for a test sail of this new 36-foot folding trimaran from the Corsair group. I sailed an early Corsair in light air and I found it too sedate. But I've watched these boats race around Puget Sound enough to know they can be very fast. The early Corsairs were designed by Australian

Corsairs can be found all over the world. This company is doing something right.

designer Ian Farrier, but now Corsair uses in-house designers along with some out-house consultants. I'm not sure that at 36 feet and 5,500 pounds this boat fits into the reasonably frequently trailerable category. But with the amas folded in, it does fit within the 10-foot-beam "special" limit.

Beam overall is 25 feet, 7 inches, but the beam of the main hull itself is almost 10 feet, which is just 8 inches shy of the beam of a new 35-foot monohull to my design. You might be inclined to think of this trimaran almost as a monohull with training wheels. Certainly an L/B of 3.6 is not narrow by any current standard. Numbers, however, can be misleading, especially when comparing different sailing types. Look at the midsection of the Corsair and you will see that below the deck level the topsides are shaved away for a narrow BWL that's about 50 percent of maximum beam, at most. A normally ballasted monohull with this narrow of a BWL would just flop over on its side and die. The daggerboard and retractable rudder give the Corsair some real beach-hugging ability. D/L is 57.27.

This Corsair has an unusual layout in that there is an aft double berth with access through an oversized deck hatch behind the cockpit. It's very snug, but with the hatch up it should feel okay. The rest of the accommodations are pretty normal. The flared hull shape is arranged so

the accommodations take advantage of the flare without any real noticeable impact of the narrow BWL. It's a trick used in almost all trimaran designs today.

The rig uses a rotating aluminum "wing" mast. I don't see much chord length to this particular wing, but that's what the press release says. Rotating masts are nice. The mast bend and sectional shape align themselves with the sail giving a far nicer shape to the main and a much cleaner and more effective leading edge. Once you have sailed with a rotating mast a fixed mast section looks clumsy.

A long carbon fiber retractable bowsprit allows you to fly a big chute or a roller-furled code zero. The mainsail is drawn with eight full battens and a fathead-type shape. Consider that if you swapped this fathead main for a straight-leach main (heaven forbid!) you would be losing 43.7 percent of your total mainsail area. The shrouds lead to the amas, which makes it easy to get tight, unencumbered sheeting angles for your jibs. Using the data I managed to extract from Corsair and based upon a projected "estimated" displacement of 5,500 pounds and a sail area including all the roach in the main I get an SA/D of 38.9. That should take care of light-air performance.

My only complaint with the Corsair boats has been the small cockpit wells. This, however, has been addressed in the 36 by extending the cockpit seat all the way to the transom. Still, the well itself is quite short. Wide but short. I suppose the answer to this is that since you can spread yourself all over the trampolines you will spend less time in the actual cockpit on this type of boat.

Corsairs are in all but two of the states in the United States and can be found all over the world. This company is doing something right. The boats are raced and cruised. I think the Corsairs have attracted a lot of new people to sailing.

Corsair Marine, 353 N. Renee St., Eagar, AZ 85925. (877) 327-8875. **www.corsairmarine**

The latest from a veteran trimaran builder.

LOA 36'; LWL 35'; Beam 25'7" (extended), 9'10" (folded); Draft 1'8" (board up), 6' (board down); Displacement 5,500 lbs.; Sail Area 757 sq. ft. (including roach); SA/D 38.9; D/L 57.27; Auxiliary 15-hp four-stroke outboard; Water 35 gals.

Dehler 36
Performance Cruiser

I used to tell people to buy the biggest boat they could afford. That was before my love affair with my own 26-footer. It doesn't cover the distances the way a bigger boat would, but it does offer a lot of care-free fun. But the other night while sailing with my wife and son I needed to use the head, and in a chop and a 25-degree heel angle that was an athletic feat. There's just not enough room to assume the position with any style and grace. Experience with a new 35-footer of my own design has led me to start thinking that 35 feet is the perfect size for the type of sailing I do. Thirty-five feet gives you headroom and head room.

This new Dehler is designed by Judel/Vrolijk and aimed at family cruising with the emphasis on performance. Twenty years ago we would have called this model a racer-cruiser. This boat would make

> ## "I think this is my type of boat. Handsome, comfortable and fast."

an excellent and comfy PHRF racer. There is only 49 gallons of water tankage so I think this precludes the Dehler from being considered an offshore cruiser. There is 24 gallons of fuel tankage.

Twenty years ago almost all boats began looking like IOR boats. Racers and cruisers alike sported pinched ends. Today we see the same thing happening based upon the IMS-encouraged features, i.e. extremely short ends. The difference is that IOR features made no sense whatsoever on cruising boats while IMS-encouraged features lend themselves positively to any boat. The only pragmatic drawbacks to the near plumb stem are getting the anchor back on board without whacking the stem and the fact that bow overhang makes for a dryer, if slower, boat. The 36 comes with a choice of either a 6-foot, 5-inch deep fin or a shoal fin drawing 5-foot, 3-inches. The D/L for this design is 170. Note how broad the stern is.

The near plumb stem has one very distinct advantage for cruising boats. Consider a design brief where

the LOA is fixed. Now extend the waterline in the current fashion. This pulls volume and cabin sole forward making for more accommodation volume. Look at the way this V-berth is wedged up into the bow while retaining at least 24 inches of width to the cushions at the toe end. Unfortunately none of this additional volume has been used to make a bigger fo'c'sle.

The accommodation plan shows double berths for two couples. The aft head has a small hanging locker that I don't think is big enough to allow enough air circulation to dry wet gear. The galley shows those sexy Euro round sinks, but I think rectangular sinks work better for washing dishes. The icebox is minimal. There are three generous hanging lockers in this boat. The nav station is well laid out, and the saloon looks big enough for entertaining. The aft double quarter berth will require some quasi-erotic gymnastics if you need to get up during the night. Engine access looks to be excellent.

The rig is a fractional sloop rig with the spinnaker hoist slightly taller than the hounds. The spreaders are swept. The SA/D is 18.89, and that's enough horsepower per pound to keep the most demanding sailor happy. However, this is enough rig to become overwhelming for the "hacker" when the wind picks up. Some cruisers are far better off with lower SA/Ds that don't require the anticipation and sailhandling skills required by the higher-powered boat.

The cockpit benefits from the broad stern. There is a large diameter wheel with the mainsheet traveler directly ahead of it. The cockpit coamings are chopped off before they get to the helmsman, allowing him to sit on the deck. The recessed companionway makes for a snug "nook" for the person operating the halyards. There is a flush anchor well forward. Jib tracks are up off the side deck and on the chamfered bottom edge of the cabintrunk.

I think this is my type of boat. Handsome, comfortable and fast.

Dehler America, 561 Boylston St., Boston, MA 02116. (617) 536-1100. **www.dehler.com**

October 2000

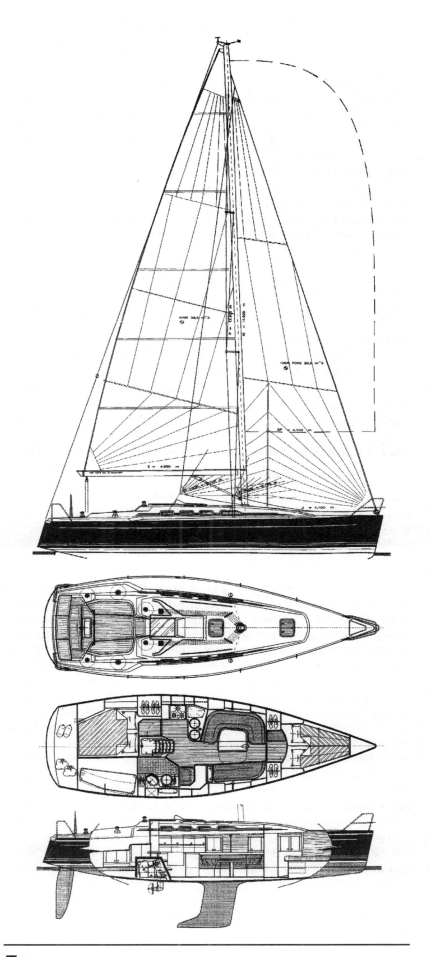

Family cruiser with style and speed.

LOA 36'1"; LWL 32'10"; Beam 11'6"; Draft (standard) 6'5", (shoal) 5'3"; Displacement 14,000 lbs.; Ballast 4,400 lbs.; D/L 170; SA/D 18.89; Sail Area 686 sq. ft.

Finngulf 41
Performance Cruiser

Here's a beautiful-looking design from Strahlmann Yacht Design in Finland and built by Finngulf Yachts. There isn't an ugly line on this entire design. It's a dual-purpose 41-footer, so by definition it will involve compromise. While I usually view compromise as a negative quality let's take a look at this design in depth and see if the compromises are balanced and justified.

This design has a beautiful, sweeping sheerline and short ends.

This is a beautifully crafted design. Clearly Mr. Strahlmann loves his work.

Beam is moderate and the stern is broad. The stem profile shows a tiny bit of convexity to it rather than the usual dead-straight line. This indicates the waterlines forward are a wee bit fuller than the straight stem type. The D/L is 168.4. Keel and rudder are exactly what you would expect for a boat intended for family racing. There are options for three different keels of 7 feet, 2 inches; 6 feet, 5 inches; and 6 feet draft. Have you noticed that the America's Cup boats all show keels with leading edge fillets at the hull, but I have not yet seen a trailing edge fillet at the hull? All in all, aesthetics aside this is a very normal looking hull.

There are two interior layouts with the only difference being the way the port side aft is treated. You can have mirror image staterooms aft with large double quarterberths. Or you can expand the head on the port side and gain a huge lazaretto. The galley is adequate with a rather small cold box outboard of the sinks. There are plenty of hanging lockers but the wet locker located in the head looks too small. You need air circulation to even approximate any dryness to wet

foulies and most wet lockers are too small. I like the main cabin with its opposing settees and aft facing chart table. I know navigating facing aft bothers some of you but I would not want to trust a navigator who felt that this was a serious challenge to his accuracy. It's a good layout.

The deck plan shows a carefully sculpted cabintrunk and a big T-shaped cockpit. The mainsheet traveler goes across the cockpit seats but it's far enough aft to still allow a decent dodger for shelter forward in the cockpit. The wheel is really big and requires a well in the cockpit sole to keep the upper perimeter at an ergonomically acceptable height. Big wheels are nice. There is a big, wide contoured helm seat that spans the breadth of the cockpit at coaming top level. This allows you to sit well outboard where you can see the entire luff of the genoa, if you are interested.

There is a deep anchor well in the bow in this design. Genoa tracks are kept off the side decks with a small molded-in riser. The chainplates are inboard enough to keep the side decks perfectly clear. There are only two hatches in addition to the companionway hatch. I'd like to see opening hatches over the aft staterooms and another one over the galley. There's something about the smell of burnt pancakes. Ventilation can be critical when cruising even in colder areas.

The rig is fractional with double spreaders swept 17.5 degrees. Running backstays are shown on the sailplan. SA/D is 20.76. This is enough power to keep the racers happy without intimidating the cruiser too much.

This is a beautifully crafted design. Clearly Mr. Strahlmann loves his work. I am anxious to see the 41 in person.

Finngulf Yachts, P.O. Box 16 FIN 10211 Inkoo, Finland, 358 **www.finngulf.com** *(0) 9-221-1703.*

March 2003

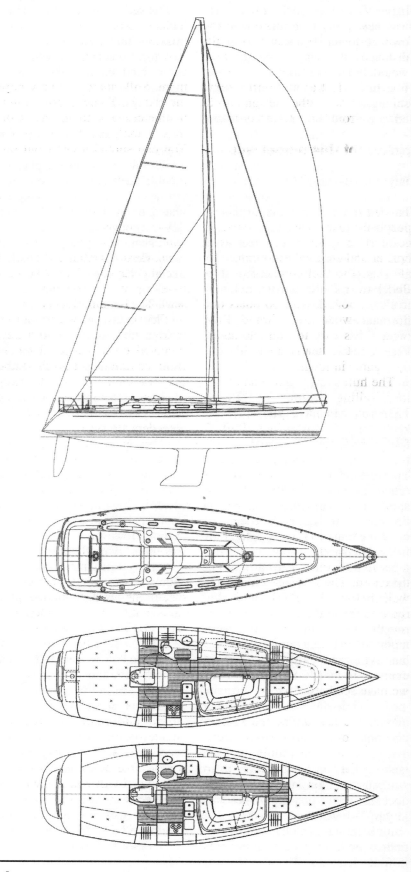

A swift boat sporting some pretty lines.

LOA 41'; LWL 36'9"; Beam 12'6"; Draft 7'2", 6'5", 6'; Displacement 18,700 lbs.; Ballast 7,040; Sail Area 980 sq. ft.; SA/D 20.76; D/L 168.4; L/B 3.28; Auxiliary Volvo Penta 40-hp; Fuel 38 gals.; Water 62 gals.

Hanse 371
Performance Cruiser

Here's a boat designed by Judel and Vrolijk and built in Greifswald, Germany, by Yachtzentrum Greifswald. Rolf Vrolijk is the designer responsible for the America's Cup boat *Alinghi*. I have been very impressed with the design work coming from this talented team.

No doubt this model will win many friends.

This new Hanse is another dual-purpose boat. There is enough comfort to qualify the boat as a cruiser and enough performance to allow you to feel competitive in a PHRF fleet. PHRF is alive and well in Puget Sound, with 60 boats out for last weekend's Grand Prix regatta. It's easy to grumble about PHRF, but in many areas it's the only game in town.

The hull shows short ends for a long sailing length. The D/L is 173. You can have your pick of keels for a 6 foot, 6 inch draft; 5 foot, 6 inch short fin draft; or a 3 foot, 4 inch integral lifting keel. That's quite a selection. I have no drawings for the lifting keel or the short fin but the deep fin has long tip chord and a bulbish shape. Note the marked leading edge/hull fillet. The rudder shows very little taper in plan form, giving it a long tip chord. The forefoot knuckle is well below the DWL and this reduces the amount of fore and aft rocker to this hull. This is a very moderate looking hull. While the beam is carried aft it is not as exaggerated as on some models we have seen recently.

The layout of the Hanse echoes the layouts of the French competition. The broad stern allows for a large double quarter-berth. There is a big lazarette to starboard that appears to be accessed from just aft of the galley. In fact, there is an option of a shower here or you can add a mirror image double berth stateroom in this space. Pity though—this door severely limits what you can do with the galley and to my eye this galley looks skimpy. Don't be expecting a balsamic vinaigrette drizzle for your pork loin if I have to cook in this galley.

The saloon looks fine if you like those chairs. I guess I'm just old school. I have never acclimatized to chairs in sailboats. Settees work better because you can sleep on them. Still, chairs are very popular these days. There is no nav station that I can see on these cryptic drawings. I don't see that as a problem. You can spread a chart out on the dining table if you need to and navigation electronics are so compact today they can fit just about anywhere in the saloon. I like nav stations, however. When you have company on board you can sit in the navigator's chair and really feel like the captain. The V-berth area looks spacious and has port and starboard hanging lockers.

This rig is designed around a self-tacking jib that sheets to a traveler mounted on a bracket. I can't tell from the drawings how far outboard this bracket allows the sheeting to go. In a perfect world it would go all the way out to the sheer. The double spreaders are swept.

Note again that this rig is not a masthead rig. There can be no question today that a well-designed fractional rig is faster than a masthead rig. Masthead rigs can be easier to sail though and I think they still deserve consideration for out-and-out cruising boats.

Styling on this boat is a bit too sedate for my taste. The boat has a clean line with moderate proportions, but there is little electricity in its look. The flattish sheerline, the short ends and the boxy cabin trunk work together well and this certainly is not a bad looking boat, I'd just like to see some more exciting styling. Having said that I am aware that many of you prefer sedate styling—blue blazers with a nice club tie. It's a good look. There is no doubt in my mind that this model will win many friends.

Hanse, Yachtzentrum Greifswald GmbH, Salinenstrasse 22, 17489 Greifswald, Germany. 49 38 34 57 92 0, **www.hanseyachts.com**

In the U.S. contact Brewer Wickford Cove Marina, 65 Reynolds St., North Kingston, RI 02852. (401) 423-9192.

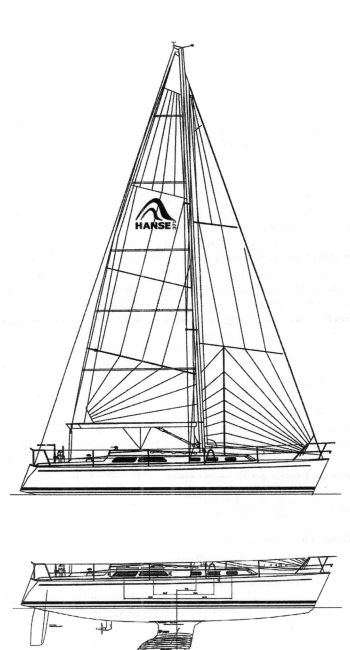

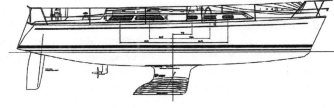

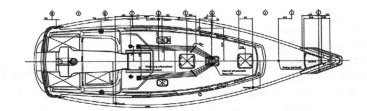

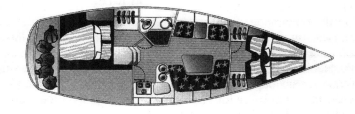

A dual-purpose boat with no pretensions.

LOA 36'11"; LWL 32'4"; Beam 11'10"; Draft 6'6" (Deep), 5'6" (Shoal); Displacement 13,120 lbs.; Ballast 4,950 lbs.; Sail Area 716 sq. ft.; SA/D 20.6; D/L 173.3; L/B 3.12; Auxiliary Volvo Penta 2030; Fuel 20 gals.; Water 60 gals.

Tartan 3700
Performance Cruiser

Of course it won't be long before you start looking at bigger boats. Those knocks and bruises get to you eventually. The Tartan 3700 would be a nice boat to move up to. Designed by Tartan President Tim Jackett, this boat is a performance-oriented cruising boat that comes with your choice of three keel configurations: a 7-foot, 3-inch fin; a 5-foot beavertail (a flat, wide tailed bulb); and a 4-foot centerboard version. That should about cover everyone's draft considerations.

The hull is consistent with the other newer Tartans. The 3700 is

> **Jackett loves to use angles in his interiors ... I think the angles may add some interest, and in some areas they can increase the apparent useful volume.**

beamy at 12 foot, 7 inches, for an L/B of 2.92. Any L/B less than 3 can be considered beamy.

In this model the beam is carried to the stern with minimal taper. This does several things, some good and some not so good, depending upon your perspective. A wide stern gives you more cockpit space and volume below for interior components like double quarter berths. Beam aft can also add form stability and sailing length.

On the down side, a wide stern increases wetted surface and makes a boat sticky in the light stuff. Heeled over, a wide, low-deadrise stern coupled with short aft overhang can give you a transom that drags and gurgles, sucking the bay along with you. It can also force the boat to roll bow down as it heels, which can give you a demanding helm. Most of these issues can be handled with prudent design, but it's tricky. I prefer a more moderate approach to beam aft.

The D/L of this design is 210 (using the displacement listed for the beavertail keel model). The range of positive stability is listed as 125 degrees, and that's textbook normal for this type of boat.

Jackett loves to use angles in his interiors. If you take the angles out, it's a pretty standard layout. I think the angles may add some interest, and in some areas they can increase the apparent useful volume. Look at that huge double quarter berth. That's why the wide stern is so attractive to the designer.

The galley is nice, but once again we see sinks with no adjacent counter space. It's natural when preparing food to do it next to the sink. The engine box is under the companionway. I like the head and shower arrangement.

This rig is a very standard masthead, two-spreader sloop type with a slight sweep angle to the spreaders. There's not much to say about a rig like this. It's simple, strong, easy to set up and tune, and versatile. The mainsail overlaps the backstay by about 6 inches. The SA/D is 18.2.

The deck plan features opening hatches in all living spaces and 12 opening ports in the cabintrunk. I know lining up opening ports like this does not look sexy, but you

> **The Tartan 3700 appears to be a boat designed to appeal to a wide range of sailors.**

can never have too much ventilation. The sheerline is accented with a solid teak toerail. There is an anchor well on the foredeck. Note the location of the primary winches.

The Tartan 3700 appears to be a boat designed to appeal to a wide range of sailors.

Tartan Yachts Inc., 1920 Fairport Nursery Rd., Fairport Harbor, OH 44077. (440) 354-3111, fax (440) 354-6162. www.tartanyachts.com

November 1999

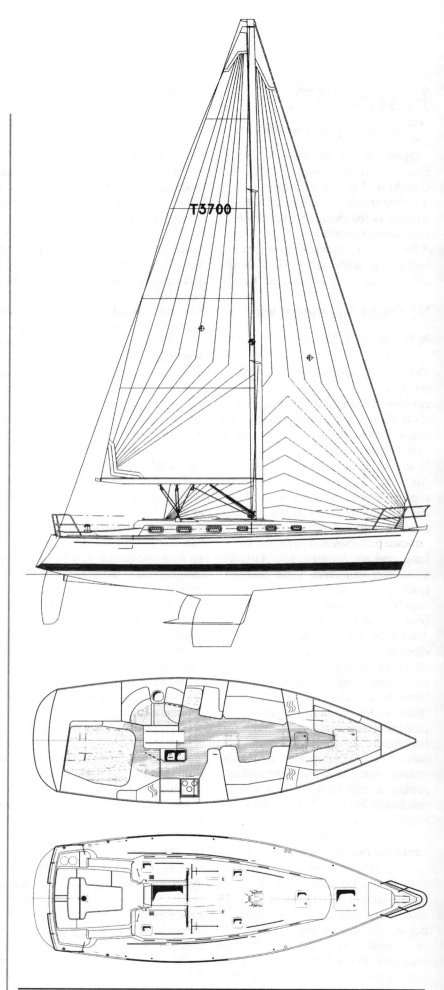

Straightforward cruiser with a simple-to-sail rig.

LOA 37'; LWL 32'6"; Beam 12'7", Draft 4' (centerboard), 5' (beavertail), 7'3" (fin); Displacement 16,350 lbs. (centerboard), 16,150 lbs. (beavertail), 15,950 lbs. (fin); Ballast 6,400 lbs. (centerboard), 6,200 lbs. (beavertail), 6,000 lbs. (fin); Sail Area 727 sq. ft.; SA/D 18.2; D/L 210 (w/beavertail); L/B 2.92; Auxiliary 38-hp diesel; Fuel 38 gals.; Water 80 gals.

Cape Fear 38
Racer-Cruiser

This light displacement racer/cruiser was designed by Bruce Marek for Cape Fear Yacht Works. Bruce was one of the Bruces of Nelson/Marek in San Diego. Bruce Nelson kept the name when Bruce Marek set up shop in North Carolina.

With a D/L of 125 you would have to consider the 38 very light for a cruising boat. Beam is 11 feet for a narrow L/B of 3.45. Draft is a modest 6 feet, which cruising owners should applaud. The profile shows a boat with short overhangs and a deep "chin" on the forefoot. Aft, the almost straight line you see in plan view across the end of the transom indicates a flat run.

Will this boat pound sailing to weather? Yes, I think so, sometimes, but so will almost every boat designed to today's modern performance parameters. Light weight and minimal rocker forward result in a tendency to pound. It's a trade-off, and in this case the designer has gone for speed-producing shapes. Note the huge rudder blade about as far aft as you could get it without having it outboard. This boat should track and maneuver well.

There is no mystery to cruising boat interiors. Displacement means volume and volume means accommodations and stowage. Take away displacement and you will pay in the area of accommodations. This means that items that some cruisers consider requirements will have to be left ashore on the 38. The boat could take the weight, but there is simply not the volume to carry large amounts of cruising gear like generators, washer-dryers, massive battery banks and A/C. This is not necessarily a bad thing. I'm a nut about simplicity and a simple cruising lifestyle.

Where this light displacement will take a bite out of your cruising convenience is in the area of tankage. We seem to have become tankage manic in the last few years. The tank capacities for the 38 will be 50 gallons for fuel and 25 gallons for water. (Let them drink wine!) Keep in mind that if your boat is a sprightly sailer you will motor far less. The tall fractional rig has an SA/D of 24.2. Racers will love the

horsepower it will produce. Cruisers will like that too, but may have some concerns about handling this much sail area when shorthanded. In their favor is the fact that the headsails do not overlap the shrouds and, of course, can be fitted with roller furling (which racers may opt for as well, since sail changes are minimized by the nonoverlapping jibs).

Note the huge rudder blade about as far aft as you could get it without having it outboard. This boat should track and maneuver well.

A smaller, nonmasthead spinnaker can be used, as well as a full masthead chute. The spinnakers are asymmetric and tack to a short bowsprit. This will be an exciting boat to sail under masthead spinnaker in surfing conditions.

The deck and cockpit are nicely laid out for efficient sail handling.

Cape Fear will build you a custom interior. The interior shown in the drawings features a large double V-berth and a minimal quarter double berth. The galley is adequate, but the stove shown is a small, light, two-burner type, which given the state of my own cholesterol level is probably just fine. Note the large lazarette, or as labeled in the drawings, "mechanical room." Missing from this layout are lockers. Apart from two hanging lockers there are few small compartments for stowage.

This is a design that puts a premium on sailing performance. Racers expect that. Cruisers who are willing to trade a certain amount of luxury for sailing speed, nimble handling and light-air performance that will keep the engine silent most of the time will appreciate it too.

I look forward to seeing this interesting new design at the boat shows.
Cape Fear Yacht Works, 111 Bryan Road, Wilmington, NC 28412. (910) 395-0189, **www.cfyw.com**

December 2001

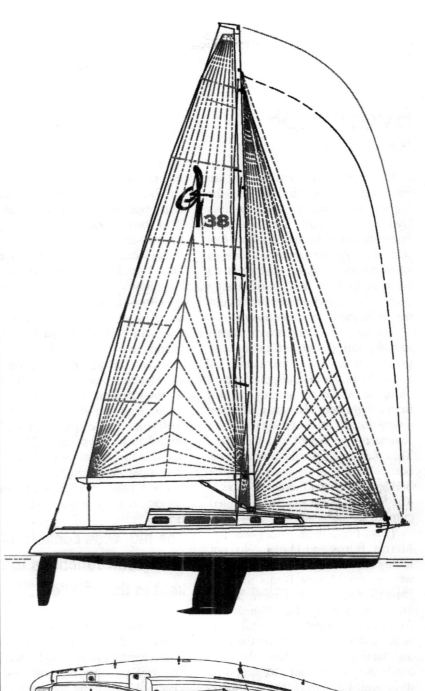

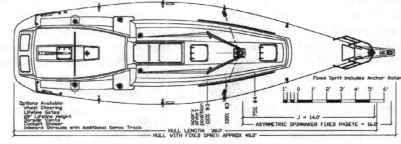

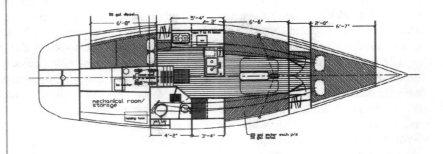

A serious attempt at racer-cruiser "perfection."

LOA 38'; LWL 34'; Beam 11'; Draft 6'; Displacement 11,000 lbs.; Ballast 5,075 lbs.; Sail Area 750 sq. ft.; SA/D 24.2; D/L 125; L/B 3.45; Auxiliary Yanmar 27-hp Saildrive; Fuel 50 gals.; Water 25 gals.

Sydney 38
Racer Cruiser

If you enjoy your cruising but are intent on being the first one into the harbor you might consider this Sydney 38 built by Bashford International of Australia. I think this really is a race boat, but the drawings show a comfy layout so there's no harm in looking at it as a cruising boat. It does make an interesting contrast with the other boats this month.

The most dramatic areas of departure for this design are in the displacement and the distribution of beam. At 11,575 pounds, the Sydney 38 has a D/L of 118 and this puts it in the "light boat" category, drawing a very distinct line between it and the Jeanneau, the Najad and the Elan. This difference would probably be best reflected in the techniques the builder uses to get the weight down. The Sydney 38 uses vacuum-bagged composite bulkheads.

This boat was designed by Murray Burns and Dovell. No, not to be confused with the Aussie doo-wop group Murray Burns and the Dovells. This is an Australian design office headed by Ian Murray of America's Cup fame. The hull form is not tailored to any particular racing handicap system with the idea that boat speed in itself is timeless in its appeal: I'd second that. Compare the plan view of this design with that of the other boats this month. You will quickly see that this design is much finer forward with the deck line from the point of max beam being almost a straight line to the stem. The cutwater of this design is very sharp, and although the L/B is 3.14, which is certainly not narrow, I would guess that the BWL of this design is considerably more narrow than the others and the topsides are quite flared.

The keel shown here is apparently not the "real keel" as the brochure says the keel is a bulbed fin. Draft is a confidence-building 8 feet, 8 inches. I would think that with the Sydney 38 you would have at least a knot in boat speed on any point of sail in any condition over the other three boats.

You had better appreciate that extra knot of boat speed because below you will not have the sumptuous veneered interior that the other boats show.

The galley is minimal, and I don't see any reefer space at all. "Oh boy! Warm Vegemite and cheese sandwiches." There are individual cubby holes for personal gear like Chap Stick, sun block, sunglasses and bandages. Despite the simple layout of this interior, it's amazing just how comfy and cozy you will feel after you beat your friends in by two hours.

This is a tall fractional rig and once again a clear sign that this boat is not intended to be put into the same category as the other three. The SA/D of this design is 26.45. The spreaders are swept about 22 degrees and there is no babystay. This is the only boat this month with a keel-stepped mast. The designers have decided that the extra weight of the

The big, wide cockpit will allow crew functions to be kept in the middle.

two-spreader mast section will be offset by the reduction in windage over a lighter three-spreader section. The two-spreader rig will also be easier to tune. The mainsail roach appears to overlap the backstay by about 16 inches, and although it seems contradictory, with its small, 109-percent jib and big mainsail, the Sydney 38 may be the easiest boat of the four to sail.

This is a racing boat deck layout because this is really a race boat. Six are currently scheduled to be delivered to the Chicago area for one-design racing. The big, wide cockpit will allow crew functions to be kept to the middle. The splayed cockpit well with its narrow side decks will keep the helmsman well outboard.

If your style of sailing includes some club racing and you want to give your local PHRF racing committee fits, bring in a Sydney 38.

North American Distributors for Bashford International are Active Yacht Sails, 29939 S. River Rd., Ste. A, Mt. Clemens, MI 48045. (586) 463-7441. www.activeyachts.com

April 2000

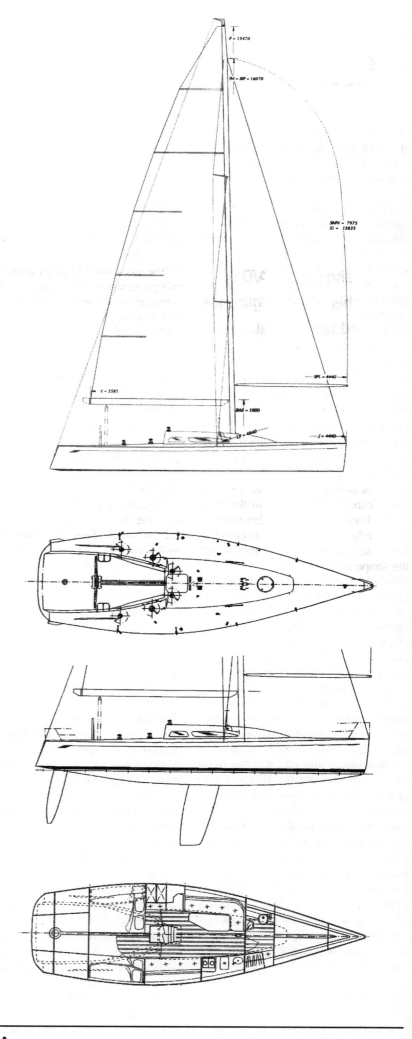

Australian design puts "businesslike" accommodations in a powerful hull shape.

LOA 38'6"; LWL 35'3"; Beam 12'3"; Draft 8'8"; Displacement 11,575 lbs.; Ballast N/A; Sail Area 848 sq. ft.; SA/D 26.45; D/L 118; L/B 3.14; Auxiliary Yanmar 38-hp saildrive; Fuel 26 gals.; Water 52 gals.

Farr 395
Performance Cruiser

This design speaks to me loud and clear. It reflects a combined effort of the Farr design office, the boatbuilding skills of Barry Carroll's crew and the Farr International company's impressive marketing power. The aim is a comfortable and fast club racer i.e., dual-purpose boat. Given the team, I

The rig shows an SA/D of 24.35. This a good figure for a spirited family boat.

think we should expect a fabulous boat, so let's put on our picky hats and look for shortcomings.

I don't think I'll pick on the hull. It has the look of just about everything else we have seen coming out of the Farr office over the last five years. Its IMS origins are obvious with the minimal bow overhang and the flattened canoe-body profile in the way of the keel. The bow in plan view is not overly fine. The stern is broad. I think we can assume that this is not the shape the Farr office would have drawn if it didn't have accommodations to think about.

The D/L is 136. This boat weighs 12,500 pounds and has the same DWL as a Valiant 42. Beam is moderate at 12 feet, 1 inch. You can have either the deep-draft keel at 7 feet, 10 inches or the shoal at 5 feet, 10 inches. Obviously this boat would be much happier with the deeper keel if you were to expect the full performance potential.

The keel is the typical Farr type with a bulb tip and a large fillet radius at the leading edge/hull intersection. The sheerline is very flat. If there is any spring to it at all it can't be more than 2 inches. Still, Farr has always had a way with his distinctive sheerlines, and this one looks good. Remember, a straight-line sheer is only a straight line when your eye is exactly at 90 degrees to the sheer.

The accommodation plan for this 40-footer is laid out for three couples. The V-berth double is shoved way up into the bow, but there's still enough room to keep from being too cramped in the toes.

Considering I have my picky hat on, I would say that this boat doesn't have many lockers. There are two minimal hanging lockers and no wet locker. Note that there are no lockers outboard of the settees. These settees are carried as

far outboard as hull shape will allow. There is just no volume left for storage space. I can't see a handy spot for my guitar.

I like this settee arrangement with the drop-leaf table. Drop-leaf tables aren't sexy, but they are usually the best solution. The galley is fine. There is actually counter space each side of the range.

The deck plan features a nice big cockpit with the traveler right in front of the wheel. There appear to be shallow line lockers over the quarter berths but not much of a lazarette. All lines are led aft and the mainsheet is on a double-ended system led to the secondary winches.

The side decks are clear as there is only a short length of jib track adjacent to the mast. The carbon fiber bowsprit for the asymmetrical chute is retractable into the hull. The flag pole (not shown) is also made of carbon fiber.

This is a good deck layout. Most cruising boats have cockpits that are too small. This cockpit is large, and while it does encroach on the headroom aft, this seems a reasonable compromise to me. There is a transom swim step. I can't find anything to be picky about with this deck layout.

The rig shows an SA/D of 24.35. This a good figure for a spirited family boat. It's far more horsepower per pound than you would have found in a similarly oriented boat from the '70s but still far short of today's hot rods. The jib has a small amount of overlap, but there are no genoas intended for this design. The chainplates are aft and show a 19-degree sweep angle. The sheeting angle from the tack point to the jib track is 13 degrees. The asymmetrical chute flies from the masthead.

In current fashion this design is being promoted as a "one design" with class management by Farr International, in part to "ensure true Corinthian amateur owner driving." I guess it's come to that today. To my eye this just looks like a nice all-around PHRF racer/cruiser. It kind of makes you long for the days when dad drove, mom did the tactics and the crew was made up of the kids and their friends. That sounds like fun.

Farr International Inc., 613 Third St., Suite 11, Annapolis, MD 21403. (410) 268-1001. **www.farr395.org**

January 2001

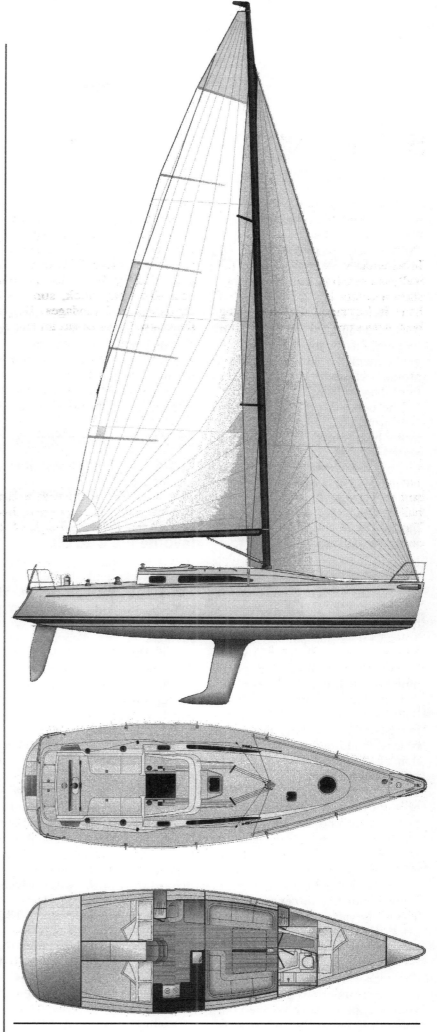

Comfortable all-around boat with plenty of horsepower.

LOA 39'4"; LWL 34'6"; Beam 12'1"; Draft 7'10" (deep), 5'10" (shoal); Displacement 12,500 lbs.; Ballast 4,000 lbs.; Sail Area 820 sq. ft.; SA/D 24.35; D/L 136; L/B 3.27; Auxiliary Volvo MD2040 40-hp diesel; Fuel 38 gals.; Water 40 gals.

X-Yacht IMX 40
Racer Cruiser

I'm a fan of Niels Jeppesen's X-Yachts designs. They are good-looking, fast boats, although I did get a chuckle when I opened the promo package for this newest boat from the company.

The new 40-footer is labeled a "performance cruiser/racer." Now in my book, there is a huge difference between a "performance cruiser" and a "racer." The characteristics that make a boat a successful performance cruiser will not help it when it crosses the starting line in a fleet of racing boats.

I have no problem with this boat. It's just that I have a problem with the ad campaign. I guess my problem is with the term "performance cruiser" and the fact that this label has also been attached to the Valiant 40/42 and similar stalwart cruising boats for the past 27 years. Maybe it's time I updated my definition of performance cruiser.

Let's look at this design from both perspectives: racing and cruising. Start with cruising. The interior is well laid-out in a minor variation of "basic plan A." There are two double quarter berths that can be closed off and have single upper berths overhead. These compartments (there's no way I'll call them "staterooms") are a little tight for my taste. I'm not claustrophobic, but I do like some room for air movement around me when I sleep. I'd be inclined not to enclose these berths. Privacy would suffer, but even the word "privacy" needs redefinition on a 40-foot boat.

This galley is too small for me. The icebox is dinky, and there is minimal counter space. I'd end up putting cooking stuff on the companionway ladder. "Could you get your foot out of my batter please!" This is not a cruiser's galley.

The rest of the layout looks fine. There is a 24-gallon fuel tank and almost 40 gallons of water tankage. This is a little on the anemic side for a true cruising boat. On the other hand, this is more interior than you would want on a racing boat.

The hull looks racy, but it's quite beamy with an L/B of 3.17. Draft is 7 feet, 11 inches and that will work quite nicely on the race course. The

Twenty-five years ago we had dozens of boats like this, including the Pearson 35, Islander 36 and my old favorite the C&C 39.

rudder is a knifelike blade, well aft. The D/L of the hull is 165. The auxiliary is a Volvo 40-horsepower with a saildrive. I have a Volvo saildrive on my own boat, and I love it. There is very low drag from these units.

The keel is a two-part unit with the top fin portion being cast iron, which is then attached to a lead bulb. The bulb attachment is designed to allow a quick and easy change of bulbs. "Would you hand me that heavier bulb dear?"

The rig is a fractional type with 11-degree swept spreaders. I don't have I, J, E and P so I can't tell you the precise SA/D of this rig. It's my guess that it's around 22.5. This is a very standard rig with the traveler placed right in front of the wheel where it belongs. I hate midboom sheeting.

I like this boat. I don't know what to call it, but 25 years ago we had dozens of boats like this, including the Pearson 35, Islander 36 and my old favorite the C&C 39. Some called them "racer/cruisers." I just called them boats. This new X-Yacht is a nice boat.

X-Yachts USA, Foot of Washington Blvd., Stamford, CT 06902. www.x-yachts.com (203) 353-0373.

December 2000

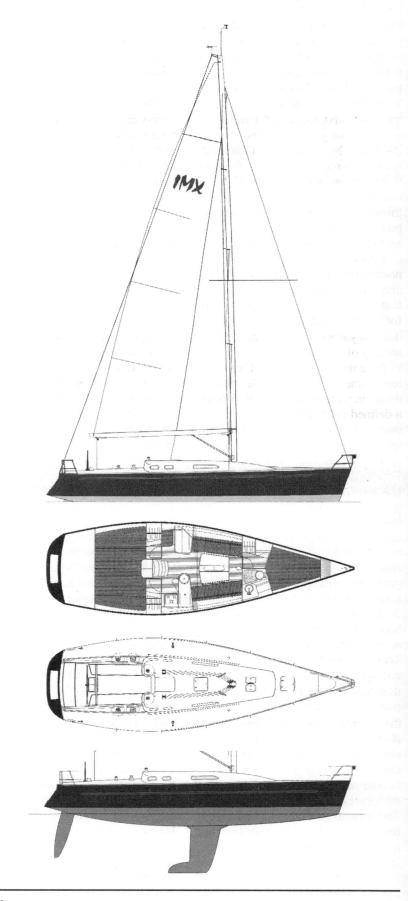

Another fast, comfortable racer/cruiser from Denmark.

LOA 39'8"; LWL 34'5"; Beam 12'6"; Draft 7'11"; Displacement 15,051 lbs.; Ballast 6,393 lbs.; Sail Area 860 sq. ft. (estimated); SA/D 22.5; L/B 3.17; Auxiliary Volvo 40-hp saildrive; Fuel 24 gals.; Water 40 gals.

C&C 121
Racer-Cruiser

Years ago, maybe 30 years ago, a couple of young Canadian designers started a company called Canadian Northern. They produced some very fast boats and, for reasons unknown to me, changed the name of the company by combining their last-name initials so that George Cuthbertson and George Cassian became C&C. Working with a group of Canadian builders C&C gradually grew to be one of the biggest production boatbuilding companies in North America. It pioneered the use of cored laminates and introduced the now universal aluminum toerail. It was responsible for elevating the aesthetics of production yachts in general through the quality of its designs.

Like many builders C&C ran into hard times during the late '80s, I think, in part, because it lost sight of a defined market "target." The boats were no longer racers, but they

It's good to see that the traditions initiated by Cuthbertson and Cassian are being maintained.

didn't make the transition to cruising boats gracefully. C&C gradually shut down and was subsequently bought by Fairport Yachts, builders of the Tartan line. C&C is still a strong market identity. Combined with the design efforts of Tim Jacket, it appears to be making a comeback.

This new C&C 121 is typical of the historical C&C type: the family club-racer/cruiser. The aesthetics are pure C&C. The cabintrunk is very contoured and sculpted with crisp facets. There are no ports forward of the big fixed windows. This saves the builder money and also reinforces the C&C look. All in all, this is a very handsome boat.

The hull shape features an extremely wide transom. It's too wide for my eye, but this beam aft benefits the cockpit layout and the aft cabin accommodations. Is this shape bad? or slow? No, I don't think so. Sometimes when you get a boat with too much beam aft the

waterlines go quite asymmetrical when the boat heels over giving it a multiple personality, i.e. it's balanced and well-behaved when sailed upright, but a real unbalanced bear when it's heeled. I would think that a designer of Jacket's experience has taken this into consideration. Note how far aft the keel is. This will help. Certainly almost all boats sail better with heel angle minimized.

The rest of the hull shape is really nice. There is a definite V to the forefoot and this V is carried aft with a 12-degree deadrise angle. This deadrise gradually fairs out as you approach the transom. Starting at station 9 the run is quite flat. The lines plan shows almost a knuckle where this transition from deadrise to flat occurs. With the big wide transom I would be concerned that this transom might slap in some moorage situations. That aside I think this boat will be quite fast. The D/L is a moderate 141. Three keels are available drawing 8 feet; 6 feet, 6 inches; or 5 feet.

This is an amazing interior for a 40-foot boat. There are berths for two couples, a large head with shower stall aft and a well-laid-out galley and nav station. The saloon area features a drop-leaf table and room for at least four people to dine. I like to see a table overlap the seats by 3 inches, but this one looks like it stops short of the settee fronts. Clearance over the aft berth is 30 inches. I wouldn't consider this clearance generous, but it is adequate. The engine is tucked into the box at the foot of the companionway. Note there is counter space on both sides of the range. There is also a lot of locker space in this design.

The rig is normal with an SA/D of 23.16 and an 8-degree sweep to the spreaders. The main overlaps the backstay by about a foot.

It's good to see that the traditions initiated by Cuthbertson and Cassian are being maintained.

C&C Yachts, 1920 Fairport Nursery Rd., Fairport Harbor, OH 44077. **www.c-cyachts.com** *(440) 354-3111.*

July 1999

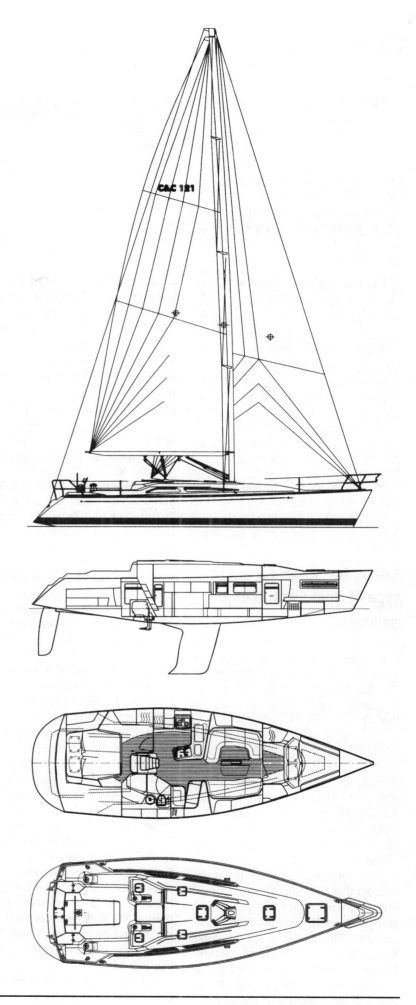

Roomy and fast family racer-cruiser.

LOA 40'; LWL 35'6"; Beam 13'1"; Draft 10'11"; Displacement 14,100 lbs.; Ballast 5,500 lbs.; Sail Area 845 sq. ft.; SA/D 23.16; D/L 140.7; L/B 3.05; Auxiliary Volvo MD 2040 with 120 S-D saildrive; Fuel 35 gals.; Water 80 gals.

Quest 40
Performance Cruiser

Holby Marine, builder of Quest boats, has added this new Rodger Martin design to its line. It is yet another performance cruiser, and in this case the pedigree of the other Quest models is there to back up the claim of performance. To me it's a handsome but not beautiful boat, although that's a very subjective area, and it wouldn't surprise me if you found the Q40 beautiful. I'd call this design a "fusion" type where you can see that the line between racing boat characteristics and cruising boat characteristics has been blurred to produce a true dual-purpose boat.

Rodger Martin likes very rounded hull shapes. They work well for him. In this case, while the BWL is narrow, the beam on deck is wide so that the L/B for this model is 2.94 indicating a very beamy boat. As you can plainly see in the deck plan the beam is carried aft to produce a very wide transom.

The ends are short giving this 40-footer a DWL of 36 feet, 6 inches and a D/L of 117 with its 12,750-pound displacement. This hull is all effec-

I think the Quest 40 is the type of boat I would enjoy sailing.

tive sailing length. Two keels are available, but I'd lean heavily toward the deeper keel with its 7-foot, 11-inch draft over the optional shoal keel that draws 5 feet, 11 inches.

The rig is a tall fractional type with nonoverlapping headsails, masthead asymmetrical chute and a loose-footed, extended-roach main. My guess is that this roach laps the backstay by 30 inches. This can make tacking in the light stuff less than elegant as the roach will inevitably hang up on the backstay as the main tries to pass through. Imagine this main without that overlapping roach, however, and you can see that you would give up about 18 percent of the mainsail area. That's a lot of off-the-wind horsepower to lose. If I use I, J, E and P, I get an SA/D of 24.83, but if you use the 105 percent jib and all the mainsail area including the roach I get a SA/D of 30. Be sure when you compare these ratios that you are using the same base data.

Spreaders on the Quest are swept 15 degrees with the chainplates right at the hull edge. Genoa jibs have all but disappeared on modern performance-oriented rigs, making inboard chainplates unnecessary. This cleans up the side decks while reducing the compressive load on the mast. This is a direct trickle-down effect from racing and works very well for cruising boats.

The interior is laid out for two couples or a family. There is one head with a shower stall aft. The galley is on the puny side for me and the centerline counter that holds the sinks is really the engine box. The aft double berth extends athwartships under the cockpit and it's huge. I'm not sure I would want to be the one sleeping aft in this berth. The forward double berth is a standard V-berth, but with plenty of room at the toes. This layout is a wee bit short on hanging locker space, but when you have only 12,750 pounds of displacement, i.e. volume, to work with you do have to give up something. What you are not giving up in this design is boat speed.

The deck plan shows a racing-style cockpit with the wheel just aft of the mainsheet traveler. The large diameter wheel requires a well to keep the top of the wheel within ergonomic limits. The aft end of the cockpit can be left open to the swim step or closed off with a feature labeled on the drawings as "cooler seat." My wife has heated seats in her Subaru. I think a cooler seat would work well in the summer. There are toe-Bensons molded into the cockpit sole to help you retain your footing when the boat heels. These work well when heeled, but they're a pain when you are flat on the hook. Note that the halyards all lead aft under a cowling.

I can't remember the last time a new client asked for a slow boat. "Faster in the light stuff, faster in the heavy, able to point higher and foot faster," is the usual design directive. Going fast is fun and going slow is okay when it's by choice and not just because of a restrictive or poor design. My dark secret is that I like to zip around the bay at 50 mph like an idiot in my Boston Whaler imagining I'm Bill Muncey.

I think the Quest 40 is the type of boat I would enjoy sailing.

Holby Marine Co., 97 Broad Common Rd., Bristol, RI 02809. **www.holbymarine.com** *(401) 253-1711.*

September 2002

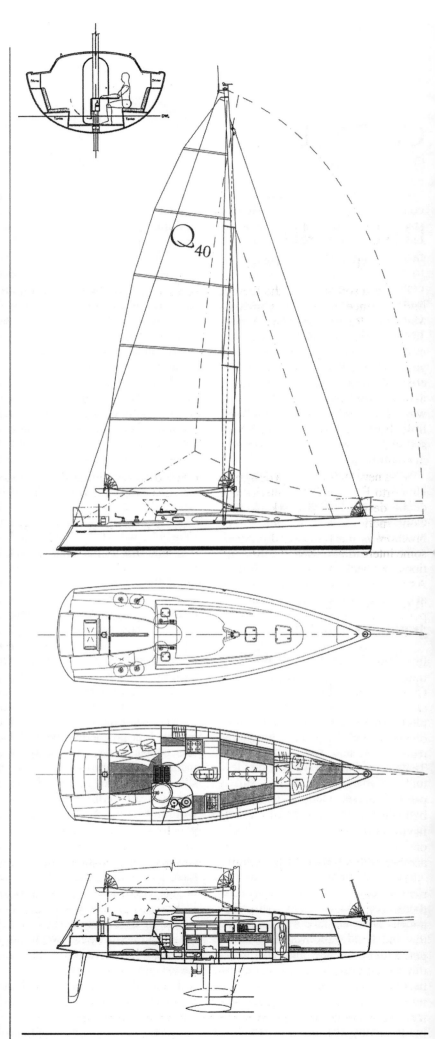

A hybrid racer-cruiser for performance in all conditions.

LOA 40'; LWL 36'6"; Beam 13'7"; Draft 7'11"; Displacement 12,750 lbs.; Ballast 5,300 lbs.; Sail Area 1,023 sq. ft.; SA/D 30 (with roach); D/L 117; L/B 2.94; Auxiliary Yanmar 3GM; Fuel 30 gals.; Water 80 gals.

Dufour 40
Performance Cruiser

I have a soft spot for the Dufour line. I once sailed a Chicago-Mackinac Race in a Dufour Arpege 30. We were the slowest rated boat in the fleet and the light winds that year did not favor our underpowered little boat. Insects were faster than we were, plaguing us the entire way. Still it was a very interesting little boat well suited to offshore sailing, a style we seldom see today in small boats.

This new Dufour 40 is a design by Umberto Felci with the interior and deck design by Patrick Roseo. Construction is French. The brochure is marvelous and contains some interesting technical contradictions, but heck, it's only advertising. As I see it, the new 40 is an attempt at a comfortable and quick dual-purpose boat, something we are seeing frequently these days.

The hull shows short ends and lots of beam aft. The L/B is 3.17 and that indicates a beamy boat. Carrying that beam aft adds stability and sailing length but more importantly, I think, makes for more interior volume aft. You see this feature regularly today. The D/L is 165. There is nothing unusual about this hull shape that I can see from the profile and plan view. The canoe body maximum depth looks pretty far aft. There are two keels available: one with a 5-foot, 3-inch draft and another with a 6-foot, 11-inch draft.

You can choose from three interior layouts. The center portion of the interior—the galley, nav area and saloon—remain the same but the end treatments differ. You can get three staterooms and two heads, three staterooms with one head or two staterooms with one head. The three stateroom versions are ideal for chartering or cruising with big families. There is a choice of forward stateroom layouts and I prefer the one with the berth to the side as it affords a much larger fo'c'sle for stowage. You pay for this with a slightly smaller double berth. If

you go with the two stateroom layout you get a big lazarette to starboard, a nice shower stall and the large fo'c'sle.

The deck-stepped, fractional rig is supported by swept spreaders. I don't trust brochure "sail area" figures; I trust I, J, E and P dimensions. I have a sail area listed for the 40 as 958 square feet and this works out to a SA/D ratio of 24. This looks like an artificially high number to me so I would conclude that the SA listed includes mainsail roach and perhaps

The new 40 is an attempt at a comfortable and quick dual-purpose boat.

even some genoa LP in addition to the regular J dimension. This is common in brochures but doesn't help us in comparing rig figures. Using the actual I, J, E and P numbers I get a SA/D of 18.32. One of the benefits of the fractional rig is that it gets the mast farther forward than it would be with a masthead rig. This puts the mast or compression post, in this case, where it doesn't interfere as much with the saloon layout.

This is a handsome boat. The flattish sheerline compliments the contours of the cabintrunk. I don't have a deck plan but I would imagine that with that much beam aft the cockpit would be very spacious.

Construction is similar to what we see in many of the French production boats with a single skin laminate below the DWL and a cored laminate above the DWL. The deck is laid up using the Resin Transfer Molding (like Scrimp) method for significant weight savings. The shoal draft keel is cast iron.

Dufour Yachts USA Inc., 1 Chelsea Court, Annapolis, MD 21403. (410) 268-6417. On the Web at **www.dufouryachts.com**

December 2002

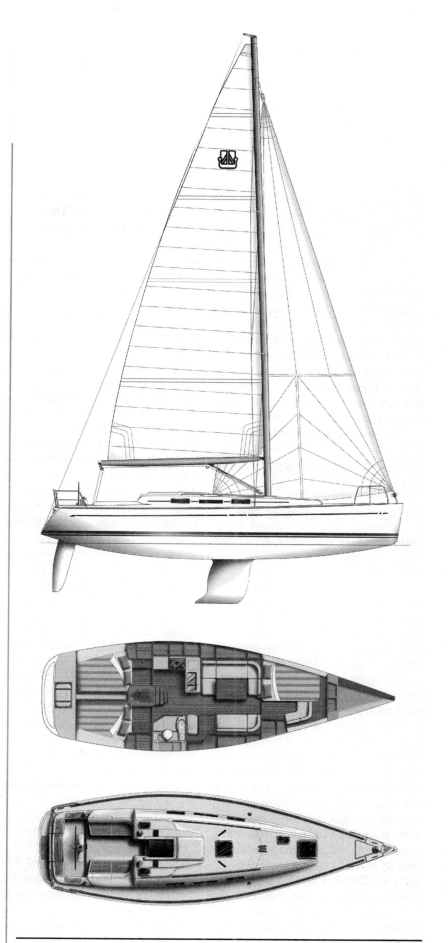

A handsome, comfortable boat with moving power.

LOA 40'8"; LWL 35'2"; Beam 12'10"; Draft 6'11" (deep), 5'3" (shoal); Displacement 16,133 lbs,; Ballast 5,967 lbs.; Sail Area 958 sq. ft.; SA/D 24; D/L 165; L/B 3.17; Auxiliary Volvo Penta 40 hp; Fuel 42 gals.; Water 92 gals.

Bavaria 41
Performance Cruiser

This new Bavaria 41 is a J&J design. The D/L is 171, L/B is 3.14 and the ballast-to-displacement ratio is 34 percent. "Whatever happened to the old rule of thumb that ballast-displacement ratios should be 40 percent?" That rule of thumb is obsolete. Cruising boats have undergone a dramatic change in the last 30 years, in large part because of what is now considered a "normal" complement of comfort-oriented gizmos. In 1966

This is a good looking, very moderate boat.

the average 45-footer would have had one battery for the house and one battery to start the engine. The typical genset of today, with its own dedicated starting battery, would have been out of the question, let alone a 600-amp hour battery bank and a powerful inverter. Ground tackle? Hah! This old 45-footer would have had a 45-pound Danforth with 20 feet of chain and 200 feet of rode.

Today there would be three anchors with at least one of them on 300 feet or more of 3/8-inch chain at 1.78 pounds per foot. Then there is refrigeration, air conditioning, a plethora of navigation instruments (in duplicate), stereo, television, computer, hair dryer, coffee grinder, microwave, blender (for margaritas), multiple roller-furling systems and a variety of additional gear. The designer must compensate for the weight of all this additional gear by cutting back on ballast in order to hit the original displacement target. Today I use 34 percent as the rule of thumb for ballast.

The good news is that we now know how to shape keels to get the VCG as low as possible so there will be no reduction in stability. The key is not the amount of ballast but its location. This Bavaria 41, for exam-

ple, shows a keel with a bulb, and a root chord that is shorter than its tip chord. Both these features help lower the vertical center of gravity. You can have either a 6-foot, 10-inch draft model or the shoal-draft model at 5 feet, 7 inches.

The rig is a fractional type with double swept spreaders. The mainsheet is midboom and while this gets the mainsheet out of the cockpit I still don't like it. Do this experiment the next time you are sailing on a boat with midboom sheeting. When hard on the wind reach up and grab the outboard end of the boom and try to move it with your hand. It's amazing how easy it is to move the boom that way. (Maybe not on the 75-foot *Pyewacket*, but on most boats under 40 feet it's relatively easy.) Now try the same thing at the midboom position. It takes a lot more force to accomplish the same thing. Still, people like to get the cockpit clear of hardware and lines. The other advantage to moving the mainsheet and traveler forward is that it frees up space for a nice dodger.

There are two interior layouts for the 41. You can have either two mirror-image quarter cabins with double berths and hanging lockers, or a single quarter cabin.

The single aft stateroom model has the galley aft to starboard. This is a good galley layout. In this layout the nav station is adjacent to the dinette. There is a large shape just forward of the nav station, but due to the cryptic nature of the drawing I can't tell what it is. The heads and the V-berth are common to both layouts.

This is a good looking, very moderate boat.

Bavaria Yachts/Yacht Sails West, P.O. Box 3415, Annapolis, MD 21403. **www.bavariayachts.com** *(401) 990-0007.*

November 2002

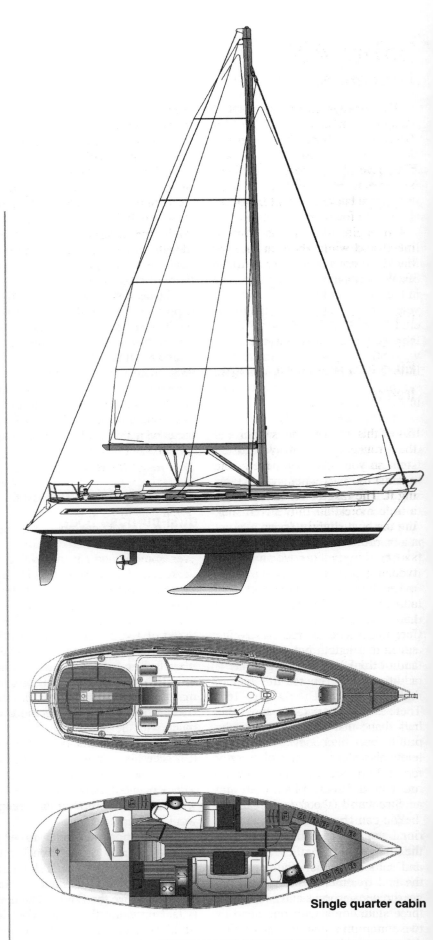

Single quarter cabin

Comfort and performance in a 'moderate' hull shape.

LOA 41'2"; LWL 36'4"; Beam 13'1"; Draft 6'10" (standard), 5'7" (shoal); Displacement 18,298 lbs.; Ballast 6,285 lbs. (standard), 5,621 lbs. (shoal); Sail Area 952 sq. ft. (including genoa); SA/D 21.9 (including genoa); D/L 171; L/B 3.14; Auxiliary Volvo Perkins D2-55 with saildrive; Fuel 50 gals.; Water 80 gals.

Sabre 426
Performance Cruiser

I've always liked Jim Taylor's design work and I like this new Sabre model. Sabre has given us a long series of good all round boats that have always been attractive. I see several areas in this design where they have bucked current trends and I'd like to focus on those areas.

To begin, look at this bow. It's raked and while short in its overhang, it's not as truncated as we are used to seeing today. The real bene-

It's interesting to watch the cross-pollination of Euro and American design trends.

fits of this type of bow is that it gets the ground tackle away from the stem so you don't bang the anchor against the boat when you are raising it. The raked bow also provides a little more flair to the bow, making the boat slightly dryer.

Of course you do give up a bit of sailing length forward with this type of bow. If we imagine this bow more close to plumb we could gain a theoretical additional 10 inches of DWL, bringing the DWL from 36 feet to 36 feet, 10 inches. Using a speed-to-length ratio of 1.34, this additional DWL would give us an additional .132 knots of theoretical hull speed.

The stern is certainly more narrow than we would see on a comparable French design. There is an elongated skeg forward of the rudder. I have not seen a skeg drawn out this far before.

Structurally the skeg can be a big help in stiffening what would be a long flat panel. Another benefit of this long skeg is that it increases the builder's options of shaft angle and shaft log arrangement. This is a minor item on the surface but it can pay big dividends when it comes to designing the engine installation. The D/L is 230.

You have your choice of two keels. The deep draft keel draws 6 feet, 10 inches. The shoal draft keel is a winged-keel and draws 5 feet. The keel wings are swept and of relatively high aspect ratio. Short fat wings work as well as short fat

keels. There is a small keel fin protrusion below the wings presumable to help protect the wings in case of grounding or setting on the hard.

All in all I think what we see when we look at the Sabre 426 hull is an intelligent amalgam of features that the builder has learned work well for pragmatic construction details in addition to providing the boat owner with a more user-friendly boat. The rig differs from the current crop of fractional rigs in that this one is a masthead rig. The three spreaders are slightly swept. The mainsheet is forward of midboom and will require a strong boom section to resist the bending moment imposed by this sheeting arrangement. Note that the mainsheet loads are spread out over three blocks to help with this load. I'd much rather see end-boom sheeting.

The SA/D is 17.7. This is not enough for blistering light air speed, but you won't have to reef when the wind gets to 18 knots either.

Jim Taylor designed the hull, appendages and rig for the 426. The rest of the design work was an in-house effort by Sabre's design team. For obvious reasons I'm partial to the outhouse approach, but in this case the Sabre designers have given the 426 a great interior layout. It's a two stateroom boat, so if there are more kids you will have to put them on the settees in the cabin for the night. I miss the days of pilot berths. I really like the symmetrically opposed settees, which make the saloon seem inviting and a comfy place to sit and go over the action of the day. The nav station is big as is the galley. This is a good example of the modern aft-cockpit interior layout. The focus is definitely on two-couple cruising.

It's interesting to watch the cross-pollination of Euro and American design trends. This clean looking Sabre gives us a Euro-style interior while maintaining the big lazarette aft. The hull and rig show details that have disappeared from most of the Euro boats. I find this a very interesting design.

Sabre Yachts, Box 134, South Casco, ME 04077. (207) 655-3831. www.sabreyachts.com

December 2002

A purposeful array of features in an attractive, user-friendly boat.

LOA 42'6"; LWL 36'; Beam 13'5"; Draft 6'10" (deep), 5' (shoal); Displacement 24,000 lbs.; Ballast 8,400 lbs.; Sail Area 920 sq. ft.; SA/D 17.7; D/L 230; L/B 3.22; Auxiliary Westerbeke 55A; Fuel 60 gals.; Water 120 gals.

Sweden Yacht 42
Performance Cruiser

With no prevailing universal rating rule, builders and designers are interested in getting as much mileage out of a given design as possible. Hence the swing toward comfort. Among other things, cruising designs are more "market durable."

This boat isn't light by today's standards, and in fact, despite its racy looks, the Sweden is surprisingly heavy.

This boat will make a good, quick and comfy cruiser.

The Sweden 42 was designed by Peter Norlin and Jens Ostmann. The hull form shows a deep canoe body with pronounced rocker. The forefoot knuckle is well below the DWL. The counter aft is quite elevated with a generous overhang. In plan view take a look at the curve made by the end of the transom. See how rounded this line is. This indicates soft bilges aft and a gentle, arced shape to the stern sections. All in all the Sweden hull looks very conventional, almost retro. The D/L is 199.57.

The rig is drawn as a fractional type with a full-hoist, self-tacking working jib. The sailplan drawing does not indicate any genoa, but I think I can see genoa tracks on the deck plan. The spreaders are swept, and there are two sets of them. The mainsheet is midboom, which frees up the cockpit but puts tremendous loads on the mainsheet and housetop traveler.

The SA/D is 20.56.

The interior is laid out for three couples with three double berths. This means that six people must be able to sit around the large dinette and dine in comfort. I'm not sure this dinette is that big, but you could always pull up a folding chair. The galley is dinky. I don't like it. If the icebox is outboard of the sink, it *can't* be big enough. Much of the food preparation will need to be done in the sinks as there is precious little counter space.

The nav area, on the other hand, is expansive. The forward head has a shower stall that intrudes into the fo'c'sle area. The aft head is generous in size, but has no enclosed shower stall.

The deck plan shows a long cockpit with benches big enough to stretch out on. The cockpit opens up aft into a T-shape with the seats cleverly pushed outboard to get the helmsman into the best position to see the luff of the jib. This also allows an open passageway through to the transom swim step. There appears to be a recess for the dodger to fold down into, X-Yacht style.

This is a good boat. The galley is not my style, but the rest of the design looks just fine. This will make a good, quick and comfy cruiser.

Sweden Yachts, Box 80, SE-444 21 Stenungsund, 46 303 77 06 40, **www.swedenyachts.se**. *In the U.S. call (203) 861-6578.*

September 2001

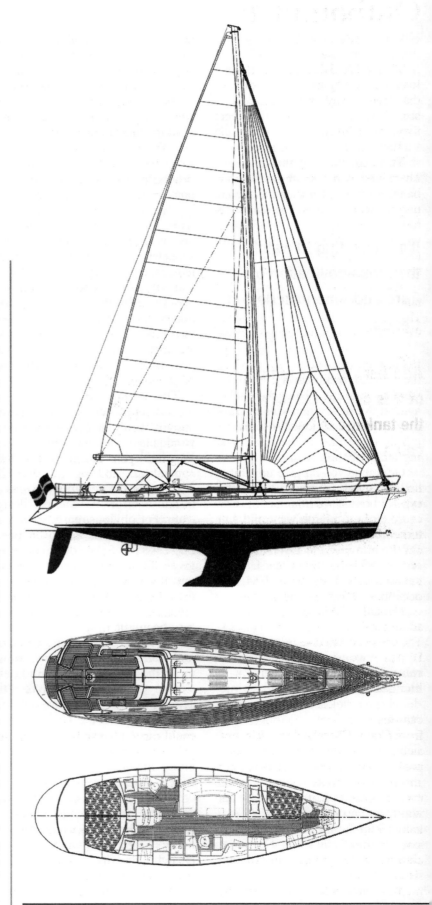

Fast, easy-to-handle cruiser with a clever cockpit.

LOA 42'6"; LWL 35'6"; Beam 12'9"; Draft 6'11"; Displacement 20,000 lbs.; Ballast 8,400 lbs.; Sail Area 947 sq. ft.; SA/D 20.56; D/L 199.57; L/B 3.32; Auxiliary 55-hp Volvo Penta; Fuel 52 gals.; Water 105 gals.

Outbound 44
Performance Cruiser

This Carl Schumacher design was built in China. Hull No. 1 was delivered to Oakland. This boat is aimed at the ex-racer who now wants to go cruising.

This is a very handsome boat with short ends and moderate beam. There is enough overhang to the bow so that you won't bonk your anchor on the stem when you raise it. The rudder is skeg-hung and supported with bearings at the heel, hull and the underside of the deck. This is a strong way to do it.

The keel is a bulbed, low-aspect-ratio fin with a 6-foot, 4-inch draft. The hull is molded in one piece with the bulk of the ballast internal in the

Another interesting feature of this design is that all the tankage is below the cabin sole.

fin. The bulb is formed by bolting on two lead cheek pieces to the outside of the molded fin, then glassing over these. You just can't pull a bulb shape out of a one-piece mold. The beauty of the molded-in fin is that it gives the 44 a very deep sump. This keel combines the best of both worlds.

The D/L of this design, using the advertised displacement, is 189. The difference between D/Ls of the IP 420 and the Outbound 44 is a reflection of the 44's greater water-line length.

I like this interior. The original drawings for this layout come from Craig Chamberlain. It's not as angular as the IP's layout, but I prefer its more conventional spaces and shapes. Obviously the raised saloon feature, with big windows and elevated cabin sole, lets in a lot more light than the typical "buried" interior. Note the counter space each side of the sinks. The reefer is not very convenient, as you will need to keep the counter space beside the stove clear during cooking. Maybe the reefer could have gone under the center island and been accessed with both top and front opening doors. This would keep the counter

top clear. Then the stove could have crept forward enough to have counter space each side of it so you can put your pots there when cooking. Keeping the cook happy is very important.

There is no shower stall in either head. I'm sure you can arrange a shower curtain in the aft head, but people have come to expect stalls. The forward head features a pullout type basin over the toilet.

There is a watertight bulkhead forward with a big fo'c'sle. There is also a huge lazarette. Another interesting feature of this design is that all the tankage is below the cabin sole. This gets it out of the accommodations, i.e. under settees, and also helps keep the boat's overall VCG down.

The deck design uses deep bulwarks capped with an aluminum toerail. This is the ultimate in security and looks good too. The cockpit is long and opens directly to the swim step. Cabintrunk lines are clean and void of any clutter with teak trim. There is a short extension to the bow in the form of an anchor roller. This is tied down to the stem with a short bobstay, so that the genoa can be flown from this tack point. I wonder why the bow could not have been extended an additional 8 inches to eliminate this extension? That would have been better.

The rig is a textbook double-spreader sloop type, with provision for both inner and outer forestays. There is minimal sweep to the spreaders, and with the genoa roller furled on the outer headstay, you could carry a hanked-on staysail for heavier air. Some owners may wish to roller furl both headsails. The SA/D of this design is 18.44.

I'm certain working in China has provided its own level of excitement for the Outbound group, as if bringing out a new design is not exciting enough on its own. Now the boat is here. The boat is sailing and it's time to see what the market thinks.

Superior Yachts West, 29 Embarcadero Cove, Oakland, CA 94606. (510) 534-9492, fax (510) 534-9495.

October 1999

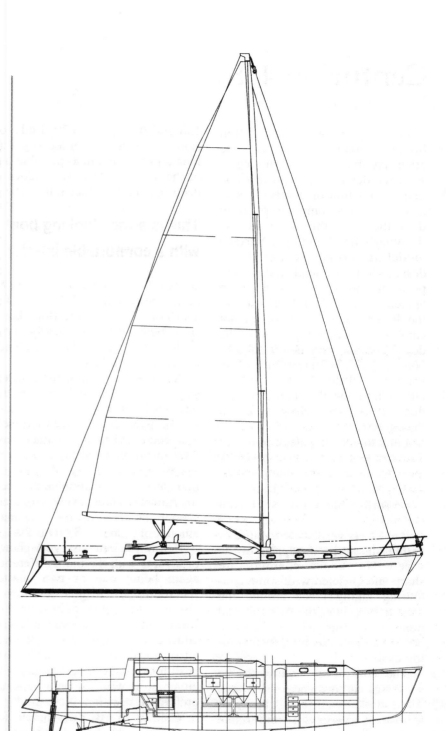

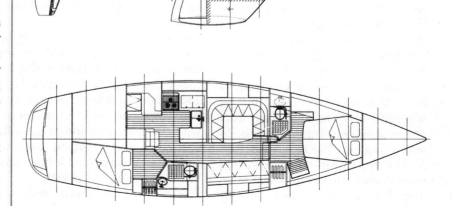

A comfortable boat for the retired racer.

LOA 44'11"; LWL 40'5"; Beam 13'4"; Draft 6'4"; Displacement 28,000 lbs.; Ballast 10,151 lbs.; Sail Area 1,063 sq. ft.; SA/D 18.44; D/L 189; L/B 3.37; Auxiliary 75-hp Yanmar; Fuel 160 gals.; Water 200 gals.

Centurion 45S
Performance Cruiser

My right hand man, Ben Souquet, made a comment the other day that we are beginning to see deck designs that appear to be more a function of a specific surface modeling computer program than they are the work of the designer's hand and eye. Surface modeling programs can be a designer's best friend and a very powerful tool that you can use to "picture" the boat while it is still in the design stage. But if you are not careful, the tail begins to wag the dog. This handsome new Wauquiez boat designed by Berret/Racoupeau shows a little of this effect, although to give the designers their due, it could be exactly the effect they were after.

Let's look at this deck in detail. The contours of the cabintrunk have to blend or complement the spring of the sheer. This design has some spring, but to my eye it's not enhanced by that flattened cove stripe. The cove stripe curvature or spring must echo the spring of the sheer. The house contours are sharp and chiseled with some contouring taking place around the mast to help bury the halyards and other lines running aft under a hoodlike piece, keeping the cabintop clean.

The cockpit is large with the coamings cut away near the wheel. This works well and gives the helmsman a variety of comfortable perches. The big wheel sinks into a well in the cockpit sole to keep the top of it in the ergonomic comfort range. The mainsheet traveler is directly forward of the wheel, making quick adjustments easy.

There appears to be a toe benson on the cockpit sole for footing while heeled. These cockpit seats are just about long enough to stretch out on. The helm seat connects to the face of the transom and hinges down to form a swim step. The life raft is tucked directly underneath the helmsman. In an age where cockpits have shrunk to make room for more accommodations, it's good to see that Berret/Racoupeau have resisted that trend and given us a real sailor's cockpit.

The hull looks fast. The D/L is

158 and the L/B is 3.29. Ends, of course, are short in order to get as long a sailing length as possible out of the 45-foot LOA. The rudder is deep and high aspect ratio. There

This is a racy looking boat with a comfortable interior.

are two keel models: one for an 8-foot, 2-inch draft and the other for a 6-foot, 5-inch draft. Both keels show bulbs at the tip, nearly vertical leading edges, and marked leading-edge hull fillets.

Again we see a rig with the headstay going almost all the way to the masthead. I'm certain that this feature keeps the head of the asymmetrical chute, hoisted to the masthead, away from the headstay to make it easier to fly and jibe. A stiff top mast section will eliminate the need for runners. Three swept spreaders support the mast drawn with a small amount of prebend. SA/D is 20.7.

Below you can have your choice of layouts with the main difference again being one or two quarter staterooms aft. In this design you also have the option of how the forward stateroom is arranged with either a centerline double with head aft or a Pullman style double with head forward. I see no advantage to either, so it will just be a personal preference decision. Note the large fo'c'sle with its own hatch for access from the deck. This is a very handy feature. I like the big galley.

A 55-horsepower Volvo Perkins with a saildrive is tucked under the companionway. I like saildrives and have one on my own boat. There is tankage for 66 gallons of fuel and 132 gallons of water. The hull has a balsa core, and the laminate is done with the resin infusion process for optimum glass-to-resin content. Vinylester resin is used for the outer layers of the hull sandwich.

This is a racy looking boat with a comfortable interior. I don't know what more you could want.

Wauquiez USA, 24 North Market St., Ste. 201, Charleston, SC 29401. **www.wauquiez.com** *(843) 805-5000.*

November 2002

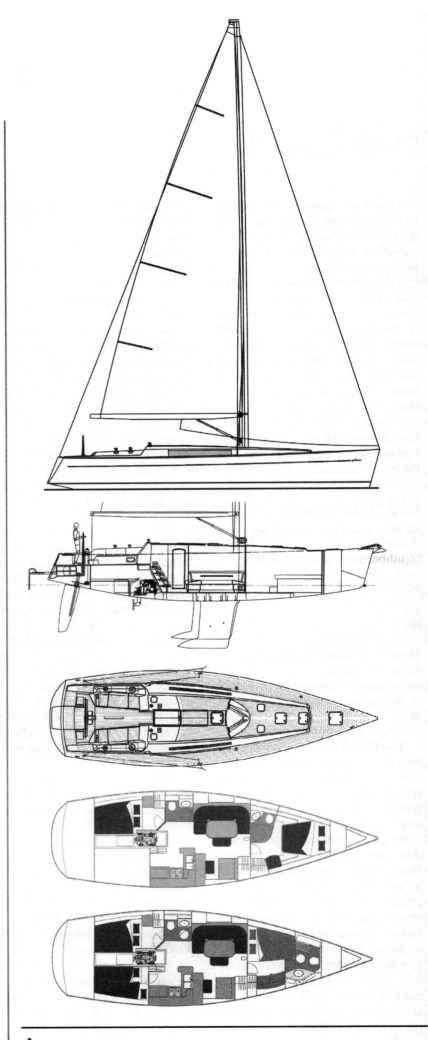

A racy cruiser that's a sailor's boat.

LOA 45'; LWL 40'3"; Beam 13'8"; Draft 8'2" (standard), 6'5" (shoal); Displacement 23,148 lbs.; Ballast 8,488 lbs. (standard), 8,818 (shoal); Sail Area 1,050 sq. ft.; SA/D 20.7; D/L 158; L/B 3.29; Auxiliary Volvo 55-hp; Fuel 66 gals.; Water 132 gals.

Firefly
Racer-Cruiser

Chuck Paine's Morris-built *Reindeer* turned a few heads in 1999 when it showed the racing fleet that Chuck knew a thing or two about what makes a boat fast. In the wake of *Reindeer* comes *Firefly*, designed for Patrick Wilmerding. The new boat will sail in "fun races" and be a comfy cruising boat the rest of the time. Construction is at Tom Morris' yard with all the structural parts being supplied by my old pal Mark Lyndsey at Boston Boatworks. Hull and deck are vacuum bagged and oven cured.

Let's start out with this mysterious sailplan. I called Chuck to ask him why the minimal headstay offset. Why not just make this a masthead rig instead of a 15/16ths rig as drawn? Chuck gave me various nebulous reasons why fractional rigs had performance advantages, but I don't question that. What I do question is the performance advantage of this tiny offset.

This one's a keeper. It will be fun to see what this design can do on the race course.

In this case I would have liked to see at least the spinnaker hoist go to the masthead. But this spinnaker is just above the hounds and still about 10 inches short. To my eye this looks to be a sailmaker's decision. Having said all that, this is still a very handsome boat and that's what we would expect from Chuck Paine.

The SA/D is 21.36. Note that both a racing mainsail and a cruising main are drawn. The cruising main is slightly shorter on the hoist and has less roach. Mast and boom are carbon fiber from GMT. The shrouds are in-line and runners and checkstays will be required to keep this mast in column.

The hull lines show a boat with short ends and a long sailing length. There is a hint of hollow in the entry and the forefoot sections have deadrise. This deadrise carries through the entire length of

the boat and almost fairs out to a tangent at the transom, but not quite. The keel is a large planform fin-and-bulb type with an upper fin portion made of welded 316L stainless steel. It is imperative if you are chasing modern performance speed targets that you do a keel like this. There is no substitute for a low VCG.

The D/L for this design is 146 and that puts this design in the slightly lighter than moderate category. The rudder is a huge, carbon fiber semi-balanced spade with what looks to be about a 20 percent balance area. I like big rudders. I have never had a client call and tell me his rudder was too big. With the prop forward and this clean run, this boat should back up under power like a dream.

This is a very conventional interior layout and close to perfect in my book. The galley is large with plenty of counter space. There is counter space on each side of the sink and each side of the range. You need counter space to hold pots on while you are cooking. The ice box is located where crewmembers can get their own beverages without disturbing the cook.

The saloon is down a step with settee berths flanked by pilot berths. I presume there could be a V-berth filler to convert the forward V-berths into a double. The aft stateroom has quarter berths and an athwartships berth section that I think is designed to allow you to use it as a double berth. Maybe it's just a place to throw sails. This is a simple and effective layout.

Chuck's notes call this an "heirloom quality" yacht. I think that is fancy talk for a structurally durable boat designed to pursue that timeless target of comfort and speed. Quality design combined with quality construction always manages to remain in style. This one's a keeper. It will be fun to see what this design can do on the race course.

C.W. Paine Yacht Design Inc., Sea St., Camden, ME 04843, (207) 236-2166. **www.chuckpaine.com**

June 2000

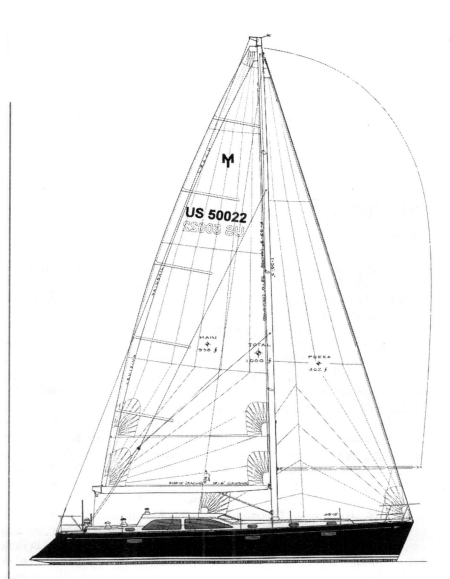

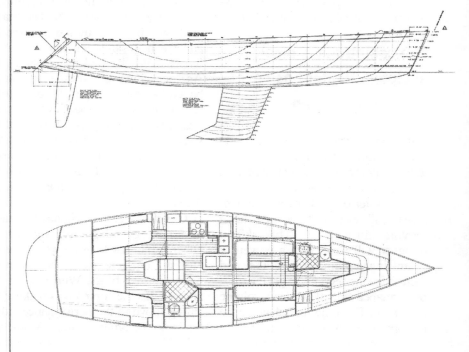

Fast, comfortable successor to *Reindeer*.

LOA 45'2"; LWL 39'7"; Beam 13'3"; Draft 8'; Displacement 20,500 lbs.; Ballast 8,600 lbs.; Sail Area 1,000 sq. ft.; SA/D 21.36; D/L 146; L/B 3.4; Auxiliary 51-hp Yanmar; Fuel 60 gals.; Water 82 gals.

Swan 45
Racer-Cruiser

The design of this Swan 45 was drawn by the Frers office. This is a great looking boat with an aggressive appearance that, upon closer inspection, hides a fairly moderate approach to hull form.

By "moderate" I refer to displacement, which in this case is at the light end of moderate. Gentle reader, let me explain one more time in answer to the many letters that I get: "Displacement" and "weight" are the same thing. A boat displaces its own weight in water, and that's why we call it displacement. Since the 45 has a displacement of 19,510 pounds, it weighs 19,510 pounds. This weight (measured "light," i.e., without gear, crew, fuel or stores) gives the Swan a D/L of 140.2.

We have a curious mix here of IMS-style, short-ended hull shapes, with a heavier hull than is usually found on race-type boats. Look at the rocker forward and the way it dramat-

The cabintrunk is nicely sculpted. Nautor has never built an ugly Swan.

ically curves up to the elevated and exposed forefoot knuckle. Also look at the way the Swan's rocker flattens out around the keel area.

The water doesn't see two-dimensional hull shapes. It sees a volume moving through it. The skilled designer will work with a proven or promising volume/area curve and then shape the sections to get the most performance out of a given volume and DWL. This requires balancing the performance components to fit the desired overall personality of the boat.

Look at this unusual rudder shape. There is a definite, gentle S-curve to the leading edge. This may be a function of simply increasing the chord length at the top or "roof" of the rudder so that there is a thicker foil there to accommodate a bigger rudder stock. Whatever the reason, it sure looks odd. But then most advances in

yacht design look odd when we first see them. The keel is an I-shaped fin and bulb. Draft is 9 feet, 2 inches.

I like the look of this boat. The sheer is flattish but goes well with the short ends. The cabintrunk is nicely sculpted. Nautor has never built an ugly Swan. The cockpit is arranged for racing with a big wheel and no coamings aft. Side decks are very broad. The mainsheet traveler is on the cockpit sole, where it should be. The mainsheet is double ended and leads to the winches just forward of the wheel. The open transom will work well for cruising.

Look at three of the four boats this month and you will see fractional rigs with swept spreaders. This is definitely the rig of the day. Big jibs are out and small jibs are in. Big mainsails with lots of roach overlapping the backstay are almost standard. On this rig the backstay is shown as a removable stay (dotted line) so that backstay loads will be taken by the mainsheet and the mainsail leach much of the time making the backstay redundant. Another drawing shows a backstay batten like on a Melges 24 to lift the stay away from the roach when tacking. It sounds scary but consider the sweep of the spreaders and the aft moment provided by the swept shrouds. The SA/D is 26.3. That's enough to keep you on your toes and the boat on its ear.

Clearly in the past Nautor has had a hard time deciding if its Swans were either fish or fowl. Usually they were "fowsh," not quite race boats and not quite cruising boats. With this 45 it appears that the company is making a strong move to the performance side while not ignoring comfort. Aesthetically Nautor has set the pace since the early '70s to the point where "Swan" has become almost a genre in itself. Swan quality is also legendary. I look forward to seeing the 45 in person.

Nautor, P.O. Box 10, Fin-68601 Pietarsaari, Finland. 358 6 760 1111. **www.nautorgroup.com**

September 2001

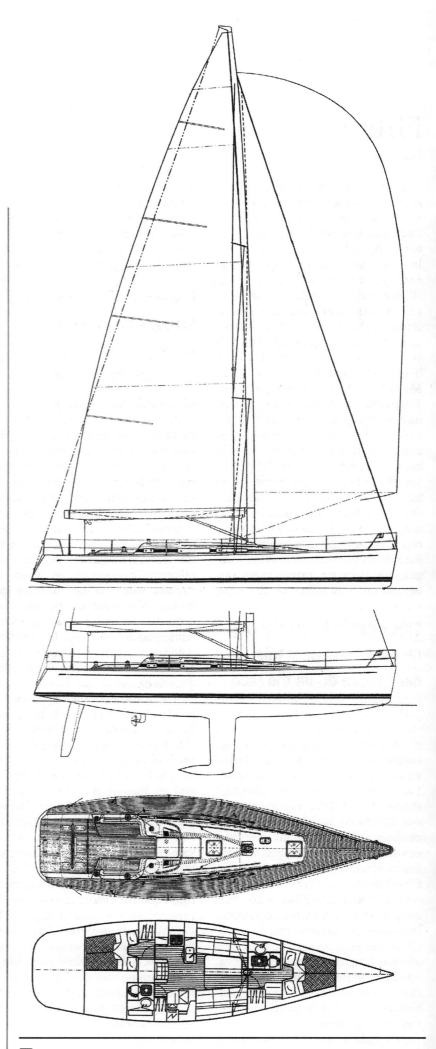

The latest Swan, with extra emphasis put on performance.

LOA 45'4"; LWL 39'7"; Beam 12'10"; Draft 9'2"; Displacement 19,510 lbs.; Ballast 9,092 lbs.; Sail Area 1,191 sq. ft.; SA/D 26.3; D/L 140.2; L/B 3.52; Auxiliary 50-hp saildrive; Fuel 39.6 gals.; Water 92.5 gals.

X-46
Racer-Cruiser

X-Yachts are always fun to review. Niels Jeppesen is a good designer and the boats are well built and beautifully finished. The new 46 is aimed at comfortable cruising and racing. It's another dual-purpose design.

The hull profile shows a lot of rocker, especially aft. The D/L is 156. The bow is quite fine and the stern is not overly broad. The L/B is 3.38, indicating a beamy boat. The rudder profile shows an interesting reverse in the trailing edge. Note how far aft this rudder is with almost the entire root chord of the rudder clear of the waterplane. You can pick from four keel choices: standard at 7 feet, 11 inches; shallow No. 1 at 6 feet, 11 inches; shallow No. 2 at 6 feet, 2 inches; and sport at 8 feet, 11 inches. In Puget Sound the deep sport keel would work great. The deep keel shows pronounced fillets at leading and trailing edge and it's my guess that all the keels will fit into the same recess and you will see smaller fillets on the shoal keels as their root chord will be longer. The specs say the keel has a cast iron fin and a lead bulb but I don't know if this refers to all four keel choices.

There are interior options that let you chose from a three- or four-stateroom layout. You can also choose what configuration you want in the saloon. The "classic" layout has the galley aft and the "modern" layout has the galley adjacent to the dinette forward. I would definitely go with the classic layout as it gives more room for lounging and provides for a more efficient offshore galley. That fourth stateroom seems a bit cramped to my eye but it would work if you had two kids who really needed to be separated. The interior is finished in teak veneers.

I like the looks of this boat. The deck is carefully sculpted and there is a recessed section running down the center of the cabintrunk forward. I don't think this recess really does anything but it's nice eye candy and the teak decking extends up into the recess. X-Yachts has been using this dodger base detail now on several models. It allows the dodger to be folded down into a recessed groove so it virtually disappears when down. It's a nice detail but in Seattle no one ever lowers their dodger. Maybe they would if they could hide it.

The cockpit seats are long enough to sleep on if you don't

I would go with the classic layout as it gives more room for lounging and provides for a more efficient offshore galley.

mind the mainsheet traveler digging into your heels. The large diameter wheel allows the helmsman to sit well outboard. The 46 has an optional anchor system, a maxi-yacht-style anchor launching system that allows the anchor to be hidden in the foredeck well until needed. This is really aesthetically effective as adequate anchor roller fittings with anchor in place are hardly things of beauty. They are more like a wart on the nose of a supermodel. This 46 has a very clean appearance because this mechanism is hidden. Cleats and stanchion bases are mounted outboard of the teak toerail and I like this look too. You do give up a wee bit of side deck but with the topsides color-wrapped over the sheer the look is very attractive.

The rig is the same rig we see on 95 percent of today's boats. It's fractional with swept spreaders. The furling drum for the headsail is tucked in the well below deck level to clean this up and get the tack down next to the deck. The specs indicate "purpose designed mast and boom sections" and I take this to mean that both sections were custom tooled for this design. That's impressive.

You can choose from a 55-horsepower or 75-horsepower Volvo diesel auxiliary. There is tankage for 100 gallons of water and 52 gallons of fuel.

In the U.S. contact X-Yachts USA, Foot of Washington Blvd., Stamford, CT 06902. (800) 926-2878. **www.x-yachts.com**

January 2004

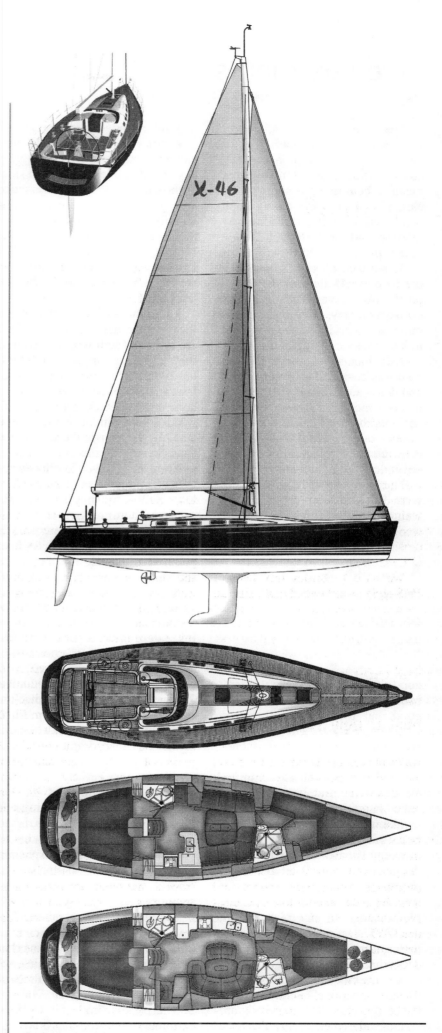

A fast boat with some slick design features.

LOA 46'; LWL 40'4"; Beam 13'7"; Draft 7'11" (Standard); Displacement 22,929 lbs.; Ballast 9,921 lbs.; Sail Area 1,115 sq. ft.; SA/D 22.1; D/L 156; L/B 3.38; Auxiliary Volvo Penta 55-hp; Fuel 52 gals.; Water 100 gals.

Sweden Yachts 45
Performance Cruiser

The Sweden Yachts 45 represents a more mainstream type of design. It's advertised as a "fast cruising" yacht and to my eye that means a boat that has some of the earmarks of a modern racing yacht combined with a cruiser-friendly interior and deck layout. While PHRF in its ideal form will allow any boat to compete, it's boats like the Sweden 45 that are more fun on the race course than the strict cruiser variety. Remember, it's more fun to cruise a race boat than it is to race a cruising boat.

This handsome, sleek-looking boat was designed by Peter Norlin and Jenss Ostermann. I'll let you in on a secret; my own boat was designed by Peter Norlin! I know, I know, but it's a long story and to give you the short answer, my wife fell in love with it. So there.

The sailplan reveals a yacht with its aesthetic roots in the Nautor and Baltic lines. The wedge-shape deck always looks

A self-tacking jib is not optimal in terms of shape control, but it sure is convenient.

good. It prohibits the use of many opening ports and that's not too good, but it's aesthetically clean with low windage. The side decks are broad, and there is an anchor well, recessed into the foredeck. The cockpit is big and combines an area with seat backs with an area without seat backs so the helmsman can get outboard. The helm seat hinges over to make a boarding platform. There is no mainsheet traveler and the main sheets to a point on the cockpit sole just forward of the binnacle like it does in my own Norlin design. The cockpit dodger nestles into a fairing to get it out of the way when racing.

The interior of the 45 is done in typical, beautiful Scandinavian-styled joinerwork. The details are subtle and rich-looking. The galley counter is a wraparound solid Corian-type unit. It's way too small for me and my penchant for cooking big meals, but it sure is pretty. "Would you like your

Vegemite sandwich warmed up?"

I don't like the dinette area either. At this size the designers have trouble integrating both sides of the saloon into one conversation area. In this case there is seating on only one side of the saloon and then a navigation area and "counter of mystery" on the other. I would much rather see opposing seating areas to make the boat at least feel big.

Twin mirror-image staterooms tuck back under the cockpit. They are tight and will work fine, but at the expense of a reasonable lazarette. The owner's stateroom is forward with the berth pullman-style and the head all the way forward. I like this. The aft head is also big. To my eye the saloon gets shortchanged in this layout.

The D/L is lower for this design than the others this month. At a D/L of 206 we may see why the accommodation plan is a little tighter on this boat. There is sufficient overhang forward to keep you from banging the anchor on the stem as you raise it. I don't understand why the forefoot knuckle is so hard. The keel shows big fillets at both leading and trailing edge intersections with the hull. You have your choice of a shoal, wing-keel option with a 6-foot, 6-inch draft or the standard 7-foot, 6-inch draft keel. The spade rudder is deep and partially balanced. Note the saildrive unit, further reducing drag.

This rig features a self-tacking jib. You can sheet the jib to a track or you can sheet it to the athwartships traveler allowing self-tending. A self-tacking jib is not optimal in terms of shape control, but it sure is convenient, especially today when I am nursing a very painful torn muscle in my right shoulder. The rig is almost masthead with swept spreaders. The SA/D is 19.2. There is sufficient jib track to let you fly a large, overlapping genoa, but I would think you would get accustomed to the self-tacking jib in a heartbeat.

The photos show this to be an extremely good-looking boat.

Sweden Yachts, P.O. Box 580, Riverside, CT 06878. (203) 861-6578. www.swedenyachts.se

March 2000

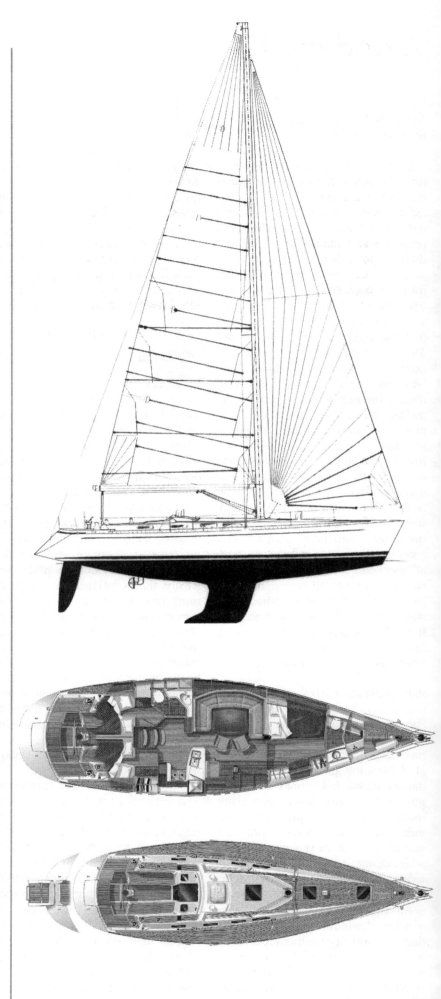

A fast, elegant cruiser in the Scandinavian style.

LOA 46'5"; LWL 39'; Beam 13'7"; Draft 6'6" (wing keel), 7'6" standard keel; Displacement 27,400 lbs.; Ballast 11,500 lbs.; Sail Area 1,090 sq. ft.; SA/D 19.2; D/L 206; L/B 3.44; Auxiliary 78-hp Volvo Penta TMD 22; Fuel 72 gals.; Water 113 gals.

Aerodyne 47
Performance Cruiser

This is a very well-thought-out boat, and I really don't have the space here to do it justice, so if you find it interesting why don't you write for Aerodyne's substantial and informative promotional package. I'll focus on the elements of this Rodger Martin-Steve Koopman design that I find interesting. The idea behind this boat was an "ultimate cruising boat" for a couple. We could sure argue over the definition of ultimate, but let's just acknowledge that it's a very subjective term.

Aesthetically this is not a classically beautiful design. The ends are truncated, the sheer is flat and the transom goes on forever. Then again we don't see too many classically beautiful boats anymore. Just look at the boats in this month's reviews. Overhangs are a thing of the past. Every designer wants to maximize sailing length for a given LOA. While we can wax on about the contribution that overhangs make or do not make to sailing length there is no argument over the benefits of waterline length. The photos of the Aerodyne 47 show it to be a very handsome if not beautiful boat. I'm certain the owners of this boat will find it beautiful.

The 47 is moderately beamy with an L/B of 3.25, and the beam is carried aft. The bow does not appear to

You are going to be very comfortable on this boat.

be very fine, at least not on deck, and that will help keep the boat dry. Fore and aft rocker is flat and the D/L is 152. We could have a long and drawn out argument over "ideal" D/Ls for cruising boats, but it all comes down to sailing style and individual approach. Heavier boats have their advantages as do lighter boats. In most conditions the lighter boat will be the faster boat while the heavier boat will be the most comfortable.

It takes a skilled builder with a dedicated approach to lightweight construction to produce an offshore cruising boat with a D/L as low as this one. The cruiser needs to balance weight against durability. Lightweight structures can be extremely strong, although strength and durability are not necessarily synonymous. The rudder is huge and the long fin has a bulb. Draft is only 6 feet. Martin likes nearly circular hull sections with a fairly narrow BWL.

The 47 is laid out for a couple with another couple as guests. It's a good layout with a huge galley and lots of counter space. Remember the cook is the most important crewmember. It's better to be lost and well fed than it is to know where you are and be hungry. You are going to be very comfortable on this boat.

The rig is unusual in that it combines a big main with the mast set well forward with a nonoverlapping, self-tacking jib on a Gary Hoyt-type jib club. This type of club is far better than other types of self-tending jib arrangements. With this club you don't need to vang the club or move sheet leads or adjust clew boards to maintain proper trim as you bear off. Of course, you do have this thing obstructing the foredeck, but I suppose you could swing it to one side when you are anchored or at the dock. It's not a pretty feature, but having a boat with this style of club myself, I can assure you that it is very efficient.

The promotional material goes to great lengths to prove the point that a moderate SA/D is better than either a low one or an overly ambitious higher number, and I would agree. It's great to have a big rig when everything is nice, but on a boat like the 47 you should be able to see at least 20 knots apparent before you are forced to reef. With the forward mast location of this design you can probably sail it effectively under main alone. A unique track system allows the self-tacking jib to be reefed while staying on the club. Drawings and photos show a loose-footed main and about 15 inches of roach overlap on the split backstay.

This deck style is the exact opposite of the deck on the C&C 99. This deck is all soft shapes and radii. This does reduce windage. The hard dodger covers about half the cockpit. Halyards are all led aft and the photos show sissy bars at the mast. There is deck access to the huge lazarette and forepeak areas. The self-tacking jib club wipes the deck clean of genoa tracks and associated gear. A short, pipe frame-type bowsprit gets the anchor away from the nearly plumb stem. The transom opens to the large swim step.

Aerodyne Yachts, 54 West Point Road, Webster, MA 01570. www.aerodyneyachts.com (508) 943-8776.

February 2002

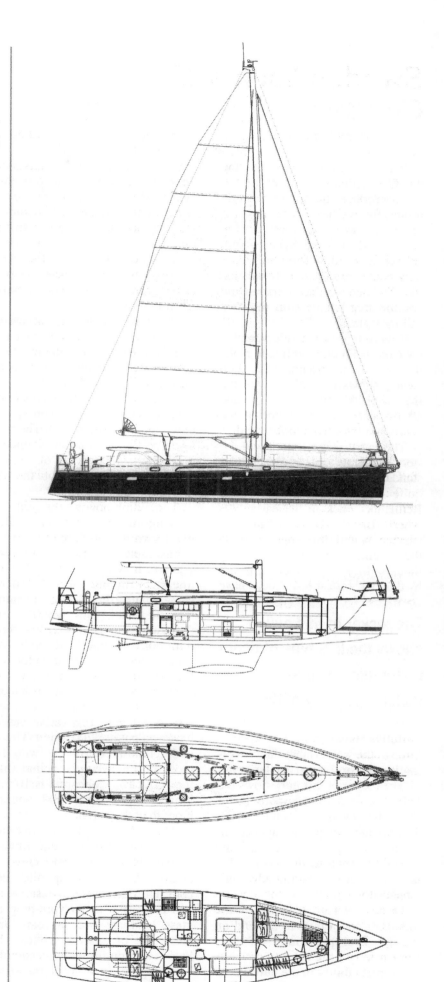

A cruiser with performance and comfort.

LOA 46'7"; LWL 42'1"; Beam 14'4"; Draft 6'; Displacement 25,370 lbs.; Ballast 10,330 lbs.; Sail Area 990 sq. ft.; SA/D 18.2; D/L 152; L/B 3.25; Auxiliary 56-hp Yanmar 4JH3-E; Fuel 100 gals.; Water 200 gals.

Concordia 47
Racer Cruiser

Bruce Farr, Carroll Marine and the Concordia yard have teamed up to produce this interesting 47-footer. Below, this boat has the appeal of an out-and-out cruiser, while on deck it's a hybrid racer-cruiser. I'm certain that this would be a great boat to own. It has that blend of performance features and comfort that I think suits my own sailing style.

This design is a development of the Corel 45 hull, modified to make it more cruiser friendly. The hull clearly shows the influence of the IMS with its snubbed-off bow and aft overhang. This may be a rule aberration but it sure looks good.

The entry is very fine, and the stern moderate in beam by today's standards. The bow sections are quite slablike to reduce drag. Remember back in the early '70s when Bill Lapworth and Brit Chance would use huge radii on their stems? I wonder what they thought they were accomplishing by this. The fastest boats today have

The rocker of this hull shows the IMS-type of depth distribution with the flattening in way of the keel

knifelike bows that cut cleanly through the water rather than mushing it aside or straight up the stem.

The rocker of this hull shows the IMS-type of depth distribution with the flattening in way of the keel. The counter aft almost appears to go hollow in profile. There is considerable sweep to this keel and a large fillet at the leading-edge hull intersection.

Draft is 9 feet, 6 inches. With this draft and a bulb at the end of the fin keel providing stability, there is very little need to develop any form stability in the hull. Form stability is drag. The D/L of this design is 111.

This is a nicely sculpted deck. Obviously the designers needed more cabintrunk than on a pure race boat to give headroom forward and conform to IMS racer-cruiser requirements. Still, challenges like this can produce excit-

ing results, and I think this is a very handsome boat. Full, standing headroom will begin to disappear at the mast, and the cockpit shows the effect of the racer-cruiser requirements with its seats, cockpit coamings and seat backs. Did you ever think we'd see the day when even decks had to pass rule requirements?

The twin wheels make access to the swim step easy. Note that the lines running aft from the mast are led under a popped-up portion of the coachroof.

The interior features a couple of curved bulkheads as you come down the companionway. The galley to port is spacious and would be ideal if it had 11 inches of counter space aft of the stove. Note the wet locker to starboard.

The plumb bow works great for shoving the interior forward. This big forward double will be very comfortable. The two heads show you just how far this design leans toward cruising. The drawing shows the aft head door swinging into the head. This won't work. Otherwise this is an excellent layout, conventional and effective. There is tankage for 60 gallons of fuel and 100 gallons of water.

If you were inclined to put the Concordia 47 in the same racer-cruiser category that Tartan would have you put its 3700, don't. This is a different breed of cat with far more horsepower per pound than the 3700. The Concordia is 10 feet longer and weighs 600 pounds more than the Tartan.

This hull is laid up with wet pre-preg, epoxy E-glass and Kevlar, vacuum bagged and post cured in an oven. The core is Superlite balsa core. The deck uses vinylester resin and E-glass with wet pre-preg E-glass laminate over a foam and balsa core of varied densities. The keel is an iron fin with a lead bulb. The engine is a 47-horsepower Yanmar saildrive.

I think it would be nice to find this boat under the Christmas tree.

Carroll Marine, 91 Broad Common Rd., Bristol, RI 02809. (401) 253-1264, fax (401) 253-5860.

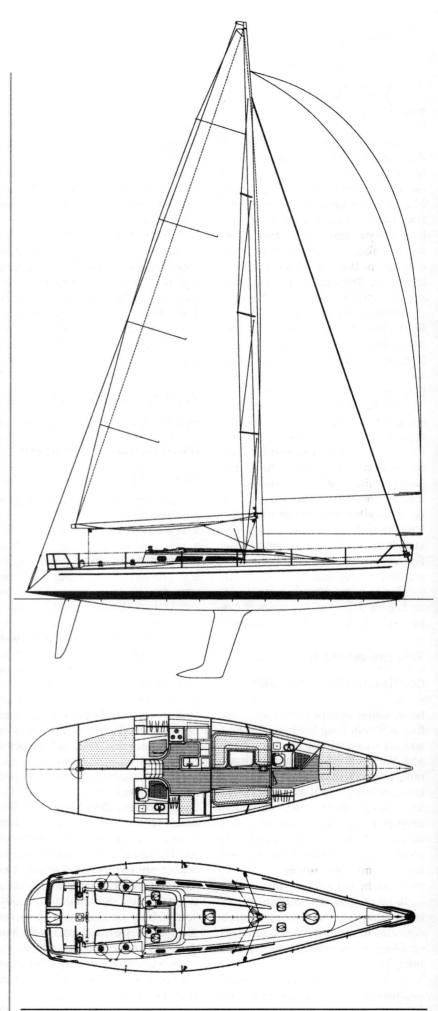

The Farr-designed Corel 45 turned high-powered cruiser.

LOA 46'10"; LWL 40'8"; Beam 13'7"; Draft 9'6"; Displacement 16,750 lbs.; Ballast 7,950 lbs.; Sail Area 1,345 sq. ft.; SA/D 32.8; D/L 111; L/B 3.4; Auxiliary 47-hp Yanmar; Fuel 60 gals.; Water 100 gals.

Wyliecat 48
Performance Cruiser

Tom Wylie is one of the real individuals in the world of yacht design. As far back as I can remember, back to the *Animal Farm* days, Tom has always done it his own way and Tom's own way has always been a good way.

No, Tom is not a fastidious draftsman. But Tom is a very good designer. It's easy to get the notion, looking at Tom's hurried drafting, that the end product for Tom is not the design but the boat. This biggest of the Wyliecat series is built by Wyliecat on a hull built by Westerly Marine. I've seen this boat, and I like it.

Tom knows how to draw a fast boat. This sparse 48-footer is slender and light with a D/L of 110. The hull is beautifully fair and without surprises. The sheer is not quite flat. Bow overhang, while not faddishly plumb, is very sensible and not at all slow. The keel is a welded steel fin with a bolted-on lead bulb. The hollow steel fin does double duty as a 65-gallon fuel tank. Draft is 9 feet, 6 inches.

The interior is simple. There are two quarter berths that are on the narrow side for legitimate doubles but wonderfully roomy for singles. The galley is skimpy but adequate. The head is ... a head. The wraparound settees have narrow pilot berths outboard. There is a wide double berth forward of the settees. This big double is divided by the mast near the foot. There are far more berths in this layout than there are places for people to sit while eating. I think if a boat is going to sleep eight then it should be able to dine eight. This layout needs some fine tuning.

I watched this boat sail up and down the Oakland estuary for three days during the Sail Expo show. I was very impressed. It's the ultimate singlehander. I kept thinking, "That's the boat for me."

This is a very good-looking boat that handles like a big dinghy. I know this cockpit can easily hold a crowd. It's a long cockpit with plenty of room for passengers to sit comfortably out of the way of sail handling.

Sail handling? What sail han-dling? This big cat boat has a hal-yard and a mainsheet. That's it. Okay, there's an outhaul, choker and boom lift, but once up you can leave these lines alone. There is no vang. There is no traveler. This is the epitome in self-tacking rigs.

Years ago I asked Lowell North what he thought the fastest rig was, and he said "a giant Laser rig." Even on San Francisco Bay there has been no need to reef the big cat, as the carbon-fiber mast falls off as the wind builds, easing pressure up top.

Sail handling? What sail handling? This big cat boat has a halyard and a main-sheet. That's it. Okay, there's an outhaul, choker and boom lift, but once up you can leave these lines alone.

The 48 can beat a Santa Cruz 50 upwind in 25 knots. The PHRF rating is 15. This boat moves and is very close winded.

I'm sure there are drawbacks to this rig, but I don't know what they are. Maybe downwind in light air you'd feel the lack of a chute. Perhaps you'd like to keep your crew busier with more strings to pull. If going the fastest for the leastest amount of effort is the key then we have to carefully consider this approach.

The SA/D is 26.28 without roach or luff round. Adding roach and luff round raises this number to 35! There is 1,300 actual square feet of sail in this big mainsail. I've seen this sail come down, and it comes down fast and falls neatly, self flaking into the web between the carbon fiber wishbone legs. You do not need sail ties.

If Tom is right with this boat, the rest of us should consider jumping on the Wylie wagon.

Thomas Wylie Design Group, 86 Ridgecrest Rd., Canyon, CA 94516. (925) 376-7338, fax (925) 376-7982

October 1999

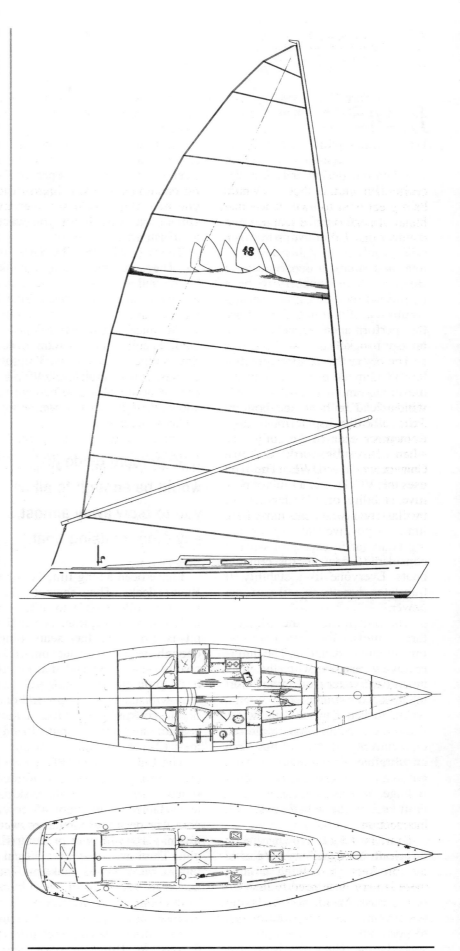

A fast, easy-to-sail cruiser.

LOA 47'6"; LWL 40'; Beam 13'; Draft 9'6"; Displacement 14,500 lbs.; Ballast 6,536 lbs.; Sail Area 1,300 sq. ft. (with roach and luff round); SA/D 26.28; D/L 110; L/B 3.65; Auxiliary Yanmar 3GM 30 hp; Fuel 65 gals.; Water 25 gals.

J/145
Racer-Cruiser

When this design arrived at the office Tim looked at it and said, "They just keep drawing the same boat over and over." I can see that if you look only at the profile, but when you consider this design in total, it's almost a departure for J Boats. The 145 appears to be a hybrid that combines the cruising comfort of J's cruising line with the performance aspects of J's bowsprit rockets.

The key to this combination is a low VCG made possible by a cast nickel-aluminum-bronze keel fin with a lead bulb on the bottom. The ballast-to-displacement ratio is 44 percent, and a draft of 8 feet, 11 inches results in a VCG 2 percent below the DWL. The 145 uses this VCG to get a limit of positive stability of 135 degrees. In the last two years we have seen limits of positive stability for racing boats far in excess of what is considered adequate for cruising boats. Everyone likes stability. It translates directly to sail carrying power.

The hull form of the 145 features a midsection with a surprising amount of deadrise. The hull is relatively narrow with the max beam carried forward in an effort to make the boat more benign when pushed hard off the wind. This is not a shape you would see on a current IMS type of hull with an ultrafine entry. Deadrise fairs out to a flattish run aft. The rudder is huge. You can choose a shoal-draft keel option with 7-foot draft. The D/L of this design is 110.

This is a very interesting interior layout. Note the V-berth/double pushed forward, leaving a large sail stowage area directly forward of the mast. Aft of this, the layout is conventional with a pilot berth to port, outboard of the opposing settee berths. The galley is big, but I would have turned the icebox 90 degrees to allow the range to come forward, providing counter space each side. It's a personal taste thing, but I do a lot of cooking and I know galleys. I surprised last

week's crew with my super three-cheese lasagna. Nitpicking aside, this is a great layout. Numerous options are available if you want to "plush up" the interior.

This is a big rig. The SA/D is 29. The spreaders are minimally swept, and runners and checkstays will be needed to keep the standard Hall Spars carbon stick in column. The mainsail is raised on a 2:1 halyard. The bowsprit is retractable. The sailplan shows overlapping genoas, but for cruising, a 95-percent blade jib would be enough to allow you to blow away almost any other cruising boat.

A 95-percent blade jib would be enough to allow you to blow away almost any other cruising boat.

I have been a long-time fan of J Boat's decks. They seem to suit my own sailing style to a T, and the 145 is no exception. The cockpit is long and has seats long enough to stretch out on. The coamings are low and that could be a problem for lounging, but they will make getting in and out of the cockpit easy. I like a low coaming at the wheel, but I like at least 12-inch coamings forward.

The 145 is built in TPI's patented Scrimp method with unidirectional carbon and E-glass skins over Baltek's Superlight 45 core. The engine is a 56-horsepower Yanmar 4JH3CE with a saildrive unit. There is tankage for 90 gallons of water in two tanks and 75 gallons of fuel.

Designer Rod Johnstone has given us a J Boat cruiser that in focus is not far from my own *Icon* design. As Bill Lee once said: "Fast is fun."

J Boats, Box 90, Newport, RI 02840. **www.jboats.com** *(401) 846-8410.*

May 2000

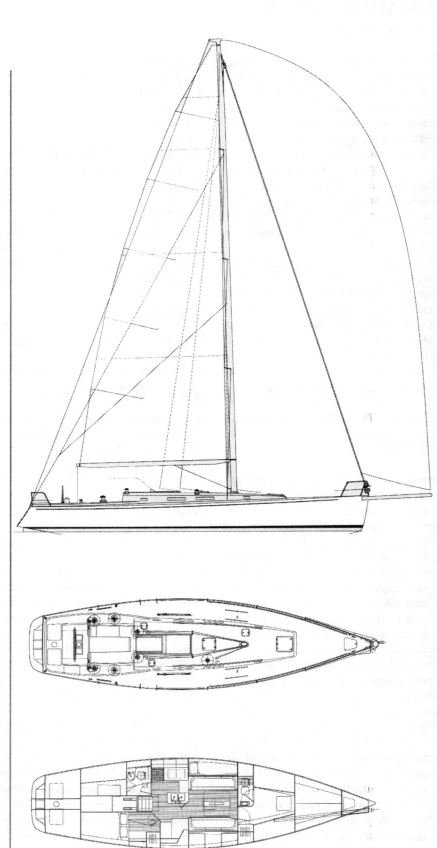

Fast design makes full use of cutting-edge technology.

LOA 48'1"; LWL 42'6"; Beam 13'; Draft 8'11" (standard), 7' (shoal draft); Displacement 19,000 lbs.; Sail Area 1,295 sq. ft.; SA/D 29; D/L 110; L/D 3.7; Auxiliary 56-hp Yanmar 4JH3CE; Fuel 75 gals.; Water 90 gals.

Hunter 50
Performance Cruiser

This 50-footer from Hunter Marine surprised a lot of people at the last Annapolis Boat Show. Essentially, I think people were not expecting Hunter to come out with such a specialized cruising boat. This project actually started several years ago and was connected to one of my stereo-gear heroes, Julian Vereker of NAIM Audio fame, who died recently. Working with Hunter, Julian developed a very similar boat based upon a B&R design, which he called the Windex 49. Although Julian didn't live to see his version of the boat completed, Hunter has gone on to produce the 50, which it is offering as a stock boat to cruisers looking for something a little different.

This is a specialized vessel from its reversed sheer to its unusual rig.

Unfortunately, I am working from very scant drawings and I have nothing that shows the underbody of the hull and nothing at all that describes the current keel—shoal and deep—configurations. It's kind of like trying to appreciate a centerfold model from just a head shot.

Warren Luhrs has the first boat of this series and his boat has a custom keel with a canting wing on the back end of a long bulb. The production boat will have a no-bulbed 8-foot, 6-inch draft keel or a bulbed 6-foot draft keel. Neither will have the movable wings.

The Vereker version featured the mysterious B&R venturi-effect hull slots. Based upon the lightship displacement, the D/L is 78.38. Stability will be enhanced by 2,700 pounds of water ballast on each side.

This is an interesting rig. It uses the B&R-style spar with the tripod support struts at the deck level going up to the gooseneck. The boom height is fixed by a solid vang. The mainsail is loose footed and has lots of roach made possible by the absence of any backstays, standing or running. The boom is scalloped in profile to help the deep foot of the mainsail flip over in tacks. The mainsail sheets to a traveler on top of the aft radar arch.

I don't understand why the clews of the jibs are so high. I like jibs to be deck sweepers. Maybe the clews are high so the clew rings don't beat up the forward rig strut during each tack.

The extreme sweep of the spreaders may make chafe a problem on long offshore passage, but Hunter assures me that this has been addressed by using rounded spreaders and well-placed chafe patches. The SA/D is 25.5.

The interior seems to work well. I'm not so sure you need what the brochure calls a "day head." Is the other head a "night head?" Is there a photo-sensitive lock to prevent you from using the day head at night?

The galley is very well-laid-out and adjacent to a comfortable dinette that actually has some corners. Considering that the water ballast takes up a lot of room and this boat weighs only 16,000 pounds, there is quite a bit of useable interior volume. The nav station is gimbaled, allowing the navigator to stay level up to 20 degrees of boat heel. The chain locker is aft at the base of the mast where the weight of the ground tackle will do the least amount of performance damage. There is a small cuddy or covered area aft of the house to provide shelter for the on-deck crew.

This is a specialized vessel from its reversed sheer to its unusual rig. It's so different that I think a two-dimensional design analysis probably does not do it justice. This is a boat you would have to live with a while to fully appreciate. Julian Vereker's NAIM stereo gear looked strange too. I own a bunch of it and you certainly would not buy it on style points alone. But it sounds fabulous. Julian was a bit of a rebel, a free-thinker, and I think this new Hunter conveys that spirit quite well.

Hunter Marine Corporation, P.O. Box 1030, Alachua, FL 32615. **www.huntermarine.com** *(904) 462-3077.*

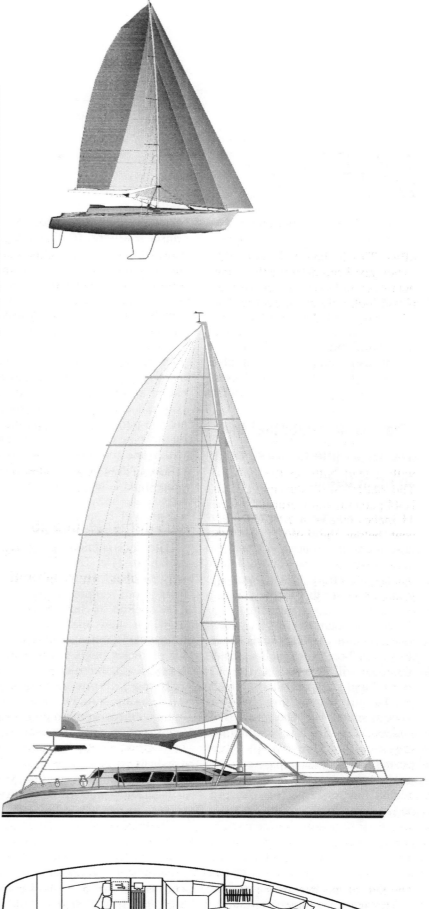

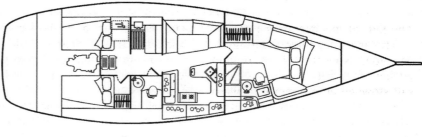

Radical departure for Hunter Marine.

LOA 50'; LWL 45'; Beam 15'; Draft 5'10"; Displacement 18,000 lbs.; Ballast 5,600 lbs.; Sail Area 1,274 sq. ft.; SA/D 25.5; D/L 78.38; L/B 3.33; Auxiliary 38-hp Yanmar; Fuel 150 gals.; Water 50 gals.

CBTF 52
Racer-cruiser

As I read the promotional material on this new canting keel model from the DynaYacht team I kept looking for the part where they said it could "leap tall buildings in a single bound." Perhaps this is best summed up in the last sentence in the brochure's introduction: "It represents the biggest step forward in yacht design since Herreshoff introduced the fin keel in the late 1800s." This is pretty hyperbolic, but in fact

There is no doubt that this will be a "line honors" boat in most fleets.

is based upon the documented performance of the firm's previous offerings, the Schock 40 and the one-off *Red Hornet*. The brochure makes an effort to convince the potential buyer that the new 52 is a combination racer-cruiser.

With a beam of 13 feet, a displacement of 14,000 pounds and an LOA of 52 feet, there is little doubt this boat will be a rocket. The D/L is 64.2 and draft is 10 feet, 7 inches. The lift, usually provided by a keel, is shared between fore and aft rudders. The "keel" is basically just a strut to hold the canting ballast bulb. With the canting keel, the seemingly low ballast-displacement ratio of 29 percent can provide tremendous stability.

CBTF stands for Canting Ballast Twin Foil technology. The ballast bulb cants up to 55 degrees from centerline. There are both manual and hydraulic cant control systems with ballast position controls and indicators located in the cockpit. The rear foil (rudder?) can be independently operated. I wonder how it feels to drive this boat. Does it feel different to have fore and aft rudders? I suspect it does. I would imagine that having rudders like this would give you tremendous maneuverability around the dock. The hull shape is very dinghylike. With a displacement this low, it's hard to imagine an undinghylike hull form.

The interior, despite the

brochure's claims, is not really a cruiser's delight. It's basically the same layout you would see in most racing yachts, with a small galley forward, a semi-enclosed head and no visible dining table. There are no provisions for sleeping privacy and no double berths. Maybe you just pull your sleeping bag over your head. Still, it's a reasonable interior considering the overall nature of this design. Of course, you can cruise with this interior, but the performance levels offered by this type of design have to come with some comfort compromises.

The SA/D of this design is 30.46 using I, J, E and P. There is a retractable bowsprit and spinnakers will be masthead. The spreaders are swept 26 degrees.

The deck is laid out in pure race boat style. There are only two hatches. Cruising boats need more ventilation than that. The cockpit is huge, and the drawings show one layout with twin wheels and another with a big diameter single wheel. The specs also list a tiller.

Using Finite Element Analysis the structure has been optimized for strength and weight. Construction materials include carbon fiber, E-glass, epoxy and vinylester resins.

The brochure says that you will be able to outsail 70- and 80-footers in the new 52. I guess we'll see about that. There is no doubt that this will be a "line honors" boat in most fleets. For certain it will give PHRF handicappers a fit and most probably begin its life with a punitive provisionary rating.

"But it's just a cruiser-racer," you say at the start of the season. "Yes," the race committee says, "but the brochure says it will outsail 80-footers so how about if we start you with an 80-footer rating?"

I'd love to sail this boat.

DynaYacht Incorporated, 8148 Ronson Rd., Suite P, San Diego, CA 92111. **www.dynayacht.com** *(858) 277-4551.*

March 2001

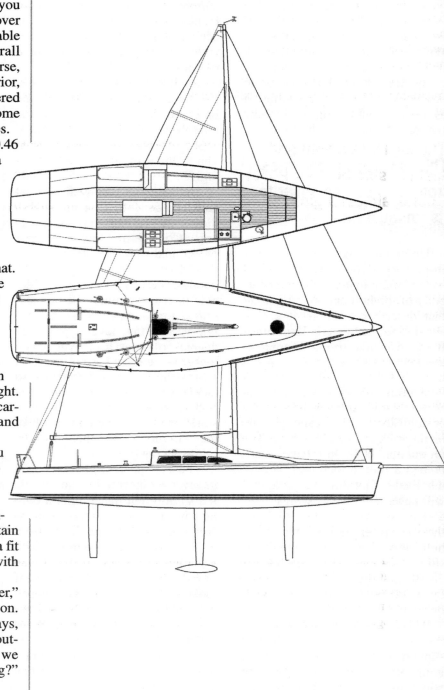

The biggest step forward since the fin keel?

LOA 52'; LWL 46'; Beam 13'; Draft 10'7"; Displacement 14,000 lbs.; Ballast 4,000 lbs.; Sail Area 1,106 sq. ft.; SA/D 30.46; D/L 64.2; L/B 4; Auxiliary 51-hp Yanmar Saildrive; Fuel 23 gals.; Water 10 gals.

Clarke 56
Racer-Cruiser

I have had the pleasure over the years of having students come to my office for work-study periods or internships, which are often required by their schools for graduation. Most of these students come from the Westlawn program, The Landing School or the Southampton Institute. My current right hand man, Ben Souquet, came to my office from Southampton. This is the only four-year yacht design school in the world, and its graduates are top notch. After a summer internship at my office Ben returned to England to finish his degree. I was sorry to see him go, but very happy when six years later I had the opportunity to hire him full time.

Students are fun. They can be frustrating and I have been accused of being "abusive." I probably

The idea was a light and fast cruising boat for Puget Sound, almost a glorified daysailer.

deserve it. It's very important to me to have the student leave my office with tangible signs of progress. Despite the nuisance factor I will continue to take in students. I owe it to the industry. And it's enjoyable for me. Kids keep you young.

I can't ask students to work on ongoing office design projects so what I do is to lay out an independent assignment for them. Last summer Dan Clarke came from The Landing School in Maine. He arrived at the office early—that's important—appearing somewhat Gothic with very long hair, tatts and all-black garb. I knew I had a musician on my hands, so I was certain we would get along. I warned Dan of my abusive nature then laid out the assignment. "You are going to design my dream boat." I gave Dan a long list of parameters then sat back to watch the design progress over the next two weeks. I think when you look at the result of Dan's Landing School experience and his time in my office you will be impressed. Eric Goetz was impressed enough to hire Dan immediately. I was sorry to see Dan go.

The idea was a light and fast cruising boat for Puget Sound, almost a glorified daysailer. The hull shape shows a firm turn to the bulge to help

with initial stability. The boat is narrow with an L/B of 4.66 so anything you can do to help stability is probably a good idea. Dan designed a keel drawing 9 feet with a bulb to further help stability. The near vertical transom is a good way to maximize both deck space and sailing length. This boat fits into what I call the "cruising sled" category.

The rig is fractional with a 110 percent working headsail. The jib is hanked on. This makes headsail changes easier. I like watching my wife scramble around on the spray-soaked foredeck changing jibs. The headstay tack is well aft of the stem. I asked for runners and checkstays because I like the idea of having lots of control over the mast bend. The mainsail roach just barely overlaps the standing backstay. The SA/D is 24, well below that of current hot rods, but enough to keep this boat moving well in light air. The shorter rig was chosen with an eye for stability.

I was emphatic in my accommodation requirements. Above all I wanted simplicity, with joinerwork details doing double duty as structural stiffeners. The big nav table has the reefer/freezer under it. There is a bulkhead-mounted wood burning stove to take the chill off the Northwest mornings. Just forward of the port quarter berth is a dedicated guitar locker. Main settees are extra long. I wanted elbow room.

The deck was designed around a big cockpit and tiller steering. Putting a tiller on a boat of this size is a bit of a stretch, but along with my fantasy for this design was the reality that my funds would be limited, so I thought a tiller would be cheaper than a wheel. If the boat is well balanced a tiller will work fine. Side decks are broad and there's a high enough seat back in the forward end of the cockpit to sit and be comfortable while reading. An open transom and swim step were included to make boarding the dinghy easy.

If Dan's work on this project is any indication we will be hearing more from him in the future.

Dan Clarke, 438 Middle Hwy., Barrington, RI 02806. **www.rapidmarineprototype.com** *(401) 245-2153.*

March 2002

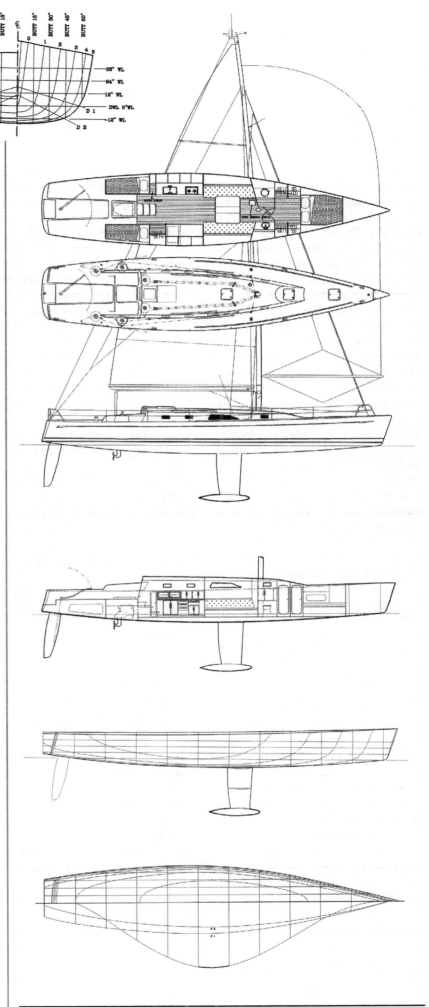

An intern designs Bob Perry's dream boat.

LOA 56'; DWL 50'; Beam 12'; Draft 9'; Displacement 19,500 lbs.; Ballast 7,000 lbs.; Sail area 1,103 sq. ft.; SA/D 24; D/L 71; L/B 4.66; Auxiliary Volvo 59-hp MD22; Fuel 40 gals.; Water 40 gals.

X-562
Performance Cruiser

Here is a new X-Boat from designer Niels Jeppesen. This is a big boat and would fall into the "ultimate cruiser" category for most of us.

This hull is obviously based on race-boat proportions. The ends are short. Beam is pulled aft, and rocker is moderate. The D/L is 163, and the L/B is 3.5. It's a pretty normal-looking hull. The hull lines show sections that go flat amidships. The keel is a deep, 9-foot, 4-inch, bulbed fin, and there is a shoal keel available. There are extended leading and trailing edge root fillets shown on the keel. Note the curved leading edge to this fin.

This is a sexy-looking boat with a wedgelike cabintrunk and enough opening ports to provide good ventilation below. There are wheels port and starboard to open up access to the transom swim step. Of course you will have to step over the traveler on your way aft, but considering the rest of this deck design, there is no other place for it to go. It will work better aft anyway.

Look at that big, wraparound coaming forward of the companionway. This coaming houses the dodger in its retracted position. This has been used on other X-Boats and is a nice feature.

Note the fixed cockpit table forward of the traveler. My only concern with this cockpit is that, although it looks long in profile, in plan view there is minimal seating forward of the traveler. What would normally be seat area has been taken up by the extension of the cabintrunk into the cockpit area to provide headroom in the quarter cabins. I prefer big cockpits.

You have your choice of three interior layouts with this boat: A2, B1 and A3. All three layouts have three heads and a fo'c'sle big enough for pipe berths. The main difference in layouts is in the number of staterooms. Layout A3 has four staterooms with upper and lower berths in the additional small forward stateroom. A2 and B1 differ in the forward owner's stateroom layout. You can have your double berth off to the starboard side with fixed Streisand chairs to port, or you can have the centerline, symmetrical berth layout flanked by small settees. Symmetry is comforting so I like the centerline double-berth arrangement.

In the saloon you can have the Streisands to port with a small table between or the more practical settee berth. This boat is beamy enough to accommodate extra chairs around the dining table. I guess this is good, but to my eye it detracts from the "boatness" of the interior. Maybe loss of boatness is the price you pay when the LOA exceeds 50 feet.

With an SA/D of 21.91 this rig is big for a cruising boat and small for a racing boat. That seems to fit right into the overall character of this hybrid design. The triple spreaders are very slightly swept, and there are running backstays and a babystay. The masthead con-

I like all the X-Boats. They seem to be well designed and offer the cruising sailor good performance.

figuration was probably chosen over the fractional type because it may require less critical tuning. It simplifies things when you offset the headstay loads with a standing backstay. Note that the backstay chainplate is on centerline at the end of the swim step area. The backstay will provide a convenient handhold when you are checking the wake.

The engine is a 100-horsepower Yanmar, and there is tankage for 227 gallons of fuel and 272 gallons of water in two tanks. There is a total of 864 amp hours of battery power, all under the cabin sole.

I like all the X-Boats. They seem to be well designed and offer the cruising sailor good performance along with very handsome looks.

X-Yachts, 7002 Channel Village Ct. #202, P.O. Box 3316, Annapolis, MD 21403. **www.x-yachts.com** *(410) 268-8098.*

December 1999

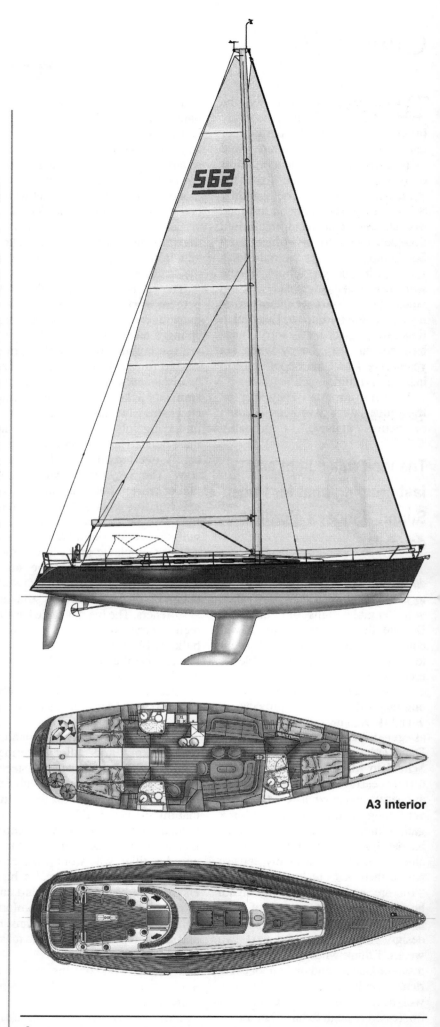

A3 interior

A big, comfortable cruiser that is capable of making quick passages.

LOA 56'6"; LWL 48'7"; Beam 15'11"; Draft 9'4"; Displacement 41,887 lbs.; Ballast 16,314 lbs.; Sail Area 1,653 sq. ft.; SA/D 21.91; D/L 163; L/B 3.5; Auxiliary 100-hp Yanmar; Fuel 227 gals.; Water 272 gals.

Turner 56
Performance Cruiser

It wasn't too long ago that sailboat types were seen as fairly exclusive. A motorsailer could not be a good pure sailer. A race boat would not make a good cruiser and you couldn't race a cruiser. Then we learned that the features that gave us speed under power were not necessarily detrimental to speed under sail. Lightweight construction meant your accommodation weight did not necessarily preclude the boat from racing. Combining a comfortable interior with a racing hull-form and rig

Say hello to the "performance cruiser" of 2002.

could produce an exciting and rewarding cruising boat. Improved sailhandling systems and the death of the genoa have also helped tame the racing rig and make it attractive to the short-handed cruiser. We now see a whole new class of boats designed to sail very fast while offering cruiser comfort. This 56-footer designed by Bill Tripp Jr. and built by Turner Yachts in Ontario, Canada, is just such a yacht. Say hello to the "performance cruiser" of 2002.

There's not much point in arguing the true definition of "cruising boat." It means different things to different sailors. The interior layout of the Turner 56 is total cruise. The hull is total race. The rig and deck layouts are hybrids. You should also be aware that this will be a somewhat demanding boat to cruise in that it's a high-powered boat with an SA/D of 29.2. You will sail fast and things will happen quickly. This is not a stiff boat given its large rig and light and narrow hull, but this does not preclude it from being a cruiser. You can always reduce sail, but a design like this needs the power to sail at optimum speeds throughout the entire wind range if it is to be competitive on today's race course.

This is a handsome boat. The sheer is nearly flat and there are minimal overhangs. I like the way the bow knuckle sits above the DWL, although photos show the boat floating a good 6 inches lower

than the flotation plane indicated in the drawings. The keel raises and lowers hydraulically reducing the draft from 12 feet, 6 inches to 7 feet, 6 inches. I think you will keep the keel down all the time while sailing. The D/L is 116.7 and the L/B is 3.82. The rudder is big and shows a planform with very little taper.

The stem radius is reduced to a working minimum at the knuckle and photos show the 56 cleaving the water cleanly. If there is a bone in her teeth it's only a chicken bone. In fact, there is none. A big frothy bow wave piling up against the stem may be photogenic, but it's also very slow. The large-radius stems we used to see in the work of Bill Lapworth and Bill Tripp Sr. have gone away. In plan form the distribution of beam in this beautiful design is entirely normal.

There are two layouts available, with the difference being in the treatment of the owner's stateroom forward. You can have a centerline double with head aft or a Pullman-style double to port with the head forward. I like both, but in my experience most people would prefer the centerline double so no one will have to sleep under the side deck. That's understandable.

Wow! We have a galley with counter space on both sides of the sink and both sides of the range. The reefer/freezer compartment is big, and there's plenty of counter and locker space. The keel trunk is nestled against the galley and virtually disappears in this layout. There are mirror-image double-berth staterooms aft with a head to port. The dinette is raised up two steps while the nav station is kept down so it can tuck under the side deck.

While one part of the old racing fleet turns to all-out one-design racers with minimal accommodations, another segment looks to retaining and even improving comfort while not giving up on blistering boat speed. That sounds good to me.

Turner Yachts U.S.A., 53 America's Cup Avenue, Bowen's Wharf, Newport, RI 02840. www.turneryachts.com (401) 846-4222.

April 2002

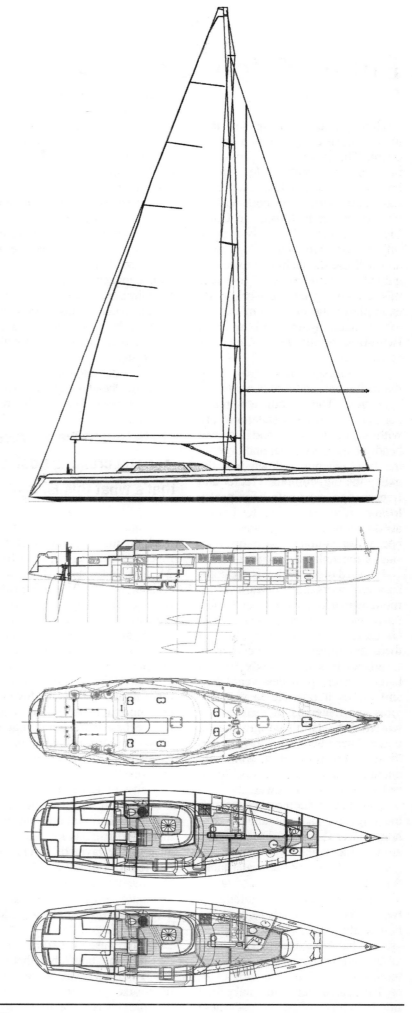

State-of-the-art performance cruiser.

LOA 56'8"; LWL 48'8"; Beam 14'10"; Draft 12'6" (keel down), 7'6" (keel up); Displacement 30,100 lbs.; Ballast 11,140 lbs.; Sail Area 1,766 sq. ft.; SA/D 29.2; D/L 116.7; L/B 3.82; Auxiliary Yanmar 100-hp 4JH3-HTBE; Fuel 150 gals.; Water 150 gals.

Rutter 57-foot Cruising Sloop
Performance Cruiser

Here's a new cruising boat that my office has designed for a Seattle client. The task was to provide a fast, safe and comfortable cruising boat for Dave and Gay Rutter to travel the world. The boat will be built by Westerly Marine in Costa Mesa, California. Westerly is fresh off its two America's Cup boats and will use the technical expertise gained in those projects to make this cruising yacht a world-class example of the breed. I'm excited to be once again working with Lynn Bowser and the capable crew at Westerly.

Most cruising boats grow from the inside out, and this boat was no exception. The layout features a comfortable owner's stateroom aft, with a double berth and adjacent head. There is a washer and dryer in the head. Stepping down into the galley the big, combined reefer and freezer is to port with huge pantry lockers over a second reefer-freezer at counter height. The galley to starboard has counter space on each side of the sinks and the range.

Forward of the galley is the combination workshop-forward stateroom, with a long workbench to starboard and copious lockers and drawers for tools and spare parts. To port there are upper and lower berths. Overhead is a large 30-by-30-inch hatch, which provides ventilation and makes it possible to move in tools and materials. If there is any feature that sets this design apart, it is the sheer number of drawers and lockers. Forward of a watertight bulkhead there is a large fo'c'sle for sail and scuba-gear stowage.

The raised saloon makes room in the bilge for tankage and the 88-horsepower Yanmar diesel. There are two fuel tanks for a total of 370 gallons of fuel, and two water tanks for a total of 300 gallons of water. There is 80 gallons of holding in two tanks located adjacent to the two heads.

This hull was designed for good all-around performance. Displacement is on the light side with a D/L of 103, calculated with tanks half filled. In my office we call these boats "cruising sleds" and have done several in this style. The forward sections are U-shaped, fairing into a midsection with 8.5 degrees of deadrise. This deadrise provides a natural sump area in the bilge and

helps with longitudinal stiffness. There is a slight hollow to the waterline forward. The deadrise is carried aft to help prevent a counter that slaps at anchor.

The keel is a bulbed fin, and the rudder is a deep carbon fiber spade. The beauty of a carbon fiber rudder for a cruising boat is that the rudder and stock are essentially monocoque, indestructible and very light. By eliminating a skeg we give the rudder balance, take some of the load off the Edson steering gear and make a boat that backs up with predictability.

The sail-handling systems may be at the heart of the success of a cruising boat. Despite the remov-

I hate to use the expression 'serious cruising boat' but that's what this is.

able inner forestay for a storm jib, I think the mast location qualifies this rig correctly as a sloop. The SA/D is 24, and that's pretty healthy for a cruising boat while it diminishes the need for overlapping headsails. We are using the Leisure Furl in-boom furling system for the mainsail. This is the slickest trick since self-tailing winches. I've specified the Leisure Furl three times. I love it. My wife loves it, and the owners love it. You get a normal main with draft, unlimited reefing increments, roach and, most importantly, battens. The mainsheet traveler is on the bridgedeck.

Construction is composite with a Divinycell core, vinylester resin and unidirectional and bidirectional knitted E-glass fabrics. There is an 8-ounce layer of Kevlar on the outside for durability. The cruising sled must combine toughness in its laminate with panel stiffness. There is a full length topside hat-section stringer.

I hate to use the expression "serious cruising boat" but that's what this is. There was no attempt to maximize market appeal in this design. This is a boat for the Rutters.

Robert Perry Yacht Design, 5801 Phinney Ave. North, Suite #100, Seattle, WA. (206) 789-7212, fax (206) 789-7214.

December 1999

A large, fast cruiser tailored to its owners' tastes.

LOA 57'; LWL 51'2"; Beam 15'; Draft 8'6"; Displacement 32,500 lbs.; Ballast 11,000 lbs.; Sail Area 1,530 sq. ft.; SA/D 24; D/L 103; L/B 3.8; Auxiliary 88-hp Yanmar diesel; Fuel 370 gals.; Water 300 gals.

X-612
Racer-Cruiser

I can't find any mention of the designer in the material on the X-612, but I think it's safe to assume this is the work of Niels Jeppesen and the X-Yachts design team. These guys are on roll. Their boats win races and win my votes for some of the best-looking production models available today. The 612 is an "ultimate" boat that combines a race-course hull with a full cruise interior.

For fun let's briefly compare this design to my double-ended 56-footer. They both share the same waterline length. The 612 has a significantly lower D/L of 157 based on a displacement of 49,606 pounds, but a similar B/D ratio of 40 percent. To achieve this latter ratio the 612 will have to be built with very high strength-to-weight

Here's a beautiful boat that can race from time to time and cruise with style and grace.

materials and methods. The 612 is a foot beamier than my 56 and draft is 9 feet, 6 inches. That's a bit much for most cruisers in the United States, but it sure will make this boat climb to weather. A shallow draft keel is available, but it would be a shame to cripple the boat with a stubby keel.

The forefoot knuckle is immersed and the stern is quite broad. The sheerline is sweet and subtle, and fore and aft overhangs, while short, are not minimized. There is enough overhang in this bow to keep the anchor from whacking the stem. Note the extended, shallow skeg preceding the big spade rudder. The keel shows pronounced leading- and trailing-edge fillets with the hull.

This layout features mirror-image staterooms with adjoining heads aft. The staterooms show double berths with an upper berth over. There is a small hanging locker in each stateroom along with a bureau. The galley is skimpy. I mean, look at the S&S galley in that 46-footer. It's bigger than the galley in this 60-footer. So much of cruising revolves around meals that I feel attention

must be paid to the galley so that there is sufficient counter space for a cook to work. You guys just sit there sipping your drinks while I stand here, day in day out, slaving away at meal preparation. The least you could do is give me some counter space and a decent reefer. It was explained to me once as, "In Europe we eat ashore." Fine. The saloon is really comfy with a big dinette and room for six (I thought you were eating ashore!), including the three swivel chairs. Forward of the saloon is a stateroom with a double berth, what look like reading chairs and an adjacent head with a large shower stall. There is a fo'c'sle big enough for two pipe berths and an exposed head. Curiously, while there is room for these reading chairs there doesn't seem to be enough room for a large hanging locker. In a 60-footer I would also like to see one hanging locker dedicated to foul weather gear.

The deck layout shows beautiful tooling and a fully inflated dinghy can be stowed in the stern garage.

Powered winches will make sail handling easier for a short-handed crew. Winches are not within easy reach of the helmsman, but on a boat this size there is sufficient directional stability to allow you to get to the winches without panic if you, by chance, are sailing the boat by yourself. The interior fit and finish is impeccable in satin-varnished teak.

In a world of fractional rigs, the designer has chosen a masthead rig for this boat. The spreaders are only very slightly swept and the drawings shows runners, checkstays, a babystay and an inner forestay for a staysail. The backstay is split to open up the transom for the garage entry. SA/D is 22.17.

Here's a beautiful boat that can race from time to time and cruise with style and grace the rest of the time. Sure the purist racer will see compromises as will the purist cruiser, but you have to look pretty hard. I see a well-balanced design that, like the J/109, was designed to give us a good all-around boat.

X-Yachts, Foot of Washington Blvd., Stamford, CT 06902. (203) 353-0373. www.x-yachts.com

May 2002

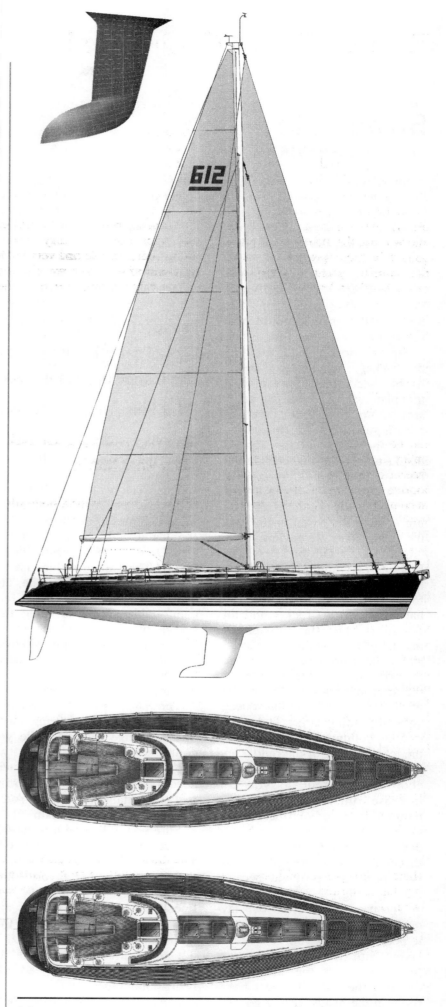

Yet another good-looking racer-cruiser from X-Yachts.

LOA 60'; LWL 52'1"; Beam 16'8"; Draft 9'6"; Displacement 49,606 lbs.; Ballast 20,060 lbs.; Sail Area 1,870 sq. ft.; SA/D 22.17; D/L 157; L/B 3.59; Auxiliary 110-hp Yanmar; Fuel 205 gals.; Water 180 gals.

Swan 601
Offshore Racer-Cruiser

Swan found a way around the "no reigning rating rule" problem. They had German Frers design a "global" one-design racer with 60 feet LOA. Now the trick will be to convince your buddies to all buy Swan 601s so you can race as a class and forget about the limitations of rating rules. This new Swan is designed for pure boatspeed first and then the Nautor group has worked hard at putting the package together with a very livable accommodations plan. If the plan was to turn out an all around attractive yacht they have done a good job. I'm attracted.

I'm inclined to use the "loaded" displacement for my calculations but so many builders publish unnaturally low displacements that I think I'll use the "light" figure to keep the Swan in line with the other boats we review. Using "light" I get a D/L of 119.6 and a L/B of 4.03 and a buttwater-to-beam ratio of 77 percent. With this low D/L you are going to eliminate fore and aft rocker and this design is very flat through the middle of the profile. The sheer is about flat with about 5.56 inches of spring across 60 feet. Note how the forefoot knuckle is lifted clear of the DWL. The keel has a dead-vertical leading edge. There is a curious hollow right at the top of the leading edge of the rudder and I would bet this is to increase the chord at the root so you can increase thickness to what's required for a carbon fiber rudderstock. With 11 feet, 10 inches of draft and that huge bulb I suspect this boat will have a lot of sail-carrying power and it should, because that rig is big.

You can choose from two layouts and each has it's own, specific deck design. If you go with the layout with two heads aft you get the deck with the bridgedeck dividing the cockpit to get headroom in the heads. If you go with the one with the nav station on centerline aft you can forgo the bridgedeck as headroom is not required at the nav station. If your proclivities run more to racing you

should go with the no-bridgedeck layout as it provides a better racing cockpit. If you are more cruising-oriented take the two heads aft version and learn to live with the big bridgedeck. It's about 12 feet from the wheel to the forward pedestal winch so you will have to

I suspect this boat will have a lot of sail-carrying power and it should, because that rig is big.

shout "Put your back into it dear" when you are cruising. It's a bit like a giant Melges 24.

This is a long, narrow, light boat but there are few compromises when it comes to the layout. Three couples would be very comfortable. Or, it would be perfect for my family. The galley is fine and the heads are more than adequate. The owner's stateroom forward is very comfortable. The one thing that strikes me is that there are no hatches aft of the companionway except for the big lazarette hatch. Maybe there are opening ports in the side of the cockpit seats.

The SA/D is 28.79. Don't fool yourself. Even in cruising mode this is a huge rig and while you could sail this boat with two strong and skilled sailors, you will need four good people on board to feel comfortable under sail. You'll need four to flake the mainsail.

Sure you will need to scramble for crew when you want to go out, and sure you won't be able to enter some of your favorite harbors, but I'll bet the crew will lineup to sail on this boat, and heck, you didn't need to go to that harbor anyway. The Swan 601 is not about anything practical, it's just about raw boat speed and heart-pounding beauty.

Nautor Swan New York, Swan Building 12-B, Foot of Washington Blvd., Stamford, CT 06902. (203) 425-9700. **www.swan-newyork.com**

May 2004

Sailors get a choice of deck designs on this sleek racer.

LOA 60'1"; LWL 52'11"; Beam 14'10"; Draft 11'10"; Displacement 39,700 lbs.; Ballast 18,700 lbs.; Sail Area 2,088 sq. ft.; SA/D 28.79; D/L 119.6; L/B 4.03; Auxiliary Volvo Penta 72-hp; Fuel 79 gals.; Water 106 gals.

Wally 60
Performance Cruiser

I think I saw my first Wally boat about 10 years ago. Immediately, what I thought of Euro styling took a huge leap forward. The Wallys have come to represent a highly refined approach to sensible sailing yachts—they are simple, they are fast, they are comfortable and they are elegant beyond comparison. Oh yes, they are expensive too. This new Wally 60 has a hull and rig by Farr but I'm going to go out on a limb here and say that the rest of the design is by the Wally design team.

The hull is typical Farr and there is little of interest there except that I'm sure it's very fast. Draft is 13 feet, 1 inch. The L/B is 3.74 and the D/L is 118. Thirty-eight percent of the displacement is ballast in that deep, bulbed fin.

This deck fascinates me. In plan view it gives the impression that it's all straight lines and 90-degree angles but in reality there is subtle curvature to the sides of the house, but not much. The beauty of this deck is in its simplicity. There is room for guests to sit with seat backs in the cockpit but the twin helms have the helmsman sitting on the deck and well outboard so he can get a good view of the slot or the waves to weather. Wally decks are more about what they do not have than what they have.

Jib tracks are located on the top edge of the cabintrunk. Note that the cabintrunk has a large recessed section, teak covered, sunken about three inches below the top of what appears to be the top edge of the house. There is also athwartships track for a self-tacking jib. There is a well at the companionway. Side decks are absolutely clean. Chainplates are outboard. None of the drawings show cleats of any type on deck but it's my guess that there are some pop-up-type mooring cleats hidden in that teak deck.

To my eye the Wallys have never been about accommodations. I have seen them more as luxurious daysailers with some accommodations below "just in case." There are staterooms, two aft with singles and one forward

with a double berth. There are three heads. The forward stateroom has a shower stall. The galley is tiny for a 60-footer. The nav station is large. The focus of this layout is entertaining after a day's sail. And to this end the symmetrical settees are about 9 feet long. No dining table is shown. That

The beauty of this deck is in its simplicity.

rectangle forward of the nav area is probably a reefer. Note the total lack of angles in this layout; 90 degrees seems to work well for this interior designer. I hate seeing angles for the sake of angles.

The mainsheet treatment is the most interesting aspect of the rig that I can discern from these overly simplified drawings. It's hooked to a hydraulic ram either below deck or in the boom. The jib sheets are also hydraulically controlled. That's why you don't see any sheet winches at the cockpit. I'm not sure what you do when the chute goes up; "Here, dear, hold this." Maybe those winches at the companionway are for the chute sheets and guys. This seems less than ergonomically optimal to me.

Ground tackle—I assume, because it's not shown on any of the drawings—will be handled "submarine style" through the bottom of the boat so you will see nothing on deck.

The Wally 60 was built by Carroll Marine. Barry closed his doors after this project and that's a loss to all of us. The company produced many fine yachts. But according to my sources at Sailing Anarchy—Lesbian Robot and Doug—all of the finishing work on the 60 was completed at Carroll Marine short of the cushions. Maybe it's fitting that Barry's last project was this spectacular 60-footer.

Wally Yachts, Seaside Plaza, 8, Avenue de Ligures, Monte-Carlo, MC 98000 Monaco. 377-93 1000 93. **www.wally.com**

December 2003

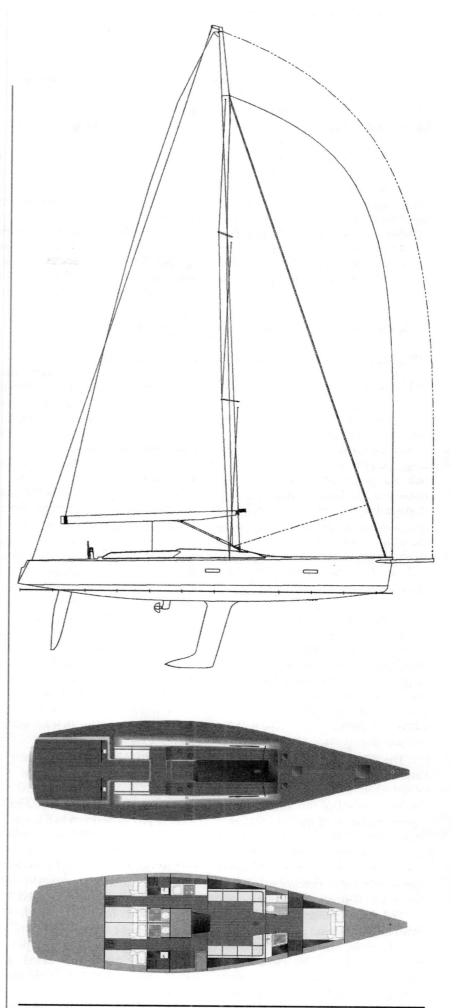

Clean lines define this elegant 60-footer.

LOA 60'6"; LWL 52'2"; Beam 16'2"; Draft 13'1"; Displacement 37,479 lbs.; Ballast 14,330 lbs.; Sail Area 2,260 sq. ft.; SA/D 32.3; D/L 118; L/B 3.74; Auxiliary Yanmar 88-hp; Fuel 132 gals.; Water 132 gals.

Santa Cruz 63
Racer-cruiser

Bob Smith of Santa Cruz Yacht designed the new Santa Cruz 63 to be a comfortable and fast dual-purpose boat. I'm sure that, given the track record of this yard, you can count on a race version being produced at some time. But the initial drawings show a boat fully outfitted for cruising. Some of you will not recognize Bob Smith's name, and I don't know Bob personally, but he has been an integral and effective part of the Santa Cruz design scene for many years. Bob was very involved with the Santa Cruz 52 project, and you can see the same ideas carried over to this new design.

The 63 represents that wholesome blend of speed and comfort.

Unfortunately, to my jaundiced eye, the aesthetics were carried over a little too much. This boat is pretty ordinary looking, and I can see no reason for that. The sheerline is flattish with a total of about 5 inches of spring overall. The cabintrunk is boxlike and could have benefitted by some clever geometry tricks. The long, straight cockpit coaming could have also used a dash of imagination. While this is a handsome boat, why not make a 63-footer exciting visually? Headroom is no problem. Freeboard is no problem. Perhaps there was a conscious attempt to keep the 63 in the same aesthetic style as the 52. I just like to see the playful side of our nature displayed in the boats we choose to sail. Make them safe, make them fast and make them beautiful. We aren't talking "sensible shoes" here.

The 63 has a wonderful interior layout. The owner's stateroom is forward with a Pullman-style double berth. Forward of this is a head that spans the beam of the boat and after that a shower. Having the shower this far forward puts pressure on the cabintrunk to extend forward to provide the necessary headroom. That's always an aesthetic challenge.

The saloon features a big dinette with a center-island seat for an additional couple. There are port and starboard pilot berths, which would make perfect places to stow your guitar. The galley has lots of counter space and lots of stowage space. I'd cook braised lamb shanks in a wine sauce. The extended center leg of the galley counter makes it perfect for preparation and serving. If the icebox were moved into this center leg it would be

great for crew access to cold drinks.

There are two more heads aft and quarter staterooms with double berths and plenty of locker space. The starboard stateroom has direct access to the starboard head and shower. I think these boats will be customized to specific owner requirements. If you don't want three heads you can have yours with two heads. The designer has provided a layout with two heads using the additional space for a washer-dryer combo and a linen locker. Suffice it to say you will be very comfy on this boat.

The hull is light with a D/L of 92.9 and a beam of 16 feet, 5 inches. The ends are short, and fore-and-aft rocker is as minimal as you would expect with any light boat. The rudder is a deep, all carbon fiber, semibalanced spade. The keel features a cast steel fin with a lead bulb. We have come to an agreement that we want all the stability we can get, and you can't do this with a traditional, all-lead keel, especially on a lightweight boat where you do not have the luxury of a high ballast-to-displacement ratio. To optimize stability you need to get the lead as low on the keel as possible.

The rig for the 63 is a fractional type with the cap shrouds going almost to the masthead. The spreaders are swept. The mainsail overlaps the backstay by about 8 inches, and there is no provision for sheeting a large genoa. The bowsprit will be deck mounted. The drawings show an inner forestay, but the angle on this is so steep I can't imagine it would be used for a staysail unless it is a very small storm staysail. The SA/D is a healthy but not terrifying 27.6.

The 76-horsepower Yanmar 4JH2HTBE turbo diesel should push the 63 along at close to 10 knots. Total fuel tankage is 220 gallons. If you slow down to 8 knots this will give you a 1,000-mile cruising range. Water tankage is 230 gallons.

The Santa Cruz yard has always done a nice job with its boats. The interiors are very well finished and the boats have had enough speed to make them threats in just about any fleet. The 63 represents that wholesome blend of speed and comfort that should ensure its long-range success.

Santa Cruz Yachts, 453 McQuaide Dr., La Selva Beach, CA 95076. **www.samtacruzyachts.com** *(831) 786-1440.*

March 2001

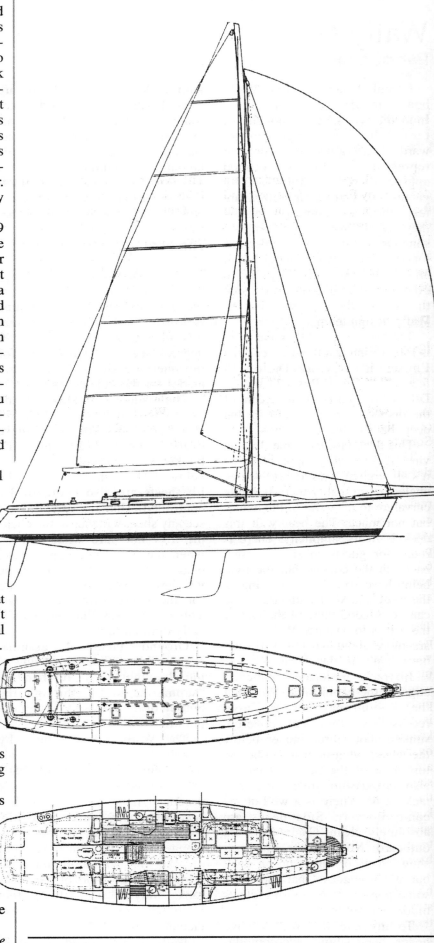

West Coast speedster with plush accommodations.

LOA 63'1"; LWL 54'; Beam 16'5"; Draft 9'1"; Displacement 32,640 lbs.; Ballast 13,000 lbs.; Sail Area 1,763 sq. ft.; SA/D 27.6; D/L 92.9; L/B 3.8; Auxiliary 76-hp Yanmar; Fuel 220 gals.; Water 230 gals.

Farr 645
Performance Cruiser

The hull, appendages and rig are designed by Farr but the styling and the interior are from an outside design house; in this case Design Unlimited. The boat is built in Sweden by BSI Marine. The idea here appears to be combining the performance pedigree of a Farr

Regardless of the interior layout, you'll be comfortable on this one.

design with the comfort and styling of a big Euro-type cruising boat. Sounds good to me.

The less-than-extreme state-of-the-art construction techniques: furniture, tankage, gensets, reefers and freezers (two in this case) and all the wild variety of gear that many cruisers find indispensable account for the huge 60.5 ton displacement. This is a big boat with an elaborate interior and a high level of outfitting.

The D/L for this design is 154. The hull form in plan view is very normal but slightly less fine forward. There is more freeboard and more hull rocker to the 645 as you would expect with the greater displacement. The fore and aft rocker is flattened amidships where the keel is bolted on. There is enough overhang forward to keep the anchor from banging against the stem. Standard draft is 10 feet, but there is an option of a shoal-draft keel with unspecified draft. I would suspect they could do a custom keel to any draft requirement you might have, within reason.

I think this is a good-looking boat. The deck structures are nicely styled and with that high freeboard there is no need for anything but a low wedgelike trunk forward. The cockpits are separated by a walk-through that keeps the guests forward while those who are actually working the boat can congregate aft where the wheels and winches are.

The center section of the transom folds down to form a swim step.

There are four standard interior layouts. Saloon, galley and nav station remain the same for each but the layout and number of staterooms changes. I prefer layout D with V-berths and a bigger fo'c'sle than the other layouts. They are all fine layouts, but some are a little congested for my taste. I don't like that rabbit warren feel. In the saloon there is a dog-legged settee to port and an angled or faceted settee to starboard. I prefer harder corners. Watch people as they go below and make themselves comfortable. People seek corners. But corners aren't sexy unless you are Wally's interior designer.

Regardless of the interior layout, you'll be comfortable on this one. I'll just sit in the nav station where I have my own corner.

The triple spreader, fractional rig has the spreaders swept 21 degrees at the chainplates. This rig uses the hydraulic mainsheet system like the Wally. There is no traveler. The boom is really high and I suspect it will clear the head of a tall man standing on the cockpit seats. That's okay, but I hate to have to go up in a bo'sun's chair just to attach the halyard. In-boom furling is an option. Headsail furling is Harken push-button hydraulic. Genoa sheets run under the deck but the drawings don't show any detail on this. The SA/D is 23.2.

I have a picture of an almost finished deck plug for this boat. It's beautiful.

Farr International (UK), Hamble Point Marina, School Lane, Hamble, Southampton, Hampshire SO31 4NB. 44 23 8045 6545. **www.farr-int.co.uk**

In the U.S. contact Boat Sales International, 312 Third St., Annapolis, MD 21403. (410) 269-6229. **info@boatsalesus.com**

December 2003

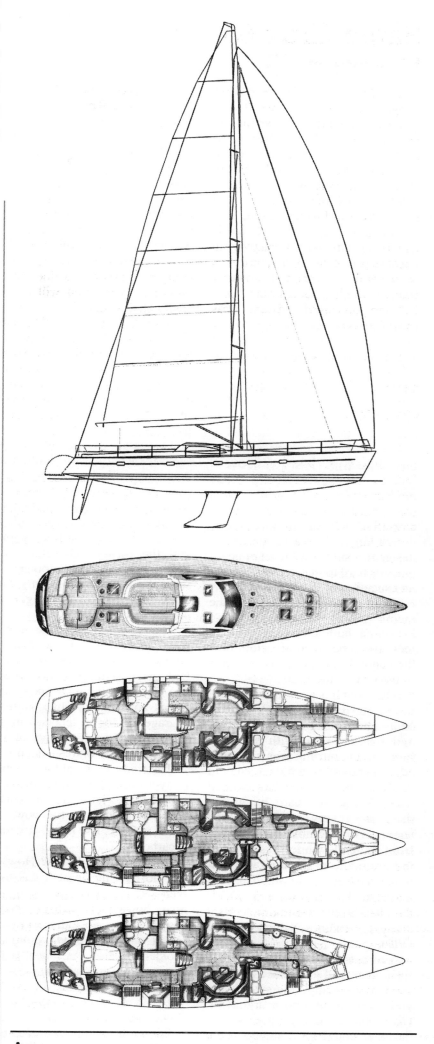

All the comforts of a cruiser in a fast hull.

LOA 64'4"; LWL 55'11"; Beam 17'2"; Draft 10'; Displacement 60,500 lbs.; Ballast 19,580 lbs.; Sail Area 2,231 sq. ft.; SA/D 23.2; D/L 154; L/B 6.4; Auxiliary Yanmar 150-hp; Fuel 26 gals.; Water 156 gals.

Dolphin 65
Performance Cruiser

I strive to be objective in the reviews. But it's hard. There is so much subjectivity in yacht design. Over the years I've developed my own preferences, and I would be shortchanging the reader if I did not share what I have learned.

This new Luca Brenta design is a perfect example of subjectivity in yacht design. Clearly this design is an offshoot of the spectacular Italian Wally boats that have become so visible. Brenta has designed several of the Wally boats, so it's only natural that the Wally approach would carry over into this design. Clearly the owner wanted a very fast and very comfortable boat with only modest accommodations. You might be tempted to look at this boat as a big

Do I like this design? How can you not?

daysailer. Given the objective design target, Brenta has taken this design to a subjective level of beauty that's hard to match in its exquisite execution of detail.

The hull owes its shape to the racing yachts of today with an IMS-type bulb on a fin with 11 feet, 10 inches of draft. Note how the canoe body profile is flattened in the way of the keel.

This boat has a lot of freeboard. I suppose it was either freeboard or a cabintrunk to get headroom, and in order to stay with the Wally look the cabintrunk was eliminated. Freeboard is windage, but in this case the designer has avoided unnecessary freeboard by giving the boat a very subtle reversed sheer. This removes freeboard from the ends while preserving it in the middle of the boat where it is needed for headroom. The L/B is 3.74. I don't have a DWL length, but I'll approximate it at 57 feet, 6 inches, which gives a D/L of 93.

You could see the choice of a flush deck and a reversed sheer as subjective design elements, and you would have a good argument. Given the design parameters the designer could have stopped here and delivered a pretty normal 65-foot glass/Kevlar/carbon pre-preg daysailer. But Brenta detailed the deck in a style that I can only relate to automobile styling—*Italian*

auto styling.

Flush is the word, except for the big windows in the side of the rounded cabintrunk. Here, where you would expect flush windows, the designer has deeply recessed them about 4 inches. This recess is carried right down to the deck, where it is used to route and hide lines leading aft into the long coaming and back to the winches in the cockpit. Every effort has been made to keep the deck clean. There are pop-up style recessed cleats, and the large, fixed hull ports virtually disappear on the dark blue topsides. The detailing at the twin wheels is jewelry quality. How can you maintain objectivity when faced with a design like this?

This is an interesting interior. I see no "owner's cabin," although I do see two mirror-image staterooms aft with small adjoining heads and no double berths. There is a large stateroom forward, but still no double berth. It's my guess that the owner will either sleep ashore or aboard the "mother ship" when he is racing his *Only Lu*. I think these sleeping arrangements are for paid crew.

The saloon looks like a great place to relax after the race. Of course, given that this boat will be built as a semiproduction model, I'm certain you could modify your layout any way you like. Note the "garage" aft for the tender. I am surprised at the small number of deck hatches that are in this design.

The rig is a typical tall, fractional type with three sets of swept spreaders. There is a carbon bowsprit hidden in the bow. The SA/D is 28.4. The mast, of course, is carbon.

Do I like this design? How can you not? At the least it has to be seen as impressive. At the same time, however, whether or not a design pushes an individual's own set of sailing lifestyle buttons is another question. As much as I do admire this spectacular design it doesn't "speak" to me.

Don't tell my Grandpa, Angelo Dante Guiseppe Nanelli.

Studio Associato Luca Brenta & Co., Via Salaino 7, 20144, Milano, Italy. **www.lucabrenta.com** *39 02 43995071.*

November 2001

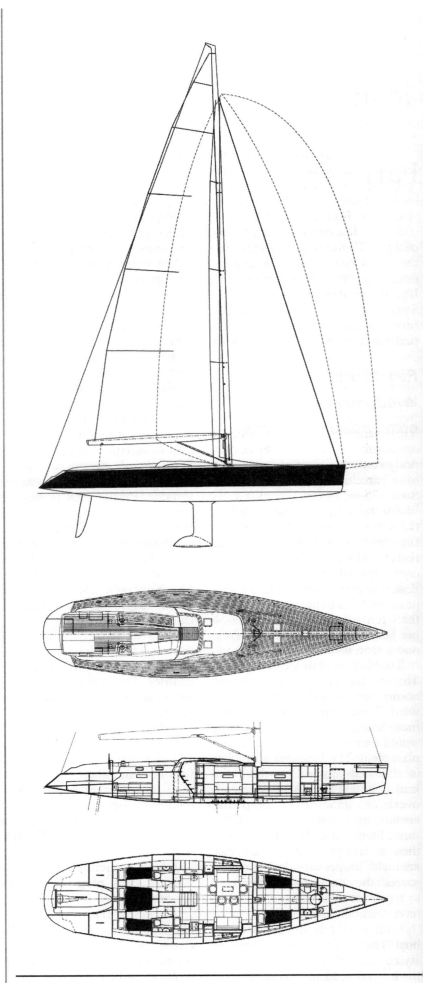

A spectacular variation on the Wally theme.

LOA 65'; LWL 57'6" (estimated); Beam 17'5"; Draft 11'10"; Displacement 39,600 lbs.; Ballast 18,000 lbs.; Sail Area 2,062 sq. ft.; SA/D 28.4; D/L 93; L/B 3.74; Auxiliary 125-hp; Fuel 208 gals.; Water 208 gals.

Icon
Racer-Cruiser

My office has had fun with the challenge of preparing this custom cruising sled design for Seattle sailors Dick and Bonnie Robbins. Dick and Bonnie's current boat is the beautiful S&S veteran heavyweight 50-footer *Charisma*. *Icon* will be a very comfortable cruising yacht that will be competitive with the best of the grand prix racers.

This design features a lifting keel that varies the draft from 8 feet, 6 inches with the keel up, to 13 feet, 8 inches with the keel down. The engineering for this lifting keel was done by my right- and left-hand man Tim Kernan in conjunction with Efficient Machinery's Peter Hammerschlag. This is a complex mechanism that is driven by an electric winch-motor and lifts the keel on recirculating ball nuts riding on two 1.75-inch worm screws running down inside the fin. The fin itself is 17-4 Ph stainless steel forged by Jorgenson Forge in Seattle. Tim and I watched the forging process wide eyed. The ballast bulb is lead. *Icon's* D/L is 68.

Icon's personality is split between racing and cruising. I think we have achieved a balance in features that makes this boat a truly refined hybrid vessel. Note the interior is laid out for a couple with room for a second couple and perhaps a grandchild or two. The interior shows a big galley with counter space on either side of the molded-in carbon fiber sinks. There is also counter space on either side of the range. Copious locker space will make this galley a cook's dream. The 76-hp Yanmar engine is located in a box within a box on the centerline portion of the forward galley counter. The aft cabin features a full queen-size double and large lockers.

Note that one of the drawings is computer drawn while the others are hand drawn. I feel very strongly that the hand-drawn drawings are far more interesting, even if they are more cluttered and difficult to read. Hand drawings convey the creative style of the designer. I'd be interested in your comments on this.

The saloon has a big dinette to starboard with a minidinette to port. This minidinette will convert to sea berths for offshore racing. Forward of the keel trunk is the owner's stateroom with head and shower stall. There will be fold-up crew berths in the fo'c'sle. We will use carbon fiber throughout the interior to reduce weight and add glossy black styling accents. The step at the aft end of the forward double is part of the anchor chain stowage system, which keeps weight aft.

The rig is huge and uses a carbon fiber mast and boom. The SA/D is 33.25 and the spreaders are swept 19 degrees. No overlapping headsails will be carried. Doug Christie of Seattle's Halsey-Lidgard sail loft has been very instrumental in helping us design this rig. A Leisure Furl boom will be fitted for cruising.

The deck plan shows wide side decks, a large sliding foredeck hatch, a buried anchor chain pipe and a recessed windlass well adjacent to the mast. The cockpit is big with high cockpit coamings forward and seats long enough for sleeping. There are two coffee grinders. The forward one will be removed while cruising to be replaced by a cockpit table. The aft grinder powers the mainsheet winch. Primary and secondary winches will be electric. All cockpit winches will be recessed into the deck. Halyards can be led to winches adjacent to the mast for racing or led aft for cruising.

Icon will be built by Marten Marine in Auckland, New Zealand, and the launch date is spring 2001. The project manager is Jim Roser of Seattle. Construction details have been engineered by Tim Kernan of my office working with High Modulus of New Zealand. The boat will be built from pre-preg carbon over a Nomex core and oven cured. Further information can be seen on the project Web site **www.iconsailing.com**.

Performance cruising remains a moving target and my office is taking a good lead on that target with *Icon*.

Robert H. Perry Yacht Designers Inc., 5801 Phinney Ave. N., Ste. 100 Seattle, WA 98103. (206) 789-7212. **www.perryboat.com**

May 2000

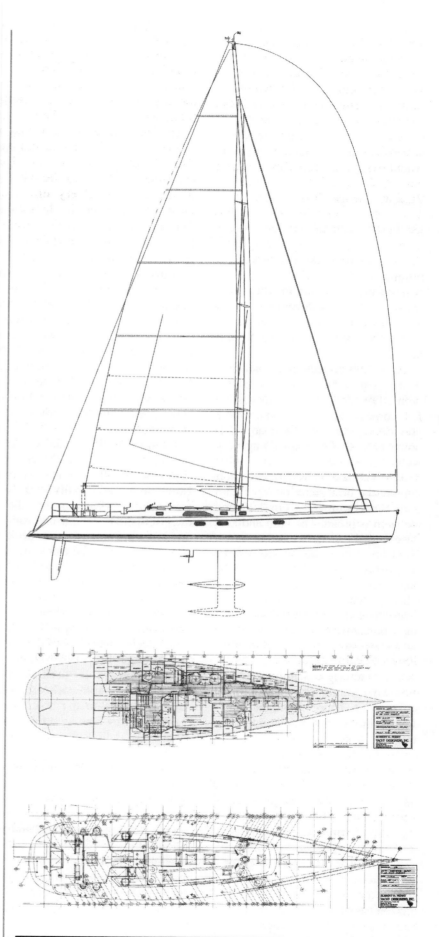

Hybrid combines high speed with cruising comfort.

LOA 65'11"; DWL 56'10"; Beam 14'10"; Draft 8'8" (keel up), 13'8" (keel down); Displacement 27,700 lbs.; Sail Area 1,906 sq. ft.; SA/D 33.25; D/L 68; L/D 4.44; Auxiliary 76-hp Yanmar; Fuel 150 gals.; Water 200 gals.

Tripp 77
Performance Cruiser

We are going to have to do something about this "performance cruiser" label. I may have invented the label, but I did not invent the type. The problem as I see it is that today the label is being fixed to a very wide variety of performance potential yachts. Every designer sees his designs as performance oriented, whether they deserve the term or not.

This is an exciting performance cruiser.

My job in writing these reviews is to remind you to keep the definition of performance fluid and to adjust it to the latest high-performance boats. This is a complex boat designed to cruise the Pacific comfortably and very quickly.

At 80,000 pounds (half load) this boat appears to be no lightweight. But with a DWL of 69 feet, 6 inches the D/L comes out at 106.3, and any time you can get a cruising boat's D/L down near 100 you are doing very well. The canoe body shows some rocker, and the ends are cut short without the bow being plumb. Beam is moderate with an L/B of 4.25, and the stern is broad. The bulb and keel raise from 12 feet, 3 inches to 6 feet, 10 inches. I presume the keel will be all the way down while sailing. The boat carries 20,000 pounds of ballast, which I expect is almost all in the torpedo on the keel fin. The rudder appears stubby, but that's because it has to be restricted to the depth of the retracted keel.

The ketch rig was chosen to give the owner the maximum number of sail options. There are no backstays or any kind of triatic stay on this rig, and the spreaders are swept 28 degrees to take up the load.

There is a retractable bowsprit for the asymmetrical chute and a mizzen chute is shown on the drawing. An inner forestay allows for high-aspect-ratio staysails to be set for heavy air. The working jib looks to have an LP of about 100 percent and sheets to short tracks right up against the cabintrunk. Roller-furled mizzen staysails are set on a stay that is anchored on the aft bulkhead of the pilothouse. Both mainsail and mizzen use Leisure Furl booms by Marten Spars of NZ. It's a complicated rig that offers a world of sail combinations to suit any condition. If we use just I, J, E, P, Py and Ey,

we get a total sail area of 2,492 square feet and an SA/D of 21.47. This, however, ignores the added area of the extreme roach on both the main and mizzen. The mizzen boom doubles as a davit for the big inflatable dinghy.

This is a nice layout. There is inside steering in the pilothouse along with a big dinette and settee. The keel trunk is neatly hidden in the layout. There are five staterooms and the owner's stateroom aft has a big queen-sized berth and direct access to the deck. There is another double-berth stateroom forward. I'm not wild about the saloon. This area has a large dinette to port with a center-island seat. The galley is to starboard and is very spread out and wide open. My biggest galley critic, the diminutive and very experienced Robin Roser would hate this galley. She yells at me because I size galleys to my body and not hers.

Considering the complexity of this rig, the decks have been kept very clean. The cockpit is raised enough to make visibility over the pilothouse no problem, and the low, wedgelike cabintrunk running forward makes the deck more interesting. The trunk aft of the cockpit is cleaved to allow a form fit for the inflatable. This cleaved area is directly over the aft double berth, so it will not impact headroom. The cockpit features twin wheels on an elevated level and a large drop-leaf dining table. There are 16 deck hatches. There are port and starboard spiral stairways down to the boarding or swim platform. The symmetry here is attractive. I find this to be a very good looking boat.

There is a retractable bow thruster forward, the auxiliary is a 315-horsepower Yanmar, and the gen set is a 20kW Northern Lights. There is tankage for 1,000 gallons of fuel and 500 gallons of water. Carbon fiber is used to reinforce this Aramid/E-glass composite hull. The rudder is carbon fiber and all interior panels are cored.

This is an exciting performance cruiser.

Tripp Design, Oyster Bend Marina, 23 Platt St., East Norfolk, CT. **www.trippdesign.net** *(203) 838-2215.*

September 2002

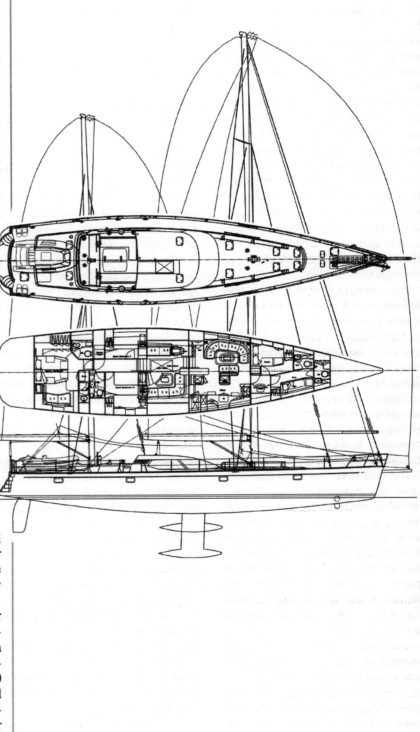

A performance cruiser with the emphasis on performance.

LOA 77'; LWL 69'6"; Beam 18'1"; Draft 6'10" (keel up), 12'3" (keel down); Displacement 80,000 lbs.; Ballast 20,000 lbs.; Sail Area 2,492 sq. ft.; SA/D 21.47; D/L 106.3; L/B 4.25; Auxiliary Yanmar 315-hp diesel; Fuel 1,000 gals.; Water 500 gals.

Briand 100
Performance Cruiser

I want to dedicate the review of the Briand 100 to the memory of my old friend Larry "Uncle Bumps" Hutson. If there is a heaviness to this month's review we can blame Larry. Larry, like the Briand 100, was bigger than life.

Unfortunately Larry's bigness took a toll on his heart. Larry liked fine wines, great cigars, old movies and good music. He liked good food too much. Larry wasn't a sailor, but on board he could be counted on to cheerfully do the right thing at the right time when asked. The Briand 100 is Larry's kind of boat. "Do you have that in 120 feet and in blue?"

This design is based upon the Briand design *Mari-Cha III*, the current transatlantic record holder and winner of the Superyacht Society Design Award. What's not to like about this boat except the moorage bill?

The concept is for a very fast cruising yacht built in either aluminum or carbon fiber. The accommodation plan is laid out in two distinct areas, with accommodations for the owner's party forward and the layout for the paid crew aft. I'd settle for either end, but if you are lucky enough to be with the owner, you will have your choice of a double stateroom to port or a twin single berth stateroom to starboard.

The saloon is huge. I'm sure you could seat a dozen of your friends around it without cramping. Larry would put a double magnum of '70 Lafitte right in the middle of that big table and challenge anyone to a sea chantey contest. Larry's best sea chantey was the extemporaneous "Ballad of the Advertising Account Executive." "Ohhhhh, I've been to New York and I've been to L.A. ...."

The crew quarters begin with the galley to starboard. There is a dinette and crew mess adjacent to the galley. Aft of this is a big nav station on centerline, flanked by crew cabins with upper and lower berths. The crew head does not have a shower stall. Maybe they'll just splash on even more cologne.

This hull is very slender with a narrow BWL and lots of flare to the topsides. There is water ballast—11,299 pounds per side. I would guess these tanks are designed to augment the stability provided by the modest draft and ballast bulb. These tanks do not come up to the deck. They stay below shelf and settee height so they don't interfere with the interior.

Using the "loaded" displacement, I get a D/L of 107. Draft is only 10 feet, 10 inches, with a bulbed and winged fin with an adjustable trailing edge. This trim tab will help compensate for the minimal amount of planform of this small fin.

Just to keep this boat in perspective, the mast height above the sheer

Suffice it to say, if you can imagine it on a sailboat, this one has at least one of them.

is 137 feet, 10 inches. I don't have I, J, E and P, but needless to say the SA/D is quite high, with maximum upwind sail area at 5,016 square feet and maximum downwind sail area at 8,719 square feet. You had better be sure which sail you want before you have your wife haul a 300-pound spinnaker on deck. (Oh, that's what those pungent guys in back with the striped t-shirts are for.)

The main halyard runs to an electric reel-winch located below deck at the maststep. There is a recessed jib track in the foredeck for a self-tacking jib. The drawings do a wonderful job of showing all the features clearly. Suffice it to say, if you can imagine it on a sailboat, this one has at least one of them.

If Larry were still here, he'd show up, late, with a pocket full of Montecristos, leave his big, black Humvee idling at the quayside in the no-parking zone, step aboard without introducing himself to anyone, hold out his hand in correct anticipation of receiving a glass of chilled Le Montrachet and take his seat behind one of the wheels. "Sailing anyone?"

I hope they finally have that wine chilled to perfection for you now Larry.

Philippe Briand Yacht Architecture, 41 Ave. Marillac, 17042 La Rochelle Cedex 1 France. (33) 5 46 50 57 44, fax (33) 05 46 50 57 94 or e-mail **100445.1543@compuserve. com.**

October 1999

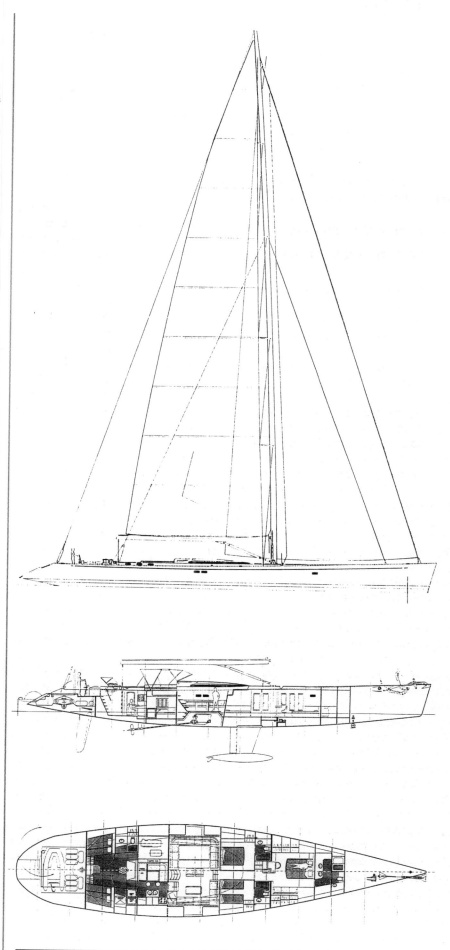

Custom-built, high-speed luxury from France.

LOA 98'5"; LWL 88'7"; Beam 23'; Draft 10'10"; Displacement 166,601 lbs. (loaded displacement); Sail Area 3,982 sq. ft. (working jib and main); SA/D 21 (based on working jib and main figures); D/L 107; L/B 4.27; Auxiliary 310-hp.

RACING DESIGNS

Piper 24
One-design

It's time for another yachting history lesson. Sit up straight, spit out your gum and pay attention. This is important.

In 1938 a young Scottish designer named David Boyd made his mark with the outstanding 6-meter *Circe*. *Circe* came to the United States to face the fastest of the American 6s, the famous S&S-designed *Goose*, in the Seawanhaka Cup. *Circe* did beat *Goose*, and Mr. Boyd's career was well on its way.

In 1958 the British challenged for the America's Cup in a David Boyd-designed 12-meter called *Sceptre*. They lost to the venerable S&S-designed *Vim*. In 1964 they again challenged with another David Boyd boat, *Sovereign*. They lost again, although to my youthful eye they won on style points. *Sovereign* had teak decks and a graceful sheer even if it did receive a drubbing at the hands of *Constellation*, the S&S twelve. (We did a lot of drubbing in those days.) I relied on my old pal and yachting historian Scott Rohrer to fill in the blanks on this background material. *Sovereign* was the last I heard of the tall and elegantly handsome David Boyd. Until now.

In 1966 Boyd designed the Piper class for fiberglass construction and one-design racing on the Clyde. All told 57 Pipers were built. In 1985 a moss-covered and neglected Piper was discovered by Frank Collam, the builder of the Cornish Crabber line. Collam saw through the grime and verdigris and recognized a classic. Plans were made with the Cornish Crabber yard to start a new fleet of Pipers. The look and mood of the little Piper fit right in with the Cornish Crabber yard's style of building.

How can you not love this boat? It looks like a mini version of the Boyd 12-meter *Sovereign*. It has the overhangs, the sheer and the cutaway full keel with attached rudder. With an LOA of 24 feet, 5 inches the overhangs reduce the DWL to a scant 16 feet, 3 inches. The D/L is a whopping 370. Approximately 59 percent of the displacement is in lead ballast, carried low and encapsulated in the keel. I would imagine that the Piper is quite stiff.

These overhangs don't do much if anything for boat speed, but they certainly are beautiful. If you compare the quarter buttock angle at the DWL (you can use the hull profile angle if you like) of the Piper with that of a modern racing yacht you will see that this angle is much steeper on the Piper. If there is anything to be gained from an overhang it must be kept closer to the water at a less steep angle where it will immerse at moderate angles of heel. Piper looks great from any angle.

The rig is a moderate-aspect-ratio fractional type that has been modernized with an adjustable rigid vang and a roller furling genoa. The 5:1 mainsheet is fixed on a thwart just above the cockpit sole. The genoa winches appear to be either the old-fashioned, bottom-action type with the handle below the deck or maybe just snubbing winches without handles. The genoa lead is a "twinger" type arrangement that is adjustable under the deck. The SA/D is 15.1 using the

How can you not love this boat?

company's figure of 220 square feet for the sail area. I don't know if this includes the area of the genoa or is based on I, J, E and P.

The deck design features a smallish, deep and non-self-bailing cockpit. The intended crew is three, but this cockpit looks tight for three. The brochure calls the Piper a "sit in" keelboat, but almost all the photos show the crew sitting on the side deck. This is fine except for the fact that there is a two-inch teak coaming around the cockpit that would bite into the back of your thighs eventually. There is a teak splash guard forward of the mast to help keep water out of the cockpit. I think in any chop at all you had better wear your foul weather pants or you will soon have a wet seat in this ride. The low freeboard, while beautiful, would make this deck a damp sitting area.

The Piper 24 is one of those boats that I think would be ideal for teaching the grandchildren about sailing. You are not going to tip over. The kids won't tumble out of the deep cockpit. And you will be introducing your little darlings to sailing in a style that will bring them into contact with the timeless aesthetic of yachting.

Cornish Crabber Ltd., Rock, Wadebridge, Cornwall PL27 6NT, England. 44 1208 862666. www.crabbers.co.uk

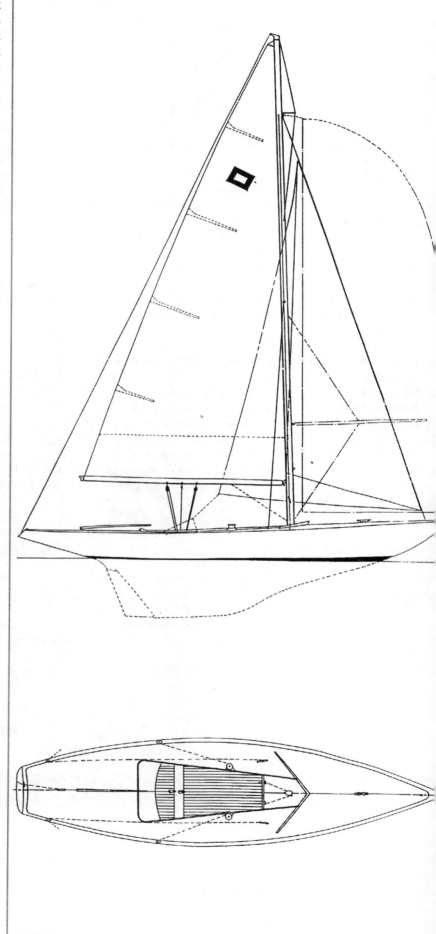

A new breath of life for a classic design.

LOA 24'5"; LWL 16'3"; Beam 6'3"; Draft 3'6"; Displacement 3,560 lbs.; Ballast 2,100 lbs.; Sail Area 220 sq. ft.; SA/D 15.1; D/L 370; L/B 3.9.

Pro25
One-Design Racer

It's not dinghy sailing weather in Seattle right now but if it was this new Pro25 would be a nice boat to race for a weekend. It's not exactly a dinghy in that it does have 704 pounds of ballast in a keel bulb. I classify boats as dinghies if they do not have ballast. But the concept for this boat appears to be to be a big, ballasted dinghy designed for one-design racing. This new boat is built in the Netherlands and designed by Judel/Vrolijk.

To my eye, what separates this model from the pack is that there is no cuddy cabin and no concession whatsoever to accommodations, however token or sparse. The layout is totally focused on what it takes to race the boat with a crew of four. This means a huge cockpit, access to the mast without getting up on deck and the ability to easily get all the

> I would guess that somewhere in the local rule where the boat in the photos races there is a clause saying 'Hiking allowed as long as legs are under the lifelines.'

crew weight forward without leaving the cockpit area. The helmsman sits well forward up against the main-sheet and traveler. On the drawings, sail control lines come out of a low console immediately forward of the traveler and while I have many good photos of the boat I can't see this detail. Suffice to say you can make all needed major sail shape adjustments from the high side. Sheet winches are well forward, putting the trimmer where he can see the entire luff of the jib. Jib tracks run athwartships allowing for a wide range of sheeting angles.

The photos show a curious lifeline and stanchion arrangement with the lifelines running from stern to bow about 7 inches above the deck in the way of the cockpit, then tapering down to nothing at the bow. Hmm? I would guess that somewhere in the local rule where the boat in the photos races there is a clause saying "Hiking allowed as long as legs are under the lifelines." After working so hard to make this boat crew friendly they add that lifeline, which must make it much harder to get your legs outboard and then back inboard.

The hull shows generous wetted surface and considerable flare to the topsides. This flare is accentuated by a kink just below the sheer inducing a slight hollow. This is undoubtedly to help get crew weight outboard. The photos show the Pro being sailed upwind with a heel angle less than 20 degrees with then entire crew on the rail. The D/L is 60.54 and ballast-to-displacement, not counting the crew, is 43 percent. In that crew weight is about half the weight of the boat it might be interesting to note that if I include crew weight with the ballast weight, also adding crew weight to the boat's "displacement," I get a ballast-to-displacement ratio of 60 percent. The retractable keel fin is carbon and draft is 6 feet, 3 inches. The rudder appears to be a straight blade but if you look very carefully and use a straight edge you can see that there is balance area forward of the pivot point on this rudder. The photos show the 25 planing along nicely under chute without a single white-cap in sight.

The SA/D is 41.2 without factoring in crew weight. The mast and boom are carbon. All sheets and control lines are Spectra and halyards are Vectran. Standing rigging is dyform.

With its design pedigree and impressive numbers there is no way this boat cannot be fast and a lot of fun to race.

Pro Marine, Kennemerboulevard 716 1976 ES Ijmuiden, Holland, 31 255-526811, **www.promarine.de**

March 2004

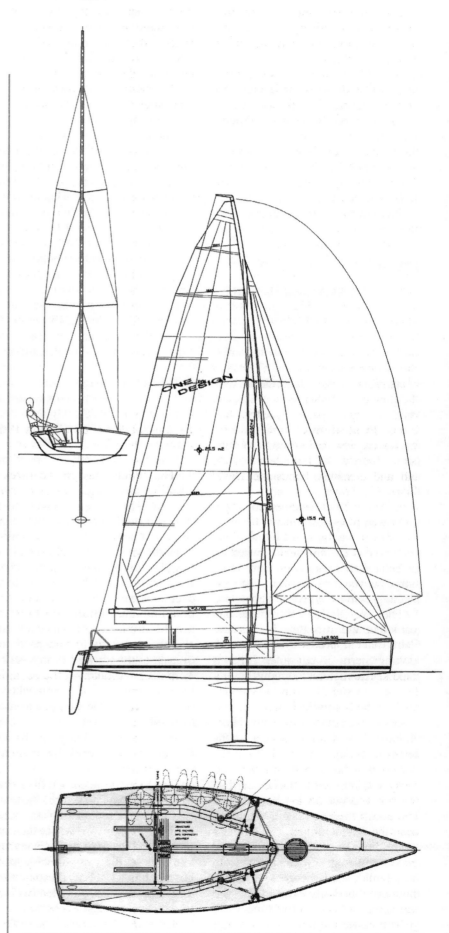

A quick keel boat with the look and feel of a competitive dinghy.

LOA 25'7"; LWL 23'; Beam 8'10"; Draft 6'5"; Displacement 1,650 lbs.; Ballast 704 lbs.; Sail Area 360 sq. ft.; SA/D 41.2; D/L 60.54; L/B 2.89.

Sierra 26
Daysailer

When I was a kid in the '60s I would hitchhike down to Leschi Park marina on Lake Washington on one-design race days and go up to the race tower and tell them I was "available crew." The race committee in the tower would announce that there was crew available. I would sit on the dock and before long some dinghy would come by and pick me up. I always got a ride. Somebody always needed crew.

I usually performed my crew duties with gusto if not consummate skill and this got me on several "regular crew" lists. Before long I had the

The spinnaker is huge and raises the sail area to more than 700 square feet.

pick of which dinghy I would crew on. I sailed on Stars, Thistles, International 14s, 110s, Geary 18s (Flatties), Lightnings, Snipes, Penguins, Dragons, Evergreens, six-meters, PCs and my all-time favorite, the Raven. The Raven was a 24-foot open dinghy with a minimal foredeck and a big, wide-open cockpit with long seats. On a good day with the wind hitting 20 or better we could get the Raven onto a full plane. I have a soft spot in my heart for big daysailers. I owned a Soling and I owned an Etchells. I raced each on rare occasions, but for me they were just nice big, aggressive daysailers.

The Nelson/Marek office has teamed up with Jim Betts of Truckee, California, to produce this exciting looking Sierra 26 daysailer. It has a fixed keel so it's not a dinghy, but it's easy to see this design as a development of the Soling/Etchells type. The beauty of the fixed, deep, bulbed keel is that you will not have to be concerned with capsizing.

You will have to sit on the side decks as there are no seats inboard so in effect you will always be "hiking." The cockpit itself is deep enough to keep the grandchildren safe. Almost all the lines are led discreetly under the cockpit sole to a control console in the middle of the cockpit where they can be easily reached by the helmsman. There is a fine tune and a gross tune for the mainsheet coming off the aft end of the console. Headstay tension, vang and mast-bend controls are also led to the console. There is no mainsheet traveler but instead a double-ended bridle

does the job. The spinnaker sheets are led from the block aft under the deck to exit in the cockpit walls just forward of the console. Even the spinnaker pole downhaul leads back to exit at the console. Jib sheets are led so they can be adjusted from the weather side.

The hull form is unusual in that it almost develops a hard chine in the last 26 percent of the LOA. I say "almost" because there is a sharp turn just above the waterline, but it never goes completely hard. This feature is combined with a skifflike midsection to promote planing. At the dock the boat weighs about 1,200 pounds with a 250-pound bulb at the bottom of an aluminum fin. The keel is removable for trailering. Draft is 5 feet, 6 inches.

It probably makes sense to include the crew weight with the boat's displacement for the D/L. Note that the boat is drawn sitting at the "with crew" flotation. Say three crewmembers weighing an average of 175 pounds each: This raises the displacement to 1,750 pounds and gives us a D/L of 77.7. This is in the ultralight range.

The rig uses carbon spars and there is a long slot at the partners allowing for a wide range of mast rake. In a breeze the mast will go forward. In the light stuff it will come aft to add helm and feel. Rig tension is handled by the adjustable headstay. Mast bend is handled by a Star-class-type mast ram. The jib has some overlap and can be barberhauled with proud-mounted cheek blocks. If we use the displacement with crew and add the roach to the mainsail and overlap to the jib we get an SA/D of 37.46. That should keep you ghosting along nicely. The spinnaker is huge and raises the sail area to more than 700 square feet.

Jim Betts is building this boat to race on Lake Tahoe. He has in mind a one-design class of these boats. The hulls and decks are carbon fiber skins over honeycomb core.

There are a lot of strings to pull on this one if you want to get the most out of it. That may bother some but like stick-shifting and double-clutching an old MG, these adjustments do deliver performance dividends. If you are lazy you can just set everything on "automatic." You will still be fast.

Nelson/Marek Yacht Design Inc., 2820 Canon St., San Diego, CA 92106. (619) 224-6347.

January 2001

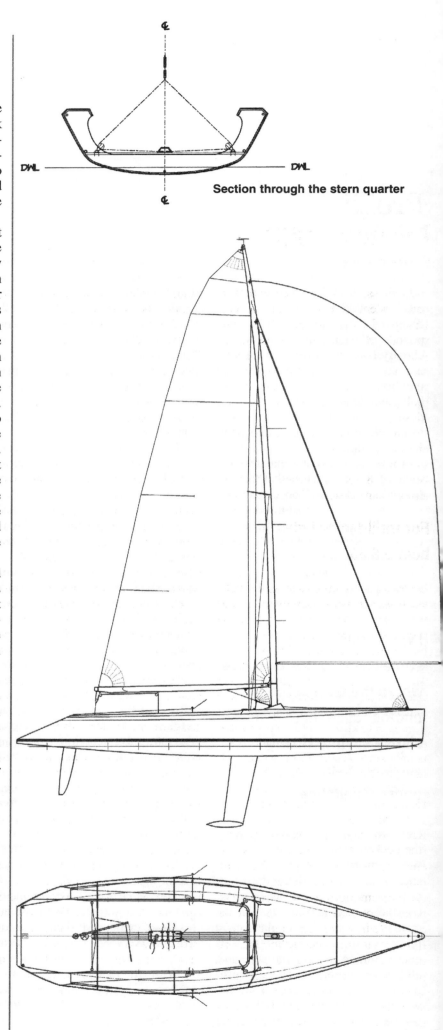

Section through the stern quarter

A fast, fun boat for daysailing and racing.

LOA 26'2"; LWL 23'; Beam 7'11"; Draft 5'6"; Displacement 1,200 lbs.; Ballast 250 lbs. (bulb weight); Sail Area 340 sq. ft.; SA/D 37.48; D/L 77.7; L/B 3.31.

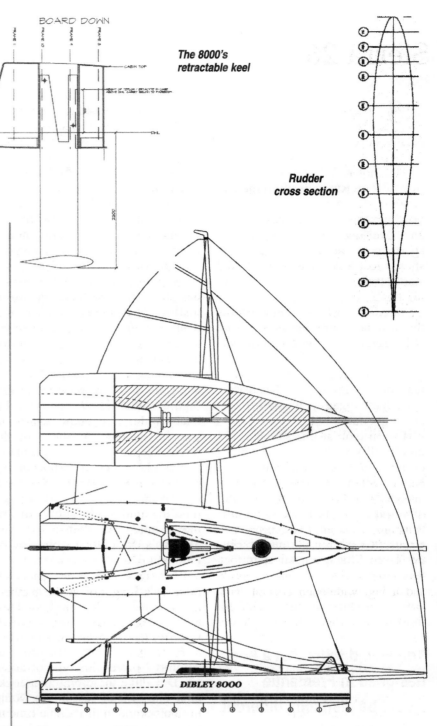

The 8000's retractable keel

Rudder cross section

Dibley 8000
Racer

Let's leap back into 2001 with this new trailerable rocket from Kevin Dibley of New Zealand. This boat was designed for a couple in Cairns, Australia, and is aimed at good all-around performance with plenty of stability. The first of these boats is being built in Cairns by Shayne Young.

This is a very sexy hull shape. The entry is slightly hollow and the topsides flare out quickly to a maximum beam of 8 feet, 2 inches. There is almost some deadrise in the forefoot,

For thrill factor I give this boat a 9.38.

but this quickly fairs away into a flattened section with slack bilges and a very narrow BWL. The beam at deck shows almost no taper as it goes aft from maximum beam. This will help keep the crew's weight well outboard. This is a very low-wetted-surface shape that will be a bit on the tippy side initially. Obviously the shape of this boat is intended to promote planing performance. The shape certainly does nothing to enhance form stability at moderate heel angles. The D/L is 77.

Draft with the keel down is 7 feet, 2 inches, and that's where the sail carrying power will come from. The keel fin is a hollow fabrication with two box-section stiffeners running full depth. The lead bulb is bolted to a flange plate at the bottom of the fin. The fin is deeply notched at the top end to allow the fin to be retracted for trailering. With the keel up the bulb is almost snug with the hull. The rudder is a very deep blade hung outboard and also retractable. There is a distinct hollow to the last 15 percent of the rudder foil. I prefer to choose rudder foils without any hollow to the section.

The deck is exactly what you would expect from a modern racing yacht. All the hard edges, including the sheer, have received generous radii. This

should make hiking comfortable, almost. The house is a bubble shape, and the cockpit seat edge has been greatly softened for seating comfort. The plan form of the cockpit features a very wide well with minimal side decks. Every effort has been made to keep the crew's weight out of the stern for reduced pitching. The mainsheet traveler is on the cockpit sole.

There is no interior on this boat. Sure the drawings show four "berths," but there is no headroom and no room for a head. If that's a porta potty dotted in next to the keel trunk, you had better bring a big paper bag with you to put over your head, 'cause that's the only privacy you'll get on this boat. I wonder why you would even bother with a cabintrunk on a design like this.

This is a monster rig. The SA/D is 44. There is a retractable "prod" for asymmetrical, masthead spinnakers. A chute can be flown from the hounds in heavier weather. The mainsail has lots of roach, which is made possible by the lack of a standing backstay. The spreaders are swept and carry the cap shrouds to the masthead. With a rig this size you are going to really need that deep bulb plus all the crew weight on the rail to even begin to keep this boat on its feet. Maybe the "Cairns couple" consists of two, 250-pound, toothless ex-rugby players.

The rig numbers keep getting bigger, the hulls lighter, the keels deeper and the bulbs bigger. Make no mistake, this is not your mom's trailerable boat. A novice skipper and crew would probably find themselves in harm's way before they cleared the breakwater. Still we live in a world of "X-treme" sports and the quest for an ever-escalating adrenaline rush. For thrill factor I give this boat a 9.38. Nice work Mr. Dibley.

Dibley Marine Architects Ltd., P.O. Box 46-167, Herne Bay, Auckland, New Zealand. 64-9-303-3678. **www.dibleymarine.com**

March 2001

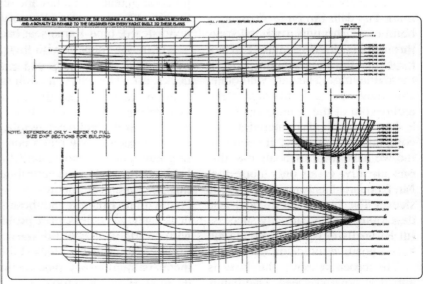

A reproduction of the 8000's original lines drawings.

High-octane rocket from Down Under.

LOA 26'3"; LWL 24'10"; Beam 8'2"; Draft 7'2"; Displacement 2,645 lbs.; Ballast 880 lbs.; Sail Area 527 sq. ft.; SA/D 44; D/L 77; L/B 3.2.

R8

Racer

This hot rod design is designed by Malcolm Runnalls of Fremantle, Australia. According to the brochure this boat was designed as an "exciting inshore trailerable sports boat, an IRC-friendly offshore racer as well as a roomy and stable twilighting and family picnic boat."

Sure, it's all those things, and if the designer really believes this he will have no trouble letting me include it as a small cruising boat this month. "It's a floor wax." "No, it's a dessert topping." It has berths, a head and a galley. It smells like a cruising boat to me.

Take a look at this sailplan. If I didn't tell you this was a Runnalls design you might think it was a Nelson/Marek design, or a Farr design or the work of any number of designers all using the same software to produce their drawings. Excuse me while I curmudge a little. I see little personal stamp on this design work. Maybe that's good. Maybe it means that this boat will be as good as any boat from those other offices. It's just that I

You would think that a boat designed in Fremantle would be distinctly different.

miss the days when a designer's hand came through loud and clear through his drafting style. I'm not knocking the presentation style of these drawings. They are well done. But they are antiseptically clean and devoid of the human touch.

Mr. Runnalls has entered a very competitive field here. It seems to me we have a lot of boats like this one already. I can only hope that Mr. Runnalls has some tricks up his sleeve. The fact that this boat is a development of an already successful Runnalls design, the Fremantle 8, is a positive indicator.

The brochure says the boat is aimed at upwind speed. Overhangs are kept to a minimum and the forward waterlines show only a hint of hollow. The midsection is arclike with soft bilges and a narrow BWL. The sections flatten toward the stern going tangent by the time they reach the transom. The D/L is 77.85. The

rudder is huge and almost 80 percent of the fin area of the keel.

Do you remember watching the America's Cup when it was held in Fremantle? It blew hard enough every day for it to be near survival conditions for a lot of sailors I know. You would think that a boat designed in Fremantle would be distinctly different from a boat designed for, say, San Diego, California. Specifically, I would expect a small rig and lots of ballast to contend better with the "Doctor." With its light displacement and high SA/D of 31.69, however, this boat would be at home and effective just about anywhere in the world. We really are on the brink of losing all local color and becoming a big dull gray world. I'm not faulting Mr. Runnalls. I'm just saying I miss the quirky local types, kind of like I miss golf swings like Lee Trevino's, Ray Floyd's and Arnold Palmer's. Do any of you remember a CCA race boat from the early '60s called *Hoot Mon*? Now there was a weird but effective boat. How about that silly IOR winner *Cascade*? There was a wacky boat.

Back to cruising. In terms of comfort I prefer this type of cockpit. Dogs like these big open cockpits. The lack of seat backs would not bother me until it came time to relax and read a book, and even then it's very easy to rig removable, upholstered, pipe-frame seat backs.

My major concern with this particular deck is the width of the side decks aft. The cockpit well gets wider as it goes aft and by the time you reach the helm position you have a side deck/seat width of about 14 inches. My butt's not getting any smaller, and I don't think I'd be comfortable for very long in this cockpit. The photos show a boat with no lifelines and these side decks would be less of a problem with no lifelines. Still I'd like some lifelines for cruising. Heck, I'd like them for racing. My race committee would like them too.

Malcolm Runnals Naval Architecture and Yacht Design, 141 Petra St., East Fremantle 6158, Australia. 61 8 9339 0441. **www.runnallsdesign.com**

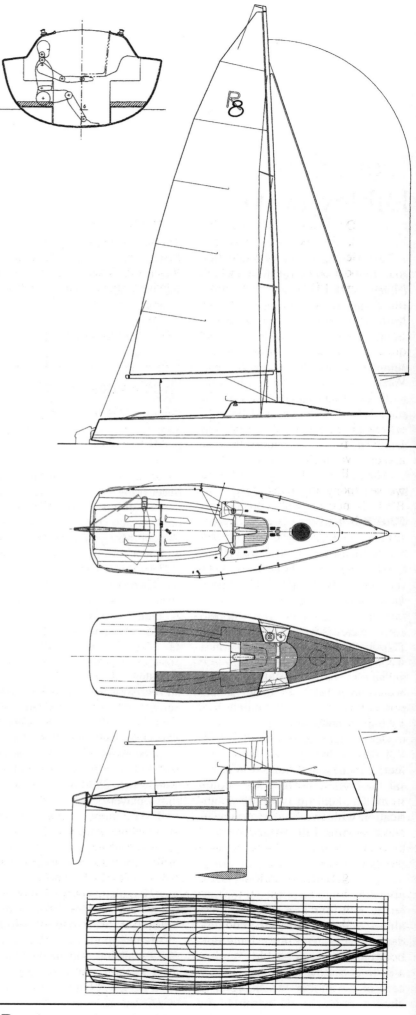

Pocket rocket from Down Under.

LOA 26'3"; LWL 23'5"; Beam 8'2"; Draft 6'4" (keel down), 1'5 (keel up); Displacement 3,000 lbs.; Ballast 1,386 lbs.; Sail Area 413 sq. ft.; SA/D 31.69; D/L 77.85; L/B 3.2.

Donovan 27
PHRF Racer

Jim Donovan of Annapolis, Maryland, designed this 27-footer for Mr. Bert Carp with the intention that the boat be competitive in both MORC and PHRF races. Competition is very stiff in this size range, but early races in the Annapolis Fall Series proved the Donovan 27 to be quite fast, finishing third, second and first in its first three outings. In a Key West series the Donovan 27 finished sixth in a hotly contested fleet. The class was won by my old pal Leif Bailey's B-32. Good on ya Leif. The Donovan is a very handsome boat and deserves a close look.

The hull is pretty typical of what we see today in racing boats. The BWL is narrow with considerable flare to the topsides. The bilge turn is firm and there is a wee hint of deadrise to the midsection. There is plenty of rocker to this canoe body and that's a function of the displacement. Using a removable 600-pound internal ballast piece, the displacement jumps from a light PHRF weight of 3,700 pounds (D/L of 130) to a MORC weight of 4,300 pounds (D/L of 151.17 using the same waterline length). In either ballast configuration, this is not a light boat by today's standards.

The entry is very fine and while the plan view drawing appears to show a fairly full line at the deck, the photos do not. Photos show the bow cleaving the water. The 1,500-pound keel is a straight fin with no bulb and 6 feet of draft. Note the curvature on both the leading and trailing edges of the keel.

This rig is big but not crazy big like we are seeing on some one-designs. In MORC configuration the SA/D is 22.2 and in PHRF configuration 24.55. The mainsail is loose footed with about 6 inches of overlap on the backstay. For MORC racing the spinnaker will be hoisted about 24 inches above the hounds, but for PHRF you can go with a bigger, masthead spinnaker. The spreaders are only slightly swept and mainsail draft adjustments will be made with the backstay.

This is a nice sized boat for racing. The spinnaker goes up fast, hand over hand, and it comes down fast too. When the flotsam hits the fan it's a relatively small chunk of flotsam that is easily overcome with well applied

This boat would be fun to race. You can get it ready in five minutes and put it away with a wash down in 10 minutes.

manpower. Mast and boom are both carbon fiber.

An alumnus of Bruce Farr's office, Donovan knows a thing or two about deck layouts on racing boats. Fashions come and go, but ergonomics remain constant. This cockpit layout has been perfected over the years and today it's almost universal on racing boats. Its key is to make lines lead logically so a new crewmember can acclimate to the boat quickly. Crew weight is kept in the most advantageous position (out of the stern) and crew movement is minimized. This is a big cockpit for a 27-footer, but that's a function of ergonomics and not LOA.

The small, bullet-shaped cabintrunk covers a couple of settee berths. The head is in the fo'c'sle. There has been no attempt to make this interior cruiser-friendly. This is a sails-and-sandwiches interior layout.

A 20-horsepower Yanmar diesel with saildrive gives this boat an honest 7 knots under power.

This boat would be fun to race. You can get it ready in five minutes and put it away with a wash down in 10 minutes. Unfortunately it enters a niche in the market chock full of good boats.

Time will tell if the Donovan 27 is anything special.

JP Donovan Design, P.O. Box 4992, Annapolis, MD 21403, (410) 263-3732 **www.jpdonovandesign.com**

April 2001

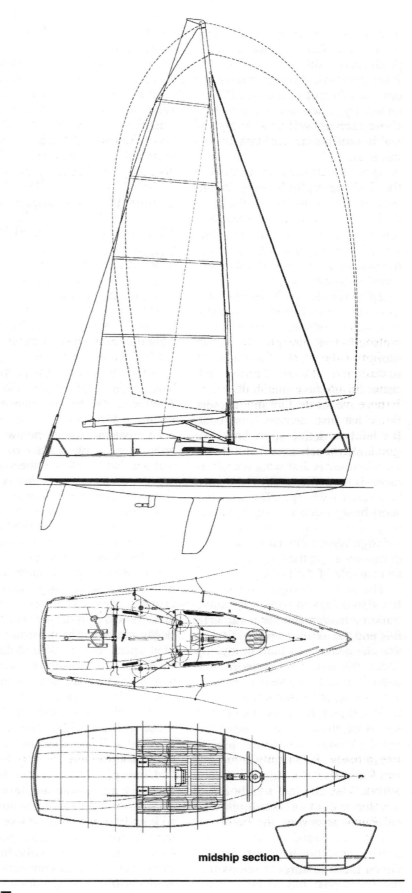

Fast and sailor-friendly racer.

LOA 27'; LWL 23'4"; Beam 8'7"; Draft 6'; Displacement 3,700 lbs. (PHRF), 4,300 lbs. (MORC); Ballast 1,500 lbs.; Sail Area 367 sq. ft.; SA/D 24.55 (PHRF), 22.2 (MORC); D/L 130 (PHRF), 151.17 (MORC); L/B 3.13; Auxiliary Yanmar 20-hp diesel.

Columbia 30
Sport Boat

Boy, does that name conjure up memories or what? Columbia was one of the founding West Coast production boatbuilders and it built a lot of boats. The Columbia 26, designed by Bill Tripp, Sr. will certainly go down as a production classic. When I was a kid Tripp was my favorite designer. He did all the Columbias. This new Columbia is designed by Morrelli and Melvin of Newport Beach, California. If you look down at the title block on these drawings, in the "drawn by" box, you will see the initials TK. TK is Tim Kernan. Tim was my right-hand man for five exciting years. We did some great boats together. Tim moved on and now works for Morrelli and Melvin. You probably think of high-powered multihulls when you think of Morrelli and Melvin so it should not surprise you that this is the design firm's first monohull.

If you want to start an argument in the bar just mention sport boat. It's hard to define sport boat. We can pretty much agree on what a racer-cruiser is and what a cruiser-racer is and these days the race boats are easy to spot. But what is a sport boat? I don't know. I think it may be more a frame of mind than a design type. Let's take a stab at a definition using the Columbia 30 as an example of the type.

The hull is designed for speed. It's also designed so that it can be trailered from regatta to regatta. To this end the extra-deep keel lifts so that the beaver tail bulb nestles up under the hull for transport. The deep, knifelike rudder is removable. Beam is less than the 10-foot limit at 9 feet, 6 inches. The D/L is low at 81.56. Overhangs are eliminated to maximize sailing length. BWL is reduced to lower wetted surface while the flared topsides will help make crew weight effective for stability. This dinghylike hull form also provides beam aft where crew weight will again be used for stability advantage. Given these features it seems that the sport boat has to be a high-powered, trailerable boat designed to maximize speed, including planing potential, for a given LOA while relying upon an active crew as an essential component of the boat's stability.

Rig-wise we see a rig similar to most high-performance racing boats. The headsail is small with minimal overlap. The spinnaker will be asymmetrical and fly from a retractable carbon bowsprit. The mainsail is a near "fathead" type with a loose foot and two full-length upper battens. The SA/D is

The hull is designed for speed. It's also designed so that it can be trailered from regatta to regatta.

30.6. By definition the sport boat will have a big rig and require a knowledgeable sailor to keep the boat on its feet and under control. Maybe this is the "sport" part.

The sticky part of this definition involves the accommodations and comfort level inherent in the design of the sport boat. Some would argue that the "down below" of a sport boat is only a place to throw sail bags and foulies. Others would argue that you need some type of sleeping arrangements and a head. The Columbia has a head tucked under the aft end of the V-berth.

What I like about this cockpit are the short coamings forward. These will keep the crew comfy and secure when they are in the cruising mode. This is a pretty cruisy cockpit for a sport boat. Side decks are clear. The mainsheet traveler spans the cockpit sole and there are foot bensons to help you stay up to weather. The cabintrunk is beautifully shaped. I'd like to see a softer corner on the aft end of those cockpit seats. The cockpit edge is well rounded for comfort while at the helm.

I like the blend represented by this boat and I think it will be a lot of fun to sail. The Columbia 30 will enter a very competitive market where even the slugs are rocket fast. It will be especially fun for me, given my Tim connection, to watch how this design does.

Columbia Yachts, 1048 Irvine Ave., #252, Newport Beach, CA 92660. (949) 631-6898. www.columbiayachts.com

March 2003

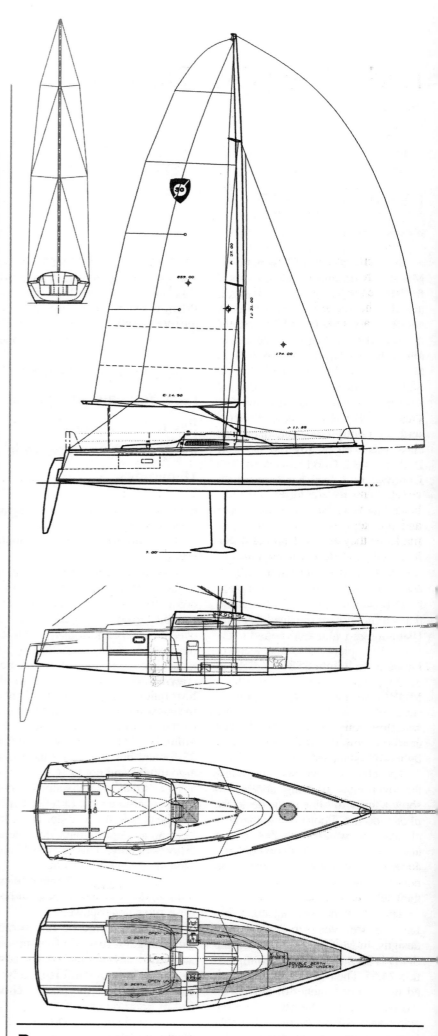

Built for speed this boat defines what a sport boat should be.

LOA 30'; LWL 26'6"; Beam 9'6"; Draft 7' (keel down), 2' (keel up); Displacement 3,400 lbs.; Ballast 1,400 lbs.; Sail Area 433 sq. ft.; SA/D 30.6; D/L 81.56; L/B 3.18; Auxiliary Honda 9.9; Fuel 20 gals.; Water 20 gals.

Endeavour One Design

Racer

There was a time when few boats were introduced as one designs. Of course, this was not true in the dinghy classes, but once you got larger than 20 feet, one-design classes grew spontaneously from boats that distinguished themselves as outstanding boats. The Soling and Etchells classes came from a call for a new three-man Olympic keelboat to replace the loggy but cute Dragon. In fact, the Etchells did not exactly fit the established parameters, so the Soling was chosen. Since that time, however, the Etchells has proven itself such a fun and quick boat to sail and race that it has developed into the more enduring of the two classes. I'm an ex-Etchells owner and an ex-Soling owner. Both of these boats are fun to sail.

There are one-design classes that exist only in regional pockets of the country and usually these are older boats that were built in a limited run and are kept as much as historical marks as they are evidence of excellence in yacht design. These include the stalwart Knarrs in San Francisco, the Ensigns in the Great Lakes, Florida and Long Island Sound, and

It's hard to look at this boat and not want to go racing.

the beautiful IODs in North East Harbor, Maine, and Marblehead, Massachusetts. The venerable hard-chine Thunderbirds that began in Seattle have gone on to establish a very active international class.

Probably the most recent example of this sequence is the J/24. I have talked about the J/24 several times in these reviews and am well aware that opinions vary greatly about the significance and quality of this boat. From my perspective as an ex-J/24 owner, I can say with personal certainty that the J/24 offered a welcome relief from cramped and cranky IOR Quarter-Tonners. A perfect example of this IOR type that had gone on to become a strong one-design class was the Bruce Kirby-designed San Juan 24. For a big guy this was not a fun boat to race. There were just a lot of them, and it was natural for them to form a one-design class. The SJ24 class did not survive long after the introduction of the J/24.

Today, the advent of a new, nondinghy one-design class is usually heralded with much hype. In my own area, one builder actually rented billboard space on the road leading to the marina turnoff. That class has yet to take off, but it was a very nice picture to have on a billboard. Simon Rogers, in England, has designed the Endeavour to be a new one-design class. The idea is that sailors tired of their Dragons, Solings, Etchells and Stars will see this as a more exciting alternative. It certainly will be a more expensive alternative. You can buy an older Etchells for around $6,000. A new Endeavour will cost close to $60,000.

From the look of it, I would think this design will comfortably outsail any of the other targeted classes. This looks to be a very fast boat modeled on what appears to be an IACC hull type. The boat is narrow with an L/B of 4.15. The D/L is 87.9 based upon a deceptively short DWL of 24 feet, 5 inches. Draft is a modest 5 feet, 11 inches. The rudder is a tiny, knifelike blade. The keel lifts for transporting. The keel is an "SG/steel/carbon composite blade with a lead bulb." "SG" could be "sand and gravel." I really don't know what "SG" stands for. There is an inboard engine, a Yanmar 1GM. Hull construction is balsa core with E-glass.

The inspiration for the rig comes from the 49er class. Note there is no backstay with the aft vector to support the rig instead being provided by the 22-degree sweep of the spreaders and the mainsheet. The jib is self-tacking and the bowsprit retractable. It's a very sexy looking rig and has an SA/D of 24.14. This excludes the area added by the roach of the mainsail, which in this case is considerable. If we use the total area of the mainsail with roach (say 225 square feet, i.e., 133 percent of the .5 E x P area) we get a total sail area of 362 square feet and an SA/D of 28.75. Whether or not you include the mainsail roach has to be a judgement call.

It's hard to look at this rig and this expansive cockpit and not want to go racing on this boat.

Endeavour Yacht Design (UK). **www.endeavouronedesign.com** *44 7767 821300.*

July 2001

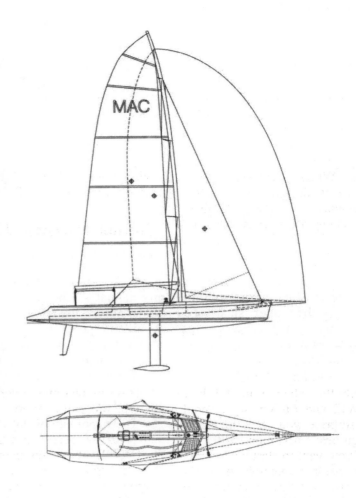

The latest one-design keelboat will sail circles around older designs.

LOA 30'11"; LWL 24'5"; Beam 5'11"; Draft 5'11"; Displacement 2,860 lbs.; Ballast 1,287 lbs.; Sail Area 362 sq. ft. (with main roach); SA/D 28.75; D/L 87.9; L/B 4.15; Auxiliary Yanmar 1 GM.

Sydney 32
One-design

Designed by Murray Burns & Dovell the Sydney 32 is the "little sister" to the super successful Sydney 38 from the same design team. According to the brochure this is an "entry-level yacht" and has been designed to be fast, comfortable and, like any good little sister, "well behaved."

This sheerline is as close to flat as you can get without being flat.

This will be a fast little boat designed to shine in fast company.

This has advantages in a smaller boat. By reducing sheer spring you maintain interior volume and headroom under the side decks without adding freeboard overall. You should always keep in mind that a flat sheer, especially on beamy boats, will usually only appear flat in the drawings. In three dimensions the overall shape of the hull will impart its own spring to the sheer, which will be further exaggerated when the boat heels under way.

This hull, like many today, is very short-ended to preserve sailing length. The D/L is 134.5 and the L/B is 3.02, which is beamy, again in keeping with the proportions du jour. The sectional shape shows flat topsides, a moderate BWL, firm bilges and a flattish bottom, although it never goes totally flat. Fore and aft rocker show a little flattening around the keel, which we'll see more of on the next page. Keel and rudder are pretty typical.

For cruising I can imagine a better layout. With its three double berths the boat can sleep six,

but I can't see more than three eating at that surfboard of a dining table. Maybe the table will double as an emergency rudder. The nav station looks well designed. A head is included in the forward stateroom. The drawings show the double V-berth in a dotted line, which I would read as meaning this berth is optional.

The rig is fractional with no overlapping headsails and no runners. The spreaders are swept 20 degrees. Masthead and fractional chutes will be carried. The SA/D is 24.84 and the brochure says that this was kept low in the interest of the entry-level nature of the boat. Let me tell you that even at 24.84 this is plenty of rig.

Looking at the cockpit it's clear to me that this design is a racing boat first then a cruising boat. The cockpit has very low coamings and no seats at all. The helmsman can sit outboard on the side decks aft of the coamings. The transom is open and there is a toe-grab type of rib down the middle of the cockpit sole to help with footing. You won't snuggle up in a corner of this cockpit with a book. The crew on this boat belongs on the rail. Most of my cruising boat clients would say, "Pardon me? You want me to sit where?"

This will be a fast little boat designed to shine in fast company. The pedigree is all there for a family wanting to start competing. One-design rules are already in place.

In the U.S. contact Nelson Yachts on the West Coast at (510) 337-2870, **www.nelsonsmarine.com** *On the East Coast contact Eastport Yachts at (410) 263-6358. Sydney Yachts,* **www.sydneyyachts.com**

April 2002

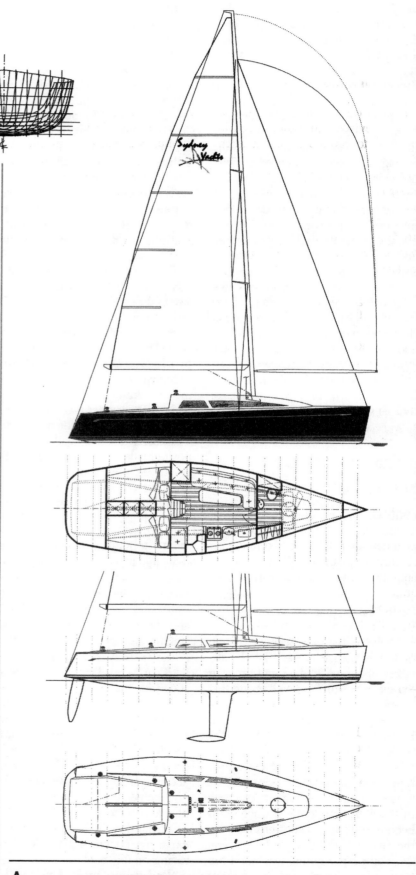

An 'entry-level' hot rod from Down Under.

LOA 31'9"; LWL 28'4"; Beam 10'6"; Draft 6'9"; Displacement 6,850 lbs.; Ballast 3,200 lbs.; Sail area 560 sq. ft.; SA/D 24.84; D/L 134.5; L/B 3.02; Auxiliary 18-hp Yanmar: Fuel 25 gals.; Water 50 gals.

T-10
Offshore One-design

It's not often that we see an old favorite revised and reintroduced in an effort to capture a new market. It's a tough go once a boat has ceased active production. Somehow the builder must convince the market that this is truly a "new" boat and can compete with the latest design offerings. T-10 Boats and Soca Marine have redesigned the classic Tartan Ten and introduced it as a new Ten.

If you go back 25 years you'll remember that the J/24 told the sailing world, loud and clear, that the IOR was not the way to produce the most boat speed for a given LOA. IOR boats were initially tippy, broad

The T-10 addressed the ills of the IOR.

beamed, relatively heavy, narrow in the ends and had disproportionally large foretriangles. This combination produced boats that, while fast upwind, especially in light air, were not much fun reaching and running in a breeze where their hull form limited them to displacement speeds and a rare, white-knuckled burst of surfing.

These tendencies were accentuated by the fact that sailmakers had us all convinced we needed to fly a blooper to gain that extra downwind speed. The only effective way of keeping a blooper filled was to sail the boat low, with the apparent aft of 160 degrees. Sailing low and at hull speed, the IOR boat was perched on its volume-challenged ends. The result was a boat that could round up or down at a moment's notice. Kind of like riding a football.

Rounding up is fine. Rounding down is another thing. With the spinnaker pole dragging through the water, the boom pointing skyward and the crew scrambling to the new high side, the skipper would usually give a command of "Aaaaaaaeeiii!" There had to be a better way to sail.

The S&S-designed Tartan Ten

was introduced as a one-design that addressed the ills of the IOR type. The hull was narrow with plenty of volume in the ends, including a stern that was much broader than typical IOR types. The rig was a small foretriangle fractional rig and the boat had a D/L of 136 instead of the 190 of a typical IOR half-tonner class. It wasn't long before Tartan was building hundreds of Tens (more than 400) and the boats were being raced under every conceivable handicap rule (IOR excepted) and doing well. In 1999 there were still 35 boats competing for the North American Championships, and the class expects 45 boats at this year's nationals.

On the surface the biggest design change for the new Ten is the addition of a cabintrunk. This trunk doesn't intrude into the large cockpit area of the original. Certainly this large cockpit is one of the best selling-features of this design. The transom has been modified, without increasing the LOA, to include a short swim step. The mast, boom, keel and rudder are all interchangeable with the original Ten components. Among the 34 changes listed in the brochure are longer bunks, an enclosed head and a redesigned galley. The Ten has always been pretty Spartan below.

If you look at the current one-design classes you will see plenty of features that were used on the original Tartan Ten. The rig uses swept spreaders, no runners and a working jib. (Genoas are forbidden when racing one-design.) The advantage the new Ten has is that there is already a very well-established and active one-design class. The plug for the new Ten was the current North American champion *Dora*. It will be fun to watch and see if the new boats compete equally with the original boats.

T-Ten boats, 2222 N. Elston Ave., Chicago, IL 60614. (773) 384-2831. **www.t-tenboats.com**

February 2001

Sailplan of the original Tartan Ten
(shown with a genoa)

Reborn one-design ready for another run.

LOA 33'; LWL 27'; Beam 9'3"; Draft 5'10"; Displacement 6,700 lbs.; Ballast 3,340 lbs.; Sail Area 486 sq. ft. (jib and main); SA/D 21.8; D/L 152; L/B 3.56; Auxiliary 18-hp Yanmar; Fuel 13 gals.; Water 15 gals.

Classic 36
Daysailer

Nelson/Marek designed this outstanding daysailer for a very lucky Japanese yachtsman. The boat, christened with the name *Karen*, was built in New Zealand through the combined efforts of Marten Marine and Lloyd Stevenson. The engineering was done by High Modulus. I think it's difficult to imagine a more perfect daysailer. This boat will be a rocket.

To begin with, this boat is 36 feet long and weighs 8,200 pounds. The beam is minimal at 6 feet, 11 inches and draft is optimized at 9 feet. This boat would be right at home in the deep, choppy waters of Puget Sound.

The topsides are slabby, and this is not pretty. But with all the righting moment being provided by a 3,760-pound lead bulb on the bottom of a 970 pound steel fin, this boat does not need stability help from topsides flare, especially since flare on its own just adds resistance and is slow.

The L/B of this design is 5.22 and that's the lowest I have ever calculated. This boat is proportioned like a big Etchells or a meter boat. By the way, we should congratulate Mr. Nelson for his recent second-place finish at the Etchells world championship in San Diego. He knows how to draw them and drive them.

Karen with its short ends is all sailing length with a D/L of 121. The daggerlike rudder and keel come right out of N/M's work with America's Cup boats. Note how symmetrical the fore-and-aft rocker is on this boat. To my eye the stern is a little on the chunky side, but it's a problem combining the right shape for boat speed with the aesthetics of a traditionally raked transom. If the stern bothers you, just look at the bow. It's deliciously beautiful.

The rig is a carbon fiber mast by Matrix Masts of New Zealand, painted to look like a wooden spar. The boom is a Park Avenue type, which means it is quite wide on top. This allows the lazy jacks to move outboard so that they don't hang up on the headboard when you are raising the main on its 2:1 halyard. The fall of the main halyard is routed to remain below deck. The mainsheet is a 3:1 purchase without a traveler that is led forward under the deck to exit at a pod-mounted

winch in the cockpit. This pod also houses the engine controls and the hydraulic headstay adjustment cylinder. Outhaul, vang and reef controls are all up near the gooseneck. The swept spreaders eliminate the need for a backstay and rig depowering will be done with the

I've got to stop here so I can wipe the drool off my keyboard

hydraulic headstay. Pump it up for heavy air and ease it off for light air. The jib is 106-percent LP. The SA/D is 27.54.

There's a head in the cuddy cabin along with seats, but that's it for "accommodations." This is a true daysailer. This design was conceived for transport in a standard 40-foot shipping container so that it could be taken anywhere in the world. The mast breaks down into two pieces.

I have a design under construction at Marten Marine in New Zealand. In fact my youngest son just spent his summer down there with hospitality provided by Steve and Wendy Marten.

Marten Marine is as good a high-tech yard as you can find. I was lucky to get the odd photo or two of *Karen* along with photos of my own project. I never did get a photo that showed *Karen* in its entirety though. We only saw a detail or two. But that was enough to tell us that here was a very special yacht being produced by a fastidious work crew.

The hull is a sandwich using kauri wood and e-glass skins with epoxy vacuum bagged over PVC foam. The kauri skins are on the inside giving the interior of *Karen* a spectacular look. Carbon fiber is used to stiffen the hull and deck in way of the keel, mast and chainplates. Internal stiffening is a molded e-glass/carbon/foam composite. The cockpit features teak decking.

I've got to stop here so I can wipe the drool off my keyboard.

Nelson/Marek Yacht Design Inc., 2820 Cañon St., San Diego, CA 92106. (619) 224-6347.

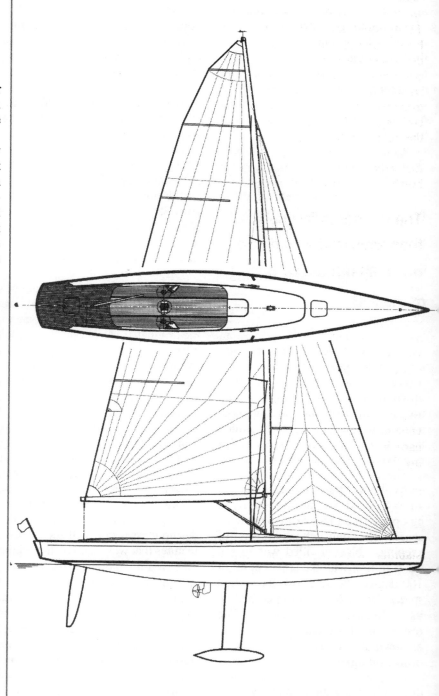

A high-tech daysailer that will stand out in a crowd.

LOA 36'; LWL 31'2"; Beam 6'11"; Draft 9'; Displacement 7,500 lbs. (light), 8,200 lbs. (sailing); Ballast 970 lbs. (steel fin), 3,760 lbs. (lead bulb); Sail Area 700 sq. ft.; SA/D 27.54; D/L 121; L/B 5.22. Auxiliary Yanmar 2GM20C diesel; Fuel 20 gals.

Seaquest 36
Racer

Reichel/Pugh has been responsible for some exciting fast racing yachts recently, including Roy Disney's *Pyewacket* and the 86-foot *Zephrus*. They also did the Team Dennis Connor America's Cup boats. Add to these a slug of line honors-type big and exotic boats like *Shockwave*. Clearly they work in rarified but pleasant air. This new 36-footer built in the UK by Seaquest yachts brings R/P down to earth somewhat. The 36 is primarily a racing yacht but it has interior features that could make it a comfortable cruising boat if your cruising preferences lean toward the light and the quick.

This hull shows a tight turn at the bilge and a pronounced flat bottom that fairs out toward the

The interior is far more than what you would find on an all out racing boat.

transom. By the time you get to the transom the sectional shape is almost round. The topsides are very flat with almost no convexity to them at all. The angle of entry for this fine bowed yacht is 17 degrees. If you mentally heel this shape over 20 degrees it creates a very symmetrical shape with a narrow heeled BWL. It looks to my eye like the LCB is quite far aft on this.

The D/L is 124, making the 36 light, but not ultra light. The ballast/displacement ratio is 46 percent and that should ensure good stability with the 7-foot, 2-inch draft bulb keel. This flattened bottom, bulb fin combo is what we call an L-shape keel with the bulb hung off the leading edge of the fin. This shape eliminates the need for a complex kelp cutter, although kelp can still stick to that vertical leading edge. The drawback to the L keel is that there is quite a twisting moment on the fin imposed by having the CG of the bulb aft of the center of the fin. To take this load the fin is cast iron while the bulb is lead. The sheerline is a straight line but this works well with the relatively high freeboard and the short

ends. R/P was kind and confident enough to provide me with a set of lines for this boat.

The interior is far more than what you would find on an all out racing boat. There are double quarterberths and if I'm reading the drawings correctly you can shut these quarterberth areas off with a door. That would make for some tight and difficult to ventilate sleeping areas. I'd prefer to leave these berths open to the saloon and forget about privacy. The galley is small but adequate and the nav station is generous. The V-berths look skimpy to me but they would be fine for kids. The interior is a molded liner type.

The tall fractional rig has spreaders swept 18 degrees and two spreaders. There are no runners. The sailplan indicates prebend to the mast. The mainsail leech barely overlaps the backstay. It's very interesting that this 36-footer has about the same rig size as the 40-foot Najad. The difference is the 17,000-pound difference in displacement. Think of SA/D as horsepower-per-pound. The SA/D of the Seaquest is 26. You will be able to sail this boat aggressively and efficiently in light air. The other edge of the sword is that you will have to reef early if you want to keep the Seaquest on its feet. Having said that I think many cruisers would be surprised at the stiffness of this high ballast-to-displacement yacht. But for racing there is simply no substitute for sail area, unless it's a gift rating.

The Seaquest 36 is a nice break from the boring dual-purpose boats that I have been swamped with lately. Many of us daysail our boats and take occasional cruises and once and a while we enter a local race. I'll go out on a limb here and say it's a lot more fun to cruise a racing boat than it is to race a cruising boat.

Seaquest Ltd., Unit 9, Parkengue Road, Kernick Industrial Estate, Penryn, Cornwall TR10 9EP, England. 44 (0)1326 377006. www.seaquestyachts.com

July 2003

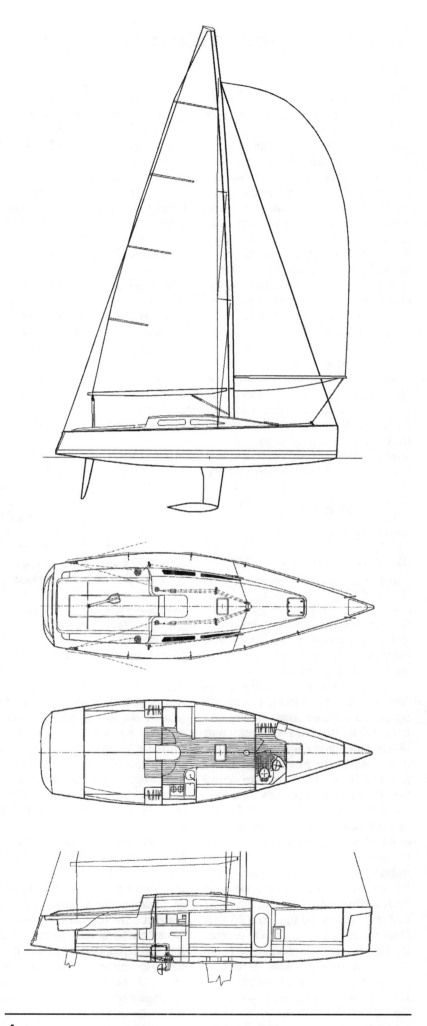

A powerful racer with the potential for cruising.

LOA 36'; LWL 32'10"; Beam 10'10"; Draft 7'2"; Displacement 9,799 lbs.; Ballast 4,538 lbs.; Sail area 745 sq. ft.; SA/D 26; D/L 124; L/B 3.32; Auxiliary diesel 20hp; Fuel 16 gals.; Water 52 gals.

36-foot one-design by Farr
Racer

When the emphasis switched to larger one-design racing classes a lot of things changed. All of a sudden we saw boats evolving at a more rapid rate since there were no rating rules to inhibit development. If it's faster, let's do it; headroom, accommodations, cockpit volume and stability requirements are things of the past; hull-shape anomalies are history. In a one-design class the designer's only job is to provide the fastest boat possible within the overall parameters. Of course, if the boats intend to mix it up with local racing fleets, and they generally do, there are some pragmatic considerations that still need to be addressed. In the case of this Farr 36-footer this is evident in the inclusion of lifelines and "accommodations."

I didn't expect to get hull lines from the Farr office. That would make it too easy to copy the hull shape, and I understand completely: Hull shapes should be proprietary.

I'm sitting here trying to imagine the acceleration out of a tack with that much horsepower.

It's difficult to make definitive statements based on the profile and plan views alone. But I'm going to take a stab at it anyway.

To my eye the hull shape looks "normal" in plan, although in profile the rocker appears deep forward and flattened amidships. The deepest part of the canoe body is right under the mast, and overhangs are absolutely minimal. This boat is not narrow and weighs only 6,695 pounds for a D/L of 84.69 and an L/B of 3.15. I think that the beam must be there for stability. With a lead bulb on a carbon fin and 8 feet, 6 inches of draft the righting moment at one degree is 810 foot-pounds. As I recall—and it's been a while—that's about the same RM that you would find on a 36-foot One-Tonner circa 1978. Of course, the One-Tonner weighed about twice as much as does this new 36-footer.

Note the shape and location of the keel-fin and its area relative to that of the rudder. This rudder is about 82 percent of the actual keel-fin area. The fin is well aft and that reflects the size of the mainsail and the keel's role in balancing the rig. It also puts the weight of the ballast much closer to the overall longitudinal center of gravity of the boat, which reduces pitching. I see no indication of a kelp cutter on the drawings. The keel mounts in a sleeve that goes to the bottom of the cockpit sole.

The promotional material talks briefly about the interior. I call this interior "Camp X-ray." It's not laid out for crew. It's laid out for detainees. There are four berths per side to keep the crew weight outboard. There is a head, sink and two-burner stove forward. I'm not sure why there is a layout. You couldn't sleep your crew below at regattas. The condensation from their breath while sleeping would require daily drying out since the extra weight would make you uncompetitive. I think on a long race dinner would be protein bars with Juicy Fruit gum for desert. I once experimented with dried German sausages stowed in my sea bag, but I smelled like a delicatessen for a month.

The rig is all carbon fiber. Heck, this entire boat is carbon fiber. The rig is big. Using I, J, E and P, I get a sail area of 773 square feet. If you add the roach of the main to that you get a total sail area of 877 square feet. Let's use the big number, which gives us an SA/D of 39.5. That should turn your cap backwards. I'm sitting here trying to imagine the acceleration out of a tack with that much horsepower. The masthead asymmetrical chute will add another 1,319 square feet. Or, if you are not feeling brave, you can go with the fractional chute. Either way, off-the-wind horsepower is no problem. There are no runners. Spreaders are swept 24 degrees, and there is a standing backstay with a wand to help the roach clear the backstay in tacks.

Boats like this are all detail and have to be built with no shortcuts. Barry Carroll's Carroll Marine work crew has become the industry leader in building these kinds of yachts. Carroll Marine turns out gems. Given the strict one-design nature of this boat, quality control will be very tight to ensure competitive tolerances. A boat like this could even rekindle my own interest in racing. I had better get in line now.

Farr Yacht Design, 613 Third St., Ste. 11, Annapolis, MD 21403. (410) 268-1001. www.farr395.org

April 2002

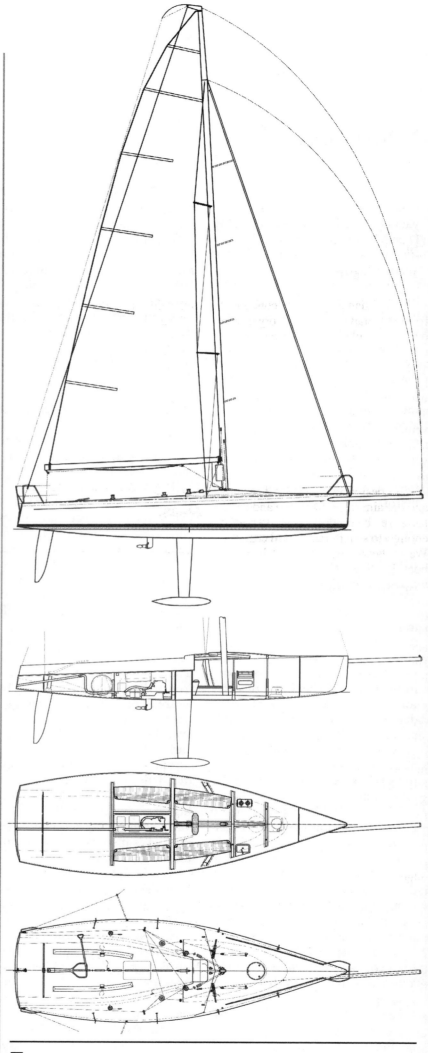

T̲he latest red-hot one-design from the Farr office.

LOA 36'1"; LWL 32"10"; Beam 11'5"; Draft 8'6"; Displacement 6,695 lbs.; Ballast 3,253 lbs.; Sail area 877 sq. ft. (with roach); SA/D 39.5; D/L 84.69; L/B 3.15; Auxiliary Yanmar 2GMSD20: Fuel 11 gals.; Water 14 gals.

Solaris 36
One-Design

This Italian project was conceived from the start as a highly organized one-design class to race in a tour format with charter options available. With help from the Dentesano family and the yard, Serigi, a company was formed, Alpe Adria Sailing Tour, to establish a series of race venues and the means to transport this one-design fleet from venue to venue. Twenty Solaris 36s were built to get the series started.

The design is by Studio Lostuzzi and the aim was a fast, safe and comfortable boat that was versatile enough to satisfy racers and cruisers. We've heard that before. I like this boat. It's like a lot of the other boats we see today aimed at one-design racing but in the classic Italian way this design shows some style. My helper Ben came in, took one look and said, "They're all the same." He's right but every designer worth his salt thinks he can do it better.

The hull has a D/L of 91.58. Shape-wise it's pretty generic but remember, small details, such as changes in sectional shape and in distribution of volume can be important, and it's what makes one hull different from the other. The Solaris shows a full deck plan view forward but the entry is very fine. There is a reasonably firm turn to the bilge, BWL is not overly narrow and there is no deadrise from what I can see from this simplified lines perspective drawing. In profile the hull shows a fairly deep chest around station 4. One drawing shows a T-type keel/bulb configuration and the other shows an L keel/bulb configuration. I suspect the T-bulb is the current keel.

The rig of the Solaris is a tall fractional rig with the headstay going quite high on the mast. The chute flies from a halyard about 15 inches above the hounds and there is a retractable carbon bowsprit. The SA/D is 33.25. The vang is a line and block type with what appears to be a GRP spar "spring"

that will hold the boom up. The mainsail is loose footed and the jibs show minimal overlap. The shrouds are swept 28 degrees, eliminating the need for any backstay on this

While the deck configuration is quite simple there is again that touch of elegant Italian styling that shows in all areas.

carbon mast built by Pauger. The mainsheet is an interesting double or "course/fine" adjustment type done with two independent systems. The fine-tune lines exit the foot braces on the cockpit sole and can be adjusted from either side.

The deck plan shows a very carefully thought out design. While the deck configuration is quite simple there is again that touch of elegant Italian styling that shows in all areas. Even the aft side of the small cabintrunk is gently cambered rather than just being flat. The big wheel makes sense if you consider that there is just no room for a tiller aft of the mainsheet.

The interior of this boat looks very nice. By most standards you would not consider this a cruising interior but I see no reason why you could not cruise this boat comfortably.

The hull is built from unidirectional and biaxial E-glass over a PVC core with epoxy-vinylester resins. This sandwich is laid up with the infusion method. The keel is a stainless steel fin with lead bulb. This will be covered with a composite skin to ensure fairness and fit.

Solaris, Cantiere Serigi di Aquileia S.r.l., Via Curiel, 49 33051 Aquileia (UD), Italy. 39 0431 91304. **www.solarisyachts.com**

January 2004

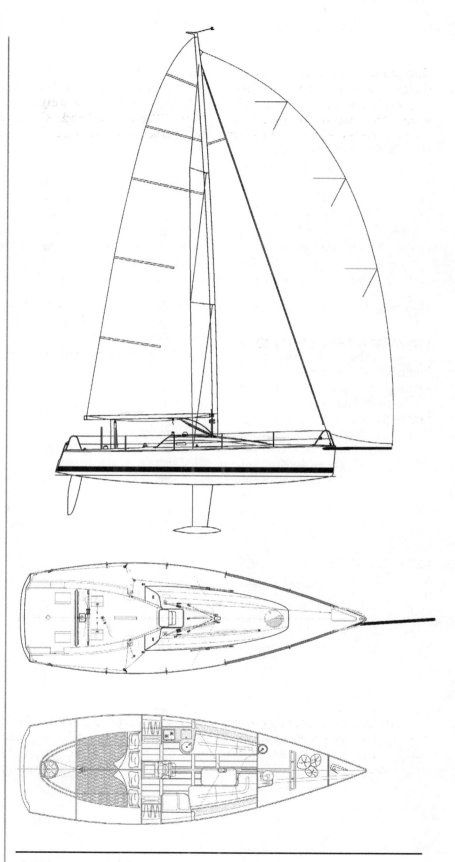

A one-design with fine Italian lines.

LOA 36'1"; LWL 33'2"; Beam 11'10"; Draft 7'6"; Displacement 7,480 lbs.; Ballast 2,640 lbs.; Sail Area 796 sq. ft.; SA/D 33.25; D/L 91.58; L/B 3; Auxiliary Lombardi 30-hp; Fuel 14 gals.; Water 42 gals.

Jutson IMOC 40
Racer

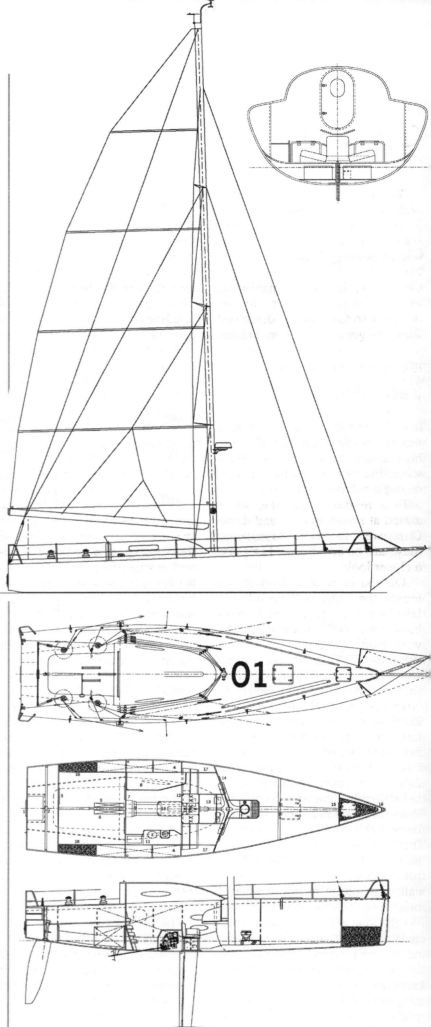

This new 40-footer was designed by Australia's Scott Jutson to race around the world singlehanded to the latest IMOC (International Monohull Open Class Association) rules. I think most of us get some kind of vicarious thrill following the exploits of these daring sailors in their 50- and 60-footers. Now there is this smaller class for those of you on a tighter budget. This design will compete in the Around Alone 2002/2003 race.

I'm glad this boat is entering a race and not a beauty contest.

The rules for this class are pretty loose. You will need to carry the same gear required on the 50- and 60-footers, which will make the 40-foot class proportionally heavier than the bigger boats. You can have any hull shape you want as long as you stay below the LOA limit. You must prove the boat to have a limit of positive stability of not less than 127.5 degrees through actually inclining the boat. Your water ballast or "active stability system" can induce a heel of no more than 10 degrees. The boats must physically prove they can re-right themselves from an inverted position.

Curiously this is done in smooth water, with the boat stripped and the mast removed. Makes you wonder what this test has to do with the reality of being capsized at sea in a storm, fully loaded with your rig hopefully intact. During this test the skipper must use his active ballast system to right the boat and considering that in reality there is a strong chance the skipper may be injured there is further doubt placed on the validity of this test. Scott Jutson goes so far as to say the test is "meaningless" but "critical" to the design. In the case of this Jutson 40 the deck shape is designed to make the boat so unstable at 180 degrees that the boat will right itself unassisted. I am not scoffing at these stability tests, just wondering how valid they are when performed in such a benign environment.

The first thing that leaps off the page when you look at this design is that it is not very beamy when compared to most solo racers, which is presumably, at least partially, a function of the stability goals. This 40-footer has a beam of 11.21 feet, which gives an L/B of 3.57 and means there

is no need for twin rudders. Twin rudders are only useful if you have so much beam the rudder pulls out of the water when the boat is heeled. When that happens it will suck air down its low-pressure side causing it to ventilate and lose its grip on the water. Twin rudders ensure that at least one rudder will stay immersed. Of course, twin rudders also double the chance of having something hit the rudder and damage it. One rudder also means less drag, less wetted surface and better reliability due to the reduced complexity of the steering system.

There is a very generous radius to the sheer of this boat and lots of deck camber, again, I'm sure, aimed at the stability goals. Note also the extremely straight line to the hull rocker forward. For the first 30 percent of this boat that rocker is a dead straight line. There are 198 gallons, or 1,700 pounds, of water ballast each side.

I had a nightmare last night that the reviews were starting to sound like Frank Deford's morning sports commentaries on NPR. "Tell them some real stuff," the critical voice in my dream trailed off. Okay. Look at this keel fin. Draft is 10 feet, 6 inches and there is a full-depth trim tab on the keel to improve lift. The area of the rudder planform is 92 percent that of the keel fin planform. Note how far aft the keel is placed. To reduce pitching you would want to have all the weights centered around the LCB (Longitudinal Center of Buoyancy) to reduce the polar moment of inertia. That's tough to do with a cruising boat, but there is so little inside this racer that it's possible to move the keel aft. This in turn allows the rig to move aft providing a larger fore triangle and a wider chainplate base.

There is tankage for 26 gallons of fuel and 26 gallons of water. The laminate for the hull has Kevlar on both sides of the foam core. The rest of the laminate is E-glass in epoxy. The boat is heavily reinforced through the mast step, keel and chainplate area. With a centerline longitudinal running to the forward watertight bulkhead. There are a total of four watertight bulkheads.

I'm glad this boat is entering a race and not a beauty contest.

Jutxon Yacht Design, Box 132 Manly, NSW 1655, Balgowlah, Australia. **www.jutson.com** *62 2 9948 1512.*

May 2001

Grand prix solo racer for the budget minded.

LOA 40'; LWL 40'; Beam 11'3"; Draft 10'6"; Displacement 9,038 lbs; Ballast 2,777 lbs. (keel plus bulb); Sail Area 1,300 sq. ft. (main and genoa); SA/D 47; D/L 65; L/B 3.57; Auxiliary 18-hp Yanmar; Fuel 26 gals.; Water 26 gals.

Open 40
Offshore Racer

You've seen photos of Open 60s and Open 50s. These boats are box-rule boats designed primarily for short-handed racing. If you are not familiar with box rules you can think of them as a set of measurements, including maximums and minimums, given to the designer so that a box is described. The designer must then balance

It's not a pretty hull.
It doesn't have to be.

the features of his design to fit in the box while extracting the most boat speed. Boats can be downwind-oriented or upwind-oriented or some balance of the two performance modes. This new 40 is aimed at speed upwind and down. Compared to dad's Ericson 38 these are bizarre boats. Let's take a closer look.

Obviously with a 40-foot box length the LOA will be 40 feet. Displacement boat speed being limited by DWL means that DWL will also be 40 feet. In plan form this hull looks almost like the forward half of an 80-footer. The rule allows for a huge rig so the designer must devise ways to keep the 40 on its feet under that huge press of sail. This is done in two ways: extreme beam—in this case 14 feet, 4 inches (L/B 2.78)—for form stability and a hydraulically canting bulb keel. With the keel canted to weather to increase righting moment the keel fin becomes quite inefficient so this 40 uses a jibing daggerboard just forward of the mast. You can call it a tacking board or a jibing board but the results are the same. When you tack, the board will automatically swivel so that it takes on a positive angle of attack to increase lift. This is very common in many high-performance dinghy classes. In the inboard profile it appears that the daggerboard and canting keel are right next to each other but in reality when on the wind the canting keel will be out to weather well away from the daggerboard.

The 40's draft is 11 feet, 10 inches. It's a clam crusher. The BWL will be minimal. It's not a pretty hull. It doesn't have to be. There is no spring to the sheer. Twin rudders are canted outboard about 10 degrees. The D/L at "lightship" is 50.56. There will be trimming tanks forward and aft so that the longitudinal trim of the boat can be altered to suit the conditions and point of sail. I suspect upwind they will sink the bow and downwind they will sink the stern to affect preferred changes in prismatic coefficient.

The meat of this design is the rig and the deck plan. The chainplates are on the sheer and swept 29 degrees. You will not square the pole on this boat. There is no standing backstay. There are runners from the masthead to support masthead chutes and reaching sails and there are runners from the hounds to support jib loads. The bowsprit is a pivoting type and it's notched into the bow so the top of it is flush with the deck but I don't have enough detail to see how it's pivoted. The gooseneck is on the deck or very near the deck but I'm not sure how this boom is vanged. The traveler spans the broad transom but I guess you will need a vang lead to the rail to get any real purchase on this huge mainsail.

There is 882 square feet in that main, and that's more sail area than in the entire rig of a Valiant 42. If we add that area to the area of the No. 1 jib we get a total sail area of 1,317 square feet for an SA/D of 56.2. The SA/D and D/L are almost the same number! I can't remember ever calculating an SA/D that high. Suffice it to say that this is a high-powered boat aimed at speeds off the wind that would intimidate most of us or at least demand our full attention.

This is a purpose-built boat. Things will happen fast on board and you had better be very skilled to keep this rocket on its feet and under control. Raise your hand if you would like to go for a ride.

Owen Clarke Design Group, Lower Ridge Barns, PO Box 26, Dartmouth, Devon, TQ6 0YG, United Kingdom. 44 1803 770495. **www.owenclarkedesign.com**

September 2003

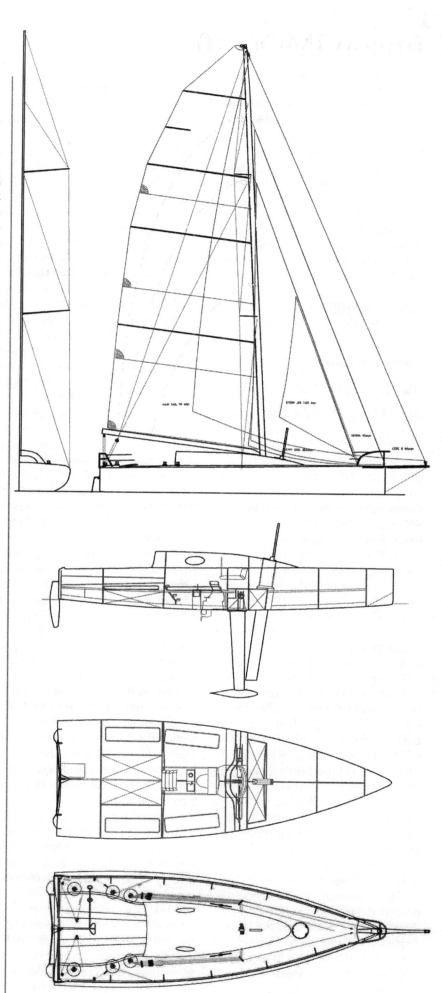

A powerful, affordable alternative to the Open 50s and 60s.

LOA 40'; LWL 40'; Beam 14'4"; Draft 11'10"; Displacement 7,260 lbs.; Ballast 2,640 lbs.; Sail Area 1,317 sq. ft.; SA/D 56.2; D/L 50.56; L/B 2.78; Auxiliary Yanmar 20-hp; Fuel 16 gals.; Water 26 gals.

Dehler 41 DS
Performance Cruiser

The Judel/Vrolik office has been doing a lot of impressive design work lately. Whoever is in charge of aesthetics is doing a nice job as is evident in this Dehler 41 DS. While the styling is definitely "Euro" and may not be to your liking, the designers have drawn a well-proportioned yacht. I'll tell you one way to spot Euro styling quickly. See those horizontal bars immediately aft of the big windows in the side of the house? For some unknown reason those bars are showing up way too frequently for my comfort. "Euro bars" I call them. Designers from Ron Holland to Bill Dixon, from Ed Dubois to Alan Warwick feel com-

If you are looking for a fast cruising boat with a unique layout this may be the one for you.

pelled to add these little bars in some form right aft of the windows. Somewhere out there is a designer with enough imagination to leave that space alone. As a movie director once said to Clint Eastwood, "Don't just do something, stand there!"

The Judel/Vrolik team has designed a lot of fast boats, so there is every indication that this new 41 will be a good sailer. It's a moderately beamy boat with an L/B of 3.18. The ends of the hull are short but don't look truncated, and beam is carried well aft. There is the option of a shoal keel drawing 5 feet, 5 inches and a deep keel drawing 6 feet, 5 inches. Ballast is the same for both keels. The rudder is huge, clearly at least 46.23 percent of the keel-fin's planform area. The D/L is 171. By today's standards, the range of what we call a "moderate" D/L is dropping. I called Ted's 33-footer "textbook moderate" at 275. Well, that must be an old textbook. Today's moderate D/L would, in fact, be closer to 200.

The interior of this boat is designed around a large raised dinette, which dominates the layout. Across from the raised dinette is a raised nav station that if equipped with an autopilot joystick would provide inside steering. Aft and to port there is a snug quarter berth stateroom with two single berths and a large hanging locker. The galley is two steps down, forward of the dinette and adjacent to a very large head. There is access to the head from either the galley side or

the V-berth stateroom.

The most unusual aspect of this layout to my eye is the fact that there is very little open cabin sole area, since the interior is broken up into small spaces of varying levels. This might give the feeling of a small-boat layout. I think the head has the largest cabin sole area. When I go below on any boat I feel certain needs in a layout that probably have as much to do with my emotional approach to sailing as they do with ergonomics. Maybe. I have never been aboard this Dehler. The photos show this layout to be beautifully detailed.

The rig is a tall fractional rig with a high boom and a self-tacking jib. The sailplan shows spreaders swept 21 degrees and a stay coming from almost exactly halfway up the middle mast panel to a chainplate on the 33-degree line. This stay would inhibit the boom from going out very far, and maybe that's why the boom is so high. I have never seen this type of staying before. This stay may be more of an intermediate backstay intended to support the staysail hounds instead of running backstays. The SA/D is a healthy 19.47.

The deck plan shows a big cockpit punctuated by an oversized wheel wrapped around a mammoth pedestal. This pedestal contains all the instruments you will need for sailing: communication gear, GPS, compass and microwave oven. You have to keep the helmsman happy. I think this pedestal is silly.

The self-tending jib track is recessed into the cabintop, but I don't see any provision to take the jib leads outboard for when you bear off. The photos show steps down the transom, but no real swim step. I don't understand this. The real beauty of a swim step is that it allows you to get in and out of the dinghy in safety, preferably with room on the step for someone to stand and grab you. In deference of the design team, the drawings show an entirely different transom step/boarding platform detail.

This is a handsome boat—even with the Euro bars—especially in the dark hull color. Deck tooling details are superb. The forward ports wrap over the corner of the house top. If you are looking for a fast cruising boat with a unique layout this may be the one for you.

Dehler America, 561 Boylston St., Boston, MA 02116. (617) 536-1100.
www.dehler.com

July 2001

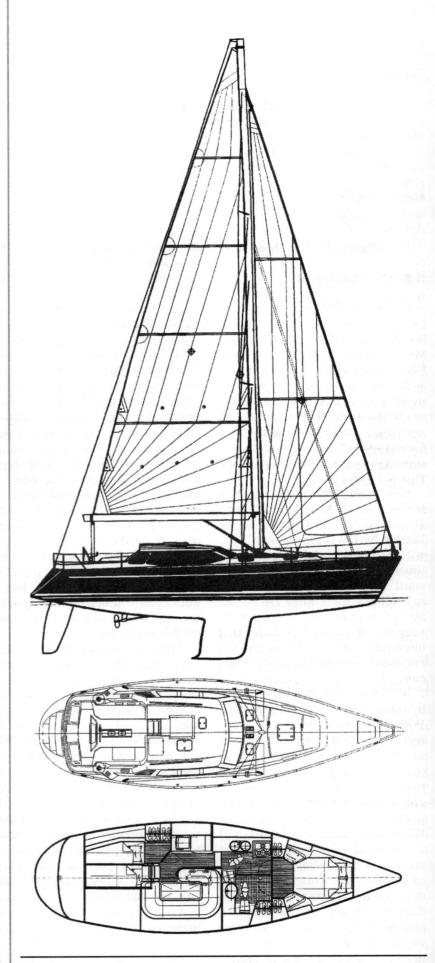

E‍uro-styling and Judel/Vrolik-designed speed combine to make a unique cruiser

LOA 40'10"; LWL 36'3"; Beam 12'10"; Draft 6'5" (standard), 5'5" (shoal); Displacement 18,302 lbs.; Ballast 7,277 lbs.; Sail Area 883 sq. ft.; SA/D 19.47; D/L 171; L/B 3.18; Auxiliary 48-hp Yanmar diesel; Fuel 42 gals.; Water 112 gals.

Dibley 46
IMS Racer

I understand that there are many of you who will forego comfort in favor of pure boat speed. Mr. Kevin Dibley has been around a while and doing much of Laurie Davidson's working-drawing drafting. Here we get to see Mr. Dibley's work without Laurie's helping hand. (Laurie is busy with America's Cup work right now.) Kevin's 46-footer raises the zzz factor to -9.031. A zzz factor of -10.00 is windsurfing naked, on bare feet (no board) with the mast stuck in your navel. This is a racing boat.

Our DWL divided by LOA factor for this design is .83. It's interesting that the one, real race boat of the four this month has the longest overhangs. This might indicate that there is more

The keel is unusual in that it features a small nip aft in the planform just above the beginning of the bulb.

to gain from short ends for cruising boats than there is for racing boats. It also may be a factor of how IMS treats the overhangs. This is a very sexy hull shape with minimal BWL, very slack bilges and soft, arclike sections throughout. Wetted surface is as low as it can get in this design. I can't wait to see how this boat performs against more normal shaped competition.

It's nice that Kevin is confident enough in his work to send full hull and keel lines for this design. My attitude is: "Only fear those who don't want to copy you." This design has a prismatic coefficient of .54, which is textbook normal, and a D/L of 130. There is no hollow to the waterlines forward, but that may be a function

of the extremely narrow BWL amidships.

The keel is unusual in that it features a small nip aft in the planform just above the beginning of the bulb. At this point the otherwise typical foil is changed to a foil with a sharp leading edge, almost like the designer is trying to reduce all lift and drag at the intersection. This may be in an effort to reduce interference drag between the two bodies, i.e. fin and bulb. The bottom of this large bulb is dead flat. I've done flat-bottomed bulbs, and while I think you can justify them on paper, they never look quite right to me. I worry about those hard edges mushing along. As Sterling Burgess once said, "If it looks right, it is right."

Kevin's rudder looks big in planform. The problem with a too-big rudder is that there is no way the boat is going to tell you that the rudder is too big. It'll sure tell you if the rudder is too small or too thin in section. A big, fat, large planform rudder will work great. It's just more wetted surface and drag than you may want to carry.

This big, fractional rig is unusual in that there are no shrouds going to the hounds, just the runners. The cap shrouds go to the masthead to support the masthead asymmetrical chute loads. The SA/D is 29. No overlapping headsails will be carried so the shroud base is well outboard. The sheeting angle, splitting the difference between the two tracks, is 11.5 degrees.

I think this boat is going to be a light air rocket.

Dibley Marine Architects, P.O. Box 34-769, Birkenhead, Auckland, New Zealand. 64-9-303-3678, fax 64-9-309-8010. **www.dibleymarine.com**

September 1999

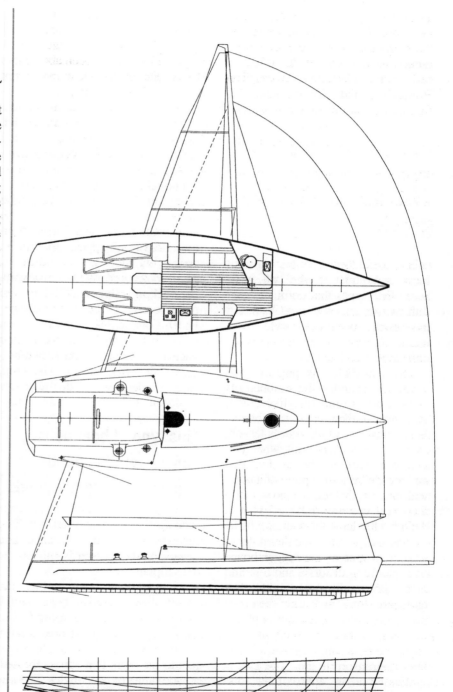

An exciting racer from New Zealand.

LOA 46'; LWL 38'3"; Beam 13'7"; Draft 10'4"; Displacement 16,424 lbs.; Sail Area 1,171 sq. ft.; SA/D 29; D/L 130; L/B 3.38.

W-46
Offshore One-Design

At the end of the first season of racing for its two 76-foot W-Class boats, Padanaram Yacht Company President Donald Tofias announced that he was commencing construction of two 46-foot, nostalgia-oriented versions, which would be designed by Bob Stephens of the Brooklin Boat Yard. From the waterline up (rig aside) these boats will have the look of the classic racing boats of the 1920s. Like the W-class 76-footers, they will be built of cold-molded wood.

These striking boats are in marked contrast to the "all business" IMS types that dominate current racing, and why not? Yachting has always been a lifestyle statement, so why not explore the styling options.

Do you give up performance when you abandon the snubbed-off ends and suppositorylike deck structures of the modern race boats? Yes, you do, if LOA figures largely in your assessment. But what you gain is a piece of functional art and an "escape" vessel capable of taking you out of this digital world and returning you to a time of what is perceived at least to be analog bliss.

The hull form of the 46-footer is similar to that of the bigger boats, with plenty of deadrise and fore and aft rocker to the canoe body. The ends are long and fine; beam is pushed forward, and there is plenty of flam to the bow sections. The sheerline is sprung with confidence, and the transom is tiny. The D/L is 199 based on an "approximate" displacement of 16,000 pounds. Beam is narrow with an L/B of 4.18. You can consider any boat with an L/B of 4 or greater as being narrow. For fun, the DWL is 72 percent of the LOA. Look at the X-562 in these reviews. It has an DWL/LOA of 86 percent, i.e. more sailing length for its LOA. Draft is 8 feet with a moderate-aspect-ratio bulbed fin. The carbon fiber rudder is a semibalanced spade with a long chord.

We've come full circle with the

rig. The fractional rigs of the past are now back in fashion. Of course this particular rig features swept spreaders and a carbon fiber mast and boom. An asymmetrical chute will be carried from the masthead. The SA/D of this design is 24.3, and that is certainly in keeping with modern designs.

The deck plan features a "period" cabintrunk. I'd prefer to see a little more shape to this item. Even some older boats had shapely deck structures. This trunk appears to have no taper to the sides at all, and to my eye, it looks authentic but awkward. The cockpit is long and T-shaped to make room for the large-diameter wheel. Look at that expanse of deck aft of the cockpit. This is a good place for a noninvolved crewmember to sit while racing. The long, flush foredeck won't do much for headroom below, but it sure looks

This type of boat usually has a beautiful, gentle and balanced feel to the helm.

great and will make sail handling forward easy. The elegance and beauty of this design is obvious in the sailplan.

If you have been sailing fat, squatty, high-freeboard boats, I think you would be amazed at the feel of the W-46. This type of boat usually has a beautiful, gentle and balanced feel to the helm that carries through a wide range of heel angles. The low freeboard means that sitting to leeward you will be close to the water rushing by, and that enhances the feeling of speed. In a one-design or PHRF setting, I don't think the small price you pay in boat speed for this aesthetic is relevant.

Padanaram Yacht Company, Reservoir Place, 1601 Trapelo Rd., Waltham, MA 02451. (781) 890-5511. **www.w-class.com**

December 1999

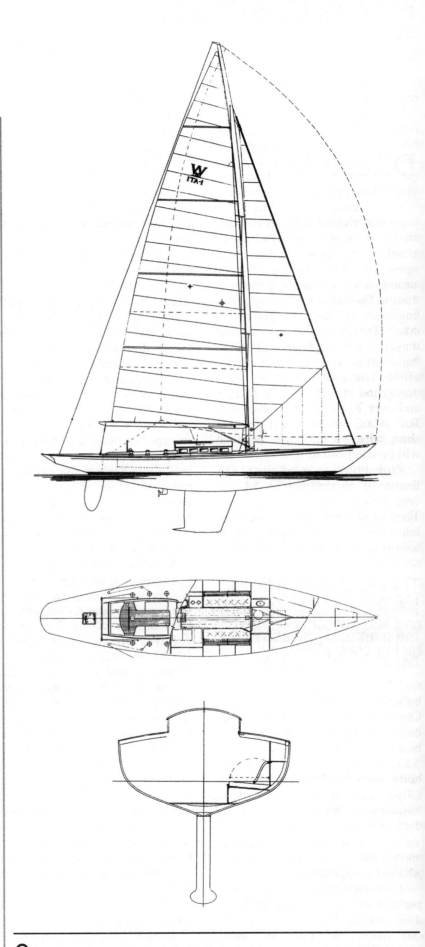

Classically influenced racer combines nostalgia with performance.

LOA 46'9"; LWL 34'; Beam 11'; Draft 8'; Displacement 16,400 lbs.; Ballast 8,400 lbs. (weight of keel); Sail Area 981 sq. ft.; SA/D 24.3; D/L 199; L/B 4.18; Auxiliary 30-hp Yanmar diesel; Fuel 30 gals.; Water 60 gals.

Farr 52 One-Design
New One-Design

It's nice to get back inside the box and look at the newest collaboration between the Farr design office and Barry Carroll's Carroll Marine. The partnership's Farr 40 class has been a resounding success. Now the market wants a bigger offshore one-design boat built to the same philosophy as the 40.

In this endeavor the Farr office has a big advantage. It has computer files on the performance of almost every race winner in the world. This reduces guessing and allows it to target its own benchmarks on the computer. If you believe everything the designer's comments say about the new 52, the only thing it can't do is leap tall buildings in a single bound. Farr's office claims the 52 will be faster downwind in winds under 5 knots and over 20 knots than the current ILC Maxi World Champion. In short, whatever the venue, this boat will be competitive.

Probably the most stand-out feature of this design is its 54-percent ballast-to-displacement ratio. There will be a small amount of internal ballast that can be used to trim the boat to the one-design class limit, and external ballast

The deck plan is all business and laid out for maximum racing crew efficiency.

will be in a steel fin with a lead bulb at a draft of 10 feet, 8 inches. Obviously the end product of this ballast-to-displacement ratio combined with narrow beam (L/B 3.57) is high limit of positive stability, specifically 141.9 degrees. (And this figure hasn't been fudged by adding the effect of the cabintrunk and mast!)

Notice how rudders and keels are approaching each other in area. If you didn't feel a healthy tug of weather helm on this rudder, I suspect it would not be doing its job as a big part of the boat's overall lift component. We can thank carbon fiber rudder stocks for making this type of rudder physically possible.

The keel bulb is big, and the fin is swept aft 16 degrees. To keep the appendages clean you have the option of installing

viewing windows in the hull at keel, prop and rudder. In plan view the hull is unremarkable in its distribution of beam. The real secrets to this hull form are in volumetric distribution and sectional shapes. Unfortunately there's no way we can discern these from the drawings at hand.

The deck plan is all business and laid out for maximum racing crew efficiency. There are coffee grinders in the cockpit for 2:1 mainsail and jib-spin sheets. The idea here is both power and speed in getting the sail in. The forward grinder faces fore-and-aft so he can watch the jib. The aft grinder faces athwartships so he can watch the mainsail.

There are no overlapping headsails so the chainplates are well outboard on the 14 degree line. The next time you find yourself mushing up the sound and struggling to make some ground to weather, consider this. The Farr 52 can probably sail to weather with a true wind angle of 32 to 34 degrees. This means an apparent wind angle of around 21 degrees. You will tack through 64 degrees. This is what high performance means.

The SA/D is 34.19. The mast is a Hall Spar carbon fiber section along with a carbon fiber spin pole and boom.

If you design a boat to weigh 20,277 pounds with 11,206 pounds of ballast you had better pick a builder who can monitor every drip and sniff of resin. It requires very careful construction to hit one-design weight parameters even at more moderate weights. The 52 is built with carbon fiber and a wet, pre-preg process, vacuum bagged and cured in an oven. "Superlight" balsa is used in the high impact areas forward, and various densities of Corecell foam are used in the rest of the vessel. There is an aluminum frame to take the keel and rig loads.

I told you we were going to be diverse this month.

Farr Yacht Design Ltd., 613 Third St., Suite 20, P.O. Box 4964, Annapolis, MD 21403. (410) 267-0780, fax (410) 268-0553. www.farrdesign.com

February 2000

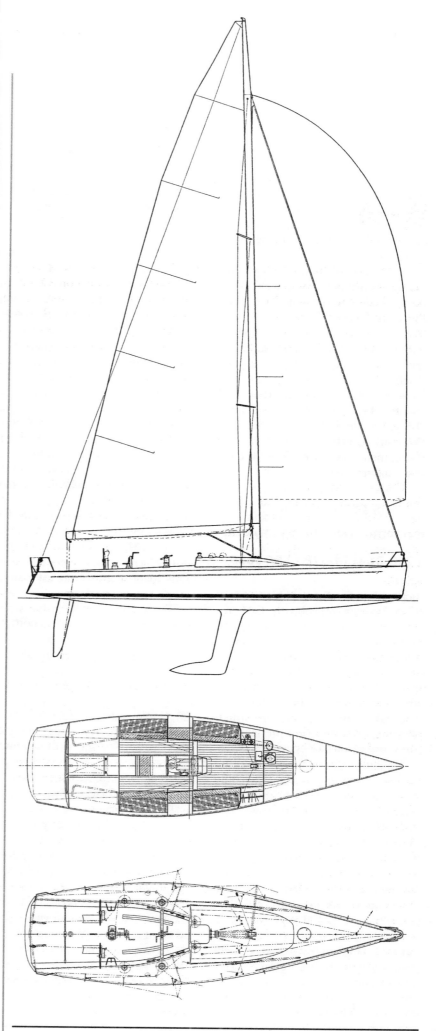

Latest high-tech one-design bid from the Farr office.

LOA 52'; LWL 45'6"; Beam 14'7"; Draft 10'8"; Displacement 20,277 lbs.; Ballast 11,206 lbs.; Sail Area 1,588 sq. ft.; SA/D 34.19; D/L 96.1; L/B 3.57; Auxiliary 56 hp Yanmar diesel; Fuel 45 gals.; Water 80 gals.

Pyewacket
Racer

How about this for a dream project? Take one of the world's best design offices noted for fast boats, Reichel/Pugh. Bring in an experienced and competitive owner with pockets as deep as the Grand Canyon, Roy Disney. Give the project to probably the best boatbuilder in the United States, Eric Goetz, and have the project managed by a world-class racer, Robbie Haines. Now to spice up the mix, add liberal portions of exotic support experts such as Frank DeBord of Scientific Marine Services, Bruce Rosen of South Bay Simulations, Giovanni Belgrano and SP Systems, Dr. Warren Davis Jr. of Northrup Grumman Aerospace. Then have the care and feeding of the finished prod-

This is probably the most spectacularly good looking race boat I have ever seen.

uct put into the ultracapable hands of Greg Hedrick, probably the best professional skipper on the West Coast. This was not a seat-of-the-pants effort. How can you lose?

Well, according to early race results you can't lose. The first race for *Pyewacket* was the '99 Miami-Montego Bay Classic in which *Pyewacket* placed first in class and first overall on IMS corrected time. It averaged 10.5 knots over the entire course, missing the record by only two hours. In the recent Newport-to-Ensenada race *Pyewacket* was first to finish and first in the sled division. Second place in that class was one of my own designs *Stealth Chicken*. (Yeah Bob!) Clearly *Pyewacket* will be the boat to beat for some time to come on the West Coast.

While in San Diego I got to have a good look at her, up close, and this is probably the most spectacularly good-looking race boat I have ever seen. It's perfect in every way. To begin with, it's beautiful. The hull lines are sensuous and svelte. The entry is long and hollow. The forefoot knuckle is well out of the water with about 24 inches of overhang showing below the knuckle. The sheerline is dead straight. But blended with the hull lines, it still looks great.

Note how far aft max beam is on this design and how fine the deck line is forward. The half angle at the deck is only 11.25 degrees. This boat is a needle. The D/L of this design is 48.54. *Pyewacket's* hull lines are a product of exhaustive performance simulation computer analysis combined with tank testing. L/B is minimal at 4.71.

On deck this boat is very clean. Crew weight is kept well forward in the long cockpit. There are two coffee grinders, one oriented fore and aft and one oriented athwartships. I presume the fore and aft grinder is used for trimming the headsails and the athwartships grinder trims the mainsail. The deck is totally "eroded" aft of the twin wheels to reduce weight. Sheeting angles for the small jibs are 8 degrees and 10.5 degrees for the genoas.

The SA/D is 36.94. Spreaders are in line. The spar is carbon fiber by Hall Spars. There is modest mainsail overlap on the backstay.

The interior is all business. The big nav station is aft of the companionway, under the low bridge deck and faces aft. The galley is adequate and uses the engine box for the sink counter. There is an enclosed head forward. That's one head for at least 20 crewmembers. "Take a number please." There are dedicated crew bins to port of the companionway where the crew can stow their personal items like Chap Stick and crash helmets. The forward third of the hull is all sail stowage.

Pyewacket is primarily designed as a Transpac record beater. This race is near and dear to Roy Disney. In his old Santa Cruz 70 *Pyewacket*, Mr. Disney broke the 20-year-old course record. If all goes according to plan the new *Pyewacket* will make short work of the new course record.

This is an amazing project. I doubt we will see another race boat effort soon that will match the intensity and thoroughness of this project. Congrats to all involved.

Reichel/Pugh Yacht Design Inc., 2924 Emerson St., Ste. 311, San Diego, CA 92106. (619) 223-2299. **www.reichel-pugh.com**

July 1999

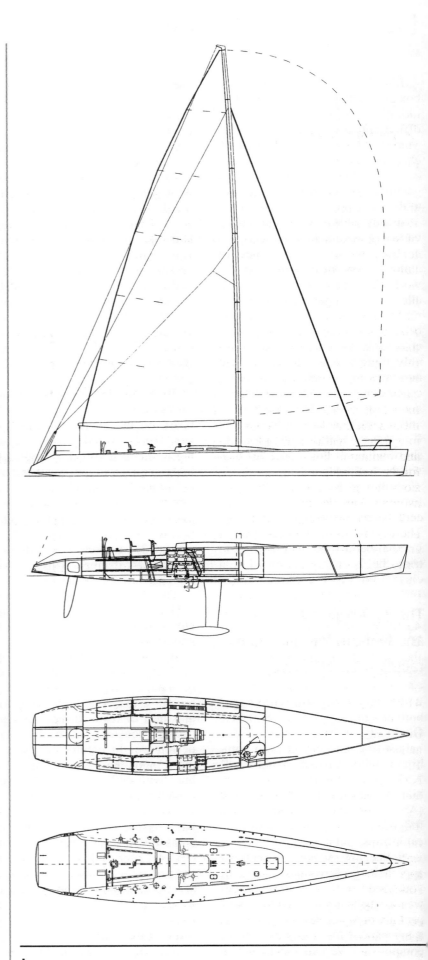

Latest turbo sled is a sexy record-breaker.

LOA 71'8"; LWL 62'11"; Beam 15'3"; Draft 12'3"; Displacement 27,060 lbs.; Sail Area 2,081 sq. ft.; SA/D 36.94; D/L 48.54; L/B 4.71; Auxiliary Yanmar 4JH2-HTE 75 hp diesel with saildrive; Fuel 40 gals.; Water 200 gals.

Zephyrus V
Racer

It's a stretch to get a clear perspective on this new design by Reichel/Pugh for owner Bob McNeil of San Francisco. In many ways it's a logical extension of the current popularity of one-design classes and the new Transpac "box" rule 52-foots boats. It's just bigger—a lot bigger.

McNeil and Roy Disney, of *Pyewacket* fame, thought that rather than battle the vagaries of a measurement rating rule they would go with a box type rule and apply it to a boat capable of breaking any and all monohull records. By "box" rule I mean a rule that describes a box within which the hull must fit. Maximum and minimum dimensions are given for the hull while maximum dimensions are given for the rig, which assumes correctly that every owner will go for the biggest rig the rule allows. There is no question that this is the most exciting monohull racing yacht I have seen in some time.

The rule allows for boats displacing between 41,800 and 46,200 pounds. And *Zephyrus V* displaces 43,127 pounds. I don't have a waterline length, but I'm going to guess that with the plumb bow and the stern overhang we would get a DWL of 77 feet, 3 inches for a D/L of 41.72. Beam, while not listed in the specs, scales off to the max allowed by the rule at 17 feet, 11 inches for an L/B of 4.81. The boat also carries 1,321 gallons of water ballast. Draft is maxed out at the rule limit of 14 feet, 7 inches with a T-shaped bulb keel and fin with a very short chord. The rudder is extremely high-aspect-ratio and is tucked under the counter well forward of the buttwater (my term to describe the opposite of the cutwater).

The deck layout shows a huge cockpit, open at the stern and with five winch pedestals, three athwartships and two fore-and-aft. Short jib tracks run athwartships, and the mainsheet traveler is well aft of the two wheels. There are only four hatches on this 86-footer, and that includes the companionway. The bubblelike cabintrunk blends beautifully into the deck and disappears in photos for an extremely clean and sexy look. I laid my straightedge along the sheerline, and it appears to have a tiny bit of spring to it.

The interior shows berths for the crew flanking a centrally located nav station and engine box just aft of the

This is the most exciting monohull racing yacht I have seen in some time.

companionway ladder. There is one head (take a number, please) and the galley shows a centerline sink island with no counter space on either side of the sinks. (I imagine dirty dishes will be a rarity on this boat. Paper plates are so much lighter and easier to clean.) There is a huge reefer/freezer area to starboard. Note the water ballast tanks that run from the mast all the way aft to the radial quadrant.

This is a monster rig with more sail area than an America's Cup Class yacht. The rule limits the boats to 6,456 square feet in the biggest spinnaker and 2,346 square feet in the mainsail. If we use the rule limits for the foretriangle using ISP instead of I and add this to mainsail area we get an SA/D of 55.07. My guess is that this includes the mainsail roach area. Even if we are a hair off here, we can rest assured that we are looking at a very high-powered boat.

Built by McConaghy Boats in Australia using the latest high-tech techniques and materials, *Zephyrus V* and its competition in the maxZ86 class will be truly spectacular. In July, just a few weeks after its launching, the boat was first to finish in the West Marine Pacific Cup drag race to Hawaii. We may have to get used to seeing that kind of performance in the months and years ahead.

Reichel/Pugh Yacht Design Inc., 2924 Emerson St., Ste. 311, San Diego, CA 92106. (619) 223-2299. www.reichel-pugh.com

September 2002

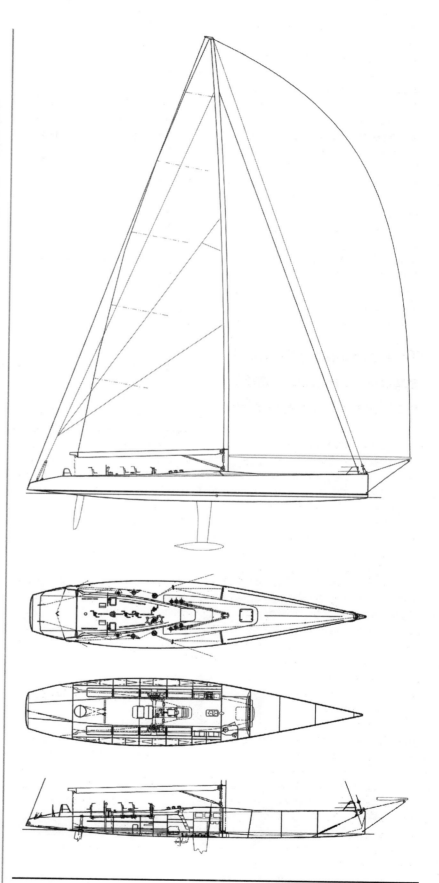

The ultimate sled for West Coast racing.

LOA 86'; DWL 77'3"; Beam 17'11"; Draft 14'7"; Displacement 43,127 lbs.; Ballast 21,385 lbs.; Sail Area 4,230 sq. ft.; SA/D 55.07; D/L 41.72; L/B 4.81; Auxiliary 125-hp Yanmar ; Fuel 100 gals.; Water 308 gals.

MULTIHULL
DESIGNS

Cheshire Cat and Inter 17
Multihull Speedsters

These two boats are interesting in that they are aimed at similar markets, but come from different eras.

The **Cheshire Cat** was originally introduced in 1965, but production was stopped in the mid '70s. The enthusiasm for small cats just wasn't enough to justify keeping this 14-footer in production. Things have changed and multihulls have never been more popular, so I.F.G. decided to reintroduce the Cheshire Cat at the last Annapolis Boat Show. While most small cats tend to be "dumbed-down" versions of racing cats, the little Cheshire was originally designed as a true high-performance cat with the features found on many of the bigger, exotic cats.

It's a narrow cat with an L/B of 2.15. The hulls are deep-chested forward with a soft and dated-looking bow profile. This rocker is exaggerated forward, then flattens out aft of the mast. This deep forward area will help keep the Cheshire Cat from burying its bow.

The centerboards are well aft and quite small. Draft with the boards down is 2 feet, 1 inch. All-up weight is a modest 185 pounds.

The rig features a rotating mast. It's interesting that if you use full battens in a 40-footer you get four and maybe five battens, but in this 14-footer you get seven if you include the foot batten. I wonder if that is a function of rating rules only allowing four battens. I had five battens on my Valiant 40.

The Cheshire Cat is designed as a singlehanded cat. It can take a crew of two, but it's at its performance best with a crew of one. The most interesting feature of this cat to me is the capsize righting method. There is a 5-foot pole called the "righting bar" that stows on the underside of the trampoline. This pole is swung down to be 90 degrees to the tramp and you use it to lever the cat back into the upright position.

If you want to step up in performance and price in a singlehanded cat, you might look at the brand new **Inter 17** built by Performance Catamarans, which also builds Nacra Cats. This is a big, muscular cat-rigged cat (no headsails) that features 4-degree canted hulls that stay on their optimum sailing lines even when you are flying a hull. The stems are plumb and the entries very fine with U-shaped sections that carry enough buoyancy forward to resist pitchpoling. All-up weight is 295 pounds. Note the difference in rocker distribution in this cat compared to the Cheshire. The rocker of the 17 is very flat. Note also how deep the high-aspect-ratio board is. Draft with board down looks to be about 4 feet.

The big, fat-head mainsail has eight battens and is Mylar. Although I called this a cat rig, there is a 183-square-foot asymmetrical spinnaker that will really increase the off-the-wind horsepower.

There is also a racing version of the boat that comes with a tall carbon-fiber mast and a 170-square-foot main. Hull construction is foam cored vinylester resin laminate.

This is a serious cat for serious speed-minded sailors.

I.F.G. International Fiberglass, 2212 S. Miami Ave., Durham, NC 27703. **www.intl-fiberglass.com** *(919) 596-2887.*

Performance Catamarans Inc., 1800 East Borchard Ave., Santa Ana, CA 92705. (714) 835-6416. **www.performancecat.com**

August 2000

Inter 17

I-17

USA

Cheshire Cat

The righting bar in action

Two takes on performance multihull singlehanders.

CHESHIRE CAT
LOA 14'; Beam 6'6"; Draft 5" (board up), 2'1" (board down); Weight 185 lbs.; Sail Area 135 sq. ft.

INTER 17
LOA 17'5"; Beam 8'2"; Weight 295 lbs.; Sail Area 160 sq. ft. (main), 343 sq. ft. (with spinnaker).

Windrocket
Multihull Speedster

When I was 15 years old my dear old Dad dropped me off at Bill Garden's office early one Saturday morning. I had a nice visit with Bill and left with an armload of old prints and a box full of magazine cutouts that went back to the '20s. I think someone had dumped the box on Bill and he just wanted it out of the office.

That box contained article after article of radical and innovative sailboat designs. The history of sailing is rife with exotic approaches to sailing fast. Most die an agonizing and slow death on the beach after their first sail trial. In some cases the radical designs just didn't work. In other cases the sailing public watches the experimental craft whizz by and says, "So what?"

Still, just look around and you'll see that the quest for speed under sail is alive and well and may have nothing whatsoever to do with market acceptance. There are designers like Ken Fry of the Windrocket program who are convinced the sailing world is waiting for a way to go faster, easier.

In the last couple of years we have seen the TriFoiler make some market headway and the foil-borne Rave has seen some acceptance. I have seen the Rave out in Seattle, but I have yet to see it rise up on its foils.

The primary problems with this approach are complexity and wetted surface. You need a healthy breeze to get these foil-borne boats to take advantage of their foils and break loose. If your area is like Seattle, you can count on 7 to 8 knots with gusts to 13 knots on most summer days. Foils aren't going to be much fun in these conditions. In fact, glued to the water in 5 knots, the foil-borne boats can be clobbered by a good monohull dinghy like a Tasar, International 14 or the exceptional 49er.

Ken's unique approach uses a narrow, planing center hull and two buoyancy pods at the end of 10-foot winglike akas. Max beam is 20 feet. The Windrocket will need to be sailed dead flat so that the pods do not create drag.

The Windrocket is still in the prototype stage and hull No. 1 has not been sailed yet. It has, however, been motored with a small outboard and the designer says that it must be sailed balanced on the center hull. I'm skeptical. I just can't see keeping this craft with its 20 foot wingspan balanced on a 30-inch-wide center hull in light air. Of course, in a breeze it will be easier to keep the hull balanced, but I wonder about dipping the leeward ama and perhaps even dipping portions of the leeward aka. What happens during a tack or jibe?

The rig is a solid wing with a flap,

The designer sees people dumping their jet skis and buying Windrockets in droves.

and an endplate and midpoint "fence" to help keep the flow attached. If the boat heels over to rest on one of the pods while docked, the wing sail will swing to leeward and develop some angle of attack. Upright, the wing will just cock to weather. To prevent the wing from swinging over, a 30-pound weight has been added to counter the weight of the wing. The pivot point of the wing is at 20-percent chord.

All-up weight of the Windrocket is projected at 300 pounds. The wings pivot around 90 degrees for trailering. Ken is very optimistic. He sees people dumping their jet skis and buying Windrockets in droves. What a thought. I hate to be a curmudgeon, but I have seen a lot of experimental craft come and go, which has given me a "build one and show me" attitude. It's one thing to envisage this boat screaming along in perfect balance in the middle of the bay, but there are other areas that need to be equally as gracefully conquered, like docking. Windrocket was scheduled to undergo sea trials in mid-June.

I wish Ken the best of luck and all the success in the world.

Windrocket, 3705G Airport Circle, Wilson, NC 27896. (252) 399-7577. **www.windrocket.com**

August 2000

Radical design with a unique approach to sailing speed.
LOA 16'; Beam 20'; weight 300 lbs.; Wing Area 110 sq.ft.

Aquilon 26
Multihull Cruiser

After more than 20 years of writing these reviews I've seen just about everything that qualifies as a "sailing boat." I've seen some iterations far too many times, and these near clones stretch my ability to write something new. That's usually when I pop in a recipe or wine recommendation. I also try not to be too narrow-minded, although as I see boats come and go it can be a struggle. At first glance this little cruising cat built in France made me groan, but I fought through that initial reaction, and I think when we look closer we will find a unique little cruising multihull that may find a market in the United States.

Why would you want a small cat? They don't heel much and for some people that's enough to open up the prospect of sailing. The brochure says this is a fast boat and that certainly has an appeal. The light weight means it's trailerable (the boat can be disassembled in about three hours or transported as is with a width permit), which opens up a lot of inland lake sailing. These pragmatic aspects may be enough to lure sailors to this type.

This cat is also a natural step up for Hobie Cat sailors who have no interest in monohulls, or newcomers to sailing who may be intimidated by any boat smacking of the traditional approach to the sport. The total lifestyle of sailing with its jargon and seemingly complex sail-handling systems may be overwhelming for some. Purchasing a catamaran establishes from the start that the multihull sailor is not buying into the esoteric world that so many of us hold dear. There's a "fun factor" here that sets these boats apart. I think the J-Boat group has done a good job of trying to bridge that gap. Just the word "catamaran" conjures up a whole different philosophy of life on the water.

This 26-footer weighs 1,875 pounds giving it a D/L of 60.55. That's light enough to hint at some good speed potential. The keels are strange-looking, low-aspect-ratio shapes that will protect the rudder when you beach the cat. But to my eye will do very little to aid in VMG to weather. I'm not wild about the big radius on the bows. I prefer a leaner and sharper cutwater. When you see a photo of a boat and there is a plume of water shooting up at the stem that's resistance. I like to see a bow slice through the water.

This accommodation plan uses the cockpit as the saloon. There's a full bimini to keep the crew out of the weather and a table in the cockpit. Down below you have a dinette and galley in the starboard hull and a stateroom with a double berth and head in the port hull. This is anything but a conventional layout. But that might be its appeal. The bulbular cabintrunks allow for a very

This is an unusual boat but carefully thought out.

unusual window arrangement. It's kind of like sitting in a bus, but there is a lot of light below and visibility is superb.

The rig is conventional with the exception of the boomless mainsail. The bowsprit allows a large asymmetrical chute to be carried. I think the rig is big enough on this light cat to give it good boat speed. The brochure claims an "average 10-knot cruising speed," which is impressive, although I'd have to see it for myself. The brochure also says the boat will do 25 knots on a beam reach in a "lively breeze." Forty knots is lively.

This is an unusual boat, but carefully thought out. It's not my cup of tea, but I don't mind heeling.

Performance Multihull Production Inc., 41 Sutter St., PMB 1089, San Francisco, CA 94104. (510) 625-0000, fax (510) 625-0001. **www.stanek-marine.com** *E-mail aquilon@earthlink.net.*

August 1999

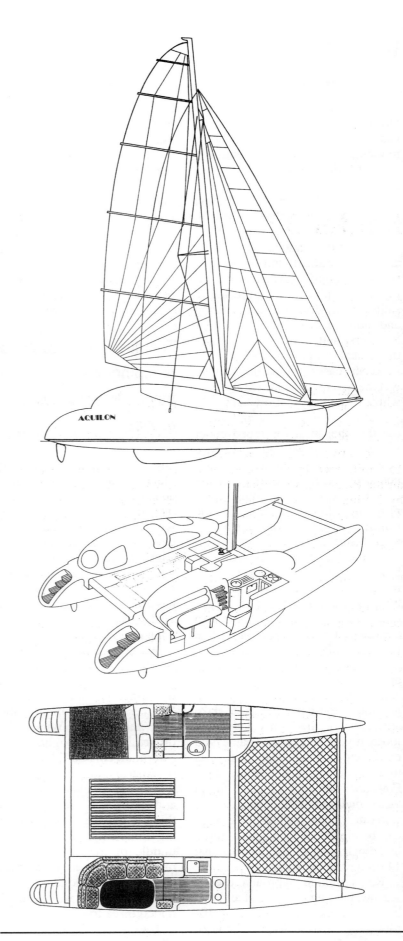

A unique multihull with speed potential.

LOA 26'2"; LWL 25'; Beam 14'9"; Draft 2'; Displacement 1,875 lbs.; Sail Area 367 sq. ft. (with working jib and full-roach main); SA/D 28.62; D/L 60.55; Auxiliary Yamaha T9.9 ultra-long-shaft outboard; Fuel 6 gals.; Water 52 gals.

Raider 30
Multihull Performer

This Raider 30 comes from Australian designer Tony Grainger. This boat already has an impressive track record with several offshore racing wins including a 330-mile event in which they beat, boat for boat, 22 multihulls and 50 monohulls. The only boats that beat the prototype Raider were an Open 60, a 56-foot carbon racing cat and a 60-foot racing cat. That is indeed impressive. In a recent 15.5-mile race in Florida in light air the Raider beat a Stilleto 23 cat by 2 minutes, 7 seconds and an F-31 by 10 minutes, 56 seconds.

The idea behind the trailerable Raider 30 is performance and comfort. Well, I agree that this boat has more comfort than many racing cats but it has some disadvantages in terms of comfort when you compare it to a 30-foot monohull. The Raider has four berths. They are generous in size but none can convert to a double. This is simply a function of the narrow hull.

The galley is equal to what you would find in many 30-footers and the head is even bigger than one in a typical 30-footer. The head is essentially part of the forward berth area with no privacy. The problem with this layout is that there isn't a saloon. There are opposing seats in the port hull but you would be sitting knee to knee with other crewmembers. I suspect this boat is intended for areas where it is warm and sunny and dining and other saloon functions will occur on deck. Trampolines are comfortable to lay on but not very comfortable to sit on for long periods but this cat does have extended cockpits in both hulls.

The hull form for this cat shows rocker that stays flat from amidships forward but kicks up sharply around station 7.5. There appears to be plenty of volume forward to help prevent the lee bow from burying. L/B is 7.54 for each hull. If we use overall beam, BOA, L/B

The idea behind the trailerable Raider 30 is performance and comfort.

is 1.54. I estimate DWL to be 29 feet and that gives us a D/L of 54.9. Note that there are molded GRP hiking racks fixed aft, which do not show up on the drawings. From the photos I would estimate these racks allow the crew to get about 20 inches farther outboard. Daggerboards are canted so when the cat heels the board will be 90 degrees to the water surface. The rudders are retractable.

The Raider comes in two models, standard and grand prix. The grand prix model has an additional 61 square feet of sail on a rotating mast that is 3 feet, 6 inches higher than the fixed mast on the standard model. The mast is well aft in this design. There is a bowsprit for flying a large screecher. Using the sail area numbers (not I, J, E and P) for the grand prix model we get a SA/D of 48.15. That's a lot of horsepower per pound.

Raider will introduce a cruising model later this summer with a hard deck instead of the trampoline, a higher boom and roller-furling headsail.

ASA Yachts, Southern Ocean Yacht Sales, 18495 South Dixie Hwy., #142, Miami, FL 33157. **www.southernoceanyachtsales.com** *(305) 609-8250.*

August 2003

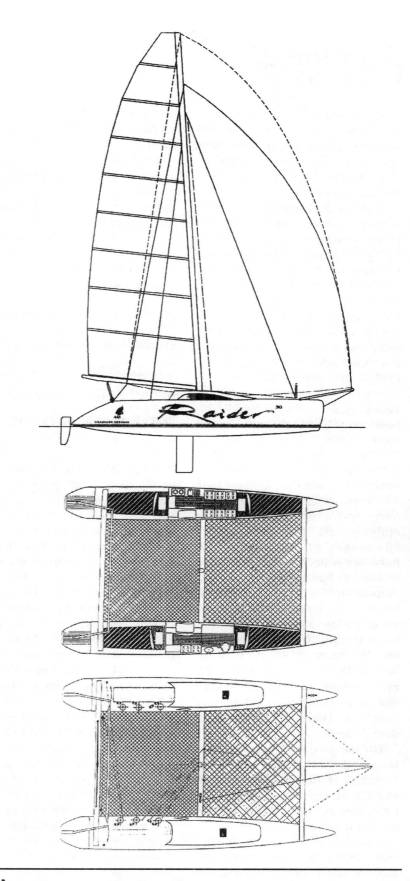

A compact cruising cat with speed to burn.

LOA 30'2"; LWL 29'; Beam 19'7"; Draft 5', 1' (boards up); Displacement 2,950 lbs.; Sail area 565 sq. ft.; SA/D 44.06 (standard); D/L 54.9; L/BOA 1.54; Water 20 gals.

Conser 30
Cruising Multihull Performer

In almost every case, the initial appeal of a multihull is boat speed. If you concentrate on *PlayStation* and its ilk, you should be convinced. But there is a world of difference between the racing cats and their cruising cousins, which can be summed up by two design features: weight and wetted surface.

The fast cats are light, and with that light weight comes low wetted surface. Heavy cruising cats are often no faster than the monohull LOA equivalent. John Conser has designed a new 30-footer that bridges the gap between the off-the-beach speedsters and the heavy, cruising "condo cat." This new cat will be built by Sperry Boats in Hulls, Massachusetts.

The Conser 30 is a development of a previous Conser design, the Warrior. Conser built 17 Warriors 25 years ago. This new 30-footer is designed to embody all the performance advantages of the Warrior, but have better accommodations.

The 30 has hulls with enough volume for a head and double berth in the starboard hull, and a small galley and single berth in the port hull. Consider, however, that the beam at the deck of the hull is 48 inches, and the double berth cannot be 48 inches wide due to the tapered hull shape and structure. This is a very narrow double berth.

On the positive side, the head is wonderfully spacious. The "saloon" is the cockpit with its molded-in seats and table. The table covers the housing for the outboard motor.

The D/L of this design is 48. I don't have any drawings that indicate hull shape beyond the simple profile and deck plan. I can tell you that the prismatic coefficient is .599 and that's quite high. The rudder is very high-aspect ratio, and the boat comes with either high-aspect-ratio daggerboards or low-aspect-ratio keels. The rudders are the kick-up type for beachability. Of course, they won't have to kick up very far if you forget to raise the daggerboards first.

The rig uses a rotating carbon fiber spar and a self-tacking jib. The wide beam of cats makes self-tacking headsails work quite

One of the most attractive aspects of this design is that it is trailerable. It is very hard to find a 30-foot trailerable boat that also sails well.

well. The mainsail on this design is boomless and I'm less sure about that. What happens when you ease the sheet? Considering the wide beam of the traveler, I suppose you could still get a decent mainsail shape so long as you kept your jibing angles up above 120 degrees. But there's no way of reducing mainsail twist as you can't move the lead forward.

One of the most attractive aspects of this design is that it is trailerable. It is very hard to find a 30-foot trailerable boat that also sails well. The Conser 30 uses a patent-pending system to reduce beam to highway-legal dimensions. The brochure says this can be done by a "small adult." The displacement of 2,471 pounds makes the Conser an easy tow load for most cars. (Yes folks, displacement IS weight). I don't know how this cat folds down, but it sure makes it attractive to those of you who move your boats from lake to lake.

Sperry Boats, 43 Farina Road, Hull, MA 02045. (781) 925-9186.
www.sperryboats.com

August 2000

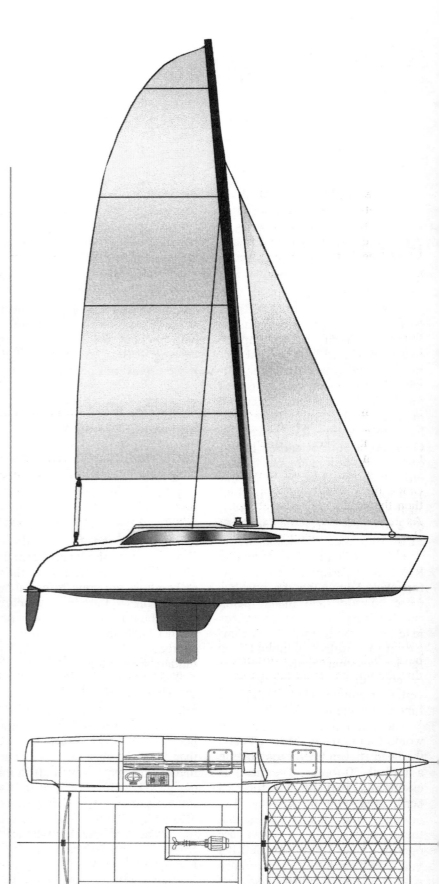

A boat that bridges the gap between racers and cruisers.

LOA 30'6"; LWL 28'5"; Beam 16'8"; Draft with keels 2'6"; Draft with daggerboards 1' (boards up), 4' (boards down); Displacement 2,471 lbs. (light); Sail Area 470 sq. ft.; SA/D 33.3; D/L 151; L/B 1.83.

Seaon 96
Multihull Cruiser

Folding trimarans are a fixture in just about every marina by now. They are a successful type and many give a very good accounting of themselves on the race course. I think the trailerability of these boats is attractive to a lot of sailors who like the option of traveling to different cruising areas and inland lakes. The Seaon is from Sweden and was designed in-house by Stefan Tornblom.

As is typical with these tris, the main hull is designed so that volume is maximized where you need it for accommodations then pared away to reduce BWL. Using the max beam of the main hull I get an L/B of 4.00. I do not have a section through the main hull or any data on BWL. I find the underwater profile and rocker distribution of this main hull very interesting. Note how the point of maximum canoe body depth is quite far aft then the rocker kicks up abruptly. As in the Raider cat this rocker shape may be a function of trying to move volume aft to preserve the desired fore and aft trim.

In a monohull you can move the keel forward and back on the drawingboard while playing with the geometry of the keel in order to balance the boat. Multihulls do not have a ballasted keel so volumetric distribution has to account totally for fore and aft trim. The rocker of the amas looks very normal. Amas will just kiss the water when the

The most unusual feature of this layout is the elevated dining area.

boat is sitting dead even. There are big daggerboards located in the amas. If we extend the amas the L/B is 1.31. You can retract the amas for mooring in a slip but you need to detach them from the arms to stay within the trailerable limit. The D/L for this tri is 46 based upon a displacement I think may be wee bit optimistic.

The accommodation plan is not complex. Lack of beam prevents the designer from getting too creative with the layout of the tri. The

Seaon has a double berth forward with a W.C. tucked under its head. There are settee berths port and starboard separated by a minigalley. Folding counter leaves add to the available counter space on the port side of the galley. I have the same forward head arrangement on my own boat. There are disadvantages, unless, late at night, in a quiet anchorage you don't mind breaking the pristine silence and marine ecological balance with that deafening sound that might as well be a fire hose. But, given the tube-like nature of this tri, I don't see an option for the head unless you were willing to give up the only double berth on board. I would not. There are no hanging lockers and no drawers.

The most unusual feature of this layout is the elevated dining area. The cabin sole is raised about 14 inches in the way of the main settees. This gets you up where you can see out the windows and it opens up a large stowage space below the sole. It also eliminates standing headroom in this area. Photos show the interior of the Seaon to be beautifully finished, sparse but very attractive and tasteful.

The cockpit of the Seaon is pretty large and extends all the way to the stern. The cockpit is bisected by the bridge for the mainsheet traveler, and while this is less convenient for movement it is perfectly convenient for controlling the mainsail. This tri has lots of sail area and if I use their figures for sail area I get a SA/D of 49.6. Of course this includes roach area of the main.

I have a neighbor on the next beach who keeps his folding tri on a mooring. He must like this boat. He daysails it by himself all the time. He always seems to be moving quite well and he covers a lot of ground. There is no question that these folding tris can be quite fast. Some day I'm going to paddle down in my kayak and ask him for a ride.

Seaon, Positionen 106, 115 74 Stockholm, Sweden. 46(0)8 23 65 55. www.seaon.com

August 2003

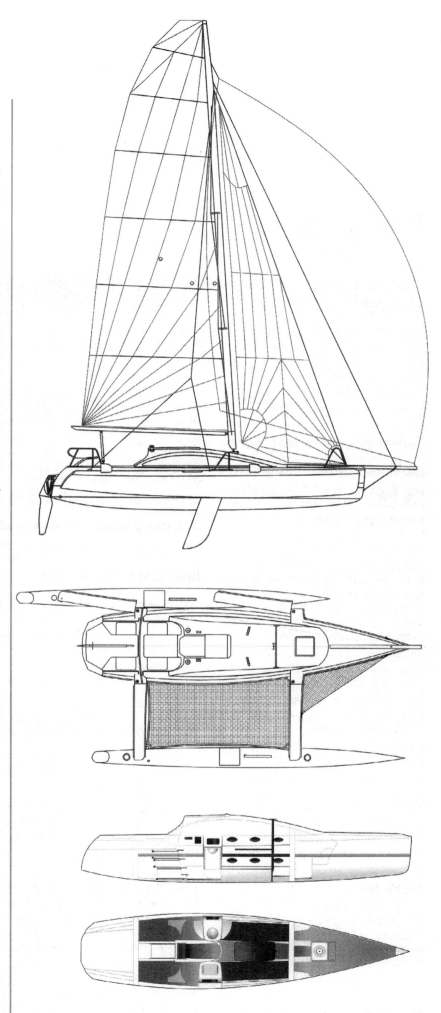

A simple but attractive interior graces this fast folding trimaran.

LOA 31'6"; LWL 31'1"; Beam 24', 11'2" (folded); Draft 5'4", 1'3" (boards up); Displacement 3,080; Sail area 659 sq. ft.; SA/D 49.6; D/L 45.8; L/BOA 1.31; Auxiliary 8-hp outboard; Water 16 gals.

F-33
Multihull Cruiser

Ian Farrier sent the information on this new trimaran. Ian has become well known for his Corsair series of tris, but this tri is built by Farrier Marine. I can't get ahold of Ian Farrier. He lives nearby but he is currently working out of his Australian office. I can't find anything in the copious printed material

Farrier boats are fast, good looking, refined and given the trailerability, appealing to a lot of sailors.

I have on this or on the Web site that tells me where these boats are built. I am going to assume they are built in Australia or you can buy the plans and build them yourself. There is every indication in the printed material that we are dealing with a stock or production boat, judging by the options list. The origins of the new F-33 were as a custom design but soon there were orders as the boat proved itself a winner.

I don't know who invented folding tris. I remember a Bill Nightingale in Seattle doing one about 25 years ago. He called it the VBT (variable beam trimaran). We just called it the BLT. I saw it sailing a couple of times with the weather ama flapping in the breeze. None were sold despite aggressive marketing. Soon I recognized the center hull with a very deep keel being marketed as a high performance monohull. The training wheels were gone. None were sold. It really doesn't matter who folded the amas first, today we associate folding tris with Ian Farrier. His designs have set the pace and established the market worldwide. His boats are fast, good looking, refined and given the trailerability, appealing to a lot of sailors.

Let's look at the numbers. The D/L is 86 with the boat fully loaded.

Max beam in the unfolded configuration is 23 feet, 5 inches, and folded 9 feet, 6 inches. Draft with the daggerboard up is 1 foot, 5 inches, and down 5 feet, 11 inches. The amas are well forward on the main hull to keep the lee bow from burying. The rocker of the main hull is quite flat through the middle of the boat then kicks up sharply toward the stern. I don't have sectional drawings but the pictures show a convoluted sectional shape designed to reduce beam at the waterline (BWL) while providing beam at seat tops and counters.

These are fast boats. Farrier tris have racked up impressive race records the world over. There have been a number of capsizes too, one recently in my area. While we could go on and on with caveats about these capsizes, the fact is that these types of tris will turn over and stay over. The good news is they will float capsized. Most of us would never push a tri hard enough to have it turn over but if you have a big chute up and you are driving the tri hard, and you get hit by a heavy puff, it can happen.

You can go with an aft cockpit model or an aft cabin model. Obviously for two couples the aft cabin version has the better layout, but if you favor a bigger cockpit for racing or daysailing you might prefer the aft cockpit layout. The daggerboard trunk divides the interior and forms the inboard bulkhead for the head. Given the current common hull proportions of monohull 33-footers, I would not call the Farrier spacious, but it in no way seems cramped.

Construction is carbon, Kevlar and glass composite over PVC foam core. Epoxy resin is used throughout. Daggerboards are all carbon.

Farrier Marine, P.O Box 40675, Bellevue, WA 98015. (425) 462-5349. **www.f-boat.com**

November 2003

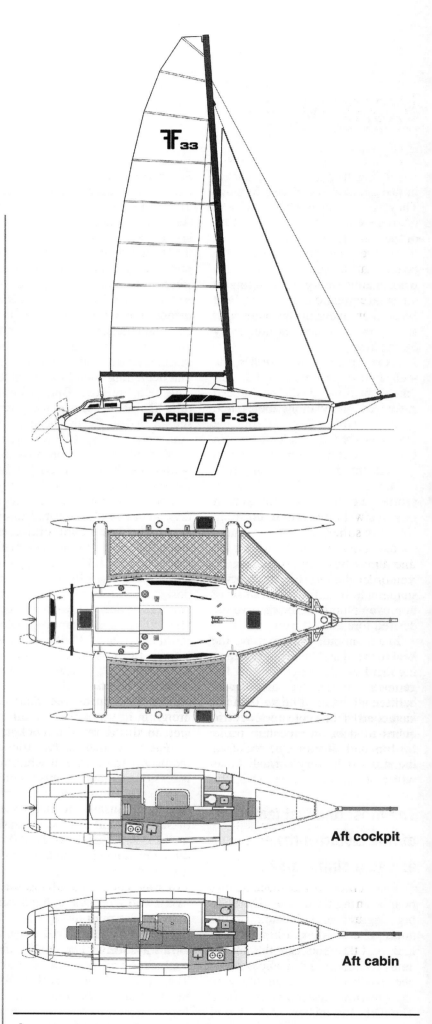

Aft cockpit

Aft cabin

A powerful trimaran that folds for easy trailering.

LOA 33'; LWL 31'4"; Beam 23'5", 9'6" (folded); Draft 1'5" (board up), 5'11" (board down); Displacement 5,900 lbs.; Sail Area 673 sq. ft.; SA/D 33; D/L 86; L/BOA 1.41; Auxiliary Honda 20-hp outboard or 12-hp inboard; Fuel 12 gals.; Water 20 gals.

Reynolds 33
Performance Cruiser

At the other end of the "off-the-beach craft" scale is this sharp new cat from Randy Reynolds and the design office of Morelli and Melvin. Okay, maybe it's a wee bit too big to be an off-the-beach boat, but it has the look of a big beach cat to me and while the drawings go to great lengths to show accommodations, I see this boat as an exciting daysailer with the option of some spartan cruising. Someone else must agree

The R-33 offers crew comfort combined with all the speed a sane sailor could want.

because these cats are selling quickly with more than 20 boats on order so far.

The boat has a 33-foot LOA and a max beam of 14 feet, unless you order the tall rig and then you get an additional two feet of beam for more sail-carrying power. Orders to date have strongly favored the tall rig with additional beam. Using my scale I get an L/B of 14.72 for a single hull. By any criteria this cat has high speed written all over it. The hulls can be detached from the connecting tubes to stow on a custom trailer within the 8-foot beam limit. Total estimated time, with practice, for assembling the R-33 for sailing is 35 to 40 minutes.

The R-33 weighs 2,250 pounds. If we use our standard formula for D/L we get a D/L of 27.94. But the brochure also lists "displacement" at 3,500 pounds. This is a bit confusing. A boat will displace its own weight in water so the two numbers should be identical. I called Randy Reynolds and his explanation was that although the boat as built weighs 2,250 pounds, it was designed to "displace" 3,500 when crewed and loaded with gear. This changes our D/L to 43.48.

Deep daggerboards are angled outboard so they are closer to vertical when the cat has a 10-degree heel angle. The rudders are dead vertical, deep and narrow in chord. The 14-foot-beam

model provides 280 square feet of combination mesh and waterproof vinyl trampoline area. Specially designed molded seats with tall seat backs provide comfort for the crew.

The tall rig gives you 525 square feet of area, and using the 3,500-pound displacement figure, this gives us an SA/D of 36.4. There is an additional 998 square feet of sail in the spinnaker and 718 additional square feet in the code zero headsail, a sail that you can think of as a hybrid genoa-spinnaker, i.e. flatter than a chute but fuller than a genoa while still classified as a spinnaker.

We could have some fun with these accommodations. The drawings are simply presented with bodies shown in the sleeping position in the hulls. It reminds me a lot of those old prints of how to load a slave ship. There is no doubt you could cruise this boat and sleep in it at night. But I find the "galley" and "dinette" arrangements a little fanciful. For instance, in order to leave the table the person sitting forward at the tiny dining table would have to lie down on his back, scootch along the berth like a tunnel rat and then exit the boat through the forward hatch. The only other option is clearing the table and hinging it up while asking the person sitting aft to move first.

The head is directly under the berth where the person sitting aft at the table sits. This will be handy for cruising those remote Mexican ports. I think you cook and eat on deck on a boat like this.

The R-33 tries to bridge the gap between off-the-beach type cats and the more luxurious cruising cats. The off-the-beach types are fast but can be scary and are certainly very wet. The big cats are heavy and slow, but oh, so comfy. The R-33 offers crew comfort combined with all the speed a sane sailor could want. Sailors are lining up for this handsome cat. I want a ride.

Reynolds Sailing 16835 Algonquin St. #216, Huntington Beach, CA 92649. (800) 366-8584. **www.r33.com**

August 2002

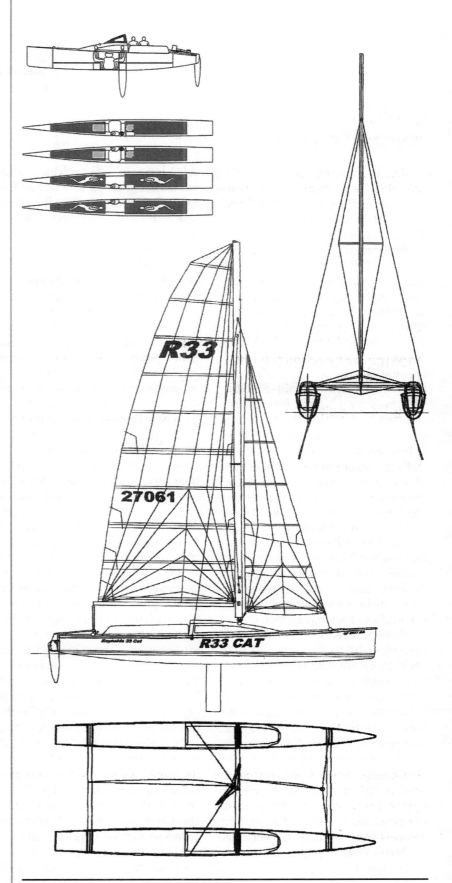

Fast new cat for racing and cruising.

LOA 33'; LWL 33'; Beam 14' (standard rig), 16' (tall rig); Draft 5'11" (board down); Displacement 3,500 lbs. (crewed and loaded); Sail Area 400 sq. ft. (standard rig), 525 sq. ft. (tall rig); SA/D 27.8 (standard rig), 36.4 (tall rig); D/L 43.48 (loaded displacement); Auxiliary single outboard.

Gulfstream 35
Cruising Multihull Speedster

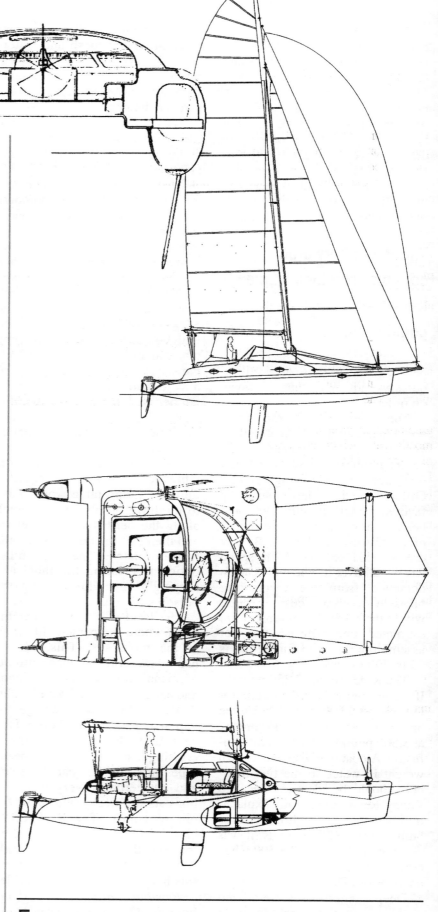

This sprightly 35-foot catamaran from designer Peter Wormwood. Construction is by Wormwood Performance Yachts in Palmetto, Florida.

Stroll around any big marina. There tucked in a corner you will inevitably find an old Stiletto cat with its jet fighter canopies and knifelike hulls. These old boats are still being raced and enjoyed. The Stiletto represents Peter Wormwood's introduction into cruising cats. Believe it or not, built in the very early '70s, the Stilettos were built with Nomex honeycomb and pre-preg E-glass hulls. Thirty years later these hulls are still near state of the art.

Peter's new cruising cat is this 35-foot racer-cruiser. Weight is the enemy in any boat design, but even more so with cats. This cat weighs 7,300 pounds for a D/L of 86.68. If cats get heavy they gain wetted surface and can become light-air dogs. Consider that a comparable, high-performance monohull with the same weight would have about 185 square feet of wetted surface (without keel and rudder). Put this displacement into two hulls and you get 220 square feet of wetted surface. This is an 18-percent increase. In light air it's almost entirely a wetted-surface battle. You can balance this a bit with the knowledge that in Peter's design the boards are fully retractable, whereas in our hypothetical monohull, the keel would almost certainly be fixed. Curiously enough, the difference in wetted surface between the cat and the monohull is almost precisely the area of the hypothetical monohull's fixed keel.

I see some of the goofiest, yes, "goofiest," looking keels on multihulls. Peter has avoided this by using high-aspect-ratio centerboards toed slightly in. This angle helps get the board trunk out of the accommodation volume. Board-up draft is a convenient 16 inches, but board down

you get a solid 7 feet of draft ensuring excellent speed to weather. The rudder is retractable, allowing you to beach this cat. Outboard motor power also facilitates this draft reduction for beaching.

The accommodations for this boat feature a layout designed for warm weather. The galley is essentially in the cockpit. My favorite quote from Peter's designer's comments refers to the galley as "not being pretentious enough to compete with romantic evenings ashore dining in some quaint, local

The SA/D of this design is an intimidating 34.44.

restaurant." That's an interesting way to put it. The hard dodger blends the accommodations with the cockpit. You can enclose the whole thing with a Bimini-curtain if the weather turns wet.

This rig is tall with a high-aspect-ratio "fat head" mainsail sporting no less than 11 battens. The mast is a rotating type to further increase the big mainsail's effectiveness. There are seven battens in the jib. Battens help control the back half of the sail and ensure a smooth exit in contrast to the "speed curl" we see along the leech on so many in-mast furling sails. The SA/D of this design is an intimidating 34.44. Not to worry, this boat can be sailed under mainsail alone when the wind pipes up. An asymmetrical chute tacked to a short, articulating bowsprit is provided for off-wind power. In light air you can ease the pole to leeward and fly a big screecher outside the shrouds.

This looks like a fun ride to me.

Wormwood Performance Yachts, 1311 Riverside Dr., Palmetto, FL 34221. www.wormwood.com (941) 729-2489.

February 2000

Fast, fun multihull from the creator of the Stiletto.

LOA 35'3"; LWL 33'6"; Beam 19'5"; Draft 7' (boards down), 1'4" boards up; Displacement 7,300 lbs.; Sail Area 810 sq. ft.; SA/D 34.44; D/L 86.68; Auxiliary 50 hp outboard; Fuel 65 gals.; Water 65 gals.

Sailrocket
Multihull Speedster

The world of multihulls shows a split personality. On one hand we have speed-oriented cats and tris employing the latest in technology and materials, and breaking speed records around the world. Most recently the Miami-to-New York record fell to the mighty *PlayStation*. With two back-to-back daily runs of more than 500 nautical miles *PlayStation* broke the record by almost 17 hours, covering the distance in 2 days, 5 hours and 55 minutes.

And *PlayStation* isn't even the fastest boat around. This past winter *Club Med* set a 24-hour speed record of 655 nautical miles on its way to winning The Race.

On the other hand we have volume-oriented cruising cats and tris, mostly cats, which are designed to offer the most living space for a given LOA. These boats are relatively heavy and while having the look of speed, seldom live up to the reputation enjoyed vicariously by all multihulls. Multihull designer Kurt Hughs made an interesting point while we were discussing cruising cats. He said that the cruising cat comes the closest to pushing an entire "house" through the water. I like that.

Whatever the draw, multihulls continue to gain in popularity. I suspect for some it is the lure of sailing without heeling. For others it might be the huge expanses of deck lounging area. For a special spartan group it is the promise of blistering speeds. So if we really use our peripheral vision we can see the performance of multihulls totally encompassing the world of monohull performance, i.e., they can be slower and they can be faster.

I reserve reasonable caveats. Me? I like cats and tris, and I've sailed quite a few. But I'm a monohull kind of guy. I like bow ties too, but I leave wearing them to Will Keene. It's hard to avoid or deny that element of personal style.

A Southampton-based speed sailing team is looking to build a craft capable of breaking the world sailing speed record, currently held by the Australian planing proa *Yellow Pages Endeavour* at 46.5 knots. (Whatever happened to names like *Flying Cloud*?) Designer Malcolm Barnsley has put 15 years of research and testing into this project. Models have been tested along with a full-size craft, with most of the work based on the ideas in the book **The Forty Knot Sailboat** by Bernard Smith, which

Performance targets call for speeds of 50 to 52 knots in 20 to 23 knots of true wind speed. The 1/5 scale model has already gone 14 knots.

was published 30 years ago. Performance targets call for speeds of 50 to 52 knots in 20 to 23 knots of true wind speed. The 1/5-scale model has already gone 14 knots, and this was done while experiencing control problems with the servo sheeting the sail. Speeds of 20 knots are expected from the model once this problem has been fixed.

The "hull" features a type of three-point suspension with a foil on the windward pontoon. I suppose the length of the weather ama is designed to give the vessel some directional stability. This boat will not tack, but will always sail on the port tack. The stubby leeward ama has no foil. The controllable angle of the rig is designed to create lift to reduce drag and to make up for the lack of buoyancy in the leeward ama.

Barnsley is looking for cash sponsors to help him complete this project. If we all send him $10 he would be sitting pretty. I'll do it. Maybe as a sponsor I would get a ride. Maybe for $20 I'd get to drive.

Sailrocket, 21 Chafen Road, Bitterne Manor, Southampton, Hampshire UK, SO 18 1BD. 44 2380 368283. **www.sailrocket.fsnet.co.uk**

August 2001

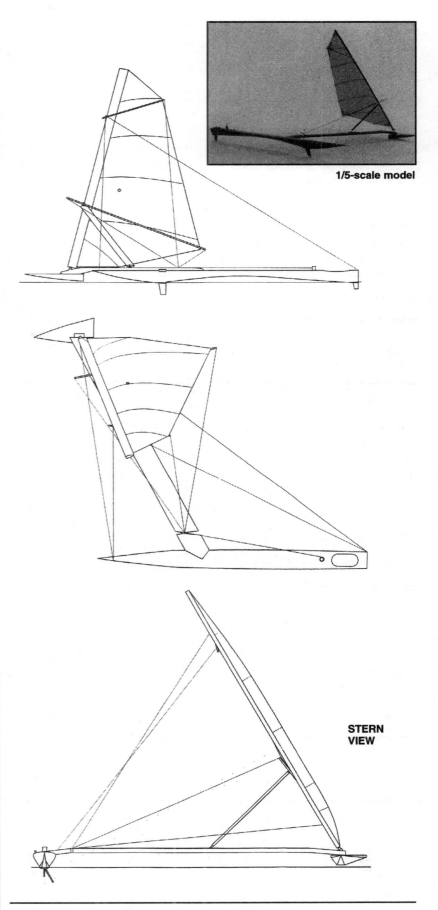

1/5-scale model

STERN VIEW

Exotic speed machine from the United Kingdom.

LOA 36'1"; Beam 26'11"; Sailing weight 550 lbs.; Sail Area 234 sq. ft.

Fastboats 38
Multihull Cruiser

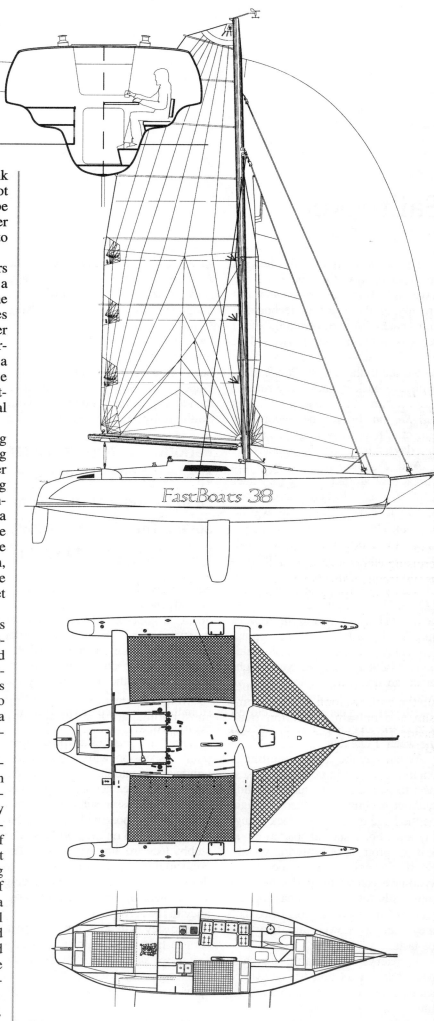

I look at multihull magazines from time to time and am struck by the wide variety of design skill levels I see. Often I'm shocked. It seems a world dominated by amateurlike work. Competition is keen for plan sales and this has resulted in the handful of skilled multihull designers having to compete with an army of unskilled, part-time designers for the commissions. I suppose competition is good, but what I see here is the entire process being reduced to the lowest common denominator and driven down by unreasonably low prices. I know what it takes to make a living as a designer, and you can't do it at these levels.

One of the experienced and skilled multihull designers is Kurt Hughes. Kurt lives in Seattle (yes, he's a friend) and has been at his work for the last 20 years. Here is a fast trimaran designed by Kurt and aimed at the cruising family.

This tri has 200-percent-buoyancy amas. This means that the volume of each ama (outrigger) is

Kurt has been fitting interiors into these challenging shapes for a long time and he's good at it.

twice the volume of the overall displacement. This provides stability and resists burying the leeward hull. Note that the amas are almost full length, and in fact, extend forward of the main hull's bow. This helps prevent pitchpoling. "Hang on kids!" The center-hull design is extremely contoured to provide the maximum interior volume while providing the lowest drag. The centerboard is set off to starboard about eight inches to help with the interior layout. The D/L of this design is 58.16. The prismatic coefficient for the main hull is .611. The tiny footprint of the tri's waterplane gives this boat a very low pounds-per-inch immersion number. In this case it's 567 pounds, which means that for every 567 pounds

you load on the boat it will sink one inch. For a typical 38-foot monohull, the number would be closer to 900 pounds. The rudder is a kick-up type to allow the tri to be beached.

Kurt has been fitting interiors into these challenging shapes for a long time and he's good at it. The flared and stepped hull topsides are used to get berths and counter space. There is really nothing normal about this layout. There is a double berth adjacent to the dinette and the nav station is located forward. It's unconventional below but functional.

The rig features a rotating mast that simplifies the rigging arrangement, allowing for a lighter mast and improving overall rig efficiency. A near masthead spinnaker will be carried along with a 7/8 screecher. The only jib is the 100-percent blade. If we use the area of the mainsail, with roach, and add the area of the blade we get a sail area of 765 square feet and an SA/D of 34.

The Achilles heel of most tris is the cockpit, and this one is no exception. I think four people would find themselves crowded in this hot tub-sized cockpit, although there's always the area of the trampoline to consider. Certainly the deck area of a tri is far greater than that of a corresponding LOA monohull.

Kurt has lots of exciting multihull designs. This is just one in a long list of tris Kurt has developed. The tri offers the stability required to apply the horsepower to a big rig. Sail area in itself is not enough to ensure boat speed. You need sail-carrying ability to convert the energy. If you compare this boat with a similar-sized monohull you will see that, without lead ballast and despite the amount of area and materials, the tri is still the lighter boat. This becomes a performance advantage.

Kurt Hughes Sailing Designs, 6121/2 W. McGraw St., Seattle, WA 98119. (205) 284-6346, fax (206) 283-4106. **www.multihull designs.com**

August 1999

Fast, stable and well-designed tri.

LOA 37'10"; LWL 37'4"; Beam 31'9"; Draft 1'8"(foils up), 8'4" (daggerboard down); Displacement 6,810 lbs.; Sail Area 765 sq. ft. (mainsail and blade jib); SA/D 34; D/L 58.16; Auxiliary 9-hp Yanmar inboard.

Maine Cat 41
Multihull Cruiser

What separates the Maine Cat 41 from most other 41-foot cruising cats is the general layout of the deck and accommodations. This layout is called an open bridgedeck design. In short, there is no cockpit and there is no saloon spanning the two hulls. Cockpit and saloon have been morphed together into one large "great room"—15 feet, 6 inches long by 11 feet, 6 inches wide. I like this. For sunny weather cruising where shutting the boat up is not frequent this is perfect.

You have the option of closing the Strata glass acrylic windows that are set in Sunbrella frames but this is not like a rigid cabin-trunk in terms of insulation. Still, when the weather is good this configuration allows you to open up the entire saloon while keeping sun and or rain protection overhead. This hard top is composite GRP set on aluminum tubing supports. It does not look very good on the two dimensional drawings but in the photos it virtually disappears and doesn't look bad at all. Being a Seattleite I'm more

Your Maine Cat will soon become the party boat.

comfortable sitting in drizzle than I am sitting in the sun. I would like this arrangement.

From this great room you step down four steps into the hulls. The starboard hull is the owner's stateroom with the head aft and a double berth forward. There is a dressing area forward of the head and there is an office area forward of the double berth. There is a single berth in the bow of each hull. You can access these single berths

through a deck hatch or you can walk through the other stateroom to get to them. Daggerboard trunks in the hulls interfere somewhat with access to the double berths, but what are you going to do? You must have decent daggerboards. Those stupid, stubby little molded in keels just do not work at all. The port hull has a very nice galley and another two staterooms.

The saloon and cockpit area has mirror image, large settees and a centerline console steering station. I can't tell from the drawings where the dining table comes from or if it is fixed. This is a cockpit/saloon capable of being a comfortable place to entertain a large group. Your Maine Cat will soon become the party boat.

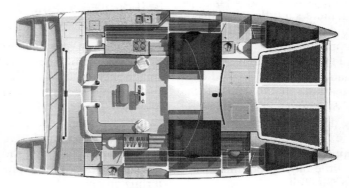

Weight studies are probably the most boring part of any design project but they are possibly the most important. Careful construction detailing gives the Maine Cat a designed displacement of 12,200 pounds. Add to this a 7,000-pound payload to put the boat in cruising trim. I think we will use the sum of these two weights, 19,200 pounds, for our ratios. The D/L is 134 and the L/B for the individual hulls is 10.5 and L/BOA is 1.8. The prismatic is on the high side at .656. This insures plenty of volume in the ends of the hulls.

The next step is to put the printed information aside and sail this cat against its more conventionally laid out competition to see if this design approach rewards the owner with better sailing performance.

Maine Cat, P.O. Box 205, Bremen, ME 04551. (888) 832-CATS. **www.mecat.com**

August 2003

A warm-weather cruising cat with a unique layout.

LOA 41'; LWL 40'; Beam 23'; Draft 7', 2'6" (boards up); Displacement 19,200 lbs.; Sail area 1,000 sq. ft.; SA/D 22.31; D/L 134; L/BOA 1.8; Auxiliary twin Yanmar 27-hp; Fuel 60 gals.; Water 120 gals.

Privilege 435
Multihull Cruiser

This is a great-looking cruising cat. Okay, maybe it does fall into the condo cat classification, but designer Marc Lombard has done a good job with the styling, an excellent job with the interior layout and a masterful job with the deck plan. This is one of those designs that just makes you want to go for a cruise.

I'm not a multihull guy. I recognize all the technological advantages of digital CD sound, but I prefer to listen to my records played through a Lyra Clavis de Capo moving-coil cartridge. My ears just like that analog sound. I also recognize the advantages of cats, but there's a little voice inside me that keeps saying, "Bob, you are a monohull guy."

Still I try not to let that cloud my appreciation of well-designed cats. Given the bulk of this big cat, the styling of the deck contours and shapely deckhouse give this boat a very sexy look. Without that dimension of depth the profile looks a little blocky, but this disappears in the photos.

The D/L of this cat is 112 using what the brochure calls "displacement light." If you use what the brochure calls "displacement maxi" the D/L is 167. The latter isn't even light in the world of monohulls anymore. The L/B is 1.88, making it the proportionately beamiest of this month's cats. Draft is provided by stubby fixed keels drawing 4 feet, 4 inches in one version, or by daggerboards that extend draft down to 8 feet, 2 inches.

The rig is tall and fractional. A drifter genoa and an asymmetrical chute can be flown from the fixed bowsprit. One of the real beauties of these big cats is the broad foredeck. This makes handling headsails much easier. And the fact that the cat won't heel more than a few degrees also helps. It's nice to be able to wrestle the chute down in a squall without having to worry about sliding out under the lower lifeline. I don't have I,J,E or P, so calculating an SA/D would not be relevant.

This boat has a great saloon. There are big windows all around for 360-degree visibility. Someone out there must like round dinettes because here's another one of them. The circular dinette sure looks good in this layout. The gal-

This boat has a great saloon. There are big windows all around for 360-degree visibility.

ley is also in the deckhouse, but down one step. There are mirror-image accommodations in the hulls with double berths forward and aft, and two heads. Eight people and two heads might create a bit of a log jam at rush hour. I have another layout drawing that shows one queen-size double forward on centerline and an additional head.

I like this cockpit. You can have the wheel forward in typical cat style or you can have twin wheels aft more like a monohull. You either look over the house with the single wheel model or you look down the side decks with the twin-wheel model. I'd like the twin wheel model, although this puts you out from under the protection of the big bimini. Either way it's a super cockpit with plenty of space for a crowd to gather and party.

There are tanks for 106 gallons of fuel and 198 gallons of water. The auxiliary power is a pair of 40-horsepower Yanmars.

The Catamaran Company, 4005 North Federal Highway Suite 200, Fort Lauderdale, FL 33308. (954) 566-9806. **www.catamarans.com**

August 2000

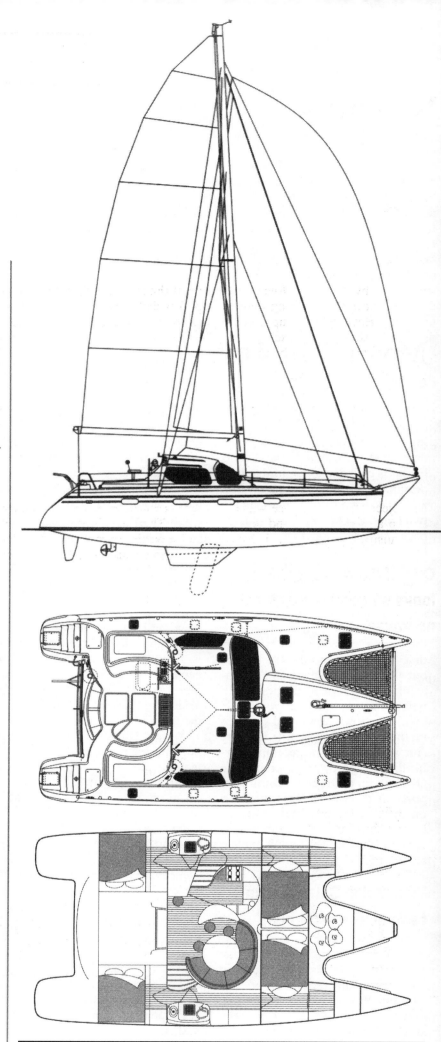

A big cat that's begging to be cruised.

LOA 43'8"; LWL 41'3"; Beam 23'2"; Draft fixed keel 4'4"; Draft daggerboard version 3'9" (board up), 8'2" (board down); Displacement 18,300 lbs. (light); Sail Area 1,195 sq. ft. (main and genoa); SA/D 27.5 (estimated); D/L 112; L/B 1.88; Fuel 100 gals.; Water 180 gals.; Auxiliary Twin 40-hp Yanmars.

Novara 44
Cruising Multihull

I think this design/promotional package is the most interesting I have ever received. A lot of time and effort went into amassing a tremendous amount of high quality material. I was particularly taken with the section suggesting a combination of business and pleasure usage by using the Novara cat as a platform for "floating dental lectures." Hey! Sign me up immediately for several of those.

The Novara cat is the brainchild of Dr. Martin Mai, a Viennese dentist, (who'd a thunk it?) and several other designers including the Coventry Polytechnic Department of Industrial Design. I can't tell exactly who has contributed what in this package. It appears that most of the hull design work was done by Phil Morrison of Southampton. The object of this exercise was to develop a series of fast and versatile cruising catamarans. I have

One of the reasons this cat looks so good is that it has no house.

spectacular photos of the first of these cats being launched by a giant crane off the autobahn, over a wide riverbank and into the river. At 44 feet, 3 inches LOA and with a 31-foot, 6-inch beam it's easy to see how this was a traffic stopper. With that amount of beam I would imagine this cat's stable enough for most dental procedures.

It's a spectacular looking design with near flush decks and a clear bubble covering the nav station. If you could get those lamb patties positioned perfectly under that bubble on a sunny day they would be cooked in no time. There is a flush sliding hatch in the bubble that is done well enough to be completely invisible in the photos. If I owned one of these I'd name it *Beam Me Up Dr. Mai*.

The hull shape was a result of tank tests using a John Shuttleworth-designed Tektron 50 as a benchmark. Test runs were run to explore the effects of volumetric distribution and BWL. If I am reading the brochure correctly the hull form chosen was the one with the least BWL and the deepest canoe body. The topsides fair

out above the DWL and there are two chines that add to the volume where you most need it for interior components. There is one deep daggerboard to starboard only.

When I first looked at the photos I thought what a great looking cat this was. Then I realized that one of the reasons this cat looks so good is that it has no house. (You can hardly count that nitrous oxide bubble as a "house.") There are no accommodations in between the two hulls. Okay, the berths extend inboard a bit in pilot berth fashion, but there is no deck saloon at all. This boat is all cockpit and working deck between the hulls.

There are three staterooms, two to starboard and one to port, each with a double berth. On the port side, in place of another stateroom, there is a dinette. It's a very clever layout. There are three heads, a nav station on the starboard side under the bubble and a galley to port without a bubble.

I'm not kidding when I tell you that the photos show a high-tech dental chair in one of the stateroom areas. "Go below Fred and whip up some lunch, and while you're at it, take out Ben's wisdom teeth."

The rig is huge. That's where all that beam comes in handy for sail carrying power. Of course, you can customize your own Novara with a smaller rig if you like, and in fact the one photo that I have of the boat in any wind does show a shallow reef in the main. If we go on faith and use the published displacement and the areas for mainsail and No. 2 jib we get an SA/D of 24.89. This includes mainsail roach. The mast appears to be a rotating type.

When I first opened this package, which consisted of two large brochures complete with a myriad of versions of the boat, I had my doubts. I had the sense that someone had spent too much time in the bubble with the gas turned on. But the more I studied the information the more impressed I became with this effort. At this point I'd have to say that the Novara is one of my very favorite large cruising cats.

Katamaran Konstruktions, A-1230 Vienna-Büttnergasse 1, Austria. 43 1 615 66 33.

August 2001

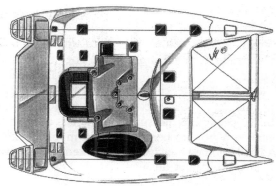

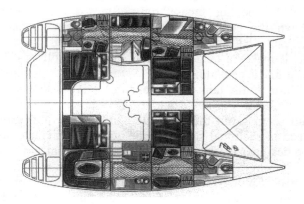

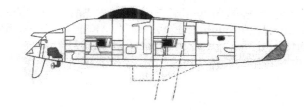

A fresh and novel approach to performance multihull design.

LOA 44'3"; LWL 43'4"; Beam overall 31'6"; Displacement 21,560 lbs.; Draft 2'11" (board up), 10'8" (board down); Sail Area 1,205 sq. ft. (with roach and genoa); SA/D 24.89; D/L 118; Auxiliary 2 50-hp Yanmar saildrives.

Hughs 46
Cruising Multihull

Designer Kurt Hughs works in Seattle and has an extensive and very well prepared catalog of multihull designs for both power and sail. This 46-footer was designed as a custom project for a client and is currently nearing completion.

The overall beam of the Hughs cat is 28 feet, 11 inches. The sectional shape is flared out above the DWL and double-chine topsides to

This new cat appears to provide the comfort advantages offered by cat proportions with the performance benefits of modern multihull design.

increase useable interior volume. The sectional shape below the DWL has a deadrise angle amidships of 8 degrees.

Have I lost you? Well, consider deadrise as the angle the section makes with the centerline measured off horizontal. A V-bottom boat has deadrise. A flat-bottomed boat has no deadrise. I have no idea at all what the etymological origins of this term are. A boat with rounded sections and no distinct "corner" or "crease" running down the centerline has no deadrise, and I call this "going tangent" as it makes a tangent with a horizontal line at centerline.

The four hulls tank-tested by Novara were all without deadrise. It would seem given the dramatic difference in sectional shapes here that one designer is "right" and the other is "wrong." Maybe. I look at it this way. Since you drag your hull through the water most of the time with a yaw angle due to leeway it doesn't make much sense to drag a corner through the water. The vortex off that corner will just create drag. Double that drag for a cat. It's far better to just let the water from the high pressure side of the hull slide over effortlessly to the low pressure side. At high, planing speeds the flatter bottom will also help the boat get up on a plane quicker. For a cruising boat, deadrise is a strong shape that adds longitudinal stiffness and creates a natural sump to gather any bilge

water that might accumulate. I suppose you could also argue that in a boat with minimal append-ages the corner of the deadrise hull will help the boat go to weather by minimizing leeway. But I'd rather see less deadrise or none at all and better boards.

This cat weighs 18,603 pounds and has a D/L of 91.14. Kurt provided a well prepared and highly documented weight study to verify this weight. You can have either fixed low-aspect-ratio keels or you can have lifting daggerboards. You will get about half the lift with the keels while incurring about the same drag. Keels will be cheaper to build and require less maintenance.

This is a well-styled boat. Given Kurt's statement about shoving a house through the water you can imagine that he considers windage very important in the design of a cruising cat.

The interior has three staterooms. This cat has a deckhouse, and the dinette, lounging area and nav station are all in this structure. There is even an inside steering station in this deckhouse. The galley is tucked all the way aft in the port hull. I don't like this, since it means you have to do your cooking down a level from the dining area, five steps down to be exact, and fairly steep steps at that. I would worry about the new potatoes and parsnips rolling off the platter as I made my way up from the galley carrying the roast. You just couldn't do it. Am I being picky? No, I think this is a serious shortcoming of this design. Having said that I'm quite certain that this was probably a client-driven feature. For me, I'd want the galley on the same level as the dining area and much closer to the cockpit. There is a shower/tub in the starboard, forward stateroom.

Kurt's an old hand with multihulls. His designs have been built all over the world. This new cat appears to provide the comfort advantages offered by cat proportions with the performance benefits of modern multihull design.

Kurt Hughs Sailing Designs, 612½ West McGraw St., Seattle, WA 98119. **www.multihulldesigns.com** *(206) 284-6346.*

August 2001

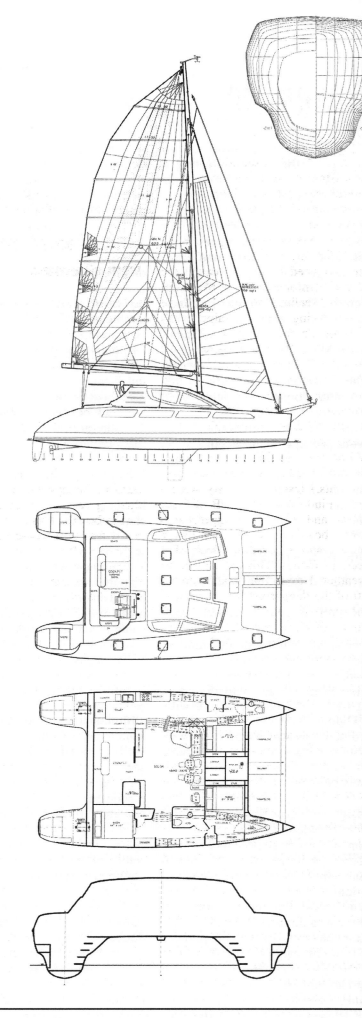

A combination of multihull comfort and performance.

LOA 46'3"; LWL 45'6"; Beam overall 28'11"; BWL 4'4" (each hull); Draft 1'7" (daggerboard model/board up), 7'9" (daggerboard model/board down), 4'3" (fin keel); Displacement 18,603 lbs.; Sail Area 1,531 sq. ft. (with genoa and including roach); SA/D 34.9; D/L 91.14; L/B 10.5 (each hull); Auxiliary Yanmar 3JHZ-TBE; Fuel 160 gals.; Water 160 gals.

Switch 51
Multihull Cruiser

If you want to sail a cat but are unwilling to give up comfort, I would suggest you look at this good-looking design, the Switch 51. Have you ever noticed that some foreign names don't translate so well? Twenty years ago there was a car produced in Taiwan called the "Deer." Unfortunately in Mandarin deer is "feeling," so you had these cars driving around Taipei with Feeling on their trunks. I don't know what "Switch" denotes, but I do know I like this boat designed by Van Peteghem and Lauriot-Prévost, and built by the Sud Composites company of France.

This 51-footer has a D/L of 183 using the published displacement. (Although I'm always skeptical of the published weight of these cruising cats.) Using my trusty scale I get an individual hull L/B of 5.96. Deep and effective daggerboards give a board-down draft of 8 feet, 6 inches and a board-up draft of 3 feet, 11 inches. This cat will go to weather. I think that small minifin aft of the daggerboard is to protect the prop if you choose to beach your Switch. Photos of the boat at rest show the transom well clear of the waterplane.

You can take your pick from a variety of layouts that primarily change the number of berths, although there are options in the galley location as well. I'll focus on the "standard" layout. In this layout there are three staterooms with large double berths, with the area forward on the starboard hull reserved for stowage. The galley on this version is a bit skimpy, and it appears that meal preparation could spill over to the nav area. I need room to work when I prepare my magical, high energy macaroni-and-cheese dish: three eggs, 20 ounces of pepperjack and cheddar cheese, and 2¹/₂ cups of heavy cream. You'd love it. Your arteries would hate it. I prefer the galleys on the "Charter 1" and "Grand Croisiere" layouts. Still, these are all comfy layouts and custom layouts are also available.

Big cats are about deck space and in that area the Switch is great. A dozen friends on board for happy hour would not burden this deck layout. The wheel is up against the bulkhead as it is on most big cats,

and for me there is something a wee bit too "powerboaty" in this wheel position. I like a wheel I can sit alongside. Sheeting angles are

This is a sexy-looking boat from all angles.

tight, and winches are well located for nearly effortless sail handling. The traveller spans the entire beam of the boat aft. Davits allow the dinghy to be tucked up between the two hulls where it has no adverse effect on the look of the boat. The life raft is stowed directly below the davits. Teak decks enhance the look of the Switch.

This is a big rig with an SA/D of 23.9, using the brochure's lower number for upwind sail area. With this rig and the high-aspect-ratio daggerboards, I think this would be a cat that you would enjoy racing against other cruising cats. Of course, with a reasonable handicap system you can race anything. It's just a lot more fun to race a boat you can sail aggressively.

As usual the profile drawing and sailplan of this cat show a strange-looking, lumpy boat. This is what happens when you compress that amount of beam into a two-dimensional graphic representation. But the photos show an exceptionally handsome vessel with attractive hulls capped with a minimally cambered deck and a well-sculpted deckhouse. This is a sexy-looking boat from all angles.

Multihull vs. monohull debates rage on for some reason. I really like all boats as long as they show well-thought-out and refined design. In the end, while we could debate the various advantages of both types, it just comes down to sailing style. I have clients that love to bury the rail! Maybe your family doesn't like to heel. You'll spill far fewer drinks on this cat.

Sud Composites, Z.A.Z. No. 2, 34540 Balaruc-Les-Bains, France., **www.sudcomposites.com** *33 4 67 43 01 82. In the U.S. contact The Catamaran Company, 4005 N. Federal Hwy., Ste. 200, Ft. Lauderdale, FL 33308. (854) 566-9806.* **www.multihullcompany.com**

August 2002

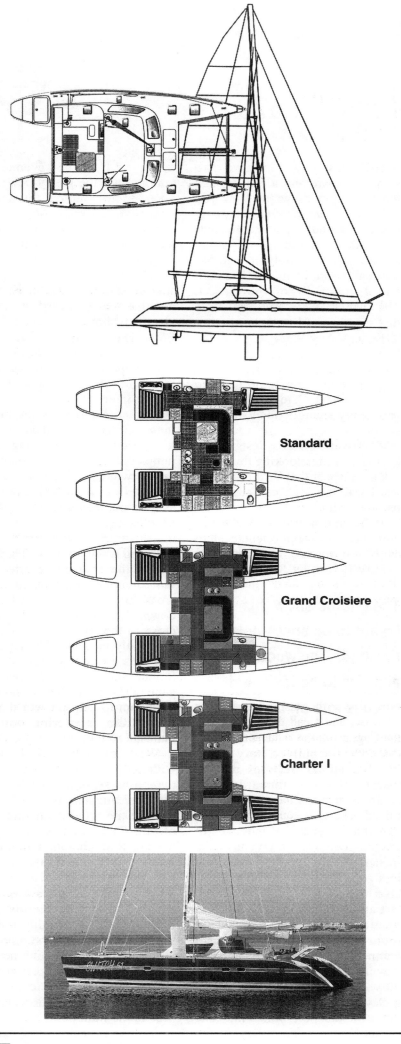

Standard

Grand Croisiere

Charter I

The best in cat comfort and style.

LOA 50' 6 "; LWL 47'2"; Beam 24'11"; Draft 8'6" (boards down), 3'11" (board up); Displacement 28,600 lbs.; Sail Area 1,399 sq. ft.; SA/D 23.9; D/L 121; Auxiliary 30- or 60-hp Saildrive; Fuel 115 gals.; Water 115 gals.

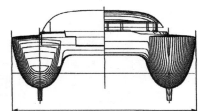

Lagoon 570
Multihull Cruiser

Let's just say you have two weeks to spare and a sail through the BVIs sounds good. Now you need to decide how you are going to sail. You could charter a 36-footer and do it all yourself or ... you could go for this fully crewed 56-foot cat. Hmmmmm, that's a hard one. I think I'll go with the cat. That way I won't spill the drink that someone just brought me.

Designed by Van Peteghem and Lauriot Prevost, the Lagoon 570 is possibly the perfect charter platform. Overall beam is 30 feet and draft is 4 feet, 7 inches. You can practically snuggle this baby right up to the beach. The rudder is well forward on this design. The keel is a strange looking thing, but I don't suspect that VMG to windward was too high on the design parameter list.

Individual hull waterline maximum beam is about 6 feet, 3 inches. If you divide this number into the DWL you get 8.32. This puts

The photos show this layout to be spectacularly finished. The wood appears to be teak, and there is lots of it.

the Lagoon in the relatively beamy category. The hulls are very shapely, with arclike sections aft and marked deadrise forward. Once again, overhangs have been minimized. The D/L is 105. Clearance from the water to the underside of the bridgedeck or "slam pan" is 36 inches. Photos of the 570 sailing in a good breeze show no discernable heel angle.

Lagoon builds several different interiors ranging from a five-stateroom charter layout with skipper's cabin to a three-stateroom "owner's layout." Three of the layouts share the same saloon and galley arrangement with the galley down in the port hull while one layout features the galley in the "up" location to starboard in the saloon. As the cook, this "up" version appeals to me. This way I can be included in the festivities as I do my meal preparation. "Now

where did I put the Vegemite?" If you go with the galley down, you open up the saloon for a more expansive conversation area and nobody will see the cook tasting the sauce. "More Vegemite!"

You can get lots of heads on your Lagoon, but if you want a shower stall you will have to go with the "owner's version." I think you just shower on deck in the BVIs. The photos show this layout to be spectacularly finished. The wood appears to be teak, and there is lots of it. By any standard this is a great interior.

The sailplan shows the big cat in two dimensions and cats seldom look good in this drawing. What jumps out at me are those vertical saloon windows. They are hard to ignore. But as aesthetically brutal as they are, they do offer pragmatic advantages in that they maximize interior volume without reducing room on deck. They also reduce the greenhouse effect and that's very important in sunny areas. Look where the mast comes down. It's deck-stepped and as close to the front of the house as physically possible. The rig is big and uses a heavy air staysail on a Solent stay inside the working genoa. There are Benson struts on the boom to help prevent the lazy jacks from interfering with the mainsail shape.

Water capacity is 264 gallons with 198 gallons of fuel for the two 56-horsepower diesels.

I'm sitting here in Seattle looking out the window at rain. Lots of rain. The brochures in front of me are a combination of charter promo material and sales material for the Lagoon 570. In the brochures the people are smiling, wearing shorts or bikinis, donning scuba gear, leaping into the water, dining on sumptuous, multi-course meals and toasting each other with apparent wild abandon.

What do I get? The sound of tires in the rain.

Lagoon America, 105 Eastern Avenue, Suite 202, Annapolis, MD 21403. **www.cata-lagoon.com** *(410) 280-2368.*

February 2002

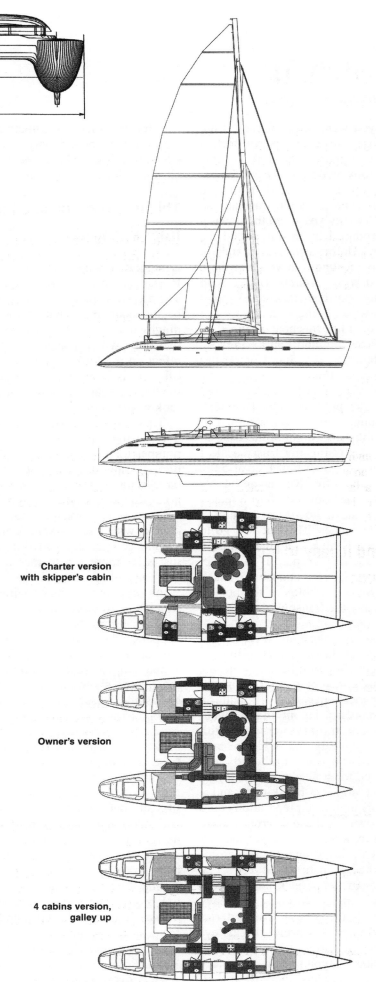

Charter version
with skipper's cabin

Owner's version

4 cabins version,
galley up

The perfect escape for a rain-soaked Seattle yacht designer.

LOA 55'4"; LWL 52'; Beam 30'; Draft 4'7"; Displacement 33,069 lbs.; Sail Area 1,500 sq. ft.; SA/D 23.3; D/L 105; Auxiliary Two 56-hp diesels; Fuel 198 gals.; Water 264 gals.

Perry Cat
Multihull Cruiser

Paul Reed Smith and I met a year ago to discuss a new boat for him. His goal was simple; the resulting boat was not. Paul wanted a sailing boat that was capable of reaching the bonefish fishing grounds off the Bahamas. He wanted a boat that could get there quickly and provide a stable platform for fly fishing. He also wanted this "mothership" to hold two rigid skiffs capable of getting right into the shallows where the bonefish live. Paul had already designed and built two of the high-speed skiffs himself so he knew exactly what the stowage requirements were.

Sometimes you sit and listen to a client's want list and the first thing that jumps into your head is, "This is impossible." The more I listened, smiled and nodded to Paul the more I was convinced it was impossible. But Paul's an innovator and convincing. He is a famous and respected guitar builder. He will run the problem through every conceivable solution,

I found it easy to bond with this boat.

whether practical or fanciful, before giving up. And he doesn't give up.

Given the stability requirement and Paul's preference for a multihull, I chose a catamaran design based upon an earlier 55-footer I had done. With 28 feet, 10 inches of beam and 26,000 pounds of displacement we would have a stable platform. With a waterline beam for each hull of 4 feet, 6 inches we would have boat speed under both sail and power. Max hull beam is 5 feet, 9 inches, with asymmetrical daggerboards in each hull to help going to weather. These were extremely effective in my previous design. I gave the boat a flat sheerline to help with crew movement while fishing. Beauty is as beauty does.

The biggest challenge with this design was the deck layout. Paul wanted to be able to walk across the stern of the cat while fishing. This required a solid deck aft spanning both hulls rather than the typical deck cutaway between the hulls where you can tuck away a dinghy. From a design standpoint the biggest problem with this type of deck is that it moves the center of gravity aft and big cats already have a tendency to trim by the stern. I added hull volume

and flattened the hull rocker aft to help deal with this. Transom rake was reduced to expand available deck space and help with the fishing requirements. With the mainsheet and boom removed, the entire aft end of the boat can be clear for fly fishing. The entire cockpit is on main deck level.

The cockpit seat/helm seat detail was designed specifically around the requirements of housing the two 14-foot, 6-inch skiffs while providing a comfy and efficient lounging and dining area. The center console houses a large ice box/reefer for fish. There is a lot of stowage in the cockpit seats. Adjacent to the cockpit dining table there are hatches in the seats to allow access to the stowed skiffs. These skiffs will be run under the stern of the boat with the driver on board. The driver will attach the skiff to the lifting mechanism then climb out through the seat hatches. That's the plan anyway. We will have to do some fine tuning once the boat is launched, but I'm convinced it can work. When the dinghies are nested snug under the deck there will be a 30-inch clearance from the skiff bottom to the water. The outboard motors will remain in the deployed position. Fun huh?

The accommodations feature staterooms for four couples, and there is an inside steering station next to a large nav station that also houses an electric piano keyboard for jam sessions on board. A large subwoofer will be housed under the dinette settee.

This was an unusual design job with an unusual outcome. I got my new guitar and I love it. Paul got a unique fishing boat. Aesthetically this boat was a challenge, and while I think the boat works well, I would hesitate to call it attractive. My hope is that when finished the bulk of the cockpit structures will be hidden by the overall bulk of the entire boat. Two-dimensional cat profiles are seldom attractive. I found it easy to bond with this boat during the design process.

Robert H. Perry Yacht Designers, 5801 Phinney Ave. North #100, Seattle, WA 98103. (206) 789-7212. **www.perryboat.com**

December 2001

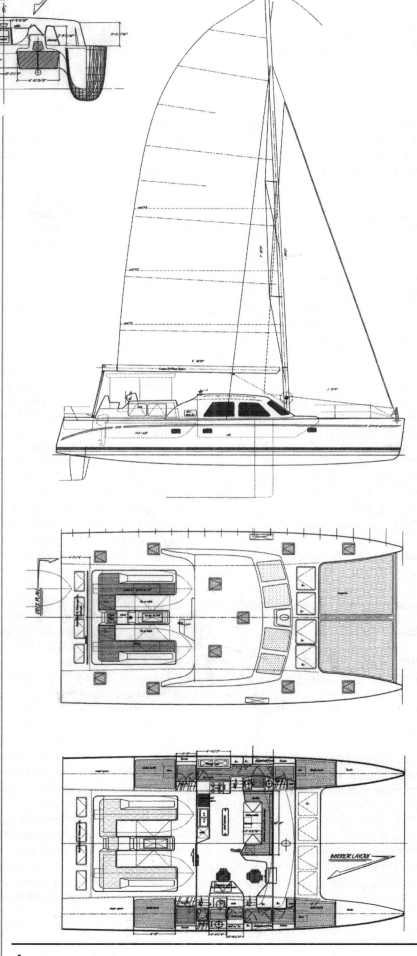

A unique cat for fishing and sailing.

LOA 56'2"; DWL 54'4"; Beam 28'10"; Draft 4'3" (board up), 7' (board down); Displacement 26,000 lbs.; Sail Area 1,385 sq. ft.; SA/D 25.2; D/L 72.4; L/B 9.8 (each hull); Auxiliary twin 75-hp Yanmars; Fuel 200 gals.; Water 150 gals.

Gunboat 62
Multihull Cruiser

When Peter Johnstone, a long-time monohull sailer, wanted a boat for world cruising he turned to Morelli and Melvin to design him a cruising cat. Peter had owned a large monohull, a racing sled he had converted to a cruising boat before he felt the comfort and stability aspects of the big cat were more to his family's liking. Peter has sailed on a lot of big cats, including *PlayStation* and *Team Adventure*, so he knew exactly what he was getting into. Soon there were two other people interested in sisterships and the Gunboat 62 was born as a semi-production model built in South Africa by Jaz Marine.

This is a pretty bland looking big cat. I would have liked to see a little more styling effort put into it. The sheer is a dead straight line.

Twenty-eight feet of beam buys you a lot of stability.

While this is not aesthetically very satisfying it is practical considering the great expanse of deck you are dealing with here. The cabintrunk is pretty ordinary in profile but there is a cockpit cut into the front of the house that will add some three-dimensional variety to the shape.

Let's look at that forward cockpit. There are doors leading from the saloon on each side of the inside steering station to this cockpit. Halyard winches flank the cockpit and the windlass is just forward of the cockpit. You can work here in safety. The doors will have to be strong and extra watertight as they will see some serious spray. The axle for the inside wheel can be run through the bulkhead and you can have another wheel in the forward cockpit. Hull No. 2 of the 62 is built that way.

In fact, this is not hull No.1, Peter's boat. This layout is for hull No. 3. There are four staterooms, and three of them have double berths. I presume the owner's stateroom is to starboard and forward. This stateroom has a mini "office" attached with desk and file drawers. The most interesting feature to

this layout is the lone aft head in the starboard hull. You can enter this head from the swim step. There are twin washbasins and twin showerheads. The galley is up in the saloon. All interiors for the Gunboat 62 are owner customized.

The hulls show an L/B of 9.0 when I scale the individual hull beam at 2.1 meters. L/BOA is 2.2 and 28 feet of beam buys you a lot of stability. The canoe body rocker shows the hull depth quite shallow forward with the forefoot knuckle above the DWL. This indicates that the longitudinal center of buoyancy may be aft, which suggests the boat needed volume aft to float the accommodation and mechanical weights. The D/L is 77.62 if I use the "max load" displacement. The retractable rudders are the cassette type, and with them retracted, the boat will float in less than 2 feet of water. Note that the saildrives are twisted off vertically so they protrude through the side of the hull at a diagonal angle, thus reducing prop draft and vulnerability to prop damage while also helping to reduce minimum draft.

The rig is pretty standard for a big cat. Marstrom of Sweden is building all the spars in carbon. Standing rigging is all Aramid covered in PVC and all halyards are Vectran. All blocks are lashed to the spars with Spectra lashings and all running rigging is "tapered." The jib is self-tacking and the beam of the cat makes it possible to have a very wide sheeting angle if needed for the self-tacking jib lead. This is always a problem with monohulls. A masthead screecher will add a lot of sail area. There is too much roach to this main to just use E and P for our SA/D so I have multiplied the .5E by P number by 1.4 to account for this roach-added sail area. This gives a mainsail area of 930 square feet and a SA/D of 29.45.

Gunboat has already sold three of these big cats.

Gunboat Multihulls, Box 951, 3 Narrows Road, Wareham, MA 02571. (508) 295-1337. **www.gunboat.info**

August 2003

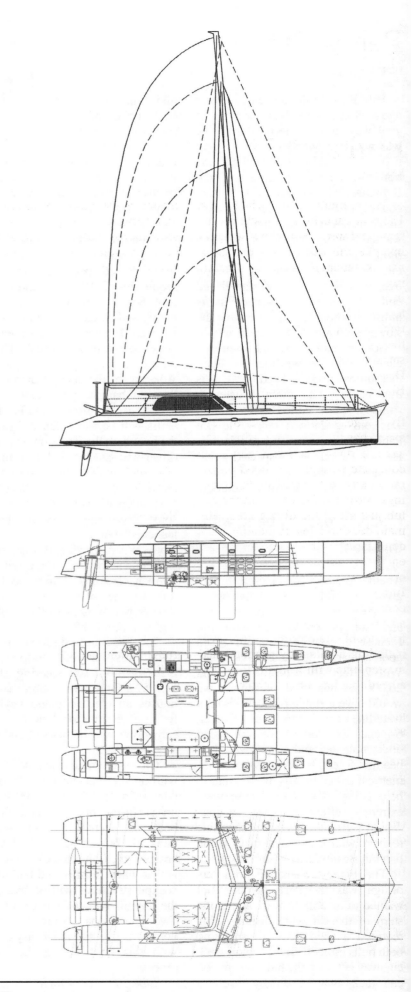

Bigger is better in this semicustom cruising cat.

LOA 62'; LWL 58'; Beam 28'3"; Draft 8'6", 2'3" (boards up); Displacement 34,000 lbs.; Sail area 1,932 sq. ft.; SA/D 29.45; D/L 77.62; L/BOA 2.2; Auxiliary twin Yanmar 56-hp; Fuel 280 gals.; Water 160 gals.

Blubay 132
Multihull Cruiser

The promotional material for this 132-foot cat calls it "a yacht for the real seafarer." Somehow I can't imagine life aboard this extraordinary catamaran as being "seafaring." In my books "seafaring" involves sweat, eye patches, parrots, torn T-shirts and rum. I imagine the typical crew list for this cat requires that you look and smell like you just stepped out of a Ralph Lauren add. Design work is all in house by Blubay Yachts of Cannes, France.

You have to call it the top level fly bridge. This upper level of deck space has the steering stations and a large dining and lounging area complete with bar and food preparation area, if I'm reading the drawings correctly. Don't forget the hot tub just aft of the dining area. The main deck area features another bar configured so the bartender can be enclosed and surrounded by seafarers enjoying their rum drinks. Inside the deck house there is a conversation area off to port and another huge dining area. There are four double staterooms on this level including a palatially proportioned master suite with walk in closet and a head that has a big bathtub.

The best I can tell is the accommodations down in the hulls themselves are intended for the big cat's professional crew. There are staterooms for eight, an office, galley, crew dining area and copious stowage areas. Three heads in the hulls are directly accessible from the stateroom on the main deck level.

Rest assured you will be comfortable on this boat.

The hulls are long and skinny. Scaling off the drawings I get an individual hull beam to length ratio of 9.53 percent. Overall beam is 51 feet, 2 inches. D/L is 43.11. If you assume the bows are absolutely slab sided you get a half angle of entry of 5.5 degrees. Cruising speed under power with twin 450-horsepower engines is 16 knots. Deep, high aspect ratio daggerboards will insure excellent performance on the wind. The rudders are well forward in the hulls. With two long, narrow hulls tracking will not be a problem and I suppose you would use power assist in close-quarter maneuvering.

It takes a monstrous rig to move a monster of a boat and this cat has

Rest assured you will be comfortable on this boat.

a big rig. The drawings indicate a rotating carbon fiber wing-section mast. The mainsheet is led to the traveler located on that cantilevered overhang on the main deck. I was going to say that this might pose an interesting engineering problem, but then this entire design requires very skillful engineering. The small, working jib is self-tacking. All winches are hydraulic, captive line in type. Given the overall proportions of these hulls combined with the big rig I expect this will be a very fast boat under sail. The sheet loads could be terrifying but I guess I could get used to it.

Size aside I think this is a very well styled design. It does take a while to warm up to the multilevel or "layered" look of the topsides. But once your eye adjusts to the bridgedeck height this design begins to look very good. Note the swelling in the cabin top immediately forward of each steering station on the upper level. There is a lot of sculpture going on here.

Chances are I'll never go cruising on this boat. It's too small for me. I have my eye on the Blubay 170 also featured in the brochure. But I can still admire the design work and marvel that we are in an age where cruising catamarans can be taken to this level. I look forward to at least seeing pictures of this boat sailing.

Blubay Yachts, 130 rue d'Antibes, 06400 Cannes, France. 33 4 97 06 20 20. **www.blubay.com**

January 2003

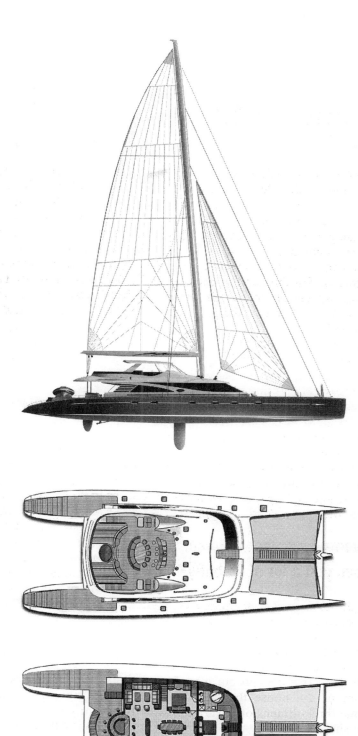

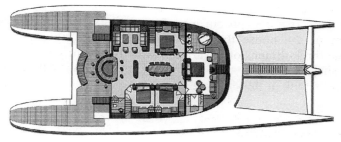

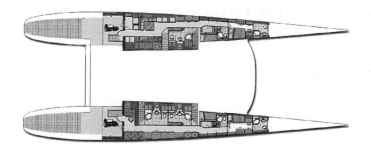

A well-appointed giant cat that's rigged to move.

LOA 131'6"; LWL 122'2"; Beam 51'2"; Draft 13'1" (boards down), 8'2" (boards up); Displacement 80 tons; Sail Area 1,980 sq. ft.; SA/D 10.14; D/L 43.11; Auxiliary Caterpillar 450hp; Fuel 4,267 gals.; Water 1,125 gals.

CLASSIC DESIGNS

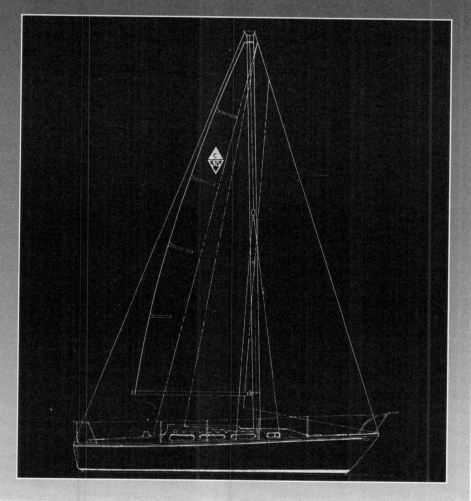

Beetle Cat
Classic Daysailer

Let's say you want to listen to some music. Options abound, but first you turn on your tube-powered amplifier and wait a half an hour for the tubes to warm up and stabilize. You check each tube to determine that it's working properly. You can even start by polishing the pins to ensure perfect contact.

Then you start your turntable and search through your venerable record collection. Let's see, should I listen to a baroque trumpet concerto by Beiber or Elvis Costello?

With the tubes glowing and giving off a shimmer of heat, you check your cartridge and delicately brush off the needle, back to front only. You clean off your brush, then wipe the LP surface. Then, with steady fingers, you ease the needle down into the first groove and sit back. Sure, the record pops and crackles on occasion, but the sound is analog exquisite and transports you back to predigital days. Is it better or worse than a solid-state muscle amp powering a Wadia CD player? Beats me, but it sure is different and fun to have this degree of tactile involvement with the music. When audiophiles get

Despite its genetic quirks, the little Beetle Cat just seemed to be the most fun. It's stiff as a church and revels in a breeze.

bogged down in technical discussions, someone usually puts an end to the argument with the taunt, "It's the music, stupid."

Triode-power-tube-powered amps and Beetle Cats are not high-tech. They are "untech." You have to haul up the throat halyard along with the peak halyard to get the gaff angle and throat tension just right so the sail sets properly. There's no vang. There's no traveler. There are no jib leads. There's no crying in catboats. The centerboard is big and crude. The rudder is about as silly a shape as you can imagine. Heavy? This 12-

foot, 4-inch boat will weigh well in excess of 560 pounds when you are aboard. Balance? Beetle Cats defined weather helm. We won't even discuss the speed issue.

But if the tube amp-turntable combination can truly express the ultimate in listener-involved music reproduction, then the Beetle Cat can express the ultimate in the personal sailing experience. This is not about high-tech. "It's the sailing, stupid." This is about enjoying an afternoon of sailing. This is about sailing along with your head about 2 feet off the water, tiller in one hand and mainsheet in the other. I know of no boat better able to convey the joy of sailing than the Beetle Cat.

I'll tell you some Beetle Cat stories. When I was about 22 years old, I rented a houseboat on Seattle's Lake Union. My dock neighbor was Dick Wagner and he had an eclectic fleet of small wooden boats he rented out. These included a Concordia sloop, several clinker-built Scandinavian sloops and two Beetle Cats. I would work on the boats in my spare time in exchange for sailing time. I sailed all the boats, but quickly chose the Beetle Cat as my ride of choice. Despite its genetic quirks, the little Beetle Cat just seemed to be the most fun. It's stiff as a church and revels in a breeze.

Jaime Barerra, a boatbuilding friend of mine, and I decided to race Beetle Cats around Lake Union after work. We bet a six-pack on the outcome. I used every trick to get my Beetle to go. Board up, board down, board partway up. More peak halyard, less throat halyard. I worked that boat and managed to beat Jaime by about 250 yards after sailing a 2-mile course. Back on the dock I asked Jaime if he had pulled his board up when he was off the wind. Jaime said, "Pull it up? I never put it down."

It was a blustery fall afternoon, and I decided I'd take a Beetle Cat out. Barreling along, I thought I'd light my pipe. I was in the middle of the lake so I just steered with my

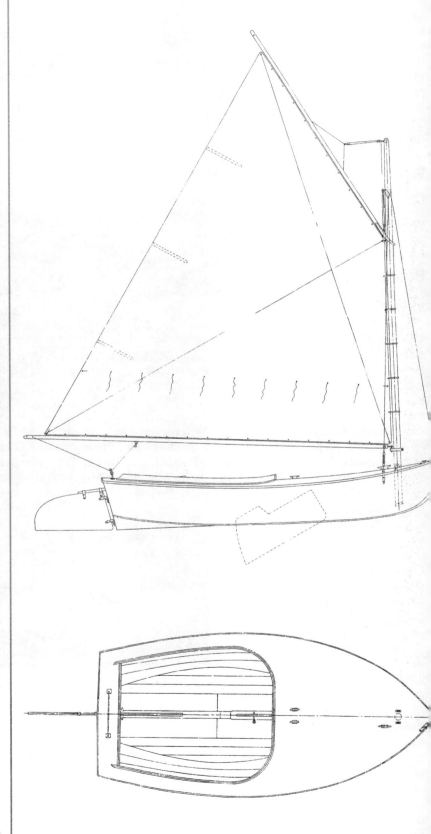

foot and ducked my head under the foredeck to get out of the wind. This took some time, but eventually I had a blaze going in my bowl when … Bam! The boat came to a jarring halt. I had run head-on into a big, black, steel navigational buoy. I was probably doing Beetle Cat hull speed—all of 4 knots—at the time. The boat was fine. The steel buoy had a dent in it and some of its paint

When you first sail a Beetle Cat, you will be impressed with its big-boat, solid feel. I don't think you could tip a Beetle over without a lot of concerted effort.

was rubbed off onto the cast bronze stem pieces of the Beetle Cat. Beetle Cats are very strong.

I've got more Beetle Cat stories, but let's take a look at the history of the boat. The Beetle Cat was designed in 1921 by the Beetle family of Clark's Point, New Bedford, Massachusetts. The Concordia Co. bought the rights to the Beetle Cat in 1946. In 1960 Concordia's Beetle Cat Division was moved to South Dartmouth. Leo Telesmanick was the foreman and stayed with the project until his retirement in 1983. Charlie York was trained by Leo and in 1993 bought the rights to the Beetle from Concordia. Leo still looks in on the shop. Today there are more than 3,500 Beetle Cats.

Beetle Cats are true to the traditional Cape Cod catboat model. They are fat and heavy. They have no overhangs. The strange-looking rudder is designed to give you control in a very shoal-draft boat. Unfortunately, this puts the center of pressure on the rudder blade way aft which exaggerates any helm pressure. The stern is broad. The mast is in the eye of the bow. I'm not going to quote numbers. This is not about numbers.

When you first sail a Beetle Cat,

you will be impressed with its big-boat, solid feel. I don't think you could tip a Beetle over without a lot of concerted effort. I certainly never even came close to capsizing one, and I sailed them in lots of breeze. You sit down low in the Beetle, so the sense of speed is exaggerated. The expansive cockpit is roomy enough for two big adults. You could even sail a Beetle with a crew of four if you wanted.

The big gaff mainsail looks great. The gaff sail has a nice, if not the most efficient shape. Off the wind, the sail presents a good amount of sail area. Upwind, the gaff falls off, inducing a lot of twist to the mainsail. Note the way the low boom overhangs the transom. You will learn a lot about controlled jibing sailing a Beetle. The rig is not a weatherly rig, but then again, the hull and board are not weatherly either. If it takes you six extra tacks to get back home, that's just six extra tacks of fun.

This is a fabulous-looking boat. Beetle Cats are built in the plank-over-frame method of wooden boat-building. No, there are no GRP Beetle Cats. Beetles are planked with Atlantic white cedar over white oak frames. The seams are caulked (pronounced "corked") with cotton. The deck is framed in white pine with cedar planking covered with canvas. The fastenings and hardware are all bronze. The spars are fir.

(That was fun.)

There's a place for Mumm 36s and 600-watt Krell solid-state amplifiers. They are a blast. There's also a place for 15-watt single-ended tube amplifiers and Beetle Cats. I imagine taking a future grandchild sailing. I'd like to introduce the child to sailing in a simple, old-fashioned boat that emphasizes the romance and unique experience of sailing. If you want high-tech, go sit at your computer for three hours. If you want to go sailing, find a Beetle Cat.

Beetle Inc., 3 Thatcher Lane, Wareham, MA 02571. (508) 295-8585. www.beetlecat.com

Designed by the Beetle family in 1921 and built in Massachusetts—first in New Bedford, then South Dartmouth—for 77 years, the Beetle Cat is still actively sailed and raced on New England and Cape Cod waters.

Beetle Cats are planked with Atlantic white cedar over white oak frames, and the seams are caulked with cotton. Here, now-retired Beetle employee Leo Telesmanick paid a visit to the operation he ran for 47 years.

SAILING pictures by Steven Borns

Sturdy, traditional catboat with a lively personality.

LOA 12'4"; Beam 6'; Draft board down 2', board up 8"; Weight 450 lbs.; Sail Area 100 sq.ft.; SA/D 74.27; D/L 23.47; L/B 2.06.

J/24
Classic One-design

There have been many boats over the last 20 years that have left an impact on sailing, but few have carried with them the shock wave of the J/24. The J/24 was so successful that it spawned the J-Boat boats ranging from the 24 to the 40. There are also numerous clones on the market. More than a type of boat, the J/24 represents a style of sailing.

As the IOR gathered momentum, boats like the Ranger 33 were pushed aside and the only viable

Exceptional one-design deserving of its success.

weapon on the race course was a boat specifically designed to exploit the complex IOR measurement system. This in itself was predictable, after all, the IOR was never intended to be a handicap rule. The problem started when the IOR boats began approaching the extremes. Today's IOR boat is a fairly subdued yacht compared to the contorted IOR boats of 10 years ago. The emphasis was squarely on rated speed and boat speed for a given length was irrelevant. By the time this approach was contracted down to the Quarter Ton level, the boats began to get a little radical. The pinched end that worked on the Two Tonner gave us a tiny stern and midget cockpit on the Quarter Tonner.

Well, along came this guy Rod Johnstone who was part way through a correspondence school for yacht design. He didn't plan on designing a big one-design class; he just wanted to have a good all-around boat that he could race under various local rules, particularly the MORC rule. The boat was fast and Rod blew away the local competition. In 1975 Rod won the MORC National Championship with John Kolius placing second. Before long J/24s were in production and dominating MORC fleets everywhere.

This continued to such a degree

that the natural extension was a one-design fleet. This aspect of the J/24's success was expertly orchestrated with the best modern advertising methods. But it worked. The Johnstone brothers had an exceptional boat and it met with exceptional success. The J/24 could demolish the hottest Quarter Tonner and compete very successfully with the best Half Tonners. The Johnstone brothers have sold more than 4,300 J/24s and it is now the largest one-design keelboat class in the world.

There are two key areas to this success. The first is pure boat speed. The J/24 is a stiff boat with lots of horsepower and sailing length. The hull lines are very clean and wetted surface is at a minimum. The J/24 is not an ultra-light. It has a D/L ratio of 150, which puts it just on the edge of "medium." This has the advantage over the ULDB approach of giving the boat sufficient displacement for good sail carrying power. J/24s love a breeze upwind or down. The J can carry a full main comfortably up to 20 knots true wind speed. The keel is a fairly high aspect ratio keel and the rudder is outboard with no balance at all. There is some flare to the topsides, and overall I'd say that this is a very attractive hull shape.

The general deck configuration and rig is the second area that has contributed to the J's success. The key here is simplicity and this translates to the most knots for the buck. The fractional rig combined with the powerful hull minimizes sail inventory, and the strict one-design organization limits sophisticated deck gear. The sweptback spreaders eliminate the need for runner. The plain, flush deck leaves lots of room for a racing crew of four or five. The J/24 is a lot more fun to sail than the typical Quarter Tonner.

The J/24 is the boat that I chose to teach my sons sailboat racing.

J Boats, P.O. Box 90, 557 Thames St., Newport, RI 02840. (401) 846-8410. **www.jboats.com**

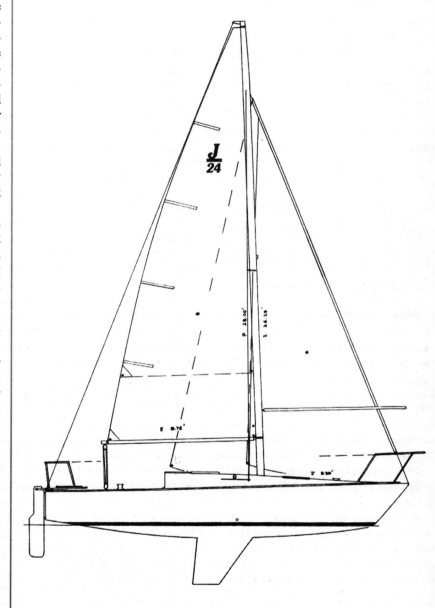

Roger Lean-Vercoe photo

LOA 24'; LWL 20'; Beam 8.92'; Draft 4'; Displacement 2,700 lbs.; Ballast 935 lbs.; Sail Area 261 sq. ft.

Santa Cruz 27
Classic Cruiser-Racer

The brochure says "Fast is fun." This phrase sums up the philosophy behind the Santa Cruz 27 designed by Bill Lee. Personally I have been so impressed with this yacht that I have given serious thought to buying one myself.

Bill Lee carved a niche very early in his career as the designer of very fast ULDB yachts. (ULDB stands for Ultra Light Displacement.) His first successful design was *Magic*. *Magic* was followed by *Witchcraft*, *Chutzpah* and *Panache*. Without doing some research I cannot tell you exactly which of these yachts won which events, but let it suffice to say that these yachts proved exceptionally effective in the long, off-the-wind ocean races, such as the Transpac. *Chutzpah* won the biennial Transpac twice in a row (1973, 1975), and *Magic* has won the Mazatlan. After winning the Transpac the first time, *Chutzpah* fell prey to that disease common to all unusually fast yachts called "establishment rulitis." The last Transpac was run with a formula added to the conventional IOR design specifically to discourage this type of off-the-wind specialty craft. You all know that I am not opinionated enough to offer a judgement on that type of ruling, but it seems a strange way to reward a designer who hits the magic design combination for a particular kind of race.

The Santa Cruz 27 was designed to provide very fast and exciting sailing at a minimal cost and without consideration given to any particular rating rule. She is extremely light. The displacement to length ratio of the 27 is 97! Her actual displacement is 3,000 pounds. Imagine this on a 24-foot waterline, and you have a very easily driven hull form. Her bow is quite fine, and her run is very flat. She has very low wetted surface and is the epitome of the clean lined yacht. As you might guess, she is not looked upon very favorably by the IOR rule. The Santa Cruz 27 has no humps, bumps or hollows, whatsoever. In short, her hull form is very much like a big planing dinghy. The IOR rating is about 24.5. This is the Three Quarter Ton limit. It may interest you to compare this design with that of a typical 3/4 tonner. You will note many differences. Incredibly enough, it is not unusual for a Santa Cruz 27 to sail up to this high rating and many times sail on a boat for boat basis with yachts as large as one tonners. The list of Santa Cruz 27 wins include many

IOR firsts overall. The 27's rating under the MORC rule is 26.5 approximately. Indeed the most efficient point of sail for these yachts is off the wind in a breeze. In these conditions, the Santa Cruz 27 can actually plane, and I would imagine from the photos I have seen that she requires about 15 knots of breeze.

The key to the performance of this design is the absence of superfluous

... Designed to provide very fast and exciting sailing at a minimal cost ...

weight. The interior has been designed to utilize all components as structural members where possible. There are two quarter berths, a small chart table to starboard, galley to port and V-berths forward. All joinerwork scantlings are relatively light but carefully detailed to achieve a maximum strength from a minimum weight. A very critical sailmaker friend of mine recently told me how impressed he was with the quality of workmanship in the Santa Cruz 27.

Despite the small rig of the 27, the numbers are very misleading. The rig only seems small if compared to the overall length. If you look at the rig relative to the displacement you will see that the Santa Cruz 27 has a sail area to displacement ratio of 23.15! The "small" rig begins to look very powerful if viewed from this perspective.

The deck plan is quite simple. There is a large cockpit with a watertight lazarette aft and a bridgedeck mounted traveller. Halyard winches are located on the cabin trunk adjacent to the companionway. The cabin trunk has been kept quite short resulting in a fairly large and unobstructed foredeck.

The construction of the Santa Cruz 27 features a balsa core hull lay-up of exceptional strength-to-weight characteristics. The cabin trunk has flush mounted "solar controlled bronze windows"—what are those?

Bill Lee has bridged the gap between the high performance dinghy and the small offshore racing yacht. I know some will say this is a "suicide machine," but, as my friend Jay Benford says, "Different boats for different folks."

Santa Cruz Yachts, 453 McQuaide Dr., La Selva Beach, CA 95076. **www.santacruzyachts.com** *(831) 786-1440.*

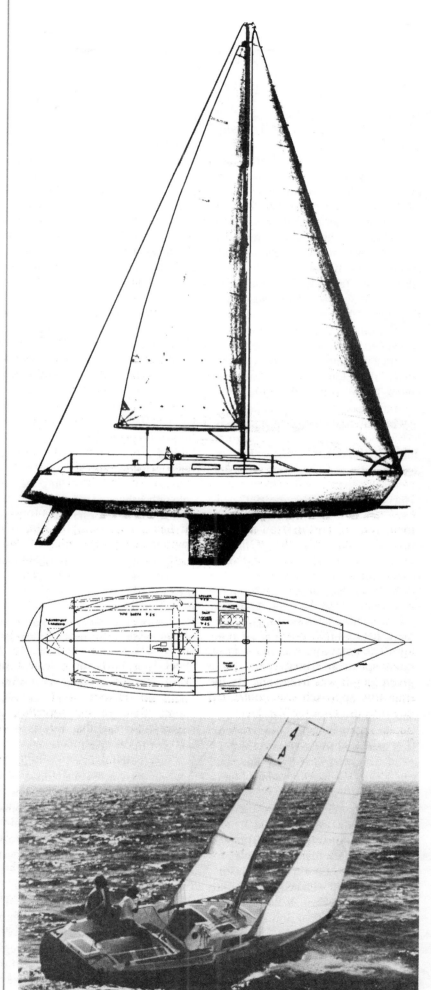

LOA 27'; LWL 24'; Beam 8'; Draft 4.5'; Displacement 3,000 lbs.; Ballast 1,500 lbs.; Sail Area 400 sq. ft.

Tartan 27
Classic Cruiser-Racer

Now 1961 was an exceptional year in France and a bottle of 1961 Bordeaux is something to be treasured. 1961 was also the year that the Tartan Marine Co. started. Their first product was the Tartan 27. I vividly remember the beautiful perspective drawing of the hull lines that appeared in the Tartan 27 ads at the time. I am lucky enough to have a print of that very drawing in front of me with the other material that Tartan forwarded. (I think I will file that drawing away in my Sparkman and Stephens file and not return it to the editor.) The Tartan 27 has lead a life similar to Sherlock Holmes. Every time the builder has tried to remove the 27 from the market, the fans have demanded its return. It can be safely said that nothing speaks better for a design than longevity, but unfortunately Tartan Marine finally has discontinued production of this favorite.

The date of the original sail plan is November 7, 1960. The original Tartan 27 was available as a sloop or a yawl. I do not have a copy of the original sloop rig, but I will assume it is the same as the rig on the 1977 version. In studying the design you should remember that this design has undergone some changes and updating. Several of the structural details have been modernized and the cabin trunk with raised doghouse has given way in favor of the straight cabin trunk. Pity though. The original house was a little stubby, but it was short and very well suited to the rather stubby lines of the hull. The new cabin trunk is very well designed and looks more up to date, but I prefer the vintage look of the original.

It is a rare treat to have a set of S&S lines sent to me. I have the perspective drawing and I also have the actual working lines drawing. I cannot make out the initials at the bottom of the drawing, but two people worked on this drawing and it is a masterpiece of marine drafting. I would speculate that at least part of the drawing was done by Al Mason. I'm sure you are well acquainted with Mr. Mason's work. It is hard to mistake his meticulous drafting style. The lines reveal a stout hull with well proportioned overhangs. There is a soft turn to the bilge and the garboards are quite hollow. The waterline has a slight hollow to it forward of station 2. In plan view the Tartan 27 shows the beam carried well into the ends to enhance stability and room below and on deck. The dis-

placement to length ratio of this design is 293. This figure was neatly printed on the original, dated June 6, 1961, so that shows you that displacement to length ratios have been used for a long time to help predict performance. Of course, compared with a modern yacht with a fin keel and spade rudder, the Tartan will seem an anachronism. While not setting the world on fire with its speed, the Tartan 27 will be a safe and comfortable small cruising yacht. Draft again was a key consideration in this design and with the board up the 27 draws 3'2".

As you study the sail plan of the modernized Tartan 27, I think you will agree that this is a handsome yacht. It does not reflect any of the cuteness or toyishness of many small yachts. Note that the actual sheer is the same while freeboard was added above the hull to deck joint to increase the useable space below. This was done with very little adverse effect on the looks of the hull. The sail area to displacement ratio is 15.84. The Tartan does have the mast coming down into the head area rather than the main cabin. A very small point but worth noting is the use of the facet on the edge of the cabin top. This area is traditionally treated with a large radius which could make a small yacht look heavy. S&S has used a flat facet to reduce the bulk of the housetop without removing useful headroom. The detail is not as apparent in the drawings as it is in the photos.

The accommodation plan of the Tartan 27 shows a very complete yacht including an enclosed head. Remember that the Tartan 27 weighs 7,400 pounds and that is as much as some of the radical one tonners. This is a heavy and voluminous hull. The interior drawing is well done and I think the features are easily discernable. Note the chart table to starboard.

I am often bothered that as designs go below 30 feet they are not given the same treatment of integrity that is used on the larger yachts. Certainly the offshore sailor in the 27 foot yacht needs the same safety factors as the sailor in the larger yacht. The Tartan 27 appears to be a tried and proven yacht for the beginning sailor who is interested in offshore cruising or the sailor who simply prefers the smaller yacht.

Tartan Marine, 1920 Fairport Nursery, Fairport Harbor, OH 44077. **www.tartanyachts.com** *(888) 330-3484.*

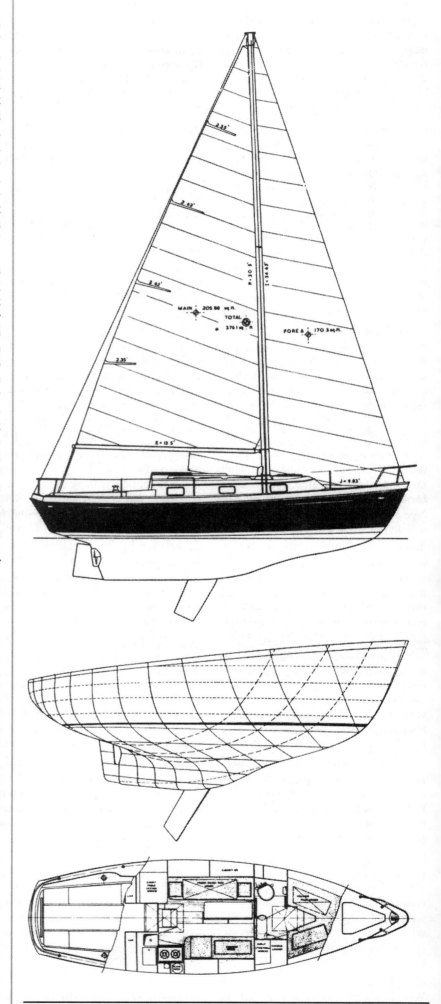

LOA 27'; DWL 21'5"; Beam 8'7-1/2"; Draft 3'2" - 6'4"; Displacement 7,400 lbs.; Ballast 2,400 lbs.; Sail Area 376.2 sq. ft.

F-27
Classic Multihull

We don't get a lot of multihulls to review, but there are definitely more and more of them appearing. We can debate the merits of multi versus monohull, then add light displacement versus heavy and throw in transom stern versus canoe stern. The fact is we all have our own sailing style and that style may have little to do with VMG.

I have noted over the years that odds are the more high-tech the sailor's occupation, the more low-tech the style of the boat. I have one character styled boat owned by an astronaut and pictures of an F-14 on the wall taken by a pilot of another F-14 who owns a Tayana 37. It may be the down vest-pickup truck syndrome. The CPA, after spending a brain-breaking day at the office, comes home, puts on blue jeans, a work shirt and a down vest. He hops into his pickup truck and heads out to the grocery store for a nice bottle of young and spicy Cabernet. The fighter pilot may want to go for a sail without watching the dials all afternoon. One way or another, we enjoy escaping on our boats. I don't look for logical, three decimal place arguments for justifying boat selection any more. I did once. Now I am happy just getting out on the water and the type of boat has little to do with it if I am just out for a nice day-sail.

So I sit there, bobbing along in my friend's Blowfish 29. There is little to do other than try and make the boat go faster. Okay, let's ease the genoa halyard and pull the traveler up to weather a bit. See, there's an additional half a knot. The quest for speed and sailing efficiency becomes a centering device for the rest of life at sea. With this in mind, it is easy how many sailors are attracted to the world of multihulls with their sometimes delivered promise of higher speeds. The move from mono to multihull seems to be more of a philosophical move than a VMG decision.

I don't think I have seen any multihull design capture the attention of monohull sailors as the F-27 has. The F-27 combines unusual features that, while none is new, blend well together in this design to produce an attractive vessel. Probably the most important aspect of this design is trailerability. My pal John owns an F-27 and he keeps it on the trailer all the time. From the road to under way, sailing takes about half an hour. This opens up a new world of potential cruising grounds without resorting to a charter. Of course, the trailerability of this design is made possible by the folding outriggers and the resultant trailerable beam of 8'6". One of the major drawbacks to this is the difficulty of finding dock space. This is a non-problem with this vessel.

The F-27 is not cheap nor is it available tomorrow at your local dealer. You are going to have to pay around $66,000 for a well equipped F-27 and unless you can find a dealer willing to sell his demo, you may have to wait six months for delivery. This and the fact that more than 100 F-27s have been sold in the last 12 months indi-

cates something is happening here.

The dealer of the F-27 is New Zealander Ian Farrier who settled in Queensland, Australia, and started with a folding 18-footer. Farrier now lives in Southern California and runs Corsair Marine.

When you bring up the subject of performance and trimarans you will invariably hear, "They don't go to weather and they capsize." Given the right circumstances, you can most probably capsize any unballasted boat regardless of the number of hulls it has. I once capsized a keelboat I owned that had a 50 percent ballast to displacement ratio. "We'll be up in a second, mates." Right. The Swan 65 *Sayula* capsized as did the C&C 61 *Sorcery*. They did, however, pop back up on their own with *Sayula* going on to win the race. F-27s have completed numerous ocean passages and ocean races with 250-mile days being commonplace.

I called my friend John and asked him about the speed of the F-27. Everybody has the day when they hit 27 knots as they beam reached across the sound in their Blowfish 29. I was not interested in optimum max speeds. I was interested in one thing. "Tell me which boats you sail boat-for-boat with on the race course." We both race in the same local fleet so benchmarks were easy to establish. On a typical Puget Sound day, the F-27 would sail boat-for-boat with the J/35 and easily outsail a J/40. Speeds of over 15 knots are well documented and easily achieved in a breeze. Upwind speeds of nine knots and better are also claimed. Heel angle rarely exceeds 12 degrees, making movement on board the F-27 easy.

Does this design have drawbacks? Weighing only 2,800 pounds, it should not surprise you that the F-27 is not roomy and spacious. Nor does it have a lot of storage space or copious tankage. You should not put two anchors on the bow and carry 300 feet of 5/16ths chain with your F-27. The accommodations are tight and roughly equivalent to a 26 or 27-foot monohull.

The unballasted and unsinkable F-27 is built with PVC core using S-glass, with Kevlar and carbon fiber in the stressed areas. The laminate is "vacupressured" to optimize the structural properties. The outriggers are held in place with one bolt each, although the bolt is not needed due to the loads being absorbed by the folding struts beneath the outrigger arms. This folding system was designed by Farrier in 1973 and has proven trouble-free.

John just called. "Do you want to go for a sail?"

"Well, it's blowing zero to three knots and I'm deep into these reviews so I will pass for now."

I promise, dear reader, that I will take John up on his offer soon and give you a detailed account of my sail aboard the F-27.

Farrier Marine, Ian Farrier, P.O. Box 40675, Bellevue, WA 98015. (425) 462-5349. **www.f-boat.com**

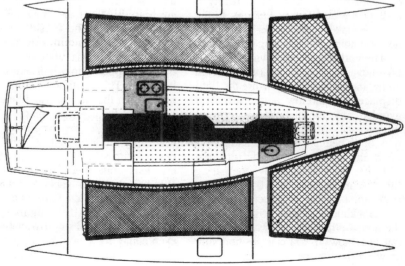

LOA 27'1"; LWL 26'3"; Beam 19'1"; Folded Beam 8'5"; Draft 1'2" - 4'11"; Displacement 2,300 lbs.; Sail Area 456 sq. ft.

Islander 28
Classic Cruiser-Racer

I was retained by Islander Yachts to design their new 28 auxiliary. The concept they were after was a fast, raceable and very comfortable, small family cruising yacht. There was the feeling from the beginning that we should not give IOR domination over the design of the yacht. With the shaky grounds that the IOR is on in many parts of the country, we thought that a better approach would be to design a yacht with good boat speed and to put IOR rated speed second.

Along with this concept was the desire to design a high powered yacht that would be at home in the many areas that have predominantly light air. Toward this end we decided to offer two rigs: the standard tall rig and the shorter San Francisco rig. I prefer to have them called the tall rig and the standard rig, but the tall rig is the standard one and the short rig, which is not really short, is the optional rig. Either one used in the areas they were intended for is a high powered rig for this yacht.

The interior was to be so good that it would set a new standard for small yacht interiors. Islander asked me to put in an interior that would do justice to a 32-footer and without good to the bulging topsides look. I knew this was going to be difficult, but I had not counted upon the help I would receive from the Islander management staff.

Two last requirements on the design were that it be of relatively light displacement, and that it have a maximum beam of 10 feet. This last requirement interested me immensely because it would be a challenge to design a good performing 28-foot yacht with this beam.

I designed the hull with relatively short overhangs and a wider than normal IOR style transom and stern. The reason for the wide transom is that I determined a minimum size space for a comfortable cockpit with benches long enough to sleep on etc., and designed the stern to accommodate this cockpit. This feature does not suit the IOR but in reality it adds power and reserve stability to the yacht. It makes for better performance in heavy running and reaching conditions.

The midships section was chosen to take advantage of the maximum beam and at the same time to ensure the light displacement and low wetted surface. I avoided any tumblehome to prevent the necessity of a split mold. I put the maximum beam at the sheer and gave a good amount of flare to the topsides. This can be imagined by comparing the maximum beam of 10 feet to the waterline beam of 7.32 feet.

An additional feature of this shape is the added affect of crew ballast on the rail in a blow. If you can position your crew on the weather rail, and the combined center of gravity is .5 feet further outboard than your competitor, you have gained an additional 720 pounds of righting moment. I used four crewmembers weighing 180 pounds each. It was intended that the Islander 28 fit into the Half Ton class. If you intend to race in this competitive class, the extra foot pounds of righting moment become very important. Apart from affecting performance, this great beam on deck gives the yacht a good amount of side deck and creates a more open feeling below.

The rudder is faired into a partial skeg and is a semi-balanced type. I did not use a full length skeg for a number of reasons. It is very difficult to lay-up a skeg and still ensure the integrity of the hull. When you use a one-piece mold, a skeg does detract from your light air performance due to the increase in wetted surface and a few other minor reasons. The design problem was to utilize enough of the hull as a skeg to eliminate the torque on the rudder from prop wash. This is a very annoying feature of some yachts with balanced spade rudders. It was also hoped that the partial skeg would impart better tracking qualities to the yacht than a true spade rudder. The displacement to length ratio of the yacht is 220. This is based upon a displacement of 6,000 pounds and a waterline length of 23 feet. I have sailed the Islander 28, and I can report on the relative success of this feature. It is a fast boat in light airs and very responsive.

The first Islander 28 was raced in Newport Beach, California, and did very well. Initially the yacht was a little tender, so we added 300 pounds of lead to the ballast and increased the draft 3 inches. This has been an excellent improvement. The helm is extremely light and well balanced. The yacht tracks well, although not as well as a yacht with a full skeg. We have almost eliminated the feel of the prop wash. When you apply a lot of rudder angle, you can feel the torque a little, but it's not enough to whip the tiller out of a relaxed grip and spin the rudder into the turning propeller.

The interior is really the high point of the Islander 28. I feel it's the best interior of any yacht of this size, but I am biased. I'll let the drawings speak for themselves. The finish is all teak, and the interior is built into the yacht rather than being a fiberglass module that is dropped into a hull and glassed in place. This method ensures better integrity of the structure and better utilization of the available space.

As I gain more experience as a designer, I am learning that some of my designs surpass my expectations and others don't quite meet my expectations. When I design a yacht, I retain the designer's ideal of the finished product. I don't mind saying that only rarely does the product exceed my expectations, or even equal my ideal. Happily I can say that due to the input from the people at Islander, and my own perseverance, the Islander 28 has surpassed all my expectations. I am very pleased with the yacht.

Islander Yachts, **www.yachts.com/builders/sailing-yachts/Islander-Yachts.html**

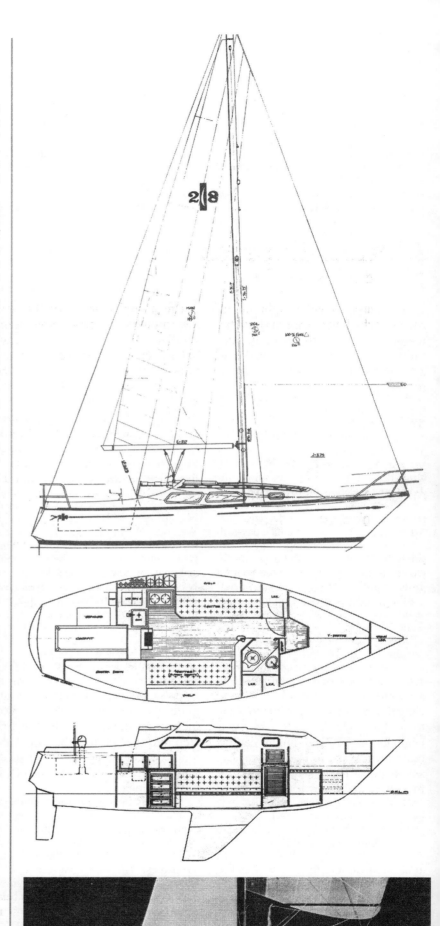

LOA 27'11"; DWL 23'; Beam 10'; Draft 5'3"; Displacement 6,000 lbs.; Sail Area 361 sq. ft. (standard rig), 326 sq. ft. (San Francisco rig).

Alerion-Express
Classic Daysailer

It is easy to get caught up in Mega yacht fever. Rare and exotic materials punctuated with gold fixtures and objects of art for ambiance work skillfully together to remove any feeling at all that you are on a boat. Wait a minute! I thought we wanted to feel like we were on a boat. I wonder what goes

... A boat that has the romance of yesterday and the performance of today ...

through the head of a mega yacht owner as he sits on the upper fantail and watches Russell Upsomerup zoom around the bay, singlehanded in his Alerion-Express. "Gosh, I wish I had one."

There's a lot to say for the feeling of power and megalomania that comes with steering a huge yacht in a breeze, but the best way to appreciate the joys of sailing is to reduce it to its basic elements. If you are a beginner, an El Toro dinghy can do quite nicely. I have to drape myself across the little eight-footer with my feet usually dangling in the lee wash.

Take it up a notch and you can tackle a Laser dinghy. You will get some wet lessons on how to jibe in a breeze and your tummy muscles will spring back to life. When the Laser begins to bore you I suggest a windsurfer. Now you are physically part of the hardware of sailing. The slightest change in body attitude will result in performance changes that you will feel from head to toe.

These simple approaches to enjoying life under sail will reacquaint you with the basics that probably were responsible for your initial attraction to sailing, i.e., working with the elements, self-sufficiency and that strange feeling that comes with having mastery over wind and wave.

I'm going to try over the next few months to bring you some smaller boats and the Carl Schumacher designed Alerion-Express is a great example. The general aesthetic model for this design is straight out of Nat Herreshoff's 1916 design *Alerion*.

The gentle sweep of the sheer is balanced by moderate overhangs and freeboard that is low by today's standards. Beam is narrow, and the hull shape looks to be moderate in all aspects. The D/L ratio is 168. Below the waterline the design shows a modern fin keel and a semi-balanced spade rudder. To me this is the most exciting mix of design features. Take an attractive, dated topsides look and blend it with performance characteristics below the waterline. The result is a boat that has the romance of yesterday and the performance of today.

You could cruise the Alerion-Express. The accommodations are quite spartan, but there is a w.c. tucked under the V-berth. The first step into the cabin is the top of the icebox and a camp stove would do nicely. A Yanmar diesel is available as an option.

The rig is a fractional rig with self-tacking jib. The mainsheet leads forward from the Harken traveller to a barney post in the middle of the cockpit. The SA/D ratio is 20.97. I think that this sail area coupled with a healthy ballast-to-displacement ratio will result in a stiff and fast ride.

The Alerion-Express is currently being built by Tillotson-Pearson in Rhode Island. All gear is first rate and the overall look is one of a sophisticated and refined small yacht.

Pearson Yachts, 373 Market St., Warren, RI 02885. (401) 247-3000. **www.pearsonyachts.com**.

Designer Carl Schumacher, 1921 Clement Ave., Bldg. 13A, Alameda, CA 94501.

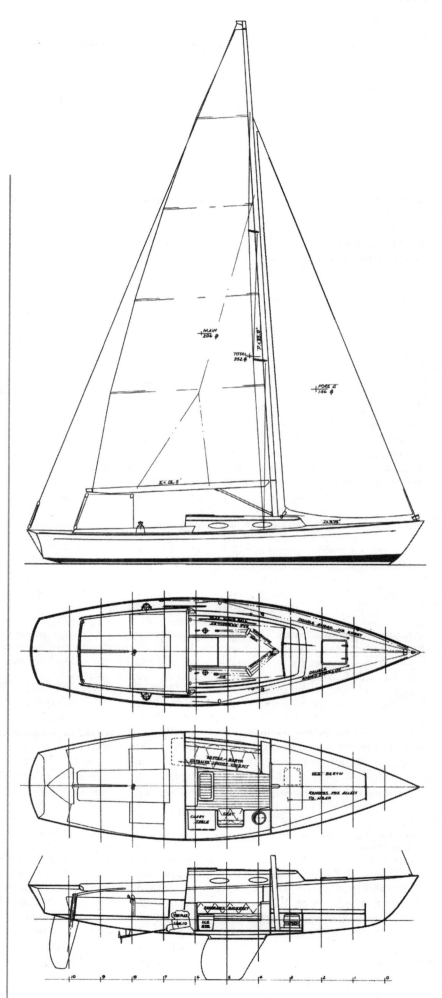

LOA 28'3"; LWL 22'10"; Beam 8'2"; Draft 4'6"; Displacement 4,400 lbs.; Ballast 2,000 lbs.; Sail Area 352; SA/D 20.97; D/L 168; Auxiliary Yanmar JGM 10.

Catalina 30
Classic Cruiser-Racer

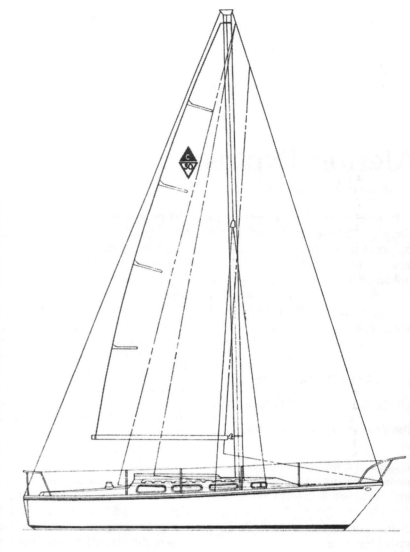

It is not often that a brand new design aimed at the cruiser-racer market starts off its career by winning the "biggest" ocean race in the world. By biggest I mean having the largest number of entries and I am, of course, referring to the Newport-Ensenada race. The 1976 Ensenada race was won by a Catalina 30, *So Long IV*, and it was not merely a victory in an obscure cruising class but first overall. This is very impressive considering the relatively short overall length of 29'11".

The displacement to length ratio of Frank Butler's Catalina 30 design is 291. From the plan view of the interior you can get a feeling for the immense beam of the Catalina 30, 10'10". The estimated IOR rating is 23.4 and there are two versions available. The standard model has a draft of 5'3" and the shoal draft model has a draft of 4'4". I would surmise from the healthy displacement figure and the large amount of beam that the Catalina 30 would be a very stiff boat and at her best in a breeze.

The deck layout features a very large cockpit with good access to the lazarette and comfortably deep seat backs. The mainsheet traveller is located aft of the main cockpit seats and this frees the top of the cabin trunk for a huge sliding hatch. I can honestly say that it is probably the largest sliding companionway hatch I have ever seen. There is another hatch molded into the cabin trunk forward and a flush anchor well in the bow. The genoa track runs along the rail which by my estimation gives a sheeting angle of about 11 degrees. I would prefer to see this angle closer to 7 or 8 degrees. My main criticism of this deck plan would be that the width of the

main hatch makes it almost impossible to lead lines aft on the house-top. On the plus side, the cockpit appears to be exceptionally comfortable.

In surveying the interior layout of the Catalina 30, there is very little omitted. There is a large double

The cockpit appears to be exceptionally comfortable.

size quarter berth to starboard opposite a comfortable and well laid out U-shaped galley, double sinks are standard. The chart table is rather small, but still adequate and certainly better than nothing at all. The dinette is large and the table stows against the forward bulkhead. The auxiliary engine space is under the aft end of the settee and there is the option of Atomic 4 or diesel power. The Catalina 30 is built with a fiberglass interior liner and a substantial amount of teak joiner work.

Once in a while I am reminded of the contributions that racing yacht design has made to cruising yacht design. Rating rules such as the CCA and the IOR with their emphasis on beam have provided the impetus for the designers to learn how to employ wide beam without paying a substantial price in performance. In fact, in some cases outstanding racing boats have been exceptionally "fat," i.e. *Finisterre* and *Aggressive II*. The Catalina 30 employs wide beam and enjoys a spacious deck and comfortable interior and at the same time has proven herself to be a very able performer.

Catalina Yachts, 21200 Victory Blvd., Woodland Hills, CA 91367. **www.catalinayachts.com** *(818) 884-7700.*

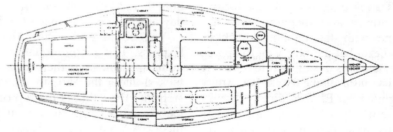

LOA 29'11"; LWL 25'; Beam 10'10"; Draft 5'3", (shoal draft 4'4"); Displacement 10,200 lbs.; Ballast 4,200 lbs.; Sail Area 446 sq. ft.

Hobie 33
Classic Cruiser-Racer

In the back of my mind I can visualize a vintage "All in the Family" scene with Archie Bunker complaining that "the ULDBs are moving in and takin' over the neighborhood." I hear harbingers of this at the various groups I talk to. I think we can relax and watch with interest as the ULDB movement takes its appropriate place in the yachting world. After all, meter boats, scows, IOR boats, planing dinghies, etc. have all found their niches. It still remains a fact that for speed around an Olympic course in a variety of wind conditions, it is hard to beat a boat with a displacement to length ratio of around 160 to 200. The present crop of "grand prix" IOR boats represents excellent blends of proportions.

Still the urge for more knots per foot of overall length is very powerful. There is something satisfying in sailing a small boat on a speed par with bigger yachts. As a designer it pleases me to see constant change and stimulus for design improvement and the ULDBs have certainly stretched our conceptions of suitable displacement numbers.

The Hobie 33 shows quite rounded sections and little effort to capture much form stability in the hull shape. This is offset by the use of a bulb keel. The sail plan shows the profile of the bulb well and it does surprise me that the bulb is as fat as is shown. It looks like the maximum thickness of the bulb is about 30 percent of the chord length aft. With stability ensured by this keel configuration, the designers have drawn a hull shape with low wetted surface and arc-like sections. This hull shape is distinctive to that of Bill Lee's work and certainly different from that of the Olson 30. Beam and hull power have been carefully carried aft to station 8, then the hull tapers fairly abruptly. The displacement to length ratio for the Hobie 33 is 59.79. Let's just stop here and put that figure into historical perspective. The classic Westsail 32 had a D/L of 435, the Valiant 40 is 264, the Cal 40 is 242, the S&S Flyer 202 and the Olson 30 are 75.

I am often asked if there isn't a sacrifice in safety and strength associated with ultra-lights. Ultra-lights require very careful construction and there is no room for sloppy glass and joinerwork. Remember that while there is less holding the boat together, there is less to hold together and rig size and loads are relatively proportionate to the displacement. I raced on a Santa Cruz 33 one night and this sailboat had been heavily cam-

paigned for the past four years. I looked the boat over carefully and found it to be structurally as sound as the day it was launched.

Lessons learned with the Hobie catamarans probably led to the 33 being kept to an eight-foot beam to allow trailering. This becomes a major design consideration and probably is the culprit that led directly to the bulb keel. The keel is retractable to help with trailering and the boat can be launched from a ramp. The benefits of this are obvious. For instance you can bring your boat home to work on it during the off season.

Hobie Alter played with this design of his for several years. The finished product is the result of strenuous prototype testing. This is something that many manufacturers cannot afford to get into. Many of my own new designs are built verbatim from the plans and it is my job to get it right the first time. with a prototype program you can get the boat right the first time then go ahead and get the boat better. Keel shapes can be evaluated and the rig can be refined and optimally mated to the hull characteristics. The Hobie has a large foretriangle fractional rig. The mast is very slightly aft of station 4. The spreaders are swept aft approximately 28 degrees and there are single aft lowers. No running backs are shown and I would guess that the sweep angle on the spreaders will help keep the luff of the jib from sagging. Off the wind the large foretriangle allows a huge spinnaker with a nice low aspect ratio, ball-like shape. This is a powerful sail and a relatively easy spinnaker to use compared to a tall, sausage-like spinnaker. Until I sail on this yacht, I can't say how the balance of upwind and downwind performance compares but I can assure you that this boat will be very fast off the wind. The sail area to displacement ratio is 28.

As you might guess, the Hobie 33 has minimal headroom under that sleek cabin trunk, but the accommodations look comfortable and include a galley that folds into the settee back. There will not be many legs of lamb cooked aboard Hobie 33s.

Hobie Alter established the state of the art in multihulls and this is his first venture into monohulls. If we were to stop and count the number of ULDBs on the market in 1982 when this came out, I would guess that we would get a number around 30. Be careful, I heard there was one moving in down the dock from your boat.

Hobie Cat, P.O. Box 1008, 4925 Oceanside Blvd., Oceanside, CA 92054. (888) 462-4321. **www.hobiecat.com**

Design Review Postscript
Sailing the Hobie 33

My friend Tom Ling called and asked if I would like to skipper a Hobie 33 in a local race. "Would I?" Of course, I would. The race was held under the PHRF system and we corrected to second place after finishing first.

I found the boat a masterpiece of manufacturing and an exceptionally responsive and rewarding boat to sail. Upwind we were fast and very close-winded but with a disconcerting touch of lee helm. It was fun to walk over Olson 30s for a change. The boat has a feeling of power despite its light displacement. Once we turned the weather mark and cleared our air, the boat walked away from the com-

petition with ease. I am not Dennis Conner on the wheel, but the Hobie made me feel as if I were for a while.

I found the outboard motor system and the lifting keel arrangement worked out extremely well and real advances in the field of trailerable yachts. The detail to the tooling was well done.

I have two complains. I prefer a slight weather helm to the lee helm this particular Hobie showed. This could possibly be tuned out with adjustment to mast rake or possibly the mast will have to be moved very slightly. I found the position at the tiller quite tiring and would have preferred wider cockpit coamings or wider side decks. Now the coamings and side decks are about equal in width and neither is wide enough to sit on comfortably.

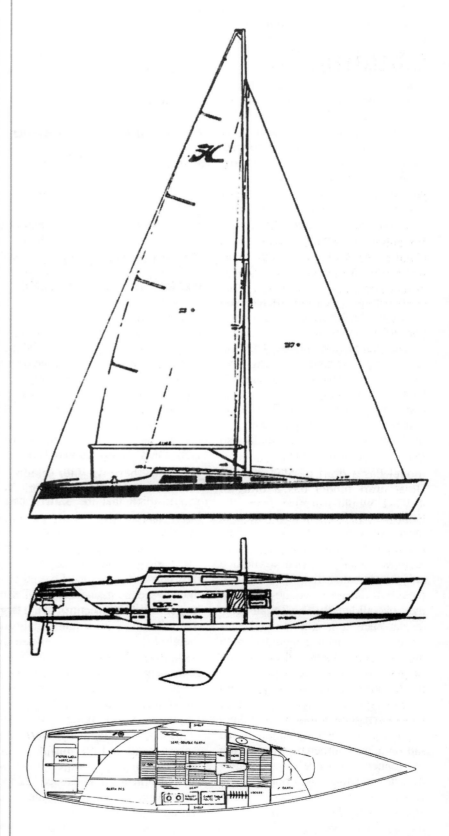

LOA 33'; LWL 30'6"; Beam 8'; Draft 5'6"; Displacement 3,800 lbs.; Ballast 1,800 lbs.; Sail Area 429 sq. ft.

Tartan Ten
Classic One-design

It should be obvious now that there is a distinct move toward the one-design racing concept. without the restrictions of rating rule, this allows the designer to create a yacht that has all the emphasis on speed and comfort. This new S&S design, to be built by Tartan Marine, is an innovative "day-racer" conceived in the tradition of the popular but slowly waning type as exemplified by international One-Designs on the East Coast and PCs on the West Coast.

I suppose the European equivalent would be the Dragon class. I love these old designs, but they are past the "state of the art" level in terms of design efficiency. The Tartan Ten while innovative in terms of concept today, utilizes proven hull form and a widely accepted rig. These features are directly developed from other designs. Yet, the total package presents an original picture. Of course one could argue that it is an updating of the IOD and the PC, but the resultant personality of the Tartan Ten is very fresh.

In racing on various yachts with Jill, my wife, I have come to reason that 30' is about the largest yacht a woman can race and not be at a physical strength handicap. In my own case I found Jill to be a very effective half ton crewmember but of dubious assistance on a two tonner. The Tartan Ten could be sailed quite competitively by two couples. It would also make a dandy singlehander.

Again, while this is not an IOR design, there is some hint of influence in the hull shape. This I do not attribute to IORisms but in general to recent advancements in hull design. Basically, the hull is 3/4 ton size although the displacement would fit a half tonner better. Keep in mind that most IOR designs are quite heavy for their overall length. The Tartan Ten's displacement to length ratio indicates lightness. The displacement to length ratio is 136. I like the rakish lines of the hull. They are accentuated nicely by the flush deck molding. If I were asked to give a relative indication of the performance of this design I think that I would expect the Tartan Ten to sail on a level somewhere between a 3/4 tonner and a one tonner with a definite advantage over both in light conditions.

As you might expect, the accommodations are minimal, but they are functional. There is a small galley forward of two settee berths. The head area appears to be surprisingly roomy and it is opposite a good-sized hanging locker. There is a large double berth forward in the V-berth position. Sitting headroom is about the most you will get with this design. But the positive side of that compromise is the good looking profile achieved with the flush deck.

The cockpit has been given full priority on this design. The long seats are contoured and there are consoles port and starboard for sailing instruments. This convenient division of the cockpit makes for a helmsperson's

The designers have chosen a 4/5s rig to avoid the cost of a complex headsail inventory.

area. I would suppose that one-design rules for this class would prohibit hiking of any sort. The Tartan Ten's cockpit design should make for very comfortable sit-in type sailing as opposed to sit-on type sailing.

One advantage over the older designs that puts the Tartan Ten way out ahead is the inclusion of inboard power. I know there are some of you that feel engines do not belong in this type of yacht, but sailing on Puget Sound with its strong tides may make a believer out of you. I heartily endorse the inboard. The engine used is the OMC 15 horsepower head with a Saildrive gear unit. If my experience with this engine is any indication, I should think that the Tartan should have enough speed under power to make your socks roll up and down.

Again, the designers have chosen a "4/5s" rig to avoid the cost of a complex headsail inventory. I would have liked to see the mainsheet traveller be longer to aid in the control of the large main. As it is, it is quite small and merely bridges the span between the cockpit seats. The sail area to displacement ratio is 23.3 which definitely accelerates my desire to sail one of these exciting yachts.

Standard equipment includes: inboard power, fuel and water tanks, icebox, head and 56 amp hour battery. The only option offered will be spinnaker gear. As an Etchells 22 fan, I can confidently say that this yacht should be fun to sail and race.

Tartan Marine Co., 1920 Fairport Nursery, Fairport Harbor, OH 44077. (888) 330-3484. **www.tartanyachts.com**

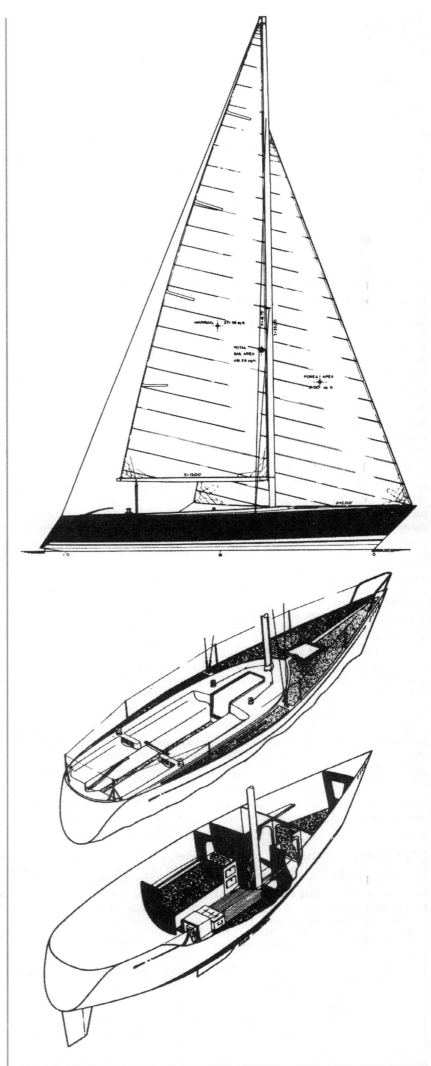

LOA 33'; DWL 27'; Beam 9'1"; Draft 6'; Displacement 6,000 lbs.; Sail Area 481 sq. ft.

Sabre 34
Classic Cruiser-Racer

The Sabre 34 is an interesting blend of somewhat "softened" IOR hull shape and a rather cruisey interior. The design is by Roger Hewson and the yacht is built by Sabre Yachts of South Casco, Maine. In perusing this design you should keep in mind that we are in a blending period now. In the next few years you will see various elements of IOR design used in the design of yachts with no intention of racing under that particular rule. The Sabre 34 looks to be a relatively fast yacht that might fair well in local club races. Overall, however, she appears to be a blend, an attempt at marrying the desirable IOR features with cruising parameters. I am sure that some of you are scratching your heads and asking "What are the desirable IOR features?" Wide beam is certainly one, another would be a relatively long waterline and resulting higher hull speed. Improved keel and rudder shape for performance and control can certainly be considered positive aspects of the rule. Also, the deep chested forward sections and the filled out bustle area allow, respectfully, more cabin sole forward and more room for engine location aft. Consider these features along with the overall additive of very efficient performance on the wind and you have components that can add design value to any cruising yacht. It is each particular designers job to decide how he will combine and modify the all out IOR manifestation of these features. Mr. Hewson's approach to the design of this high performance cruising yacht leans heavily toward a pure IOR approach.

To generalize you could say the hull form of the Sabre 34 was quite "Petersonesque." I do not have a copy of the lines, therefore, I cannot speak with any authority of the sectional shape of the Sabre 34. But, I can surmise by the specified dimensions of the hull profile that her shape would closely resemble something between a Peterson style Three Quarter Tonner and a One Tonner. The reason evades me why the builders chose this in between size. It may have something to do with a common feeling in the yachting industry right now that building a production ton yacht is the kiss of death for a builder. By hitting this intermediate size Sabre Yachts can avoid being labeled a has been one tonner or three quarter tonner. There again it may be, when we look at the interior, that may be, when we look at the interior, that we will find the real reason this overall size was chosen. There is a problem here, I am trying to determine the displacement/ length ratio and using the figures in the brochure, I keep coming up with 361. It is not unusual for me to punch wrong numbers on my Hewlett-Packard but I have come up with the same answer three times. Ah ha! I think I found it, the manufacturer lists the waterline length at 23'6", but using my trusty tie-strip I determine the waterline length to be closer to 26. This gives a revised displacement/ length ratio of 266 which is more in keeping with yachts of this type.

As I mentioned before, a glance at the interior may reveal the reason that the designer and builder chose this in between ton level size. There appears to be very little omitted from this interior. While it is certainly the epitome of the standard interior in terms of its layout, it displays good taste in its straightforwardness. The galley is U-shaped and opposite a larger quarter berth and navigation station. The main cabin table stows against the bulkhead and the head is large enough that you could shower in it comfortably. There is a bilge sump in the keel fairing. This is a feature often left out of racing yachts. If you have spent much time with a sponge in one hand and a bucket in the other crawling around on your knees trying to sop up the bilge, you will appreciate the bilge sump.

The sail area to displacement ratio is 16.91. This indicates a relatively high powered yacht that should perform very well in light air. While the rig in general appears to be a pure IOR derivative, the use of double lower shrouds is one exception. In a yacht of this size I feel the sloop rig is still the most suitable for cruising shorthanded. It is clean, simple, and will reward you with excellent performance.

Sabre Yachts prides themselves on a perfectionist approach to their building. The standard auxiliary engine is an Atomic 4. There is a 20 gallon aluminum fuel tank and two 19-gallon water tanks under the main cabin berths. Oiled Burma teak is used on all visible surfaces and the cabin sole is striped teak.

There seem to be fewer and fewer yachtsmen who are willing to invest their money on a yacht with insured obsolescence and questionable resale value. The all out racing yacht is an exotic pet that potentially can turn on the owner. The Sabre 34 seems a very sensible alternative.

Sabre Yachts, P.O. Box 134, South Casco, ME 04077. (207) 655-5050. **www.sabreyachts.com**

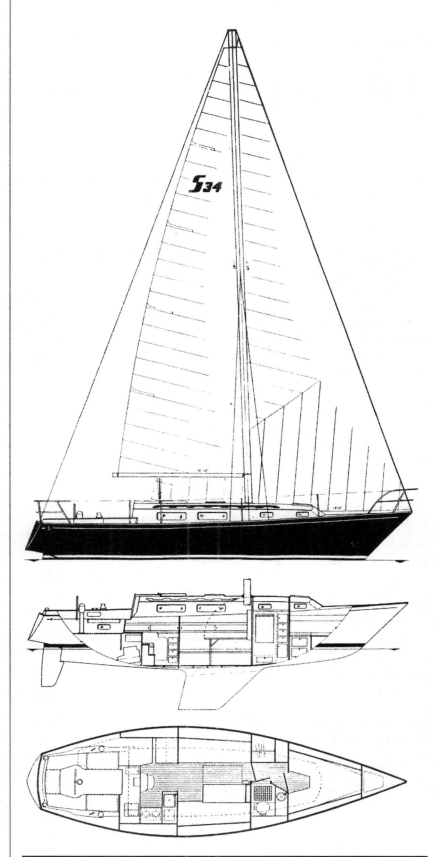

LOA 33'8"; LWL 26'3"; Beam 10'6"; Draft 5'6"; Displacement 10,500 lbs.; Ballast 4,400 lbs.; Sail Area 507 sq. ft.

Alberg 35
Classic Cruiser-Racer

The drawings are dated 1962 and 1963. The designer is Carl Alberg, and the yacht is the classic Alberg 35 built by Pearson.

The Alberg 35 represents a very successful production yacht from both sales and performance aspects.

The Alberg 35 was designed toward the tail end of the CCA era and at a time when the distinctions between the offshore racing yacht and the racer-cruiser were not as well marked as they are today. There was still that feeling that an offshore racing yacht should possess certain wholesome qualities, and that the sport of sailboat racing should take place in a gentlemanly manner. The Alberg 35 fared well under the CCA rule and shows some of the earmarks of a CCA "designed to the dots" boat, i.e. rather slab topsides, short waterline, powerful ends and a squatty rig. But, this was a true dual purpose yacht, and this is substantiated by the fact that I have three friends all living aboard Alberg 35s at this time. They are indeed a loyal and loving group of boat owners. While there is little question regarding the rather dated design of the Alberg 35, the relevance of this boat comes from the Alberg's subtle blend of proportions that make it work very well under all conditions.

As I previously mentioned, this hull was designed to the CCA rule and represents a state of the art racer-cruiser for 1962.

The beam is narrow by today's standards at 9'8". It is rare when a 30-footer today doesn't have 10 feet of beam. Note the manner in which the beam is drawn out into the ends of the Alberg. The bow is quite full and the stern overhang shows excellent shoulders to help extend the sailing length when the boat is heeled. The underbody shows the cutaway keel with an attached rudder on a raked rudder post.

Dick Carter's *Rabbit* and *Tina* were just around the corner and would soon put an end to the full keel approach to racing yachts. We should make a distinction between this type of keel configuration and the Atkin INGRID type of full keel. While the Alberg's rudder is attached to the keel and the keel itself could hardly be called a fin, this is still stretching the definition of a full keeled yacht. Perhaps "cutaway full keel" would be more accurate. The displacement to length ratio of the Alberg 35 is 406. There is some danger in trying to relate this displacement to length ratio to a modern racing yacht's D/L ratio. The D/L ratio of the Alberg is

distorted toward the high end of the scale to accommodate a better rating in the same way IOR boats tend to be distorted toward the low end of the scale. The measuring of the actual DWL, under the CCA rule tended to shorten the DWL. Under the IOR, the DWL is not measured at all and girths are used to determine sailing length.

In studying the interior of the Alberg 35, I am initially struck by the large cockpit with a true lazarette hatch aft of the mainsheet traveller. The layout of the accommodations is very straightforward and it would be helpful to compare this interior with that of the Islander 36 designed in 1970 after the introduction of the IOR. There is little I can say about the layout of the Alberg. Obviously it works well.

The Alberg 35 was available in two rig configurations. The CCA permitted a mizzen staysail to be carried without any penalty to the sail area measurements. The mizzen staysail was free. This feature of the rule produced a lot of yawl rigs, especially in areas where there was a lot of reaching involved in the racing. So, I'm sorry to disappoint some of you, but the mizzen was actually a rule beating feature of the Alberg similar in intent to the bumps and creases that IOR boats display.

Both the sloop and the yawl used the same mast location, and a quick look at the interior plan will show that the mast was stepped on a bridge between compression posts. Note that the mast is rather forward on the Alberg resulting in a small foretriangle and a large low aspect ratio mainsail. This conveniently put the mainsheet traveller behind the cockpit and got the chainplates out of the main cabin. The small foretriangle gave us 170 percent genoas and quite small winches to handle the genoa. As winches developed, the foretriangles became larger and mainsails were reduced to almost token helm trimming sails. We have now seen the reversal of this trend with the advent of the competitive IOR fractional rigs.

One of the benefits of the Alberg's rig was that the boat could be sailed effectively under main alone in a breeze. This is quite a trick with a modern IOR sloop with ribbon main. The sail area to displacement ratio of the Alberg 35 is 16.1.

The Alberg 35 has been fun to review. Gil, Betty, Joe and Mr. Abraben, you have nice boats.

Pearson Yachts, 373 Market St., Warren, RI 02885. (401) 247-3000. **www.pearsonyachts.com**
Designer: Carl Alberg.

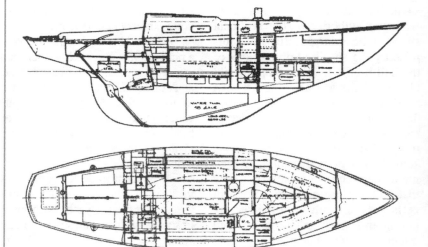

LOA 34'9"; LWL 24'; Beam 9.8"; Draft 5'2"; Displacement 12,600 lbs.; Ballast 5,300 lbs.; Sail Area 545 sq. ft. (sloop), 583 sq. ft. (yawl).

Ericson 35, C&C 35
Classic Cruiser-Racers

For a change, I have decided to combine these two 1983 boats into one review. This will make a comparison much easier and it should be fun. Both C&C and Ericson have done 35s before and these newer versions are both very different than their predecessors. Are these boats both intended for the same market and is a direct comparison really fair? The answer to the first part of the question is no. They are not intended for the exact same market. The answer to the second part of the question is also no, but close enough.

The main difference is that the C&C appears to be much more oriented toward the IOR and can be considered a racer-cruiser, while the Ericson with its smooth midships section is more of a cruiser-racer. Although the difference in actual boat speed may be slight, the difference in rated speed might give the C&C the edge on the race course.

I think the relevance in comparing these two similar yachts is in taking a look at two very different answers to almost the identical problem. There is little doubt that C&C has been the most successful production yacht builder in the past few years. They have tooled many different models but have maintained a very consistent approach to design.

Ericson has been a little quieter recently but they have added energy to their line by splitting it into a racing line designed by Ron Holland and a cruising line designed by Bruce King. The C&C line has progressed much like the Mercedes-Benz line of automobiles. The changes are slight and the parent style is maintained through each model change. Ericson has been less consistent with their design direction because they do not have the benefit of in-house design teams. This does not mean that C&C produces better boats than Ericson, it simply means that the numbers show C&C to be the more successful, and as a designer I want to know why.

Any time you line up a C&C against another production yacht and judge the two by looks alone, I think the C&C will win. While the Ericson is a very good-looking yacht, I prefer the balance and

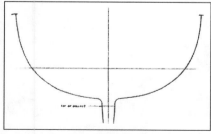

Ericson 35 station 5

general aesthetics of the C&C. This is purely my opinion and subjective but I can find no fault at all with the aesthetic balance of the C&C. Cabin trunk, bow profile, stern shape and sheer spring are all near perfect.

The Ericson with its raised counter and more pronounced overhang aft does not appeal so much to my eye. The Ericson does carry the cabin trunk fur-

ther forward and with more height. This has a positive effect on the accommodations by providing extra headroom but a negative effect on the appearance. It is very difficult to argue with headroom.

The basic canoe-body profiles of the two boats show some contrasts with the Ericson having more rocker and a steeper angle to the run as consequence. To my eye it is doubtful if that degree of overhang aft at that distance from the DWL will do much good when it comes to extending the DWL under sail. The Ericson's rudder has been pulled forward under the bustle and the C&C rudder is aft and butts up against the counter to use

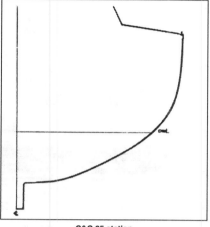

C&C 35 station

it as an end plate. The displacement to length ratio for the Ericson is 241 and the C&C is 220.

The keels are quite different. The Ericson comes with a shoal keel or a deep keel. The deep keel is a typical Bruce King style keel with the trailing edge raked forward. This may help to make the maximum thickness line more vertical and improve the general performance of the keel. The C&C keel rakes the trailing edge aft and shows little difference between the chord length at the root and the chord length at the tip. This may reflect an effort to get more lead weight lower in the fin and increase stability.

When you compare the interiors it becomes obvious that the Ericson is the bigger boat in terms of interior volume. The Ericson shows a very clever layout, leaving nothing to be desired with the possible exception of more hanging locker space aft. The C&C has a more conventional approach to the layout and follows the basic layout "A" play. I would have to give the nod to the Ericson for interior design while at the same time realizing that they had more room to work with.

If I have made people in either camp mad I can only hope that I have made them equally mad on both sides. Comparisons are fun.

Ericson Yachts, 1301 E. Orange-thorpe Ave., Fullerton, CA 92831. **www.ericsonyachts.com**.

C&C Yachts, 1920 Fairport Nursery Rd., Fairport Harbor, OH 44077. **www.c-cyachts.com** (440) 354-3111.

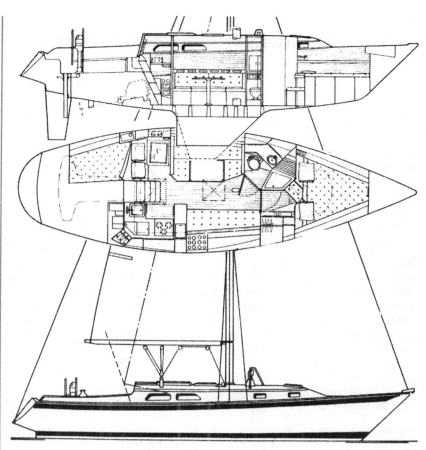

Ericson 35

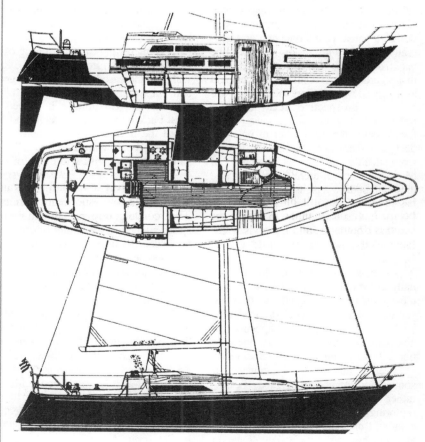

C&C 35

ERICSON 35
LOA 35'6"; LWL 28'10½"; Beam 11'4"; Draft 4'11½" or 6'2"; Displacement 13,000 lbs.; Ballast 5,800 lbs.; Sail Area 598 sq. ft.

C&C 35
LOA 34.65'; LWL 28'; Beam 11.16'; Draft 6.42'; Displacement 10,825 lbs.; Ballast 4,354 lbs.; Sail Area 571.5 sq. ft.

Pearson 35
Classic Cruiser-Racer

Wines are my hobby and I think about them a lot and from time to time I am presented with rather dull designs to review, and in the process, my mind often wanders to more pleasant subjects, such as wine. It might interest you to know that wine making and yacht designing are similar in many ways. Both can be considered art-sciences because while many of the components involved can be quantified objectively, the final result, i.e., the feel of the yacht and the taste of the wine, involves nuances far beyond the calculated data. I use a very sophisticated computer program to produce almost every imaginable hydrostatic component. The program runs complete stability analysis and prints out the variations in stability that coincide with variations of trim that I compute. Yet, when a new design is launched,, rigged and the sails are hoisted for the first time, the resultant personality goes far beyond the numbers.

I know it bothers some people to hear yacht design referred to as an art-science. As they go off watch on a particularly rough night they would like to think of it as all science, but the problem with this kind of thinking is that it assumes art is subordinate to science. Any fool with a calculator and two years of high school algebra can perform the calculations to design a yacht. In interviewing and generally talking with scores of would-be yacht designers, it has become evident that an artistic appreciation of yachts and a highly developed art discipline will carry the prospective yacht designer much farther than college calculus. In fact, usually, the most bitter of potential designers seem to be those with degrees from MIT and the University of Michigan in naval architecture who find they cannot draw a pleasant sheer. All this has little to do with the Pearson 35, but I'll get to that later. In the meantime try and find a bottle of 1975 Eyrie vineyards Pinot Noir produced by David Lett in Oregon.

The Pearson 35 was introduced originally in 1968. I don't know how many of these yachts have been built, but they persevere as a popular shoal draft cruising yacht. I'm not surprised. I happened one afternoon to enter a long channel and noticed five yachts grouped rather closely, beating and obviously engaged in some kind of informal race. Feeling rather lethargic that afternoon, I was motoring along in *Ricky Nelson* quite content. Before long, I realized the boats ahead of me were four Valiant 40s and a Pearson 35. Of course, pride got the better of me so I motored into a comfortable weather position on the trailing V-40, hoisted my sails and reluctantly joined in the beat up the channel. Initially, I was pleasantly struck by the fact that here was a group of simple cruising boats all beating in a 15-knot breeze on their way back to Seattle. I was told by one designer I worked for that, "Cruising yachts don't have to go to weather because cruisers would rather motor than beat." So much for that theory. These cruising yachts were obviously enjoying the stiff beat up the narrow channel. It did make me feel good that four of the boats were Valiants, but I was mildly surprised at the performance of the Pearson 35. With perhaps a 185 percent genoa up the Pearson 35 was on its ear, but it was moving well.

The shoal draft configuration of the Pearson is indeed a factor in its popularity. Bill Shaw designed that yacht with the East Coast in mind and 3'9" draft appeals to a lot of people. The overhangs are pleasantly proportioned and the cabin trunk is not overly long. The displacement to length ratio of this design is 371, but beware of comparing this number to that of more modern designs. The Pearson 35 was designed before a rule was introduced to the racing fleet that encouraged "weak ends." The Pearson has powerful ends and can extend its useful sailing length very quickly as it heels. Note also the moderate beam of the 35. The 10-foot beam would be considered quite narrow for a 35-foot yacht today, but it does give the 35 speed and endearing handling characteristics. Bob, a dock neighbor of mine, owns a Pearson 35. I asked him if he would write a short owner's report. He said, "No." He did say, however, "I like it."

It is interesting to study the rig of the Pearson 35. As foretriangles got bigger with the increased technology of genoa and spinnaker design, the mast moved aft. This did two things. It shoved the mast back into the main cabin and hindered the accommodations, and it also made the boats with the large "J" measurements more critical to main trim and reefing. The rig of the Pearson 35 shows the mast forward of the main cabin and a large, low aspect ratio main. This main gives the 35 good reaching and running speed and keeps the center of effort low to reduce the heeling moment. You seldom see new designs with the mainsheet traveller located at the aft end of the cockpit. Note also that the Pearson 35 does have a very big cockpit.

Going below you will notice that the interior seems small for a 35-foot yacht. This is a function of the moderate beam and the rather low displacement of 13,000 pounds. I am not going to explain this layout as it is simple and quite standard, and it works very well.

Vintage 1968 wasn't a good year for wines in France. It was a very good year in California. A bottle of 1968 Beaulieu vineyards, Cabernet Sauvignon (George de Latour private reserve) is a California wine that will reward you with a very pleasant evening. 1968 was also a good year for Bill Shaw and Pearson. The Pearson 35 has aged well and looks like it has a few moe good years in the bottle.

Pearson Yachts, 373 Market St., Warren, RI 02885. (401) 247-3000. **www.pearsonyachts.com.**
Designer: Bill Shaw.

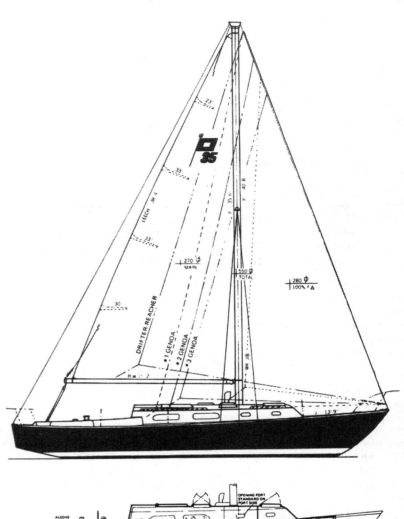

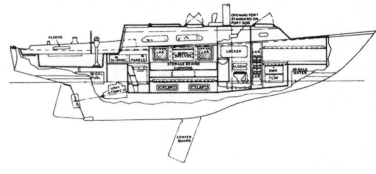

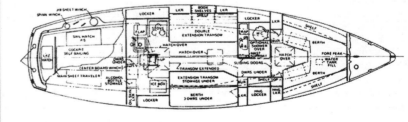

LOA 35'; LWL 25'; Beam 10'; Draft 3'9" - 7'6"; Displacement 13,000 lbs.; Sail Area 550 sq. ft.

Swan 36
Classic Cruiser-Racer

Here is a new boat from Nautor. There. I thought that would get your attention. This is not only a new Swan, but it establishes what I think is a new direction for Nautor: away from the quasi racer-cruiser types produced in the past toward a more cruise oriented boat.

Swan taught us all how beautiful semi-flush decks could be. They established the benchmarks for svelte decks and were copied all over the world. "Swan deck" became a generic term and while the designers changed, the Swan deck remained a constant design element and product of Nautor's factory styling team.

We have seen the offshore racing scene taken over by no compromise, all-out racers and the days when a family racer-cruiser could win are gone. As Nautor built their boats with more and more complex and luxurious interiors, it became increasingly difficult to keep the boats competitive. The new Swan 36 seems to accept the dual role more honestly than the older models which carried freeboard to new heights in order to combine the Swan deck with a full headroom cruising interior.

This design is from German Frers. Freeboard is lower than previous Swans, but the general look of the hull still owes a lot to race boat heritage. I am sure that Frers has in mind competitiveness under the IMS with this design.

We don't have any hull lines for this model, but I think it is pretty easy to imagine the general shape from the plan and profile views. The keel has curved leading and trailing edges as does the balanced spade rudder. The transom features the double radius treatment that Frers has used so often. This knocks the corners off the transom and gives it a very shapely look. Beam-wise, the boat has plenty of it at 11.98 inches, but this will give stability, deck space and useable interior volume. Draft is 6'9", but I would not be surprised to see a reduced draft model available soon. The D/L of this design is 214. Note the high bootstripe.

When you look at the sail plan you should notice the subtle interplay between sheerline, cove stripe and the double bootstripe. I would guess that Frers has drawn the bootstripe at least eight inches above the DWL. This all works together to accentuate and lower the freeboard. The sheer spring is subtle and beautiful. Few designers have as good an eye for a sheer as does Frers. The cabintrunk is interesting in that it fairs to a knuckle forward of the mast. This maximizes interior volume and headroom while keeping deck space.

I guess the big bomber window is okay. This big window works also as a skylight. Gone is Swan's extended bridgedeck, and this model shows a more conventional cockpit design with a low bridgedeck. The cockpit coamings don't appear wide enough to sit on comfortably. The traveler is right in front of the wheel. There is no provision in these drawings for a tiller option.

The rig is a tall sloop with runners, baby stay and two sets of spreaders. The chainplates are tucked in on the 12.5-degree line. The mast appears to be exactly on station 4. The sail area to displacement ratio is 18.44. Note the headstay is pulled aft of the stem about 10 inches. All halyards are led aft to two winches, one each side of the companionway.

This interior layout is basic plan A with a French style quarterberth tucked behind the engine box. The icebox has been reduced in size, but this is not an offshore cruiser. The edge of the table leaves seems a long way from the edge of the settees. I like to see the table come very close to overlapping the settees if possible. The chart table is small and features a swing-out stool. Note the double access to the head.

Nautor's leadership in deck design was paralleled by Nautor's leadership in interior finish quality and detail. "It's as good as a Swan" became the worldwide standard and very seldom matched. It's tough to go below in a Swan and not feel that smile creeping onto your face. They always felt perfect with a careful blend of functional and attractive design combined with a detail approach that obviously pointed to a long prototype development period.

While we all can sit around and extol the virtues of our personal favorites, the owner of this new Nautor 36 has only to say, "It's a Swan." All Nautor has to do is maintain the image by keeping the quality at the top.

Nautor Yachts, P.O. Box 10, Fin-68601 Pietarsaari, Finland. 358 6 760 1111. **www.nautorgroup.com**
Designer: German Frers.

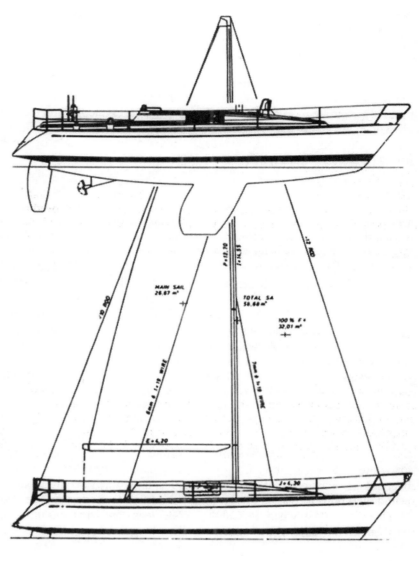

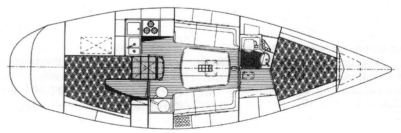

LOA 36.61'; LWL 29.72'; Beam 11.98'; Draft 6.9'; Displacement 12,600 lbs.; Ballast 5,600 lbs.; Sail Area 624 sq. ft.; SA/D 18.44; D/L 214; Auxiliary Volvo 2003R; Fuel 31 gals.; Water 63 gals.

Cal 40
Classic Cruiser-Racer

The year 1964 gave us the Beatles, the baby IOR and the Cal 40. It is probably accurate to say that the Cal 40 won more major races than any other production boat. Bill Lapworth had been working toward this design for some time, and his Lapworth 36 certainly shows the beginnings of the features that were to make the Cal 40 a knockout success.

Seattle enjoys a very close knit and competitive Cal 40 one-design class. This class is made up of conservative, disgruntled with the IOR, yacht racing gentlemen. They collectively view the Cal 40 as the last of the wholesome, racer-cruisers, and the most adamant of the Cal 40 owners will tell you that all racing boats designed since the Cal 40 are dangerous freaks. I think it is quite significant that many of these owners have raced in the IOR class and even owned IOR boats larger than the Cal 40. These owners simply gravitated toward the Cal 40 because it was an excellent all-round dual purpose yacht.

There was a day when the Cal 40 was seen as the harbinger of undesirable things to come. Ted Turner was first seen big boat racing in the Cal 40 *Vamp X* and this, of course, meant that dinghy styled crewing was coming to the big boats. It is unfortunate for the Cal 40 that it was introduced at the same time the IOR was getting its footing in Europe. The IOR would not be kind to the Cal 40 with its light displacement, full ends and relatively narrow beam. In fact, I think you could say that the IOR killed the Cal 40's production run at the early age of 170 boats, approximately. The Cal 40 with its displacement to length ratio of 242 was considered light, and below the waterline was the radical fin keel and spade rudder. These features were being questioned by the conservatives who were being irritated by the 40's proclivity to winning big races. For three years the Cal 40 was king. Again you will note the CCA earmarks.

The Cal 40 interior is as unaffected as the Alberg's. There are no tricks to the layout, just a simple, symmetrical layout with port and starboard pilot berths in the main cabin. Note again the long cockpit and the large lazarette. The emphasis in this interior is on practicality while racing, while still maintaining comfortable cruising accommodations.

The mast is stepped on the keel of the Cal 40, and the chainplates are outboard on the inside of the hull. Note that the small foretriangle puts the mast forward of the main cabin and thusly opens up the space in the main cabin. The Cal 40 shows the squatty rig preferred under the CCA. There are many similarities between the proportions of the Cal 40 rig and that of the Alberg 35. The shortness of this rig is further emphasized by the fact that the Cal 40 has only centerline lower shrouds and there are no baby stay or running backs.

It is interesting how one's sense of beauty in yacht design evolves. I was never fond of the Cal 40's looks when it was introduced, but today I find the Cal 40 a very attractive design. Perhaps it is because so many features on modern yachts have been tortured past the point of aesthetic acceptance. Regardless, I see the Cal 40 as an attractive design today. The cabintrunk is modest in size and the side decks are wide and uncluttered. The long cockpit coamings stretch out the lines of the Cal 40 and the end result is a very sleek yacht compared with something like a Coronado 35.

The Cal 40 surfed. It surfed easily and with excellent control. This was a breakthrough for large boats and the race results bear this out. Perhaps if the Cal 40 had been less effective on the race course, we would have been able to preserve the CCA and would have left the IOR to the other side of the Atlantic. I would hypothesize that many boat owners backed the adoption of the IOR just so they would not have to deal with the Cal 40. In many ways the Cal 40 epitomizes exactly the type of design that the early IOR was designed to discourage.

The Cal 40 represents a significant milestone in yacht design. Bill Lapworth established himself as a very innovative designer with the Cal 40 and still produces very high performance designs for the Cal line by Jensen Marine.

Jensen Marine, 200 Kalmus Dr., Costa Mesa, CA 92626.

Designer: C. William Lapworth, Landfall, 32341, Del Obispo, San Juan Capistrano, CA 92675. (949) 443-9750.

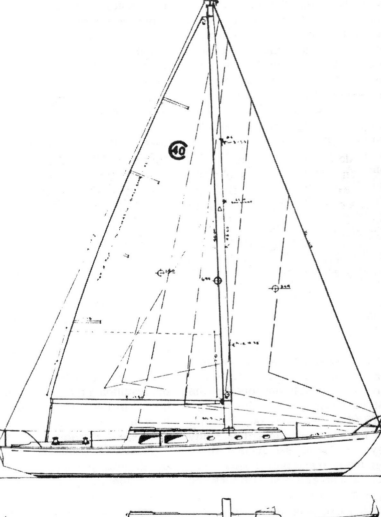

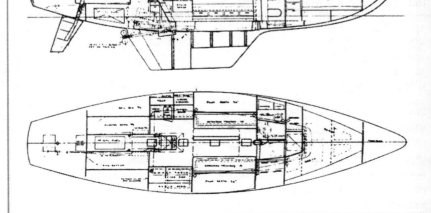

LOA 39'4"; LWL 30'4"; Beam 11'; Draft 5'7"; Displacement 15,000 lbs.; Ballast 6,000 lbs.; Sail Area 700 sq. ft.

Bermuda 40
Classic Cruiser-Racer

The Bermuda 40 is a very interesting design from 1959. Unfortunately, this design came with little reference material so our review will suffer and I will have to guess now and then. I will resort to my own library for some background on the B-40. If the history of yacht design interests you, you might try these two books, **Choice Yacht Designs** by Richard Henderson and **The Great American Yacht Designers** by Bill Robinson. This will give you an excellent perspective of design development.

When I was 15 years old few things excited me more than the designs of Bill Tripp. He produced successful designs with more than the usual amount of personal style manifested. His designs were very easy to recognize. There was the strong bow, the exaggerated stern counter truncated by a sometimes vertical or near vertical transom and lots of sheer. *Ondine*, designed in 1960, will remain one of my own favorites along with the striking, flush deck *Touche*. The beginnings to the Bermuda 40 are found in the Vitesse Class yawls. This design used fiberglass successfully and was finally marketed as the Block Island 40. It was a short design jump from the Block Island 40 to the Bermuda 40 that Tripp designed for Hinckley. Regardless of your present design philosophy, it's hard to not admire the beauty of the Bermuda 40 and the fact that these boats are still built is the best credit possible to the original design. Consecutive Bermuda 40 changes are superfluous modifications to the rig and interior.

With an overall length of 40'9" and a waterline length of approximately 28'10", you can see the extreme result of the CCA's waterline measurement. The waterline was measured, and then 4 percent of the DWL above the DWL the length was measured, thanks Ted Brewer, and this is responsible for the hollow in the stern counter of the B-40. The B-40 had a center-board and drew 4'1". The sections show a very full shape extending down into a wide keel. The rudder stock is vertical. Due to the measurement of the ballast to displacement ratio of these CCA boats, tanks and other heavy items were placed as low as possible in the boat in order to lower the center of gravity of the design without resorting to a rating penalty due to a high ballast to displacement ratio. The CCA was not without its genetic defects and rule cheating features. The displacement to length ratio of the B-40 is close to 400, although this reflects rule oriented distortion. The Bermuda 40 is 1959 at its finest.

The rig of the B-40 has been raised and the boom shortened to be consistent with current design practices. The original rig was a squatty sloop and often yawl configuration. The yawl rig was another way of capitalizing on a CCA rule loophole.

Part of the reason the B-40 is so beautiful is the wide side decks and the resultant small cabin trunk. The house is low and trim leaving a large fore deck and a huge cockpit. Of course, the interior volume is about equivalent to an Islander 36, but there is a large lazarette and a very useful forepeak. The layout is very standard and I do admire the symmetry of the main cabin with the port and starboard pilot berths.

It is difficult for me to wax on about boats that preceded my own professional involvement in yacht design. I called Ted Brewer this morning for some background and could have listened for hours. Again, I suggest doing some of your own homework with the books I mentioned if you are interested in these boats. It is fascinating to watch design features reappear and move through the current phases of the design cycle.

The Hinckley Co., 130 Shore Rd., Southwest Harbor, ME 04679. **www.thehinckleyco.com** *(207) 244-5531.*

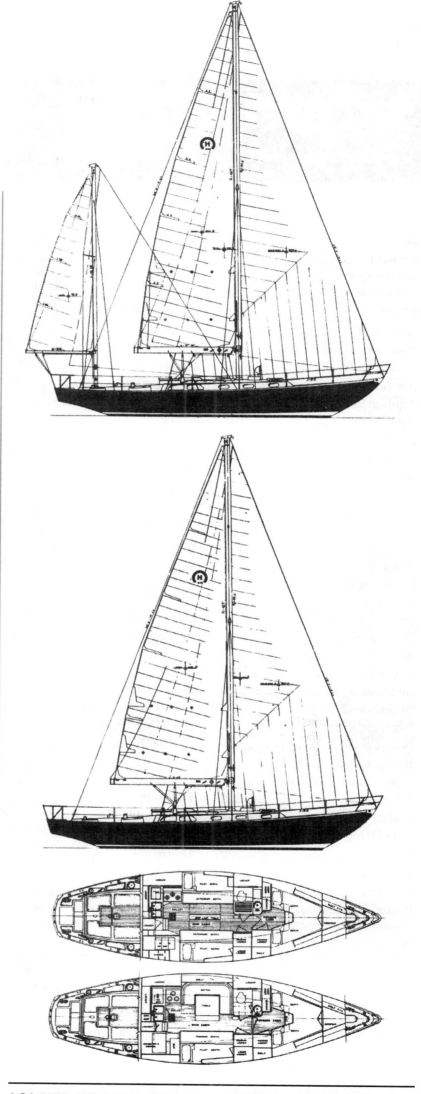

LOA 40'9"; LWL 28'10"; Beam 11'9"; Draft 8'9"; Displacement 20,000 lbs.; Sail areas: yawl 782 sq. ft., sloop 727 sq. ft.

DESIGN INDEX

CATEGORY INDEX

Design Evaluation Formulas

The displacement to length formula is:
displacement in long tons divided by one percent of the waterline cubed

or

$$\frac{\text{displacement in long tons (2,240 lbs.)}}{[(.01)\,(DWL)]^3}$$

The sail area to displacement formula is:
the sail area in square feet divided by the displacement in cubic feet to the two-thirds power

or

$$\frac{\text{sail area in sq. ft.}}{(\text{displacement in pounds}/64)^{2/3}}$$

Directory of Boatbuilders and Designers

A

Active Sports Boats, P.O. Box 441, Constantia 7848, Western Cape, South Africa. 27 21 715-2531. www.activesportsboats.com

Active Yacht Sails, 29939 S. River Rd., Ste. A, Mt. Clemens, MI 48045. (586) 463-7441. www.activeyachts.com

Aerodyne Yachts, 54 West Point Rd., Webster, MA 01570. (508) 943-8776. www.aerodyneyachts.com

Alan Andrews Yacht Design, 259 Marina Dr., Long Beach, CA 90803. (562) 594-9189. email: andrewsyacht@compuserve.com

Andrews, Alan, 241 A. Marina Dr., Long Beach, CA 90803. (562) 594-9189.

Antonio Dias Design, 171 Cedar Island Rd., Narragansett, RI 02882. (401) 783-4959. www.diasdesign.com

Areys Pond Boat Yard, P.O. Box 222, South Orleans, MA 02662. (508) 255-0994. www.areyspondboatyard.com

ASA Yachts, Southern Ocean Yacht Sales, 18495 S Dixie Hwy, #142, Miami, FL 33157. (305) 609-8250. www.southernoceanyachtsales.com

Avalon House, RR1 Belfast, Prince Edward Island, Canada C0A 1A0. (902) 659-2790. www.norseboat.com

B

Back Bay Boat Works, 629 Terminal Way, Ste. 4, Costa Mesa, CA 92627. (949) 515-2733. www.backbayboatworks.com

Baltic Yachts Ltd., 53 America's Cup Ave., Newport, RI 02840. (401) 846-0300. www.balticyachts.com

Barracuda Yachts Inc., (954) 327-9888 fax, (954) 791-6555.

Bavaria Yachts USA, P.O. Box 3415, Annapolis, MD 21403. (410) 990-0007. www.bavariayachts.com

Beetle Inc., 3 Thatcher Lane, Wareham, MA 02571. (508) 295-8585. www.beetlecat.com

Beneteau USA, 1313 Highway 76 West, Marion, SC 29571. (843) 629-5300. www.beneteauusa.com

Berret/Racoupeau, 3 Bis Avenue des Ameriques, 1700 La Rochelle France, 33 546 45 79 79. www.berret-racoupeau.com

Blubay Yachts, 130 Rue d'Antibes, 06400 Cannes, France. 33 4 97 06 20 20. www.blubay.com

Boat Sales International, Hamble Point Marina, School Lane, Hamble, Southampton, S031 4NB, England. 44 23 8045 7966. www.farr-pilothouseyachts.com

Bootsbau Rugen/International Yachting Center, Hwy. 64 West, Columbia, NC 27925. (252)796-0435. www.inter-yacht.com

Brewer, Ted, P.O. Box 48, Gabriola Island, BC, Canada V0R 1X0, (250) 247-7318. www.tedbrewer.com

Brewer Yacht Design Ltd., P.O. Box 48, Gabriola Island, BC, Canada V0R 1X0, (250) 247-7318. www.tedbrewer.com

Brooklin Boat Yard, P.O. Box 143, Brooklin, ME 04616. (207) 359-2236.

Bruckmann Custom Yachts, 2265 Royal Windsor Dr. Mississauga, ON, Canada L5J 1K5. (800) 254-7618.

Buehler, George, P.O. Box 966 Freeland, Whitbey Island, WA 90249. (360) 331-4262. www.georgebuehler.com

Burns & Dovell, P.O. Box 729, Newport Beach, NSW 2106 Australia. 61 29979 6202. www.murrayburnsdovell.com

C

C Design, 1`3113 Brandon Way Rd., Gaithersbury, MD 20878. (301) 926-1755. www.blueheronyachts.com

C&C Yachts, 1920 Fairport Nursery Rd., Fairport Harbor, OH 44077. (440) 354-3111. www.c-cyachts.com

C. W. Paine Yacht Design Inc., Sea St., Camden, ME. (207) 236-2166

Camp, Mike, General Delivery, Comox, BC, Canada V9N 8A1. (250) 339-5521

Cape Fear Yacht Works, 111 Bryan Rd., Wilmington, NC 28412. (910) 395-0189. www.cfyw.com

Caroff, Gilbert, 69 Rue de Clichy, 75009 Paris, France. 33 148 7823 43

Carroll Marine, 91 Broad Common Rd., Bristol, RI 02809. (401) 253-1264, fax (40l) 253-5860.

Catalina Yachts, 21200 Victory Blvd., Woodland Hills, CA 91367. (818) 884-7700. www.catalinayachts.com

Channel Cutter Yachts, 3300 Bissel Rd., Ladysmith, BC, Canada V9G 1E4. (250) 722-3340. www.channelcutteryachts.com

Charlie Ward, Traditional Boats Ltd., Tides's Reach, Morston, Nr Holt, Norfolk NR25 7AA. 44 1263 740377, fax 44 1263 741424.

Chesapeake Light Craft, 1805 George Ave., Annapolis, MD 21401. (410) 267-0137. www.clcboats.com

Clark/Ames, Steve/Bob, 8854 Blue Sea Dr., Columbia, MD 21046. (443) 745-8908.

Clarke, Dan, 438 Middle Hwy., Barrington, RI 02806. (401) 245 2153. www.rapidmarineprototype.com

Columbia Yachts, 1048 Irvine Ave. #252, Newport Beach, CA 92660. (949) 631-6898. www.columbiayachts.com

Com-Pac Yachts, 1195 Kapp Dr., Clearwater, FL 33765. (727) 443-4408. www.com-pacyachts.com

Compass Classic Yachts, P.O. Box 143, South Orleans, MA 02662. (508) 240-1032. www.compassclassicyachts.com

Contest Yachts North America, Box 12-B, The Swan Bldg., Ste. 2, Washington Blvd., Stamford, CT 06902. (203) 348-9100. www.contestyachtsna.com

Cornish Crabbers/Britannia Boats, P.O. Box 5033, Annapolis, MD 21403. (410) 267-5922. www.britanniaboats.com

Cornish Crabber Ltd., Rock Wadebridge, Cornwall Pl 27 6NT, England. 44 1208 862666. www.crabbers.co.uk

Corsair Marine, 353 N. Renee St., Eagar, AZ 85925. www.corsairmarine.com

Covey Island Boatworks, Petite Riviere, Nova Scotia, Canada B0J 2P0. (902) 688-2843.

D

Dehler America, 561 Boylston St., Boston, MA 02116. (617) 536-1100. www.dehler.com

Dewitt, Jim, 1232 Brickyard Cove Rd., Point Richmond, CA (510) 235-0912

Dias, Antonio, 171 Cedar Island Rd., Narragansett, RI 02882. (401) 783-4959

Dibley, Kevin, P.O. Box 46-167, Herne Bay, Auckland, New Zealand. 64-9-303-3678. www.dibleymarine.com

Dibley Marine Architects Ltd., P.O. Box 46-167 Herne Bay, Auckland, New Zealand. 64-9-303-3678. www.dibleymarine.com

Dieter Empacher Designs, P.O. Box 194, Marblehead, MA 01945. (781) 631-5-705. www.dieterempacher.com

Discovery Yachts Ltd., Harbour Close, Cracknore Industrial Park, Marchwood, Southampton S040 4AF, UK. 44 2380 86 5555. www.discoveryyachts.com

Dixson, Bill, Graydon, School Rd., Southampton

Dongray, Roger, Town Arms Stables Guildhall Ln., Lostwithiel, Cornwall PL22 OBW, 01208 873648

Donovan, Jim, P.O. Box 4992, Annapolis, MD 21403. (410) 212-6114. www.jpdonovandesign.com

Drawbridge Marine, 592 Birch Ct., Sebastian, FL 32958. (561) 388-2832. www.raidersailboats.com

Dufour Yachts USA, 1 Chelsea Ct., Annapolis, MD 21403. (410) 268-6417, fax (410) 268-9739. www.dufouryachts.com

Dyna Yacht Inc., 8148 Ronson Rd., Ste. P, San Diego, CA 92111. www.dynayacht.com

E

Eastland Yachts, 33 Pratt St., Essex, CT 06426. (860) 767-8224. www.eastlandyachts.com

Eastsail Yachts, 553 Rte. 3A, Box NH 03304. (603) 224-6579. www.eastsail.com

Elan Marine, SI-4275 Behunje na Gorenjskem, Slovenia. 386 4 535 13 70. www.elan-marine.com

Ellis, Mark, 11 Mews Rd., Fremantle, Western Australia 6160. 61 8 9430 570. www.markellisdesign.com

Empacher, Dieter, P.O. Box 194, Marblehead, MA 01945. (781) 631-5-705. www.dieterempacher.com

Endeavour Yacht Design, (UK) 44 7767 821300. www.endeavouronedesign.com

Ensign Spars Inc., 736 Scotland St., Dunedin, FL 34698. (727) 734-1837. www.ensignspars.com

Erdevicki, Ivan, 400-1200 West Pender St., Vancouver, BC Canada V6E 2S9. (604) 879-0363. www.ivanerdevicki.com

Ericson Yachts, 1301 E. Orangethorpe Ave., Fullerton, CA 92831. www.ericsonyachts.com

ETAP-USA, 9 Timber Ridge, Freeport, ME 04032. (866) 382 -7872. www.etap-usa.com

Etap Yachting, N.V., Steenovensstraat 2, BE-2390 Malle. (207) 865-1855. www.sail-la-vie.com

F

Fairport Yachts Ltd., 1920 Fairport Nursery Rd., Fairport Harbor, OH 44077. (440) 354-3111. www.c-cyachts.com

Farr, Bruce, 613 Third St., Ste. 11, Annapolis, MD 21403. (410) 268-1001. www.farr395.org

Farr International, Hamble Point Marina, School Lane, Hamble, Southampton, Hampshire SO31-4NB. 44 23 8045 6545. www.farr-int.co.uk

Farrier Marine, P.O. Box 40675, Bellevue, WA 98015. (425) 462-5349. www.f-boat.com

Fauroux, Jacques, Immeuble La Suquetane, 16-18 Rue des Suisses, Cannes, France 06400. 33 4 92 59 09 10

Finngulf Yachts, P.O. Box 16, FIN 01211 Inkoo, Finland, 358-9 2211 703. www.finngulf.com

Fontaine, Ted, 92 Maritime Dr., Portsmouth, RI 02871. (401) 682-9101. www.fontainedesigngroup.com

Fontaine Design Group, 92 Maritime Dr., Portsmouth, RI 02871. (401) 682-9101. www.fontainedesigngroup.com

Frers, German, Guido 1926-1, Piso-1119 Buenos Aires, Argentina, 54 802 0568

Fusion Sailboats USA, 1388 Cornwall Rd., Ste. D, Oakville, ON, Canada L6J 7W5. (416) 543-1064. www.fusion15.com

George Buehler Yacht Design, P.O. Box 966, Freeland, WA 98249. (360) 331-5866. www.georgebuehler.com

G

Gerard Dijkstra & Partners, Kruithuisstraat 21, 1018 WJ, Amsterdam, Holland. 31 20 6709533. www.gdnp.nl

Gib'Sea/Dufour Yachts, 1 Chelsea Court, Annapolis, MD 21403. (410) 268-6417. www.dufouryachts.com

Gib'Sea/Dufour Yachts, 1 rue Blaise Pascal-17185 Perigny, France. (410) 268-6417 US contact

Groupe Finot, 1 Rue Pierre, Vaudenay, Jouy en Josas, France

Gunboat Multihulls, Box 951, 3 Narrows Rd., Wareham, MA 02571. (508) 295 -11337. www.gunboat.info

H

Hake, Nick, 4550 SE Hampton Ct., Stuart, FL 34997. (772) 287-3200.

Hake Yachts, 4550 SE Hampton Ct., Stuart, FL 34997. (772) 287-3200. www.seawardyachts.com

Hallberg-Rassy, Varvs AB, Hallavagen 6, SE-474 31, Ellos, Sweden. 46 304 54 800. www.hallberg-rassy.com

Hallberg-Rassy USA, 33 Pratt St., Essex, CT 06426. (860) 767-8224. www.eastlandyachts.com

Hanse, Yachtzentrum Greifswald GmbH, Salinenstrasse 22, 17489 Greifswald, Germany. 49 3834 57 92 0. www.hanseyachts.com

Hanse North America, Brewer Wickford Cove Marina, 65 Reynolds St., North Kingston, RI 02852. (401) 423-9192. www.hanseyachts.com

Henderson, Glen, www.hendersonyacht.com

Herreshoff Design, 1 Burnside St., Bristol, RI 02809. (401) 253-5001. www.herreshoff.org

Hinckley Co., 130 Shore Rd., Southwest Harbor, ME 04679. (207) 244-5531. www.thehinckleyco.com

Hobie Cat, 4925 Oceanside Blvd., Oceanside, CA 92056. (888) 462-4321. www.hobiecat.com

Holby Marine Co., 97 Broad Common Rd., Bristol, RI 02809. (401) 253-1711. www.holbymarine.com

Holland, Ron, P.O. Box 23, Kinsale, Cork, Ireland. 353 2 177 4866

Hoyt, Garry, Newport R&D Inc., 1 Maritime Dr., Portsmouth, RI 02871. (401) 683-9450. www.alerionexpress28.com

Humphreys, Rob, Lymington Marina, Bath Rd., Lymington, Hampshire, UK

Hunter Marine Corp., Rte. 441, P.O. Box 1030, Alachua, FL 32615. (800) 771-5556. www.huntermarine.com

Hylas Yachts Ltd., E5-7 Westminster Bus. Square, Durham St., London, SE11 5JH. UK. 44 (0) 207834 8651. www.hylasyachts.com

I

I.F.G. International Fiberglass, 2212 S. Miami Ave., Durham, NC 27703. (919) 596-2887. www.intl-fiberglass.com

Imagine Yachts Ltd., 980 Awald Dr., Ste. 201, Annapolis, MD 21403. (410) 268-0102.

International Yachting Center, Hwy 74 West, Columbia, NC 27925. (252) 796-0435. www.inter-yacht.com

Island Packet Yachts, 1979 Wild Acres Rd., Largo, FL 33771. (727) 535-6431. www.ipy.com

Islander Yachts, www.yachts.com/builders/sailig-yachts/Islander-yachts.html

J

J Boats Inc., P.O. Box 90, 557 Thames St., Newport, RI 02840. (401) 846-8410. www.jboats.com

J&J Design, Pot na Lisice 2, 4260 Bled, Slovenia. 386 4 5353 646

Jeanneau North America, 105 Eastern Ave. Ste. 202, Annapolis, MD 21403. (410) 280-9400. www.jeanneauamerica.com

Jensen Marine, 200 Kalmus Dr., Costa Mesa, CA 92626.

Johnson, Bob, Island Packet Yachts, 1979 Wild Acres Rd., Largo, FL 33771. (813) 535-6431

Johnstone, Rod, RD1, Box 107, Stonington, CT 06378. (860) 535-2680.

JP Donovan Design, P.O. Box 4992, Annapolis, MD 21403. (410) 212-6114. www.jpdonovandesign.com

Jude/Vrolijk, R&J Design, Vismara Yacht Design and Baltic Yachts Am Seedeich 45, 27572 Bremerhaven, Germany. 49 471 97 123 95. www.judel-vrolijk.com

Jutson, Scott, P.O. Box 132, Manly, Australia 1655. 61 2 9948 1512. www.jutson.com

Jutson Yacht Designs, P.O. Box 132 Manly, Australia 1655. 61 2 9948 1512. www.jutson.com

K

Kanter Yachts, 9 Barrie Blvd., St. Thomas, ON, Canada N5P 4B9. (519) 633-1058. www.kanteryachts.com

Katamaran Konstruktions, A-1230 Vienna-Buttnergasse 1, Austria. 43 1 615 66 33.

Ketterman and Nils Bunkenberg, Greg, 4925 Oceanside Blvd., Oceanside, CA 92056.

Killing, Steve, RR #1 Midland, ON, Canada L4R 4K3.

Koper, Chris, Toronto, Canada. (905) 608-8994.

Kurt Hughes Sailing Designs, 612-1/2 W. McGraw St., Seattle, WA 98119. (205) 284-6346, fax (206) 283-4106. www.multihulldesigns.com

L

Lagoon America, 105 Eastern Ave., Ste. 202, Annapolis, MD 21403. (410) 280-2368. www.cata-lagoon.com

Lapworth, C. William, Landfall, 32341, Del Obisp, San Juan Capistrano, CA 92675. (949) 443-9750.

Laurent Giles Design, P.O. Box 130, Lymington, Hampshire, SO41 0YR, UK. 44 1590 641777. www.laurentgiles.co.uk

Lombard, March, Rue de la Trinquette, La Rochelle, France

Lyman Morse Boatbuilding, 82 Water St., Thomaston, ME 04861. (207) 354-6904. www.lymanmorse.com

M

MacGregor Yacht Corp., 1631 Placentia, Costa Mesa, CA 92627. (949) 642-6830. www.macgregor26.com

MacNaughton Yacht Designs, P.O. Box 190, 35 Clark St., Eastport, ME 04631. (207) 853-6678. www.macnaughtongroup.com

Maine Cat, P.O. Box 205, Bremen, ME 04551. (888) 832-CATS. www.mecat.com

Malcolm Runnals Naval Architecture & Yacht Design, 141 Petra St. East Fremantle 6158, Australia. 61 8 9339 0441. www.runallsdesign.com

Malo Yachts & Hans Leander, AB Kunsviken, S 47399 Henan. 46 304 59 600. www.malyachts.se

Malo Yachts, AB Kungsviken, S 47399 Henan. 46 304 59 600. www.maloyachts.se

Marek, Bruce, 5420 Collinwood Ct., Wilmington, NC 28403. (910) 799-9245.

Mark Ellis Design Ltd., 77 Bronte Rd., Oakville, ON, Canada L6L 3B7. (805) 825-1107. www.markellisdesign.com

Martin, Rodger, P.O. Box 242, Newport, RI 02840. (401) 849-2390

Mason Yachts International, 400 Harbor Dr., Ste. C, Sausalito, CA 94965. (415) 332-8070. www.masonyachts.com

Melges Performance Sailboats, P.O. Box 1, Zenda, WI 53195. (262) 275-1110. www.melges.com

Mike Camp Designs, General Delivery, Comox, BC, Canada V9N 8A1. (250) 339-5521, fax (250) 339-5855.

Mills, Clark, 1028 Sunnyside Dr., Clearwater, FL 33755

Moody America, 335 Lincoln St., Hingham, MA 02043. (781) 749-8600. www.moddy-america.com

Morrelli and Melvin, 412 29th St., Newport Beach, CA 92663

Morris Yachts, P.O. Box 395, Grandville Rd., Bass Harbor, ME 04653. www.morrisyachts.com

Morrison, Phil, 42 Victoria Rd., Exmouth, Devon EX8 1DW, UK 44 1395 224731

Mortain and Mavrikious, Galerie de l'Aquarium, Avenue du Lazaut, 1700 La Rochelle, France. 33 5 46 44 4822. www.mortain-mavrikious.com

N

Najad, SE-473 31 Henan, Sweden. +46 304 360 00, fax 46 304 311 79. www.najad.se

Nautor Yachts, P.O. Box 10, Fin-68601 Pietarsaari, Finland. 358 6 760 1111. www.nautorgroup.com

Nautor Swan New York, Swan Building 12-B, Foot of Washington Blvd., Stamford, CT 06902. (203) 425-9700. www.nautorgroup.com

Nelson Yachts, West Coast: (510) 337-2870. East Coast: (410) 263-6358.

Nelson/Marek Yacht Design Inc., 2820 Canon St., San Diego, CA 92106. (619) 224-6347.

Newport R & D, One Maritime Dr., Portsmouth, RI 02871. (401) 683-9450. www.alerionexpress28.com

North Wind Yachts, Pso Juan de Borbon s/n, Moll de Llevant, 08039 Barcelona, Spain. 34 93 221 6056. www.northwindyachts.com

Northshore Yachts Ltd., Itchenore, Chichester, West Sussex, PO 20 7AY, UK. +44 1243 512611. www.northshore.co.uk

O

Ocean Yachts, 6 Afxediou Str., Alimos 174 55, Greece. 30 210 985 5518. www.ocean-yachts.com

One Boat AB, Box 45 SE 590 83 Storebro, Sweden. +46 492-303-40. www.oneboat.com

Owen Clarke Design Group, Lower Ridge Barns, P.O. Box 26, Dartmouth, Devon, TQ6 0YG, UK. 44 1803 770495. www.lowenclarkedesign.com

Oyster Marine Ltd., Fox's Marina, Wherstead, Ipswich, Suffolk, IP2 8SA. 44 1473 68 88 88. www.oystermarine.com

P

Padanaram Yacht Co., Reservoir Place, 1601 Trapelo Rd., Waltham, MA 02451. (781) 890-5511. www.w-class.com

Paine, Chuck, P.O. Box 763, Camden, ME 04843. (207) 236-2166. www.chuckpaine.com

PC Sailing, P.O. Box 139, Jamestown, RI 02835. (401) 481-3811. www.sailabongo.com

Pearson Yachts, 373 Market St., Warren, RI 02885. (401) 247-3000. www.pearsonyachts.com

Performance Catamarans Inc., 1800 East Borchard Ave., Santa Ana, CA 92705. (714) 835-6416.

Performance Multihull Productions Inc., 41 Sutter St., PMB 1089, San Francisco, CA 94104. (510) 625-0000, fax (510) 625-0001. www.stanek-marine.com

Performance Sailcraft, 2555 Dollard, Unit 14B, Lasalle, QB, Canada H8N 2A9. (514) 363-5050. www.megabyteclass.org

Perry, Robert, 5801 Phinney Ave. N. Ste. 100, Seattle, WA. (206) 789-7212. www.perryboat.com

Perry Yacht Design, 5801 Phinney Ave. North #100, Seattle, WA 98103. (206) 789-7212. www.perryboat.com

Phelps, Simon, Primrose Cottage, 23 Above Town, Dartmouth, Devon, England Q6 9RG. 44 1803 835 242. www.amaryllis.uk.com

Philippe Briand Yacht Architecture, 41 Ave., Marillac, 17042 La Rochelle Cedex 1 France. (33) 5 46 50 57 44, fax (33) 05 46 50 57 94. email: 100445.1543@compuserve.com

Pro Marine, Kennemerboulevard 716, 1976 eS Ijmuiden, Holland. 31 255-526811. www.promarine.denelson

R

B. Yacht Sales, P.O. Box 9204, 145 Pearl St., Noank, CT 06340. (860) 536-7776. www.finngulf.com

Raider Sailboats, Drawbridge Marine, 592 Birch Ct., Sebastian, FL 32958. (561) 388-2832. www.raidersailboats.com

Reichel/Pugh Yacht Design Inc., 2924 Emerson St., Ste 311, San Diego, CA 92106. (619) 223-2299. www.reichel-pugh.com

Reynolds Sailing, 16835 Algonquin St., #216, Huntington Beach, CA 92649. (800) 366-8584. www.r33.com

Rio House, 76 Satchell Lane, Hamble, Southampton SO31 4HL, England. 23 80 45 4722.

R (continued)

Rogers Yacht Design, 68 High St., Lymington, Hampshire, SO 41 9AL, UK.44 (0) 1590 672000. www.rogersyachtdesign.com

RS Racing Sailboats, Trafalgar Close, Chandlers Ford, Eastleigh, Hants SO 53 4BW, UK. 44 2380 27 4500. www.ldcracingsailboats.com

S

Sabre Yachts, P.O. Box 134, South Casco, ME 04077. (207) 655-5050. www.sabreyachts.com

Saga Marine, St. Catharines, ON, Canada. (800) 560-7242. www.sagayachts.com

Sail Extreme Pty. Ltd., 53 Aitken St., Williamstown, VIC 3016, Australia, 61 3 9399 9009. www.sailextreme.com

SailAus Pty. Ltd., P.O. Box 323, Maclean NSW, Australia 2463. 61 2 6645 5088. www.kaycottee.com

Sailrocket, 21 Chafen Rd., Bitterne Manor, Southampton, Hamshire UK, SO18 1BD. 44 2380 368283. www.sailrocket.fsnet.co.uk

Santa Cruz Yachts, 453 McQuaide Dr., La Selva Beach, CA 95076. (831) 786-1440. www.santacruzyachts.com

Schumacher, Carl, 1921 Clement Ave., Bldg. 13A, Alameda, CA 94501.

Sea Craft Yacht Sales, 927 N. Northlake Way, Ste. 100, Seattle, WA 98103. (206) 547-2755. www.seacraft.com

Sea K Designs, #24-3265 S Millway, Mississauga, ON, Canada L5L 2R3. (805) 608-8994. www.sea-k-designs.com

Seaon, 106, 115 74 Stockholm, Sweden. 46 (0) 8 23 65 55. www.seon.com

Seaquest Ltd., Unit 9, Parkengue Rd., Kernick Indust., Est.,Penryn, Cornwall TR10 9 EP, England. www.seaquestyachts.com

Shannon Yachts, 19 Broad Common Rd., Bristol, RI 20809. (401) 253-2441. www.shannonyachts.com

Siltala Yachts, OY, Lallintie 92, FIN-21870, Riihikoski, Finland. 358 2 486 400. www.nauticat.com

Silver Phantom Yachts, 244 Parfitt Way SW, Bainbridge Island, WA 98110. (206) 780-2391. www.silverphantom.com

Solaris, Cantiere Serigi diAquileia S.R.L., Via Curiel, 49 33051 Aquileia, Italy. 39 0431 91304. www.solarisyachts.com

Sparkman & Stevens, 529 Fifth Ave., New York, NY 10017. (212) 661-1240, fax (212) 661-1235. www.sparkmanstephens.com

Sperry Boats, 43 Farina Rd., Hull, MA 02045. (781) 925-9186. www.sperryboats.com

Spirit Yachts Ltd., Ipswich Haven Marina, New Cut East, Ipswich, IP3 OEA. 44 1473 214715. www.spirityachts.com

Stanyon, Paul, Masthead Way, Sanctuary Cove, QLD 4212 Australia, 07 5514 8222.

Stanyon Marine Design, Gold Coast City Marina, Coomera Qld 4209, Australia. 07 5573 6300. www.stanyonmarine.com.au

Steve Killing Yacht Design, P.O. Box 755, Midland, ON Canada (705) 534-4016.

Studio Associato Luca Brenta & Co., Via Salaino 7, 20144, Milano, Italy. 39 02 43995071.

Sud Composites, Z.A.Z. No. 2 34540 Balaruc-Les-bains, France. 33 4 67 43 01 82. www.sudcomposites.com

Superior Yachts West, 29 Embarcadero Cove, Oakland, CA 94606. (510) 534-9492, fax (510) 534-9495.

Sweden Yachts, Box 80, SE-44421 Stenungsund. 46 303 77 06 40. www.swedenyachts.se

Sweden Yachts USA, P.O. Box 580, Riverside, CT 06878. (203) 861-6578. www.swedenyachts.se

T

Tartan/Fairport Marine, 1920 Fairport Nursery, Fairport Harbor, OH 44077. (888) 330-3484. www.tartanyachts.com

Tboat, P.O. Box 34540, Birkenhead, Aukland, New Zealand, 649 419 6032. www.tboat.com

The Catamaran Company, 4005 N. Fereral Hwy. Ste. 200, Ft. Lauderdale, FL 33308. (854) 566-9806. www.catamarans.com

The Laser Centre, 6 Riverside, Banbury, Oxon, OX16 5TL UK. 44 1295 268191

The North Wind Group, 100 Seconds Ave. S, Ste. 200, S St. Petersburg, FL 33701. (727) 709-0611. www.yachtmarketinggroup.com

Thomas Wylie Design Group, 86 Ridgecrest Rd., Canyon, CA 94516. (925) 376-7338, fax (925) 376-7982.

Timeless Marine Inc., 5355-C 28th Ave. NW, Seattle, WA 98107 (206) 782-4650, fax (206) 782-4066

Tony Castro Ltd., Rio House, 76 Satchell Ln., Hamble, Southampton S0314HL, England. 44 2380 454 722. www.tonycastroyachts.com

Triangle Marine Engineering Ltd., P.O. Box 208, North Kingstown, RI 02852. (401) 295-7773. www.trimareng.com

Tripp Design, Oyster Bend Marina, 23 Platt St., East Norfolk , CT (203)838-2215. www.trippdesign.net

Tripp Jr., Bill, 44 Post Rd., Westport, CT 06880

T-Ten Boats, 222 N. Elson Ave., Chicago, IL 60614. (773) 384-2831. www.t-tenboats.com

Turner Yachts USA, 53 America's Cup Ave., Bowen's Wharf, Newport, RI 02840. www.turneryachts.com

U

Ultimate Sailboats, 565 McQuaide Dr., La Selva Beach, CA 95076. (800) 724-5820. www.ultimatesailboats.com

US Dewitt Dinghy Assoc., 1230 Brickyard Cove Rd., #200, Pt. Richmond, CA 94801. (800) 398-2440.

V

Vanguard Sailboats, 300 Highpoint Ave., Portsmouth, RI 02871. (800) 966-7245. www.teamvaguard.com

W

Walker Bay Boats, 607 W. Ahtanum Rd., Union Gap, WA 98903. (888) 449-2553. www.walkerbay.com

Wally Yachts, 8 Avenue de Ligures, Monte-Carlo, MC 98000 Monaco. 377-93 1000 93. www.wally.com

Wauquiez International, ZI Du Vertuquet, 59535 Neuville-en-Ferrain Cedex, France. www.wauquiez.com

Wauquiez USA, 24 North Market St., Ste., 201, Charleston, SC 29401. (843) 805-5000. www.wauquiez.com

WindRider Sailing Trimarans, 3761 Old Glenola Rd., Trinity, NC 27370. (800) 311-7245. www.windrider.com

Windrocket, 3705G Airport Circle, Wilson, NC 27896. (252) 399-7577. www.windrocket.com

Wolstenholme, Andrew, The Flint Barn, Westbourne Rd., Coltishall, Norfolk NR12 7HT, England. 44 1603 737 024. www.wolstenholmedesign.com

Wormwood Performance Yachts, 1311 Riverside Dr., Palmeto, FL 34221. (941) 729-2489. www.wormwood.com

X, Y

X-Yachts, Fjordagervej 21, Box 115, 6100 Haderslev, Denmark. 45 7452-1022. www.x-yachts.com

X-Yachts USA, Foot of Washington Blvd, Stamford, CT 06902. (203) 353-0373. www.x-yachts.com

Yarmouth Boat Company Ltd., Saltern Wood Quay, Yarmouth, Isle of Wight, PO 41 OSE, England. 44 1983 760521. www.yarmouth23.com